thomson.com

changing the way the world learns℠

To get extra value from this book for no additional cost, go to:

http://www.thomson.com/wadsworth.html

thomson.com is the World Wide Web site for Wadsworth/ITP and is your direct source to dozens of on-line resources. *thomson.com* helps you find out about supplements, experiment with demonstration software, search for a job, and send e-mail to many of our authors. You can even preview new publications and exciting new technologies.

thomson.com: *It's where you'll find us in the future.*

SUZANNE I. BARCHERS

Teaching Reading From Process to Practice

W Wadsworth Publishing Company

I T P™ An International Thomson Publishing Company

Belmont, CA · Albany, NY · Bonn · Boston · Cincinnati · Detroit · Johannesburg · London
Madrid · Melbourne · Mexico City · New York · Paris · Singapore · Tokyo · Toronto · Washington

Education Editor:
Joan Gill

Assistant Editor:
Valerie Morrison

Marketing Manager:
Jay Hu

Project Editor:
John Walker

Print Buyer:
Barbara Britton

Permissions Editor:
Peggy Meehan

Production:
Dovetail Publishing Services

Interior and Cover Designer:
Seventeenth Street Studios

Copy Editor:
Luana Richards

Illustrator:
Dovetail Publishing Services

Compositor:
Dovetail Publishing Services

Printer:
R. R. Donnelley & Sons

**Library of Congress
Cataloging-in-Publication Data**

Barchers, Suzanne I.
  Teaching reading : from process to
practice / Suzanne I. Barchers.
    p.   cm.
  Includes bibliographical references
and index.
  ISBN 0-534-53856-8
  1. Reading (Elementary)—United
States. 2. Literature—Study and
teaching (Elementary)—United
States. 3. Vocabulary—Study and
teaching (Elementary)—United
States. 4. English language—
Composition and exercises—Study
and teaching (Elementary)—United
States. 5. Content area reading—
United States. 6. Reading compre-
hension—Study and teaching
(Elementary)—United States.
  I. Title.
  LB1573.B358 1998
  372.4—dc21   97-37398

For more information, contact
Wadsworth Publishing Company,
10 Davis Drive, Belmont, CA 94002,
or electronically at http://www.thom-
son.com/wadsworth.html

International Thomson Publishing
  Europe
Berkshire House 168-173
High Holborn
London, WC1V 7AA, England

Thomas Nelson Australia
102 Dodds Street
South Melbourne 3205
Victoria, Australia

Nelson Canada
1120 Birchmount Road
Scarborough, Ontario
Canada M1K 5G4

International Thomson Publishing
  GmbH
Königswinterer Strasse 418
53227 Bonn, Germany

International Thomson Editores
Campos Eliseos 385, Piso 7
Col. Polanco
11560 México D.F. México

International Thomson Publishing
  Asia
221 Henderson Road
#05-10 Henderson Building
Singapore 0315

International Thomson Publishing
  Japan
Hirakawacho Kyowa Building, 3F
2-2-1 Hirakawacho
Chiyoda-ku, Tokyo 102, Japan

International Thomson Publishing
  Southern Africa
Building 18, Constantia Park
240 Old Pretoria Road
Halfway House, 1685 South Africa

DEDICATED TO DAN—
WHO KEPT EVERYTHING TOGETHER THROUGH IT ALL.

Contents

CHAPTER THIRTEEN:
THE LITERATE ENVIRONMENT

CHAPTER FOURTEEN:
BUILDING READING
AND WRITING UNITS

Preface

You are about to embark on one of the most rewarding journeys a teacher travels: that of learning how to teach reading. Reading, such a vital component of every aspect of education, can be a profound source of pleasure for you and your students. It can also be frustrating as you try to meet the needs of many students with varying abilities.

According to a reading/language arts survey of classroom teachers, reading teachers, media specialists, and computer coordinators conducted by Education Market Research in late 1995, nearly 75 percent of respondents follow a basal program (one that uses commercially prepared textbooks), but only 17.7 percent indicated they used it as their primary resource (Resnick 1996). At the same time, 75.9 percent of the respondents reported that they use the whole-language approach (a philosophy that emphasizes learning through use of authentic materials), while simultaneously providing phonics instruction or using basals to guide instruction. More than 90 percent teach using themes to integrate the curriculum. As Robert M. Resnick once said, "Teachers are eclectic. They may use basals, but they also use literature. They may practice whole language, but they also teach phonics" (April 3, 1996).

Clearly, teachers use a variety of resources in the reading classroom, demonstrating that they search far and wide for ways to meet a variety of instructional needs. *Teaching Reading: From Process to Practice* addresses the challenge of understanding the philosophical underpinnings of a variety of reading theories, choosing effective practices, and making the best use of available resources.

Tackling as vast a subject as reading instruction creates an interesting challenge. **Developmental reading** is defined by Charles W. Bonds and Don Sida as sequential reading instruction given by regular classroom teachers to the average or near average grade-level children and in the content areas (1993, 4). Of course, teaching reading would be easier if these were our only students. However, we are often also responsible for **corrective reading instruction**, which integrates diagnosis with teaching to eliminate skill deficiencies that could become problematic (ibid.). **Remedial reading instruction** is for students who need intensive diagnosis and tutoring and is usually taught by a resource or remedial reading teacher who works with small groups of children or who works collaboratively with the classroom teacher (ibid., 5). This text centers on the developmental reader, with suggestions for working with learners with special needs, such as those needing corrective reading instruction.

Reading instruction is quite necessarily integrated into nearly everything a teacher does, so organization is critical for busy students and teachers who need easy access to information and ideas. Therefore, *Teaching Reading* first provides a context with discussions of theories and instructional approaches. Teachers need to know how it all begins; therefore, the chapter on emergent literacy explores learners' early reading and writing experiences. Chapters 4–6 address the specifics of word identification, vocabulary, and comprehension before exploring the many uses of literature plus the reading-writing connection in following chapters. Because teachers in every subject area teach reading, Chapter 11 addresses strategies that can be used in the content areas, as well as in the reading class. Chapter 12, on reading evaluation and assessment, also provides the teacher with strategies that can be applied in other subject areas. The next chapters deal with the creating the literate environment and how to build a unit, including a sample unit on the Civil War. Recognizing that many teachers combine their literature program with basals, the final chapter addresses how to pull everything together, with an emphasis on combining, adapting, and extending a basal program with literature.

Teachers also need to know how to implement theory. Therefore, features called "Spotlights" appear throughout much of *Teaching Reading*. These sections provide examples of how teachers can use literature to teach phonics, comprehension, skills, writing, and so forth. Features entitled "Something to Try" provide further ideas that can enhance field or classroom experiences. Management suggestions, integrated into many chapters, provide a new teacher with practices that can be used on the first day or on days when a new approach is needed. Sample units, book lists, readers theatre, and other supplemental information can be used by both new and experienced teachers, who will appreciate material to refresh existing programs. Although recommended grade levels are given, the sample units can easily be adapted to other grade levels.

Recognizing that most classrooms have many diverse learners, strategies for working with second-language or learners with special needs appear throughout the text. Dealing with special populations in depth is beyond the scope of this text, and readers are advised to seek out additional sources of information that appear in related references. In recognition of limited resources, such as paraprofessionals, readers will also find a variety of suggestions for involving parents as participants in the reading process as well as ideas for involving adults as classroom volunteers.

Teaching Reading: From Process to Practice provides both teachers who are studying to become elementary or middle school teachers and experienced teachers with the basic information, strategies, and encouragement necessary to develop an effective reading program that combines the best of both basal readers and literature.

REFERENCES

Bond, Charles W., and Don Sida. "A Reading Paradigm to Meet the Needs of All Students." *Reading Improvement* 30, no. 1 (Spring 1993): 2–8.

Resnick, Robert M. *National Survey of Reading/Language Arts: Whole Language and Multimedia Product Needs, Grades K–6.* Rockaway Park, N.Y.: Education Market Research, 1996.

ACKNOWLEDGMENTS

Grateful acknowledgment is made to Terry Rodriguez Phillippi, Marla Jacobson, Marcia Parrish, and Cheryl Singer for sharing their many great ideas. Will Hobbs was especially generous in providing me with the text of his presentation on revising. I appreciate the material shared by Donita Covey, JoAnne Piccolo, Tom Sutherland, Anthony Fredericks, and Martha Hamilton and Mitch Weiss. For their direction, vision, and support, my thanks go to Bob Jucha, Joan Gill, Valerie Morrison, Luana Richards, Joan Keyes, and the many generous reviewers. Dick Scott deserves a medal for his thoughtful reading of the manuscript. Thanks also go to the many students throughout the years who have inspired me. Once again, I must express my heartfelt appreciation to my family who understood when I had to meet another deadline.

Reviewers

Mary Lou Meerson
San Diego State University

Rosemary Winkeljohann
Northern Kentucky University

Sam Sebesta
University of Washington

Patricia DeMay
University of West Alabama

Bonita Miller
Spring Arbor College

Ramon Serrano
St. Cloud State University

June Barnhart
Northern Illinois University

Anita L. Corey
Radford University

Mina Bayne
University of Wyoming

Gayle Flickinger
Illinois State University

Eileen S. Kelble
University of Tulsa

Susan M. Martin
University of South Florida

Lupe Martinez
Metropolitan State College

Maureen O. Oates
University of Northern Iowa

Marilyn M. Ohlhausen
University of Nevada, Las Vegas

Billie Robbins
Adelphi University

Idalia Rodriguez
University of Texas, El Paso

Masha K. Rudman
University of Massachusetts, Amherst

Lana Smith
Memphis State University

William Earl Smith
Ohio University

Debra L. Stahle
Brigham Young University

Laverne Warner
Sam Houston State University

Mary Lou White
Wright State University

Philip M. Wishon
University of Northern Colorado

Penelope R. Speaker
Tulane University

Rob Whaley
Concord, North Carolina

Leah S. Smith
Stephen F. Austin State University

George H. Willson
University of North Texas

Jan LaBonty
University of Montana

Sarah Nixon-Ponder
Kent State University

Carol L. Mack
Portland State University

Nedra Nastase
Indiana University of Pennsylvania

Pamela Adams
Dordt College

Carolyn E. Dankers
California State University, Chico

Jeanne M. Harrington
University of Nebraska, Omaha

Jeanette Parsons
Jersey City State College

Barr W. Taylor
East Carolina University

Lane Roy Gauthier
University of Houston

Nancy Bacharach
St. Cloud State University

Sharon Kane
SUNY, Oswego

1

Early History and Theories of Reading

FOCUS QUESTIONS

1. What is the history of early reading texts in North America?

2. What is the role of a Directed Reading Activity in reading texts?

3. How do I define reading?

4. What is the bottom-up theory of reading?

5. What is the top-down theory of reading?

6. What is the interactive theory of reading?

7. What is the transactional theory of reading?

8. What do I think about reading?

When asked to identify the first reading texts in America, many people will identify McGuffey's Readers, pictured on page 1. Others might think of the characters Dick and Jane from the Scott Foresman books as the first symbols of reading instruction. Take a minute to reflect on how you learned to read. Did your parents teach you at home? Did you learn in first grade using a reader with a collection of stories? Did you read library books? Were you taught phonics? Was learning to read a gradual process, or did you just suddenly understand how reading worked?

In an effort to describe where our reading instruction fits historically and the choices we face as reading teachers, this chapter presents a brief overview of the history of reading instruction in North America and a discussion of current theories of reading.

A Brief History of Reading in North America

For the early Jamestown settlers, the primary purpose for reading instruction was to further religious growth (Townsend 1983, 21). Literate women gathered the children together in their kitchens, and at these "Dame Schools" the children read from *The New England Primer*, a combined ABC and catechism, or from hornbooks. A hornbook, a thin strip of wood with a sheet of paper attached, contained the alphabet, syllables, and the Lord's Prayer. A thin sheet of semitransparent horn protected the paper. Children drilled on their ABCs, practicing spelling until they could put fragments together, finally progressing to reading religious passages (Gray 1963, 43).

Webster's *American Spelling Book*, popular from 1782 to 1845, included the alphabet, drills for combining vowels and consonants, and lists of spelling words. Essentially, people believed that if one could spell, one could read. Thus children often used this speller from first to eighth grade, perhaps finally being allowed to read four fables at the end of the book (ibid., 46).

In 1838, educator Horace Mann criticized the alphabet method and introduced the word method, which came to be known as the "look-say" method.

Hornbooks were used to teach early readers.

He asserted that children see words in use and have associations with words such as "candy" and that this is a natural way to learn to read, as opposed to learning letters that have no associations. Mann also encouraged teachers to ask questions of the students, directing them to read silently to obtain the answer before they read it orally (ibid., 48), a practice that continues today.

Popular in the late 1800s, McGuffey's Readers, primarily lessons in prose and poetry, included the alphabet and syllables, plus writings from the Bible, Washington Irving, Daniel Webster, Shakespeare and others. Rather than practice with a speller for several years, students used graded readers with stories that William Holmes McGuffey purportedly tried out on a group of neighborhood children (ibid., 49).

McGuffey was the first to use repetition systematically and also to monitor the number of new words introduced on each page, influences that continue today (Berger 1995, 32).

In 1908, Edmund Burke Huey wrote:

School readers, especially primers, should largely disappear, except as they may be competent editings of the real literature of the mother tongue, presented in literary wholes, or as they may be records of the children's own experiences and thoughts, or as they may be books needed for information in the everyday life of the school. The children should learn to read books, papers, records, letters, etc., as need arises in their life, just as adults do, and they should be trained to do such reading effectively (Huey 1908, 381).

(Collections of tales, essays, and poetry from historic readers have been developed into a series, *Classic American Readers*, edited by Jeanne S. Chall, providing teachers and students with a fascinating glimpse of the enduring nature of using literature in reading programs.)

Yet, Americans were ready for an educational overhaul at the end of the nineteenth century, and Scott, Foresman and Company, founded in 1896, introduced one of their first successful series, *Grammar School Readers*, authored by William H. Elson (Luke 1987, 100). These readers primarily included previously published works; the *Elson Grammar School Reader, Book Four* (eighth grade), included poetry by Henry W. Longfellow, stories by Lord Byron and Edgar Allan Poe, and excerpts from *Hamlet* (Elson and Keck 1909, 3–4).

The success of the industrial age brought prosperity (or dreams of such) to many Americans, and people such as Rockefeller and Carnegie were widely admired. Organizational systems for management and efficiency, along with the profit motive, drove change in public institutions (Goodman et al. 1987, 11). Scientific principles were applied in many areas of everyday life. The advantages of an advancing technology were recognized and courted as Americans began to appreciate what assembly-line production could do for the economy and therefore for the prosperity of the individual.

Meanwhile, Edward L. Thorndyke [also spelled Thorndike] studied psychology and education to determine how teachers might best provide for the students, reasoning that by the time children entered school they were already profoundly affected by their environment (1912, 94). Thorndyke formulated several principles that he felt should be in place for teaching to be successful. He believed that readiness for learning must be present for the instruction to be effective; this he called the **Law of Readiness**. He believed that exercise strengthened the relationship between a situation and the response; this is the **Law of Exercise**. Further, this relationship strengthened with an increased level of satisfaction; this is the **Law of Effect**. Thorndyke also recognized the selectivity of human behavior; that is, a person may respond to an isolated portion of an experience as well as to the whole experience. Thought, feeling, and conduct are intricately connected (ibid., 100). Thorndyke also studied the effect of practice on learning, concluding that using a variety of methods with appropriate motivation can lead to improvement and that the improvement of one desirable ability generally helps another (ibid., 113). Accepting practice as key to learning fostered the development and use of ancillary materials such as workbooks, word cards, and charts.

As assembly-line production became more effective and profitable, educators looked for ways to use scientific management methods in the school setting. Educators studied instructional practices and learning environments, testing to see which methods were most effective. They believed that once the most successful elements of instruction were identified they could be used by all teachers, guaranteeing widespread student success. Thus as educators such as William S. Gray, a student of Thorndyke and later a professor of education at the University of Chicago, isolated the elements of a successful **curriculum**, the text publishing industry expanded, marrying educational theory and scientific management principles in carefully sequenced textbooks.

Law of Readiness
The belief of Edward L. Thorndyke that readiness for learning must be present for effective instruction.

Law of Exercise
The belief of Thorndyke that exercise strengthens the relationship between a situation and the response.

Law of Effect
The belief of Thorndyke that an increased level of satisfaction improves the effect of exercise.

Curriculum
All planned learning experiences.

FIGURE 1.1

First Story from
*The New Fun with
Dick and Jane*

Look Up

Dick said, "Look, look.
Look up.
Look up, up, up."

Jane said, "Run, run.
Run, Dick, run.
Run and see."

"Look, look," said Dick.
"See Sally.
See funny Sally and Father."

"See, see," said Sally.
"Sally is up, up, up.
This is fun for Sally."

Gray, William S., A. Sterl Artley, May Hill Arbuthnot, and Lillian Gray. *Guidebook: The New Fun with Dick and Jane.* (Chicago: Scott, Foresman and Company, 1951) 6–8.

The addition of Gray to the editorial staff at Scott, Foresman and Company gave a stronger voice to the concerns of educational psychology, and the collaboration of Elson and Gray resulted in the Elson–Gray readers, which were the forerunners of the modern reader. These readers incorporated varied literary selections from authors of the day, such as poetry, essays, and short stories, units focusing on social environment or subjects of special interest to children, and instructional suggestions (Elson and Gray 1931, 3).

The first and most familiar of the modern readers was produced in the 1940s and introduced generations of American school children to Dick, Jane, Sally, Father, and Mother—the first archetypal basal characters. **Basal textbooks**, readers prepared for elementary grade levels, provided the basic system for reading instruction. These early basals were part of the Curriculum Foundation Series, a successful package begun with the Elson–Gray readers that continued for more than 40 years (Luke 1987, 101). These readers were the first to use colorful illustrations. However, the poetry, folk tales, myths, and fables of the turn-of-the-century readers gave way to carefully constructed stories of everyday life, created with controlled vocabulary so that students could build competence in a systematic manner. The first story from the 1951 Scott Foresman primer, *The New Fun with Dick and Jane*, appears in Figure 1.1.

■ **Basal textbooks**
Readers prepared for elementary grade levels that provide the basic system for reading instruction. A basal reading program includes student texts and workbooks, teacher's manuals, and supplemental materials.

With the emphasis on research as the basis for curriculum development, it is not surprising that textbook publishers next turned their attention to developing guidebooks for teachers. These manuals, which flourished with the Scott Foresman readers, provided instructional guidance and comprehension questions for each story (Shannon 1989, 25). The manuals, still used today, reflect the most widely accepted scientific management principles as well as the American respect for businesslike management. Clearly stated goals and objectives for reaching them are outlined in detail. Patrick Shannon points out that guidebooks are a direct application of Thorndyke's psychology. The guidebook directs teachers along a carefully constructed path of instruction. The daily lesson plans provide skills practice, and teachers see a direct connection between this approach and improved achievement and increased test scores (ibid., 25–26). Instructions for teaching the preceding story, "Look Up," are summarized in Figure 1.2.

Scott, Foresman enjoyed enviable popularity and growth as the company added texts for science, art, social studies, arithmetic, and health. Many school-age children of the 1950s used these texts. However, publishers once again had to reckon with continuing research and changing times. **Phonics** and the speech sounds they represent appeared as an integral component of many reading programs. With phonics, students are taught that a letter such as *t* has an identifiable sound (*tuh*), and that the sound of this letter can be combined with other sounds to identify a word. Phonics differed from the alphabet-spelling method seen in Webster's *American Spelling Book* because phonics emphasized the isolated sounds such as *tuh* for *t*.

Linguistics became the basis for a reading system that advocates learning words with a pattern such as *sat*, *rat*, and *fat* in groups. Leonard Bloomfield, a linguist from Yale University, and Clarence L. Barnhart, one of the leading lexicographers of the English language, collaborated on a linguistic approach that emphasized identifying words from patterns; this cumulatively builds independence and competence (1961, 7). This approach is based on **alphabetic writing** in which each character represents the **phoneme**, the smallest speech sound that can be distinguished. The graphic representation of the phoneme is a **grapheme**. Some phonemes have more than one grapheme: *f* and *ph* can represent the same phoneme.

Bloomfield and Barnhart believed that one must be able to recognize the graphemes and also to produce the phonemes they represent (1961, 26). Therefore, to begin to read, children should first learn to recognize the letters of the alphabet and be able to read them successively from left to right. They should then be introduced to simple words in which every letter represents one single phoneme, such as *pin*. Children are asked to read the names of the letters and then are taught to pronounce the word. The key point distinguishing this approach from phonics is that the student does not produce sounds of the letters, such as *tuh* for *t*; instead the student spells and then pronounces the

---

Phonics
An approach to reading instruction that teaches students to recognize the relationships between letters or letter combinations and the speech sounds they represent.

Linguistics
The study of sounds that humans make when speaking to each other.

Alphabetic writing
A system of writing in which each character represents a unit speech sound.

Phoneme
The smallest speech sound that can be distinguished.

Grapheme
The graphic representation of a unit of sound.

Preparing for Reading

Establishing background: Introduce the idea of solving a mystery and changing personal appearances.

Presenting vocabulary: Use the pocket chart and cards to introduce words, phrases, and sentences. Have students read the lines silently and orally.

Checking the presentation: Ask questions about the words in the pocket chart and introduce the story.

Interpreting the Story

Guided reading: Review previously read stories, discuss the text and pictures on each page, reading silently and orally.

Rereading: Have students retell and reread the story from differing points of view.

Extending Skills and Abilities

Memory of word form: Work on recognizing words with word cards, memorization skills.

Comprehending sentence meaning: Use sentences on the board or in the pocket chart with missing words.

Developing phonetic skills: Use rhyming words.

Meeting individual needs: Work on rhyming words.

Think-and-Do Book: Use two pages of the workbook.

Extending Interests

Art activities: Draw a picture as if riding on someone's shoulder.

Dramatizing a story: Dramatize the story with masks.

Enjoying literature: Read or play song-games, Mother Goose rhymes, or poems.

William S. Gray, A. Sterl Artley, May Hill Arbuthnot, and Lillian Gray. *Guidebook: The New Fun with Dick and Jane.* (Chicago: Scott, Foresman and Company, 1951) 61–66.

word in full. Charles Fries published *Linguistics and Reading* in 1962 with the message that instruction should emphasize word families. He felt that phonics instruction created unnecessary difficulties because the sounds of letters in isolation are at odds with the sounds of letters in the context of words.

Shortly thereafter, Jeanne Chall, in her book, *Learning to Read: The Great Debate*, outlined the controversy between early reading instruction (which stressed learning the code), sound-based phonics, and meaning-based methods (1967, 78). She noted that although inconclusive, research from 1912 to 1965 appears to indicate "that a code-emphasis method . . . produces better results, at least up to the point where sufficient evidence seems to be available, the end of the third grade" (ibid., 307). Chall thus recommended earlier phonics instruction, particularly using words that could be readily **decoded** using a knowledge of phonics. In a 1989 article, Chall asserts that research from 1910 to 1988 indicates that children need to be familiar with phonics or letter-sound correspondence to learn to read English text successfully (1989, 533). In the third edition of *Learning to Read*, Chall demonstrates how a more interactive approach has become acceptable and emphasizes that in reading, *both* meaning and the use of the alphabetic principle are essential (Introduction, 1996).

Though linguistic principles were incorporated into some basal series, the more pervasive and enduring effect resulted from Chall's recommendations. Phonics instruction continued to be an integral and often dominating component of basal series. The debate over the role of phonics instruction continues in the literature and will be addressed further in Chapter 4, Identifying Words.

■ **Decode**
Literally meaning to break the code, it has come to mean identifying words through a letter-sound relationship.

Directed Reading Activities and Modern Basal Readers

Emmett Betts's ideas on basal instruction began to affect reading methodology in the middle of the twentieth century, and his influence continues to the present. In *Foundations of Reading Instruction* (1957), Betts outlined five essential steps for **Directed Reading Activities**. These steps are included here because they are the underpinning for many commercial reading programs.

■ **Directed Reading Activities**
According to Betts, reading instruction that includes readiness for reading, silent reading, discussion to develop comprehension and word recognition skills, rereading, and follow-up activities.

1. Students should be prepared for reading a selection (ibid., 430). The teacher should consider student backgrounds; develop concepts or understanding through discussions, questions, pictures, other stories, or additional information; relate the reading to previous reading; introduce names of characters or special words; and motivate the students to read.

2. Students next read the selection silently, and the teacher follows with questions that check facts, verify opinions, compare and contrast characters, and identify situations (ibid., 431). Children are encouraged to seek help on word identification or the understanding of the story.

3. Comprehension and word-recognition skills should be developed during and immediately following the introductory reading (ibid.).

4. The oral or silent rereading is motivated by the need to find information, answer questions, find details, determine the main idea, or develop fluency (ibid.).

5. Follow-up activities should be keyed to the interests and needs of the students, developing organizational skills and efficient study habits (ibid.). Workbook

materials are used to solve specific problems and are not for every student (ibid., 550).

According to Betts, the Directed Reading Activity, now often referred to as the Directed Reading-Thinking Activity, takes about 20 minutes in the primary and 30 minutes in the intermediate grades (ibid., 538). Students who are not working directly with the teacher can pursue the follow-up activities or complete other assignments. Note that this process can be applied to novels, content-area textbooks, and so forth.

STEPS OF A DIRECTED READING ACTIVITY

Today's basal lessons have not changed significantly since the introduction of Betts's Directed Reading Activity. The typical steps of a basal lesson include the following.

PREREADING

Prereading
All lessons and activities that prepare and motivate students to read.

Prereading essentially includes all lessons and activities that prepare and motivate students for their reading. During this section the teacher asks questions to determine the students' familiarity with the reading's subject matter so that they can be given information they may lack that will enable them to complete the reading assignment successfully. The questions may delve into technical information, feelings, or interests of the students.

The teacher may also present new vocabulary words that will be encountered in the selection. These words may be presented in the context of the anticipated reading, in isolated form, or as an activity such as matching words with definitions. The vocabulary may be presented on cards, on the board, or on a worksheet, and the presentation may emphasize word-recognition skills. Alternatively, the presentation may primarily emphasize meaning.

Information gained from the questioning and vocabulary discussion guides the development of activities that relate to other aspects of the curriculum. For example, if the reading is an African folk tale, examining maps of that country would enable the teacher to use geography to stimulate interest in the reading.

Setting the purpose for reading continues to be an integral part of the reading instruction. These purposes may be indicated by looking at an illustration and encouraging the students to speculate with a leading question such as "What do you think will happen when the mother fills the swimming pool?" The purpose for the reading can also be revealed with a statement such as "Read to find out what will happen when the children ask if they can go swimming."

DURING READING

■ **During reading**
Questions, activities, and discussions that encourage comprehension.

Comprehension is the main goal, of course, whether students are reading orally or silently. The **during reading** section, which focuses on comprehension, has changed in many basal texts during the past few years. Previously, the teacher formally assembled the reading group at the reading table and then closely monitored each student as he or she read aloud, perhaps a page or two, regularly interrupting the reading to ask comprehension questions. This method of instruction has been referred to as "Round Robin" or "Barbershop" reading. The teacher can easily assess how well students recognize words and then assist them with the troublesome ones. More recently, students silently read the entire text or a major portion of it with little or no interruption. The reading may be interrupted only upon occasion to pose a prediction question about what might happen next, to clarify misconceptions that have developed through the reading, or to provide additional information that will enable the students' continued success or understanding in the reading process.

■ **Strategies**
Specific systems or approaches to reading.

Students who need assistance with reading can be taught several **strategies**. For example, Maribeth Cassidy Schmitt and James F. Baumann recommend that the students stop reading periodically to check their understanding. Summarization or prediction can occur at logical points in the story, such as when a scene changes or a new character is introduced. Students can be encouraged to consider what they know about the context of the story, thereby activating their background knowledge. Finally, Schmitt and Baumann recommend that students generate their own questions as they read the text; this will increase their involvement in, and comprehension of, the story (1986, 30–31). Additional strategies will be discussed throughout this text.

POSTREADING

■ **Postreading**
All lessons and activities that follow the reading.

Basal readers typically begin the **postreading** lesson by suggesting a series of questions that determine the level of student comprehension. Basals were previously criticized for asking primarily factual questions. Research by B. S. Bloom and D. R. Krathwohl (1956) led basal developers to vary the questions, including inferential or evaluative level questions. Some basals indicate in the teacher's manual the type of question being asked.

Lillian Gray, formerly an author for Scott, Foresman, described this instructional stage as "skills and drills." Examples include rereading for information or clarification, practicing consonant substitutions, drilling on vowel rules, improving vocabulary, improving oral reading, and discussing workbook pages that might follow (1963, 193–194).

Students may be given suggestions for additional reading using trade books or reference materials in the library. Writing is most often addressed during the postreading. Students might be asked to write a letter, poem, or paragraph about a related subject. The assignment is generally brief and may be labeled "Optional" or "Extension" in the text.

Today's basal texts, more commonly referred to by publishers as reading programs, usually include a wide variety of stories, poems, biographies, articles, and essays from previously published trade books for various graded reading levels. Additionally, a scope and sequence of skills and objectives for the reading process may be included, as well as a teacher's manual, which provides carefully scripted directions for instruction; extension activities; tests developed from the basal series itself; and a management system for recording student progress.

Many of today's reading texts appear to have come full circle. In contrast to the carefully constructed stories of Dick and Jane, many readers now include selections from the best of current children's and young adult literature, just as the Elson readers included contemporary works. These selections are often excerpted and, due to space constraints, don't always include every illustration (Goodman 1994, xvii; Goodman, Maras, and Birdseye 1994). The role of basals is discussed more thoroughly in Chapter 2, Instructional Reading Approaches.

The Mystery of Reading

Now that you have a brief historical overview of early reading texts, read the following story and answer the questions in complete sentences.

Billy's Darpnold Baj

Billy was chinging darpnold. The skaver skaved the nold to Billy's rel. Billy baj the nold with the rel. Billy dup marfly to blig darp.

1. What was Billy chinging?
2. What did the skaver do?
3. What did Billy use to baj the nold?
4. How did Billy dup?

(Inspired by Kenneth Goodman's "The Marlup.")

If you haven't stopped to answer the four previous questions, take time to do it now. How did you do? Do you think your answers are correct? Was it easy? Were you frustrated? Did you understand what you read, or did you simply give up? Try to remember how you learned to read. Did your mother teach you with picture and story books? Did you learn in school from textbooks such as those described earlier in this chapter? Was learning to read a slow, deliberate accumulation of skills and knowledge, or did you just suddenly know how?

For many students, reading remains as frustrating to them as "Billy's Darpnold Baj" does to us. They use what they know of spoken language to get by, but they don't fully understand what they read. Take a minute to list the cues you used to answer the questions. You probably first used what you know about **graphophonics** to decide how to pronounce the words. Perhaps the *ing* and *ed* endings gave you clues to verb tense. Maybe you decided that the answer to question 4 is "marfly" because you know that *ly* often indicates an adverb. You probably relied on **syntax** knowing that in simple text, nouns precede verbs. The **semantics** probably didn't help you much, except for words such as *Billy, was, with,* and *the,* but those simple words confirmed the syntactics. Meaning is so critical to the understanding of text, that identifying only one key word in "Billy's Darpnold Baj" makes reading the paragraph and answering the questions much easier. Take some time to wrestle with what *darpnold* might mean. The answer is given later in this chapter.

Reading has always been mysterious to me. I don't recall how I learned to read, but I vividly recall my first Scott Foresman reader, where I marveled at the repetition of one of the first words, *look.* I was fascinated by the pocket chart, wishing I could handle those cards with words on them. I learned quickly, but found the instruction to be tedious and slow. I never could understand why I had to listen to others read aloud when I had already read the story silently, usually in much less time. As teachers of reading, I am sure that reading continues to fascinate us all, so before we begin to examine the process of reading, let's explore some definitions of reading.

- **Graphophonics**
  According to Ken Goodman, a combination of cues that readers and writers use, including sound system (phonology), graphic system (orthography), and the system that relates them (phonics).

- **Syntax**
  Patterns of phrases and sentences.

- **Semantics**
  Meaning of text.

Definitions of Reading

Why should we define reading? To be effective and responsive reading teachers, we must know what reading is and what good readers do (Fowler 1993, 109). Further, as Ned D. Marksheffel has observed, although we may never agree on one definition, the process is important for several reasons:

1. *Reading is taught as it is defined* (1966, 9).

2. *Reading or any other phenomenon must be defined before it can be measured* (ibid.). Even though some facets of reading may not be measurable, skills such as word recognition, skimming rapidly, or varying reading rate for the purpose can be measured.

3. *Agreement on a definition of reading must be reached by those who write about reading and those who teach reading in order that confusion over method, or methods, be decreased* (ibid.). Many people are involved in a student's education: parents, teachers, specialists, administrators, and textbook publishers. It would be

A young reader enjoys studying striking photos.

useful if those of us who are involved with reading instruction were to reach consensus as to what we think reading is, although total agreement is likely to remain elusive.

4. *Tests of reading do not always measure reading* because test designers, lacking an acceptable definition of reading, test only minor facets of the reading process (ibid.). Breaking the reading process into measurable skills provides only pieces of the picture. For example, when students were asked to build, extend, and examine text meaning, the National Assessment of Educational Progress considered four orientations: initial understanding, interpretation through inferences and connections, personal response, and critical stance or considering how the author crafted a text (Mullis, Campbell, and Farstrup 1992, 2).

Consult a dictionary and you will find that reading is defined as the act of examining and understanding written material. However, students have a somewhat different view. The elementary student may define reading as work, but a teenager may define it as comprehending words that are written down. These two views reveal a great deal about the students' reading programs. The elementary student is involved in a program that uses many worksheets; consequently, the student views reading as "work." The teenager appreciates the role of understanding because she is often asked to write essays about what she has read.

What do you think reading is? Review the following definitions and decide whether one fits your ideas about reading:

- Reading is a process by which children can, on the run, extract a sequence of cues from printed texts and relate these, one to the other, so that they understand the message of the text (Clay 1991, 22).

- Reading begins with the registration of the printed words in the brain by the visual and perceptual processes, with the brain converting the written symbols to language, and with cognitive and comprehension processes, adding meaning by relating the symbols to the reader's prior knowledge (Dechant 1993, 69).

- Reading is a purposeful reconstruction of an author's printed message for recreational, aesthetic, or functional purposes (Duffy and Roehler 1993, 36).

- Reading is a complex, dynamic process that involves the bringing of meaning to, and the getting of meaning from, the printed page (Rubin 1993, 5).

Do any of these definitions fit your ideas of what reading is? If not, try to revise one or create your own. To help you in this process, return to "Billy's Darpnold Baj" on page 11. Substitute *baseball* for *darpnold* and read it again. Now you can probably translate the entire story easily, just knowing that one word. How does this process affect your definition of reading?

Theories of the Reading Process

A theory can be defined as "a system of assumptions, accepted principles, and rules of procedure devised to analyze, predict, or otherwise explain the nature or behavior of a specified set of phenomena" (*American Heritage Dictionary* 1985, 1260). You may have developed a definition of reading you are comfortable with, but you may still be unclear as to how the reading process works. There are many theories on the reading process; we will examine those that relate most closely to the instructional practices commonly found in today's schools: bottom-up, top-down, interactive, and transactional.

BOTTOM-UP THEORY OF READING

- **Mainstreaming**
Placing students with special learning needs in a regular classroom.

Mrs. J. teaches first grade in a school that **mainstreams** students with special needs as much as possible. Her class includes one student with cerebral palsy who uses a wheelchair, one student with limited English skills, and one student who is hearing-impaired, all of whom leave the classroom part of the day for individualized help.

Because Mrs. J. believes that students who have a strong understanding of the relationship between letters and sounds will be successful when they encounter unfamiliar words and complex sentences in books, she provides a variety of experiences that help her students thoroughly understand grapho-phonics. The students not only use worksheets (which allow them to practice identifying letters) but also use paints, the sand table, letter cards, and clay, which they use to explore letters and their sounds. When a student has difficulty with a letter or sound, Mrs. J. spends time with that student reteaching the relationship, then follows the lesson with extra practice.

Mrs. J.'s teaching is based on a theory you may have encountered when you learned to read or perhaps when you learned to type, a most useful skill for college students! If you took a high school typing class, you probably learned the home row first (letters *a, s, d, f, j, k, l, ;*), practicing striking the eight keys under your fingers until you mastered these strokes with a high degree of accuracy. You also learned a few necessary functions, such as the space bar and return lever or key. You then progressed to other nearby letters, forming words that were easy to type. During the class and after dedicated practice, you progressed to less frequently used symbols, such as the exclamation point or numbers. The objective of this practice was to enable you to use your basic typing skills automatically. Once you mastered the basic skills, you could type from copy, perhaps eventually in excess of 40 words per minute. With continued practice, you were able to type fluently as you composed letters, reports, or papers—you no longer consciously thought about how to type, except to correct mistakes or change text.

It's easy to see the bottom-up theory and the principle of automaticity (where we internalize a process until it is so automatic it no longer requires our attention) at work in this instructional sequence. Typing students begin by practicing individual letters, building to more letters and words until they can type without consciously thinking about the process. Can you think of other times when you learned something using the bottom-up model? Figure 1.3 diagrams the bottom-up theory.

Like Mrs. J., many kindergarten and first grade teachers use the bottom-up model to teach beginning reading. They usually spend several weeks ensuring that all the students understand the relationship between letters and their sounds. They begin with the consonants that are easy to articulate and identify, adding a few short vowel sounds next. The students practice using these sounds until

FIGURE 1.3
Bottom-Up Theory of Reading

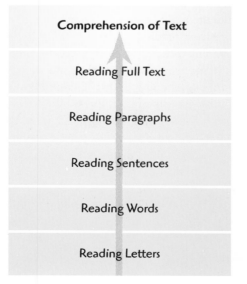

Comprehension of Text

Reading Full Text

Reading Paragraphs

Reading Sentences

Reading Words

Reading Letters

they identify the letters and related sounds easily. After practicing short words with a consonant-vowel-consonant (CVC) pattern, such as *cat, ant, hat,* or *hop,* they proceed to preprimers, small illustrated books that have just a few words or a short sentence on each page. As students move through these early readers, the teacher sorts students into groups that need more or less practice, and they continue to build a repertoire of words, sentences, and paragraphs through carefully sequenced stories. Intermediate students use the bottom-up process when they determine the meanings of unknown words by analyzing prefixes, suffixes, and root words.

The process of mastering graphophonics (the relationship between the letters and sounds) and systematically building letter-by-letter, word-by-word, and sentence-by-sentence exemplifies the bottom-up theory. One of the goals, automaticity, underscores the belief that once students can read the words and sentences easily, they can attend to the meaning of the text. This process aims for early mastery of the "parts" of reading, giving students the tools to decode text by identifying words through the letter-sound relationship.

TOP-DOWN THEORY OF READING

Walk into Mr. B.'s first grade room and you find the classroom walls covered with stories, poems, lists, and charts written by Mr. B. and his students. A tepee and scattered pillows on a small rug provide a reading area near the classroom library. Students work on projects in small groups, play at the grocery store, or explore one of several learning or activity centers. Mr. B. moves about the room, offering advice and redirecting students. Periodically, he assembles a group of students, and they read from a big book so oversized that it allows all the students to see the text and pictures easily. He follows this activity by having the students reading small versions of the book. Then they discuss how they will use their reading, perhaps writing their own version of the book or creating new illustrations after copying the sentences. A large rug dominates the room; the entire class can be found there several times a day writing experience stories, listening to Mr. B. read aloud, and talking about what they are doing in all aspects of their lives.

Each day begins with the entire group discussing and recording "News of the Day," which may include current events, personal events, the weather, and plans for the upcoming day. This is displayed and referred to frequently. Just before the students go home, they reread the "News of the Day" and create another bulletin that sums up what they've accomplished today. A volunteer parent compiles and photocopies these reports for the students to take home on Friday. Parents are asked to have their children read the news bulletins to them or with them over the weekend.

Mr. B.'s class includes two students who are being tested for possible learning disabilities. Students with physical limitations join the regular classroom only during special classes, such as music and art. Mr. B. enjoys drawing on the children's experiences for much of their instruction. He endeavors to provide rich group experiences, such as a field trip to a nearby aquarium that would prepare his students for a reading unit on sea animals. He also builds instruction around words they already know. For example, the grocery store center capitalizes on the many food labels the children could already read. After a few months, this center will become a fast-food establishment.

Those of you who have raised children know that preschoolers have a vast knowledge of how printed symbols work. They recognize in print the name of the stores and restaurants they and their parents frequent, plus the names of their favorite toys, stuffed animals, and games. When a curious 3-year-old asks someone to identify a word, generally the whole word is identified. My son at age 3 pointed to the word on the underside of the toilet lid and asked what it was. Like most parents, I didn't stop and explain the sound of a *b* and the other letters. I simply supplied the word, he learned it, and then he generalized it—somewhat inappropriately—to other toilets. For several years, a toilet was called a "Bemis."

Top-down reading models capitalize on the experiences and knowledge that a child brings to the process, coupled with the child's purposes. Supporters of this theory believe that just as children learn to speak by experimenting, taking risks, guessing, and refining their utterances, so can they learn to read by using their experiences and knowledge of print to make sense of what they are reading. Instead of focusing on building precise sound-symbol relationships, words, sentences, and so forth, children can be taught to read by using what they know to approximate the meaning of the text. The more they know about what they are to read, the less they need to rely on exact interpretation of the symbols. Figure 1.4 shows how this model works.

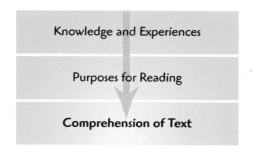

FIGURE 1.4
Top-Down Theory
of Reading

If you think about how you read "Billy's Darpnold Baj," you may find that you used sound-symbol relationships as your "going-in" strategy. But until you figured out that *baseball* could be substituted for *darpnold*, the story held little or no meaning for you. This process of finding meaning in the reading is key to the theory of top-down reading.

INTERACTIVE THEORY OF READING

The environment in Miss M.'s class combines aspects of the previous two classrooms. Commercial materials, such as charts that remind students of letter-sound relationships, are posted alongside lists of words created by students. Books are found in the classroom library, in various interest centers, and on every student's desk. Miss M. also has three children in her class who leave periodically through the day for special instruction for speech delays.

Miss M. begins the day reading aloud from *The Wee Little Woman* by Byron Barton. As she reads, she points to each word. After discussing what *wee* means, writing it on the board, and talking about the sounds of the letters, Miss M. reads from the book again, asking the students to raise their hand every time she reads the word *wee*. She discusses how *w* is the letter of the day, what it looks like, and that today the students will use the letter *w* for several activities. She then splits the students into groups. While some students practice making *w*'s or *w* words in the art center and others reread familiar stories silently, one group meets with Miss M. These students brainstorm all the words they can think of that begin with the letter *w*. When someone suggests *wild*, several volunteer "Like in *Where the Wild Things Are!*" and they take a moment to be wild things. After making a chart of their list, the students are told how to complete a worksheet that gives them practice matching the letter to pictures such as *water*, *wing*, *wire*, and *wolf*. They are told that after they finish the worksheet they should choose a *w* word to illustrate for a class *w* book. When someone suggests making a "Wild Things" book instead, they all agree this would be more fun to do. Miss M. concludes by telling the group that the next time they meet, they will be reading a story that has many *w*'s in it, so they should be thinking about words that start with *w*.

Miss M. smoothly combines the use of commercial materials, such as worksheets, with both the students' previous experiences with books and their personal interests. Knowing that some of her students need more practice with graphophonics than others, she provides a mix of instruction. She plans instruction carefully so that it builds knowledge sequentially, and she is always open to student suggestions for follow-up activities, such as creating a "Wild Things" book.

Miss M. combines aspects of both the top-down and bottom-up theories into the interactive theory. This theory suggests that student readers use their background knowledge and their decoding skills simultaneously to find meaning in text. The reader begins with some ideas about the text while processing the print. If the student has a fair amount of background knowledge about the subject, the reading will be much easier than if she has little or no knowledge about the topic. To illustrate, try reading the following:

The most basic source of depth perception is retinal disparity, also a binocular cue. Retinal disparity is based on the simple fact that the eyes are about 2½ inches apart. Because of this, each eye receives a slightly different view of the world. When the two images are fused into one overall image, stereoscopic vision occurs. This produces a powerful sensation of depth (Coon 1989, 119).

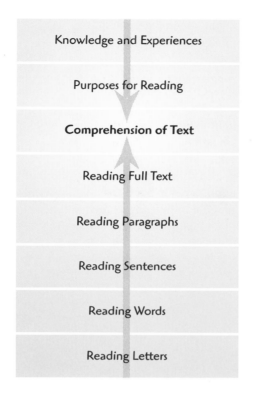

FIGURE 1.5
Interactive Theory
of Reading

Knowledge and Experiences

Purposes for Reading

Comprehension of Text

Reading Full Text

Reading Paragraphs

Reading Sentences

Reading Words

Reading Letters

For some of us, the first sentence might be rather daunting. But after reading the complete passage, most of us will understand the gist of the message. We will have successfully used our knowledge of graphophonics and some background knowledge about our eyes to gain a sense of the writer's message. Rereading, further information, or continued reading would also increase our comprehension.

In practice, teachers often use the interactive model. This enables them to tailor the reading experience to capitalize on an individual's strengths and to improve areas of weakness. A student who has traveled to Mexico and has excellent decoding skills will have little trouble reading about Mexico City. A student who has excellent decoding skills but no travel experience would benefit from seeing a video or film before reading about a new culture. A student with little or no background experience and weak decoding skills will need even more preparation before tackling the assignment. Modifying instruction to suit the needs of students is an ongoing challenge for any teacher. Figure 1.5 shows a model of the interactive theory.

TRANSACTIONAL THEORY OF READING

Mr. T. begins Monday with a class meeting of his first graders. Everyone gathers on a rug and they review the activities of the week before, exploring their agreed-upon topic: insects. Because they live in a rural area and it is late spring, students have been actively investigating which kinds of insects appear as the weather becomes warmer. Several students saw the first earthworms of the season that weekend, and they add these to a chart that has spaces for recording insect characteristics.

Next, Mr. T. reads *The Very Busy Spider* by Eric Carle aloud; this is the story of a spider who has no time to play because he is busy spinning his web. Mr. T. has garnered enough copies from various libraries so that during the second reading, the students share the book in groups of three, feeling the developing web on the pages as he reads aloud. After this second reading, Mr. T.

asks whether the students have anything to share about the book. Some students recall that they have already read two other insect books by Eric Carle, *The Grouchy Ladybug* and *The Very Hungry Caterpillar*. Another student recalls reading *Miss Spider's Tea Party* (Kirk 1994), a story in which different insects are afraid of the spider. One student wonders what kind of insects, besides flies, spiders like to eat. Another mentions how she thought it was neat to be able to feel the web. They discuss how Eric Carle's books are often unusual.

After a lengthy discussion, Mr. T. writes several possibilities on the board for follow-up activities: investigating what spiders eat; finding and sharing other books by Eric Carle; finding and sharing informational spider books; and creating a new story for a spider book that will also have a raised web. The students decide which area to investigate and break into small groups to plan how to proceed. Two undecided students try to think of another project they can pursue.

The activities in Mr. T.'s class exemplify the transactional theory, an elaboration of the interactive model, which emphasizes social context. Instead of having an interactive relationship, the reader and text are seen as having a circular relationship in which each affects the other (Rosenblatt 1991, 60). The

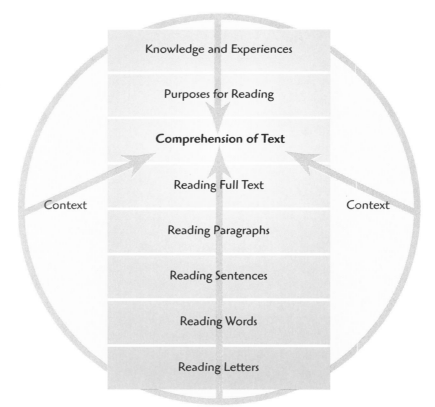

FIGURE 1.6
Transactional
Theory of Reading

reader's response to the text is flexible, and the reading event is conditioned by the context. The reader's response, either aesthetic or efferent, depends on his or her purpose in reading this particular text. For example, the armchair traveler reads an article about Paris and gains a pleasant impression of an intriguing place—an aesthetic response. A businesswoman who is about to visit Paris reads the same article for entirely different purposes and takes away different information. The soon-to-be traveler has an efferent response, as she is more concerned with retaining specific information.

In the transactional model, the context for reading—daydreaming or planning—"conditions" (affects) the content of the retained material: a pleasant impression of Paris or ideas about what to do in Paris. The writer of the article may have intended it to be primarily informational, but the armchair traveler has different intentions than the businesswoman, and thus retains entirely different information.

In Mr. T.'s class, some students were fascinated by the construction of the book, while others were curious about the spider's dietary preferences. Transactional theory places the interactive theory within the framework of context and assumes that context heavily influences the reading experience. In Mr. T.'s class, this broader context was driven by the children's fascination with insects, due in part to the school's rural setting and the natural interest in insects at this age. Figure 1.6 illustrates the transactional theory of reading.

Discovering Your Beliefs about Reading

Deciding on your personal theory of reading takes time and reflection. You may have some general ideas about which theory fits your learning style. Remember, however, that your learning style may not match those of your students. Reading is challenging to teach because it is impossible to make generalizations about individual student readers. Just when you find one or two approaches that work for most of your students, you will encounter a class where nothing seems to work.

Thinking about reading theory provides you with a starting point in your endeavor to become an effective reading teacher. Here is an activity that will help you discover your personal beliefs about reading theory. Read the statements in Figure 1.7 on the next page and note whether you strongly agree or disagree.

After deciding how you feel about each of these statements, meet with a fellow classmate and discuss which theory each statement supports. For example, supporters of the top-down theory would strongly agree with statement 1, that readers should guess at unknown words. Supporters of the bottom-up theory would agree with statement 2, that readers should carefully sound out words using their phonics skills. You will probably have some

FIGURE 1.7

Thinking about Reading Theory

Do You Agree?

Directions: Rate your feelings about the following statements from 1 to 5, with 1 indicating that you strongly disagree and 5 indicating that you strongly agree.

1. Readers should guess at unknown words. _____
2. Readers should carefully sound out words using their phonics skills. _____
3. Readers should master letters and sounds before trying to read text. _____
4. Readers should learn the vocabulary before reading new text. _____
5. Looking up words in a glossary or dictionary is important for learning new words. _____
6. Students should read only high-quality literature or materials that will improve their vocabulary. _____
7. Readers who understand punctuation marks will understand their reading better. _____
8. Readers should work in a quiet environment. _____
9. Readers benefit from talking in class. _____
10. Readers benefit from listening to good reading models. _____
11. Readers should have a lot of oral reading so they learn to read aloud more fluently. _____
12. Incorrect pronunciation should be corrected immediately. _____
13. Readers work best in a highly structured environment. _____
14. Students should have high-quality print displays for models. _____
15. Readers work better in an organized room with individual desks. _____
16. A classroom should have only student writing displayed. _____
17. Students learn best when they receive a lot of individual instruction. _____
18. Students learn best when they get to choose their working groups. _____
19. Students learn better when they can read materials they have chosen, even materials such as magazines or comic books. _____
20. Instruction should be systematically planned to cover all skills. _____
21. Instruction should be spontaneous, depending on the needs of the students. _____
22. Students should work independently so they are accountable for their own work. _____
23. Students who work with others may rely on others too much. _____
24. When students work together, both the stronger and weaker readers benefit. _____
25. Most students need careful guidance regarding their education. _____
26. It is important for students to be tested regularly so the teacher and parents know how they are doing. _____
27. All students should be tested frequently because our society judges students based on how well they perform on standardized tests. _____
28. Informal test measures are preferable to standardized tests. _____
29. Special students would do better in programs designed specifically for their needs. _____
30. Special students can learn along with regular learners given the right conditions. _____

healthy discussions about which theories some statements would support. For example, supporters of any theory might agree with the statement that students learn best when they receive a lot of individual instruction. You may find that certain statements you agree with seem inconsistent with each other.

A Final Note

If you have spent time in a classroom or have raised children, you know that behavioral theories are never the final answer. They are merely starting points. Your thoughts on reading instruction may change by the end of this course. Further, once you are ready to teach reading, you will also need to consider the expectations of your district or building. Principals often have strong ideas about what new staff members should attempt in their classrooms. They will also want the results coming out of your classroom to mesh with what staff at the next grade level must accomplish. Most importantly, you will undoubtedly need to adapt your methods to your students. If a district uses a certain basal series, as a new teacher you might want to begin with it, gradually shifting to a more interactive approach if you find that it works better for you and your students. Teachers who have been in the profession for many years have seen various practices come in and out of favor. Wise teachers continually explore new ideas, assuming that just as they want their students to grow and stretch, they too must grow and stretch. Being open to new practices that might benefit their students, even as they retain sound practices that work, is a good way to ensure a continual expansion of their teaching skills.

Summary

Examples of early readers include McGuffey's Readers, Elson Readers, and Elson–Gray readers. Beginning in the 1950s, Scott, Foresman enjoyed tremendous popularity with the Modern Curriculum Foundation Series. Basal readers continue to use Directed Reading Activities, which include prereading, during reading, and postreading instruction. Modern basal readers contain more complete literary selections, although teacher's manuals are essentially the same.

Developing a definition of reading is important because that definition often determines how you will teach reading. Most of the definitions in this book emphasize that reading is a process that involves the use of print and thinking about that print. The idea that we must understand what we read is also a key part of a comprehensive definition of reading.

Several theories of learning were considered. The bottom-up theory of reading emphasizes the acquisition of skills to achieve comprehension. The top-down theory emphasizes the student's background and experiences, using these as a basis for reading, with skills acquisition de-emphasized. The interactive theory uses skill-knowledge and the student's background and experiences to create an instructional model. The transactional theory expands the interactive theory to include the influence of social context on comprehension.

Teachers in the process of defining a personal theory of reading should consider their personal beliefs, features of the various theories, requirements of their district or building, and the individual needs of the students. Theories of reading are not the final answer, but they are a starting point for developing an approach that works for your students.

References

American Heritage Dictionary. Boston: Houghton Mifflin, 1985.

Barton, Byron. *The Wee Little Woman*. New York: HarperCollins, 1995.

Berger, Allen. "Nothing Comes from Nowhere: The Story of the National Federation of McGuffey Societies." *Reading Today* 12, no. 6 (June/July 1995): 32.

Betts, Emmett A. *Foundations of Reading Instruction: With Emphasis on Differentiated Guidance*. New York: American Book, 1957.

Bloom, B. S. and D. R. Krathwohl. *Taxonomy of Educational Objectives*. New York: Longmans, Green, 1956.

Bloomfield, Leonard, and Clarence L. Barnhart. *Let's Read: A Linguistic Approach*. Detroit, Mich.: Wayne State University Press, 1961.

Carle, Eric. *The Grouchy Ladybug*. New York: Thomas Y. Crowell, 1977.

_____. *The Very Busy Spider*. New York: Philomel, 1985.

_____. *The Very Hungry Caterpillar*. New York: Collins World, 1969.

Chall, Jeanne S. *Classic American Readers*. Kansas City, Mo.: Andrews & McMeel, 1994. (Titles in series include *About Animals and Plants*, *Ancient Myths and Legends*, *A Book of Tales*, *Life in Early America*, *Selections of Famous Writers*, and *Stories of the American Revolution*.)

_____. *Learning to Read: The Great Debate*. New York: McGraw Hill, 1967.

_____. *Learning to Read: The Great Debate*, 3rd ed. New York: McGraw Hill, 1996.

_____. "Learning to Read: The Great Debate 20 Years Later—A Response to 'Debunking the Great Phonics Myth.'" *Phi Delta Kappan*, 70 (March 1989): 521–539.

Clay, Marie. *Becoming Literate: The Construction of Inner Control*. Portsmouth, N.H.: Heinemann, 1991.

Coon, Dennis. *Introduction to Psychology: Exploration and Application*, 5th ed. Minneapolis, Minn.: West Educational Publishing, 1989.

Dechant, Emerald. *Whole-Language Reading: A Comprehensive Teaching Guide*. Lancaster, Pa.: Technomic, 1993.

Duffy, Gerald G., and Laura R. Roehler. *Improving Classroom Reading Instruction: A Decision-Making Approach*, 3rd ed. New York: McGraw Hill, 1993.

Elson, William H., and William S. Gray. *Elson Basic Readers, Book Four*. Chicago: Scott, Foresman, 1931.

Elson, William H., and Christine Keck. *Elson Grammar School Reader, Book Four*. Chicago: Scott, Foresman, 1909.

Fowler, Teri. "Fluency in Reading: Risk Success." *Reading Improvement* 30, no. 2 (Summer 1993): 109–112.

Fries, Charles C. *Linguistics and Reading*. New York: Holt, Rinehart & Winston, 1962.

Goodman, Kenneth. "Foreword: Lots of Changes But Little Gained." In *Basal Readers: A Second Look*, edited by Patrick Shannon and Kenneth Goodman, xiii–xxvii. Katonah, N.Y.: Richard C. Owen, 1994.

Goodman, Kenneth, Lisa Maras, and Debbie Birdseye. "Look! Look! Who Stole the Pictures from the Picture Book?" In *Basal Readers: A Second Look*, edited by Patrick Shannon and Kenneth Goodman, 35–56. Katonah, N.Y.: Richard C. Owen, 1994.

Goodman, Kenneth S., Patrick Shannon, Yvonne S. Freeman, and Sharon Murphy. *Report Card on Basal Readers*. Katonah, N.Y.: Richard C. Owen, 1987.

Gray, Lillian. *Teaching Children to Read*, 3rd ed. New York: The Ronald Press Company, 1963.

Gray, William S., A. Sterl Artley, May Hill Arbuthnot, and Lillian Gray. *Guidebook: The New Fun with Dick and Jane*. Chicago: Scott, Foresman, 1951.

Huey, Edmund Burke. *The Psychology and Pedagogy of Reading*. New York: Macmillan, 1908.

Kirk, David. *Miss Spider's Tea Party*. New York: Scholastic, 1994.

Luke, Allan. "Making Dick and Jane: Historical Genesis of the Modern Basal Reader." *Teachers College Record*, 89, no. 1 (Fall 1987): 91–116.

Marksheffel, Ned D. *Better Reading in the Secondary School.* New York: The Ronald Press Company, 1966.

McGuffey, W. H. *McGuffey's Eclectic Primer.* New York: Van Nostrand Reinhold, 1881.

Mullis, Ina V. S., Jay R. Campbell, and Alan E. Farstrup. *NAEP 1992 Reading Report Card for the Nation and the States.* Washington, D.C.: U.S. Department of Education, 1992.

Rosenblatt, Louise. "Literary Theory." In *Handbook of Research on Teaching the English Language Arts* edited by James Flood, Julie M. Jensen, Diane Lapp, and James R. Squire, 57–62. New York: Macmillan, 1991.

Rubin, Dorothy. *A Practical Approach to Teaching Reading.* 2nd ed. Boston: Allyn & Bacon, 1993.

Schmitt, Maribeth Cassidy, and James F. Baumann. "How to Incorporate Comprehension Monitoring Strategies into Basal Reader Instruction." *The Reading Teacher* 40, no. 1 (Oct. 1986): 28–31.

Shannon, Patrick. *Broken Promises: Reading Instruction in Twentieth-Century America.* New York: Bergin & Garvey, 1989.

Thorndyke, Edward L. *Education: A First Book.* New York: Macmillan, 1912.

Townsend, John Rowe. *Written for Children.* New York: J. B. Lippincott, 1983.

2

Instructional Reading Approaches

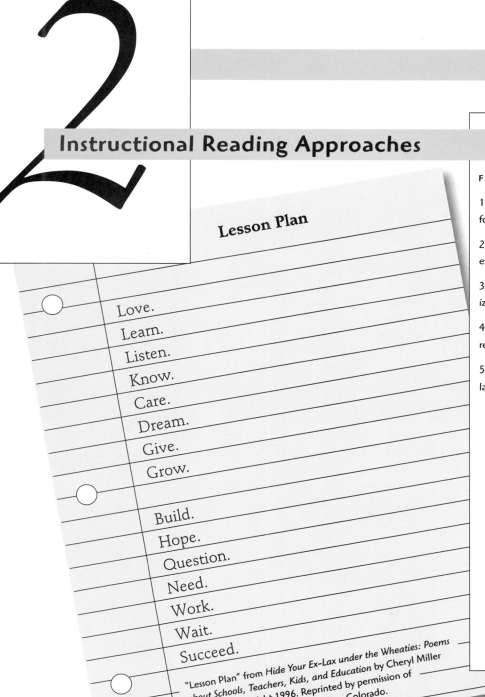

Lesson Plan

Love.
Learn.
Listen.
Know.
Care.
Dream.
Give.
Grow.

Build.
Hope.
Question.
Need.
Work.
Wait.
Succeed.

"Lesson Plan" from *Hide Your Ex-Lax under the Wheaties: Poems about Schools, Teachers, Kids, and Education* by Cheryl Miller Thurston. Copyright 1996. Reprinted by permission of Cottonwood Press, Inc., Fort Collins, Colorado.

FOCUS QUESTIONS

1. How are basals used for instruction?

2. What is the language experience approach?

3. What is an individualized reading program?

4. What is a literature reading program?

5. What is whole language?

"Instruction refers to what someone or something does or says that has the potential to teach one or more individuals what they do not know, do not understand, or cannot do" (Durkin 1990, 472). During my teaching career in classroom, clinic, and resource room, I have taught using basal readers, the language experience approach, individualized reading, linguistics, a literature-based program, and whole language. Like many experienced teachers, I believe I have been on a journey, with many stops along the way. Each of these "layovers" has included a set of experiences and understandings that I've absorbed and taken along to the next stop, as I built a repertoire of practices that I could then match to the needs of my students.

You may have a clear sense of how you prefer to learn and teach, perhaps because of your experiences as a learner. Or you may find the prospect of teaching reading intimidating. Either way you will soon find out that you too have embarked on a career-long journey, and at each layover, you will find yourself endeavoring to keep the best of what you know even as you add something new to your repertoire. It is important that you develop a basic understanding of various instructional methods if only to be able to use the vocabulary common to your profession; however, it is more important that you understand what choices will be available to you and also that many of these choices overlap. Further, you may find that what works in one setting or with one individual or group doesn't work in another setting. The following discussions are drawn from a variety of experts and from my own experiences as a classroom teacher and reading specialist. Each section addresses the following aspects of the program or philosophy: environment; grouping; skills; direct, indirect, planned, and unplanned instruction; collaboration; responsibility; evaluation; and teaching diverse learners. Some of the details will overlap, and many topics, such as evaluation, will be developed more fully in subsequent chapters. However, this chapter should clarify the choices available to you as you become an effective reading teacher.

Teaching Reading with Basal Texts

Chapter 1 provided a historical overview of reading textbooks. If you think back to the evolutionary nature of these textbooks, you will recall that the readers of the 1800s often included written work from writers of the times. In contrast, basal readers of the mid 1900s featured carefully constructed texts. Now we see that readers have largely returned to the practice of using **literary wholes**.

Literary wholes
Complete stories, poems, and articles rather than excerpts or adaptations.

Briefly, today's basal textbooks feature collections of stories, essays, articles, and poetry written or chosen for a specific grade or reading level. The stories may be drawn from current children's or young adult literature and may be excerpted or included in wholes. Vocabulary development is carefully monitored, and word analysis is taught deliberately. Comprehension is taught throughout the elementary and middle school grades in a systematic sequence. The texts are presented with attractive, full-color layouts, although sometimes illustrations from storybooks are eliminated due to space constraints, altering their interplay with the text (Goodman, Maras, and Birdseye 1994, 46–47).

The teacher's manuals that accompany today's basal readers provide detailed, minute-by-minute instructions, and management suggestions and usually emphasize mastery learning. Auxiliary materials include such items as CD-ROM software, videodiscs, workbooks, reproducible worksheets, posters, cassettes, Big Books, word cards, letter cards, project cards, films, enrichment materials, assessment measures, software, and teacher resources (Goodman 1994, xxi–xxii). Tests that have been developed from the materials enable the teacher to monitor student progress. A recent development, the **portfolio** system, is gaining popularity with teachers, students, and parents (see Chapter 12). Writing is also a part of these programs, but the activities are often driven more by the skills being taught than by the process of communication and self-expression (Maras 1994, 84).

Portfolio
A collection of a student's best work over time.

Basal reading programs cannot be characterized as using one instructional approach. Different basals emphasize different theories of learning. For example, one program may focus on a bottom-up theory of reading, while another presents an interactive approach. This said, they do have common components, but before we examine them, a few comments on the advantages and disadvantages of the commercial programs will give you some perspective.

As noted, teacher's manuals leave little to the teacher's imagination. Every stage of instruction—from readiness to extension—is carefully scripted. The teacher is told exactly how to teach the lessons and often even what to say. In general, one need only progress through the many discrete steps of the lesson—lesson plans or systems of accountability are almost not necessary. Some teachers (and their students) will find such a directive program stifling. However, for the inexperienced teacher they can provide valuable on-the-job training (McCallum 1988, 207).

The commercial programs provide a vast array of materials for instruction, practice, review, remediation, supplementary instruction, and evaluation. The materials also include management techniques and systems, support for teachers, and research. Many education majors take only one course in reading and only one course in language arts methods. To expect inexperienced teachers to devise an entire reading program for a class of 25 or 30 students risks failure for both the students and the teacher. Teachers who use basal readers in a critical manner can provide students with sound reading instruction, especially if they are willing to adapt or abandon components as necessary, evaluate the success of the lessons, and consult alternative resources for additional information.

ENVIRONMENT

Typically, teachers who use basal texts primarily will organize their rooms to accommodate those materials. Various textbooks will be grouped on the shelves to correspond to the reading groups. Workbooks for each text or unit may be stacked on shelves or kept in the students' desks. Worksheets may be stored on shelves or in filing cabinets. Auxiliary materials, such as charts, posters, or student guidelines, will be provided by the publisher rather than be student-produced, although student-created materials may be in evidence. Because basal materials are relatively expensive and require much paper for the reproducibles, there may be few supplementary picture books or novels in the classroom. However, some teachers use only the basal texts, preferring other activities over workbooks, worksheets, or expensive auxiliary materials. Students usually sit at tables or desks, with a small table in another area with a chalk board, pocket chart, or chart paper nearby for reading-group instruction.

GROUPING

For efficiency, most teachers who use basal materials traditionally divide their class into three instructional groups. This usually includes one group that reads more fluently, one at the designated grade level for the basal series, and one that reads easier texts. Some teachers work together, pooling their students to create five or six groups that accommodate achievement levels more closely. This practice requires careful scheduling and can thus limit flexibility. Decisions regarding placement in groups are normally determined by beginning-of-the-year tests provided by the program. Because students often progress unevenly, groups should be flexible to allow for change throughout the year.

SKILLS: DIRECT, INDIRECT, PLANNED, AND UNPLANNED INSTRUCTION

Basal materials rely primarily on direct, planned instruction to teach reading skills, and they generally include between 150 and 200 separate skills in the elementary program (Crawford and Shannon 1994, 7). With the best of intentions, publishers have endeavored to provide materials that will be successful with all teachers and all students. The public perception that students are not learning the "skills" of reading has led to increasing emphasis on ensuring that *all* the necessary skills are taught, practiced, and evaluated. The result—a potentially overwhelming emphasis on skills mastery—can elicit dismay at the preponderance of exercises that take away time that could be spent experiencing the magic of reading and writing (Edelsky 1994, 33).

A skills-based curriculum is based on several premises: that children need to learn the rules of spoken language for correct usage; that they should use texts that have familiar vocabulary and sentence structure; that they should demonstrate mastery of a skill before moving on to another skill or assignment; that drill and practice reinforce reading and writing skills; and that mastery of the conventions of print is critical to success.

Attempting to teach such an extensive list of skills puts pressure on teachers, on administrators, and ultimately on students. Aside from the reams of worksheets that demand completion from day to day, the implication is that teachers must ensure that each and every student achieves adequate mastery at each and every grade level. Because the materials are expensive and constitute a signficant financial commitment on the part of the district, it is difficult for teachers to choose not to use them. Also, some teachers have been trained to believe that such materials are the basic elements of the language arts program—therefore, they must be used.

Many basal reading programs emphasize seatwork. This is not always the best choice; many lessons are more effective when they are taught orally (Veatch 1978, 144). The most important criticism of seatwork is that it takes up valuable time that could be spent actually reading and writing.

Finally, teachers of skills-based series relinquish control of the instruction and student learning to the publishers of the series. As Patrick Shannon emphasizes, the publisher has made the decisions regarding the components of the lessons; all that is left to teachers is to determine the pace of the class (1989, 627). For example, when the program is based on the bottom-up theory of carefully building skills knowledge, instruction is systematically planned. The teacher's manual provides a carefully scripted sequence of questions to ask, activities to implement, and worksheets to assign (Crawford and Shannon 1994, 17–18). For example, the manual might provide a lesson on how *gh* is silent when a selection features several words such as *light*, *night*, or *sight*, and the worksheets provide practice using this rule. Students are taught in small groups with reteaching integrated into the program through frequent **criterion-referenced tests** (see Chapter 12).

■ **Criterion-referenced tests**
Tests based on comparing performance to a standard, such as demonstrating mastery at the 80 percent level.

This systematic presentation of teaching skills can also be seen as an advantage, as Robert C. Aukerman found in his review of 15 basal reading series. Here are some of the advantages he cited: the sequential programs of vocabulary development, the developmental plans of word-analysis techniques, the developmental sequencing of comprehension skills throughout the entire elementary grades, and well-developed management systems assuring mastery learning (1981, 333). In basal programs, assessments of progress are ongoing and easily documented through the assignments. Seatwork can be modified to fit individual needs; assignments can be eliminated or extra practice added. Worksheet assignments also provide the student with directions and assignments similar to that found in standardized tests. Good worksheets ensure that students practice needed skills, follow directions, work independently, and use a variety of test formats.

Teachers who use commercially prepared materials should critique each assignment carefully. Although duplicating masters on many topics or with various activities can be purchased readily, not all of them have merit. For example, let's consider word searches, typical activities found in many programs. The word searches are keyed not only to the text, but also to such subjects as books that have won the prestigious Newbery award. However, there is little educational value in completing a word search. Methodically checking each row for possible words going up, down, or at angles involves only persistence and dedication to a tedious task and does not promote critical thinking skills. When a poorly duplicated word search is assigned to a child with visual difficulties or learning disabilities, it becomes a painful process. Indeed, assigning such a chore borders on the irresponsible. Before you assign seatwork, ask yourself whether the skill can be taught more effectively in another form. If the seatwork is the only practical choice, ask whether the assignment has value for the learner.

Some teachers find basal programs confining; others use them as a framework for individual creativity. Some teachers feel pressure to cover everything; others find it comforting to know that everything in the curriculum is planned and provided. Good teachers use these materials selectively, omitting repetitious assignments and adapting activities and questions for their groups. Experienced teachers also know that indirect or unplanned instruction (discussed more fully in later sections) is necessary for effective learning.

COLLABORATION

Because of the carefully scripted instructional program, basal series do relatively little to foster collaboration among students. Students work in small groups only to review and discuss an assigned story; the groups are directed by the teacher who is in turn following instructions in the teacher's manual. Students usually read silently and complete the worksheets at their desks, but they rarely work in pairs or small groups where they are responsible for the outcome. Opportunities for collaboration generally occur only when the teacher determines that students have time for one of the extensions, such as developing a story into a play, completing an art project, or writing a group story.

RESPONSIBILITY

The teacher holds primary responsibility for students' progress. Although students complete the worksheets and read the stories, responsibility for success remains with the teacher. Students rarely have ownership of the process because they don't participate in deciding what stories they will read or how they will practice skills.

EVALUATION

Evaluation
Collecting and using information to determine how a student learns and to monitor the student's progress and achievement.

Checklists
Informal records that allow teachers to check off student accomplishments, skills, interests, and progress.

Informal reading inventory (IRI)
Graded passages of reading that can be used to determine students' strengths and weaknesses in recognizing words and comprehending text.

Evaluation is both frequent and formal in basal programs. Teachers ask many questions during discussions of the stories, articles, and poems, and many series have placement tests, end-of-unit, end-of-book, end-of-level, and individual skills tests. Typically, skills mastery is expected to be at the 80 percent level before students move to the next level or unit. When reteaching or retesting is necessary, teachers can select from a variety of published materials, or they can supplement with teacher-made materials. School districts may have criterion-referenced tests (see Chapter 12) closely tied to the basal programs. These tests are often administered on a schoolwide basis two or more times per year.

Some teachers adapt basal evaluation materials. For example, they can elect to use end-of-unit tests before they begin a unit; then they can skip teaching skills students have already mastered. Good teachers also use informal evaluation measures to supplement those in basal programs, and to meet these needs, some basal series now provide **checklists**. The program may also include **informal reading inventories** (IRIs) and other informal measures (Murphy 1994, 104). However, the frequency with which formal measures occur makes it challenging to manage many additional informal practices.

TEACHING DIVERSE LEARNERS

STUDENTS WITH SPECIAL NEEDS

The Individuals with Disabilities Education Act stipulates that students with disabilities be placed in the least restrictive environment so that they will have opportunities to be educated with children who do not have disabilities (Sawyer, McLaughlin, and Winglee 1994, 204). With the possible exception of students with mental retardation or serious emotional disturbance, data indicate that an increasing number of students with disabilities are being served in the general classroom (ibid., 212). With mainstreaming continually increasing, teachers are looking closely at how well basal materials serve all students.

Because of the individualized nature of special students who have academic or physical challenges, it is difficult to make generalizations about the effectiveness of basal materials for these students. However, the personalized instruction often required by these students is one area in which basal programs are not particularly strong. The standard tests inadequately diagnose reading difficulties, and students may perform poorly due to the very nature of the tests. Still, Ruth Lyn Meese emphasizes that a basal's early emphasis on phonics skills and sight word recognition may be useful for remedial readers (1994, 210). For some students, the repetition and carefully sequenced progression of a basal may be just right; for others, more repetition on particular skills or practices may be necessary, and the teacher will need to customize the instruction to provide adequate instruction.

Potential areas of concern can even include components as fundamental to the program as the worksheets and group learning. For students with handwriting difficulties, the constraints of the worksheet blanks can be very frustrating. Other special students may have difficulty concentrating during the small- or large-group instruction that occurs frequently with basal texts.

Some students may simply need more help than the classroom teacher can reasonably provide. It is not unusual to find a grade-level achievement span of three or more years in a regular classroom. Students with learning challenges may read two or more years below their grade level, and continued placement in an inappropriate reading group will affect their self-esteem and limit their sense of accomplishment. In the past, students with this great a discrepancy received help from reading specialists, but with shrinking budgets and mainstreaming, classroom teachers often find themselves responsible for a least a portion, and perhaps all, of a special student's reading instruction.

Another category of students with special needs—those identified as gifted—may not have many outside resources available to them either, and they too will need ample opportunities to advance, to pursue independent research, and to read literature independently of the basal program. Given the diversity of learning needs in today's typical classroom, it is more important than ever to monitor reading groups and to provide a variety of experiences—experiences that inspire all students to become avid readers.

TEACHING MULTICULTURISM

Basal readers should be carefully analyzed for their portrayals of cultures, sexes, professions, ages, and so forth. Critics of basal readers have pointed to their stereotyped images, particularly their emphasis on white males. In response, basal series have added multicultural children's literature and lessons. However, because of the very nature of basal texts, excerpts often present only a brief exposure to a particular culture, thereby shortchanging the reader. In a survey of how one publisher treated a story for first graders about an African-

American child and an Anglo-American child, Elaine Schwartz found that the multicultural ideas were lost in the more than 50 lessons and activities that accompanied the story (1994, 95). Schwartz concluded

Basals continue to represent linear, Western perceptions of ways of knowing, learning, and doing, while multiculturalism requires [that] other voices and ways of knowing be validated. Without serious consideration of Eastern philosophy, women's ways of knowing, and native transcendentalism, basals provide a tourists' sweep through other cultures and ways of thinking and acting (ibid., 101).

It is easy to dismiss the biases in basal texts by assuming that teachers will monitor and neutralize bias and that they can make a significant difference in how children interpret what they read. However, Cathy M. Roller contends that communication patterns in basal texts contribute to the sorting and stratification process that perpetuates and maintains our class- and race-stratified society (1989, 493). Basal lessons are dominated by the **IRE model**. In this model, the teacher dominates and controls the discussion, and the children communicate the essentials, reflecting what the teacher expects to hear. The students who can achieve within this system are "successful"; those who do not are sorted into middle and low reading groups. Roller points out that these interaction patterns can be influenced by class and race; children in the lower groups spend proportionately more time in the teacher-dominated interaction patterns (ibid., 498). Further, Peter Freebody and Carolyn D. Baker contend that children's readers are an early introduction to the school culture, mediating and shaping the relationship between children and school (1985, 396).

Recently, publishers have increased the number of multicultural selections in basals. Elaine Schwartz found that Harcourt Brace Jovanovich and Silver Burdett-Ginn have added specific statements on multiculturalism and multicultural children's literature by well-known educators (1994, 93). While she commends the publishers for no longer including multiculturalism as an afterthought, she expresses concern that the many exercises accompanying the selections lessen the positive effect of incorporating more balance (ibid., 95). As with other issues, the teacher must work to ensure a balance in a basal reading program.

> ■ **IRE model**
> The teacher **i**nitiates through a question; the student **r**esponds; and the teacher **e**valuates.

Language Experience Approach

> ■ **Language experience approach (LEA)**
> An early language arts approach based on students' experiences.

The **language experience approach** (LEA), an approach based on the top-down theory of reading, emphasizes the experiences that children talk about, translate into written text, and read (Stauffer 1980). Because these reading experiences develop from children's early speaking, listening, and life experiences, LEA serves as a natural starting place for reading. It can be an effective bridge to basal readers, literature, and trade books, or a component of a whole-language program (Dechant 1993, 83).

The experiences of an individual student or of the entire class comprise the starting point for LEAs, with the teacher instigating a discussion of these experiences. According to Roach Van Allen, the following characteristics distinguish this approach:

1. Word recognition and vocabulary growth develop from the oral language background of the children.

2. Reading vocabulary and words of high frequency are introduced through natural language.

3. Individual growth is emphasized.

4. Grouping is used for specific needs.

5. Language experiences stimulate the activities, selection of materials, and learning events.

6. Word recognition skills are closely related to writing and spelling.

7. Children use a variety of books and other materials, such as films, photographs, art, and music.

8. Children express themselves through a variety of media.

9. Reading is a process of reconstructing oral language that has been written (1976, 19–22).

In practice, briefly, the individual or group decides what should be written down. Depending on the experience or the children, this written record might be a story, chart, list, poem, or reflections. Students dictate while the teacher writes or do their own writing. Finally, the students read what has been written. Using the written pieces, the teacher provides instruction based on the piece in its entirety, as well as on sentences, word meaning, word recognition, and the relationships of phonemes to graphemes. This approach emphasizes a top-down approach as the student moves from reading of the whole to focusing on graphophonics.

The language experience approach is primarily used in the early instructional stages such as preschool through first or second grade. As you will see, the emphasis on individual or whole-group experiences makes this an effective approach for students with special needs, because children begin by reading and writing about their own experiences. Many LEA teachers move students into a literature-based program or a basal series when students have the requisite sight words and skills.

A teacher writes a
story on a chart.

ENVIRONMENT

The LEA environment is generally more informal than a traditional textbook-dominated classroom. The classroom hums with students involved in activities that relate to and inspire their experience stories. Roach Van Allen advocates a variety of centers, such as the Discussion Center, the Arts and Crafts Center, the Cooking Center, the Discovery Center, and the Language Study Center, to name a few (1976, 66). The Discussion Center can be used for such activities as introducing new topics, sharing, solving problems, and planning. The Discovery Center features materials that encourage students to explore and name things, such as a microscope for looking at plants or insects (ibid., 69). There may be a post office area that inspires role-playing in addition to writing letters that will actually be mailed. The Language Study Center provides opportunities to acquire sight vocabulary and functional grammar (ibid., 71). The environment should inspire spontaneous free play, while providing areas for whole- and small-group instruction. These might include a carpeted area, small tables, or movable furniture. (See Part Two of *Language Experience Activities* by Roach Van Allen and Claryce Allen for an abundance of activities that can occur in the centers.)

The classrooms include a wide variety of print materials: books, magazines, newspapers, comic books, and so forth. Labels help organize the room and encourage independent reading and writing. Student-written stories are posted around the room, and students are encouraged to reread them frequently. Writing materials are available everywhere in the room. Students may write in the theme areas, such as the post office or grocery store, at a writing center, in the book area, on the chalkboard, or on chart paper. Writing is a functional part of each day—stories are written to record spontaneous events, and directions, checklists, and "how-to" charts are written whenever an opportunity presents itself.

GROUPING

Groups change regularly in the LEA classroom, in part due to the nature of the experiences. On any given day, one group explores a common interest, one group works on a skill, and another works toward a goal they have identified, while the teacher makes plans for a whole-class experience.

Whole-class experiences are particularly important for students who come to school without rich experiential backgrounds. The teacher may plan something simple, such as blowing bubbles, then have the students write a whole-class story about the event on chart paper. The students practice rereading the experience stories as a group. Individual versions, sentence strips, and word cards drawn from the story may be replicated for repeated independent readings. Emerald Dechant lists the following steps for developing a language experience story:

1. Provide for commonality of experience (for example, a field trip) or identify an experience that the children have shared as a group. The experience story may grow out of a simple picture.

2. Have children discuss and describe their experiences. Children have a natural inclination to want to talk about their experiences, either as individuals or as a group. They love to tell about a mountain trip, fishing at a lake, planting a garden. . . . The teacher helps children to identify significant ideas, to decide on the sequence, and to choose appropriate vocabulary. . . .

3. Record the story of narrative on the chalkboard. The story in the early grades may be short, consisting of perhaps three or four lines. At beginning reading levels, each new sentence should begin on a new line. After the first draft has been written, assist children in revising their sentences. Ringler and Weber (1984, 96–102) describe three types of experience charts: the personal experience or narrative chart; the work or directions (how to do it) chart; and the reading strategy or skill-teaching chart (e.g., summarizing of text).

4. Read the narrative as a whole, moving one hand from left to right in a smooth flowing motion under each word.

5. Have the children read the whole story aloud with the teacher.

6. Have individual children read the story one sentence at a time. Children's memory spans are usually adequate to "read" back simple sentences.

7. Transcribe the story onto chart paper (the experience chart). Make two charts: one of which becomes a part of the children's book of stories and the second of which is used for teaching purposes.

8. Cut the story from one of the charts into sentence strips and help pupils to read the sentences fluently.

9. Isolate parts of the story for specific emphasis, such as the teaching of a specific word, of a specific grapheme-phoneme correspondence, or of a specific meaning or comprehension skill.

10. Have the children read the story again as a whole. This may take the form of silent, choral, or individual oral reading.

11. Make a file of experience charts and label them Our (My) Big Book.

12. Begin a card file of sight words, help children develop a picture dictionary, and start each child's phonogram book. The card file or word bank, consisting of a 3 × 5-inch file box with index cards, may contain word categories for such diverse groupings as words for things, people, or animals; words for days of the week; words for weather; and words for different colors. It may contain groupings of question words, or words that tell when, where, how many, and words that describe actions.

13. Have children reread the stories occasionally.

(Reprinted with permission from *Whole Language Reading: A Comprehensive Teaching Guide* by Emerald Dechant, 1993, Technomic Publishing, Lancaster, Pa., 345–346.)

Not every whole-class experience results in a story. After visiting a zoo, a group of first grade students may want to list all the animals they saw and sort them by various categories (mammals, reptiles, and so forth). Or they may decide to collaborate on a newsletter that describes everything they saw during the field trip, sending copies of the newspaper home to parents.

SKILLS: DIRECT, INDIRECT, PLANNED, AND UNPLANNED INSTRUCTION

Teachers use the language experience approach to provide both direct and indirect skills instruction, with emphasis on the latter because it encourages students to discover the relationships and understandings themselves. Although a teacher may have a general direction in mind, much of the instruction is unplanned—it evolves from the needs of the students. This practice is in sharp contrast to basal readers where textbooks develop mastery by building on a carefully planned sequence of skill instruction.

Returning to our *gh* example, the LEA teacher notices that a student is having trouble reading the word *straight* in written form. The teacher writes *light* on a piece of paper or the chalkboard, discusses how this word has the same feature, and asks the student to think of others. They might discuss other featured words; the teacher points out how the *gh* is silent in all of them. The student then transfers these words to a personal list to help remember them. In this unplanned, *direct* instruction, the teacher demonstrates the distinction directly.

In contrast, during unplanned, *indirect* instruction, the teacher may, for example, take a moment during the reading to ask the student to recall another word with *gh*, knowing that the student can now read the word *light*. Usually, the student responds with "I get it! You don't hear the *gh*, just like in *light*!" After acknowledging the correct conclusion, the teacher moves on with the reading. Here the teacher, upon realizing the problem, sets up a situation where the student can recognize the relationship between the words independently.

When a student or group needs further instruction, the teacher may plan for indirect or direct instruction to occur at another time. For example, the teacher reads a Big Book story aloud because it has the *gh* pattern, commenting afterward that you don't hear the *gh* with these words. In a more direct approach, the teacher reads the story aloud and follows it with a discussion of all the *gh* words, listing them on the board and discussing how they feature these silent letters.

COLLABORATION

In an informal sense, collaboration is central to the LEA classroom. The very nature of this approach, with its group-experience stories, role-playing, and functional writing, fosters collaboration. Students are generally not assigned to groups to perform specific learning tasks; instead, they are encouraged to form spontaneous groups to pursue an interest, to create a story inspired by a common experience, or to discuss a project. The entire group works together more often than in most reading models, because much of the reading and writing is driven by whole-group experiences or common interests.

RESPONSIBILITY

Students in the LEA classroom have a tremendous amount of ownership in their learning. Most of their reading and writing activities are directed from their personal backgrounds and eventually from school. Although the development of the group stories is managed by the teacher, the students take responsibility by guiding the content and rereading the product. Students also take responsibility for creating much of the print that is displayed around the classroom, such as directions, lists, or a record of plant growth.

EVALUATION

Evaluation in the LEA classroom should include processes that help students look at themselves and where they stand in relation to their schoolwork (Veatch 1978, 519). Jeannette Veatch emphasizes the role of student conferences throughout this literacy model. Not only do students and teachers confer about words and books, they also evaluate progress daily. The teacher listens to students read a selected passage aloud and helps them improve their read-aloud skills. Conference records may be brief or detailed; they are kept to help determine report card grades if required.

Although there are many informal measures, such as checklists, informal reading inventories, and teacher-made tests, teachers may also be required by the district to give standardized tests, both criterion-referenced and norm-referenced (see Chapter 12). These test results must be considered in light of the entire learning program and can be supplemented by a variety of informal measures.

TEACHING DIVERSE LEARNERS

This approach is ideal for the young multicultural classroom. It fosters a gradual transition from the home language environment to school and other formal environments, allowing students to adapt more naturally. The language experience approach recognizes the first language as an important contribution to the student's background. Using the student's listening and speaking skills as the source of reading and writing experiences and instruction further validates the individual's cultural background. Because students make their own texts from their own written material, they not only learn that what they say can be represented in print but also that what they say has value. Students can choose books that are of interest to them and can work in groups that share their interest. They can thus investigate their culture's customs, leaders, or historical events, further validating their personal histories.

Special students with learning or physical handicaps usually thrive with this approach because of its highly personalized nature. The student chooses areas of interest to pursue; this is highly motivating. This can be especially effective for the gifted student who enjoys working independently.

Mismatches between the student's oral language and written materials are prevented, diminishing the gap between reader and text (Dechant 1993, 82). Students reap benefits in other ways because they enjoy reading what they have written. Indeed, resource or remedial reading teachers who take the students out of the classroom for individualized or small-group instruction often use this approach, particularly if the classroom teacher uses basal texts.

Individualized Reading Program

> **Individualized reading**
> An approach to reading that emphasizes student selection of reading materials, self-pacing, small-group work, and conferences.

Individualized reading programs, an approach based on the top-down theory of reading, make use of the notion that children are highly motivated to learn and that they will naturally seek out learning experiences that are appropriate and necessary. Therefore, self-selection and pacing are integral to these programs. Students are encouraged to follow their interests, determine their course of action, and pursue the learning with a high degree of independence, choosing their own books and reading at their own pace.

Teachers of this approach agree with Richard L. Allington, who stresses that children should be allowed to read in increasing amounts and without interruptions (1977). This personalized approach of allowing students to choose their own materials can be especially satisfying for students who like ownership in the process. Many teachers will build early reading skills through the language experience approach and move students into individualized reading once they can read beginning books independently.

Of all the reading programs, the individualized approach is probably the most demanding on the teacher. Conferences, integral to the program, provide direction, feedback, and a source of records for evaluation. The teacher may meet for only 5 or 10 minutes with each student, but meeting with every student individually is demanding. Because of the individualized nature, this program involves a large amount of paperwork and management. Teachers also need to have a strong background in literature, although they can certainly learn the literature along with the students. Students who have difficulty working independently or pacing themselves may make poor choices for this program. They may drift through the day, requiring structure such as checklists or contracts. However, many principles of individualized reading endure in classrooms today.

ENVIRONMENT

The environment for an individualized reading program using literature is very similar to that in the language experience classroom. Shelves hold a minimum of four to five books per student for reading, research, and writing. There may be centers for writing and content areas, but theme-related centers are not as common. Instead, energy is directed toward organizing the vast amount of materials necessary for independent work. Therefore, print displays that organize the room and provide directions are important for both students and teacher.

The physical arrangement of the classroom reflects the independent work approach. Students may work at desks or small tables, but small- and whole-group instruction occurs less frequently than in other models. The teacher spends more time with individuals than with groups and usually has students come to a small table or the teacher's desk for conferences.

GROUPING

Because instruction is personalized, small-group instruction occurs less frequently, usually when the teacher realizes that several students need direct instruction on the same skill. A visitor to this classroom will see students working at their desks or at centers with relatively little interaction. Most teachers will still have some whole-class activities, such as reading aloud or group story writing after an experience such as a field trip. Generally, the emphasis is directed at independent progress.

SKILLS: DIRECT, INDIRECT, PLANNED, AND UNPLANNED INSTRUCTION

In exemplary individualized reading programs, skill instruction emphasizes indirect and unplanned instruction when students need help, and evaluation determines whether they have successfully mastered the skills. Skills are taught in conferences when it becomes clear that the student needs assistance to continue to progress, although small groups are formed occasionally for planned instruction. Commercial or teacher-created worksheets may supplement the reading, and students usually work independently on skills when difficulties are diagnosed. Teaching skills on an entirely individualized basis can be particularly challenging with a large class.

COLLABORATION

Because of the independent nature of the learning, collaboration during the instruction phase of this program is less evident. However, for an individualized reading program to be successful, students provide informal support and must work together to keep the room organized and functional. Though students may not work in pairs or small groups to accomplish this, they have an investment in maintaining a smooth routine. This means not only taking individual responsibility for managing books and materials but also keeping the needs of the group in mind.

RESPONSIBILITY

A key principle of the individualized reading program is the assumption that students will take great ownership in their progress. Students choose their reading, manage their pacing, and determine extensions to their reading. One interesting strategy used in this program is the "Rule of Thumb" for book selection. The student opens a book to the middle and reads a page of text, putting down a finger for each unknown word encountered. If the student puts down all four fingers plus the thumb, the book is too hard. No fingers down indicates the book is too easy, and two or three unknown words indicates the book is approximately at the student's instructional level. Although not necessarily always accurate, this method provides students with a way to assess a book's difficulty by themselves.

The teacher guides and recommends during conferences, but usually the ultimate responsibility falls on the students. Because some students prefer not to take responsibility for conferences, teachers often require a minimum number of meetings per month or schedule some routine conferences interspersed with opportunities to sign up for additional consultations. Students who are accustomed to a more structured, teacher-directed model, may feel overwhelmed when they first assume responsibility for their own learning. These students will initially need support in managing their progress, perhaps with checklists or contracts negotiated with the teacher.

EVALUATION

Evaluation is ongoing in an individualized program, with the form of evaluation reflecting the materials in use. A teacher using literature will have more informal evaluations during reading conferences, perhaps asking the student to read a passage aloud to check word recognition skills or asking questions to determine understanding. Criterion-referenced tests required by the district will be useful only if they are linked to students' independent reading levels. This complicates administration, because these tests generally require generous amounts of administrative time. If the teacher cannot give individualized tests, some students may perform poorly and feel unsuccessful. Further, the standardized test results will not be as useful in planning further instruction.

TEACHING DIVERSE LEARNERS

An individualized reading program can be especially useful for students from other cultures. In a program that uses literature, students can pursue their own interests, often finding familiar stories that help smooth their transition from personal experience to school. The program can be structured so that students learn meaningful skills that help them with practical needs, such as reading signs, buying groceries, or reading menus. Conversely, the individualized nature of this program can further isolate students who would benefit from higher levels of social interaction. Thus the teacher must work hard to ensure that second-language learners have many opportunities to interact and converse.

Students with learning disabilities or physical limitations often find an individualized program more attuned to their needs. They usually appreciate the personalized nature of the reading conferences and feel less stigma than when they are relegated to the "low" reading group. However, some students with learning disabilities have difficulty assuming responsibility for day-to-day tasks and long-term progress. Distractible students may need to use study carrels or have individual management systems; these may involve contracts or behavioral modification. Gifted students often enjoy the opportunity to choose their literature, projects, or research topics. However, these students also need ample opportunities for socialization. As with any program, you must tailor this program to fit the needs of your students.

Literature Reading Program

The literature reading program, drawn from transactional theory, uses children's and young adult trade books as the primary source of reading materials. Although similar to the individualized reading program, which emphasizes individual reading and teacher conferences, this program strives to elicit reader response. To do this, the teacher and students discuss books and share what they have read. Louise Rosenblatt emphasizes that the transaction between reader and text can be powerful. The literary work "gains its significance from the way in which the minds and emotions of particular readers respond to the verbal stimuli offered by the text" (1976, 28). Student readers bring their personalities and experiences to bear on the text, and they take away images and messages that relate to them personally. These elements prompt the student responses, a rich source

A student uses a guide while reading a chapter book.

that provides an endless variety of material that teachers can incorporate into their instruction (ibid., 31). Literature and the student responses become the content and context for discussion and skills development; this transaction between the student reader and the text also inspires many extensions or follow-up activities. Proponents believe that children learn to read by listening to, reading, and discussing authentic literature (that is, literature that is drawn from quality children's literature and magazines), and that students must therefore be immersed in reading entire books (not merely excerpts) of high quality and with rich vocabulary. In this program, students select the books, participate in frequent group discussions, routinely confer with the teacher as an ongoing activity, and take a high degree of responsibility for their work.

The key feature that sets the literature program apart from individualized reading is the stress placed on the importance of sharing what one reads with other students. Students in the literature program read as an emotional outlet and for entertainment. They also read to gain knowledge, to solve problems, to escape, and for many other reasons. They may find themselves immersed in novels, author studies, or in a series of books with similar themes. Through discussion groups, they learn how others react to, interpret, and appreciate the literature they are reading. "Every time a reader experiences a work of art, it is in a sense created anew" (Rosenblatt 1976, 113). In this approach, how students respond to the text is more important than their determining exactly what it means.

ENVIRONMENT

The literature classroom, dominated by trade books, also includes multiple copies of books, magazines, newspapers, reference materials, and miscellaneous print. Because the literature reading program requires an abundance of books, the classroom library is usually supplemented by school and public library books, as well as by the teacher's and students' personal libraries. As in the individualized reading program, organization is a critical factor, because students choose their reading and work independently for extended time periods. Print displays, such as labels and lists, assist with organization, and students learn to keep materials in reasonable order.

Because conferences and group work are also critical in the literature reading program, the teacher will usually organize the room accordingly. A small table may be set aside for individual and small-group conferences or for informal discussions about the different books currently being read. Because reading aloud is important, a large area, usually with a rug, is reserved for whole-class listening and discussion. Students can use these areas for informal discussions, **paired reading**, or other related activities.

■ **Paired reading**
When two students of approximately the same achievement level read together collaboratively.

GROUPING

Grouping changes frequently in the literature-based program. Pairs of students will work together to discuss books they are reading. A group of students will read the same novel and meet to discuss it; these are often called Literature Circles. (See Chapter 9 for a more detailed discussion.) The entire class may occasionally read a novel, although it can be difficult to purchase 25 or 30 copies of many books. Whole-class groupings also occur when the teacher reads aloud or for practical reasons, such as reviewing or planning the day's schedules. Often when other work is completed, students will choose a book for independent reading. In this situation, they will confer with the classroom teacher periodically and pursue some enrichment activity upon completion of the reading.

SKILLS: DIRECT, INDIRECT, PLANNED, AND UNPLANNED INSTRUCTION

A strong component of literature reading programs includes unplanned instruction, which may be direct or indirect. Because students read from trade and informational books, much of the skills instruction evolves from the reading and occurs during these group discussions or conferences. The teacher may notice that several students are struggling with a feature of a book, such as the use of flashback. This device will immediately be discussed, perhaps by asking students to share titles of other books that use this method and by asking them how they could tell when the story was in the present or in the past.

When literature is the major source of instruction, it is tempting to teach everything possible through a story. A simple story such as "The Little Red Hen" might be read and discussed repeatedly to teach grammar (for example, when to use "not I"); dialogue; the use of quotation marks; sequencing and gardening (growing wheat from seeds); seasons; vocabulary (thresh, harvest, mill, ground); and social issues (responsibility, collaboration, the rewards of work). A logical wrap-up activity, baking bread, can be used to teach fractions, measurement, organization, and even scientific principles (for example, how does bread dough rise?). Alternatively, "The Little Red Hen" can also be enjoyed for its delightful simplicity and gentle story. Here the teacher would discuss the message, ask a few questions, reread the story so the students could appreciate its repetition and rhythm, and then students would reread the story individually if they so chose. Literature should not be overused to teach skills. You will be able to maintain a balance between eliciting responses to the literature and using it to teach skills as you become comfortable with the abundance of opportunities you will have to work with literature in this program.

COLLABORATION

■ **Sustained silent reading (SSR)**
A period of independent silent reading. Synonymous to SQUIRT (**s**ustained **q**uiet **u**ninterrupted **i**ndividualized **r**eading **t**ime), DEAR (**d**rop **e**verything **a**nd **r**ead), and USSR (**u**ninterrupted **s**ustained **s**ilent reading).

When novels are read in small groups, collaboration occurs in the discussions and follow-up activities, and can be fostered during the reading through activities such as paired reading. Groups may trade materials, share books, share discussions, and come to consensus on what direction to pursue in the course of reading a novel. The entire class needs to work together to keep the classroom running smoothly. Books and materials must be organized, and this requires the participation of everyone. Students may have extended periods of individualized reading as well, particularly if the teacher or school encourages **sustained silent reading** (SSR) advocated by Lyman C. Hunt as a powerful tool for motivating students (1997).

RESPONSIBILITY

Students in the literature reading program have a high degree of responsibility for the program itself. First, they choose the novel they will read for their literature group; when their group meets, they must be ready to contribute to the discussion. Leadership roles are clearly defined in such activities as Literature Circles (see Chapter 9); leaders of these circles are usually responsible for keeping records throughout the discussion of a novel. It is the group that decides how to complete a project that follows the reading of the novel; all manner of collaborative skills are required here. Grading may depend in part on whether the student takes responsibility for the group's efforts. If students are also reading individually chosen books, they may be the ones who decide when they need a conference to determine follow-up projects, further reading, research areas, and so forth.

EVALUATION

As with the individualized program, evaluation in the literature reading program is ongoing and personalized. Most evaluations occur during the reading conference, with unplanned instruction immediately following diagnosis. Informal record keeping usually includes anecdotes, checklists, or simply notes. Portfolios, a collection of a student's representative work, may be the preferred choice for evaluation. (See Chapter 12 for a discussion of portfolios.) Some teachers keep a notebook with a section for each student, recording the conference highlights during or after consultation. When working in groups or Literature Circles, students may be expected to participate in self-evaluation or group evaluations, reaching consensus with other students and with the teacher on grades. At report card time, students will be involved in reviewing their progress and discussing which grades are appropriate. Because formal testing occurs rarely, students required to take standardized tests may need help understanding the format and expectations.

TEACHING DIVERSE LEARNERS

The variety of materials found in a literature reading program can be advantageous for students from various cultures. Because students can choose to read books about their culture or in their native language, they find affirmation for their backgrounds through reading. This, of course, can be highly motivating. Students' discussion skills and their social skills are enhanced as they work in groups to read and discuss their readings. The research and/or activities inspired by novels provide further opportunities for personal exploration and growth. And, shared experiences strengthen the learning of the entire class.

Both second-language learners and remedial readers can benefit from listening to tapes of books while reading silently. Auditory learners, perhaps not remedial or second language, will also benefit from the use of tapes. Students who have learning difficulties may thrive in Literature Circles, as the group interaction and collaborative activities present different paths to learning that may fit their needs more closely. Knowing others are mutually interested in a particular topic can motivate the student who wants to keep up with the group.

After trying several methods, Marilyn D'Alessandro, who teaches special education students in Brooklyn, found that a literature reading program was especially effective for her emotionally handicapped students. Her 8- and 9-year-old students came from chaotic homes, where they had not learned such basics as their birthdays or appropriate foods. In D'Alessandro's program, her students read aloud extensively and she found this helped them become more attentive, with improved behaviors. Because of the richness and length of her chosen stories, she was able to base many rewarding activities on them—activities that extended the learning. Best of all, her students became readers, and they continued to read after leaving her classroom (1990).

When self-selected independent reading is a component of the literature program, mainstreamed students are not singled out as being slower or needing special treatment because everyone is reading a variety of materials during those times. Indeed, the very best reader in the class may decide to spend a week reading nothing but comic books, an acceptable choice in a literature reading program (Krashen 1993, 56). The line blurs among the gifted, remedial, and regular students, a rare occurrence in our stratified society and a rewarding experience for all involved. As with any self-directed program, some students may need help keeping on track during independent work.

Whole Language

Whole language
A philosophy that
language is acquired
through use and that
advocates using au-
thentic materials,
such as children's lit-
erature, and genuine
literacy events, such
as writing letters.

Proponents of **whole language** believe that all learning experiences should be taught in an integrated manner (as opposed to teaching categories). Thus teaching reading includes teaching listening, speaking, writing, and viewing, *and* all content areas, such as math, social studies, science, art, and music. Depending on the philosophy of the teacher, the interactive or transactional theories of reading may be used to present the whole-language program. Similar to the literature program, the whole-language program is grounded in the belief that children learn best by reading and writing with authentic materials and having legitimate purposes for their reading. Whole language may include elements of the language experience approach, individualized reading, and literature-based reading.

Because the philosophy is broad, reading experts have struggled with finding a common definition. Frank Smith states that whole language "is the instructional philosophy that reflects most consistently the view that meaning and 'natural language' are the basis of literacy learning" (1988, 301). Dorothy Watson emphasizes keeping language whole during instruction and avoiding fragmentation through isolated drill (1989). Ken Goodman writes that whole language "is not a dogma to be narrowly practiced. It's a way of bringing together a view of language, a view of learning, and a view of people, in particular two special groups of people: kids and teachers" (1986, 5).

Though definitions may vary, there is general agreement on the principles that characterize whole language, and the following list is built from the works of Ken Goodman (1992), Dorothy Watson (1989), Brian Cambourne (1988), Frank Smith (1988), and Constance Weaver (1994):

1. Readers construct meaning for themselves by drawing on clues, prior experiences and learnings, and personal purposes as they read. They predict, hypothesize, confirm, and self-correct as they interact with print. Comprehension is the primary goal of readers.

2. Writers strive to include enough information and detail to make their writings comprehensible to their intended audience. They draw on their prior experiences and learnings to write effectively and functionally.

3. Learning is enhanced when learners actively interact with other learners, books, materials, artifacts, and the world.

4. Learning is a social act that involves collaboration in a community that is dedicated to learning and supports exploration and taking risks.

5. Learning that is purposeful and significant to the learner is more effective and enduring than learning that is imposed by outside forces. When learners are

intensely interested in the topic, they are more likely to risk, achieve, and grow.

6. Literacy develops from whole to part and from known to unknown.

7. Literacy has neither a defined hierarchy of subskills, nor an identifiable sequence. Learning is a personal process that is largely unpredictable, perhaps even chaotic.

8. Learners are accepted for who they are, and learning is built on their experiences, backgrounds, and cultures.

Goodman explains that whole language is a grassroots movement of teachers who are dedicated to providing a democratic learning community where teachers and pupils learn together and learn to live peacefully together (1992, 196). The resulting program integrates educational concepts and movements, including:

Process writing and the National Writing Project

Developmentally appropriate experience

Multigrade and family grouping

Cooperative and collaborative education

Language across the curriculum

Language experience reading

Theme cycles and thematic units

Literature-based reading instruction and literature sets

Questioning strategies for students and for teachers

Child-centered teaching

Critical pedagogy

Critical thinking

Nongraded schools

Emergent literacy (see Chapter 3)

Authentic assessment (see Chapter 12)

Conflict resolution (ibid., 196)

Most researchers agree that a successful whole-language program contains a variety of components. However, Goodman believes that whole language *excludes* some practices as well: (1) outcome-based education, because it imposes often narrow and specific goals on learners; (2) phonics-only reading programs or any other program that reduces learning to a simple, isolated skill sequence; (3) models that assume learning only occurs because of direct teaching; and (4) direct instruction that is equated with a focus on skills (ibid., 197).

ENVIRONMENT

The principles of whole language influence the environment more dramatically than other practices, perhaps because they affect more than reading and writing. As with the language experience approach, literature reading programs, and individualized programs that use literature, the classroom library is extensive. Developing a library that supports language arts, science, social studies, music, art, and other area requires time and money. Therefore, teachers rely on a variety of sources to provide and maintain the necessary resources; these include school, public, and professional libraries, as well as the teacher's and students' personal libraries. In addition to books, the whole-language classroom usually has a constantly changing supply of artifacts for science and social studies investigations, manipulatives for math, and resources for other content areas.

At first glance, a whole-language classroom may be so replete with books and materials that it appears disorganized. Upon investigation, however, visitors will recognize an underlying structure. Catherine E. Loughlin and Mavis D. Martin discuss the basic provisioning framework for the literacy environment that makes materials available to children during their learning. Among these provisions are raw materials, tools, information sources, containers, work spaces, and display facilities (see Figure 2.1). Activity centers house related provisions. Shelves are labeled so students can retrieve and return items independently. Because students create prodigious amounts of writing, nearly every surface is covered with displays of their products.

The arrangement of desks or tables reflects the preferred practices as much as the budget allows. Flexibility is important because themes change and learning pursuits vary continually. Direct instruction occurs infrequently, so desks don't need to face the traditional focus of the room, the chalkboard or overhead projector screen. Instead, tables or desks are arranged to encourage collaborative efforts; these arrangements change as themes or individual pursuits change. A large area provides for whole-class read-alouds, discussions, and planning sessions. Traffic patterns allow students to access materials freely. The teacher's desk is often used primarily for storage, with a small table preferred for individual or small-group conferences.

GROUPING

Groups continually change in the whole-language classroom. Groups form to pursue common goals, to read books together, to solve a problem, to accomplish a task, or to complete a project. The entire class might gather for discus-

FIGURE 2.1
Basic Provisioning
Categories

Raw Materials	Tools	Information Sources
Construction materials	Measuring	References
Natural materials	Joining	Communication media
Found objects	Computing	Pictures
Fabrics	Cutting and shaping	Recordings
Cords	Mixing	Natural specimens
Food	Observing and viewing	Labels
Pigments	Recording	Books
Papers	Heating and cooling	Models
Sculpture materials	Expressing and	Charts
	communicating	Living things

Containers	Display Facilities	Work Spaces
Flats	Bulletin boards	Booths
Dry deep	Cases	Mats
Watertight deep	Shelf space	Underneaths
Cages	Stands	Corners
Blank books	Frames	Flat surfaces
Racks	Racks	Vertical surfaces
Envelopes	Label blanks	
Chart papers		

sions, read-alouds, listening to writers, problem solving, demonstrations, minilessons, presentations, planning, decision making, speeches, questions, or a variety of shared experiences (Robb 1994, 283). But small groups might also form for many of these activities, as well as for writing, collaborative evaluations, paired reading, paired questioning, storytelling, research, book talks, self-evaluation, and dramatizations (ibid., 284). Students also work individually to read silently, research, reflect, write, solve problems, evaluate, and pursue independent interests and activities.

SKILLS: DIRECT, INDIRECT, PLANNED, AND UNPLANNED INSTRUCTION

A common misconception about whole language is that teachers never teach skills. This misunderstanding has probably developed because much of the instruction is indirect and unplanned. To return to the earlier examples of instruction, a teacher who is circulating when a student needs help reading the word *caught* asks the student to think about other words that have *gh* in them. Although a good whole-language teacher is always reinforcing skills, indirect instruction is often difficult for the casual observer to identify, and some whole-language teachers are so skilled in their guidance that an observer might not recognize more direct instruction. Ken Goodman points out that anything a teacher does that fosters learning is direct instruction. When whole-language advocates decry direct instruction, they are criticizing the focus on skills that can be tested for mastery, usually by objective tests (Goodman 1992, 197).

To whole-language advocates, a more acceptable form of direct instruction occurs when the teacher models effective reading strategies, perhaps during a literature discussion or a read-aloud, building a repertoire of strategies that students can use as they need them (Spiegel 1992, 41). The teacher notices that many students are struggling with writing dialogue and will thus point out how an author uses punctuation and format in a Big Book. If a student or students continue to struggle with this concept, the teacher may work with a small group, teaching the skill directly and helping students apply it to their own work.

In the whole-language classroom, direct teaching is not dictated by the scope and sequence of a skills program but occurs in direct response to the students' needs (Weaver 1994, 336). Therefore, covering all the skills can be difficult, even when in the hands of an experienced whole-language teacher dedicated to ensuring that all students show progress. A wise teacher becomes familiar with the skills generally associated with the grade level and specified by the district, and integrates them into the program as his or her students evidence need. This is important, of course, because keeping abreast of skills helps students perform well on the standardized tests, typically skills-based, that may be required by the district.

COLLABORATION

For a whole-language classroom to function effectively, everyone must collaborate. As discussed, temporary groups form continually to accomplish a wide variety of goals or tasks: research, problem solving, shared reading, discussing, and so forth. The whole-language classroom is probably the most social of all the models, because its collaborative nature fosters discussion, negotiation, developing common goals, and pursuing common interests. The wide variety of materials mandates a level of organization that requires everyone's cooperation. Students are involved in paired reading, paired questioning, storytelling, book talks, collaborative evaluations, peer writing conferences, dramatizations, and any number of projects with common goals. Students may also pursue interests or research independently; independent work is valued as much as group work.

Collaboration extends beyond the classroom and students, as a variety of adults are involved. Perhaps the most important outside collaborator is the school librarian, who needs to have an open-door policy that allows students access to the library at any time of day rather than only during scheduled periods. The whole-language librarian understands the power of independent and group investigations and plans library activities with the classroom teacher that support theme units or other research projects. The whole-language librarian gathers sets of books together, books from the school and professional libraries that support class projects. The librarian also works with students—helping them discover how to use the library to their advantage; recommending favorite or new books, and appropriate print and nonprint resources; and identifying materials that might be overlooked.

Another important source of collaborators is other whole-language teachers, particularly for those teachers who are relatively new to the whole-language concept. Just as students can be bewildered by the myriad of choices, so can teachers struggle with the complexity of this program as they attempt to determine what is just right for their classroom (Church 1994, 364). There are more than 450 formal support groups, Teachers Advocating Whole Language (TAWL), who meet to discuss issues, share strategies, and socialize, plus many other groups who meet informally (Watson 1994, 602). The teacher who is the only whole-language advocate in an entire building will especially benefit from the support such a group brings.

Other key collaborators include the building administrators and all support staff. Many administrators, in their curiosity to learn about whole language, join whole-language groups or take continuing education classes. Their understanding is crucial to help communicate with another key group of collaborators, the parents. A recent newspaper article on whole language called it "whole-word" approach, essentially equating it with a phonics approach. Phonics is one of many skills integrated into the whole-language approach, but it is definitely not the basis of whole language. Such misinformation confuses parents and others who could potentially be strong advocates of this philosophy. Most parents are delighted with programs based on the whole-language philosophy once they see the results: children who love to read, create stories, write poetry, and pursue research. Good whole-language teachers model good practices to their students, and they also model exemplary procedures through written communication, conferences, and ongoing education.

RESPONSIBILITY

Because a typical whole-language classroom has 1 adult and 25 or more students, responsibility for learning must be shared by everyone. Except for routines dictated by the building's schedule, the idea of choice is integrated into as much of the educational process as possible. The entire class chooses to pursue a theme cycle, but within that theme individuals select the books they want to read, research they want to pursue, problems they want to solve, and extensions they want to complete. Students who have difficulty making choices will need assistance; it is usually helpful to limit their choices at first. Once they realize they can take risks *and* succeed, they will naturally move to take control of this aspect of the program. And the more choices they make, the more ownership they have. Anne Genevieve Whitt, a secondary teacher who began her class's transition to whole language with theme units, found that her students far exceeded her expectations with their experiential presentations. "Students just felt so much ownership of their choices that nothing seemed too much effort for their own presentations" (1994, 490).

Students in the whole-language classroom also take responsibility for the routine tasks necessary for smooth functioning. The classroom has an abundance of materials that require organization and care. Students can be in charge of feeding pets, replacing writing materials, recording information, routine cleaning, completing forms, and other routine tasks. Whenever I felt overwhelmed with the minutia associated with a busy classroom, I would pause and reflect on tasks students could take over that would allow me more time to work with them, while not detracting from their activities. I discovered that some students loved keeping the library organized; this reinforced their alphabetizing skills. The student who was having a hard time sitting enjoyed taking messages to the office for me. The student who needed some adult companionship enjoyed staying after school for a few minutes to help tidy the room. Being intimately involved in the smooth operation of the classroom builds ownership for the entire class—that community of learners who spends at least one-third of their waking hours together.

EVALUATION

Teachers who have successfully embraced whole language recognize that grading is another piece of the teacher-student partnership. The teacher evaluates progress and achievement, and the students engage in reflection and self-evaluation. Peers may collaborate to evaluate their progress on a group project. A group may participate in the evaluation process, for example, by critiquing an individual's writing piece (Weaver 1994, 338).

Generally, the whole-language teacher is required by the district or school to administer some standardized tests. But these assessments are only a part of an ongoing evaluative process. Teachers look beyond the product to the processes learners engage in, evaluating how successfully they solve problems and apply reading strategies. Teachers also consider how the learners assess themselves. **Metacognition** becomes an integral part of the learning process,

■ **Metacognition**
Awareness of, and knowledge about, one's thinking processes.

and teachers interact with students to determine how thoughtfully they tackle challenges.

Teachers integrate assessment into the context of daily learning. Standardized tests only reveal how a student did on a particular day on that specific test. Anecdotes, observations, and artifacts (writings, projects, and other samples), combined with checklists, questionnaires, interviews, and conference notes, provide a more complete evaluation profile of the students' progress. Frequent conferences help students understand their progress, and on report card day they usually know exactly what they earned. Assessment and evaluation is discussed in depth in Chapter 12.

TEACHING DIVERSE LEARNERS

Whole language, like the language experience approach and literature-based programs, serves second-language learners well because it fosters learning with materials that have relevance for the students. Having and making choices and taking responsibility for learning further empowers students who may be bewildered by an unfamiliar environment, be it a new school or a new country. Literature that represents students' cultures or that is bilingual can be made available. The high value placed on discussion fosters language development, particularly when compared to a classroom where students are required to complete worksheets independently and quietly.

Second-language learners also benefit from whole-language content-area instruction. Betty Belcher, a classroom teacher, used a study of caves during a summer program for 10 students who had been in the United States for as little as 1 month and as long as 2 years. They read books and articles, wrote about their learnings, took field trips, listened to speakers, played games, cooked, and explored cave art. Caves have a universal appeal to children, and this meaning-filled curriculum fostered communication and growth, regardless of the students' individual language skills (Lim and Watson 1993).

The whole-language classroom also serves those students well who face learning or physical challenges. Because whole language focuses on language processes rather than on isolated skills, it targets the areas in need of development, provides more personalized instruction, values individual differences and progress, and provides multisensory experiences using a variety of materials. Students with learning disabilities who are mainstreamed benefit when teachers plan the program to support the goals of the entire class (Scala 1993). Additionally, the flexible nature of the whole-language classroom fosters more effective collaboration with support services such as speech or reading resource teachers (Zucker 1993, 661). As with literature programs or individual reading programs, gifted students appreciate the opportunity to delve into topics of personal interest and to experience a level of autonomy that is not possible in a more traditional approach.

A Final Note

In Chapter 1, you explored theories of reading and thought about your learning preferences. Now that you have read about a variety of instructional practices, you can begin to think about how these practices fit with your theory of reading. Figure 2.2 provides an overview of the various instructional methods and their features. However, this chart is far more tidy than the reality of choosing instructional practices to match your philosophy. Many whole-language classes use language experience activities throughout their program. Perhaps one of these practices suits you now, but it may not suit your students. Many new teachers begin with a basal program, incorporating components of other programs that fit their philosophy more closely. As mentioned in Chapter 1, you will need to be sensitive to the building where you will be teaching, adapting somewhat to the philosophies and materials in place. And once you are in the classroom, you will need to spend a fair amount of time observing your students to discover their learning styles. Once you have all these pieces, you can begin to assemble that fascinating puzzle we call teaching reading.

Summary

Based on the bottom-up theory of reading, reading with basal texts involves commercially produced materials, defined reading groups, planned and direct instruction, teacher responsibility, and frequent testing. Basal readers are designed to serve the majority of learners, rather than those with special needs. Teachers may need to supplement with additional practice or more personalized approaches.

The language experience approach, a top-down instructional approach, relies heavily on individualized and group experiences, an environment with many trade books, regularly changing groups, unplanned instruction, frequent collaboration, student responsibility, and informal evaluation. The language experience approach is especially suited to students with special needs because it is based on individual experiences.

Individualized reading, another top-down instructional approach, is characterized by a rich environment of print materials, flexible classroom arrangements, much independent work, occasional small-group work, emphasis on

	Basal Readers	Language Experience	Individualized	Literature	Whole Language
Features	Bottom-up. Commercial texts. Systematic instruction. Teacher-directed.	Top-down. Based on children's experiences, discussion. Student-centered reading and writing.	Top-down. Self-selection of literature. Self-pacing. Conferences with teacher are integral.	Transactional. Literature groups. Discussion groups. Reader response.	Interactive or transactional. Broad program encompassing content areas. Authentic materials and experiences. Student-centered.
Environment	Organized to accommodate instructional groups, commercial materials, auxiliary materials.	Varied centers for reading, writing, exploring, playing. Flexible arrangements for small- and whole-group work.	Many books and materials. Some centers. Promotes individual work. Some areas for small- or whole-group work.	Conference area. Small-group areas. Rich library. Also accommodates whole group.	Rich resources: books, artifacts, materials. Some centers. Areas for changing small groups and whole class.
Grouping	Usually three instructional groups. Less fluid than other approaches.	Many whole-group activities. Small groups change often to reflect goals, interest, needs. Spontaneous groupings.	More individual work or with teacher. Small groups for skills as needed.	Reflects reading choices, discussion groups, sharing. Small groups change often.	Varied groups reflect projects, goals, instructional needs. Also whole grouping at times.
Skills	Much direct, planned instruction. Systematic development of skills.	Emphasis on indirect skills instruction. Direct instruction also provided. Much unplanned instruction.	Taught in one-to-one conferences or changing small groups. Emphasis on indirect and unplanned instruction. Based on student needs.	Much unplanned instruction, which may be direct or indirect. Some changing groups for like instructional needs.	Much unplanned, indirect instruction. Much modeling of strategies, how to solve one's own problems.
Collaboration	Routine collaboration. Not promoted actively or critical focus for learning.	Emphasis on whole-group collaboration. Much spontaneous collaboration.	Minimal collaboration. Confined to routine room procedures.	Frequent discussion and reading groups. May also have paired reading, some whole-group focus. Changes regularly.	High degree of collaboration throughout program. Extends to other adults, beyond school to community.
Responsibility	Primarily held by teacher as directed by publisher.	Primarily held by students. Emphasis on whole-group experiences that drive material written and read by students.	High degree of student responsibility for learning. Students select much of learning material.	Much student responsibility for selection of materials, discussion, and so forth.	Collective responsibility for routine maintenance of classroom. Emphasizes responsibility for learning.
Evaluation	Frequent, formal, with criterion-referenced tests. Some informal measures available as supplements.	Informal, focusing on self-evaluation with frequent teacher conferences.	Much informal evaluation, often during one-to-one conferences with teacher.	Much ongoing, personalized, informal evaluation. Evaluation occurs with teacher and peers.	Much self-evaluation and collaborative evaluation. Much informal evaluation.
Special students	Designed to serve the needs of most regular students, but not special students or groups of students.	Excellent for early learning because it focuses on existing knowledge and provides personalized instruction and learning.	Can be useful for special students, though more social programs may be preferable. Very adaptable and personalized.	Shared interests and discussion can be useful to special students. Shared responsibility for learning is also beneficial.	Special students can benefit from use of authentic materials. Personalized program. Ownership in learning.

FIGURE 2.2

Comparison of Reading Methods

indirect and unplanned instruction, little instructional collaboration, a high degree of student ownership, informal evaluation, and personalized instruction for students with special needs.

Literature reading, modeled on the transactional theory of reading, features a rich print environment, frequent groupings with some individualized reading, unplanned and direct or indirect instruction, collaboration among group readings, a high level of student responsibility, more informal evaluation, and personalization for students with special needs.

Whole language features meaning-based experiences in an environment rich with books and other materials, flexible and changing groupings, a healthy mix of indirect and direct instruction, ongoing collaboration, intense student responsibility, and more informal evaluation. Depending on the teacher, whole-language programs may exemplify the interactive or transactional theories of reading. Students with special needs can be successful in the whole-language classroom because of the personalized nature of the program.

When deciding on an instructional method, consider your preferred theory of reading, the instructional practices and theories in place in your building, and the needs of your students.

References

Allington, Richard L. "If They Don't Read Much, How They Ever Gonna Get Good?" *Journal of Reading* 21, no. 1 (Oct. 1977): 57–61.

Aukerman, Robert C. *The Basal Reader Approach to Reading.* New York: John Wiley, 1981.

Cambourne, Brian. *The Whole Story: Natural Learning and the Acquisition of Literacy in the Classroom.* Auckland, New Zealand: Ashton Scholastic, 1988.

Church, Susan. "Is Whole Language Really Warm and Fuzzy?" *The Reading Teacher* 47, no. 5 (Feb. 1994): 362–370.

Crawford, Patricia, and Patrick Shannon. "'I Don't Think These Companies Have Much Respect for Teachers': Looking at Teachers' Manuals." In *Basal Readers: A Second Look,* edited by Patrick Shannon and Kenneth Goodman, 1–18. Katonah, N.Y.: Richard C. Owen, 1994.

D'Alessandro, Marilyn D. "Accommodating Emotionally Handicapped Children through a Literature-Based Reading Program." *The Reading Teacher* 44, no. 4 (Dec. 1990): 288–293.

Dechant, Emerald. *Whole-Language Reading: A Comprehensive Teaching Guide.* Lancaster, Pa.: Technomic, 1993.

Durkin, Dolores. "Dolores Durkin Speaks on Instruction." *The Reading Teacher* 43, no. 7 (March 1990): 472–476.

Edelsky, Carole. "Exercise Isn't Always Healthy." In *Basal Readers: A Second Look*, edited by Patrick Shannon and Kenneth Goodman, 19–33. Katonah, N.Y.: Richard C. Owen, 1994.

Freebody, Peter, and Carolyn D. Baker. "Children's First Schoolbooks: Introductions to the Culture of Literacy." *Harvard Educational Review*, 55, no. 4 (Nov. 1985): 381–398.

Goodman, Kenneth. "Foreword." In *Basal Readers: A Second Look*, edited by Patrick Shannon and Kenneth Goodman, iii–xxvii. Katonah, N.Y.: Richard C. Owen, 1994.

_____. "I Didn't Found Whole Language." *The Reading Teacher* 46, no. 3 (Nov. 1992): 188–199.

_____. *What's Whole in Whole Language.* Portsmouth, N.H.: Heinemann, 1986.

Goodman, Kenneth, Lisa Maras, and Debbie Birdseye. "Look! Look! Who Stole the Pictures from the Picture Book?" In *Basal Readers: A Second Look*, edited by Patrick Shannon and Kenneth Goodman, 36–56. Katonah, N.Y.: Richard C. Owen, 1994.

Hunt, Lyman C. "The Effect of Self-Selection, Interest, and Motivation upon Independent, Instructional, and Frustrational Levels." *The Reading Teacher* 50, no. 4 (Dec. 1996/Jan. 1997): 278–282.

Krashen, Stephen. *The Power of Reading: Insights from the Research.* Englewood, Colo.: Libraries Unlimited, 1993.

Lim, Hwa-Ja Lee, and Dorothy J. Watson. "Whole-Language Content Classes for Second-Language Learners." *The Reading Teacher* 46, no. 5 (Feb. 1993): 384–393.

Loughlin, Catherine E., and Mavis D. Martin. *Supporting Literacy: Developing Effective Learning Environments.* New York: Teachers College Press, 1987.

Maras, Lisa Burley. "Step One, Step Two, Step Three, Four, Five: My, This Writing Seems Contrived!: Writing Process in Basal Reading Programs." In *Basal Readers: A Second Look*, edited by Patrick Shannon and Kenneth Goodman, 69–86. Katonah, N.Y.: Richard C. Owen, 1994.

Meese, Ruth Lyn. *Teaching Learners with Mild Disabilities: Integrating Research and Practice.* Pacific Grove, Calif.: Brooks/Cole, 1994.

McCallum, Richard D. "Don't Throw the Basals out with the Bath Water." *The Reading Teacher* 42, no. 3 (Dec. 1988): 204–208.

Murphy, Sharon. "Neither Gone nor Forgotten: Testing in New Basal Readers." In *Basal Readers: A Second Look*, edited by Patrick Shannon and Kenneth Goodman, 103–113. Katonah, N.Y.: Richard C. Owen, 1994.

Ringler, L. J., and C. K. Weber. *A Language-Thinking Approach to Reading.* New York: Harcourt Brace Jovanovich, 1984.

Robb, Laura. *Whole Language, Whole Learners: Creating a Literature-Centered Classroom.* New York: William Morrow, 1994.

Roller, Cathy M. "Classroom Interaction Patterns: Reflections of a Stratified Society." *Language Arts* 66, no. 5 (Sept. 1989): 492–500.

Rosenblatt, Louise. *Literature as Exploration.* New York: Noble & Noble, 1976.

Sawyer, Richard J., Margaret J. McLaughlin, and Marianne Winglee. "Is Integration of Students with Disabilities Happening? An Analysis of National Data Trends Over Time." *Remedial and Special Education* 15, no. 4 (July 1994): 204–215.

Scala, Marilyn A. "What Whole Language in the Mainstream Means for Children with Learning Disabilities." *The Reading Teacher* 47, no. 3 (Nov. 1993): 222–229.

Schwartz, Elaine. "Patterns of Culture of Distorted Images: Multiculturalism in Basals." In *Basal Readers: A Second Look*, edited by Patrick Shannon and Kenneth Goodman, 87–101. Katonah, N.Y.: Richard C. Owen, 1994.

Shannon, Patrick. "The Struggle for Control of Literacy Lesson." *Language Arts*, 66, no. 6 (Oct. 1989): 625–634.

Smith, Frank. *Understanding Reading.* 4th ed. Hillsdale, N.J.: Lawrence Erlbaum, 1988.

Spiegel, Dixie. "Blending Whole Language and Systematic Direct Instruction." *The Reading Teacher* 46, no. 1 (Sept. 1992): 38–44.

Stauffer, Russell. *The Language Experience Approach to the Teaching of Reading,* 2nd ed. New York: Harper & Row, 1980.

Thurston, Cheryl Miller. *Hide Your Ex-Lax under the Wheaties: Poems about Schools, Teachers, Kids, and Education.* Fort Collins, Colo.: Cottonwood Press, 1987.

Van Allen, Roach. *Language Experiences in Communication.* Boston: Houghton Mifflin, 1976.

Van Allen, Roach, and Claryce Allen. *Language Experience Activities.* Boston: Houghton Mifflin, 1976.

Veatch, Jeannette. *Reading in the Elementary School.* 2nd ed. New York: John Wiley, 1978.

Watson, Dorothy J. "Defining and Describing Whole Language." *The Elementary School Journal* 90 (Nov. 1989): 130–141.

_____. "Whole Language: Why Bother?" *The Reading Teacher* 47, no. 8 (May 1994): 600–607.

Weaver, Constance. *Reading Process and Practice: From Socio-Psycholinguistics to Whole Language,* 2nd ed. Portsmouth, N.H.: Heinemann, 1994.

Whitt, Anne Genevieve. "Whole Language Revitalizes One High School Classroom." *Journal of Reading* 37, 6 (March 1994): 488–493.

Zucker, Carol. "Using Whole Language with Students Who Have Language and Learning Disabilities." *The Reading Teacher* 46, no. 8 (May 1993): 660–670.

3

Emergent Literacy

The First Day of School

The first day of school
I was shivering and whivering.
I was certainly scared.
I did not know my teacher very well.
The classroom was funny and weird,
    weird and funny.
I did not know my room number,
    but of course it is room 122.
My teacher looked nice, very nice.
But she just isn't my mom.

Julia

FOCUS QUESTIONS

1. What is emergent literacy?

2. What are the conditions for learning in the home and school?

3. How can I prepare a context for successful early learning experiences?

4. How can I develop effective talking and listening activities?

5. How can I develop effective early reading and writing experiences?

6. How can I support early reading efforts?

7. What are early-intervention programs?

8. How can I support second-language learners?

9. How can I involve parents?

"The first Day of School" expresses the excitement and misgivings young children experience when they arrive at school. By the end of first grade, Julia clearly had absorbed a rich repository of words and images that she drew upon when she wrote her poem. Her poem is a fine example of what can happen when young children are encouraged to stretch and grow with reading and writing and when they are given a learning environment that supports taking such risks. But as every parent knows, a lot happened to Julia before her first day at school.

Educators once attempted to identify children's "reading readiness" by defining developmental stages that preceded more formal instruction. If young children were categorized as needing more time in a readiness program, perhaps because of their score on a readiness test, their instruction would be delayed until they could demonstrate the requisite skills for reading (Durkin 1989, 77). As educators began to realize that learning begins very early in a child's life, the notion of **emergent literacy** developed (ibid., 100). This process has no clear beginning or ending point. As parents, we recognize this process when our toddler identifies single letters or recognizes the symbol or word for a favorite toy or food (Laminack 1990, 538; Strickland 1990, 19). As children develop oral language, more is occurring than simply learning to talk; children are already working on reading and writing processes (Strickland, 20). This is a powerful notion worth taking a moment to consider.

If we accept that young children are beginning to read and write at the same time they are learning to communicate orally, it is appropriate to provide them with a rich variety of informal reading and writing activities, in addition to their listening and speaking experiences. Many parents or caretakers naturally involve their children in reading and writing activities, such as helping with cooking, preparing a grocery list, or identifying words on billboards. These literacy events occur in interactions that take place with an interested adult or sibling who quite naturally delights in the child's accomplishments. Note that these events occur in the context of real-life experiences, an important feature when we consider how we can best foster early learning experiences. This chapter explores effective contexts for early literacy learning and makes recommendations for beginning reading instruction. More specific information about topics such as word identification, building vocabulary, and developing reading comprehension will be examined in subsequent chapters.

Emergent literacy
The time before formal reading instruction when children are building concepts about reading. This process can begin as early as 14 months of age.

If you are reading this book sequentially, this is the first chapter in which you encounter "Spotlights." Each Spotlight gives you a related teaching idea that uses children's or young adult literature. The Spotlight also provides a broader context for the skill, linking processes and philosophy with practical applications. Although grade levels are designated, many Spotlights can be adapted to other grades and are also applicable with other literature examples. I suggest that you keep a notebook both of additional ideas the Spotlights inspire and of books you will want to have on your shelves. The features called "Something to Try" are more detailed suggestions for applications that you might try in your field experiences. They are generally not linked to a specific book. Again, you will want to adapt the suggestions to your particular school or training.

Contexts for Early Literacy Experiences

Marie Clay, recognized for coining the term *emergent literacy*, emphasizes that if we could design instruction that builds naturally from what children do before they come to school, we would be far more effective teachers (1991, 26). Therefore, the first challenge to the teacher of the very young is to observe them—learn how they talk, interact, solve problems, think, and learn. (Of course, teachers of older students will also benefit from working at knowing the individuals in their classroom.) You can then plan opportunities for rich learning experiences that build on the knowledge and interests of your children and that allow them to enter in the events as equal participants. First, let's consider the impact of the home environment on early literacy experiences.

CONDITIONS OF LEARNING IN THE HOME ENVIRONMENT

■ **Conditions of Learning**

Immersion: Surrounding children with language to the point where they are practically inundated.

Demonstration: Modeling what is to be learned; also an artifact.

Expectation: Assumption that children can indeed learn.

It is important for us to know what works in the home setting as we strive to understand how to best promote reading in the classroom. Brian Cambourne (1988), an Australian researcher on the subject of literacy, has identified seven conditions for learning to talk that are intimately connected with the environment. You will see that these conditions can enhance early literacy as well.

The first condition, **immersion**, involves the wealth of stimuli that newborns are exposed to, perhaps even before birth. Babies quickly distinguish and appreciate the rhythms of spoken language or music, and so do learners. **Demonstration** occurs when a verbal request, such as asking for the newspaper, creates a response. Artifacts also serve as demonstrations of concepts; for example, a piano is an artifact that demonstrates how music can be made by striking a key. The third condition, **expectation**, refers to the assumption that children can learn. Every new parent assumes that a newborn will soon smile and (all too quickly) learn to roll over, sit, stand, walk, and talk. When children

■ **Conditions of Learning (continued)**

Responsibility: Children take ownership of their learning.

Approximation: Coming close to mastery.

Use: Employment of language.

Response: Giving children feedback.

take ownership in their learning, they are demonstrating the fourth condition of learning, **responsibility**. Parents reinforce the very youngest children for their earliest attempts at talking; new parents are utterly convinced that the slightest utterance represents "ma" or "da." This **approximation**, the fifth condition, is often celebrated as an exciting step on the road to mastery. The sixth condition of learning, **use**, involves giving children opportunities to employ language. Children need time and opportunity to hone and master their skills. Many parents have heard their children in bed experimenting with words instead of going directly to sleep. The final condition, **response**, refers to the constant informal feedback we parents give to our children's approximations. For example, when our toddler says "goggy," we don't say, "You need to work on your initial *d* sounds. The correct word is 'doggy.' Now try it." Instead, we say, "That's right! There's a doggy!" Many parents extend the conversation by adding something like "He's a big doggy!" or "What color is the doggy?" (ibid., 32–38).

In the ideal home environment, adults and family members immerse a child in language, demonstrate the function of language, assume everyone will learn to talk, foster responsibility and use of language, celebrate approximations, and respond favorably to language attempts. A review of research indicates that parents contribute to literacy development through functional spoken and written language, which takes place primarily as social interactions in everyday events, in conversation, or during entertainment (Stevens, Hough, and Nurss 1993, 344). However, some parents don't realize that their contribution is important because they assume that only more formal instruction leads to literacy. Parents need to understand that the informal learning that occurs daily is every bit as important as school learning (Goodman and Haussler 1986, 29).

CONDITIONS OF LEARNING IN THE SCHOOL ENVIRONMENT

The conditions that so effectively encourage learning in the home offer us key information for creating school environments that encourage learning naturally. Children learn language *while* they are eating, playing, listening to stories, and talking (Neuman and Roskos 1993, 102). They aren't taught all the skills of eating and then allowed to eat. Therefore, when creating a learning environment, teachers should carefully consider how they can *immerse* young children in a setting that stimulates interaction with literacy events. This may include but is not limited to books for browsing; writing materials; art, science, and building materials; and woodworking tools. Thematic play areas where children can practice reading and writing (grocery store, fast-food restaurant, office) or develop topics for exploration (astronauts, spiders, dinosaurs, or the circus) are especially effective.

Teachers *demonstrate* important functions of literacy when they run their fingers underneath the text from left to right as they read a story aloud, when they describe the steps as they write a letter or short word on the board, or when they think aloud as they solve a problem such as who should have care of the class pet over a long weekend. Cambourne emphasizes that demonstrations should be contextually relevant; that is, they should be appropriate to the literacy task the learner is trying to complete (1988, 50).

Just as parents *expect* that their children will learn to walk and talk given opportunity and encouragement, so should teachers express confidence in their students' prospects for learning. Teachers demonstrate negative expectations when they group unsuccessful learners together, make all the decisions for their students, let students know that a task is too hard, emphasize failures, or regard learning tasks with boredom or fatigue (ibid., 59). Teachers who approach new learning situations with a sense of adventure, good humor, and a willingness to take risks and who investigate right along with their students communicate their love of learning and high expectations.

Giving students increasing amounts of *responsibility* for the learning process does not mean abandoning your role as teacher. Cambourne's view recognizes the active role students can take in determining relevance, particularly in the context of authentic learning experiences. One way to increase the students' sense of responsibility involves giving them opportunities to practice making age-appropriate decisions (ibid., 68). Teachers develop responsibility when they encourage students to take risks, to try something independently before asking for help, and to look to peers for assistance with the problem-solving process. These teachers always promote these opportunities with the expectation that the learning goals will eventually be met (ibid., 66).

Approximations, better known as guesses, are essential to the learning process. As approximations in language development are verbalized, listeners' responses move the speaker closer to accuracy. The form that these responses take can affect the learner's progress adversely or move them toward success. For example, when a 3-year-old says "I love gaspetti" and the parent says "I love spaghetti too!" the child hears the correct pronunciation in the form of positive feedback. If the parent were to respond with "No, no, it's *spaghetti*," the youngster is less likely to risk such a difficult word again.

When children are not encouraged to take risks, their progress slows. This can happen in the school environment when the teacher adopts the attitude of what Cambourne calls "get-it-right-first-time" (GIRFT) teaching. The GIRFT teaching style, which is an unrealistic practice, attempts to give students everything they need to know, usually in small bits (ibid., 69–70). Teachers who value approximations recognize the merit of work that is neither perfect nor polished. They also recognize that an individual is progressing toward a larger learning goal, even though the journey meanders at times.

Just as children need ample opportunities to approximate language, so do they also need abundant opportunities to *use* language. This means that classroom settings should encourage learners to read and write. These activities must have purposes beyond the need to practice the skill. For example, copying new words from a list will quickly become boring for most learners. But adding words to a personal dictionary because the learner is about to do research on dinosaurs or write a story makes the task purposeful. When students read and write about mice because they are considering having classroom pets, they develop a focus that intensifies and solidifies the learning.

Our "gaspetti" example reminds us that we as teachers must also respond appropriately. Our responses should be meaning-centered, supportive, and natural. The teacher who reads a child's story about a pet dog and responds with "I like the way you wrote about your pet" gives a superficial response that will be recognized by the learner. In contrast, consider this teacher's response: "This story reminds me of a dog I once had. It was good to think about Bandit again. Let's talk about what might make the story even better." In this case, the teacher showed his sincere interest in, and enjoyment of, the story as he moved his student toward polishing the writing.

In discussing his conditions of learning, Brian Cambourne emphasizes the importance of engagement. "It didn't matter how much immersion in text and language we provided; it didn't matter how riveting, compelling, exciting, or motivating our demonstrations were; if students didn't engage with language, no learning could occur" (1995, 186). Therefore, he offers the following "Principles of Engagement":

1. Learners are more likely to engage deeply with demonstrations if they believe that they are capable of ultimately learning or doing whatever is being demonstrated.

2. Learners are more likely to engage deeply with demonstrations if they believe that learning whatever is being demonstrated has some potential value, purpose, and use for them.

3. Learners are more likely to engage with demonstrations if they're free from anxiety.

4. Learners are more likely to engage with demonstrations given by someone they like, respect, admire, trust, and would like to emulate (ibid., 187–188).

When the conditions of learning are met, students begin to take responsibility for their learning. Discussion and reflection become increasingly important for language learning, and students and teachers apply knowledge through collaboration and discussion (ibid.).

PREPARING THE CONTEXT FOR EARLY LITERACY EXPERIENCES

Your classroom environment will change often to reflect the activities undertaken by the children, so your year will be less hectic if you can prepare some of your materials before the school year begins. Begin by finding out what

something to try 1

Visiting Classrooms

Visit at least three primary classrooms. (Arrange through the school office in advance for these visits.) Explain that you would like to see classroom environ-ments that support early literacy efforts.

While in the class-rooms, write down all the ideas that support learning. Look for themed areas, displays of student work, supply centers, activity centers, a classroom library, gathering area, and so forth. Examine how fur-niture is used. Does its arrangement support the activities or inter-fere with them?

Make a rough sketch of each classroom dur-ing your visit. Afterward, combine the best fea-tures into one ideal classroom and then sketch it. Compare it with sketches of your fellow classmates; then make further recom-mendations based on the discussion.

exists in the classroom and what resources are available. Assess the variety and number of books available to you through the classroom, school, and public libraries. Determine what art supplies are available and if you have a budget for additional supplies. You may want to contact printing or paper supply establishments to see whether they will give you their discards. Check on the availability of audio-visual equipment. Begin thinking about how you will organize the classroom. (See Chapter 13 for more information on devel-oping the classroom environment.)

Prepare such basics as name tags, a schedule, a letter to parents regarding needed supplies, a calendar, a classroom job chart. Determine how and where you will display student work. Plan and prepare storage containers for lunch boxes, completed work, lost items, extra pencils and markers, and so forth. A multipocketed shoe bag is useful for organizing a variety of necessities (Schorr 1995, 12). Other possible projects include creating a flannel board, a message board (where students can leave and obtain messages from you and other stu-dents), a card file of favorite poems to read aloud, and blank books.

Plan for your themed areas, taking into consideration the existing equip-ment and materials available. These might include the library, housekeeping area, blocks, art area, and so forth. Consider how areas should be organized so they won't interfere with other activities. For example, placing a relatively noisy block area next to a library area won't work very well. Plan for a large area, perhaps defined by an area rug, for whole-class meetings and instruction. Create spatial boundaries by using physical cues, such as book shelves and low furniture, and symbolic cues, which utilize functional, meaningful print and pictures (Neuman and Roskos 1993, 105). Look at the room as if you were a child. Does the organization make sense? (See Something to Try 1.)

CREATING A PRINT-RICH ENVIRONMENT

Given that the first condition specified by Brian Cambourne is that of immersion, one of the first goals for creating a supportive literacy context is to provide a print-rich environment. This does not mean you should label every item in the room; it means instead that there are myriad opportunities to read and write print in a context instead that encourages such use. This might include labels of objects that help children get organized, work independently, or investigate a topic. Of course, the print-rich environment also includes ample books, magazines, reference materials, newspapers, letters, and messages that demonstrate and encourage ongoing interactions with print. Near the cage of mice, for example, there might be directions for daily feeding, a list of observations, informational and fictional books about mice, blocks for building mazes, a photograph illustrating a mouse's skeletal system, and a list of mouse-related phrases, such as "quiet as a mouse." Much of the print evolves during the year as an outgrowth of the daily activities of the students, depending on whether the class is focusing on making observations, keeping records, creating charts or directions, writing stories, or organizing information.

THE CONTEXT OF PLAY

Play belongs in the classroom. Children learn invaluable social skills from play: taking turns, sharing, solving problems, conversing, speculating, imagining, and creating. But play in enriched play environments also fosters engagement in literacy behaviors. From a review of studies on the role of play and developing literacy, Carol Vukelich found that enriching the play environment with carefully selected literacy materials results in

1. A significant increase in the amount of literacy activity children engage in during play.

2. More purposeful reading and writing behaviors.

3. Children making more connections to other interests or topics by setting up explicit contexts.

4. Children engaging in more reading and writing activities with each other.

Also, adult involvement with children while they play in literacy-enriched environments is very effective in encouraging children to engage in literacy-related behaviors (1993, 387).

Creating a themed center, such as a fast-food restaurant, encourages children to play a variety of real-life roles. As children write the menu, take orders, take money, organize and serve the food, they use a variety of problem-solving skills. Any business-related theme, such as a grocery or toy store, offers endless opportunities for reading and writing as well as for using math and verbal skills. Including cookbooks, grocery coupons, food packages, and paper and pencil in the housekeeping area invites students to use reading and writing, and to converse while they play (Neuman and Roskos 1993, 104).

THE CONTEXT OF TALKING AND LISTENING

Because educators have been intensely concerned with making children better thinkers and learners, curriculum has focused on giving skills and facts to young students. What we are finding, however, is that children need more opportunities to reflect on and discuss information that is pertinent to their personal lives (Burke 1993, 95). When children are growing up, their talk revolves around events in their lives. A toddler who says "milk" with emphasis clearly communicates a need and generally gets reinforced by receiving a bottle or cup of milk. Talk in this instance is purposeful and succinct, and it gets results. This is how the child realizes the importance and power of listening.

As a child becomes older, talk becomes an ongoing backdrop to everyday events. Parents discuss the clothes they are putting on the child, places they have been or are going to, names of things about them. All children need continual experiences in conversation as they mature, but for those students who come to the classroom without such conversational experiences, the teacher must create an especially rich environment that encourages purposeful talk and listening.

Although listening dominates a student's school activities, this skill is often taken for granted. Few teachers emphasize effective listening skills even though discussion is usually the sounding board for developing and shaping ideas (Temple and Gillet 1996, 21). The following principles can guide your instruction in talking and listening (ibid., 22):

1. *Talking and listening should be purposeful.* The effective learning context should include activities, such as planning what to include in a note home or in a get-well card to a friend.

2. *Talking and listening should be nurtured for a range of purposes.* Purposes might include communicating, explaining, or sharing feelings, information, humor, or dreams.

3. *Talking and listening should be approached in the context of the other language arts.* Spoken and written language support each other, benefitting from processes such as questioning to clarify comprehension, composing, or speaking. Further, reading literature gives students language models and discussion topics.

4. *Language should be performed, too.* Although recitation and elocution studies are no longer emphasized, public speaking benefits students, particularly in forms such as choral reading, readers theatre, and dramatizations (see Chapter 10).

5. *Children should be aware they are learning strategies for talking and listening.* Just as students understand that they are learning the content of math or history, so should they understand that they are learning effective speaking and listening strategies—strategies that will benefit them as learners and in everyday life.

DIRECTED LISTENING-THINKING ACTIVITY

Directed listening–thinking activity
Develops critical listening and thinking skills by having students listen to part of a story read aloud and then predict what will happen next based on the illustrations, what they have heard, and their own experiences and knowledge.

Listening can be enhanced by engaging students in a **Directed Listening–Thinking Activity** (DLTA). The DLTA is similar in principle to the Directed Reading Activity discussed in Chapter 1; it begins with the teacher choosing a story with a clear plot. The story should have a problem and a resolution, plus meaningful illustrations (Stauffer 1980). Depending on the story, the teacher chooses between two and four natural pauses in the story where she can elicit predictions about what will follow; she then encourages students to predict what will happen next by thinking about the title and by looking at the illustrations. Students summarize their predictions at each stopping point; it is important for the teacher to accept all predictions noncommittally, recognizing that they are what *might* happen. She eventually confirms the correct prediction by focusing on the idea rather than on the person who predicted it, and she paces the reading and discussion to keep the DLTA lively. See Something to Try 2 on page 74 for an example of a DLTA.

LISTENING THINK-ALOUDS

This activity occurs when you verbalize for your students the thought process used by effective listeners. Here is how you do this: Choose an easy book, such as Gail Gibbons' *Emergency!* Read the title aloud and then discuss your purposes for reading it: "This book is *Emergency!* by Gail Gibbons. I think it should tell me about a lot of different emergency vehicles. What do you already know about emergency vehicles? [Write those they mention on the board.] I think it might also help me decide which emergency vehicle I want to learn more about. If I want to remember something, I'm going to write it on the board."

Begin reading the book, then stop after several pages. Discuss anything that is confusing. Write down anything you want to remember. For example, for this book, you might write on the board that a utility truck has a boom and then discuss this new use of the word *boom.* Continue reading the book, noting other unusual features or facts.

After you have read the book, review your impressions. "I didn't realize there were so many important emergency vehicles. Did we list every vehicle the author included? What did we leave out? What did she leave out? I think this book gave me a lot of ideas. I was surprised to learn about the ambulances of the past, but this author only told me a little. I think I will try to learn more about those. Where do you think I should begin my research?"

Directed Listening–Thinking Activity

BOOK: *Arthur's Chicken Pox* by Marc Brown (Boston: Little, Brown, 1994).

Arthur eagerly anticipates the family's outing to the circus on Saturday until he gets sick. He decides he must get better fast. His special treatment is resented by his little sister D.W., but then the chicken pox appear. Arthur continues to get special treatment, and D.W. pretends she has chicken pox and teases him about not going to the circus. The tables are turned when Arthur gets better just in time —and his sister gets the chicken pox and must miss the circus.

1. For this book, do not show the cover or title because it gives away part of the plot. Instead, cover the book and tell the students that you are going to share a book about Arthur. They may be familiar with other Arthur books. If so, discuss the ones they've read and have them predict what this one might be about. Tell your students that you'll be reading parts of the book and letting them tell what they think will happen next. Explain that if they realize they already know the story, they should let the other students predict the story.

2. Read the first seven pages, stopping at the picture of the family at the dining table. Ask the students what illness they think Arthur has. Accept all predictions, asking why they think Arthur has that particular ailment. Respond positively to the predictions: "Yes, Arthur might have a cold."

3. Turn the page and have students confirm Arthur's chicken pox by looking at the picture. Then read the text, confirming that chicken pox is the correct prediction.

4. Read until Grandma Thora tells D.W. she'll give her a soothing bath and fix some juice. Ask students to predict what they think will happen during her bath. Accept all responses.

5. Again, use the picture on the next page to resolve their predictions. Then read the text and discuss the prediction.

6. Read to the next to the last page in which Arthur is laughing. Review what has happened in the story so far and ask students how they think it will end. Accept all predictions.

7. Use the picture of D.W. with her spots to resolve the predictions, commenting on how this story could have ended several ways.

8. This book offers a good opportunity to predict what happens beyond the story. Who will stay home to take care of D.W.? How will she handle her disappointment? Would there be another opportunity to go to the circus? Students might want to share times when things haven't worked out for them, as in this story. This book is also a good lesson in how teasing can backfire, which could be another fruitful discussion area.

Finally, take a few minutes to talk about how you used your thinking skills as you read this book to decide how useful it was and to decide what to do next. Comment on your students' contribution to the process through their careful listening. This process can be used easily with a video or film; you can stop the presentation at key points. Involve your students in determining where to stop, emphasizing that they can interrupt the process to clarify information, discuss words, and so forth.

TALKING-LISTENING GAMES

Listening games can be played to fill a few moments or to refocus the class. For the game, "I Spy," the teacher gives a clue to something students can see in the immediate area, adding more information after incorrect guesses. "I spy something that sits on a shelf. . . . I spy something that sits on a shelf and is used during writing and reading. . . ." The one who guesses correctly can lead the next game. "I Packed My Suitcase" is another alphabet game. The first person starts with an *a* word: "I packed my bag with an apple." The second person adds, "I packed my bag with an apple and a baseball." Restricting the game to topics, such as food or animals, not only adds to the challenge, but also provides an opportunity to reinforce a topic under investigation. For young children, repeat the cumulative line as a group with the student adding the new line so that everyone experiences success. (See Spotlight 1 on page 76.)

CONVERSATION

Children explore thoughts, opinions, feelings, and information through conversation; however, many of us were taught to be quiet in the classroom. In today's classroom, conversing is given more value. Informal conversation helps a teacher maintain communication with individuals. Some teachers schedule regular times for conversations, such as taking turns having lunch with individuals or small groups.

Formal conversation occurs when students share information about an assignment, work in small groups to complete a project, or work with a partner to solve a problem. The following objectives for conversation are adapted from work by Elizabeth Thorn (1974, 191–192):

1. Students talk "with" rather than "at" each other.

2. Students listen attentively and responsively.

3. Students interrupt courteously to present a new point of view or thought.

4. Students participate without monopolizing.

5. Students disagree courteously.

6. Students add interesting information to the conversation.

spot l i g h t   1

Listening/Alphabet Games

GRADE LEVELS: Kindergarten and up.

BOOK: *A My Name Is Alice* by Jane Bayer, illustrated by Steven Kellogg (New York: Trumpet, 1984).

ACTIVITY: Organized alphabetically, this book begins with the familiar chant, "A my name is Alice and my husband's name is Alex. . . ." Read the book aloud. Then organize the children alphabetically by their first names in a circle. Go around the circle, letting each child contribute a line using their first name as the beginning phrase. Use "friend" instead of "husband" or "wife." If students have difficulty, brainstorm possibilities for the names, places, and items to sell before each turn. Record their responses, but allow changes later. (With a large class, this activity may take several sessions.) After everyone has determined their lines, review the illustrations in the book, noting how the artist used the text to create the pictures. Give students copies of their lines and drawing paper to create a class Big Book. Save the Big Book to use the next year as an example of a previous class's work. Another time you can extend the lesson by looking up on a map all the places from the lines "I come from _____. . . ."

SHARING

In the early grades, sharing often takes the form of show-and-tell, telling about a book, or talking about current events. The teacher may begin the day simply by asking, "Who has something to share?" Sharing is important because this may be the only time when children can give elaborated answers to the teacher's or students' questions. Children can share out-of-school experiences and can discuss personal experiences (Cazden 1988, 8). Sharing can be valuable for everyone if the teacher works at modeling pertinent questions to keep the process lively and interesting. Asking the following questions when someone is talking about an object will help this process:

Where did you get it?

Why did you get it?

What do you do with it?

What other things do you have like it?

What other class members have something like it?

Create special sharing times by having the students bring in their favorite baby picture, collection, holiday item, pet photo, memento from a vacation, item that will fit in a pocket, and so forth. Be sensitive to the economic level of your students so that all can participate in the process.

When students share a favorite book, ask them to share a favorite page, explain what is special about the book, or show a favorite illustration. When they share favorite art, ask them what was used to create the piece, how long it took, what it felt like, and so forth.

For sharing current events, have students bring in photographs from newspapers and articles. In the beginning-of-the-year letter, encourage parents to discuss current events with their children, looking for interesting topics, such as an unusual animal being born at the zoo. Keep parents informed of any topics you are investigating through units and request that they send in related pictures and photographs during the investigation. Vary current events by having each student bring in a favorite comic strip from the Sunday newspaper.

INFORMAL LITERATURE DISCUSSION GROUPS

Everyone loves to talk about their favorite book. Begin informal discussion groups within the first few weeks of school. Model how to share books by gathering the children in a circle. One child should share the name of the book and then tell a partner something about the book. The partner asks questions about the book while others listen. Then the partner takes a turn sharing (Peterson and Eeds 1990, 56). Discuss the kinds of questions that make for good conversations about books. Have children participate in casual booktalks, then expand the discussion to small groups. As children become more comfortable, they will share more details in addition to their thoughts and feelings about their books they are reading. A first grade teacher and a Chapter 1 teacher, who worked in a federally funded program, recorded their students' discussion groups, sharing the transcripts with their students; they found this was a powerful process for the students. Five children seemed to be the optimal number for these discussion groups. Most importantly, they found that when children discussed thought-provoking books, they had meaningful discussions (Crawford and Hoopingarner 1993, 271–272).

FINGERPLAYS AND RHYMES

Fingerplays develop dexterity, cultivate appreciation for rhyme and rhythm, and help youngsters focus. Obtain a resource of fingerplays or create your own from nursery rhymes. The following example may inspire you to make others:

Little Jack Horner

Little Jack Horner.	[Make outline of head.]
Sat in the corner.	[Put fingers on palm of hand.]
Eating his Christmas pie.	[Make eating motion.]
He stuck in his thumb.	[Put thumb down on palm.]
And pulled out a plum.	[Pull thumb out, look at it.]
And said, "What a good boy am I!"	[Put thumbs in "suspenders."]

Cumulative poems, similar to the "I packed my bag" activity, give students an opportunity to listen and participate in a rhythmic pattern. The entire class can read the poem, or voices can be added with each stanza. Try the following well-known poem:

The House That Jack Built

This is the house that Jack built.
This is the malt, that lay in the house that Jack built.
This is the rat, that ate the malt . . .
This is the cat, that killed the rat . . .
This is the dog, that worried the cat . . .
This is the cow with the crumpled horn, that tossed the dog . . .
This is the maiden all forlorn, that milked the cow with the crumpled horn . . .
This is the man all tattered and torn, that kissed the maiden all forlorn . . .
This is the priest all shaven and shorn, that married the man all tattered and torn . . .
This is the cock that crowed in the morn, that waked the priest all shaven and
   shorn . . .
This is the farmer sowing the corn, that kept the cock that crowed in the morn . . .

CHORAL SINGING

Young children love to sing, and they appreciate a teacher who enjoys singing, even if your voice isn't solo quality. Most children have learned simple tunes, such as "Mary Had a Little Lamb," or the alphabet song. Consider investing in a baritone ukelele to accompany the singing. This inexpensive instrument allows you to face the children while singing. It also gives a richer sound than a regular ukelele and is pitched at a comfortable level for young voices. Learn a few basic chords (C, D, F, and G), and you will be able to "fake" almost any easy song.

Start with some familiar nursery rhymes that can be sung: "The Mulberry Bush," "Three Blind Mice," "Sing a Song of Sixpence," "Hey, Diddle Diddle." Teach the traditional verses, and then make up your own with the class. For example, the following could be sung to "The Mulberry Bush":

spotlight 2

Singing Lullabies

GRADE LEVELS:
Preschool–1.

BOOKS: *Little Donkey Close Your Eyes* by Margaret Wise Brown, illustrated by Ashley Wolff (New York: HarperCollins, 1959, 1987, 1995).

Time for Bed by Mem Fox (New York: Trumpet, 1993).

A Song for Little Toad by Vivian French, illustrated by Barbara Firth (Cambridge, Mass.: Candlewick Press, 1995).

ACTIVITY: Each of these books features animals going to sleep; however, *Little Donkey* focuses on singing as well. After reading any of the stories aloud, ask what kind of song helps your students go to sleep. Sing some familiar lullabies, such as "Hush Little Baby," "By'm Bye," or "Rock-a-Bye Baby." Talk about what is soothing in lullabies. Make up new verses and write them on chart paper. Sing them just before rest time or when you need to calm the class.

This is the way we stack our books
Stack our books, stack our books.
This is the way we stack our books
On a cold and frosty morning.

Bruce Lansky has created "gentle rhymes for happy times" in *The New Adventures of Mother Goose*. Share his new rhymes and sing them to the familiar tunes. For example, sing the following rhyme by Robert Scotellaro to "Three Blind Mice." (Adapt the first line by repeating each phrase to fit the music.) Then challenge the students to make up their own new nursery rhymes.

Three kind mice, see how they run!
They all ran after the farmer's wife,
they took out some cheese, and they cut her a slice.
Did you ever see such a sight in your life
    as three kind mice?

© 1993 Meadowbrook Creations. Reprinted from *The New Adventures of Mother Goose* by Bruce Lansky with permission of its publisher, Meadowbrook Press, Minnetonka, MN.

If you truly cannot sing, use the same process for choral reading. Write nursery rhymes or simple poems on chart paper and have small groups or the entire class read the poems together. Those students who are just beginning to recognize the relationship between words and sounds will benefit from the repetition. (See Spotlight 2 and Something to Try 3 for more ideas.)

something to try 3

Choral Singing or Reading Program

Organize a choral singing or reading program for primary students. Work with the class to learn a variety of nursery rhymes or easy songs. The songs or readings could be related by theme, such as animals, or by event, such as a holiday. Have your students practice using charts with the words so they don't feel the pressure of memorization. Plan to include one or two songs or poems that parents can sing or read at the end of the program. Set a date and invite parents to attend the sharing. Decide on an appropriate sequence of presentation and prepare a simple program with the students' names listed. Consider serving simple refreshments at the end of the program to celebrate their success.

PUPPETRY

Puppetry, effective for all ages, may include puppets you have purchased or made that relate to a variety of stories; these can be hand puppets made of felt or socks, stick puppets that are outlines glued to tongue depressors, paper bag puppets, papier-mâché and cloth creations. A tongue depressor glued to a paper plate can be used to create a variety of faces for puppet play. For shadow puppets, have children hold stick puppets between a light and a sheet. Use the overhead projector and a screen with stick puppets for an easy puppet show.

After your students have used puppets with familiar stories, such as in the puppet play example "The Three Billy Goats Gruff" beginning on page 100, encourage them to find stories they can adapt for puppetry. Young children can tape-record their version, dictate the play to a volunteer who writes it down, or create a script with a combination of temporary spelling and **rebuses**. Have periodic performances of plays you have learned, using a resource such as Denise Anton Wright's *One-Person Puppet Plays* if necessary, in addition to those plays the children have created.

■ Rebuses
Words that combine
letters and pictures.

STORYTELLING

Storytelling brings its own special magic as teller and listeners immerse themselves in the story. Children begin storytelling at an early age, often showing a sense of a beginning, middle, and end by the age of 3 years. With reinforcement from family members, 5-year-olds will begin to show distinctive personal styles, and most children at age 8 can tell several different types of stories, relating complex events (Engel 1995, 16–17). Children tell stories of personal experience, shared personal anecdotes during which another person conarrates the story, or fantasy and fiction (ibid.).

Young students
enjoy a puppet
show.

Whether children are telling or listening to others, storytelling develops receptive and expressive language skills (Kies, Rodriguez, and Granato 1993, 45). Children who love storytelling can read books looking for a story to tell. Listening to a professional storyteller can be both motivating and entertaining, but the teacher who tells stories, despite an amateur status, encourages the process by example. Ease into storytelling by telling some personal family stories, using audience participation stories, or repetitive stories (Barton 1993, 18). The following steps can be useful:

1. Choose a familiar story with interesting characters, action, suspense, a strong beginning, and a powerful climax. Consider humorous, cumulative, repetitive, or audience-participation stories.

2. Read the story several times, listing the main points repeatedly until you have internalized the story.

3. Practice the story in front of a mirror, refining the wording, inflections, pauses, and characterization through intonation and hand gestures.

4. Plan the introduction carefully, using minimal props.

5. Be sure your listeners can hear you. Maintain eye contact and vary your gestures as you have practiced. Use directed movement to refocus your listeners.

6. Evaluate the story, making notes as to where you want to further polish the story. Videotaping the story can be useful.

spotlight 3

Storytelling

GRADE LEVELS:
Preschool and up.

BOOK: *Deep in the Forest* by Brinton Turkle (New York: Trumpet, 1976).

ACTIVITY: In this wordless reversal of *Goldilocks and the Three Bears*, a young bear wanders into a log cabin, sampling the porridge, breaking a chair, tearing up a pillow, and falling asleep. When the family comes home, mama chases the cub off with a broom. The book ends with the cub safe with his mama and siblings. Share this book by just showing the pictures. Share it again, asking students to describe what is happening in the pictures. Encourage students to retell the story, using the pictures as their guide. Another wordless picture book useful for retelling is Ed Young's *The Other Bone*, the classic story of a dog who drops his bone upon seeing his reflection in the water.

Encourage young students to begin storytelling by having a joke day when everyone tells a favorite joke. If students need a resource, provide them with a book such as *The Laugh Book: A New Treasury of Humor for Children* compiled by Joanna Cole and Stephanie Calmenson or Marvin Terban's *Funny You Should Ask: How to Make Up Jokes and Riddles with Wordplay*. Consider using well-known fairy tales, favorite cumulative tales or rhymes, and favorite easy story-books for the next step. A flannel board for storytelling can be made by covering a board with flannel and propping it on an easel. Cut out figures from felt and use them to tell the story. Encourage students to try the process with their favorite stories, perhaps beginning with small groups of listeners. For a collection of 30 stories scripted for young storytellers, consult Martha Hamilton and Mitch Weiss's *Stories In My Pocket: Tales Kids Can Tell*. (See Appendix E for a sample story and see Spotlight 3 for a storytelling activity.)

DRAMA

Drama in the primary classroom does not mean putting on a play after weeks of rehearsals. Instead, drama develops from the daily play of young children (who are quite comfortable with dramatization), using setting and situation rather than a predetermined plot to stimulate their dramatic play (Sebasta 1993, 37). They come to school knowing how to assume a role, project a character's voice, and act out a fantasy. Children who build a castle with blocks, adding figures while narrating a fairy tale, are participating in dramatic play. Immerse your students in a dramatic play of a fairy tale using simple costumes

spotlight 4

Dramatizing a Folktale

GRADE LEVELS:
Preschool and up.

BOOK: *The Princess and the Pea* by Janet Stevens (New York: Holiday House, 1982).

ACTIVITY: Read this classic tale aloud. It is the story of a girl who proves she is a real princess when she can't sleep a wink due to a pea under a pile of mattresses. Ask the students what they would need to play this story: hats, jewelry, scarves, aprons, nightgown, wedding clothes, crowns, and so forth. If you have mats for resting or physical education, add several to the collection of materials. After gathering the various items, place copies of the book or other versions in the dramatic play area, and students will take it from there.

made of extra-large T-shirts with felt, ribbons, or cloth glued on to make different characters. See Joyce Harlow's *Story Play: Costumes, Cooking, Music, and More for Young Children* for costume patterns for a variety of fairy tales.

Drama with young children should be relatively unstructured, stimulated by themed areas, such as the post office or fast-food restaurant previously mentioned, or driven by children's natural love of dressing up and assuming roles. Martha Brady and Patsy T. Gleason recommend preparing for drama by considering the following: collecting sound effects on tapes; having a synthesizer; using percussion instruments; incorporating puppets; using items with strong smells (pine cones, potpourri, spices, perfumes); having a media collection of unusual poems, stories, pictures; collecting a box of makeup and clown white. You can also procure and learn how to use a video camera and photographic camera; gather fabric scraps; fill a box with props (wigs, glasses, masks, and so forth); have boxes for special spaces (dragon's cave, spaceship); and fill a bag with dress-up clothes such as shawls, scarves, gloves, costumes (1994, 16). (See also Spotlight 4.)

Early Reading Instruction

Most kindergarten and first grade students come to school with high expectations. If they have not learned to read as yet, most assume this will be their first accomplishment, preferably on the first day! Perceptive teachers capitalize on this eagerness, demonstrating to the students that they can be readers and may already know many words. The following practices help beginning, as well as more accomplished, readers.

READING ALOUD

Children in the emergent literacy stage enjoy interacting with print, listening to stories, imitating reading, and attempting to write (O'Donnell and Wood 1992, 5). In a review of the research, Stephen Krashen emphasizes the multiple effects reading aloud has on literacy development. Children who regularly listen to books participate in discussions, read more, and show gains in vocabulary and comprehension (1993, 39). Students make literary connections and begin to understand literary references, stretch their imaginations, and develop critical thinking (Friedberg and Strong 1989, 41–44). In *The New Read-Aloud Handbook*, Jim Trelease emphasizes the importance of instilling a desire to read in children by singing its praises just like McDonald's advertises its products. The best advertisement for reading is reading aloud when children are young and then reading to them all their lives (1989, 9). Further, reading aloud is not just for the primary language arts or reading teacher; it is for every subject area and every grade level.

Teachers may despair at finding the time to read aloud, claiming they have to cover the curriculum. However, just the fact that reading aloud increases vocabulary and comprehension is adequate justification for incorporating reading aloud into your daily schedule. Some teachers begin their class by reading aloud, recognizing that a good book will motivate students to arrive promptly to class. Starting with a book also allows you to segue to a unit of study or discussion topic. Others choose to read aloud during normally flat times such as after lunch. Another favorite read-aloud time is at the end of the period or day to bring closure to activities or studies.

Teachers who are not sure how to begin or what to read aloud can refer to two resources. Jim Trelease's *The New Read-Aloud Handbook* (1989) makes a strong case for reading aloud and includes a treasury of classic read-alouds, complete with annotations. Sharron L. McElmeel's *The Latest and Greatest Read-Alouds* (1994) includes an annotated bibliography of books published since 1988. Each book contains recommended grade levels and related books. Once you have selected a book, preread it before sharing it with the class. Be sure you are comfortable with the content, vocabulary, and style of writing. After you have read it aloud once, consider reading it aloud another time or two. Then make it available for your students to read independently. For additional ideas, refer to the read-aloud recommendations in Figure 3.1. And don't forget to share with students those books you are reading on your own time. You are an important role model.

A popular way to initiate early listening experiences with young children is to use oversize picture books called Big Books. This shared reading experience, advocated by Don Holdaway (1979), involves placing an enlarged book on an easel for reading aloud. The book may be a commercial version, one that is a

Read-Aloud Recommendations

1. Read the book before reading it to the class.
2. Read aloud books you enjoy.
3. Read as often as possible.
4. Allow students to be comfortable, but be sure you have their full attention.
5. Keep distractions to a minimum.
6. Vary the types of books you read. Read nonfiction and fiction.
7. Read picture books daily to all ages, even high school. When students are ready for a chapter book, read related picture books, in addition to the ongoing chapter book.
8. When reading picture books, be sure all students can see the illustrations.
9. Encourage young children to chime in and participate, especially with repetitive lines.
10. Choose books that are slightly challenging to the listener, perhaps books that your students might not ordinarily select. They will stretch for a good book, and many will read it when you have finished.
11. Pace the reading of chapter books so that they hold the students' attention from day to day.
12. Plan adequate time for longer books, but be willing to quit a book if it isn't successful.
13. Allow time for discussion when appropriate, but do not dissect the book.
14. Use expression when reading, changing voices and adding sound effects when appropriate.
15. Share information about the author.
16. Be willing to reread a favorite book. Remember that a good book is worth a second visit.
17. Read other material aloud, such as magazines and newspaper articles aloud.
18. Send home read-aloud recommendations to parents.

familiar book with new illustrations created by the students, an adaptation of a familiar story, or an original story created by the students or teacher. The teacher reads aloud the book, pointing to each word, encouraging the children to join in after the first reading. Big Books can also be used with intermediate students. Diane Snowball points out that when Big Books are used, students can begin to understand forms of writing, language style, print conventions, paragraphing, and layout of text (1991, 54–55).

TEACHING THE ALPHABET

Our jobs would be much easier if every child came to school knowing how to identify all the letters of the alphabet. In reality, some students won't know how to recite the alphabet song and others will be able to print the letters in upper- and lowercase. Some preschool or kindergarten teachers introduce a new letter a week, immersing their students in a variety of activities that celebrate words that begin with that particular letter. However well intended, taking 26 weeks to progress through the entire alphabet can be deadly for those students who are already creating their own stories. Accomplishing this approach in 26 days might be more tolerable, especially if the activities are interesting and thoughtfully developed for both the students who don't know their letters and those who do.

Alternative activities that allow for individualized responses can be incorporated into shared reading practices, discussed in the next section. Alphabet books, available on virtually any topic, can be read aloud and used to inspire student-created alphabet books. A song such as "John Jacob Jingleheimer Schmidt" can be used to reinforce the letter *j*. Play "Concentration" by turning upper- and lowercase letters face down and having students match them. Reinforce the names of letters while reading aloud: "I'm going to read aloud *'Buzz, Buzz, Buzz,' Went the Bumblebee* by Colin West. 'Buzz' begins with the letter *b*. Do you see some more *b*'s in the title?" An alphabet center can include alphabet blocks, sandpaper letters, a sand tray for tracing letters, clay for creating letters, occasional alphabet cookies, stencils, and so forth. (See Spotlight 5.)

DEVELOPING PHONEMIC AWARENESS

■ **Phonemic awareness**
The ability to recognize that a spoken word comprises a sequence of individual sounds.

Developing **phonemic awareness** in your students helps them become aware of sounds. Some awareness of sounds supports the beginning reading process, and when youngsters do begin reading, they further develop their phonemic awareness. In a review of recent research in her introduction to the third edition of *Learning to Read: The Great Debate* (1996), Jeanne Chall asserts that phonemic awareness is highly related to the ability to learn phonics; we will discuss this more fully in Chapter 4.

How does a parent or teacher know that a child is developing some phonemic awareness? When the child listening to a new story predicts a rhyming word or an alliterative word, the child shows phonemic awareness. Other signals include trying to give the initial sound of a word and trying to label drawings using **invented** or **temporary spelling**. Children demonstrate conscious attention to a phoneme when they isolate sounds as they try to spell a word or when they use the sounds associated with letters to identify words and recognize families of words (Richgels, Poremba, and McGee 1996, 633).

■ **Invented spelling**
Functional spelling that approximates the correct form. Also called *temporary spelling*.

spotlight 5

Alphabet Books

GRADE LEVELS:
Preschool and up.

BOOK: *Eating the Alphabet: Fruits and Vegetables from A to Z* by Lois Ehlert (New York: Trumpet Club, 1989).

ACTIVITY: After sharing this brilliantly illustrated collection of foods, students can choose their favorites for each letter of the alphabet and assemble their own alphabet book of preferred foods. For a class project, create a chart that lists all the foods for each letter. For example, for A, include apricot, artichoke, avocado, apple, and asparagus. Have the students vote on the class favorite and make a simple graph. Create a class favorites alphabet book, with one or two children responsible for one or two pages. (Because this book presents each word in lower- and uppercase, be sure to point out the differences.)

Many of the activities we've been discussing, such as reading aloud, choral singing and reading, and talking games, develop phonemic awareness. Literature that plays with the sounds in language is especially useful in developing phonemic awareness (Griffith and Olson 1992, 520). Read a poem with rhyming words aloud and have students raise their hands every time they hear a pair of words that rhyme. At another time, read a new rhyming poem aloud, stop before the rhyming words, and let students fill in possible answers. Give students pictures of various objects that rhyme and have them sort and match the rhyming pairs. Challenge students to post pictures of rhyming pairs on a bulletin board or word wall.

Shared reading provides the context for another process for developing phonemic awareness, entitled "What Can You Show Us?" Developed by a kindergarten teacher, this process includes four steps: preparation, previewing, student demonstrations, and applications. The teacher first selects and displays a text such as a letter, recipe, Big Book, or teacher-developed text. The text is previewed informally at first, with the teacher inviting the students to explore the text as they wish. Later, during a whole-class time, they discuss the book and briefly note its features. During the heart of the process—student demonstrations—the teacher invites the students to show the class something they know about the text. This may include identifying letters or words or reading passages. Finally, during applications, the class follows the usual three steps of shared reading: the teacher reads the selection, the class then reads it together, and the class completes selected activities or extensions. Follow-up readings and extensions may occur over several days, giving the students ample opportunities to further develop their phonemic awareness (Richgels, Poremba, and McGee 1996, 634–635). (See Spotlight 6 on page 88.)

s p o t l i g h t 6

Developing Phonemic Awareness

GRADE LEVELS:
Preschool and up.

BOOK: *Little Donkey Close Your Eyes* by

Margaret Wise Brown, illustrated by Ashley Wolff (New York: HarperCollins, 1959, 1987, 1995).

ACTIVITY: In this book, each animal is urged to go to sleep with a simple rhyme. Read each verse aloud, stopping before the end and letting the children fill in the missing word. Many of the verses end with "Close your eyes," which offers all students an opportunity to experience success.

Hallie Kay Yopp (1992, 699) suggests that you have the children decide which of several words begins with a given sound or have them say a word that begins with a particular sound. For example, you could show children a coat, hat, and pants and ask them to identify the one that begins with the /p/ sound. Conversely, children could be told a word and asked to tell what the sound is at the beginning of the word (ibid., 700). Yopp also suggests having children substitute new initial sounds, such as changing "Ee-igh, ee-igh, oh!" from "Old MacDonald Had a Farm" to "Bee-bigh, bee-bigh, boh!" (ibid., 701). Any activities for developing phonemic awareness should have an element of fun, should be conducted in groups, should respect children's curiosity and individual differences, and should be conducted informally (ibid., 702).

SHARED READING

Shared reading is the step between your reading aloud to students and their reading independently. Robert and Marlene McCracken (1986, 13) describe the "lap technique," where we hold a child in our lap while we read aloud. Shared reading is an expanded version of this enjoyable experience; the children learn by reading with a teacher who gradually allows them to assume increasing amounts of responsibility for the process.

This process, often used with an easy Big Book (or a poem on an overhead so that all students can participate), may begin with the teacher discussing the back and front covers and the title as she speculates on the story. She then reads the story aloud, allowing students to chime in if the story is repetitive. If appropriate, she might interrupt the reading once or twice to ask her students what they think will happen next, to clarify the text, or to discuss word meanings. Such interruptions should be kept to a minimum, however, so that students can appreciate the story line. At the end of the story, the teacher discusses the students' responses to the book.

During the second reading, which may occur immediately or later in the day, the teacher may point to each word, reinforcing the visual and auditory link. As students become readers, she will limit her pointing to a sweep beneath the line of text. The teacher may discuss specific words or how print conventions affect the story. Students are then asked to join in and read a particular repeated word or phrase. Or she may play a bit with a subsequent reading, using a different voice, such as an underwater, telephone operator, or opera voice (Rodriguez 1995). The next step might involve dramatizing the story, adding motions, adding music, chanting, singing to familiar tunes, distributing individual copies for reading, illustrating parts of the story, using sentences on tagboard strips, creating new sentences on strips, or creating the whole story.

Terry Rodriguez, a primary teacher and consultant, suggests that students with special needs may benefit from a "picture walk" before reading the book aloud (ibid.). In this case, the teacher introduces the book by discussing first the covers and titles and then pages through the book, inviting students to discuss what is happening. When the story is read aloud, the class can verify whether their predictions and the illustrations are consistent with the written text. Perhaps their story is even better than the written version. When using second-language materials with bilingual students, use sticky notes to put the dominant language over the book's text. Gradually remove the words during subsequent readings, incorporating additional new words.

A good book for shared reading should have an enlarged format and a predictable story pattern with strong characters. It should use spoken language naturally, have an interesting or memorable story line, hold up to repeated readings, be appropriate for fluent reading, and be age appropriate. The illustrations should be meaningful, and rhyme, rhythm, and repetition should be used liberally (Depree and Iversen 1994, 36; Rodriguez 1995). (See Chapter 7 for a discussion of predictable and pattern books.) Use an old favorite that has held up through repeated readings to teach skills such as identifying the sound of a letter. Terry Rodriguez emphasizes that one should choose a book to teach a skill because the students will need the skill to read similar books (ibid.). For example, a teacher could use sticky notes to cover up the -*ed* endings on words to demonstrate the function of past tense. This information could then be used with another shared reading book that uses past tense. A story or song such as "Bring Back My Bonnie to Me" could be used to identify the sound of *b*. See Figure 3.2 on page 90 for a sample shared reading activity.

SUSTAINED READING

A primary goal of teachers should be to inspire their students to read for an extended period of time. For the youngest students, this may begin with quietly looking at picture books for 5 minutes, with the amount of time

FIGURE 3.2
Shared Reading
Activity

Shared Reading Activity

1. Welcome or introductory comments (5 minutes)
2. Sharing favorite stories, songs or poems (5–7 minutes)
3. Minilanguage lesson, using an old favorite (5 minutes)
4. Reading a new story or poem (10 minutes)
5. Follow-up activity, such as writing new versions, creating a movable book, illustrating a section (20 minutes)
6. Independent reading (following completion of above activity) (5–30 minutes)
7. Sharing follow-up activities (10 minutes)
8. Reading aloud (15 minutes)

Terry Rodriguez. Emergent Literacy Workshop. Denver, Colo. June 21, 1995.

gradually expanded. As students look at the pictures, they learn that words and print have an important connection, that text proceeds from left to right, that illustrations often support the story, and that reading is an enjoyable pastime. Older students often participate in a more formal period of quiet reading, also known as SSR (sustained silent reading). For younger children, this is generally not a particularly quiet time; indeed, young readers will probably be trying to say some of the words out loud, verbalizing what they think is happening, or sharing something exciting or special with a friend. These behaviors should be allowed if the students are truly engaged and are not disrupting others. If the entire school participates in SSR, the period will be more formal, with everyone in the entire school, including office staff, reading quietly for a prescribed period of time.

Emergent Writers

Just as young children are fascinated with reading, so do they also love to experiment with writing. It is difficult to discuss reading as a singular language art because reading and writing develop in tandem. Dolores Durkin (1966) investigated children who read at an early age and who had little traditional instruction. She found that these youngsters were quite curious about language and very interested in writing. They wanted to write their names, scribble, and create notes. A key component of their success was an adult who fostered their interest in reading and writing by reading aloud and discussing these processes.

A student writes
about his day.

Children often begin writing by labeling their drawings with a few letters that represent words. Their writing will be vertical, horizontal, or a combination (Wilson, Mosley, and Shirley 1993, 115). Once they have shown an interest in writing, their enthusiasm can be fostered by giving them authentic reasons to write: invitations, letters, notes to their parents, reminders, lists, observations, records, and so forth. Reading provides many opportunities for writing, as demonstrated in the shared reading process when students create new sentences or versions of a story. A writing center can house materials useful for exploring writing; however, writing opportunities should also be integrated into other areas such as the alphabet center.

Sometimes teachers or parents express concern about the many invented spellings used by emergent writers. Correctness should not be the major focus at this stage. Some people believe that the writing should stand as it is, but often even the writer will forget what was intended after the passage of time. Therefore, some teachers pencil in the correct spelling so that everyone can appreciate the message. Others attach a sticky note with the correct written text. When a child asks how a word should be spelled, a teacher or parent can easily reinforce phonemic awareness by asking how the child thinks the word sounds at the beginning. When spelling a word that presents difficulties with the sound-symbol association, such as *of*, you can comment that the spelling of some words must just be memorized. Linking reading and writing is discussed more fully in Chapter 10.

Taking the Next Step

It can be difficult to know when students are ready to engage in more formal literacy activities. Ask yourself the following questions; does the student

1. Identify most letters and some sounds?

2. Appreciate rhythm, rhyme, and repetition?

3. Show enjoyment of stories?

4. Volunteer to read text aloud?

5. Correct errors voluntarily?

6. Make accurate predictions from the story and the illustrations?

7. Recognize some words in a variety of contexts?

8. Recognize basics, such as left to right orientation and how to handle a book?

9. Ask appropriate questions about print?

10. Want to read?

If you have affirmative answers to most of these questions, this student is probably ready for additional literacy experiences. However, activities such as reading aloud, sustained reading, or informal literature discussion groups continue to be appropriate even as learners advance.

Early-Intervention Programs

In an urban southern school, a first grade student entered the Reading Recovery room, a small room set up for individualized teaching, carrying an envelope with several paperback books inside. First, the teacher had him write the word "give" on the board. After sitting at the table with her, he read fluently from two favorite books, *Pancakes for Supper* and *The Three Little Pigs*. Next he read a new book, while she recorded notes regarding errors, repetitions, or omissions in a running record. This youngster was skilled at using illustrations to help with comprehension, and he carefully sounded out words. However, he made some mistakes and sometimes said words without understanding them. The teacher addressed some of the errors and then directed his practice with magnetic letters, having him find little words in big words, such as *hen* in *then*. Next, he chose to write a story sentence: *I went to get a haircut.* After printing the sentence with some direction from the teacher, he reread it.

The teacher cut up the strip (h/air/cut) and he rearranged it before placing it in an envelope. Finally he read a new book, receiving additional instruction on *gr* and *e* and on how to interpret the pictures. The lesson moved quickly, and the student maintained a high level of interest throughout.

Time is precious to a first grader who can't read as well as the peer group, and Marie Clay emphasizes that students struggling with reading should not have to wait for help (1991, 324). Reading Recovery has been shown to be effective with the lowest-achieving children and with diverse populations (Swartz and Klein 1997, 3) and appears to be promising as an early-intervention program in Spanish (Escamilla 1997, 120). Reading Recovery provides intensive, daily, 30-minute lessons that allow one student to work with one teacher on a variety of reading and writing experiences. A lesson may contain the following components in varying order:

- The student reads a familiar story.

- The teacher keeps a running record of the reading and then immediately teaches key points.

- The student works with letters to construct words.

- The student writes a message or story.

- The student reads a new book (Pinnell, Fried, and Estice 1990).

Because of the one-on-one nature of Reading Recovery, the instruction is time-intensive and expensive, both to train teachers and to maintain instruction. The program has met with success because students use their known language to gain proficiency in the semantic, syntactic, and visual cueing systems used to become independent readers (Reynolds 1993, 80). However, continued classroom instruction, reading in the home, and a rich curriculum are vital components of a complete reading program (Pinnell, Fried, and Estice 1990, 294).

In another early-intervention program, Carol Caserta-Henry organized Reading Buddies, in which first graders were paired with high school student tutors (1996). The first graders were chosen based on their early word knowledge plus a referral by the classroom teacher that indicated the children were falling behind in the language arts and were expressing frustration with reading, writing, and spelling. A 7-month commitment to training and tutoring was required of the nine tutors. The tutoring format included reading a new book each week, rereading a familiar story from the previous week, writing in a journal at least twice a week, and doing word-study activities once or twice a week. Both students and tutors achieved success and expressed great enthusiasm for this program. Involving minimal cost, it could be developed using parent or community volunteers.

Success for All, a total school program for kindergarten through third grades in inner city communities, focuses on individual tutoring and classroom support (Pikulski 1994). The program, which emphasizes reading-level groupings and direct instruction in phonics, requires intense commitment and cooperation from the whole staff (Freeman 1995/1996). The Winston–Salem Project organizes first grade instruction into four 30-minute blocks for heterogeneous instruction on writing, working with words, self-selected reading, and working with a basal program plus related literature. Students spend a total of 3 hours and 15 minutes per day in reading-related activities (ibid.). With Early Intervention in Reading (EIR), first grade teachers give an extra 20 minutes of reading instruction to five to seven of the lowest-achieving students in their class (ibid.). The Boulder Project involves Chapter 1 teachers providing instruction to a group of three students while an aide instructs another group; they then trade roles midway through the year. Both this project and EIR focus on repeated readings of predictable books and teaching word-recognition skills (ibid.).

Language Differences

Many young children come to school with different language styles or dialects, and the practices for helping these students have varied during the past decade. Some districts emphasize bilingual education programs, during which students receive instruction in both languages with an emphasis on maintaining the primary language while developing English. Other districts provide transitional programs that move students from their primary language, such as Spanish, to English as quickly as possible. Still other districts provide support for the student for a short time each day, but leave the bulk of the teaching to the regular classroom teacher.

Nonstandard dialects do not demonstrate deficiencies; rather, they indicate differences that may be derived from the dominant culture or from varying home practices (Neuman and Roskos 1993, 75–79). **Limited-English-proficient** (LEP) students who have a rich first language will generally achieve high levels of vocabulary and concepts in both languages. Those with an impoverished first-language environment will be more challenged (ibid., 80). For example, a student who can already tell time in one language will probably learn it faster in the second language than a student who cannot tell time at all (Handscombe 1989, 4). Students who have an alternative dominant language come from many backgrounds; their parents may be immigrants, refugees, international students, or second-generation immigrants (ibid., 2–3). To provide these LEP students with a quality program, Handscombe identifies these five points:

Limited-English-proficient (LEP) students
Children whose home language is not English; children who need to acquire English as a second language.

1. An orientation program should provide information to the new student and parents, preferably in the dominant language. This should include information about the school, practices, and so forth. This program also can provide the staff with information about the student.

2. A monitoring procedure includes an initial assessment, placement and program decisions, and a periodic review of progress.

3. A program of parental involvement ensures that parents are invested in the educational process and aware of the school's expectations.

4. The language program should *add* English, rather than *substitute* for it. A strong program will provide students with opportunities to demonstrate their first-language skills as they develop the second language.

5. An academic upgrading program provides students who are years behind their age group with opportunities to catch up, yet allows them to be with their peers as much as possible. A teacher or tutor should begin instruction in the dominant language and use more English as language skills develop (ibid., 6–10).

When working with second-language learners, remember that they can often understand much more than they can speak. Use movement, gestures, and pictures to enhance communication. Recognize that many of the practices that help emergent readers and writers, such as reading repetitive books or singing songs, also help LEP students. Choral reading, the process of reading or speaking poetry together, effectively involves second-language learners (McCauley and McCauley 1992). Learn a few key phrases from your students' language and ask them to teach you more words and phrases.

Involve these students in all aspects of the classroom activities, even if you think they don't understand everything about the activity or communication is difficult. I once had a student who had arrived from Vietnam 2 weeks before school began. He had virtually no English skills. After a few weeks of school, I recalled that during the Vietnam War, a pen pal soldier had sent me a custom-made dress that I still had in my closet. I brought it to school one day, and upon examining the label, this student delightedly shared that while living in Saigon he passed this shop every day on his way to school. This invaluable connection smoothed the transition for him into what must have been a bewildering experience.

Celebrate many cultures of the world, particularly those represented in your classroom. Inviting parents to share their culture not only enriches the classroom experience but also enhances the individual student's connection between home and school (Schmidt 1995, 411). For a rich resource of history on cultures and related activities, consult Carole Angell's *Celebrations Around the World: A Multicultural Handbook*.

Carole Cox and Paul Boyd-Batstone identify practices that support second-language learners: a room environment with many opportunities for reading; scheduled time for reading; reading aloud; shared reading (Big Books, charts, and so forth); buddy or paired reading; sustained silent reading; wide independent reading (1997, 61–62). These are, of course, familiar to us because such activities also support the general class in reading successfully. Cox and Boyd-Batstone also stress the importance of allowing ample opportunities for talking, responding to questions, writing in journals, and reading related books. Response opportunities (projects), reading texts as writing models, story dramatization, readers theatre, storytelling, puppetry, artistic responses, making media such as filmstrips or slides, using computers, constructions such as dioramas, and making books—all contribute to the success of LEP students (ibid., 65–66).

Collecting family stories not only involves parents but also encourages all students to explore their cultural heritages. Rita Buchoff (1995) shared family stories found in children's literature, such as Valerie Flournoy's *The Patchwork Quilt* and its sequel, *Tanya's Reunion*. Students then had a list of prompts with which they asked family members for a story. The prompts included such statements as "Tell me about the house you lived in when you were my age." After collecting the story, the student can practice telling the story before sharing it orally with the class. Family stories can also be recorded in writing, illustrated, taped, or video-recorded.

All students need rich language experiences that build on existing knowledge and immerse them in meaningful activities. Supporting your mainstreamed special learners involves providing them with many opportunities to increase their language skills. This often requires a team of professionals who are dedicated to finding the necessary mix of optional individual and classroom instruction.

Involving Parents

Parents are generally intensely interested in the early education of their children. Sadly, this interest often wanes through the passing years, so it is particularly important for teachers to develop (and hopefully "cement") involvement during the early years. Educators, parents, and community members are responding to this need. Parent-involvement programs may be part of a long-range plan, such as The Talk to a Literacy Learner (TTALL) program developed in Australia. This 18-month program entails 16 workshops for parents and further training for selected participants who become community tutors (Cairney and Munsie 1995). *A Survey of Family Literacy in the United States* (Morrow, Tracey, and Maxwell 1995) describes

something to try 4

Family Storytelling Club

Reading Is Fundamental (RIF) and the Spanish Education Development Center in Washington, D.C. developed this storytelling program to encourage parents of preschoolers to read to their children for pleasure (Morrow, Tracey, and Maxwell 1995, 24).

Begin by using a storytelling resource such as Martha Hamilton and Mitch Weiss's *Stories in My Pocket: Tales Kids Can Tell*. (See sample tale in Appendix E.) Learn a few basics about storytelling or have a professional give you some pointers. Keep in mind that you don't need to be polished! Share your story with the students and discuss what you had to do to learn the story.

Work with several student volunteers to develop their stories, encouraging them to use short, familiar stories. Folktales work particularly well. As these students share their stories, encourage other students to join the process.

Ask parents to come in and share their family stories. At first only a few may respond, but more will join in time. Have the students share their stories at the same time as the parents. Videotape the session and offer to let students take it home to share. This will encourage others to become involved. Continue to develop the club and encourage students to watch for opportunities to hear professional storytellers in the community.

more than 60 parental-involvement and intergenerational programs, plus sources for research on family literacy and a list of related agencies and associations, and *Family Literacy: Connections in Schools and Communities* (Morrow 1995) gives information on a variety of programs. (See Something to Try 4.)

Some programs not only involve parents in family literacy but also seek to develop an understanding of the challenges of families from diverse cultures. While conducting research, Lynn Moody met individually with a wide variety of parents to discuss literacy and learning and came to realize how willing they were to communicate their personal experiences, their cultural practices, their beliefs, and their life stories. "By listening to these parents' stories, I came to appreciate how my new knowledge of these out-of-school literacies and competencies could affect and inform my teaching practice" (1992, 228). She reflected on how previous teaching conferences had always been one-way transmissions of information, rather than opportunities to learn from them. To tap this rich source of knowledge and experience, she recommends planning a variety of experiences, such as informal get-togethers that would encourage mutual learning. Discussions could include topics of community, social, environmental, or educational issues. An activity, such as sharing family stories, would be an appropriate focus. She found that events that involved certain parents also improved the literacy efforts of other students from other cultures, as they all learned from each other (ibid., 232).

Involving families can be smoothly integrated into the routine of the school. In a meeting with all kindergarten parents during the beginning of the year, Marcia Parrish, a librarian in Littleton, Colorado, encourages parents to read aloud and check out books from the library. As part of their student-teacher conferences, all students in this elementary school bring their parents into the library to demonstrate the check-out procedure and on-line catalog access. To promote reading and books, she gives brief book talks or announcements at every school event, from music programs to community breakfasts. Cheryl Singer, a librarian in Baton Rouge, Louisiana, asked parents to donate stuffed animals no longer used at home. She paired these with related books, and students check out the stuffed animal and book in tote bags to take home. Teachers can reproduce pages with book-related discussion questions and activities from Anthony D. Frederick's *Involving Parents through Children's Literature: Grades Preschool–Kindergarten* for parents to use at home.

Minicelebrations at major milestones are a good way to involve parents. For example, celebrate the completion of a thematic unit by inviting the parents to come in and see what the students are sharing about their research. Have each student learn a favorite poem and have a poetry reading the last hour of a Friday, asking parents to share one of their favorites as well. Make each final Friday of the month an arts day, sharing readers theatre one Friday, a play the next, favorite songs the next, and so forth. Ask parents to volunteer, share information, "shadow" their student (spend a day doing everything with the student), come to lunch, cook for the students, read aloud, and so forth. Terry Rodriquez had students write questions in their journals for their parents to read and respond to each night. In short, use every strategy you can think of to get and keep parents involved in your program. Everyone will benefit.

A Final Note

Working with the very youngest learners takes a tremendous amount of energy but is incredibly rewarding. Young children come to school eager to learn, enjoying most authentic learning activities. They also usually love their teachers, a perk that you will treasure. However, along with their implicit trust comes a huge responsibility: As their teacher, you are entrusted with introducing them to the mystery and magic of reading and writing. Luckily, for us and for our students, there are a great many ways to do this, as you will see in later chapters.

Summary

Emergent literacy occurs during that time before formal instruction when children are building concepts related to reading and writing. These learners will most often be found in the preschool, kindergarten, or first grade. Conditions for learning include immersion, demonstration, expectation, responsibility, approximation, use, and response. Learners who are engaged in the learning process are more likely to achieve success in the school environment.

Thoughtful preparation of the context for early learning experiences promotes success. Your classroom should have ample books and print materials, themed areas, an organized use of equipment, and rich play areas. Talking and listening should be purposeful and should be fostered as an integral part of the language arts program. Listening and talking can be nurtured through the Directed Listening–Thinking Activity, Listening Think-Alouds, talking and listening games, conversation, sharing, informal literature discussion groups, fingerplays and rhymes, choral singing and reading, puppetry, storytelling, and dramatization.

For beginning reading and writing instruction, include reading aloud, alphabet activities, phonemic-awareness activities, shared reading, and sustained reading. Bridge from reading to writing, and provide a variety of authentic writing experiences. Be ready to move students into additional reading and writing activities as their skills develop.

Early-intervention programs can also be used in the school. Reading Recovery, Reading Buddies, Success for All, the Winston–Salem Project, Early Intervention in Reading, and the Boulder Project are successful examples of this approach.

Second-language students often come to school with language limitations and thus require instruction in both their dominant language and English. The program should include opportunities for valuing all cultural differences, in addition to providing instruction.

Family literacy programs can involve parents in the reading program. Celebrate the cultures of the world and provide rich language experiences. More informal efforts can be integrated into the routine of the school, particularly with the help of the school librarian. Involve parents with specific programs that train parents, such as The Talk to Literacy Learner (TTALL);

seek out opportunities to converse with these parents; and ask them to share family stories.

Puppet Play

THE THREE BILLY GOATS GRUFF

CHARACTERS: Narrator, Troll, Little Billy Goat Gruff, Middle Billy Goat Gruff, Big Billy Goat Gruff.

PUPPETS: Use stick puppets for a shadow or overhead projector presentation. Students could also present stick puppets or paper bag puppets by draping a blanket over a table and crouching beneath it.

DELIVERY: Students should practice matching voices to their individual sizes. The troll should sound very gruff. Students can join in with trip-trap noises as the goats cross the bridge, perhaps using wood blocks or simply clapping.

RELATED BOOKS

Alborough, Jez. *The Grass is Always Greener*. New York: Dial Books for Young Readers, 1987.

Hooks, William H. *The Gruff Brothers*. New York: Bantam, 1990.

Stevens, Janet. *The Three Billy Goats Gruff*. San Diego: Harcourt Brace Jovanovich, 1987.

SCRIPT

Story begins with puppet characters below or off stage. The narrator can be off to one side.

NARRATOR: Once upon a time there were three billy goats. Their name was Gruff. They wanted to eat the green grass on the hillside to make themselves fat. On the way was a bridge over a stream. Under the bridge lived a mean, ugly troll. It had big eyes and a long nose. The youngest Billy Goat Gruff set off to cross the bridge.

Youngest goat begins to cross the stage. Narrator leads audience in quiet trip-traps.

NARRATOR: Trip, trap! Trip, trap!

Troll pops head above stage.

TROLL: Who's that trip-trapping over my bridge?

Youngest goat answers timidly.

YOUNGEST BILLY GOAT GRUFF: It is I, the littlest Billy Goat Gruff. I am going to the hillside to eat the green grass and make myself fat.

Troll shakes and rumbles.

TROLL: On no you won't! For I am coming up to eat you!

Youngest goat backs up a bit.

YOUNGEST BILLY GOAT GRUFF: Oh please don't eat me! I am so little. Wait for the next Billy Goat Gruff. He is much bigger. He will make a much better meal for you.

TROLL: Well, then. Be off with you!

Troll disappears and little goat goes off to the side.

NARRATOR: So the little Billy Goat Gruff trip-trapped over the bridge. He began eating the green grass on the hillside.

Middle Billy Goat Gruff begins to cross the stage. Narrator leads audience in louder trip-traps.

NARRATOR: Soon the middle Billy Goat Gruff came across the bridge. Trip, trap! Trip, trap!

Troll pops head up near goat, speaking more loudly.

TROLL: Who's that trip-trapping over my bridge?

Middle goat answers in a medium voice.

MIDDLE BILLY GOAT GRUFF: It is I, the middle Billy Goat Gruff. I am going to the hillside to eat the green grass and make myself fat.

Troll shakes and rumbles more.

TROLL: On no you won't! For I am coming up to eat you!

Middle goat backs up a bit.

MIDDLE BILLY GOAT GRUFF: Oh please don't eat me! I am so little. Wait for the next Billy Goat Gruff. He is much bigger. He will make a much better meal for you.

TROLL: Well, then. Be off with you!

Troll disappears and middle goat goes to the side.

NARRATOR: So the middle Billy Goat Gruff trip-trapped over the bridge. He began eating the green grass on the hillside.

Big Billy Goat Gruff begins to cross the stage. Narrator leads audience in very loud trip-traps.

NARRATOR: Soon the big Billy Goat Gruff came across the bridge. Trip, trap! Trip, trap! Trip, trap!

Troll appears near goat, speaking the loudest.

TROLL: Who's that trip-trapping over my bridge?

Big goat answers loudly.

BIG BILLY GOAT GRUFF: IT IS I, THE BIG BILLY GOAT GRUFF. I am going to the hillside to eat the green grass and make myself fat.

Troll shakes and rumbles even more.

TROLL: On no you won't! For I am coming up to eat you!

Big goat advances on the troll.

BIG BILLY GOAT GRUFF: Then come on up!
For I have two horns.
I'll poke out your eyeballs!
I'll crush all your bones.

Big goat and troll butt at each other, following actions described by narrator. All characters can chime in on the closing rhyme.

NARRATOR: The troll flew at the big Billy Goat Gruff. But the big Billy Goat Gruff butted and poked him just as he promised. The big Billy Goat Gruff threw the troll into the stream and went on up the hillside. There the three Billy Goats Gruff ate and ate and ate. They got so fat they could hardly walk home. So. . .

Snip, snap, snout.
This tale's told out.

Adapted from *Readers Theatre for Beginning Readers* by Suzanne I. Barchers (Englewood, Colo.: Teacher Ideas Press, 1991) 19–21.

References

Angell, Carole. *Celebrations Around the World: A Multicultural Handbook.* Golden, Colo.: Fulcrum, 1995.

Barton, Bob. "Storytelling." In *Children's Voices: Talk in the Classroom*, edited by Bernice E. Cullinan, 17–32. Newark, Del.: International Reading Association, 1993.

Bayer, Jane. *A My Name Is Alice.* Illustrated by Steven Kellogg. New York: Trumpet, 1984.

Brady, Martha, and Patsy T. Gleason. *Artstarts: Drama, Music, Movement, Puppetry, and Storytelling Activities.* Englewood, Colo.: Teacher Ideas Press, 1994.

Brown, Marc. *Arthur's Chicken Pox.* Boston: Little, Brown, 1994.

Brown, Margaret Wise. *Little Donkey Close Your Eyes.* Illustrated by Ashley Wolff. New York: HarperCollins, 1959, 1987, 1995.

Buchoff, Rita. "Family Stories." *The Reading Teacher* 49, no. 3 (Nov. 1995): 230–233.

Burke, Constance. "Talk Within the Kindergarten: Language Supporting a Learning Community." In *Cycles of Meaning: Exploring the Potential of Talk in Learning Communities*, edited by Kathryn Mitchell Pierce and Carol J. Gilles, 79–97. Portsmouth, N.H.: Heinemann, 1993.

Cairney, Trevor H., and Lynne Munsie. "Parent Participation in Literacy Learning." *The Reading Teacher* 48, no. 5 (Feb. 1995): 392–403.

Cambourne, Brian. *The Whole Story: Natural Learning and the Acquisition of Literacy in the Classroom.* Auckland, New Zealand: Ashton Scholastic, 1988.

_____. "Toward an Educationally Relevant Theory of Literacy Learning: Twenty Years of Inquiry." *The Reading Teacher* 49, no. 3 (Nov. 1995): 182–190.

Caserta-Henry, Carol. "Reading Buddies: A First-Grade Intervention Program." *The Reading Teacher* 49, no. 6 (March 1996): 500–504.

Cazden, Courtney B. *Classroom Discourse: The Language of Teaching and Learning.* Portsmouth, N.H.: Heinemann, 1988.

Chall, Jeanne. *Learning to Read: The Great Debate*, 3rd ed. New York: Harcourt Brace, 1966.

Clay, Marie. *Becoming Literate: The Construction of Inner Control.* Portsmouth, N.H.: Heinemann, 1991.

Cole, Joanna, and Stephanie Calmenson. *The Laugh Book: A New Treasury of Humor for Children.* Illustrated by Marilyn Hafner. Garden City, N.Y.: Doubleday, 1987.

Cox, Carole, and Paul Boyd-Batstone. *Crossroads: Literature and Language in Culturally and Linguistically Diverse Classrooms.* Columbus, Ohio: Merrill, 1997.

Crawford, Kathleen, and Theresa Hoopingarner. "A Kaleidoscope of Conversation: A Case Study of a First-Grade Literature Group." In *Cycles of Meaning: Exploring the Potential of Talk in Learning Communities*, edited by Kathryn Mitchell Pierce and Carol J. Gilles, 261–273. Portsmouth, N.H.: Heinemann, 1993.

Depree, Helen, and Sandra Iversen. *Early Literacy in the Classroom: A New Standard for Young Readers.* Bothell, Wash.: Wright Group, 1994.

Durkin, Dolores. *Children Who Read Early.* New York: Teachers College Press, 1966.

_____. *Teaching Them to Read*, 5th ed. Boston: Allyn & Bacon, 1989.

Ehlert, Lois. *Eating the Alphabet: Fruits and Vegetables from A to Z.* New York: Trumpet Club, 1989.

Engel, Susan. *The Stories Children Tell: Making Sense of the Narratives of Childhood.* New York: W. H. Freeman, 1995.

Escamilla, Kathy. "Descubriendo La Lectura: An Early Intervention Literacy Program in Spanish." In *Research in Reading Recovery*, edited by Stanley L. Swartz and Adria F. Klein, 109–121. Portsmouth, N.H.: Heinemann, 1997.

Flournoy, Valerie. *The Patchwork Quilt*. Illustrated by Jerry Pinkney. New York: Dial Books for Young Readers, 1985.

____. *Tanya's Reunion*. Illustrated by Jerry Pinkney. New York: Dial Books for Young Readers, 1995.

Fox, Mem. *Time for Bed*. New York: Trumpet, 1993.

Fredericks, Anthony D. *Involving Parents through Children's Literature: Grades Preschool–Kindergarten*. Englewood, Colo.: Teacher Ideas Press, 1993.

Freeman, Matt. "Success for . . . All." *Reading TODAY* 13, no. 3 (Dec. 1995/Jan. 1996): 34–35.

French, Vivian. *A Song for Little Toad*. Illustrated by Barbara Firth. Cambridge, Mass.: Candlewick Press, 1995.

Friedberg, Barbara, and Elizabeth Strong. "'Please Don't Stop There!': The Power of Reading Aloud." In *Children's Literature in the Classroom: Weaving Charlotte's Web*, edited by Janet Hickman and Bernice E. Cullinan, 39–48. Needham Heights, Mass.: Christopher-Gordon, 1989.

Gibbons, Gail. *Emergency!* New York: Holiday House, 1994.

Goodman, Yetta, and Myna M. Haussler. "Literacy Environment in the Home and Community." In *Roles in Literacy Learning: A New Perspective*, edited by Duane R. Tovey and James E. Kerber, 26–32. Newark, Del.: International Reading Association, 1986.

Griffith, Priscilla L., and Mary W. Olson. "Phonemic Awareness Helps Beginning Readers Break the Code." *The Reading Teacher* 45, no. 7 (March 1992): 516–523.

Hamilton, Martha, and Mitch Weiss. *Stories in My Pocket: Tales Kids Can Tell*. Golden, Colo.: Fulcrum, 1996.

Handscombe, Jean. "A Quality Program for Learners of English as a Second Language." In *When They Don't All Speak English: Integrating the ESL Student into the Regular Classroom*, edited by Pat Rigg and Virginia G. Allen, 1–14. Urbana, Ill.: National Council of Teachers of English, 1989.

Harlow, Joyce. *Story Play: Costumes, Cooking, Music, and More for Young Children*. Englewood, Colo.: Teacher Ideas Press, 1992.

Holdaway, Don. *The Foundations of Literacy*. Portsmouth, N.H.: Heinemann, 1979.

Kies, Daniel, Idalia Rodriguez, and Frieda V. Granato. "Oral Language Development through Storytelling: An Approach to Emergent Literacy." *Reading Improvement* 30, no. 1 (Spring 1993): 43–47.

Krashen, Stephen. *The Power of Reading: Insights from the Research.* Englewood, Colo.: Libraries Unlimited, 1993.

Laminack, Lester L. "'Possibilities, Daddy, I think it says possibilities': A Father's Journal of the Emergence of Literacy." *The Reading Teacher* 43, no. 8 (April 1990): 536–540.

Lanksy, Bruce. *The New Adventures of Mother Goose.* Illustrated by Stephen Carpenter. Deephaven, Minn.: Meadowbrook Press, 1993.

McCauley, Joyce K., and Daniel S. McCauley. "Using Choral Reading to Promote Language Learning for ESL Students." *The Reading Teacher* 45, no. 7 (March 1992): 526–533.

McCracken, Robert A., and Marlene J. McCracken. *Stories, Songs, and Poetry to Teach Reading and Writing: Literacy through Language.* Chicago: American Library Association, 1986.

McElmeel, Sharron L. *The Latest and Greatest Read-Alouds.* Englewood, Colo.: Libraries Unlimited, 1994.

Moody, Lynn. "Conversations with Parents: Talking about Literacy and Living." In *Becoming Political: Readings and Writings in the Politics of Literacy Education,* edited by Patrick Shannon, 224–233. Portsmouth, N.H.: Heinemann, 1992.

Morrow, Lesley Mandel, ed. *Family Literacy: Connections in Schools and Communities.* Newark, Del.: International Reading Association, 1995.

Morrow, Lesley Mandel, Diane H. Tracey, and Caterina Marcone Maxwell, eds. *A Survey of Family Literacy in the United States.* Newark, Del.: International Reading Association, 1995.

Neuman, Susan B., and Kathleen A. Roskos. *Language and Literacy Learning in the Early Years: An Integrated Approach.* New York: Harcourt Brace Jovanovich, 1993.

O'Donnell, Michael P., and Margo Wood. *Becoming a Reader: A Developmental Approach to Reading Instruction.* Boston: Allyn & Bacon, 1992.

Peterson, Ralph, and Maryann Eeds. *Grand Conversations: Literature Groups in Action.* New York: Scholastic, 1990.

Pikulski, John J. "Preventing Reading Failure: A Review of Five Effective Programs." *The Reading Teacher* 48, no. 1 (Sept. 1994): 30–39.

Pinnell, Gay Su, Mary D. Fried, and Rose Mary Estice. "Reading Recovery: Learning How to Make a Difference." *The Reading Teacher* 43, no. 4 (Jan. 1990): 282–295.

Reynolds, DeEtta Kay Reynolds. "The Reading Recovery Program as It Relates to Understanding." *Reading Improvement* 3, no. 2 (Summer 1993): 76–81.

Richgels, Donald J., Karla J. Poremba, and Lea M. McGee. "Kindergartners Talk about Print: Phonemic Awareness in Meaningful Contexts." *The Reading Teacher* 49, no. 8 (May 1996): 632–642.

Rodriguez, Terry. Emergent Literacy Workshop. Denver, Colo., June 21, 1995.

Schmidt, Patricia Ruggiano. "Working and Playing with Others: Cultural Conflict in a Kindergarten Literacy Program." *The Reading Teacher* 48, no. 5 (Feb. 1995): 404–412.

Schorr, Memory Long. *A Handbook for First Year Teachers: Ready! Set! Go!* Englewood, Colo.: Teacher Ideas Press, 1995.

Sebasta, Sam Leaton. "Creative Drama and Language Arts." In *Children's Voices: Talk in the Classroom*, edited by Bernice E. Cullinan, 33–46. Newark, Del.: International Reading Association, 1993.

Snowball, Diane. "Big Books for Big Children." *Teaching PreK–8* 21, no. 8 (May 1991): 54–56.

Stauffer, Russell. *The Language Experience Approach to the Teaching of Reading.* 2nd ed. New York: Harper & Row, 1980.

Stevens, Janet. *The Princess and the Pea.* New York: Holiday House, 1982.

Stevens, Joseph H., Ruth A. Hough, and Joanne R. Nurss. "The Influence of Parents on Children's Development and Education." In *Handbook of Research on the Education of Young Children*, edited by Bernard Spodek, 337–351. New York: Macmillan, 1993.

Strickland, Dorothy S. "Emergent Literacy: How Young Children Learn to Read and Write." *Educational Leadership* 47, no. 6 (March 1990): 19–23.

Swartz, Stanley L., and Adria F. Klein. "Reading Recovery: An Overview." In *Research in Reading Recovery*, edited by Stanley L. Swartz and Adria F. Klein, 1–5. Portsmouth, N.H.: Heinemann, 1997.

Temple, Charles, and Jean Gillet. *Language and Literacy: A Lively Approach.* New York: HarperCollins, 1996.

Terban, Marvin. *Funny You Should Ask: How to Make Up Jokes and Riddles with Wordplay.* Illustrated by John O'Brien. New York: Clarion, 1992.

Thorn, Elizabeth. *Teaching the Language Arts: Speaking Listening Reading Writing.* Toronto: Gage, 1974.

Trelease, Jim. *The New Read-Aloud Handbook.* New York: Penguin, 1989.

Turkle, Brinton. *Deep in the Forest.* New York: Trumpet, 1976.

Vukelich, Carol. "Play: A Context for Exploring the Functions, Features, and Meaning of Writing with Peers." *Language Arts* 70, no. 5 (Sept. 1993): 386–392.

West, Colin. *"Buzz, Buzz, Buzz," Went Bumblebee.* Cambridge, Mass.: Candlewick Press, 1996.

Wilson, Timothy, Mary H. Mosley, and Sheri Shirley. "Emergent Literacy: Young Children's Experiments with Written Communication." *Reading Improvement* 30, no. 2 (Summer 1993): 113–116.

Wright, Denise Anton. *One-Person Puppet Plays.* Englewood, Colo.: Teacher Ideas Press, 1990.

Yopp, Hallie Kay. "Developing Phonemic Awareness in Young Children." *The Reading Teacher* 45, no. 9 (May 1992): 696–703.

Young, Ed. *The Other Bone.* New York: Harper & Row, 1984.

4

Identifying Words

The first grade class worked quietly at their tables, completing a worksheet on initial short vowel sounds. The worksheet had pictures of a variety of items, among them an egg, apple, octopus, umbrella, elephant, and underwear. The students' task was to write the letter of the initial sound in a blank below the picture. Later the teacher noticed an unusual number of incorrect responses for one student; this was surprising because she had demonstrated a strong knowledge of letters and sounds. One blank even had two letters, further perplexing the teacher. He called the student to his desk and asked her to explain her choices for each answer. The student obligingly answered. "This is a for agg [long a sound]. And a is for apple. S is for squid. B is for 'brella. E for elephant. And p and t are for panties and t-shirt. I didn't know which one you wanted."

FOCUS QUESTIONS

1. How can I capitalize on students' prior knowledge of environmental print?

2. How can I support students' developing auditory discrimination?

3. How do children learn the alphabet?

4. What is phonemic awareness?

5. What is phonics?

6. What role should phonics play in beginning reading instruction?

7. What is exemplary phonics instruction?

8. What are function and high-frequency words?

9. How can students use context to identify words?

10. How can I assess word-recognition ability?

Introduction

Teachers are always learning from their students. In the opening story, the teacher could have marked the responses as incorrect and moved on to the next paper. Luckily, he knew enough about his student to want to know more about why she made those choices. This first grader demonstrated a sophisticated knowledge of initial vowel sounds and background information, plus good problem-solving skills. She displayed a regional dialect, using the long *a* sound for *egg*. Her dropping of the first **syllable** of *umbrella* was probably a family habit. Though she didn't identify the octopus, she had learned what a squid and an elephant are. And when she saw the underwear, she decided to put two letters down to cover both options.

This example illustrates one of the major difficulties you will encounter when you use published materials that isolate skills, such as identifying initial vowel sounds. The creators of worksheets work hard to produce foolproof materials, but children come to school with diverse dialects, background knowledge, and levels of accomplishment that defy the best intentions of publishers (Harste 1989, 27). Further, as this youngster demonstrated, children are adept at problem-solving and making materials work for them.

In this chapter we explore the complex challenge of teaching students to recognize words. This challenge is complicated because of the misunderstandings, theoretical differences, and politics that accompany any discussion of **word recognition**. Ideally, the processes for recognizing words would be addressed only in the broader context of comprehending phrases, sentences, paragraphs, and longer passages of text; however, such discussions would be lengthy and cumbersome. Therefore, we will examine the topic of word recognition separately from comprehension.

Because this chapter deals primarily with beginning word recognition, many Spotlights are for primary grades. However, intermediate students also benefit from phonics instruction, and many will be using syllabication and morphemic analysis well into middle school. Think about keeping a notebook of additional ideas the Spotlights inspire or books that you will want to have on your shelves when you teach word identification.

■ **Syllable**
A group of letters forming one unit of pronunciation.

■ **Word recognition**
The process of identifying printed symbols with correct pronunciation and the association of meaning with the pronounced word.

Beginning Word Recognition and Understanding

Although children may have a wealth of knowledge about print, many come to kindergarten not realizing how much they already can read. The challenge for teachers of the very young is how to provide successful initial experiences that capitalize on what they already know about print.

RECOGNIZING ENVIRONMENTAL PRINT

Perceptive kindergarten or first grade teachers recognize that children arrive with an abundance of knowledge and skills. Many children know how to read many words, but they simply take such knowledge for granted. For example, children can often read a variety of words they see regularly in their environment. In some cases, this **environmental print** has been regularly pointed out by parents. In other cases, the children have themselves figured out what the words mean through their continual experiences with the words. Collecting, discussing, and using examples of environmental print can be an ongoing activity throughout the school year. (See Spotlight 1.)

Environmental print Words found in children's environments that they recognize, such as names of toys, food, fast-food establishments, and street signs.

Children who are read to regularly in the home often acquire a wealth of word knowledge without formal instruction. Kindergarten teachers will attest to the impressive word knowledge young dinosaur fans bring to school. The size and complexity of these words are pretty consistent with the size and complexity of dinosaurs! Yet children master these words, which challenge adults, because they are intensely interested in the topic. They may or may not have visited a natural history museum, but they have all pored over books about dinosaurs.

Many teachers ask children to bring their favorite books from home and share them in class; this helps children see how they may already be able to read many words and shows them how they can use familiar books to learn words. Margaret Wise Brown's *Goodnight Moon* is a fine example of a long-time favorite that many children memorize long before they arrive at school. (Parents and teachers will enjoy Sean Kelly's *Boom Baby Moon*, an amusing parody of Brown's classic.)

Children who have not come from print-rich environments with ample opportunities to use books, magazines, and other print especially need a classroom environment that offers a variety of opportunities for literacy experiences. Children learn best in a language- and print-rich environment that provides numerous occasions to observe, experiment, and practice all forms of communication (Taylor, Blum, and Logsdon 1986, 147). Providing a supportive environment is discussed more fully in Chapter 13, "The Literate Environment."

s p o t l i g h t   1

Using Environmental Print

GRADE LEVELS: Preschool–1.

BOOKS: *Mama, Coming and Going* by Judith Caseley (New York: Greenwillow, 1994).

A Teeny Tiny Baby by Amy Schwartz (New York: Orchard, 1994).

ACTIVITY: In Judith Caseley's book, a busy mother runs around town, trying to get through her sometimes frantic day. Amy Schwartz's book describes a baby's total control over the immediate environment. Both books contain many examples of signs found in any neighborhood. After sharing the book, students can read the signs or labels in the book. Then have them share and later collect examples of environmental print they find in their homes and neighborhoods. Use their words to create a Word Wall, a class book, or individual books.

SUPPORTING DEVELOPING AUDITORY DISCRIMINATION

Auditory discrimination The ability to distinguish among sounds.

Auditory discrimination is critical to successful language acquisition and reading development. The student in the opening story used excellent auditory discrimination skills when she determined that egg had the long *a* sound because her dialect supported that conclusion. Just as students arrive at school with varying background knowledge, so do they also arrive with differing abilities to discriminate among sounds. A student who has poor auditory discrimination will have difficulty with speaking or listening, and eventually with reading, writing, and spelling. Most students benefit from activities that improve auditory discrimination skills, but some may not develop adequate skills until age 7 or 8.

To support the development of auditory discrimination, present your students with a variety of listening activities. When you read simple books aloud, point out repetitive sounds, alliteration, and rhyming words. Share tongue twisters, such as those found in Nola Buck's *Creepy Crawly Critters and Other Halloween Tongue Twisters*; students also love to play at creating tongue twisters. Make a game of this: Have students listen to you say three words with the same beginning sound and one with a different initial sound—they then identify the different one. Play other simple listening games, such as being quiet and identifying environmental noises, taking a "listening walk," or blindfolding a student who must identify the person who is whispering.

To be truly useful to the reading process, auditory discrimination must be accompanied by understanding. We have all listened to someone speak and not gotten the message, perhaps because of distractions, lack of background

s p o t l i g h t   2

Auditory Discrimination

GRADE LEVELS:
Preschool–
kindergarten.

BOOK: *THUMP,
THUMP, Rat-a-Tat-
Tat* by Gene Baer,
illustrated by Lois
Ehlert (New York:
HarperTrophy, 1989).

ACTIVITY: A marching
band gets off the bus,
and as they approach,
the *thumps* and *rat-a-
tat-tats* get louder and
louder. Students partici-
pate enthusiastically in
the reading of this
book. After the first
reading, give students
drums for the *thumps*
and rhythm sticks for
the *rat-a-tat-tats*. Have
them practice listening
for the correct times to

join in at varying levels
of loudness. Add march-
ing activities as appro-
priate. If possible,
arrange to listen to a
marching band or to
have band members visit
the class. Discuss the
instruments and the var-
ious sounds they make.
This book is also appro-
priate for introducing
the sounds of short *a*
and short *u*.

knowledge, disinterest, or fatigue. Using children's literature fosters understanding along with listening, especially cumulative tales such as Pat Hutchins'
The Surprise Party and *Don't Forget the Bacon* (Lundsteen 1979, 112). Many
youngsters come to school without a background in nursery rhymes and will
benefit from learning the rhythms and language of these simple rhymes.
Adding fingerplay increases their involvement. (See Spotlights 2 and 3.)

LEARNING THE ALPHABET

I vividly recall my first son, before he was 2 years old, standing on an airplane
seat, pointing to and identifying the letters indicating the seats. His learning
had occurred when we sang the alphabet song and played simple games such
as pointing out letters on billboards while in the car. This is how many children learn the alphabet.

It is generally accepted that letter identification is useful for successfully
learning to read (Clay 1991, 266), but the range of accomplishment varies
widely by the time children enter school. Some students can recognize and
identify all the letters. Some only recognize those letters associated with their
names, and others begin to learn letters only when they first want to write
their names.

Many children recognize long or multisyllabic words long before they can
identify all the individual letters. At the earliest stage, letter recognition is primarily a visual process (although highly complex), particularly if a child has
learned to identify a particular letter in a variety of contexts. Nowadays, many
children begin to learn letters through a fascination with computer keyboards.

s p o t l i g h t   3

Auditory Discrimination

GRADE LEVELS:
Preschool–1.

BOOKS: *The Little Old Lady Who Was Not Afraid of Anything* by Linda Williams, illustrated by Megan Lloyd (New York: HarperTrophy, 1986).

Rattlebone Rock by Sylvia Andrews (New York: HarperCollins, 1995).

ACTIVITY: Linda Williams depicts a little old lady who is walking home to her cottage when she encounters shoes that go CLOMP, CLOMP, pants that WIGGLE, WIGGLE, and so forth. She isn't afraid until a pumpkin head appears, saying "Boo!" *Rattlebone Rock* is a rollicking good time with various spooky, yet silly, characters. Either book is especially useful for little ones who are not yet accustomed to sitting quietly. Encourage students to chime in with the words, sounds, and actions. After reading the book, have them help you choose new words for the action, such as *stamp, stamp* instead of *clomp, clomp* or *wriggle, wriggle* for *wiggle, wiggle*. Encourage students to make up new words that fit either story.

When young learners come to school, the teacher spends time observing each student's range of understanding the alphabet. Reading and writing environmental print encourages children to experiment with the alphabet. Students playing in a grocery center will create a shopping list by transferring the first letter of various food items onto a list. Names are a natural focal point for learning letters, so it's a good idea to have a repertoire of name games and activities that reinforce alphabet knowledge. Games can be as simple as saying "I'm thinking of a name that starts with the letter *S*. Who is it?" Another effective activity involves having all the students whose names start with *A* line up, followed by those whose names start with *B*. As you continue through the alphabet, you also reinforce alphabetical order. Children also love to play alphabet games as they eat alphabet soup and cereal letters.

Alphabet books are popular with children long after they have mastered the basics. Alphabet books range from very simple ones such as Kate Duke's engaging *The Guinea Pig ABC* to complex puzzles such as Bruce Whatley and Rosie Smith's *Whatley's Quest*. Students can collaborate with others or with their teacher to create new alphabet books (McGee and Richgels 1989, 223). Because of the varying abilities in any student group, many will not only know the letters of the alphabet but will also associate sounds with the letters. Pairing these children with those students who haven't quite mastered these skills can speed the progress of the entire class. (See Spotlights 4 and 5.)

PHONEMIC AWARENESS

Identifying letters may be a prerequisite to learning to read, but it is not sufficient for this complex task. As discussed in Chapter 3, phonemic awareness is the ability to recognize that a specific spoken word consists of a sequence of individual sounds. For example, a child hearing the word *dog* does not think of it in terms of three phonemes, the sounds represented by the letters *d*, *o*, and *g*. Similarly, if the family's dog eats from a dish labeled *dog*, the child does not think of those letters as having individual sounds either. Indeed, the child doesn't really care! The individual sounds are meaningless. After all, *dog* is perfectly understandable in its entirety, and young readers require little beyond understanding the word when they hear it or read it. This first stage of learning about words is referred to as **logographic** (Stahl 1992, 619). When the child begins to associate the initial sound of *d* with the word *dog*, he demonstrates phonemic awareness. When children use individual letters and sounds to identify words, they demonstrate the **alphabetic** stage (ibid.). The last stage, **orthographic**, occurs when children begin to see patterns in words and to use these patterns to identify words without sounding them out (ibid.).

Of course, now that these stages are so carefully defined, we must note that the order in which they occur is not predictable. If you have children or have spent extended time with them, you know that they simply do not follow expected patterns. Further, we will soon see that exactly what role and sequence phonemic awareness plays in the development of reading is one of the more prickly and political issues debated by reading experts. Phonemic

■ **Logographic stage of phonics**
The first stage in learning words, when children learn words as whole units.

■ **Alphabetic stage of phonics**
When children use individual letters and sounds to identify words.

■ **Orthographic stage of phonics**
The last stage of learning words, when children see and use patterns to recognize words.

spotlight   5

Alphabet Awareness

GRADE LEVELS: Preschool–1.

BOOK: *The Alphabet Parade* by Seymour Chwast (San Diego: Harcourt Brace Jovanovich, 1991).

ACTIVITY: In this word-less picture book, a parade is organized from A to Z. The students can study the illustrations and identify each of the objects. Make a list on the board of all the words, reinforcing how each word begins with the appropriate letter. Students can create their own parade with artifacts they find in the classroom or bring from home.

awareness is also largely an individual matter demonstrating an important insight into how letters and sounds work together (Adams 1991, 392). Skilled readers understand that sounds are associated with letters, and they learn to identify letters in the context of the sounds of other phonemes in a word (Griffith and Olson 1992, 516). Children with phonemic awareness recognize that the sound at the beginning of *dog* is the same as that at the beginning of *doll*.

Many of you were probably taught that if you couldn't recognize *dog* in your reading, you should isolate the sounds associated with the letters, saying something like *duh-ah-guh* and then dropping the *uh* sounds of the first and last letters as you said the three sounds quickly. Critics of this process point out the artificial nature of analyzing isolated speech sounds, especially when the very process ascribes different sounds in isolation than those found in the word itself. Take a minute and try to isolate the sound of *d* in *dog, dig*, or *dad* or *r* in the words *run, reed*, or *rat*. It's virtually impossible to separate the sound of the vowel from the *d* or *r*, and this phonological context influences how we think of the sound of initial consonants.

Because our language uses the alphabet or graphemes to represent phonemes, we have come to recognize a relationship between phonemic awareness and learning to read. The question then becomes whether phonemic awareness should be developed before reading or as part of the reading process. Having students practice identifying sounds, such as in the opening story, is consistent with the bottom-up theory of reading discussed in Chapter 1, which emphasizes skill mastery (Ediger 1995, 60–61). Teachers who agree with the top-down theory of reading believe that children will continue to develop phonemic awareness as they read, and those teachers will give students reading activities that help them develop phonemic awareness as an adjunct to the reading. Hallie Kay Yopp points out that the research supports not only the premise that phonemic awareness is a prerequisite to reading but also that the act of reading causes phonemic awareness (1992, 697). The process is thus usually an interactive or circular one. In short, students need a basic level of phonemic awareness to become successful readers, and the very process of reading itself develops phonemic awareness.

Yopp recommends that you should decide what task should be taught (such as matching words by sounds or substituting sounds in a word), then find a developmentally appropriate activity with which to learn the skill. When young children know the alphabet and are ready for this step, Yopp recommends riddles, guessing games, songs, and playful activities that encourage interaction and success with written words or letters (ibid., 702). For example, to teach easy prepositions, such as *in, under, over,* or *above,* a first grade teacher holds up a card with *under* on it and asks her students to demonstrate through movement (getting *under* something) that they can read the word. When she deals with initial vowel sounds, she might say, "I'm thinking of something that starts with *a,* has five letters, is often red, and tastes good. What is it? . . . That's right. I'm thinking of *apple.* Let's write it on the board and see what other letters *apple* has. . . ." You can make up new verses to *Mary Had a Little Lamb* that will make young students think about words that begin with a particular letter. "Mary had a brand new pet . . . and it begins with *s.*" (Accept any *s* words.) "Mary went to buy some food . . . and it begins with *b.*" Students can make up their own verses or riddles and take turns directing the simple games in small groups for extra practice. (See Spotlight 6.)

---

spotlight 6

Phonemic Awareness

GRADE LEVELS:
Kindergarten–2.

BOOKS: *In the Small, Small Pond* by Denise Fleming (New York: Henry Holt, 1993).

Ride a Purple Pelican by Jack Prelutsky, illus-trated by Garth Williams (New York: Greenwillow, 1986).

Crocodile Smile: 10 Songs of the Earth as the Animals See It by Sarah Weeks, illustrated by Lois Ehlert (New York: HarperCollins, 1994).

ACTIVITY: These books can be used to explore rhymes, alliteration, and playful uses of words.

Fleming's book features bounding, colorful words. Prelutsky's poems are reminiscent of nursery rhymes and provide examples of creating new words, such as "Timble Tamble Turkey" (48). Students can listen to the tape that accompanies Weeks's songs and then explore the rhymes and rhythms.

Strategies for Recognizing and Understanding Words

Although experts disagree on how students should be taught to read, they all agree that most students *want* to read successfully. As teachers, we want our students to have all the tools for success so they can figure out or decode any word, whether that involves phonics, using illustrations, contextual clues, or other processes discussed in this chapter. Remember that one strategy may work almost magically with one group of students, and when one process works so well, it is tempting to generalize it to all students. Also, what seems to be perfect for one student sometimes fails miserably with another. Because learners are so diverse, you need to internalize a variety of instructional strategies and be prepared to adapt them to various students. Ideally, students will learn a variety of skills that will prove useful when they encounter unknown words.

PHONICS

■ **Phonology**
The sound system of an oral language.

Phonics is the set of relationships between **phonology** and the letter symbols or graphemes. In extensive research regarding the efficacy of teaching phonics, Jeanne Chall recommends earlier phonics instruction, particularly using words that could be readily decoded using a knowledge of phonics (1967). As mentioned in Chapter 1, Chall asserts that children need to know phonics or letter-sound correspondence to learn to read English text successfully. However, she also emphasizes that teachers can overdo the teaching, relying on workbooks or neglecting to read stories (1989, 531). Arthur Heilman (1993, 35) believes that students are ready for phonics instructions once they have demonstrated auditory discrimination, visual discrimination of letters, and phonemic awareness. Teachers also look for the following: enjoyment of picture books; attention span for stories, songs, and poems; interest in writing; efforts at constructing their own spellings; interest in learning to read. However, it is not necessary for each of these attributes to be in place before phonics instruction begins. Learning is not always smooth. One student may be fascinated with letters and books at an early age but delay pursuing writing activities until much later.

The role of phonics in reading instruction is widely discussed these days. Some educators and parents even assume that phonics instruction has no place in a whole-language classroom. One common misconception is that a teacher must choose whether to teach phonics at all. This text treats phonics as one of several word-recognition strategies. Your responsibility is to understand this strategy well enough to determine where it fits in your reading program and when to teach it.

SYNTHETIC PHONICS

- **Synthetic phonics** The isolation of each sound of a letter followed by the sounds being blended together as they are pronounced.

When teaching **synthetic phonics** (usually coupled with explicit teaching), each sound associated with a letter is pronounced in isolation and then blended together (Dechant 1993, 305; Gunning 1995, 484). Earlier in the chapter, the word *dog* was identified by isolating each sound. Now try to isolate all the sounds of *cat* or *car*. The teacher would say something like "*c* goes with the /k/ sound, *a* goes with the /a/ sound, and *t* goes with the /t/ sound. Now, blend them all together: /k/-/a/-/t/." Of course, the difficulty comes when the sounds in isolation don't resemble the sound of the whole word, especially when vowels are affected by such letters as *r*. As words become longer or have more complex sounds, the task becomes even more difficult. Further, although our alphabet has 26 letters, these letters represent approximately 44 phonemes. Add in dialectical differences, and the process becomes even more complicated.

A group of students discusses uses of words such as those displayed.

However, proponents of synthetic phonics point out that *s*, *m*, and *f* and long vowels can be isolated and used to begin reading instruction. Other easy consonants include *l*, *n*, *r*, *v*, and *z* (Stahl, Osborn, and Lehr 1990, 77). Students who can sound out words are better equipped to take on unknown words alone (ibid., 88). Critics of this process usually prefer analytic phonics instruction, which analyzes the sound in the context of the word. (See Spotlight 7.)

ANALYTIC PHONICS

- **Analytic phonics** The practice of having students find sounds in the context of words.

When we teach the sound of *d* by having our students find or think of words that start with the same sound as *dog*, we are using **analytic phonics**. The sound of *d* is not isolated to *duh* because distortion occurs; rather, the values of the letters are taught in a whole-word context (Dechant 1993, 305). Students may look for examples around the room, in books, and in magazines and then compile a page or draw pictures of their choices. This is often referred to as implicit phonics instruction because the relationships of letters and sounds are

spotlight 7

Teaching Synthetic Phonics

GRADE LEVELS: Kindergarten–1.

BOOK: *Hop Jump* by Ellen Stall Walsh (New York: Trumpet, 1993).

ACTIVITY: In this easy book, a frog decides she doesn't want to hop and jump like the other frogs; she wants to dance! First, read the book to the students.

Then show students the cover and explain that you are going to talk about the first word in the title, letting them identify *hop*. Have students raise their hand every time they hear *hop* in the second reading of the book. After the second reading, write the word on the board and ask students to make the sounds of each letter individually, blending them together to make the word. Have the students sit on their haunches while you read the story again, asking them to make a little hop every time you read the word. Extend the lesson by having them write the word on paper, in sand, with paint, and so forth. You can vary this process using *jump*. This story also lends itself well to dramatization and movement, with students acting out the different parts of the frogs while the story is read aloud.

taught in the context of a whole word. However, this process can be challenging to teach when students do not come to school with some phonemic awareness (Beck and Juel 1992, 113). (See Spotlight 8 on page 120.)

COMBINING SYNTHETIC AND ANALYTIC PHONICS

Many teachers use a combination of synthetic and analytic phonics instruction with early readers, avoiding the letters that cannot be isolated easily in synthetic phonics. In his research with 7-year-old students, Thomas G. Gunning notes that their most frequent word-identification strategy was to pronounce the beginning consonant and then the whole word (*buh-bat*), even though half the class had been taught with explicit synthetic phonics and half with implicit analytic phonics. He concludes that the students divided the words into **onset** and **rime** (1995, 484). Using this natural tendency to use pronounceable word parts, Gunning suggests a system of teaching phonics called Word Building (ibid.). Briefly, the teacher and class build words by adding onsets to rimes. For example, in contrast to the example from *Hop Jump* (Walsh 1993) in Spotlight 7, the teacher writes *op* on the board and asks students to give a letter that would make the rime into a word. *Bop, cop, hop, lop, mop, pop, sop,* and *top* might be given. (See Something to Try 1 on page 121 for a more detailed example of the steps.)

■ **Onset**
The initial consonant or consonant cluster of a word.

■ **Rime**
The vowel or vowel plus consonant element of a word.

s p o t l i g h t   8

Analytic Phonics

GRADE LEVELS:
Kindergarten–3.

BOOK: *Anno's Magical ABC: An Anamorphic Alphabet* by Masaichiro Anno (New York: Philomel, 1980).

ACTIVITY: The letters and representative objects in Anno's book require a reflective cone (provided with the book) to be seen in proper perspective. The discovery on each page delights younger and older readers alike. After students have identified the letters and objects, lead them to identify other objects that could be used for each letter. Older students could try the art process as described in the book to create their own examples.

COMMON PHONIC ELEMENTS

A thorough exploration of phonics is beyond the scope of this book. However, the following information provides basic information about phonics in the English language.

Consonants   Consonant letters include *b, c, d, f, g, h, j, k, l, m, n, p, q, r, s, t, v, w, x, y, z*. These letters are often taught first because they usually have only one sound for each letter. One exception includes *y*, which functions as a vowel when it is not in the initial position (*lucky*). Another exception is the letter *w*, which can also function as a vowel or have no sound (*mow*). The letter *k* can be silent (*knit*). The letters *c* and *g* can have hard and soft sounds: *car, coast,* and *cut*; *cease* and *city*; *garage, goat,* and *gum*; *germ* and *ginger*.

Consonant Blends   A combination of two or three consecutive consonants in one syllable is called a consonant blend or cluster. Each letter has its own sound.

INITIAL POSITIONS

bl (blue)	*br (brown)*	*cl (clown)*	*cr (crown)*	*dr (drown)*
dw (dwell)	*fl (flew)*	*fr (fry)*	*gl (glow)*	*gr (grow)*
pl (play)	*pr (pray)*	*sc (scare)*	*sch (school)*	*sk (skunk)*
sl (slip)	*sm (small)*	*sn (snake)*	*sp (spell)*	*spl (splash)*
spr (spray)	*st (stay)*	*str (street)*	*sw (sweet)*	*tr (tree)*
tw (twin)				

FINAL POSITIONS

ct (affect)	*ld (held)*	*lf (shelf)*	*lk (milk)*	*lm (film)*
lp (help)	*lt (melt)*	*mp (lamp)*	*nd (land)*	*nk (sink)*
nt (went)	*sp (grasp)*	*st (west)*		

something to try 1

Word Building

STEP 1: *Building words by adding the onset* (Gunning 1995, 485). Write *it* on the board and ask what should be added to make *sit*. Form a variety of words, having students read them aloud. Discuss the relationships of the sounds to the letters.

STEP 2: *Building words by adding the rime* (ibid., 486). Present the onset, such as *p* and have the students say the sound and suggest what is needed to make *pit*. Continue building words by adding rimes to onsets.

STEP 3: *Selecting a model word* (ibid.). Choose a common, known word that can be illustrated to serve as a reminder of the pattern.

STEP 4: *Guided practice* (ibid.). Provide a variety of experiences to explore the pattern: listening to stories and poems with the patterns; creating group and individual stories and patterns; writing examples in the sand, with blocks, with paint, with markers, on charts, on 3 × 5 cards, and so forth.

STEP 5: *Application* (ibid.). Provide many opportunities for reading material that uses the pattern. Challenge students to find the pattern in other materials. Create a Word Wall that documents all the reading sources that include the pattern.

Consonant Digraphs   When two consecutive consonants represent one sound of a word or syllable, they are called consonant digraphs.

ch (chip)	*ck (sick)*	*gh (cough)*	*ng (sing)*
ph (phone)	*sc (scissors)*	*sh (ship)*	*si (mission)*
voiced: *th (thick)*			
unvoiced: *th (the)*	*ti (nation)*	*wh (when)*	*wr (write)*

Silent Consonants   The following consonants have no sound value in English in certain combinations or instances.

gh (ghost)	*gn (gnat)*	*h (herb)*	*k (knight)*
pn (pneumonia)	*ps (psychology)*	*rh (rhinocerous)*	*wr (write)*

The Ptarmigan

The ptarmigan is strange,
As strange as he can be;
Never sits on ptelephone poles
Or roosts upon a ptree.
And the way he ptakes pto spelling
Is the strangest thing pto me.

Anonymous

Vowels   Vowels include *a, e, i, o, u*. As noted, *y* may function as a vowel when it is not the initial sound of a word (*silly*), and *w* may function as a vowel when it follows another vowel (*flow*). The two most frequent types of vowel sounds include short and long sounds. Regional dialects influence the sounds of vowels.

SHORT VOWELS	LONG VOWELS
at	*ate*
end	*eve*
ill	*ice*
odd	*open*
us	*use*

Vowel Digraphs   When two consecutive vowels represent one sound, they are called vowel digraphs. These are the most common.

ai (main)	*au (auto)*	*aw (awning)*	*ay (may)*
ea (east)	*ee (beet)*	*ei (either)*	*ie (tie)*
oa (coat)	*oe (toe)*	*ow (mow)*	*ue (blue)*

Diphthongs   Diphthongs have two consecutive vowels with one sound. The tongue starts in one position and moves rapidly to another.

oi (boil)	*ou (out)*	*ow (owl)*	*oy (toy)*

Schwa   The schwa sound is an unstressed short *u* sound, "uh." It is symbolized by /ə/. All vowels can have the schwa sound in the English language. Note that these examples occur in the unstressed syllables.

A	E	I	O	U
human	*omen*	*humid*	*melon*	*humus*

SYLLABICATION

Once readers understand the sounds of groups of letters, you can begin to talk about syllables and how they can be used to analyze an unknown word. Every syllable contains a vowel sound, and a vowel can form a syllable by itself (*about*). Open syllables end in vowel sounds (*pri*mary), and closed syllables end in consonant sounds (*mid*dle). Young students also find it useful to know that words contain syllables, and they will benefit from understanding that a word, such as *little* has two distinct syllables. Teachers often introduce the presence of syllables by clapping each syllable as they say it. Teachers of intermediate or older readers may teach the use of accents with syllables and how to approximate the syllabication of words. General knowledge, rather than precise syllabication, is usually all that is required to identify unknown words and to spell words accurately.

Prefixes are syllables that precede the root word. *Dis* is the prefix in *dislike* and *like* is the root word. **Suffixes** follow the root word, such as *able* in *likeable*. **Inflectional endings** change the meaning, such as adding an *s* to make a noun plural (dog*s*), adding a *d* to change verb tense (like*d*), or adding *er* to change to the comparative form of an adjective (small*er*).

Word Building, discussed previously in this chapter, can also be used to teach multisyllabic words (Gunning 1995, 486). For example, to teach the familiar elements in words that contain the short *a*, present a known word, such as *bat*, and introduce *battle*. Then add *cattle*, *prattle*, *rattle*, and *tattle*.

Students often find Word Building helpful in understanding compound words—words made of two or more words such as *outside*. The meanings of compound words may simply be a combination of the two words, or a different (although related) meaning such as *cattail* may be created. Compound words lend themselves to wordplay (also a compound word), which can illustrate the word or create new versions. Students enjoy creating sayings such as "If we have a *chairman*, why don't we have a *deskman*? If we wear an *outfit*, why don't we wear an *infit*?" A collection of traditional and nontraditional compound words makes an intriguing bulletin board.

Students syllabicate more easily if they learn that when two consonants come between two vowels, the word generally divides between the consonants: *sum-mer*, *sis-ter*. Also, when *le* occurs at the end of a word, it combines with a preceding consonant in a separate syllable: *sta-ble*, *tri-ple*.

Teaching syllabication should be integrated into every aspect of your reading, writing, and spelling programs. However, it isn't necessary for students to memorize long lists of syllables. Figure 4.1 on page 124 lists common prefixes, suffixes, and inflectional endings. For additional examples, plus lists of many other kinds of words, consult *The New Reading Teacher's Book of Lists* (Fry, Fountoukidis, and Polk 1985). (See also Spotlight 9 on page 125.).

MORPHEMIC ANALYSIS

Students with a strong base in prefixes, suffixes, and root words might approach an unknown word such as *untouchable* by looking first for a known word. Once *touch* is identified, the student who knows that the prefix *un* gives it the opposite meaning and that the suffix *able* means "given to a certain state of being" will be able to get the sense of the meaning, "that which can't be touched." This process is referred to as **morphemic analysis**. A **morpheme** is either a prefix, suffix, or root. In our *untouchable* example, the prefix, root, and suffix each have a specific meaning. After students study a word such as *untouchable*, challenge them to think of others that fit the pattern: *uncomfortable*, *unmanageable*, *unlikable*, *unworkable*. Students will undoubtedly think of some that fit the form but are nonstandard (*unflexable*). When this occurs, have volunteers confirm the words in the dictionary and discuss the correct form.

PREFIXES

Prefix	Meaning	Example
anti–	against	antiwar
dis–, im–, il–, ir–	not	disallow, impure, illegal, irregular
inter–	together, between	interstate
pre–	before	premix
re–	again, back	reappear
un–	not, opposite	unlike
under–	beneath	underground

SUFFIXES

Suffix	Meaning	Example
–age	act or result of	marriage
–dom	position or state of being	kingdom
–ful	full of	thoughtful
–hood	state of being	falsehood
–less	without	thoughtless
–like	relating to	childlike
–ness	state of being	meanness
–tion	state of being	action

INFLECTIONAL ENDINGS

Inflectional Ending	Meaning	Example
–ed, –d, –ing	change of tense	licked, liked, licking
–er, –est	comparative	smaller, smallest
–ily, –ly	in what manner	happily, sadly
–s	plural	girls

Intermediate students particularly benefit from instruction on morphemic analysis when the elements are likely to be standard and applicable to other words. Use morphemic analysis (and perhaps a dictionary) to determine the meanings of these words: *alliumphile, animadversion, belletrists, disingenuous, disputatious, erhthrophobia, indoctrination, indurated, mystagogical, poetaster, senescence, and teleology.* Intermediate and middle school students often get hooked into a love of words by class explorations of obscure words such as these.

CONTRACTIONS

A contraction is formed by combining two words with the omitted letter(s) indicated by an apostrophe. Contractions can be confusing because the apos-

spotlight 9

Syllabication

GRADE LEVELS:
One and up.

Three Ghostesses

Three little ghostesses,
Sitting on postesses,
Eating buttered
    toastesses,
Greasing their fistesses,
Up to their wristesses,
Oh, what beastesses
To make such feastesses!
                Anonymous

ACTIVITY: Write the poem on the board or on an overhead transparency. Read it aloud, asking what is unusual about this poem. Once students have identified the use of *ghostesses* (and the other similar words) instead of *ghosts*, discuss that the poet added extra syllables to the words. Rewrite the poem with the normal plurals (*ghosts, posts,* and so forth). Is the poem as much fun to read? Explore poems that use nonsense words, such as Lewis Carroll's "Jabberwocky" or Spike Milligan's "On the Ning Nang Nong." (See the *Random House Book of Poetry for Children*, edited by Jack Prelutsky.) Encourage students to make up their own nonsense verse that uses multisyllabic words.

trophe is also allowed to show possession. Many adults confuse *its* with *it's* because the possessive form (*its*) does not use an apostrophe. (I gave the dog its bone.) The contractions shown in Figure 4.2 on page 126 are common ones students use frequently.

INSTRUCTIONAL SEQUENCE OF PHONICS

Teachers are interested in teaching phonics because they know that students who can identify words successfully in the early stages of reading will experience success as they tackle increasingly difficult material. The more students read, the better their opportunities for improving comprehension and vocabulary skills (Beck and Juel 1992, 105). If you use prepared materials, you will normally be given a prescribed sequence of instruction. However, even within this framework, you should adapt and amplify the program with other activities, such as those suggested in the Spotlights.

If you use literature for your reading program, generally you must first decide whether to use synthetic or analytic phonics instruction or a combination of the two. Your next decision concerns focusing first on consonants or first on vowels.

Teachers who favor introducing consonants first appreciate the consistency of sounds they represent in contrast to the varying sounds of vowels. Words

CONTRACTIONS

FIGURE 4.2

Contractions

not	will	is/has	would/had	us	are	am	have
can't	he'll	he's	I'd	let's	they're	I'm	I've
couldn't	I'll	here's	he'd		you're		you've
didn't	she'll	it's	she'd		we're		we've
don't	that'll	she's	they'd				
hadn't	they'll	that's	we'd				
hasn't	you'll	there's	you'd				
weren't		what's					
won't							
wouldn't							

considered easy to read often have a consonant-vowel-consonant (CVC) pattern, as in *hop, sat, pup, pet,* and *hit.* In addition to *s, m, f, l, n, r, v,* and *z,* the most consistent consonant sounds include *b, h, k, p,* and *t.* More words begin with consonants than with vowels. Further, consonants have more identifiable features than vowels. For example, you can easily read *l _ t t l _,* but *_ i _ _ _ e* is no small challenge.

In contrast, teachers who prefer to begin with vowels point out that consonant sounds cannot be isolated, while vowel sounds can be. Advocates of teaching long vowel sounds first point out that the letters directly represent the sounds (*a, e, i, o,* and *u*), making them easier to master (Heilman 1993, 87). However, short vowel sounds appear more often in beginning stories, usually in the CVC pattern. Thus, some teachers prefer to teach the short and long vowel sounds in pairs, by contrasting their sounds (CVC/CVCe): *hat/hate, hop/hope, bit/bite, cut/cute.* Another practice involves introducing a few consonants with a few vowels so that easy words, especially those with the CVC pattern, can be mastered quickly. For example, students who know *a, c, n,* and *t* can learn *ant, can, cat,* and *tan.* Which letters would you teach first? When deciding, keep in mind that although you may have a general instructional sequence in mind, if you are drawing from literature and student interest, their choices of reading material will influence your instructional sequence.

Once your students are fairly comfortable with the consonants and vowel sounds and their function in identifying words, you can begin teaching final consonants or introducing consonant blends such as *bl* or *st.* Consonant digraphs, such as *th, ch,* and *sh* are usually taught in the initial position (*thin*) and then in the final position (*math*). Silent consonants are tackled last, along with specific challenges such as the sounds of *g* and *s* and combinations such as *qu.* As students master increasingly challenging material, you can help them

A group of students works on word identification.

understand digraphs (*beak, coat*), diphthongs (*boy, oil*) and *r*-controlled vowels (*car, fur*).

As students progress through the elementary grades, they take on more sophisticated phonics instruction. Understanding suffixes, prefixes, compound words, syllabication, and related patterns helps students read increasingly complicated words. In a detailed analysis of phonic generalizations in the primary grades, Theodore Clymer found that of 45 phonics generalizations found in texts, only 18 were useful. Exceptions should be noted so that students don't make inappropriate assumptions as they try to identify unknown words (1996, 187).

PHONICS AND LITERATURE

Phonics instruction plays an important role in any reading program and is enhanced in the context of authentic reading and writing experiences. Students might explore phonics after a choral reading or as they generate rhyming words. Phyllis Trachtenburg recommends a whole-part-whole sequence that integrates phonics instruction with quality children's literature:

1. *Whole*: Read, comprehend, and enjoy a whole, high-quality literature selection.

2. *Part*: Provide instruction in a high-utility phonic element by drawing from or extending the preceding literature selection.

3. *Whole*: Apply the new phonic skill when reading (and enjoying) another whole, high-quality literature selection (1990, 649).

For example, a teacher who wants to explore the difference between the long and short sounds of *a* reads aloud from Esphyr Slobodkina's *Caps for Sale*. Afterward, he writes *caps* and *sale* on the board and discusses the different *a* sounds with the children and also how the *e* on *sale* affects the sound. Then his students might practice writing words and short sentences that demonstrate the two sounds. Finally, they listen to Eric Kimmel's *The Gingerbread Man* and find more examples of short and long *a* sounds.

Any use of literature to reinforce phonics should be done sparingly. Nothing is more frustrating to listeners or readers of any age than to have a beloved story dissected and analyzed until its beauty is lost. However, students who are reading and hearing many stories throughout the day will benefit from phonics instruction that naturally develops from the reading, especially if many forms of reading occur in class. See the list of books beginning on page 139 that lend themselves to early phonics introduction. For a more detailed, anecdotal exploration of this topic, consult *Looking Closely: Exploring the Role of Phonics in One Whole Language Classroom* (Mills, O'Keefe, and Stephens 1992) or Barbara Fox's *Strategies for Word Identification: Phonics from a New Perspective* (1996). For a resource that lists an abundance of books to use in phonics instruction, consult Karen Morrow Durica's *Literature Links to Phonics: A Balanced Approach* (1996). (See Spotlight 10.)

EXEMPLARY PHONICS INSTRUCTION

Good reading teachers incorporate phonics instruction in ways that are *interesting*, *appropriate*, and *useful*. Skilled readers identify words accurately and rapidly and thus are free to attend to comprehension (Dechant 1993, 111). Well-designed phonics instruction that develops word-recognition skills allows readers to devote less time to recognizing words and more time on understanding their reading. Stacks of worksheets that require every student in the class to identify all the words that start with the letter *b* satisfy none of the criteria of being interesting, appropriate, and useful. However, having students identify the words in Seymour Chwast's *The Alphabet Parade* (see Spotlight 5) and later create their own parade with objects they find in the classroom or bring from home fulfills all of these criteria.

"All readers (at least those who can hear) can and do use phonics. But they use it within the complex process of making sense of print as they read, and of expressing comprehensibly what they need to say as they write. And it's most useful when it's used in just the right amount: not too much, not too little" (Goodman 1993, 50). Ken Goodman emphasizes that children find their own understanding of the rules, that phonics is only one component of reading our

spotlight 10

Short and Long *i* Sounds

GRADE LEVELS: 1–2.

BOOKS: *In the Middle of the Puddle* by Mike Thaler, illustrated by Bruce Degan (New York: Harper & Row, 1988).

Whitefish Will Rides Again by Arthur Yorinks,

illustrated by Mort Drucker (New York: HarperCollins, 1994).

ACTIVITY: Read *In the Middle of the Puddle* aloud and discuss the use of the short and long *i* sounds. Reread the book and have students raise their hands when they hear either *i* sound. List these words on the board. Then have students sort them out into short and long categories. Have stu-

dents work in small groups to list rhyming words with short and long *i* sounds. Then read *Whitefish Will Rides Again*. During the second reading, have the students once again identify words with short and long *i* sounds. Discuss the different patterns of the words, helping students understand how some words, such as *ride*, are affected by the final *e*.

language, that it has value only in meaningful context, and that it is best learned in the course of learning to read and write and *not as a prerequisite* (ibid., 51). Few researchers quibble with Goodman's points. See Figure 4.3 on page 130 for a summary of recommendations for exemplary phonics instruction, drawn from the work of Marilyn Adams (1991) Ken Goodman (1993), Thomas G. Gunning (1988), Arthur Heilman (1993), and Steven Stahl (1990, 1992).

FUNCTION AND HIGH-FREQUENCY WORDS

Many words challenge early readers because they have no concrete meaning: *that, the, of, for,* immediately come to mind. They are usually noun determiners (*the, that*), verb auxiliaries (*were, had*), prepositions (*by, of*), and conjunctions (*and, or*). These structural, or function, words are difficult to define and often have similar configurations: *when, what; then, this*. A word such as *Stegosaurus* or *spider* carries more potency and opportunity for discussion and retention than the word *was*.

Many of these words are also high-frequency words—words we use repeatedly. Edward Fry has compiled a list of "Instant Words," words that are found most frequently in the English language. Also referred to as "sight" words, these words are particularly pesky because they are easily misread and difficult to analyze phonetically (try to sound out *the* or *are*) or by using configuration cues, yet they are important to comprehension. They are also important beginning spelling words because of their utility. Consider the following

Recommendations for Exemplary Phonics Instruction

1. Build on a child's ability to differentiate among different sounds in words.
2. Build on a child's ability to visually discriminate between printed letters.
3. Build on a child's understanding of how print relates to reading and writing.
4. Build on a foundation of phonemic awareness.
5. Build on existing knowledge of words found in the environment.
6. Be aware of dialectical differences that affect phonics.
7. Allow time for observation to determine what types of phonics instruction are appropriate.
8. Teach phonics as one of several strategies for word recognition, not as a prerequisite for learning to read. Be certain that students also master other strategies for word recognition and understanding.
9. Teach phonics in the context of meaningful reading and writing experiences.
10. Do not overuse or diminish enjoyment of literature.
11. Use phonics generalizations or rules only when they have a high degree of utility.
12. Be familiar with the range of phonics instruction in other grades so that you can teach phonics to students with widely varying levels of accomplishment. Refer to the scope and sequence of an adopted basal series or familiarize yourself with criterion-referenced phonics tests.
13. Avoid published materials that isolate phonics instruction, such as having students find and list all the words on a page that start with the letter *m*.
14. Discontinue phonics instruction when students can read successfully.

words: *the, is, you, was, are, they, have, from*. How many would be difficult to sound out or recognize by their configuration? Because of these challenges, these words are often taught to be recognized by sight. A word bank is usually helpful for sight words. Students use it to refer to the word in a known context (say in a poem they have learned), after which they practice writing the word (on paper, in the sand, with paint, and so forth). Some teachers use a list of sight words as a beginning point for spelling instruction, thus providing students with many opportunities to interact with the words. Practice reinforces their recognition. Fortunately, students can read many stories, poems, and other material after mastering relatively few of these words. Using books that have patterns or repetition fosters the recognition of these words, as do many of the books found in the list at the end of this chapter, "Books for Teaching Beginning Phonics."

USING CONTEXT

To make sense of print, children need more than phonics instruction. According to Ken Goodman, all readers use phonics, but they also use meaning and grammar cues (1993, 60). As previously discussed, semantic cues provide meaning to the text, and efficient readers use these cues to facilitate comprehension. Background knowledge, prior experiences, and skills represent only a portion of what a student uses to understand a passage. For example, someone with a background in geology knows what is meant in a passage about a mountain peak made of *Precambrian gneiss* and *schist*, but another person without that background may not even know how to pronounce *gneiss* and *schist*, let alone understand what they mean. The more we know about what we read *before* we read it, the more likely we are to experience successful comprehension.

Readers also use their knowledge about syntax (the structure of the text) as they determine meaning. Just from listening to conversation, we learn patterns that are fairly predictable. If you were 6 years old and you heard someone say all but the last word of a message such as "Mother went to the ____," you would know that a noun indicating place goes in the blank. Good guesses might include *store, market,* or *neighbor's house.* Syntactic information helps a reader or listener figure out what is likely to come next.

Using semantics and syntax, many readers quickly learn that not every word is necessary to understand the text. They have discovered or were told that they can read for the gist of the passage and, unless they become totally lost, they can continue reading without total recognition. Young readers can also be taught this strategy—that they can skip an unknown word, continue reading, and still understand what is going on. The word may be unnecessary, or the context may provide sufficient clues to verify the meaning of the unknown word (Smith 1988, 143).

Some students make more deliberate attempts to determine word meanings by analyzing the context of the sentence, making an educated guess as to the meaning, stopping, rereading, and confirming their choice. Before reading on, can you define the word *swale?* You may not know the word, or you may have only a general idea of its meaning. Now consider this sentence: *The road crossed a broad swale before climbing again.* The use of *swale* in this sentence may confirm your notion that it means a low area. If you decided to verify the meaning by looking it up in the dictionary, you would discover that *swale* refers to low ground that is also moist or marshy. Even more information is given in the following sentence: *The road crossed a broad swale before climbing again to dry ground.* Educators who favor a top-down approach generally emphasize the use of context over phonetic analysis because students tend to focus on the whole meaning of a passage rather than on individual words.

Students can also learn to use pictures to decide the meaning of text. Many teachers read aloud books with pictures that enable the beginning reader to narrate the text after only one or two hearings. Some books are designed so that students can predict what will happen on the next page. Many times young readers approximate the text, gradually refining their reading as skills improve and vocabulary increases. According to Brian Cambourne, approximations (discussed first in Chapter 3 and more fully in Chapter 13) are a condition of learning that involves coming close to mastery (1988). These approximations should not be perceived as "wrong" but should instead be celebrated as steps toward mastery. When approximations are recognized in a positive manner, students will continue to take risks with their learning.

Many teachers construct **cloze** materials to help students realize that enlightened guessing does work. Cloze takes advantage of our natural desire to complete a pattern that has a missing part. Words are systematically deleted from a reading passage (say, every fifth word) and students are assessed on how well they guess the missing words. For general classroom use, the teacher might choose to eliminate key words or parts of words that have been identified as problematic. When students supply words that are appropriate but different from the text, the class can discuss why authors choose certain words and how other words can also be valid. See Figure 4.4 for two examples of cloze and also Something to Try 2 on page 134.

Many students use context and phonics—for example, they use the beginning sound of the word in combination with the meaning of the sentence to determine the individual word. This supports the notion that combining approaches is effective (Nicholson 1993, 120).

■ **Cloze**
A test of reading comprehension in which the student is asked to supply words that have been systematically deleted from the text.

_____ FIGURE 4.4
Examples of Cloze

Cloze

In this example every fifth word is deleted. This would be read for meaning.

Near a great forest _____ a poor woodcutter, his _____, and his two children, _____ and Gretel. They had _____ to eat or drink, _____ when famine swept the _____ there was not even _____ to eat.

In this example function words are deleted.

Near _____ great forest lived _____ poor woodcutter, his wife, _____ his two children, Hansel _____ Gretel. They _____ little _____ eat _____ drink, _____ when famine swept _____ land _____ _____ not even bread _____ eat.

Adapted from "Hansel and Gretel" by the Brothers Grimm.

Word-Recognition Strategies for Beginning Readers

1. Look at the first letter of the word. How does the word start?
2. Do you know a part of the word?
3. Look at the context. Does the rest of the sentence give you clues about the unknown word?
4. Can you think of a word that would make sense?
5. Reread. Did you leave out an important word that would help you identify the unknown word?
6. Check the punctuation for useful clues.
7. Think of where you have seen the word (a book, your writing, a sign, and so forth).
8. Look up the meaning in the dictionary.
9. Ask a student or adult for help.
10. Look at pictures for help. (Also charts, maps, graphs, diagrams, or tables.)

Reading must ultimately be automatic, so students need to attain fluency. Students who read slowly may not retain the meaning long enough to comprehend the passage. Therefore, at some point students need to work on speed; they can ease into this by skipping difficult words or guessing at them along the way so that they can construct meaning from the passage (Fowler 1993, 110–111). Students who do not learn easily from phonics benefit from reading books repeatedly, as well as writing stories, choral reading, listening to tapes of books, and other similar activities (Carbo 1987, 432). Figure 4.5 summarizes a variety of word-recognition strategies.

ASSESSING WORD-IDENTIFICATION ABILITY

In the 1960s, Ken Goodman and his colleagues addressed what occurs when students read unfamiliar text aloud. They categorized each response to a word as *expected* (when the word is read correctly) or *observed* (what the reader said instead of the correct word). The observed responses, referred to as *miscues*, were analyzed for logic and the degree to which they supported comprehension. When teachers address the meaning behind miscues, they often find that the student's choice of a word makes perfect sense. Word-by-word accuracy becomes less important than reading for meaning. Ken Goodman's most complete miscue analysis, the Goodman Taxonomy of Reading Miscues, contains 18 questions that analyze the complex relationships between expected responses to the text and the observed responses (Marek and Goodman 1996, 21). The Classroom Reading Miscue Assessment (CRMA) takes about 10–15 minutes per student to administer and can be given during silent reading or other quiet times (Rhodes and Shanklin 1990, 252).

something to try 2

Using Context/Cloze

Choose a book, such as Constance W. McGeorge's *Boomer's Big Day*, in which Boomer, a lovable dog, has his routine terribly disrupted when his family moves to a new home. Before sharing with the children, read the book to yourself and decide which words can be predicted easily. Cut up sticky notes and cover these words. Read the book aloud and show the pictures to your students, encouraging them to fill in the missing words. Don't stop to discuss whether they are right or wrong, just continue through the story. Then remove the notes and read the book through again. Emphasize how well the students got the meaning of the text, even if their choices were different from the author's words. Discuss how they can use this strategy when they are reading independently. This strategy can be used with any book that has a simple story line.

A revised version involving only six questions collects and examines (as with earlier versions) a complete oral reading experience, after which the student retells the text. The student reads unfamiliar, but interesting and manageable text, preferably of at least 500 words in length. A tape recorder records the reading and retelling. The teacher has a triple-spaced typescript for marking the miscues, such as text substitutions, omissions, or insertions, during the reading. The student reads the entire text and then retells the story with no help. The six questions are as follows:

1. Does the miscue occur in a structure that is syntactically acceptable in the reader's dialect?

2. Does the miscue occur in a structure that is semantically acceptable within the reader's dialect?

3. Does the miscue result in a change of meaning?

4. Is the miscue corrected?

5. How much do the two words look alike?

6. How much do the two words sound alike? (Marek and Goodman 1996, 28–33)

Another variation described by Yetta Goodman, involves the students in asking questions about their miscues. They listen to their own taped readings while they follow the script and then review the entire selection or portions selected by the teacher (1996). For an overview of miscue analysis, consult "To Err Is Human: Learning about Language Processes by Analyzing Miscues" by Yetta and Ken Goodman. For a more in-depth treatment, consult Yetta Goodman and Ann Marek's *Retrospective Miscue Analysis: Revaluing Readers and Reading* (1996).

Another test, the Names Test, uses a list of 25 first and last names that look like a classroom list. The names can be decoded using commonly taught vowel rules or analogous decoding approaches and represent a good sampling of the most common English spelling patterns. Teachers use the test at the beginning of the year to gain initial impressions about students' abilities. Patterns of errors, such as being unable to decode three-syllable words or having difficulty with initial blends, can be noted so that the teacher can focus on them later. This process differs from miscue analysis in that it does not take into consideration the six questions mentioned earlier. However, though somewhat limited, it is convenient and useful for diagnosing basic word-identification problems (Cunningham 1990).

Technology and Identifying Words

In the 1980s, many people thought that computers would offer wonderful opportunities to teach students with a minimum of teacher interaction. Unfortunately, many schools could not afford much more than one computer per classroom, or the computer lab they developed had to be shared by the entire school. Many of the early programs acquainted students with computers, an important step, but the content was not much more than a workbook on a screen. Computers were not the salvation for education that many people had thought.

Multimedia
The use of more than one medium of communication, such as video, sound, graphics, and photography, to deliver a message. Also referred to as hypermedia.

With the advent of CD-ROMs, technology enthusiasts once again look with high hopes at the possibilities of **multimedia** or **hypermedia**. A CD-ROM (Compact-Disc-Read Only Memory) is a small disc, similar in size and appearance to music CDs. Played on a CD player connected to the computer, it can access vast amounts of information. One CD-ROM equals 1,500 floppy disks, making browsing a full-volume encyclopedia convenient and fast.

For word-identification CD-ROM products, one need only browse through current periodical multimedia reviews to discover the latest possibilities. *Kid Phonics* (Davidson 1994) combines distinct characters and sound effects with phonics activities, songs, and games. Users can also create a personalized dictionary with the CD-ROM. Interactive books, such as *Dr. Seuss's ABC* (Broderbund 1995), allow users to listen to and watch the story or to use the keyboard to click on words and move through the story independently. The graphics are enhanced by the animation possible in this form, and clicking on various illustrations brings unexpected surprises. This particular program also includes songs about letters of the alphabet. A similar program, *P.B. Bear's Birthday Party* (DK Multimedia 1995), uses photographs in this story of a teddy bear who celebrates his birthday with a picnic. Rebuses, interspersed throughout the text, allow students to hear and see the word for the rebus, and a click on the rebus initiates a brief animation. Because so many CD-ROM programs are coming out, use review sources, such as *Language Arts* and *School Library Journal* to help with selection. A subscription to *Classroom Connect*, published by Wentworth Worldwide Media, provides lists of educational Web sites, a glossary, media centers, and information about the Internet and products.

One example of what is available is the Sunshine Series—a CD-ROM program designed for direct reading instruction that includes books, alphabet learning, vocabulary and phonics games, plus writing activities for creating stories (Sunshine Multimedia 1995). Many CD-ROMs are bilingual, a big plus when you have several second-language students. Don't forget, however, that LEP students particularly need the social interaction that comes with working with others and should not be relegated to a computer. Computers are no substitute for rich communication and learning experiences.

Because CD-ROMs are proliferating worldwide, take care that you choose products that fit with your school's prevailing philosophy. For example, the Australian-produced *Phonics Alive* identifies the letter *b* by its sound, telling the user to find the letter "buh" on the keyboard. In the United States and Canada, most educators don't call letters by their sounds such as this program does. Some programs are marketed directly to the parents, such as IBM's *Forest Friends Reading Club*, which includes prereading lessons, alphabet development, phonics activities, games, storybooks, and workbooks.

How people feel about technology ranges from "dismay to bliss" according to Alain Dumort at MILIA, the 1996 International Multimedia Conference in Cannes, France. Some enthusiasts predict that the end of the book is near, leading D. T. Max to pose the question in a 1994 article for the *Atlantic Monthly*: "Is print on its way out?" For the school setting, the cost of CD-ROM equipment will certainly delay the demise of the book, perhaps indefinitely. A strong defense can also be made for the special role that some say only print can play. However, the use of quality programs in the instruction will sometimes intrigue a reluctant reader or provide the second-language learner with just enough support necessary to get to success. More information about using CD-ROMs in the reading program follows in subsequent chapters.

Involving Parents

I n Brownsville, Texas, where 80 percent of the parents are predominantly or entirely Spanish-speaking, the Parents as Tutors program begins with kindergartners. During the first year, tutoring provides parents with activities that support language arts and mathematics. In first grade, the parents met biweekly to discuss information topics and further activities for home tutoring. Parent training continues during second grade. The program has not only helped the students, it has also helped many of the parents study English and obtain their GEDs (Morrow, Tracey, and Maxwell 1995, 36).

Generally, information about a child's literacy efforts go from school to home. When parents or caregivers are invited to bring information about their child's involvement with print to the classroom, they actively contribute to the child's development (Lazar and Weisberg 1996, 229). Such sharing develops mutual understanding of the practices being used both at home and at school. Daily journals encourage parents to record their children's interaction with print. For example, parents might note that their child now reads a variety of advertisements when they are in the car. This information can be used by the teacher to build on the child's knowledge of those words through a variety of activities and extensions. Parents are sometimes frustrated at the perceived lack of progress by their child. Their journals can alert the teacher, providing possibilities for interventions. Further, such journals provide long-term evidence of progress.

You need not have a formal program to encourage parental involvement. Parents can develop phonological awareness in the home through a variety of singing, rhyming, and reading activities (Baker, Serpell, and Sonnenschein 1995, 246). Songs typically include rhymes, reinforcing the intriguing sounds of words. Nursery rhymes, longtime favorites of young children, also support early knowledge of the sounds of letters and words. The choral reading and singing activities discussed in Chapter 3 will encourage parents to become involved in the program. Repeatedly reading collections of poetry or books with repetitive or rhyming language is one of the easiest ways for parents to develop early word-identification skills. Encourage parents by sending home suggestions for read-alouds that support phonemic awareness, such as those found in the list on page 139, "Books for Teaching Beginning Phonics."

A Final Note

Sometimes finding the right way to teach your students to recognize and understand words may seem like "enlightened guessing." Although researchers can give you guidance about how groups of children learn to read, once you are in the classroom with 30 students, you and you alone must decide how your students can best be taught to read. When you are deciding how to teach word recognition, remember that what works for one student may not work for another. Some students recognize and understand words so quickly they need little or no phonics instruction. Others have poor auditory discrimination and find phonics frustrating. Still others will rely heavily on phonics to read and write. One effective route for you to take is to provide your students with a variety of decoding strategies and discuss with them what works best. They can help you decide which tools will make them successful at reading and writing.

Summary

Most children come to school with some word-recognition skills, having learned to identify words from environmental print or from being read to at home. Teachers can build on their existing knowledge for beginning reading instruction. Auditory discrimination, an important skill for successful learning, can be fostered through reading aloud, choral reading, and listening activities. Young learners are usually interested in recognizing the letters of the alphabet, and they benefit from associating sounds with letters.

Phonemic awareness is the recognition that a word has a sequence of individual sounds. The logographic stage is typified by children learning words as whole units. When children use individual letters and sounds to identify words, they demonstrate the alphabetic stage. The orthographic stage occurs when children see and use patterns in words for identification of unknown words. Phonemic awareness is necessary for successful reading but may also be learned during the reading process.

Phonics instruction may include both synthetic phonics, with sounds isolated, and analytic phonics, which occurs when a teacher points out words that start with a particular letter, avoiding the isolation or distortion of sounds. Common phonic elements include consonants, consonant blends, consonant digraphs, silent consonants, vowels, vowel digraphs, diphthongs, and the schwa sound. Phonics instruction should include teaching syllabication and the understanding of the role of prefixes, suffixes, inflectional endings, compound words, morphemic analysis, and contractions. Children's literature can be used to teach phonics, but books should not be overtaught.

Exemplary phonics instruction builds on existing skills, is sensitive to dialectical differences, and allows for observation time. It is taught as one of several word-identification skills and in the context of meaningful reading and writing experiences. Teachers should be familiar with the overall program, use only well-developed published materials, and discontinue phonics instruction upon reading mastery.

Function words can be difficult for students because their configurations are often similar and their meanings may be hard to grasp. Edward B. Fry's list of Instant Words is useful for reading and spelling instruction.

Young readers can also use context to identify words. Knowledge of semantics and syntax helps children make educated guesses about the unknown words. Using picture cues also helps word recognition. Cloze procedures support using context to determine word meanings.

Students should acquire enough fluency to retain meaning throughout the reading of the passage. Analyzing readers' miscues can be a useful process. Various miscue-assessment procedures can be used, depending on the time you have for this process. The Names Test can give you some initial impressions about a student's reading achievement.

Using technology such as CD-ROM programs is effective for a variety of students. Parents can be encouraged to help readers by sharing songs, poems, and books. Finally, you should be familiar with many practices to determine how best to teach a wide variety of students.

Books for Teaching Beginning Phonics

SHORT *a*

Baer, Gene. *THUMP, THUMP, Rat-a-Tat-Tat.* Illustrated by Lois Ehlert. New York: HarperTrophy, 1989.

Kimmel, Eric. *The Gingerbread Man.* Illustrated by Megan Lloyd. New York: Holiday House, 1993.

Moncure, Jane Belk. *Word Bird Makes Words with Cat.* Illustrated by Linda Hohag. Mankato, Minn.: The Child's World, 1984.

Vaughan, Marcia. *Tingo Tango Mango Tree.* Morristown, N.J.: Silver Burdett Press, 1995.

SHORT *e*

Moncure, Jane Belk. *Word Bird Makes Words with Hen.* Mankato, Minn.: The Child's World, 1984.

Snow, Pegeen. *A Pet for Pat.* Illustrated by Tom Dunnington. Chicago: Children's Press, 1984.

SHORT *i*

Brown, Marc. *Pickle Things.* New York: Parents Magazine Press, 1980.

Moncure, Jane Belk. *Word Bird Makes Words with Pig.* Illustrated by Vera Gohman. Mankato, Minn.: The Child's World, 1984.

Thaler, Mike. *In the Middle of the Puddle.* Illustrated by Bruce Degen. New York: Harper & Row, 1988.

Yorinks, Arthur. *Whitefish Will Rides Again.* Illustrated by Mort Drucker. New York: HarperCollins, 1994.

SHORT *o*

Andrews, Sylvia. *Rattlebone Rock.* Illustrated by Jennifer Plecas. New York: HarperCollins, 1995.

Asch, Frank. *Popcorn.* New York: Trumpet, 1979.

Baron, Alan. *Red Fox Dances.* Cambridge, Mass.: Candlewick Press, 1996.

Murphy, Stuart J. *Ready, Set, Hop!* Illustrated by Jon Buller. New York: HarperCollins, 1996.

Walsh, Ellen Stoll. *Hop Jump.* New York: Trumpet, 1993.

SHORT *u*

Baer, Gene. *THUMP, THUMP, Rat-a-Tat-Tat.* Illustrated by Lois Ehlert. New York: HarperTrophy, 1989.

Moncure, Jane Belk. *Word Bird Makes Words with Duck.* Illustrated by Linda Hohag. Mankato, Minn.: The Child's World, 1984.

Walsh, Ellen Stoll. *Hop Jump.* New York: Trumpet, 1993.

West, Colin. *"Buzz, Buzz, Buzz," Went Bumblebee.* Cambridge, Mass.: Candlewick Press, 1996.

Ziefert, Harriet. *Nicky Upstairs and Down.* Illustrated by Richard Brown. New York: Viking Kestrel, 1989.

LONG *a*

Cowen-Fletcher, Jane. *Baby Angels.* Cambridge, Mass.: Candlewick Press, 1996.

Hennessy, B. G. *Jake Baked the Cake.* Illustrated by Mary Morgan. New York: Penguin, 1990.

Merriam, Eve. *Train Leaves the Station.* Illustrated by Dave Gottlieb. New York: Trumpet, 1988.

Raffi. *Shake My Sillies Out.* Illustrated by David Allender. New York: Crown, 1987.

Robart, Rose. *The Cake That Mack Ate.* Illustrated by Maryann Kovalski. Boston: Little, Brown, 1986.

LONG *ar*

Jeram, Anita. *Contrary Mary.* Cambridge, Mass.: Candlewick Press, 1995.

_____. *Daisy Dare.* Cambridge, Mass.: Candlewick Press, 1995.

LONG *e*

Barton, Byron. *The Wee Little Woman.* New York: HarperCollins, 1995.

Lewison, Wendy Cheyette. *Going to Sleep on the Farm.* Illustrated by Juan Wijingaard. New York: Trumpet, 1992.

Marzollo, Jean. *Home Sweet Home.* New York: HarperCollins, 1997.

Shaw, Nancy. *Sheep in a Jeep.* Illustrated by Margot Apple. Boston: Houghton Mifflin, 1986.

_____. *Sheep Out to Eat.* Illustrated by Margot Apple. Boston: Houghton Mifflin, 1992.

Snow, Pegeen. *Eat Your Peas, Louise!* Illustrated by Mike Venezia. Chicago: Children's Press, 1985.

LONG *i*

Brett, Jan. *Comet's Nine Lives.* New York: G. P. Putnam's, 1996.

Greene, Carol. *Ice Is. . . Whee!* Illustrated by Paul Sharp. Chicago: Children's Press, 1983.

Hayes, Sarah. *Nine Ducks Nine.* New York: HarperCollins, 1996.

Thaler, Mike. *In the Middle of the Puddle.* Illustrated by Bruce Degan. New York: Harper & Row, 1988.

Yorinks, Arthur. *Whitefish Will Rides Again.* Illustrated by Mort Drucker. New York: HarperCollins, 1994.

LONG *o*

Peek, Merle. *Roll Over! A Counting Song.* New York: Clarion, 1981.

Vaughan, Marcia. *Tingo Tango Mango Tree.* Morristown, N.J.: Silver Burdett Press, 1995.

West, Colin. *"Only Joking!" Laughed the Lobster.* Cambridge, Mass.: Candlewick Press, 1995.

LONG *u*

Eversole, Robyn. *The Flute Player.* Illustrated by G. Brian Karas. New York: Orchard, 1995.

E w

Numeroff, Laura, and Barney Saltzberg. *Two for Stew.* Illustrated by Salvatore Murdocca. New York: Simon & Schuster, 1996.

Gershator, Phyllis. *Tukama Tootles the Flute.* Illustrated by Synthia Saint James. New York: Orchard, 1994.

O o

Ziefert, Harriet. *Who Said Moo?* Illustrated by Simms Taback. New York: HarperCollins, 1996.

O w

Oppenheim, Joanne. *"Not Now!" Said the Cow.* Illustrated by Chris Demarest. New York: Bantam, 1989.

O u

Baron, Alan. *Little Pig's Bouncy Ball.* Cambridge, Mass.: Candlewick Press, 1996.

Books Useful for Teaching a Variety of Vowel Sounds

Baker, Keith. *Hide and Snake.* New York: Trumpet, 1991.

Baron, Alan. *Little Pig's Bouncy Ball.* Cambridge, Mass.: Candlewick Press, 1996.

Carle, Eric. *All about Arthur (An Absolutely Absurd Ape).* New York: Franklin Watts, 1974.

Conrad, Pam. *Animal Lingo.* Illustrated by Barbara Bustetter Falk. New York: HarperCollins, 1995.

Davol, Marguerite. *The Heart of the Wood.* Illustrated by Sheila Hamanaka. New York: Simon & Schuster, 1992.

Durant, Alan. *Mouse Party.* Illustrated by Sue Heap. Cambridge, Mass.: Candlewick Press, 1995.

Fleming, Denise. *In the Small, Small Pond.* New York: Henry Holt, 1993.

Galdone, Paul. *Henny Penny.* New York: Scholastic, 1968.

Grossman, Bill. *The Banging Book.* Illustrated by Robert Zimmerman. New York: HarperCollins, 1995.

Kirk, David. *Miss Spider's Tea Party.* New York: Scholastic, 1994.

Lobel, Arnold. *The Book of Pigericks.* New York: Harper & Row, 1983.

Marzollo, Jean. *Sun Song.* Illustrated by Laura Regan. New York: HarperCollins, 1995.

_____. *The Teddy Bear Book.* Illustrated by Ann Schweninger. New York: Dial, 1989.

McPhail, David. *Pigs Ahoy!* New York: Dutton Children's Books, 1995.

Murphy, Stuart J. *The Best Bug Parade.* Illustrated by Holly Keller. New York: HarperCollins, 1996.

Prelutsky, Jack. *The Baby Uggs Are Hatching.* Illustrated by James Stevenson. New York: Mulberry, 1982.

_____. *Ride a Purple Pelican.* Illustrated by Garth Williams. New York: Greenwillow, 1986.

Seuss, Dr. *Fox in Socks.* New York: Random House, 1963.

Waddell, Martin. *John Joe and the Big Hen.* Illustrated by Paul Howard. Cambridge, Mass.: Candlewick Press, 1995.

Zemach, Margot. *The Little Red Hen: An Old Story.* New York: Farrar, Straus & Giroux, 1983.

References

Adams, Marilyn Jager. *"Beginning to Read:* A Critique by Literacy Professionals and a Response by Marilyn Jager Adams." *The Reading Teacher* 44, no. 6 (Feb. 1991): 370–395.

Andrews, Sylvia. *Rattlebone Rock.* Illustrated by Jennifer Plecas. New York: HarperCollins, 1995.

Anno, Masaichiro. *Anno's Magical ABC: An Anamorphic Alphabet.* New York: Philomel, 1980.

Baer, Gene. *THUMP, THUMP, Rat-a-Tat-Tat.* Illustrated by Lois Ehlert. New York: HarperTrophy, 1989.

Baker, Linda, Robert Serpell, and Susan Sonnenschein. "Opportunities for Literacy Learning in the Homes of Urban Preschoolers." In *Family Literacy: Connections in Schools and Communities,* edited by Lesley Mandel Morrow, 236–252. Newark, Del.: International Reading Association, 1995.

Beck, Isabel L., and Connie Juel. "The Role of Decoding in Learning to Read." In *What Research Has to Say about Reading Instruction,* 2nd ed., edited by S. Jay Samuels and Alan E. Farstrup, 101–123. Newark, Del.: International Reading Association, 1992.

Brown, Margaret Wise. *Goodnight Moon.* Illustrated by Clement Hurd. New York: Scholastic, 1947.

Buck, Nola. *Creepy Crawly Critters and Other Halloween Tongue Twisters.* Illustrated by Sue Truesdell. New York: HarperCollins, 1995.

Cambourne, Brian. *The Whole Story: Natural Learning and the Acquisition of Literacy in the Classroom.* Auckland, New Zealand: Ashton Scholastic, 1988.

Carbo, Marie. "Reading Styles Research: 'What Works' Isn't Always Phonics." *Phi Delta Kappan* 68 (Feb. 1987): 431–435.

Caseley, Judith. *Mama, Coming and Going.* New York: Greenwillow, 1994.

Chall, Jeanne. *Learning to Read: The Great Debate.* New York: McGraw-Hill, 1967.

_____. "Learning to Read: The Great Debate 20 Years Later—A Response to 'Debunking the Great Phonics Myth.'" *Phi Delta Kappan*, 70 (March 1989): 521–539.

Chwast, Seymour. *The Alphabet Parade.* San Diego: Harcourt Brace Jovanovich, 1991.

Clay, Marie. *Becoming Literate: The Construction of Inner Control.* Portsmouth, N.H.: Heinemann, 1991.

Clymer, Theodore. "The Utility of Phonic Generalizations in the Primary Grades." *The Reading Teacher* 50, no. 3 (Nov. 1996): 182–187.

Cunningham, Pat. "The Names Test: A Quick Assessment of Decoding Ability." *The Reading Teacher* 44, no. 2 (Oct. 1990): 124–129.

Dechant, Emerald. *Whole-Language Reading: A Comprehensive Teaching Guide.* Lancaster, Penn.: Technomic, 1993.

Duke, Kate. *The Guinea Pig ABC.* New York: Trumpet Club, 1983.

Durica, Karen Morrow. *Literature Links to Phonics: A Balanced Approach.* Englewood, Colo.: Teacher Ideas Press, 1996.

Ediger, Marlow. "Reading: Skills Versus Ideas." *Reading Improvement* 32, 1 (Spring 1995): 60–62.

Fleming, Denise. *In the Small, Small Pond.* New York: Henry Holt, 1993.

Fowler, Teri. "Fluency in Reading: Risk Success." *Reading Improvement* 30, no. 2 (Summer 1993): 109–112.

Fox, Barbara. *Strategies for Word Identification: Phonics from a New Perspective.* Englewood Cliffs, N.J.: Prentice-Hall, 1996.

Fry, Edward B., Dona Lee Fountoukidis, and Jacqueline Kress Polk. *The New Reading Teacher's Book of Lists.* Englewood Cliffs, N.J.: Prentice-Hall, 1985.

Goodman, Kenneth. *Phonics Phacts.* Portsmouth, N.H.: Heinemann, 1993.

Goodman, Yetta M., and Kenneth S. Goodman. "To Err Is Human: Learning about Language Processes by Analyzing Miscues." In *Theoretical Models and Processes of Reading,* edited by Robert B. Ruddell, Martha Rapp Ruddell, and Harry Singer, 104–123. Newark, Del.: International Reading Association, 1994.

Goodman, Yetta M. "Revaluing Readers While Readers Revalue Themselves: Retrospective Miscue Analysis." *The Reading Teacher* 49, no. 8 (May 1996): 600–609.

Goodman, Yetta M., and Ann M. Marek. *Retrospective Miscue Analysis: Revaluing Readers and Reading.* Katonah, N.Y.: Richard C. Owen, 1996.

Griffith, Priscilla L., and Mary W. Olson. "Phonemic Awareness helps Beginning Readers Break the Code." *The Reading Teacher* 45, no. 7 (March 1992): 516–523.

Gunning, Thomas G. *Teaching Phonics and Other Word Attack Skills.* Springfield, Ill.: Charles C. Thomas, 1988.

____. "Word Building: A Strategic Approach to the Teaching of Phonics." *The Reading Teacher* 48, no. 6 (March 1995): 484–488.

Harste, Jerome. *New Policy Guidelines for Reading: Connecting Research and Practice.* Urbana, Ill.: National Council Teachers of English, 1989.

Heilman, Arthur. *Phonics in Proper Perspective,* 7th ed. New York: Macmillan, 1993.

Hutchins, Pat. *Don't Forget the Bacon.* New York: Greenwillow, 1975.

____. *The Surprise Party.* New York: Macmillan, 1986.

Kelly, Sean. *Boom Baby Moon.* Illustrated by Ron Hauge. New York: Dell, 1993.

Kimmel, Eric. *The Gingerbread Man.* Illustrated by Megan Lloyd. New York: Holiday House, 1993.

Lazar, Althier M., and Renee Weisberg. "Inviting Parents' Perspectives: Building Home-School Partnerships to Support Children Who Struggle with Literacy." *The Reading Teacher* 50, no. 3 (Nov. 1996): 228–237.

Lundsteen, Sara. *Listening: Its Impact at All Levels on Reading and the Other Language Arts.* Urbana, Ill.: National Council Teachers of English, 1979.

Marek, Ann M., and Yetta M. Goodman. "Understanding the Reading Process." In *Retrospective Miscue Analysis: Revaluing Readers and Reading,* edited by Yetta M. Goodman and Ann M. Marek, 21–38. Katonah, N.Y.: Richard C. Owen, 1995.

Martin, Bill Jr., and John Archambault. *Chicka Chicka Boom Boom.* Illustrated by Lois Ehlert. New York: Simon & Schuster, 1989.

Max, D. T. "The End of the Book?" *The Atlantic Monthly* (Sept. 1994): 61–71.

McGee, Lea M., and Donald J. Richgels. "'K is for Kristen's': Learning the Alphabet from a Child's Perspective." *The Reading Teacher* 43, no. 3 (Dec. 1989): 216–225.

McGeorge, Constance W. *Boomer's Big Day.* Illustrated by Mary Whyte. San Francisco: Chronicle, 1994.

Mills, Heidi, Timothy O'Keefe, and Diane Stephens. *Looking Closely: Exploring the Role of Phonics in One Whole Language Classroom.* Urbana, Ill.: National Council Teachers of English, 1992.

Morrow, Lesley Mandel, Diane H. Tracey, and Caterina Marcone Maxwell, editors. *A Survey of Family Literacy in the United States.* Newark, Del.: International Reading Association, 1995.

Nicholson, Tom. "Reading Without Context." In *Reading Acquisition Processes,* edited by G. Brian Thompson, William E. Tunmer, and Tom Nicholson, 105–122. Clevedon, Avon, U.K.: Multilingual Matters LTD, 1993.

Prelutsky, Jack. *The Random House Book of Poetry for Children.* Illustrated by Arnold Lobel. New York: Random House, 1983.

_____. *Ride a Purple Pelican.* Illustrated by Garth Williams. New York: Greenwillow, 1986.

Rhodes, Lynn K., and Nancy L. Shanklin. "Miscue Analysis in the Classroom." *The Reading Teacher* 44, no. 3 (Nov. 1990): 252–254.

Schwartz, Amy. *A Teeny Tiny Baby.* New York: Orchard, 1994.

Slobodkina, Esphyr. *Caps for Sale.* Reading, Mass.: Addison-Wesley, 1968.

Smith, Frank. *Understanding Reading.* Hillsdale, N.J.: Lawrence Erlbaum Associates, 1988.

Stahl, Steven A. "Saying the 'P' Word: Nine Guidelines for Exemplary Phonics Instruction." *The Reading Teacher* 45, no. 8 (April 1992): 618–625.

Stahl, Steven A., Jean Osborn, and Fran Lehr. *Beginning to Read: Thinking and Learning about Print: A Summary.* Urbana-Champaign, Ill.: Center for the Study of Reading, 1990.

Taylor, Nancy E., Irene H. Blum, and David M. Logsdon. "The Development of Written Language Awareness: Environmental Aspects and Program Characteristics." *Reading Research Quarterly.* 21, no. 2 (Spring 1986): 132–149.

Thaler, Mike. *In the Middle of the Puddle.* Illustrated by Bruce Degan. New York: Harper & Row, 1988.

Trachtenburg, Phyllis. "Using Children's Literature to Enhance Phonics Instruction." *The Reading Teacher* 43, no. 9 (May 1990): 648–654.

Walsh, Ellen Stoll. *Hop Jump.* New York: Trumpet, 1993.

Weeks, Sarah. *Crocodile Smile: 10 Songs of the Earth as the Animals See It.* Illustrated by Lois Ehlert. New York: HarperCollins, 1994.

Whatley, Bruce, and Rosie Smith. *Whatley's Quest.* New York: HarperCollins, 1995.

Williams, Linda. *The Little Old Lady Who Was Not Afraid of Anything.* Illustrated by Megan Lloyd. New York: HarperTrophy, 1986.

Yopp, Hallie Kay. "Developing Phonemic Awareness in Young Children." *The Reading Teacher* 45, no. 9 (May 1992): 696–703.

Yorinks, Arthur. *Whitefish Will Rides Again.* Illustrated by Mort Drucker. New York: HarperCollins, 1994.

CD-ROM REFERENCES

Dr. Seuss's ABC. Novato, Calif.: Broderbund Software, 1995.

Forest Friends Reading Club. IBM in conjunction with Odyssey Interactive Media, 1996.

Kid Phonics. Torrance, Calif.: Davidson & Associates, 1994.

P.B. Bear's Birthday Party. London: DK Multimedia, 1995.

Phonics Alive. Mona Vale, Australia: Advanced Education Services, 1996.

The Sunshine CD-ROM Collection. Auckland, New Zealand: Sunshine Multi-Media, 1995

5

Teaching Vocabulary

Be Mine

I used my dictionary today
And I have something to say:

You're a magus, a hakim, a pandit, a belletrist,
a virtuoso, a mosaicist, a scholiast, an artiste,
an empress, a maharani, a czarina, a queen,
a scholar, a thaumaturge, a wit, an academe,
a regina, a siren, Aphrodite, a grace,
an exemplar, the epitome, a paragon, an ace,
a metrician, a rimer, a goliard, a poet—
How do I feel? These words show it!

Introduction

Some of you may have already stopped to find out whether all the words in "Be Mine" can really be found in a thesaurus. You may have decided this would be a perfect introduction to teaching synonyms. You may have decided it would be fun to write a parallel poem using antonyms such as *fool, oaf,* or *fop*. You may want to share Eve Merriam's poem, "Be My Non-Valentine," which inspired "Be Mine" (1986, 17). Words intrigue, amuse, inform, and entertain us. Teachers are eager to learn how to teach vocabulary more effectively, thus instilling a love of words in their students. In this chapter we examine existing information on teaching vocabulary, goals and strategies for instruction, suggestions for helping remedial readers and second-language learners, and a variety of activities for instruction.

Vocabulary and Reading Comprehension

"Vocabulary knowledge is fundamental to reading comprehension; one cannot understand text without knowing what most of the words mean" (Nagy 1988, 1). Our vocabulary (or lack thereof) can also indicate what prior knowledge we need to be able to understand a topic (Pittelman and Heimlich 1991, 37). In a discussion of the high correlation of vocabulary and comprehension test scores, Mary E. Curtis emphasizes how the vocabulary's level of difficulty and our background knowledge work together to affect the challenges the vocabulary will present us with as we read a passage (1987, 49).

The relationship of vocabulary to comprehension seems to be indisputable; a student who cannot understand the words cannot possibly understand the text. However, because vocabulary and comprehension are highly correlated does not necessarily mean that improving vocabulary increases comprehension (Beck, McKeown, and Omanson 1987, 147; Nagy 1988, 1). William E. Nagy provides two reasons for this predicament: (1) Most instruction fails to provide the in-depth knowledge necessary for improved comprehension, and (2) readers need not know *every* word to understand a passage (ibid.). Many readers become quite skilled at making educated guesses. Therefore, the challenge is to determine what kind of vocabulary instruction will improve reading comprehension. This is the challenge we will address.

Traditional Vocabulary Instruction

Those of you who learned to read using basal textbooks are familiar with the practice of receiving instruction on new words before you read a story, essay, or article. Usually your teacher wrote the word in a sentence on the board, and you then read the sentence and discussed the probable meaning of the words. After the reading, perhaps your reading group discussed the accuracy of the earlier definitions or completed a worksheet that reinforced the meaning of the vocabulary words.

In an effort to determine whether the words being taught in such programs are truly "new," a group of researchers, largely from the Center for the Study of Reading at the University of Illinois at Urbana-Champaign, investigated whether second and fifth graders already know the meanings of the vocabulary words being presented as "new" in their basal readers. In general, they found that students do not perform substantially better on words that are formally taught. In short, the students already know the words, at least partially (Stallman et al. 1990, 26). The authors of this study point out that, as indicated by an executive editor from a basal company, words may be included for additional reasons other than being "new": "key words for understanding the passage, words that could be used to apply recently learned skills, and words that are not likely to be in the students' oral vocabularies" (ibid., 27). Therefore, as a teacher making difficult choices about vocabulary instruction, usually due to time limitations, you should routinely evaluate the necessity of any textbook-prescribed vocabulary instruction. In this chapter we look at a variety of activities for teaching vocabulary that expand on traditional vocabulary practices used in reading instruction, as well as in content areas such as social studies, math, science, music, and art.

Indirect Vocabulary Instruction

Vast numbers of vocabulary words are acquired annually by children despite the presence or absence of vocabulary instruction. William E. Nagy and Patricia A. Herman believe that a major source of vocabulary development is the incidental learning of words from reading and oral context. We know that children acquire thousands of words orally before attending school, most without direct instruction. Once in school, the chance of learning a word from one exposure in text is approximately 1 in 20 (Nagy and Herman 1987, 26). However, this can, in the long run, be a sizable acquisition rate. According to Nagy and Herman's estimates, if students spent 25 minutes a day reading at a rate of 200 words per minute, for 200 days a year, they would read approximately a million words of print per year. They would

A teacher reads with her students.

encounter approximately 15,000–30,000 unfamiliar words, thus learning between 750 and 1,500 words annually (ibid.). This finding has led Stephen Krashen to posit that the most important activity for vocabulary acquisition is **free voluntary reading** (1993, 12). These reading materials need not be award-winning literature. Indeed, Kyung-Sook Cho and Stephen Krashen found that four adult second-language learners made excellent gains in vocabulary and improved their listening and speaking English while reading books from the *Sweet Valley Kids* series (1994).

Free voluntary reading
The practice of allowing students to choose their own reading materials and then to read for extended time periods.

Reading aloud to students is another important indirect source of vocabulary acquisition. Warwick B. Elley found that 7- and 8-year-olds who listened to stories where no explanations of the words were given showed vocabulary gains of 15 percent and gains of 40 percent when the stories were accompanied by explanations of word meanings. Further, Rebecca G. Eller, Christine C. Pappas, and Elga Brown illustrated the significance of incidental learning by reading stories aloud to prereading kindergartners on three separate occasions. The children were then invited to read the stories back, and they demonstrated substantial success in using the semantic and syntactic information acquired from their listening to support their "reading" (1988, 18). The success that comes with such experiences further motivates young children to continue exploring words through books and conversation.

Most reading experts agree that it is not necessary to decide between direct or indirect vocabulary instruction. Instead, teachers should strive to provide rich instructional activities along with a variety of indirect experiences (Stahl and Fairbanks 1986, 72). As Jeanne S. Chall from Harvard University con-

(New York: Trumpet, 1986).

spotlight 1

Opposites

GRADE LEVELS:
Preschool–1.

BOOK: *Opposites* by
Rosalinda Kightley,

ACTIVITY: Simple illus-
trations with bold colors
illustrate pairs of oppo-
site words, on opposite
pages, such as *high* and
low. A matching game
at the back of the book
offers an opportunity to
review the concepts.
Share the book and
help the children come
up with other examples.
Students can then act
out many of the word
pairs. Create an oppo-
sites wall or chart and
add pairs as students discover them.

cludes, "Students need to learn words through reading, and they need to learn words directly, apart from the context" (1987, 15). Teachers should make learning vocabulary an integral component of every subject throughout the entire day. (See Spotlight 1.)

Goals of Vocabulary Instruction

Michael Graves, from the University of Minnesota, discusses three major goals of vocabulary instruction: learning words, learning to learn words, and learning about words. These goals suggest the general direction instruction should take during the elementary, middle, and high school years.

LEARNING WORDS

Michael Graves breaks the first goal into six tasks:

1. *Learning to read known words.* This means learning to read words that young students already have in their oral vocabulary. Beginning reading instruction generally emphasizes these words, and by the intermediate years, average and above-average readers have generally mastered this vocabulary (1987, 167).

2. *Learning new meanings for known words* (ibid.). This means understanding, for example, that *bay* can mean "part of a sea," "a leaf used in cooking," "a reddish-brown color," "an alcove between columns," or "a wolf's howl."

3. *Learning new words to represent known concepts* (ibid.). This occurs when a student uses *famished* instead of *hungry,* or *enormous* instead of *big.*

4. *Learning new words that represent new concepts* (ibid.). This can be difficult, especially if the concepts and the words are difficult. For example, the word *serfdom*

is more easily understood when related to slavery, but a full understanding of the word requires a larger historical context than U.S. history.

5. *Clarifying and enriching the meanings of known words* (ibid., 170). This occurs when students encounter known words in a variety of contexts. Creating a semantic feature analysis, discussed later in this chapter, is an excellent way to develop an understanding of the nuances of meanings.

6. *Moving words from students' receptive (listening and reading) to expressive (speaking and writing) vocabularies* (ibid., 171). In this final task, teachers use meaningful activities to encourage an internalization of the vocabulary so that it is readily available when students speak or write.

LEARNING TO LEARN WORDS

Contextual analysis
The use of words, sentence structure, or other features to understand an unknown word.

Contextual analysis is one way we understand unknown words. Although contextual analysis has some challenges, discussed later in this chapter, it is a practical strategy for learning new words (Graves 1987, 175). When analyzing unfamiliar words, students should be taught strategies that they can rely on as they read independently. Useful strategies include making an educated guess at the meaning of the word, reading on to see whether the context helps with the meaning, returning to the word and analyzing parts of the word, and rereading the passage. If understanding the word is critical to comprehension, students can turn to an outside resource such as a dictionary, thesaurus, teacher, or schoolmate. Graves recommends that students be encouraged to develop their own personal plans for building vocabularies (ibid., 177). This can include more free reading, using resources such as a thesaurus, working crossword puzzles, developing a word bank or personal dictionary, reading about words, and playing word games.

LEARNING ABOUT WORDS

Graves identifies the last goal, learning about words, as the most ambitious, yet it probably receives the least attention in schools (1987, 177). He discusses several tasks related to learning about words. First, students need to learn what it means to know a word. For example, students might never have seen a word before—it is completely new to them. Or, they might recognize a word in one of several ways: (1) the word but not the meaning, (2) orally but not in written form, (3) the connotation but not the denotation, or (4) its full meaning.

Second, students need to learn that word meanings vary and how they vary (ibid., 178). As seen in the example of *bay*, a word can have multiple meanings, and students need to learn that context affects meaning.

Next, students need to recognize and manipulate word relationships (ibid., 178) through such activities as classification, semantic feature analysis, and webs. (See Figures 5.6–5.10 later in this chapter.) Robert and Jana Marzano have classified words into instructional clusters that encourage student recognition of relationships. For example, a minicluster built on the word *throw* includes *toss, pass, pitch, flip, heave, cast, fling, thrust,* and *flick* (1988, 67). Their resource, *A Cluster Approach to Elementary Vocabulary Instruction*, lists a variety of clusters that can be used as the basis for many of the strategies discussed in this chapter.

Recognizing and using figurative language proves to be another challenge for students (Graves 1987, 179). Reading aloud daily and discussing the use of figurative language or wordplay encourages students to internalize examples. (See "Recommended Books for Exploring Vocabulary" on page 178 for resources.) Finally, students need to learn to value words (ibid., 180). When students hear, read, and discuss excellent examples of literature, poetry, essays, and plays, they begin to appreciate the beauty of the written and spoken word.

Characteristics of Ineffective Vocabulary Instruction

Few teachers would argue with the belief that students are more successful in nearly all aspects of learning when they have good vocabularies; indeed, vocabulary is thought to be an excellent indicator of a person's intelligence (Sternberg 1987, 90). Not surprisingly, teachers go to great lengths to incorporate vocabulary instruction into their reading program and such content areas as social studies. However, some techniques for teaching vocabulary waste time and energy. Most of you will agree that memorizing lists of words or writing them in sentences did little to develop your love of words. William E. Nagy, who has studied vocabulary development at the Center for the Study of Reading at the University of Illinois, emphasizes that the most effective methods are those that foster an in-depth knowledge of the words being learned (1988, 3). Having students look up words in a dictionary or memorize lists provides neither the meaningful understanding nor the sense of excitement that is necessary for continued growth. Dictionary definitions may not fit the reading or may be incomplete (ibid.), so the student may never use the words beyond this task.

Providing written contexts for the new words is a common, but often misunderstood, practice. Textbook manuals usually include lists of sentences that present vocabulary words in context, but textbook authors cannot tailor these lists to fit the background and skills that a particular group of students brings to the examples. Textbook sentences, although useful, are generally too brief to provide the nuance that enables a student to fully understand the meaning of the word, and the sentences may even be misleading. One study suggests that not only can contextual clues be unreliable predictors of meaning, they

A teacher and student work together on vocabulary.

can also create confusion (Schatz and Baldwin 1986, 451). Further, this practice of reading a single sentence to determine meaning does not encourage the discussion that is critical to vocabulary acquisition, in part because it doesn't provoke questions of clarification that come about naturally when people converse about a particular subject. When we realize that (depending on the research consulted) the average 6-year-old's vocabulary is estimated to be between 2,500 and 25,000 words, that this same child might understand roughly twice that number of words when heard in context (Douglass 1989, 71), and that most preschoolers learn their vocabulary in oral contexts, without explicit interpretation, it is easy to see how important discussion is to continued vocabulary development (Nagy and Herman 1987, 24).

Another practice, having students write words in sentences, is an isolated exercise that does not develop the thorough understanding necessary for thoughtful expression. Camille L. Z. Blachowicz, a researcher on classroom vocabulary instruction, suggests that the common practice of having students keep a vocabulary notebook, wherein they record words, definitions, and sentences using vocabulary words, occurs because teachers know they should be teaching vocabulary, but lack alternative strategies (1986, 643). Students who are asked to memorize lists or write words in sentences generally have to demonstrate their competence by taking a test on the words. They then promptly forget the words. (See Spotlight 2 on page 156.)

Stategies for Effective Vocabulary Instruction

Although researchers disagree on specific points about teaching vocabulary, a consensus for effective instruction emerges from the research. The following 10 strategies apply not only to general vocabulary development but also to using vocabulary instruction to enhance comprehension.

■ **Schema**
A related network of concepts or existing conceptual background for learning new words. (The plural of schema is schemata.)

STRATEGY 1: **Draw upon students' *schemata*.** (Blachowicz 1985, 879; Blachowicz 1986, 644; Pittelman and Heimlich 1991, 54). Introduce unknown words in a known context; that is, relate a new word such as *quadrilateral* to known words such as *square* or *rectangle*. A student who uses written and oral contextual clues learns that *fall* not only means "to drop down suddenly" but also means "autumn" and "to come to pass or happen" (that is, *Christmas falls on Wednesday this year*). Robert J. Sternberg, from Yale University, emphasizes that before students can learn from context, they must understand the processes, cues, and moderating variables that might affect the learning (1987, 96). Contextual analysis involves more than educated guessing and using the cues in the passage. The student reader must also be able to fully understand the topic (Drum and Konopak 1987, 85). This relatively sophisticated process of learning how to "mine" the context effectively comes from prior experience with the topic and also from skillful instruction.

As you work with vocabulary words, model this practice by verbalizing what you know about unfamiliar words. Ask pertinent questions, such as

"What does this word make you think of?" "Have you ever seen this word before?" "What was the context?" "What do other words tell me?" The semantics of words can be examined as they relate to others through discussion, brainstorming, webbing, classification, or semantic feature analysis. Examples for these and other appropriate activities are discussed under the section entitled "Activities for Teaching Vocabulary."

STRATEGY 2: **Be selective when choosing vocabulary for an instructional activity.** Teachers who use textbook materials or literature-based units may be confronted with a list of 10–30 recommended vocabulary words, a daunting prospect for most learners. Marvin L. Klein suggests that teachers analyze words in relation to their purpose or function, determining whether the students need full or low-level ownership (1988, 66). Dale D. Johnson and P. David Pearson point out that vocabulary found in the content areas cannot all be taught; they suggest that teachers focus on essential words and on strategies that foster independence. When choosing vocabulary for instruction, consult the text's word lists, glossary, and boldfaced or italicized words. Consider your students' reading levels, experiential backgrounds, and the most important concepts (1984, 178–179).

In addition, Steven A. Stahl recommends considering how thoroughly the word must be taught. Some words can be taught easily because they are associated with well-known words; others require in-depth instruction (1986, 666). Stahl also recommends that if words are partially known, it may be better to concentrate on critical unknown words because clarification of partially known words will come about naturally through the reading (ibid). Activities such as a vocabulary rating (see Figure 5.3 on page 165) and vocabulary tests (Curtis 1987, 50) provide information on partially known words.

Analysis of context improves when a word appears frequently in the text (Beck, McKeown, and Omanson 1987, 149; Elley 1989, 174; Johnson and Pearson 1984, 141; Stahl and Fairbanks 1986, 72). Therefore, choosing vocabulary that occurs in both the literature and the content area is particularly effective (Blachowicz and Lee 1991, 191). Consider these three questions: (1) Will the word be important to your students in 5 years? (2) Will knowing the word help them understand related words? (3) Is the word's meaning essential for comprehending the reading passage? Adjust your teaching accordingly, focusing on long-term retention for the first two questions and short-term understanding for the third (Blachowicz 1985, 879).

STRATEGY 3: **Foster word connections.** To do this, predict with students how the words relate to the current topic. Help them notice that the structure of a reading passage helps their comprehension; for example, important words might be boldfaced, in the headings, or noted in the margins. Ask students to predict the content of the passage and the meaning of key words based on their preview of the structure. Their predictions need not be accurate (Blachowicz 1986, 644).

STRATEGY 4: **Involve your students.** As we have discussed elsewhere, when students are fully involved in the learning process, learning is always more successful. Remember that any activities for vocabulary instruction require active participation on a whole-class or small-group basis. Through questions, discussion, and related reading, students can speculate on meanings, consulting references as a final clarification when necessary (Blachowicz 1985, 879; Pittelman and Heimlich 1991, 55; Stahl 1986, 665).

STRATEGY 5: **Have students read the text in total.** Students will begin to answer the questions raised during the preceding predictive phase (Blachowicz 1986, 644).

STRATEGY 6: **Discuss the reading.** Encourage students to confirm and clarify their predictions about the words. Be ready to use appropriate reference books to clarify meanings that are still ambiguous (Blachowicz 1986, 644; Pittelman and Heimlich 1991, 55).

STRATEGY 7: **Provide meaningful opportunities for students to use the words in their reading and writing.** This is the most challenging step, because the traditional practice of recording words in sentences in a vocabulary notebook does not encourage students to truly internalize the word (Beck, McKeown, and Omanson 1987, 149; Blachowicz 1985, 879; Blachowicz 1986, 664; Pittelman and Heimlich 1991, 55). Students might instead read related fiction or informational books, newspaper articles, essays, or magazines. Related writing projects can be as complex as editorials, critiques, questionnaires, reviews, analyses, and interviews or as simple as lists, notes, comparisons, and letters.

STRATEGY 8: **Use every subject to teach vocabulary.** Integrate vocabulary instruction throughout all subjects during the entire year (Blachowicz 1985, 880; Johnson and Pearson 1984, 2). Model your enthusiasm about learning new words, regularly pointing out interesting words, subtle differences in meaning, and strategies for comprehending unknown words (Pittelman and Heimlich 1991, 56). Point out how the students can use the root word plus suffixes and prefixes to determine the meaning of new words. For example, if a student knows *conform* and is familiar with suffixes and prefixes, she will be able to figure out the meaning of *nonconformist*.

STRATEGY 9: **Celebrate wordplay.** Familiarize yourself and your students with the wealth of books available on wordplay and meanings, in addition to the standard resources such as a dictionary and thesaurus (Blachowicz 1985, 880; Pittelman and Heimlich 1991, 56). Linda Gibson Geller recommends nursery rhymes, lilting rhymes, and conversation for preschoolers; nonsense verse,

s p o t l i g h t   3

Understanding and Appreciating Words

GRADE LEVELS: 3–5.

BOOK: *Guppies in Tuxedos: Funny Eponyms* by Marvin Terban, illustrated by Giulio Maestro (New York: Clarion, 1988).

ACTIVITY: When a name becomes a word, it is an eponym. Familiar food examples include the Earl of Sandwich, Sylvester Graham, and Napoleon. Obtain several copies of the book and divide the students into four to eight groups, assigning a chapter to each group. Have the small groups create clues that identify the source of the eponym and try to stump the class. Students should not represent the item directly. For example, to do Ferris wheel, students might create pictures of George Washington, a fair, and a group of people (us) to demonstrate that the ferris wheel is named after George Washington Ferris.

rhyming verse, riddles, and jokes for ages 5–7; and exploring metaphor, more sophisticated riddles, humorous verse, tongue twisters, and parody for ages 8–11 (1985). Continue to expose your students to all the informal experiences that encourage vocabulary development—read-alouds, conversation, listening (Johnson and Pearson 1984, 2). Celebrate discoveries of new and interesting words with a word wall. Motivate students to contribute by sharing your own discoveries. Tell the stories behind words. (See Spotlight 3.)

STRATEGY 10: **Give students responsibility for their vocabulary.** Once students are familiar with a variety of strategies and activities for learning vocabulary, encourage them to become responsible for using these strategies. For example, have them preview a reading passage and select the most effective strategy for fully understanding that particular vocabulary. Students who prefer an activity such as a semantic map could work together in small groups to develop the map and learn the material. Another student might prefer to work alone on a semantic feature analysis. By providing choices, you allow your students to fully internalize activities that will become life-long learning strategies for facing unfamiliar words (Johnson and Pearson 1984, 2).

Vocabulary and Learners with Special Needs

Language use varies both within groups of speakers and between groups of speakers (Edelsky 1989, 96). Shirley Brice Heath notes that anthropologists, social historians, and folklorists have long recognized the rich verbal forms of Afro-American rhymes, stories, music, sermons, and joking; yet schools repeatedly call for more emphasis on literacy skills for young and old African-Americans (1992, 29). My fourth and fifth graders and I would often talk about how we had different vocabularies. Our "sibling vocabulary" differed from our "grandparent vocabulary"; our "playground vocabulary" certainly differed from our "church vocabulary." We discussed how easily we could shift between those vocabularies, depending on the context and the audience. Although this conversation often came up in the context of appropriate language for the school setting and respectful language for peers, despite their differences, the underlying message was a respect for the ability to vary language as needed. Edelsky emphasizes that people who learn a second language join a speech community and must learn the contexts that come with this language, along with its unique variations (1989, 99). It is therefore important to recognize and value the richness that each culture brings to the community at large.

One of our goals as teachers is to encourage our students to increase the time they spend reading. This is especially critical for those of us who teach students with reading problems or second-language learners, because their particular challenges often discourage them from reading. Second-language learners who became fluent in their primary language during their first 4 or 5 years are now confronted with a school environment that simply cannot duplicate the home environment that fostered such rapid language acquisition. Therefore, it is crucial that teachers of these students consider not only what is *there* in the environment but also *how* students use what is available to them (Lindfors 1989, 39). By constantly assessing the communication processes children use, teachers can closely approximate those early learning experiences where children aren't *taught* language, they are "*doing* language—joking, informing, arguing, inquiring, comforting, challenging, and so on" (ibid., 40).

A child's reluctance to read, coupled with minimal opportunities to converse, slows his or her acquistion of vocabulary. Students unsuccessful at reading increasingly difficult material naturally become less and less willing to spend time reading. As Steven A. Stahl and T. Gerard Shiel point out, "children who are good readers become better readers because they read more, but poor readers get relatively worse because they read less" (1992, 224).

Happily, the preceding recommendations and strategies for effective vocabulary teaching and the activities that follow this section can be equally useful in working with second-language learners and remedial readers, as well as with average or above-average students. The following recommendations should be kept in mind when teaching second-language learners or students with special needs:

■ *Every assignment should have value.* Those students who face more than the ordinary challenges in learning particularly deserve authentic learning experiences that respect their investment of time and effort.

■ *Develop activities that integrate verbal communication.* Carole Urzúa suggests activities that inspire conversation. For example, give two students a box with hand holes through which they feel something interesting inside, then encourage them to talk about what they think the object is (1989, 19).

Elaboration
Active use of prior knowledge.

■ *Foster activities that involve* **elaboration**. For example, students could work together in pairs to list what they know about a topic (Chamot and O'Malley 1994, 93). When possible, make links to the individual's cultural context (ibid., 96).

■ *Use a conversational style.* When you work with students, encourage them to talk informally with you, fostering their use of words (Urzúa 1989, 22).

■ *Read aloud to students.* (Stahl and Shiel 1992, 225). Encourage their parents, siblings, or other family members to read aloud to them daily.

■ *Teach students specific coping strategies.* These can be as varied as substituting synonyms for unknown words, rereading text, looking for known parts of unknown words, or using metacognitive strategies (for example, discussing strategies for figuring out a word's meaning with a teacher or peer).

■ *Encourage "scanning."* Help students learn to judge when words must be defined and when they can be skipped (Rhodes and Dudley-Marling 1988, 148). Convince students that they don't need to read every word by demonstrating the usefulness of skipping and scanning to find specific information. Reinforce this when you use content textbooks.

■ *Encourage students' interest in words.* Help them understand how words convey meaning (ibid.).

■ *Provide students with specific strategies.* For example, teach them to use graphs, illustrations, charts, headings, introductions, and summaries to preview material.

■ *Make connections.* Determine what the students already know; make explicit connections between what they know and what they don't know. Encourage them to hypothesize about new information (Blachowicz 1991, 299).

■ *Encourage discussion.* Discussion should occur in all activities. When it comes to vocabulary instruction, a good classroom is a talkative classroom. This is especially true for students who may learn more easily through their ears than through their eyes.

■ *Encourage responsibility.* Teach students to review and evaluate the strategies and activities they have used during their vocabulary work. Encourage them to figure out which strategies work best for them.

s p o t l i g h t   4

Understanding and Appreciating Words

GRADES LEVELS: 5–9.

BOOK: *Kites Sail High: A Book about Verbs* by

Ruth Heller (New York: Grosset & Dunlap, 1988).

ACTIVITY: Turn to the section of the book that demonstrates passive and active voice. Discuss the examples and have students brainstorm other examples and

how to change them from passive to active voice. Have students find examples of passive voice in published works and their own writings and then have students revise them to active voice. Discuss which is more "attractive."

■ *Use simple supports.* Finally, take time to analyze what simple supports might help these students. These could include charts of difficult words, miniglossaries, materials presented in two languages, picture dictionaries, use of a highlighter for important words, making marginal notes, and so forth.

Activities for Teaching Vocabulary

The following activities are useful for regular reading instruction as well as for the content-area instruction. They are arranged generally in order of increasing complexity. However, certain activities (such as "Connect Two") may be equally useful for twelfth graders as they are for second graders; a character rating can be constructed with kindergartners as successfully as it can be with sixth graders. Therefore, you must make the final judgment regarding the appropriateness of any activity for your students. Once students have internalized a variety of activities, they should be encouraged to select the ones that have proven most useful for them.

CONNECT TWO

■ **Connect Two**
A vocabulary activity in which students decide on relationships between words and then justify their connection.

Connect Two can be used successfully with all grades as a prereading or postreading activity. It provides students with a way to build connections through discussing and exploring words drawn from one or more reading sources. The teacher begins by putting a list of target words on the board or overhead transparency. The words might be taken from the boldfaced terms found in a textbook, from a vocabulary list, or from the reading assignment. Students decide individually or in small groups which words might go together and then justify why they connect the words. For example, in Figure 5.1, a student might state "I connect *soddies* and *dugouts* because *they are both*

FIGURE 5.1

Connect Two

Connect Two

Directions: Draw lines to connect the words from "Homesteading Women" that go together. Be sure you can justify your choices.

settlement	railways
Homestead Act	immigrants
persecution	zinc
soddies	dugouts
ploughing	scurvy
buffalo dung	droughts
grasshoppers	poultices
pleurisy	turpentine
bees	harvesting
husking	quilting
skunk oil	blizzards

houses." These connections are saved and compared after the reading. Connect Two builds on existing schemata to integrate new words and foster discussions of relationships. For a variation, try Connect Three. The list of words in Figure 5.1 is from "Homesteading Women," Chapter 3 of *Plains Women: Women in the American West* by Paula Bartley and Cathy Loxton. How would you connect them?

CLASSIFICATION SORT

Classification Sort
A vocabulary activity in which students sort words into possible categories.

When confronted with new information, we immediately try to understand it by looking for common characteristics and relating these characteristics to our prior knowledge or past experience (Pittelman and Heimlich 1991, 38). Teaching categorization skills helps students organize and access information. **Classification Sort** builds on existing schemata by allowing students to speculate on how to classify words. Develop a list of important words from the reading and write them on multiple sets of note cards. Before assigning the reading, give the sets of cards to small groups of students. Direct them to sort the words into logical categories and label the categories. When the groups have finished, a student representative can share the decisions from each group. As in many prereading vocabulary activities, there is no one right answer. After the reading, have students resort the cards and discuss how their decisions differ from before. See Figure 5.2 on page 164 for how one group sorted a list of orchestral instruments.

FIGURE 5.2

Classification Sort

Word List

bass drum	saxophone	bass fiddle
snare drum	bassoon	timpani
cello	triangle	clarinet
trombone	cymbals	trumpet
flute	cymbals	trumpet
flute	tuba	French horn
viola	oboe	violin

List Sorted by Instrument

Woodwinds	Brass	String	Percussion
flute	trumpet	violin	timpani
clarinet	trombone	viola	snare drum
oboe	tuba	bass fiddle	bass drum
bassoon	French horn	cello	cymbals
saxophone			triangle

VOCABULARY RATING

Vocabulary rating
A list of vocabulary words with an opportunity to respond with "can define," "have seen or heard," or "not sure."

Constructing a **vocabulary rating** is appropriate for any grade level. Read the chosen book or textbook passage and select words that challenge your students. Make a list of the words with the categories "Can define," "Have seen or heard," and "Not sure." Before students read the selection, they check off the appropriate category for each word. Then they compare their lists in small groups and discuss possible meanings. After reading the material, students rate the words again, using a different-colored pen or pencil. This is a nongraded activity effective for developing interest in the reading, making predictions about word meanings, and making connections with vocabulary. (See Figure 5.3.)

RATING SCALE

Rating scale
A grid for rating the degree of the presence of a characteristic.

In her collection of teaching strategies for reading novels, Donita Covey, a teacher-librarian from Vancouver, British Columbia, includes a **rating scale** (1991). Although her example is for use with character analysis, the principle of using antonyms for the rating can be applied to a variety of concepts. When used with small groups, this activity fosters discussion and clarification of meanings. (See Figure 5.4 on page 166.)

FIGURE 5.3
Vocabulary Rating
for *The Story of
the Empire State
Building* by
Patrick Clinton

Vocabulary Rating

Vocabulary	Can Define	Have Seen or Heard	Not Sure
landmark			
tycoons			
architect			
rubble			
monument			
ingenuity			
observatory			
port			

WORD THEATER

Word theater
Acting out the
meaning of vocabu-
lary words.

Word theater, described by Nancy Whisler and Judy Williams (1990, 119), gives students an an opportunity to combine drama with vocabulary development. The teacher prepares two lists of words drawn from the story or reading that can be pantomimed like Charades. After students read a selection, they pair up as one actor and one guesser. The actors silently act out the first word on the list, progressing to the next word as each is guessed correctly. Students should keep the reading in mind as they guess the words. Once the list is finished, they trade roles to act out the second list. See Figure 5.5 on page 167 for examples of word theater lists.

WEBS

Web
An informal map
that shows the rela-
tionships between
concepts and impor-
tant terms.

A **web** is another effective activity. There is no single correct way to create a web; the design will depend on the importance readers place on the concepts and the relationships that are emphasized. Some webs will feature cause and effect; others will compare and contrast; still others will develop the main ideas with supporting details. Younger students might construct a web from just one paragraph as seen in Figure 5.6 on page 168. Older students might use more material in which they develop major concepts rather than use the specific vocabulary shown in the web for "Taking a Spacewalk."

Webbing can be used to introduce a topic for a thematic unit or to explore possible research topics. To begin, put the main topic in large letters in a circle in the center of the board or overhead transparency. Encourage students to

FIGURE 5.4

Rating Scale

Name: _____

Title: _____

Author: _____

Who is the main character? _____

Rate the character using the scale below. Color in the squares that show the qualities the character displays in your novel. Be ready to give examples to prove that your ratings are accurate.

	Very	Some-what	Both	Some-what	Very	
independent						dependent
friendly						unfriendly
brave						cowardly
uncertain						certain
stubborn						flexible
valued						unvalued

Now make your own rating scale using the qualities that are best displayed by your character.

From *Novel Strategies for Young Adults* by Donita Covey. (Teacher Ideas Press. P.O. Box 6633, Englewood, CO: 80155-6633, 1992).

brainstorm words related to the topic and list them along the bottom or side of the board or transparency. Decide with students what the key concepts are and add them in circles that connect by lines to the main idea. Use lines to connect additional words in circles to the key concepts. Students can then discuss and modify the web.

As a postreading activity, have students read a story, passage, essay, or article and then create a web that interprets the reading logically. Webs can also be used to review major ideas and relationships in a lesson. The teacher can begin the web or provide a partially completed web for students to finish (Moore, Readence, and Rickelman 1989, 53).

SEMANTIC MAPS

■ **Semantic map** Graphic organizer that emphasizes word meaning and nuance.

A **semantic map**, similar to a web, focuses on nuance. To design a semantic map, review the reading assignment and consider your objectives for the map. Choose several key words to start the map and list a variety of related words.

FIGURE 5.5
Word Theater

Primary list for *The Very Busy Spider* by Eric Carle

blew	run	chase	spin
sleep	nap	ride	jump
swim	eat	roll	catch

Intermediate list for Chapter 1, *Avalanche* by Arthur Roth

slid	suffocate	shove	pawing
windmilling	squeezed	tightened	unshouldered
struggled	tumbling	relaxed	smother

Middle school list for pages 3–10, *Letters from a Slave Girl: The Story of Harriet Jacobs* by Mary E. Lyons

bleeding	weed	sew	floating
cry	giggling	buried	hollering
traveling	recall	marry	shivery
sweat	plop	clamp	taste

Organize the words into logical groups and label the groups. Arrange the groups on a map and evaluate how effectively they portray the relationships you want to teach. When using the map with students, solicit their input regarding additions or deletions. Once students are familiar with semantic maps, have them work in small groups to create their own maps as a postreading activity. Joan E. Heimlich and Susan D. Pittelman found semantic mapping to be effective in activating prior knowledge, building vocabulary, developing comprehension, and developing study skills (1990, 45). For further information, consult their publication, *Semantic Mapping: Classroom Applications*.

SEMANTIC GRADIENT

Semantic gradient
A classification scheme that arranges related words on a continuum.

A **semantic gradient**, described by Camille L. Z. Blachowicz (1986, 646), is a classification scheme that uses a continuum. After completing the gradients, students can use a thesaurus to construct a gradient with synonyms or one with a new theme. Note that students may disagree on the exact arrangement of the terms; discussion should be encouraged. (See Figure 5.7 and Something to Try 1 on pages 168 and 169.)

OPIN

Opin
A vocabulary strategy that involves selecting words that best fit a sentence.

Opin, a vocabulary strategy attributed to Frank Greene, has students working in groups. Groups are given a passage with key words omitted. They discuss what word would be the best choice for the sentence and why. Then the group

Taking a Spacewalk

Space is an unfriendly environment. The spacecraft provides a safe surrounding for astronauts. But human beings need a special spacesuit to survive outside the spacecraft. The spacesuit provides the correct pressure and oxygen. Safety lines connect the astronaut to the spacecraft in case of an emergency. Some astronauts use a manned maneuvering unit, a backpack that holds tanks of nitrogen gas. The astronaut can maneuver through space using gas thrusters operated by hand controls. This gives astronauts more flexibility for performing a variety of tasks outside the spacecraft.

Directions: Make a web using important words from the paragraph.

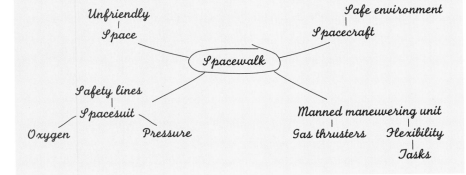

Size

Directions: Arrange these words from smallest to largest.

enormous

middle-sized

microscopic

huge

large

little

tiny

smallest

↓

largest

something to try 1

Semantic Gradient

Choose one of the following topics and create a semantic gradient:

degree of age; degree of wealth; degree of happiness; degree of health. Use a thesaurus to develop a pool of words.

Have small groups of students arrange the words. Can they come to consensus within

their groups? Do they agree across the groups? Do they agree with your assessment? Discuss how rich our vocabulary can be and challenge students to add other words to the semantic gradient.

shares their selections and justifications with the entire class. The passage can be written so that there are no correct answers—the students serve as the final arbiters for best choices. Alternatively, a passage can be selected from literature; students then compare their choices to the author's usage. (Don't be surprised if your students decide their choices improve the passage!) How would you complete the following excerpt from "Fowler's Fowl"? (Barchers 1990, 65).

There once was a _____ who would dress up as a poor _____ and go begging at _____ and capture pretty _____. No one knew what happened to the _____ because they were never _____ again. One day he came to the _____ of a man who had three lovely _____. The _____ looked pathetic and _____, carrying a _____ on his back for handouts.

Answers: wizard, man, houses, girls, girls, seen, door, daughters, wizard, feeble, basket.

STRUCTURED OVERVIEW

■ **Structured overview**
A scheme for organizing vocabulary words while analyzing concepts.

■ **Graphic organizer**
A diagram or scheme for showing the relationships among words and concepts.

The **structured overview** is a form of **graphic organizer** that focuses on concepts (Vacca 1981, 62). A superordinate concept is identified, with coordinate concepts and subordinate concepts arranged in an appropriate hierarchy. To construct a structured overview, review the material and determine the concepts. Next add familiar and unfamiliar words that support the concepts. Create a scheme with the most important word at the top of the diagram, adding other words. Evaluate the overview to determine whether it portrays the concepts and their relationships accurately. Revise as necessary, but assume that students will initiate further revisions during its use.

The structured overview can introduce a topic or help students understand the text. However, it is important that students be actively involved in the process. Structured overviews have proven to be useful as prereading organizers because they provide an overview of the material to be learned; a reference point for new material; a cue for important details in the passage; a concise review instrument; and visual aides for written and verbal information (Griffin

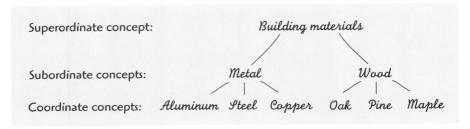

FIGURE 5.8

Structured
Overview

Superordinate concept: *Building materials*

Subordinate concepts: *Metal*   *Wood*

Coordinate concepts: *Aluminum   Steel   Copper   Oak   Pine   Maple*

and Tulbert 1995, 79–80). The example in Figure 5.8 uses building materials as the superordinate concept, with metal and wood as coordinate concepts. Note that an additional subordinate concept might be plastic and that there are a variety of possibilities for additional subordinate concepts.

Once students are familiar with this process, they can complete a diagram during or after their reading (Moore, Readence, and Rickelman 1989, 56). For more of a challenge, students can create their own structured overviews. Some hierarchies, such as the solar system, are easy to arrange because of the fixed nature of the components, and students' overviews will be similar. Other subjects generate more variability. My fourth graders worked in small groups using the boldfaced words from a science textbook chapter on pollution, and their superordinate designations ranged from pollution to environment to natural resources. Each group had valid reasons for their interpretation and, through their discussion, demonstrated their clear understanding of the concepts and related vocabulary. See Chapter 11 for more examples.

VENN DIAGRAM

Venn diagram
Overlapping circles that demonstrate relationships.

A **Venn diagram** provides a structure for comparing common elements. To prepare a Venn diagram, draw two large circles that overlap in the center. Label one circle with one element and the other circle with a different element. Students sort the words they are using into the appropriate circles; words that have both features are listed in the center. Nancy Whisler and Judy Williams suggest using this process to compare and contrast elements in literature. For example, in *Sarah Plain and Tall* by Patricia MacLachlan, the setting shifts from the sea to the prairie, offering opportunities to compare the different elements of both settings and those common to both settings (1990, 106).

SEMANTIC FEATURE ANALYSIS

Semantic feature analysis
A chart that analyzes features of a chosen category of terms or concepts.

A **semantic feature analysis** chart is recommended for vocabulary development and can be used for prereading or prewriting experiences. It is also an excellent postreading strategy for reading instruction and in the content areas (Pittelman et al. 1991, 8). To begin the process, the teacher chooses a category. The words are listed down the left side of the grid, as in Figure 5.9. The fea-

FIGURE 5.9

Semantic
Feature Analysis

	reed	wood	keys	metal	slide	strings	membrane
flute	–	+/–	+	+/–	–	–	–
clarinet	+	+/–	+	+/–	–	–	–
oboe	+	+	+	–	–	–	–
bassoon	+	+	+	–	–	–	–
saxophone	+	–	+	+	–	–	–
trumpet	–	–	+	+	–	–	–
trombone	–	–	–	+	+	–	–
tuba	–	–	+	+	–	–	–
Fr. horn	–	–	+	+	–	–	–
violin	–	+	–	–	–	+	–
timpani	–	+	–	+	–	–	+

tures can be generated by the students and are listed across the top. Students then work through the list of words on the left side, comparing features to determine whether they exist for a certain instrument. A plus sign indicates that the feature exists, a minus indicates an absence of the feature, and a question mark indicates an unknown. The grid can be expanded as students come up with additional features or think of more words for the category. Students should be encouraged to confirm their decisions by checking appropriate reference books. During the first experience, the teacher should lead the students, but they soon become skilled enough to create their own grids with minimal direction.

Semantic feature analysis can be used in all grades. The authors of *Semantic Feature Analysis: Classroom Applications* (Pittelman et al. 1991) suggest using these charts to analyze features of fruits in kindergarten, pets in second grade, character traits in third grade, stringed instruments in fourth grade, polygons in fifth grade, and early civilizations in seventh grade. This type of analysis can also be used to compare different versions of the same story, as in Figure 5.10 on page 172, which uses "Little Red Riding Hood."

ANALOGIES

Analogy
A comparison of two
similar relationships.

Analogies foster critical thinking about words and their associations. For example, a typical analogy might be: lake is to pond as river is to creek. This is usually written as lake : pond :: river : _____ (tributary, sea, creek).

FIGURE 5.10

Semantic

Feature Analysis

Little Red Riding Hood

	Red cape	Wine	Cake	Flowers	Hunter rescues
Dahl	?	?	?	?	–
Hyman	+	+	–	+	+
Montresor	+	–	+	+	?
Richardson	+	–	–	–	+
Zipes	–	+	+	+	+

BOOKLIST:

Dahl, Roald. "Little Red Riding Hood and the Wolf." In *Revolting Rhymes*. New York: Bantam, 1986.

Hyman, Trina Schart, reteller. *Little Red Riding Hood*. New York: Holiday House, 1983.

Montresor, Beni. *Little Red Riding Hood*. New York: Doubleday, 1991.

Richardson, Lee, reteller. *Little Red Riding Hood*. Carmel, Calif.: ShirLee, 1985.

Zipes, Jack, translator. "Little Red Cap." In *The Complete Fairy Tales of the Brothers Grimm*. New York: Bantam, 1987.

After introducing their second graders to the general concept of analogies, Kelly Ann HuffBenkoski and Scott C. Greenwood (1995) had them choose the word that did not belong, incorporating words from their thematic unit. Then students were given three words that related and were asked to provide a related fourth word. Divergent answers were accepted when logical. Students began to develop an understanding of word and concept relationships and were able to move to the more formal style seen in the following examples. The students concluded by creating their own analogies, trying to stump their classmates and teachers. When working with analogies, students should discuss the relationship in pairs or small groups, especially if they have trouble understanding the relationship. Here are some common analogies:

1. Part to whole
   Letter : word :: sentence : _____.
   (phrase, paragraph, clause)

2. Cause and effect
   Heat : boiling :: cold : _____.
   (cooling, steaming, freezing)

3. Antonym
   Naive : wise :: young : _____.
   (old, adolescent, juvenile)

4. Synonym
   Talent : ability :: skill _____.
   (faculty, dexterity, clumsiness)

5. Characteristic
   Cold : snow :: wet : _____.
   (rain, ice, wind)

6. Degree
   Delirious : thrilled :: tedious _____.
   (prosaic, dignified, diligent)

STORY INTRODUCTIONS

In her extensive guide to studying fairy tales, *Within the Forest: A New Approach to Fairy Tales*, Susan Ohanian recommends comparing how fairy tales begin (1991, 3). Collect several versions of "Goldilocks and the Three Bears." Students will quickly see how carefully selected words influence the impact of the story. Some selections are simple and familiar, while others take a humorous or repetitive approach. For older readers, choose a more challenging fairy tale, such as "Beauty and the Beast." Students can discuss the similarities—that is, each version emphasizes the role of the merchant father and his degree of wealth—and also the differences. Semantic feature analyses can stimulate further interpretations as seen in Figure 5.10.

Technology and Vocabulary Development

Hypertext
A process of organizing or stacking information for easy computer access.

As noted in Chapter 4, CD-ROMs that use video clips, sound, graphics, text, and animation may also use **hypertext**. A program that combines media gives students a variety of options to access and use information. Many CD-ROM programs also integrate "hot words," which students can click on for definitions, elaboration, or presentations in other media. For example, youngsters in preschool through first grade can explore and develop their computer skills by clicking on hot words in *Franklin's Reading World*, a prereading program that reinforces vocabulary, phonics, word recognition, spelling, and comprehension. Students enjoy the animation integrated into such programs, sometimes referred to as *edutainment*. An entertaining CD-ROM that involves students in word games, *Reading Blaster: Invasion of the Word Snatchers* (1995), appeals to students in grades 2–5.

Multimedia technology is most successful when it supports existing curriculum goals. For example, Jane Beaty, a fourth grade special education teacher, uses *The Semantic Mapper* (Kuchinskas and Radencich 1986), software that involves students in constructing semantic maps and brainstorming. Beaty uses this software throughout the reading program, capitalizing on her students' interest in computers (Wepner 1990, 13). Another useful tool for vocabulary development, *Merriam-Webster's Collegiate Dictionary, Deluxe Electronic Edition* combines a dictionary with a thesaurus. Students find words by entering part of the definition, utilize the spell-check program, or play word games. *Vocabulary Builder* takes players through the "Vocabulary Institute" with a coach; they participate in word duels and take quizzes (Merriam-Webster 1996). *Word Crazy*, another Merriam-Webster product, includes a variety of word games with varying levels of difficulty. Teachers should also consider such programs as *Core: Reading and Vocabulary Development* (Hamilton and Hombs 1995), a program in English or Spanish that gives guided drill and practice in the core vocabulary found in many major reading textbooks.

With the proliferation of multimedia products, choosing appropriate materials can be daunting. Many library and educational journals regularly review these products, and one trade magazine, *Kidscreen* (416-408-2300), provides information about the industry. When considering multimedia, ask yourself these questions:

1. *Does the presentation format provide opportunities for learning that other materials do not easily provide?* For example, a CD-ROM that allows students to explore additional information or have alternative experiences through the media (that is, video clips or auditory enhancements) provides more learning opportunities.

2. *Is the information layered to accommodate varying levels of achievement or prior knowledge?* Does the program inspire learners to look for more information or complete more activities? For example, can a student access additional information on a topic or play a related game that reinforces the learning?

3. *Does the program allow for diverse learners?* Does it offer multiple, complementary formats and perspectives? For example, the program that offers audio in addition to text supports students with weaker reading skills. Bilingual programs support second-language learners. Does it encourage gifted students to explore different avenues of thinking or learning?

4. *Does the program fit into a larger structure of authentic learning?* For example, creating semantic maps with software gives students another way to expand their uses of words in reports or during research.

5. *Does the program's skills or information transfer to other learning situations?* For example, completing word games through a dictionary program builds a life-long interest in words and appreciation for using a dictionary.

6. *Does the program provide opportunities to reflect critically on learning and to elaborate on knowledge gained?* For example, a program that promotes creating reports offers more learning opportunities than one where students simply fill in the blanks.

7. *Can learners use the information in the program for other purposes?* For example, could a video clip be combined with data to create a new report?

8. *When feedback is included, is the feedback useful?* For example, feedback for incidental learning should be eliminated in favor of feedback that reinforces mastery or information or skills.

9. *Does the program foster independent use?* Is it easy to use? Can students get in, get what they need, get out, and return easily?

10. *Does the program educate more than it entertains?*

Involving Parents

Not all parents will have the means to enhance the home environment with purchased books, CD-ROMs, and other learning tools on the market. Fortunately, one of the best ways parents can help their children develop vocabulary doesn't cost money. Conversing with children and reading aloud to them is still the number one way to promote literacy. Stephen Krashen emphasizes that much of what we learn about words and their grammatical properties is not deliberately taught. "Intensive methods that aim to give students a thorough knowledge of words are not nearly as efficient as reading in terms of words gained per minute" (1993, 15). It may be hard to convince parents that reading aloud can be more beneficial than copying words out of a dictionary, but books such as Stephen Krashen's *The Power of Reading: Insights from the Research* can support you in this endeavor. For those parents who are unsure what to read aloud, provide them with lists of recommended books, such as the Caldecott or Newbery winners for older students. (See Appendix D.) Most public libraries will furnish parents with updated lists of these award winners.

If you have a regular classroom newsletter, consider including a vocabulary strategy that you have introduced in class and suggest that parents use this in another application. For example, have the students check out a thesaurus and try the suggestion in the Something to Try 1 on page 169. Consider sharing

something to try 2

Parent Nights

Create a monthly parent night where you share strategies parents can use with their children. Try the following set of ideas, modifying them to suit the students' parents.

1. Begin with a favorite read-aloud. Picture books can be used with all ages, and parents will enjoy this ice breaker.

2. Model a strategy for identifying words. (See Chapter 4.)

3. Model a strategy for exploring vocabulary from this chapter.

4. Model a strategy for building reading comprehension. (See Chapter 6.)

5. Model a strategy for use in the content area, if appropriate. (See Chapter 11.)

6. Preview any new instructional strategies you will be using in the immediate future. This time could also be used for a special topic, such as test-taking skills.

7. Close with an entertaining poem or another short read-aloud.

books from the list of recommended books for exploring vocabulary found at the end of this chapter. Build a classroom library of these books by applying for district or school grants and encourage students to share them with their parents.

A Final Note

Vocabulary acquisition will always be an important feature of reading and language arts programs, and teachers will always be searching for ways to increase their students' vocabularies in an interesting and challenging manner. Wise teachers share their love of words throughout the day, noting surprising or interesting words used in poetry or during a read-aloud. They model vocabulary growth by adding new words to their personal dictionaries or word banks, by reading widely and sharing newly found words with the students, and by looking up unknown words in the dictionary. They use a variety of strategies to understand meaning during their reading. Skilled vocabulary teachers read aloud frequently and teach new words in the context of meaningful reading passages or learning experiences. They are selective in their instruction and use picture books, poetry, wordplay, and games to make vocabulary acquisition fun. Finally, they delight in finding that perfect word that expresses exactly what they want to say.

Summary

Vocabulary is highly correlated to comprehension; however, improving vocabulary does not necessarily improve comprehension. Traditional vocabulary instruction used basal textbooks where words were introduced in sentences and discussed before the reading and then explored in a follow-up discussion or worksheet.

Indirect vocabulary instruction includes such activities as free voluntary reading, discussion, and listening to read-alouds. Most reading experts agree that a sound program provides direct and indirect instruction.

Goals for vocabulary instruction include learning words, learning to learn words, and learning about words. Ineffective vocabulary instruction is characterized by inadequate contexts, isolated exercises (such as copying the definition and writing the word in a sentence) and standard seatwork (such as keeping a vocabulary notebook—be careful here, some students enjoy and benefit from this in the context of writing or exploring word usage).

Strategies for effective vocabulary instruction include the following: drawing upon students' schemata, being selective about the vocabulary taught; making connections with the topic; involving students fully in the learning process; having them read the text in total and discuss the reading; providing meaningful opportunities to use words further; integrating vocabulary instruction throughout all subjects; having fun with wordplay; and allowing students to select their preferred strategies for vocabulary growth.

For students with special needs, use all these strategies, but develop learning experiences with value. Incorporate conversation, elaboration, and the cultural context when appropriate. Emphasize reading aloud, coping strategies, piquing their interest in words, developing strategies for reading textbooks, making strong connections to what is known, discussions, and student evaluation and implementation of successful strategies.

Recommended activities for vocabulary instruction include Connect Two, Classification Sort, vocabulary rating, rating scales, character ratings, word theater, webs, semantic maps, semantic gradients, opin, structured overviews, Venn diagrams, semantic feature analyses, analogies, and story introductions.

Multimedia enable students to explore words in different contexts. Multimedia should provide opportunities for learning not easily met by existing materials, accommodate varying levels of achievement or background knowledge, and allow for students with special needs. They should fit into a larger structure of authentic learning, transfer to other learning situations, provide opportunities to reflect critically on learning and to elaborate on knowledge, and allow learners to use the information in other contexts. Finally, multimedia should provide useful feedback, foster independent use, and educate more than entertain.

Involve parents by encouraging them to converse with, and read aloud to, their children. Provide lists of suggested books and suggest teaching strategies for use with their children.

Recommended Books for Exploring Vocabulary

*N*ote: Though some of these books are easy picture books, they can be springboards to sophisticated exploration. Don't hesitate to consider using any of these for intermediate and middle school levels.

Ashton, Christian. *Words Can Tell: A Book about Our Language.* Englewood Cliffs, N.J.: Julian Messner, 1988. Grades 3 and up.

____. *101 American English Idioms: Understanding and Speaking English Like an American.* Lincolnwood, Ill.: Passport Books, a division of National Textbook Company, 1987. Grades 4 and up.

Callis, Harry. *101 American English Proverbs: Understanding Language and Culture through Commonly Used Sayings.* Lincolnwood, Ill.: Passport Books, a division of National Textbook Company, 1992. Grades 4 and up.

Chermayeff, Ivan, and Jane Clark Chermayeff. *First Words.* New York: Harry N. Abrams, 1990. Grades kindergarten and up.

Cox, James A. *Put Your Foot in Your Mouth and Other Silly Sayings.* Illustrated by Sam Q. Weissman. New York: Random House, 1980. Grades 1 and up.

Esbensen, Barbara Juster. *Words with Wrinkled Knees: Animal Poems.* Illustrated by John Stadler. New York: Thomas Y. Crowell, 1986. Grades 4 and up.

Gomi, Taro. *Seeing, Saying, Doing, Playing: A Big Book of Action Words.* San Francisco, Calif.: Chronicle, 1985. Grades kindergarten and up.

Gwynne, Fred. *The King Who Rained.* New York: Simon & Schuster Books for Young Readers, 1970. Grades 1 and up.

Heller, Ruth. *A Cache of Jewels and Other Collective Nouns.* New York: Grosset & Dunlap, 1987. Grades preschool and up.

____. *Kites Sail High: A Book about Verbs.* New York: Grosset & Dunlap, 1988. Grades 2 and up.

____. *Many Luscious Lollipops: A Book about Adjectives.* New York: Grosset & Dunlap, 1989. Grades 2 and up.

____. *Merry-Go-Round: A Book about Nouns.* New York: Grosset & Dunlap, 1990. Grades 2 and up.

Hepworth, Cathi. *Antics! An Alphabetical Anthology.* New York: G. P. Putnam, 1992. Grades 2 and up.

Hoban, Tana. *All About Where.* New York: Greenwillow, 1991. Grades kindergarten and up.

_____. *More Than One.* New York: Greenwillow, 1981. Grades kindergarten and up.

Hooper, Patricia. *A Bundle of Beasts: From <u>pride</u> of lions to <u>sleuth</u> of bears, poems about animals in groups.* Illustrated by Mark Steele. Boston: Houghton Mifflin, 1987. Grades 3 and up.

Juster, Norton. *Otter Nonsense.* Illustrated by Eric Carle. New York: Philomel, 1982. Grades 4 and up.

Kightley, Rosalinda. *Opposites.* New York: Trumpet, 1986. Grades preschool and up.

Koch, Michelle. *Just One More.* New York: Greenwillow, 1989. Grades preschool and up.

Lederer, Richard. *Anguished English: An Anthology of Accidental Assaults upon Our Language.* Charleston, S.C.: Wyrick, 1987. Grades 4 and up, selectively.

Leedy, Loreen. *Big, Small, Short, Tall.* New York: Holiday House, 1987. Grades preschool and up.

Levitt, Paul M. Douglas, A. Burger, and Elissa S. Guralnick. *The Weighty Word Book.* Illustrated by Janet Stevens. Longmont, Colo: Bookmakers Guild, 1985. Grades 3 and up.

Lowe, A. Mifflin. *Beasts by the Bunches: Illustrated Poems about the Strange-But-True Names for Groups of Animals.* Illustrated by Susan J. Harrison. Garden City, N.Y.: Doubleday, 1987. Grades 3 and up.

MacCarthy, Patricia. *Herds of Words.* New York: Dial Books for Young Readers, 1991. Grades 2 and up.

McMillan, Bruce. *Becca Backward, Becca Frontward: A Book of Concepts.* New York: Lothrop, Lee & Shepard, 1986. Grades preschool and up.

_____. *Super, Super, Superwords.* New York: Lothrop, Lee & Shepard, 1989. Grades preschool and up.

Merriam, Eve. *A Sky Full of Poems.* New York: Dell, 1973. Grades 4 and up.

Morley, Diana. *Marms in the Marmalade.* Illustrated by Kathy Rogers. Minneapolis, Minn.: Carolrhoda, 1984. Grades kindergarten and up.

Most, Bernard. *There's an Ant in Anthony.* New York: Morrow Junior Books, 1980. Grades kindergarten and up.

Murphy, Stuart J. *The Best Bug Parade.* Illustrated by Holly Keller. New York: HarperCollins, 1996. Grades preschool and up.

_____. *Give Me Half!* Illustrated by G. Brian Karas. New York: HarperCollins, 1996. Grades kindergarten and up.

Noll, Sally. *Jiggle Wiggle Prance.* New York: Greenwillow, 1987. Grades preschool and up.

Steckler, Arthur. *101 More Words and How They Began.* Illustrated by James Flora. Garden City, N.Y.: Doubleday, 1980. Grades 3 and up.

_____. *101 Words and How They Began.* Illustrated by James Flora. Garden City, N.Y.: Doubleday, 1979. Grades 3 and up.

Terban, Marvin. *The Dove Dove: Funny Homograph Riddles.* Illustrated by Tom Huffman. New York: Clarion, 1988. Grades 2 and up.

_____. *Guppies in Tuxedos: Funny Eponyms.* Illustrated by Giulio Maestro. New York: Clarion, 1988. Grades 3 and up.

_____. *I Think I Thought and Other Tricky Verbs.* Illustrated by Giulio Maestro. New York: Clarion, 1984. Grades 1 and up.

_____. *In a Pickle and Other Funny Idioms.* Illustrated by Giulio Maestro. New York: Clarion, 1983. Grades 3 and up.

_____. *Mad as a Wet Hen! And Other Funny Idioms.* Illustrated by Giulio Maestro. New York: Clarion, 1987. Grades 3 and up.

_____. *Punching the Clock: Funny Action Idioms.* Illustrated by Tom Huffman. New York: Clarion, 1990. Grades 3 and up.

_____. *Superdupers! Really Funny Real Words.* Illustrated by Giulio Maestro. New York: Clarion, 1989. Grades 3 and up.

_____. *Your Foot's on My Feet and Other Tricky Nouns.* Illustrated by Giulio Maestro. New York: Clarion, 1986. Grades 3 and up.

West, Colin. *One Day in the Jungle.* Cambridge, Mass.: Candlewick Press, 1995. Grades preschool and up.

References

Barchers, Suzanne I. *Wise Women: Folk and Fairy Tales from Around the World.* Englewood, Colo.: Libraries Unlimited, 1990.

Bartley, Paula, and Cathy Loxton. *Plains Women: Women in the American West.* Cambridge: Cambridge University Press, 1991.

Beck, Isabel L., Margaret G. McKeown, and Richard C. Omanson. "The Effects and Uses of Diverse Vocabulary Instructional Techniques." In *The Nature of Vocabulary Acquisition*, edited by Margaret G. McKeown and Mary E. Curtis, 147–163. Hillsdale, N.J.: Lawrence Erlbaum Associates, 1987.

Blachowicz, Camille L. Z. "Making Connections: Alternatives to the Vocabulary Notebook." *Journal of Reading* 29, no. 7 (April, 1986): 643–649.

_____. "Vocabulary Development and Reading: From Research to Instruction." *The Reading Teacher* 38, no. 9 (May, 1985): 876–881.

_____. "Vocabulary Instruction in Content Classes for Special Needs Learners: Why and How?" *Reading, Writing, and Learning Disabilities* 7, no. 4 (1991): 297–308.

Blachowicz, Camille L. Z., and John J. Lee. "Vocabulary Development in the Whole Literacy Classroom." *The Reading Teacher* 45, no. 3 (Nov. 1991): 188–195.

Carle, Eric. *The Very Busy Spider.* New York: Philomel, 1985.

Chall, Jeanne S. "Two Vocabularies for Reading: Recognition and Meaning." In *The Nature of Vocabulary Acquisition*, edited by Margaret G. McKeown and Mary E. Curtis, 7–15. Hillsdale, N.J.: Lawrence Erlbaum Associates, 1987.

Chamot, Anna Uhl, and J. Michael O'Malley. "Instructional Approaches and Teaching Procedures." In *Kids Come in All Languages: Reading Instruction for ESL Students*, edited by Karen Spangenberg-Urbschat and Robert Pritchard, 82–107. Newark, Del.: International Reading Association, 1994.

Cho, Kyung-Sook, and Stephen D. Krashen. "Acquisition of Vocabulary from the Sweet Valley Kids Series: Adult ESL Acquisition. *The Reading Journal* 37, no. 8 (May 1994): 662–667.

Clinton, Patrick. *The Story of the Empire State Building.* Chicago: Children's Press, 1989.

Covey, Donita. *Novel Strategies for Young Adults.* Englewood, Colo.: Teacher Ideas Press, 1991.

Curtis, Mary E. "Vocabulary Testing and Vocabulary Instruction." In *The Nature of Vocabulary Acquisition*, edited by Margaret G. McKeown and Mary E. Curtis, 37–51. Hillsdale, N.J.: Lawrence Erlbaum Associates, 1987.

Dahl, Roald. "Little Red Riding Hood and the Wolf." In *Revolting Rhymes*. Illustrated by Quentin Blake. New York: Bantam, 1986.

Douglass, Malcolm P. *Learning to Read: The Quest for Meaning.* New York: Teachers College Press, 1989.

Drum, Pricilla A., and Bonnie C. Konopak. "Learning Word Meanings from Written Context." In *The Nature of Vocabulary Acquisition*, edited by Margaret G. McKeown and Mary E. Curtis, 73–87. Hillsdale, N.J.: Lawrence Erlbaum Associates, 1987.

Edelsky, Carole. "Putting Language Variation to Work." In *When They Don't All Speak English: Integrating the ESL Student into the Regular Classroom*, edited by Pat Rigg and Virginia G. Allen, 96–107. Urbana, Ill.: National Council Teachers of English, 1989.

Eller, Rebecca G., Christine C. Pappas, and Elga Brown. "The Lexical Development of Kindergartners: Learning from Written Context." *Journal of Reading Behavior* 20, no. 1 (1988): 5–23.

Elley, Warwick B. "Vocabulary Acquisition from Listening to Stories." *Reading Research Quarterly* 24, no. 2 (Spring 1989): 174–187.

Fry, Edward B., Dona Lee Fountoukidis, and Jacqueline Kress Polk. *The New Reading Teacher's Book of Lists.* Englewood Cliffs, N.J.: Prentice-Hall, 1985.

Geller, Linda Gibson. *Wordplay and Language Learning for Children.* Urbana, Ill.: National of Council of Teachers of English, 1985.

Graves, Michael F. "The Roles of Instruction in Fostering Vocabulary Development." In *The Nature of Vocabulary Acquisition*, edited by Margaret G. McKeown and Mary E. Curtis, 165–184. Hillsdale, N.J.: Lawrence Erlbaum Associates, 1987.

Griffin, Cynthia Carlson, and Beth Lorene Tulbert. "The Effect of Graphic Organizers on Students' Comprehension and Recall of Expository Text: A Review of the Research and Implications for Practice." *Reading and Writing Quarterly: Overcoming Learning Difficulties* 11 (Jan.–March 1995): 73–89.

Heath, Shirley Brice. "Oral and Literate Traditions among Black Americans Living in Poverty." In *Becoming Political: Readings and Writings in the Politics of Literacy Education*, edited by Patrick Shannon, 29–41. Portsmouth, N.H.: Heinemann, 1992.

Heimlich, Joan E., and Susan D. Pittelman. *Semantic Mapping: Classroom Applications.* Newark, Del.: International Reading Association, 1990.

Heller, Ruth. *Kites Sail High: A Book about Verbs.* New York: Grosset & Dunlap, 1988.

HuffBenkoski, Kelly Ann, and Scott C. Greenwood. "The Use of Word Analogy Instruction with Developing Readers." *The Reading Teacher* 48, no. 5 (Feb. 1995): 446–447.

Hyman, Trina Schart, reteller. *Little Red Riding Hood.* New York: Holiday House, 1983.

Johnson, Dale D., and P. David Pearson. *Teaching Reading Vocabulary*, 2nd ed. New York: Holt, Rinehart & Winston, 1984.

Kightley, Rosalinda. *Opposites.* New York: Trumpet, 1986.

Klein, Marvin L. *Teaching Reading Comprehension and Vocabulary: A Guide for Teachers.* Englewood Cliffs, N.J.: Prentice-Hall, 1988.

Krashen, Stephen. *The Power of Reading: Insights from the Research.* Englewood, Colo.: Libraries Unlimited, 1993.

Lindfors, Judith Wells. "The Classroom: A Good Environment for Language Learning." In *When They Don't All Speak English*, edited by Pat Rigg and Virginia G. Allen, 39–54. Urbana, Ill.: National Council of Teachers of English, 1989.

Lyons, Mary E. *Letters from a Slave Girl.* New York: Charles Scribner's, 1992.

MacLachlan, Patricia. *Sarah Plain and Tall.* New York: Harper, 1987.

Marzano, Robert J., and Jana S. Marzano. *A Cluster Approach to Elementary Vocabulary Instruction.* Newark, Del.: International Reading Association, 1988.

Merriam, Eve. "Be My Non-Valentine." In *A Sky Full of Poems*, by Eve Merriam. New York: Dell, 1986, 17.

Montresor, Beni. *Little Red Riding Hood.* New York: Doubleday, 1991.

Moore, David W., John E. Readence, and Robert J. Rickelman. *Prereading Activities For Content Area Reading and Learning.* 2nd ed. Newark, Del.: International Reading Association, 1989.

Nagy, William E. *Teaching Vocabulary to Improve Reading Comprehension.* Newark, Del.: International Reading Association, 1988.

Nagy, William E., and Patricia A. Herman. "Breadth and Depth of Vocabulary Knowledge: Implications for Acquisition and Instruction." In *The Nature of Vocabulary Acquisition*, edited by Margaret G. McKeown and Mary E. Curtis, 19–35. Hillsdale, N.J.: Lawrence Erlbaum Associates, 1987.

Ohanian, Susan. "Goldilocks and the Three Bears." From *Within the Forest: A New Approach to Fairy Tales.* Chicago: Science Research Associates, 1991.

Pittelman, Susan D., and Joan E. Heimlich. "Teaching Vocabulary." In *Effective Strategies for Teaching Reading*, edited by Bernard L. Hayes, 35–60. Needham Heights, Mass.: Allyn & Bacon, 1991.

Pittelman, Susan D., Joan E. Heimlich, Roberta L. Berglund, and Michael P. French. *Semantic Feature Analysis: Classroom Applications.* Newark, Del.: International Reading Association, 1991.

Rattigan, Jama Kim. *Truman's Aunt Farm.* Illustrated by G. Brian Karas. Boston: Houghton Mifflin, 1994.

Rhodes, Lynn K., and Curtis Dudley-Marling. *Readers and Writers with a Difference: A Holistic Approach to Teaching Learning Disabled and Remedial Students.* Portsmouth, N.H.: Heinemann, 1988.

Richardson, Lee, reteller. *Little Red Riding Hood.* Illustrated by Shirley Holt. Carmel, Calif.: ShirLee, 1985.

Roth, Arthur. *Avalanche.* New York: Scholastic, 1979.

Schatz, Elinore Kress, and R. Scott Baldwin. "Context Clues Are Unreliable Predictors of Word Meanings." *Reading Research Quarterly* 21, no. 4 (Fall 1986): 439–453.

Stahl, Steven A. "Three Principles of Effective Vocabulary Instruction." *Journal of Reading* 29, no. 7 (April 1986): 662–668.

Stahl, Steven A., and Marilyn M. Fairbanks. "The Effects of Vocabulary Instruction: A Model-Based Meta-Analysis." *Review of Educational Research* 56, no. 1 (Spring 1986): 72–110.

Stahl, Steven A., and T. Gerard Shiel. "Teaching Meaning Vocabulary: Productive Approaches for Poor Readers." *Reading and Writing Quarterly* 8, no. 2 (1992): 223–241.

Stallman, Anne C., Michelle Commeyras, Bonnie Kerr, Kathryn Reimer, Robert Jimenez, Douglas K. Hartman, and P. David Pearson. "Are 'New' Words Really New?" *Reading Research and Instruction* 29, no. 2 (1990): 12–29.

Sternberg, Robert J. "Most Vocabulary Is Learned from Context." In *The Nature of Vocabulary Acquisition*, edited by Margaret G. McKeown and Mary E. Curtis, 89–105. Hillsdale, N.J.: Lawrence Erlbaum Associates, 1989.

Terban, Marvin. *Guppies in Tuxedos: Funny Eponyms.* Illustrated by Giulio Maestro. New York: Clarion, 1988.

Urzúa, Carole. "I Grow for a Living." In *When They Don't All Speak English,* edited by Pat Rigg and Virginia G. Allen, 15–38. Urbana, Ill.: National Council of Teachers of English, 1989.

Vacca, Richard T. *Content Area Reading.* Boston: Little, Brown, 1981.

Wepner, Shelley B. "Holistic Computer Applications in Literature-based Classrooms." *The Reading Teacher* 44, no. 1 (Sept. 1990): 12–19.

West, Colin. *One Day in the Jungle.* Cambridge, Mass.: Candlewick Press, 1995.

Whisler, Nancy, and Judy Williams. *Literature and Cooperative Learning: Pathway to Literacy.* Sacramento, Calif: Literature Co-op, 1990.

Zipes, Jack, translator. "Little Red Cap." In *The Complete Fairy Tales of the Brothers Grimm.* New York: Bantam, 1987.

CD-ROM AND SOFTWARE

Franklin's Reading World. San Mateo, Calif.: Sanctuary Woods, 1995.

Hamilton, Priscilla, and Barbara Hombs. *Core: Reading and Vocabulary Development.* Freeport, New York: Educational Activities, 1995.

Kuchinskas, G., and M. C. Radencich. *The Semantic Mapper.* Gainesville, Fla.: Teacher Support Software, 1990.

Merriam-Webster's Collegiate Dictionary, Deluxe Electronic Edition. Springfield, Mass.: Merriam-Webster, 1996.

Reading Blaster: Invasion of the Word Snatchers. Torrance, Calif.: Davidson, 1995.

Vocabulary Builder. Springfield, Mass.: Merriam- Webster, 1996.

Word Crazy. Springfield, Mass.: Merriam-Webster, 1995.

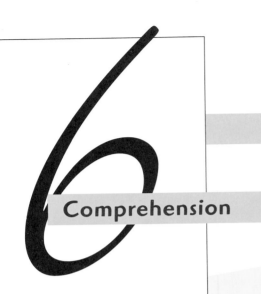

Comprehension

The Wise Woman

The people of a village in Algeria were under siege. Many had died, and with little food or water, others were losing hope of surviving much longer. The mayor called a meeting and asked the villagers to consider surrendering before all were dead.

As the villagers listened with heavy hearts, an old woman, long admired for her wisdom, came forth with a request. She asked for a calf and some corn. In spite of their weariness, the villagers searched far and wide for a calf and corn.

Indeed they found that one stingy man had hidden a calf, hoping to sell it later for a handsome price. Several villagers managed to find a few scraps of corn, and soon they had a modest sackful. The old woman took the calf and corn away, telling the people to trust that soon they would be free.

Just as she had promised, within a few hours the enemy departed.

How did the old woman save her village?

"T
he Wise Woman" is an intriguing folktale. Although it is short, it contains many elements of a good story: an unusual setting, a conflict, a heroine, and a happy ending. There is also a problem to solve—how did the old woman save the village? What did you do as you read the story? Did you think about the word *siege*, recalling that it probably meant that an enemy had surrounded the village, cutting off all food and supplies? Did you wonder why the villagers hadn't fought back? Did you wonder why the old woman asked for the calf and corn? Did you immediately guess what the old woman did? Did you read it again looking for clues to the solution? Were you (or are you) mildly frustrated because you don't know exactly how to confirm your hypothesis?

These processes demonstrate that you were engaged in your reading and were actively comprehending the text, even if you left the story unfinished to read the preceding paragraph. This is the goal of reading teachers: to engage readers in the text, thereby getting them to draw upon their background knowledge, make hypotheses, confirm or disconfirm those hypotheses, think about the information, and use it to solve problems.

As to how the old woman defeated the enemy? When she pushed the calf out the village gates, the watching soldiers collected it and took it to their king. The king wondered how the villagers could spare the calf, but decided that because they were running out of provisions themselves, they would make a feast of it. When they slaughtered the calf and discovered undigested corn in its stomach, the enemy king decided the village must have ample provisions and could easily outlast their attack, so they departed. ("The Wise Woman" is adapted from Suzanne I. Barchers' *Wise Women: Folk and Fairy Tales from Around the World*, 323–324. For collections on folk stories presented in this style, consult George Shannon's *Stories to Solve: Folktales from Around the World and More Stories to Solve: Fifteen Folktales from Around the World*.)

Because you are reading this text you are no doubt a reasonably proficient reader, but you probably don't recall how you got to proficiency. Some fortunate children suddenly start reading as they approach school age. Most of us, however, received fairly deliberate and methodical instruction and increased our skills gradually over several years. Think about what you do when you read. What strategies do you use? They are no doubt so ingrained that you may have trouble identifying them; however, list as many as you can before you proceed.

As you learned in Chapter 4, readers decode words by identifying them through their letter-sound relationship or grapheme-phoneme correspondence. In most cases, they then access their mental **lexicon** attaching the pronunciation to the written symbols. Readers sometimes need to hear the word to access the meaning; conversely, some readers understand the meanings of words without knowing how they are pronounced.

■ **Lexicon**
A personal dictionary or body of terms relating to a topic, profession, or style.

Normally with very little conscious effort, we use several cueing systems as we ascertain the meaning of the phrases, sentences, and paragraphs we are reading (Dechant 1991, 12). These cueing systems include semantics, the meanings of words; syntax, the patterns of phrases and sentences; graphophonics, the relationship between the sounds of the words and the symbols; and our schemata, the networks of associated concepts that we have collected over the years. All these elements flow together seamlessly, requiring from us varying degrees of effort, depending on a number of factors: concept density, organization, style, and readability of the reading material; our skills at decoding, encoding, and recoding; our prior experiences with the reading topic, our level of motivation, and our fluency as readers (O'Donnell and Wood 1991, 121–125); and environmental factors such as distractions, temperature, and lighting.

Teachers want their students to understand and appreciate what they read. It isn't enough to have our students go through the motions; reading without comprehension is frustrating, demoralizing, and a waste of time for everyone. Reading without pleasure, at least periodically, discourages further reading. Reading comprehension is such an important topic that entire books are devoted to the subject. University professors and researchers design experimental studies in an effort to discern exactly how students learn to understand text, and entire journal issues are devoted to the results and differing opinions of these experts. The topic of reading comprehension is vast, complex, and often perplexing, challenging us to understand what sometimes seems incomprehensible. Understanding this topic is necessary to the process of becoming an effective reading teacher; therefore, comprehension is addressed early in this book. In this chapter we discuss the contexts of reading comprehension and how to build and support reading comprehension. See the Spotlights in this chapter for suggestions for using literature to teach comprehension.

The Contexts of Reading Comprehension

When researchers want to understand a process, they typically study various aspects of it. For example, if you wanted to understand how the tongue responds to different tastes, you could place sugar on various areas of your tongue, and you would quickly realize that the front of your tongue tastes sweet items. You could repeat this process with salt, something sour, or something bitter until you had constructed a "map" of your tongue's taste buds. Understanding reading comprehension is difficult to "map" because researchers can only observe the results of comprehension or lack thereof. The following sections give a historical overview of developing theories of comprehension and a variety of definitions of comprehension. Having this background will help you make informed choices about the strategies you will use to teach comprehension.

A HISTORICAL CONTEXT OF COMPREHENSION THEORIES

In the days of colonial America when many people were just learning to read, recitation and memorization of religious material were emphasized. During the 1800s, students began to study secular works such as poetry, biography, stories, history, and science. People began to move beyond the mechanics of reading to consider the meaning of passages and rhetorical features such as phrasing and figures of speech (McNeil 1992, 2). The 1900s saw a move toward a *translation* view of reading in which the emphasis shifted away from understanding the author's voice to translating the meanings implicit in the text. Teachers began to emphasize skills such as identifying the main idea, recognizing sequence, and understanding cause and effect (ibid., 3). In the *transmission* model of education, students were considered receptacles for knowledge, and learning materials emphasized memorization of facts and mastery of skills, often in isolation (Weaver 1994, 87). Based on Thorndyke's laws of learning, described in Chapter 1, these practices continue to appear in basal reading programs.

A more *interactive* view of reading comprehension developed in the late 1970s; this view acknowledged the role of the reader's background in understanding the text (Wixson and Peters 1987, 335). Teachers recognized that readers bring a wealth of experiences to the reading, and that these experiences influence the reader's interpretation and understanding of the text. In this interactive view, teachers can build on students' existing schemata to support comprehension. (Schema theory is discussed more fully on page 195.)

Active learning The theory that learners should determine purposes and strategies for successful reading.

Active learning supports the interactive view. Students select the information to learn, commit important information to memory, make connections among ideas, and integrate new ideas with existing knowledge. Another component of the interactive view stresses developing students' metacognition skills (Graves and Graves 1994, 25; McNeil 1992, 5).

Further refinements in reading comprehension theory have led some researchers to identify reading as a *constructive* process (Tierney 1990, 37). The constructive process focuses on the role of the reader's background and

Retelling	Drawing	Writing a new version
Storytelling	Sculpting	Writing in a journal
Sharing	Constructing	Reading aloud
Acting	Discussing	Researching
Scripting	Debating	
Choreographing	Arguing	

FIGURE 6.1
Possible Responses
to Reading

the reader's desire to understand the text. The idiosyncratic nature of the reader's response to the text is emphasized, and the idea that different readers will have different responses is accepted (Graves and Graves 1994, 27; McNeil 1992, 7; Tierney 1990, 38). That authors' intentions may not match the readers' purposes is also a component of this process (Tierney and Pearson 1994, 502). Learners may focus on efferent reading or what information they will take with them. For example, a student may read about gerbils in anticipation of acquiring a classroom or personal pet. He may even take notes on how to take care of the gerbil. However, when he reads a suspense or fantasy novel, he may concentrate on the aesthetic experience, responding to the reading on a personal level, and may not remember the plot or setting at all (Rosenblatt 1978, 1991).

In the constructive approach to comprehension development, reading teachers work at developing thoughtful, expert readers who can comprehend text independently most of the time. Teachers may have students choose how they will demonstrate their comprehension, perhaps through models, written or oral reports, dramatizations, outlines, or other projects (Ediger 1995, 62). Student responses can also include discussing, writing, researching, interpreting, analyzing, generalizing, summarizing, retelling, or simply reflecting (Cooper 1993, 347). When teachers value response, students develop ownership and strive to improve and monitor their reading and writing. See Figure 6.1 for a partial list of ways students can demonstrate comprehension.

Teachers who support a constructivist view create rich learning environments that encourage students to take risks, investigate, and explore. They believe that skills, such as being able to correctly sound out an unknown word or identify the main idea, will come in the context of meaningful reading. Students have ownership in their choice of reading material and actively discuss the meaning of the text. Students spend more time developing comprehension strategies that support predicting, guessing, confirming, and self-correcting (Buikema and Graves 1993). See Figure 6.2 for a chart that compares the transmission and constructivist models as they relate to reading comprehension.

FIGURE 6.2
Models of Reading
Comprehension

Transmission Model	Constructivist Model
Reading comprehension is a separate subject.	Reading comprehension is taught as part of every topic, including math, science, and so on.
Reading, writing, listening, and thinking are often taught as separate subjects.	Reading, writing, listening, and thinking develop simultaneously.
Teacher provides schemata by providing common experiences or background information.	Students draw upon existing schemata and react to text based on personal experiences and knowledge.
Students practice skills such as finding main idea or details, choosing a title, and so on.	Students discuss motivation of characters or author, role of setting, literary features, and so on.
Students read passages and answer questions to validate that they comprehend correctly.	Students are encouraged to try different self-monitoring activities to "figure it out" independently.
Student work is assigned by the teacher, who may be guided by published materials.	Students read to investigate authentic problems and for enjoyment.

DEFINITIONS OF READING COMPREHENSION

As you review the following definitions of comprehension, decide where they fit in the context of comprehension. For example, when discussing comprehension, Emmett Albert Betts listed 32 factors, including such items as facility in using language, ability to grasp the author's intent, and ability to use context to identify the pronunciation or meaning of a word (1957, 94). His definition clearly represents the transmission view of reading that was current in the 1950s.

In 1988, Frank Smith emphasized a more holistic view. "Comprehension may be regarded as relating relevant aspects of the worlds around us—written language in the case of reading—to the intentions, knowledge, and expectations we already have in our heads" (6).

Emerald Dechant stresses the importance of thinking. "Comprehension is thinking on the highest level. It is a cognitive process. It requires inference, verifying, correcting, and confirming of expectancies about the text" (1991, 339).

Robert J. Tierney emphasizes the constructive process of reading, stressing the role of writing, believing that students who are actively writing begin to think about the role of the author and how authors get their ideas. This influences their writing and their reading as they explore, experiment, and evaluate (1990, 37–39). Reading as engagement recognizes the role of imagination, emotions, affect, and visual involvement (ibid.). You have no doubt read a book that has had a profound impact on you or that you think about periodically. Perhaps when you were a child you repeatedly asked your parents to read a fairy tale, or you have a child who enjoys the comfort of a familiar story. Finally, the view that reading is situation-based recognizes that readers explore texts in varying ways and should not be limited to single sources or interpretations. Rather, readers should become skilled at connecting and using multiple schemata to comprehend text fully (ibid., 41).

Now that you have read several definitions of comprehension, take a few minutes and write your own definition before reading the next section, which discusses some of the controversies associated with reading comprehension. Then review these definitions and think about their commonalities. Be sure to save yours; just as experienced teachers do, you may want to revise it later.

Building Reading Comprehension

Young children have a remarkable ability to connect meaning to print years before they arrive at school. They recognize names of fast-food restaurants, soft drinks, stores, and toys and attach meaning to these symbols. The sign for a favorite place has pleasurable connotations; the child understands the experiences associated with it and thus begins to "read" the sign. Their reading, in Frank Smith's words, is *purposeful, selective, anticipatory*, and based on *comprehension* (1988, 3). We adults also read for a purpose—to locate information, to learn, to reflect, and simply to enjoy. Our reading is selective because we only read what is necessary; we don't read every recipe in a cookbook when we are making beef stroganoff. Our reading too is anticipatory because we have a purpose, such as locating a street on a map, and reading helps us fulfill that purpose. Finally, our reading is based on comprehension because our need to understand drives our desire to read (ibid.).

The remainder of this chapter discusses various components of reading comprehension in an orderly fashion. Such structure, although convenient, is highly unrealistic. As Robert J. Tierney notes, there is a big difference between school-based and real-world learning and knowledge: Ideas and strategies are presented in context in the real world. Children don't learn to identify the grocery store's name by seeing it in a book or out of context. Further, in school, as in this textbook, ideas and strategies are often presented as if they were straightforward, well organized, and hierarchical.

In the real world, ideas and strategies are often ill-structured and messy, and they are rarely hierarchical (1990, 41). Therefore, keep in mind that although the information that follows is structured and hierarchical, *this is not necessarily the way children learn!* My older son didn't read much when he went to first grade, but 3 months later, he was reading chapter books and the newspaper. He didn't need phonics instruction or comprehension strategies. My other son needed structure, direct instruction on word-attack skills, phonics instruction, and guided practice to learn to read. The challenge to you as a teacher is to be able to draw upon various strategies as your students need them.

LISTENING AND READING COMPREHENSION

Of all the language arts (listening, speaking, reading, writing, and viewing), listening is probably the first one a child experiences regularly. A newborn recognizes its mother's voice and quickly responds to it. In a few short years, the child becomes a relatively sophisticated listener, even if her speaking skills are still developing. Reading and listening comprehension are similar because the listener and reader both attend to the language to gain meaning (Durkin 1989, 383). Listening to someone talk soon becomes highly interactive, with the listener displaying puzzlement, boredom, disagreement, or support through facial expressions or body language. If a speaker doesn't respond to the visual cues that signal a lack of comprehension, the listener may stop the speaker and request clarification or a restatement of the information.

A student listens attentively to a friend.

The listener attends to analogous features such as stress, phonemes, pauses, intonation, pitch, pronunciation, timbre, and amplitude. In contrast, the reader attends to features such as letters, periods, semicolons, dashes, commas, italics, capitalization, paragraphing, spelling, handwriting, and type size (Lundsteen 1979, 3). In an academic setting, mature listeners will develop outlines or take notes to enhance and focus their listening skills. Readers can reread the text, scan or skip ahead for clarification, or consult other written sources for support. In summary, Sara

s p o t l i g h t   1

Listening Comprehension

GRADE LEVELS:
Preschool–1.

BOOK: *The Listening Walk* by Paul Showers, illustrated by Aliki (New York: Harper, 1991).

ACTIVITY: A father and daughter identify sounds as they take a walk. After sharing the book, take a walk and identify all the sounds that can be heard. Assign the task of remembering the various sounds to different students. After returning to the classroom, make a list of all the remembered sounds on the board.

Lundsteen notes that listening and reading are similar in that they are receptive activities and use analogous features, vocabulary, and the common skills of thinking and understanding (ibid.)

Developing listening comprehension is important to developing reading comprehension. Reading aloud to students is an especially effective practice. While students listen, their vocabulary builds, which simultaneously supports improved comprehension (Krashen 1993, 39). Listening to stories encourages skills such as following sequence, distinguishing between fact and fancy, making inferences, visualizing settings and characters, predicting outcomes, and recognizing cause and effect. Active discussion and writing about what is heard deepens the learning even further. (See Spotlights 1 and 2.)

s p o t l i g h t   2

Listening Comprehension

GRADE LEVELS: 5–12.

BOOK: *A Sky Full of Poems* by Eve Merriam, illustrated by Walter Kafney-Kassell (New York: Dell, 1986).

ACTIVITY: Choose a poem from the section "Poet's Talk" and read it aloud to the students. Have them work in small groups to discuss the message of the poem. Compare the groups' ideas. Then read the poem again and discuss the poem as a whole class. How did their interpretations differ upon the second reading?

SCHEMA THEORY

Schema theory
Building new con-
nections and knowl-
edge on existing
experience.

As we grow and learn, we expand our knowledge of our world. How we organize this knowledge is explained in **schema theory** (Dechant 1993, 124;
O'Donnell and Wood 1991, 121; Weaver 1994, 18). This theory emphasizes
"cognition, conceptual learning, mental events, understanding, conscious
experience, thinking, reasoning, problem solving, and meaning. It provides an
explanation of how knowledge is acquired, processed, organized, stored, and
retrieved" (Dechant 1993, 124). Readers analyze simultaneously at several levels: graphophonemic, morphemic, semantic, syntactic, pragmatic, and inter-
pretive. Readers theorize what the text means, revising as further information
clarifies what they are reading.

How do you organize schemata? Take a moment to list every category of
museum you can recall. I have arranged my list in Figure 6.3. What other
museums would you add to this? Some of you may have decided to organize
your museum schema more thoroughly by creating subcategories for types of
museums. For example, a more detailed schema for art museums is found in
Figure 6.4 on page 196.

Different museums also have different, characteristic operational schemata
(Weaver 1994, 21). For example, art museums are by necessity very protective
of their art; their security systems warn us with gentle (or not-so gentle) beeps
if we come too close to a work of art. Our role as visitors in these museums is
to observe and appreciate.

Children's museums, on the other hand, are hands-on environments; they
intentionally invite children and adults to touch, experiment, role-play, and
participate. It is easy to see how different and important the schemata of art
museums and children's museums are; a child who has known only children's
museums may be unaware of the hands-off nature of other museums. The
experiences are entirely different and those experiences make up your museum schema.

Using the museum example, think about how schemata affect reading comprehension. E. L. Konigsburg's chapter book, *From the Mixed-up Files of Mrs.
Basil E. Frankweiler,* describes a young girl and her brother who run away to
live in the Metropolitan Museum of Art in New York City. At first they enjoy

FIGURE 6.3

Museums Schema

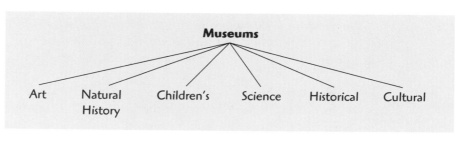

FIGURE 6.4
Art Museums
Schema

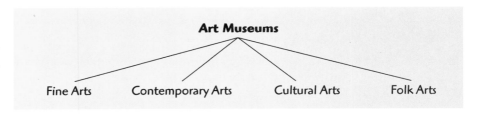

their adventure, but when they are ready to return home, they become immersed in discovering the creator of a beautiful statue. Think about how students' schemata will help them understand the references to the English Renaissance hall (1967, 40) and the act of Claudia hiding her violin case in a sarcophagus (ibid., 44). Although most upper-intermediate students will enjoy the story for its adventure, those students who have visited art museums, especially those who have visited the Metropolitan Museum of Art, will find the book even more satisfying and perhaps even easier to read. Teachers who value the role schemata play build a network of experiences for their students, such as visiting museums, creating a minimuseum in the classroom, or researching museums before reading the book.

How do your schemata affect how you interpret this sentence? "The first thing she noticed was the run." Jot down what you think the sentence means. Now substitute the word *he* for *she*. Does this change your interpretation? There are more than 100 meanings for the word *run*. *Run* can be a race, fish migrating, a run in a stocking or knitting, an amount of something produced, or a succession of notes played quickly. What other meanings can you think of? In this case, additional information provides a context, and readers evaluate and refine their schemata, discarding those that do not fit. When students do not have the appropriate schema, they cannot use their prior knowledge, or they misunderstand the text. In either case, comprehension becomes difficult, if not impossible.

Building schemata is particularly important for students who lack a wide experiential background. It is usual for preschool, kindergarten, and first grade teachers to begin the year with a unit on the community, in part because it provides common ground for the students. The class might explore community workers such as fire fighters, postal workers, and doctors, building on existing background knowledge. Once students begin developing a schema for community, this understanding feeds other literacy activities, such as reading or writing, which in turn feeds the development of more schemata. As with many areas of learning, developing schemata is a cyclical process.

Let's consider a unit where students' background knowledge is more variable. A teacher who is doing a unit on snakes may find that some students have a vast knowledge, while others have little or no background. Before having students begin their investigations, the teacher might develop a schema by

s p o t l i g h t   3

Schema and Comprehension

GRADE LEVELS: 3–5.

BOOKS: *Musician from the Darkness* by Claude Clément, illustrated by John Howe (Boston: Little, Brown, 1989).

Love Flute by Paul Goble (New York: Bradbury Press, 1992).

ACTIVITY: *Musician from the Darkness* is about the role of music in a primitive society. *Love Flute* is about a young Plains Indian man who receives a flute from the animals. Work with the music teacher to provide students with recorders or penny whistles. (A penny whistle in the key of C is easier to play because it only has six openings and simple tunes are easy to learn on it.)

After teaching them a simple tune such as "Mary Had a Little Lamb" read either of these books aloud. Invite students to ask friends and family for other examples of simple flutes and explore the use of flutes in other cultures.

bringing in snakes, visiting a zoo, showing a video or film, or having a herpetologist visit. Before these experiences, many students may have had a schema of snakes being slimy, threatening, and repulsive. After a variety of experiences with snakes, most students will have developed a new schema that recognizes that snakes feel soft, dry, and muscular, with tongues that tickle. The class might decide to acquire a snake, extending their knowledge over many additional months. Students who have long-term, in-depth experiences with a subject such as snakes read more critically and with greater comprehension than students who have a very limited schema for snakes and who are reading their first article or book on this topic. It is our job to determine whether our students have the appropriate schemata for their learning and to expand students' schemata so they can succeed. (See Spotlights 3 and 4.)

SCAFFOLDING

Scaffolding
The process of using prereading, during-reading, and post-reading activities to assist students to successfully comprehend, learn from, and enjoy a reading selection.

To build schemata, consider hands-on experiences, field trips, audio-visual materials, related read-alouds, guest speakers, brainstorming, small- and large-group discussions, and topical questions. As psychologist Jerome Bruner worked with mothers and infants, he identified the experience of building an instructional structure that assists in the learning process as **scaffolding** (Graves and Graves 1994, 2). Think about how many parents read a simple book aloud. They read the story aloud while the child listens and looks at the pictures. The parent then says, for example, "Point to the dog." Later the parent points to the word *dog* and repeats the word. Soon the child can find and

spotlight 4

Schema and Comprehension

GRADE LEVELS: 6–12.

BOOK: *Battlefields and Burial Grounds:*

The Indian Struggle to Protect Ancestral Graves in the United States by Roger and Walter Echo-Hawk (Minneapolis, Minn.: Lerner, 1994).

ACTIVITY: Use the introduction and Chapter 1 to introduce

a unit on burial practices or on Native Americans. Students can consult other chapters or the Notes for further research.

recognize the word *dog*. The parent has not directly taught the child to read *dog*, but has structured the experience so that the child is successful.

Consistent with the constructivist approach of providing an environment that encourages students to explore and learn, a Scaffolded Reading Experience (SRE) provides students with the elements of a meaningful, worthwhile reading experience. In many ways, the SRE is similar to Emmett Betts' Directed Reading Activity, discussed in Chapter 1 (1957). Possible components of the SRE are described in Figure 6.5. The SRE, however, is not an entire reading program. It does not deal with the tools of comprehension such as word identification, syllabication, word parts, and so forth. Graves and Graves emphasize that the SRE should be used in collaboration with a wide variety of reading experiences, such as Literature Circles (see Chapter 9) or free reading (1994, 16). Teachers should provide enough scaffolded experiences that students are successful without becoming bored. The example in the Spotlight 5 on page 200 might take 1 or 2 days to complete. Middle school students might take up to a week with an SRE. Consult Graves and Graves' *Scaffolding Reading Experiences: Designs for Student Success* for additional examples at varying grade levels. When reviewing these components, keep in mind that a postreading activity, such as discussion or dramatization, could also be a successful prereading activity.

UNDERSTANDING AND APPRECIATING PHRASES AND SENTENCES

In addition to bringing personal schemata to bear upon their reading experience, good readers break their oral reading into phrase units, with fewer pauses, while poor readers continue to read word by word. Reading phrases helps with comprehension because the reader does not lose the meaning of the phrase due to slow or inaccurate word identification. To develop phrase-reading skills, a part-to-whole process, students should have adequate memory for words they are reading.

Prereading Activities	During-Reading Activities	Postreading Activities
Motivating	Silent reading	Questioning
Relating the reading to students' lives	Reading to students	Discussion
Activating background knowledge	Guided reading	Writing
Building text-specific knowledge	Oral reading by students	Drama
Preteaching vocabulary	Modifying the text	Artistic, graphic, and nonverbal activities
Preteaching concepts		Application and outreach activities
Prequestioning		Reteaching
Predicting		
Direction setting		
Suggesting strategies		

FIGURE 6.5
Possible
Components of a
Scaffolded Reading
Experience

Excerpted from Michael Graves and Bonnie Graves, *Scaffolding Reading Experiences: Designs for Student Success* (Norwood, Mass.: Christopher-Gordon, 1994) 6.

Model phrase reading to students by reading aloud, perhaps with appropriate Big Books, so that you can demonstrate how the author has divided the words into phrases to go with the illustrations. Big Books are also useful for demonstrating the use of print conventions, such as commas and ellipses, to guide the phrasing. Point out transition words, such as conjunctions and prepositions, that cue phrases. Have students engage in choral reading and readers theatre to practice phrasing. Identify phrases by inserting slash marks between phrasal units in sentences. Proverbs and idiomatic phrases provide opportunities to explore how phrases can be entire thought units.

Good oral readers not only understand word meanings, syntax, and punctuation, they also read silently far enough ahead of the words they are reading out loud to adjust their comprehension even as they speak. This requires expertise that only comes with practice and time. Once students have mastered their phrase-reading ability, they can focus on sentences. Continue to build on concepts previously mentioned by reinforcing the use of qualifying words; types of sentences (imperative, interrogative, or declarative); and use of punctuation. Demonstrate and discuss how to use stress, pitch, intonation, pacing, and rhythm. Reinforce how sentences, such as compound sentences, connect, and how individual ones link within paragraphs. Help students understand more complex patterns of sentences, such as those with nonrestrictive or appositive clauses.

Remember that teaching features of sentences should not occur in isolated exercises—this is critical—but should instead be an ongoing process of awareness and discovery. Well-written sentences, both simple and complex, should

Scaffolded Reading Experience

GRADE LEVELS:
Preschool–2.

BOOK: *Moja Means
One: Swahili Counting
Book* by Muriel Feelings,
illustrated by Tom
Feelings (New York:
Dial, 1972).

PREREADING
ACTIVITIES: *Motivating*
Bring in a variety of artifacts pictured in the
book. Possibilities in-
clude bamboo flutes,
drums, thumb piano,
African clothing or
cloth, or pottery. Share
the artifacts with the
students and discuss
their origins.
   *Building text-specific
knowledge* Use a map

to locate Africa, the
countries where Swahili
is spoken (identified in
the introduction of the
book), and the Nile River.
Relate the discussion to
any Swahili-speaking
African country that
might be currently in
the news.

DURING READING
ACTIVITIES: *Reading
to students* Read the
book aloud. Have stu-
dents practice pro-
nouncing the Swahili
words. Relate the various
examples to students'
schema. For example,
find Kilimanjaro on the
map and have students
share information about
mountains they have
seen. Have students
describe counting games
they know and play
when reading about
mankala.

POSTREADING
ACTIVITIES:
Discussion Discuss the
likeness and differences
of the cultures. For
example, the women
carry their babies on
their backs in cloth
slings. How do *their*
mothers carry babies?
   Drama Share an
African folktale. Consult
Heather McNeil's *Hyena
and the Moon: Stories to
Tell from Kenya* for sto-
ries and background
information.

OUTREACH ACTIVITY:
Create an African dish
or meal. Resources
include Fran Osseo-
Asare's *A Good Soup
Attracts Chairs: A
First African Cookbook
for American Kids* or
Constance Nabwire
and Bertha Vining
Montgomery's *Cooking
the African Way.*

be noted during read-alouds, while sharing original writing, when brainstorming examples on the board, and while reading silently. Many students enjoy
keeping a journal of favorite sentences that they find particularly meaningful,
amusing, or elegant. An effective book for exploring simple sentences is Betty
Fraser's *First Things First: An Illustrated Collection of Sayings Useful and Familiar for
Children.* Some sayings may be unfamiliar, such as what to say when everyone
is bossy and nothing gets done right: "Too many cooks spoil the broth."
Curiously, this book has no end punctuation, providing an opportunity to discuss how students would punctuate the sayings. Older students will enjoy
using Marvin Terban's *Funny You Should Ask: How to Make Up Jokes and Riddles
with Wordplay* to develop additional skills with words in the context of phrases

s p o t l i g h t 6

Understanding Phrases and Sentences

GRADE LEVELS: Kindergarten–2.

BOOK: *Wind Says Good Night* by Katy Rydell, illustrated by David Jorgensen (Boston: Houghton Mifflin, 1994).

ACTIVITY: In this story, a child can't sleep because the moon is shining, a cricket is dancing, a frog is strumming, a cricket is playing, and a mockingbird is singing. The night wind repeatedly implores each one to stop, and finally a cloud agrees to cover the earth so all can sleep. After reading the story, discuss the repeated phrases and put them on the board. Then discuss the simple sentences concluding the book. Discuss other ways to add to this book by thinking of other nighttime distractions ("so branch will stop creaking"). The class could create another version based just on city, barnyard, or apartment sounds.

and sentences. Others will enjoy reading about idioms in books such as James A. Cox's *Put Your Foot in Your Mouth and Other Silly Sayings* and will often share their own families' sayings with the class (Renner and Carter 1991). (See also Spotlights 6 and 7.)

UNDERSTANDING AND APPRECIATING WORDS

Readers must not only decode a word but must also understand the semantics in its context. Readers consult their mental dictionaries and extract the meaning that fits their schema, reconciling that information with the material they are reading and with the author's message. If they find that they still do not understand the material, good readers may reread the text, consult other sources (written and human), or skip unknown words and read on for more information. Poor readers often have inadequate vocabularies. Many read so slowly that they can't patch the text together well enough to hold the thoughts long enough to understand the material. They may not use strategies to help with their comprehension, or they may concentrate so much on their recoding that they can't focus on comprehension. Many do not realize that they don't understand the text (Dechant 1991, 355).

As we saw in our discussion on schema theory, students need certain, basic concepts to fully understand written material. Although understanding words generally occurs in the context of understanding chunks of language such as phrases or sentences, increasing one's understanding of individual words is very beneficial. (Vocabulary development is discussed in detail in Chapter 5.) Beyond the obvious advantages of improved comprehension, having an appreciation for words enhances all reading. For example, it's fun to know that hamburgers appeared first in Hamburg, Germany; Limburger cheese came from Limburg, a province in Belgium; Roquefort cheese came from Roquefort, France; and cheddar cheese originated in Cheddar, England. Fortunately, writers of children's books are giving us many delightful wordplay books that offer a whole range of amusing and intriguing experiences with word meanings—it's easy to have fun with vocabulary these days.

Children begin to understand literal and figurative language at approximately 6 years of age. At this age, they can enjoy the antics and wordplay of Amelia Bedelia when she literally steals the bases in *Play Ball, Amelia Bedelia* by Peggy Parrish. Students also appreciate Fred Gwynne's collections of homonyms in *The King Who Rained*. Norton Juster has created a more sophisticated wordplay book that requires careful interpretation of illustrations for understanding in *Otter Nonsense*. Intermediate and middle school students will enjoy Marvin Terban's *Guppies in Tuxedos: Funny Eponyms* or *The Dove Dove: Funny Homograph Riddles*. They are often inspired to try writing their own fanciful stories about words after hearing stories from *The Weighty Word Book* by Paul M. Levitt, Douglas A. Burger, and Elissa S. Guralnick.

Figurative language can be especially challenging for second-language learners; thus frequent use of good literature, coupled with discussions of the meaning of the language, supports students who are just beginning to appreciate the nuances of English. Explorations of words in the context of meaning support comprehension as students begin to understand how rich our language is. (See Chapter 5 for more information on teaching vocabulary and additional recommended books.)

Supporting Reading Comprehension

As we have seen, reading comprehension from the constructivist point of view builds on a student's prior experiences and existing knowledge in an environment that supports explorations, investigations, and reading for enjoyment. Thus thoughtful, active, expert readers

- Search for connections between what they know and the new information they encounter.

- Monitor the adequacy of their models of text meaning.

- Take steps to repair faulty comprehension once they realize they have failed to understand something.

- Learn to distinguish early on important ideas from less important ideas.

- Are adept at synthesizing information within and across texts and reading experiences.

- Draw inferences during and after reading to achieve a full, integrated understanding.

- Sometimes consciously, and almost always unconsciously, ask questions of themselves, of the authors they encounter, and of the material they read (Pearson et al. 1992, 153–154).

It is exciting to witness the convergence of the various elements of reading comprehension: schemata, syntax, semantics, graphophonics. As mentioned previously, this process is idiosyncratic, depending on the individual response of the reader. This next section provides a variety of activities that help students use these elements simultaneously and with flexibility. When you introduce reading activities, provide your students with adequate opportunities to rehearse the strategy before implementing it. Some will benefit from more traditional instruction, and others will appreciate more interactive approaches (Dole et al. 1991). Adapt the activities freely to make them suitable for your students and the topic. Evaluate the effectiveness of the various activities with your students, and, once they have a repertoire they are comfortable with, encourage them to continue to use it.

PREPARING FOR COMPREHENSION

The first step in preparing for comprehension is to determine whether the students need additional experiential background for the reading. Find out through discussion and questioning how much they know about a topic.

Sometimes this can be accomplished by bringing in a variety of materials related to the topic and allowing students to browse through them. Listening to their conversations will provide insights into their knowledge. Then use concrete materials, field trips, role-playing, or audio-visual materials to introduce the material more thoroughly (Dechant 1993, 135).

Another effective way to introduce the topic or to engage your students is to read aloud easy, related picture books or short stories. Constance Weaver discusses the value of combining the reading with prediction activities by encouraging the children to draw upon their prior knowledge, prior contexts, and other cues, such as picture cues. She recommends that you demonstrate this activity in a careful sequence. First, you predict what the story is about, then you discuss predictions with your students, inviting them to participate. Finally, you read the story aloud and discuss whether your predictions were appropriate. She labels this sequence the DDID cycle, Demonstration, Discussion, Invitation, and Further Discussion, noting that the sequence may mingle or repeat (1994, 154). Consider using the Directed Reading Activity in Chapter 1 as another structure for preparing for and developing comprehension.

■ **Narrative text**
Written material that tells a story, as found in novels and short stories.

■ **Expository text**
Text that informs; usually features highly structured text, graphs and tables, and visual cues such as bold-faced or italicized words, and headings.

In contrast to **narrative text**, textbooks usually contain **expository text** (discussed more fully in Chapter 11). When you introduce textbook chapters or articles, have students preview the material by reading introductory features such as the table of contents, headings, boldfaced words, illustrations or charts, and the summary. The class can then discuss what the selection is probably about and what questions the reading might answer. These questions can be kept and reviewed after the reading to determine whether the text provided the information as anticipated.

John D. McNeil believes that reciprocal teaching of questioning processes helps students comprehend more effectively. The teacher initiates the questioning process by modeling well-designed, content-related questions and provides additional information as necessary. A truly effective question will elicit a response like this second grader's as he waved his hand vigorously: "Ooh, ooh, it's burning my tongue!" After understanding the types of questions that are appropriate, the students meet in small groups to query each other about the material to be read. Teacher involvement is phased out as students take control of their questions and of finding the answers (1992, 42).

Using graphic organizers, such as structured overviews, semantic maps, and webs, also facilitates comprehension (Clarke 1991). A thematic organizer that prompts students to think about the central theme of a passage improves reading performance (Risko and Alvarez 1986). These activities, described more fully in Chapter 5 (Vocabulary) and Chapter 11 (Content-Area Reading), are frequently used to study text that might be dense and complicated. However, several of these strategies, such as creating maps or previewing, are useful in improving comprehension.

AIDING COMPREHENSION DURING READING

If all students were highly motivated to read, teaching reading would be easy. Students who are highly motivated to read a text will process it more effectively and thus comprehend it better (McNeil 1992, 67). Gerald G. Duffy and Laura R. Roehler emphasize the importance of two factors in motivation: if there is a reasonable chance of success and if the end result is valued (1993, 60). Someone who is planning a trip to France will be highly motivated to learn as much of the language as possible before the trip and will be directly rewarded for even the most rudimentary skills. Students are intrinsically more motivated to read text that has relevance to their lives. However, Dolores Durkin (1989, 371) emphasizes that even purposeful reading like **procedural text** requires instruction, particularly for those students who have not used procedural text before.

Procedural text Material that describes the processes for doing something, such as directions for assembling a toy or a recipe.

When students are not comprehending the reading, they will usually do one of three things: (1) continue to pass their eyes over the page while thinking of other things, (2) give up and find something else to do, or (3) search for ways to understand the text. Some students will instinctively reread, ask someone for help, or turn to resources, such as a dictionary, for clarification. Others need help to stay on track; they need someone nudging them into making connections to other information, into using contextual clues or other strategies. Sometimes this is because they haven't had enough exposure to the process of reading. For example, they don't automatically know that it is sometimes necessary to put comprehension on "hold" until further information is revealed. They only know this after they have experienced it.

Some students may be able to perform a task (such as identifying the main idea or understanding difficult vocabulary) with contrived texts but will be unable to transfer that skill to the more natural texts that they will encounter in their everyday lives (Hare, Rabinowitz, and Schieble 1989; Schatz and Baldwin 1986; Stahl et al. 1989). Providing students with comprehension strategies helps them become aware that comprehension isn't always automatic. Suzanne McConnell found that adult students improved their comprehension skills dramatically by drawing their mental images before and after reading the text. Trials with primary-age children confirmed that drawing what children know before the reading prompts more involvement in the text during the reading. The drawing can also be an effective alternative to a written response to the text (1993).

Consider preparing a list of questions that will help students think about comprehension as they read. Here are some general questions:

- What is the author trying to tell me?

- What is the main idea of this (paragraph, story, chapter)?

- What details are important for understanding?
- What words could I be misunderstanding?
- Do I need to reread some of the material?
- What other resources could I consult?

These questions can be used for narrative text:

- Who is the most important character?
- How do the characters relate to each other?
- How important is the setting?
- What is the sequence of the events?
- What events have changed the direction of the story?

For expository text, the questions have a different focus:

- Is there a cause-and-effect relationship in the passage?
- Is the author comparing different ideas?
- Is the author trying to persuade me about something?
- Does the information solve a problem?
- What can I learn from charts, figures, the table of contents, and so forth?

Writers use punctuation to guide the reader, and good readers heed these typographic signals. As students progress through the grades, they will not only master these signals as they read but will also incorporate them in their writing. During reading and writing activities, point out effective uses of periods, commas, question marks, exclamation marks, semicolons, and colons. Reinforce the role of capitalization, indentation, headings, ellipses, and boldfaced words. Discuss how sequential signal words such as *first, last, before,* and *after* affect meaning. Teach signal words that indicate simultaneous events such as *while, meanwhile, simultaneously* and those that indicate cause and effect, such as *because, therefore,* and *consequently.* Pronouns such as *we, they,* and *it* can be problematic for young readers; demonstrate how they refer to other people and things in the text.

MONITORING COMPREHENSION

After students have completed their reading, a common practice is to ask three types of questions: those with answers found in the text; those with answers that are inferences derived from the text; and those with answers derived from

A teacher helps a student with her reading.

the reader's background knowledge (Durkin 1989, 364). Taffy E. Raphael has developed a strategy that enables students to deal with these questions in which the question-answer relationships are referred to as QARs (1982). Type 1 questions, text-explicit, are *right there* and are easily found and understood in the reading. Type 2 questions, text-implicit, are referred to as *think-and-search* questions. They require combining information found in the reading. *On my own* questions, Type 3, require students to draw upon background information, additional reading, or other sources of information —these questions require some synthesis. Raphael further refines QARs by adding the categories of *In the Book* and *In My Head* to the process (1986). After discussing what types of questions might be encountered, she found that upper-grade students can understand how to process the question types within a few minutes. Primary students may need several weeks of practice. Using these strategies to find information helps students locate, infer, and synthesize information more independently. Figure 6.6 on page 208 gives an overview of QARs.

Remember that not all questions or discussions need to be carefully organized or structured. I remember watching *The Piano* with my two sons, ages 17 and 19, worrying that, even though they were pianists, they wouldn't find the movie as intriguing as I had. As the movie ended, I simply said, "What did you think?" Simultaneously, they said, "It was great!" "Why?" My younger son pointed to his stomach and said, "It got me right here! Not many movies do that." Our dinner conversation revolved around various issues related to the movie, often prompted by why the movie "got" them. The discussion was spirited and meaningful, prompted by the simple question, "What did you think?" Effective book discussions can begin with just such a simple question.

If the students have previewed the text and developed a list of questions prior to their reading, consult this list to determine whether the reading answered the questions. If it didn't, the students should evaluate why there is a discrepancy. Perhaps the author's title, headings, or illustrations were misleading. Perhaps the passage wasn't as detailed as they expected. Perhaps the

FIGURE 6.6
Question–Answer
Relationships

In the Book QARs	In My Head QARs
Right There	**Author and You**
The answer is in the text, usually easy to find. The words used to make up the question and words used to answer the question are *right there* in the same sentence.	The answer is *not* in the story. Students need to think about what they already know, what the author says in the text, and how it fits together.
Think and Search (Putting It Together)	**On My Own**
The answer is in the story, but the student needs to put different story parts together to find it. Words for the question and words for the answer are not found in the same sentence. They come from different parts of the text.	The answer is not in the story. The student can even answer the question without reading the story. Students rely on their own experience.

material simply wasn't as well written as it should have been; coherent text is more likely to compensate for lack of knowledge (McKeown et al. 1992, 92). Students often assume that they—and not the author—are at fault; that is, they implicitly accept that written material is always correct, a tendency we have all participated in at one time or another. As students become more adept at questioning text, they also become more skilled at understanding the text and trusting their abilities. So, encouraging students to challenge text can be worthwhile. Students can create additional questions they would like answered and decide how to find the appropriate materials.

Students may find that they will more fully understand the material, especially expository material, if they summarize or outline it afterward. This process takes them back into the text, analyzing it more critically in order to restructure it. Joyce Eddy suggests reading aloud a selection that has a clear plot or sequential passage and demonstrating how to write succinct one- or two-sentence summaries for small segments of text. Next, write the summaries on sentence strips, rearrange them, and have the students return them to the appropriate sequence. Finally, students can make their own summary statements and check them against other students' summaries (1993, 69–71).

Many commercial achievement tests include a section on reading comprehension. (See Chapter 12 for more information on commercial tests.) Typically, students read short passages and answer multiple-choice questions. Educators express concern about comprehension tests for a variety of reasons: Questions can be answered without reading the passage; test passages are prepared using readability formulas that may be inaccurate; skills such as

spotlight 8

Comprehension

GRADE LEVELS: 4–9.

BOOK: *The Mennyms* by Sylvia Waugh (New York: Greenwillow, 1993).

ACTIVITY: A family of rag dolls functions as if they were human beings, living in a rented house, shopping, and ingeniously earning income. Their routine is disrupted when the human heir to their home writes that he intends to visit and become acquainted. Without telling the students that the book is about dolls, read aloud the opening letter in Chapter 1 plus Chapter 2. Discuss what the students think the book is about. Then read Chapter 3 aloud, which explains the premise of the book. Discuss how readers must sometimes continue reading, even though the material seems nonsensical.

comprehension-monitoring abilities are not tested; prior knowledge is not accounted for; scores are difficult to interpret and reveal little about a student's reasoning (Durkin 1989, 488). When taking comprehension tests, good readers not only look back at the text, they also use their own knowledge to figure out answers. Poor readers benefit from training in how to go back to the passage for answers and how to think about what they already know (Davey 1989). When evaluating comprehension, Leo M. Schell recommends using material whose language structure and concept load approximate those of the reader. The reader should be able to pronounce words with at least 90 percent accuracy. For a diagnosis to be valid, comprehension should be evaluated over a period of time under a variety of conditions. Finally, teachers should work at identifying specific comprehension problems. A student could be failing to look back at the passage, or could need instruction on critical words, need more meaningful material, or need instruction on self-correcting mispronounced words (1988, 15). (See Spotlight 8.)

Supporting Comprehension with Second-Language Learners

Children begin constructing meaning from the time they begin acquiring language in their native tongue (Farnan, Flood, and Lapp 1994, 136). School environments should not impede language learning, but should foster a wide range of experiences that support comprehension through listening, speaking, reading, and writing. Sara LaBrec Wyman emphasizes that curriculum should reflect the school's population when it

something to try 1

Fostering Comprehension with ESL Students

Using either Betsy Hearne's *Beauties and Beasts* or Judy Sierra's *Cinderella*, choose a variety of tales from different countries. Ask the students to share what they know about the tale you have selected—for example, "Cinderella." Write all the components on the board, including the characters, settings, problems, and so forth.

Read two stories aloud, such as the familiar Perrault tale and the less well-known "Yeh-hsien," an ancient Chinese tale in which the young girl is helped by a magic fish. Compare the varying elements and the differences in the language. Another day, read aloud "Cap o' Rushes," a tale written in dialect. Discuss how this tale varies in voice and content.

Continue reading and comparing different tales for several days. Then have students search the library for additional stories and read them independently. Discuss what they find. If time allows, create a semantic feature analysis (see Chapter 5), comparing the many variants.

includes diverse learners. For example, the literature, videotapes, maps, artifacts, and films should reflect various cultures and values (1993, 17–18). Further, materials should support those students who are just beginning to speak English as well as those who have a limited command of it (Allen 1994, 110). Materials should also be interesting, age appropriate, supportive of English acquisition, have text structure that supports understanding, and be drawn from a variety of **genres** (ibid.). For schools with largely homogeneous populations, it is just as important that materials reflect a wide variety of cultures. Activities (as well as materials) should foster the understanding of different cultures and points of view. (See Something to Try 1.)

■ **Genre**
A distinctive literary category.

Fortunately, practices that support comprehension for English-speaking students also support second-language learners. The following suggestions are summarized from the writings of specialists in teaching English as a second language. Many practices or topics are discussed more fully in other chapters.

1. Provide many opportunities to discuss what is being read. Build on existing schemata and use concrete materials that support the discussions and readings (Nurss and Hough 1992, 291, 307).

2. Discuss the material or story in prereading conferences (see Chapter 9), introducing vocabulary and new concepts as necessary (Farnan, Flood, and Lapp 1994, 141). Begin with known vocabulary and expand understanding through open-ended discussions (Nurss and Hough 1992, 307).

3. Use predictable books and patterned language (see Chapter 7) to provide students with successful early reading experiences (Allen 1994, 119; Farnan, Flood, and Lapp 1994, 140). Allen also recommends using books whose illustrations support and extend the meaning of the text and books that invite talk (1994, 120–121).

4. Choose books that have a familiar component, such as a fairy tale that might be known in another culture.

5. Choose books and materials that are "readable," books that have meaning for the students, allowing them to construct meaning from their reading (Rigg 1989, 66).

6. Incorporate storytelling, dialogue journals (see Chapter 10), shared reading, and taped books (Nurss and Hough 1992, 307).

7. Provide instruction on how to comprehend expository text as discussed in Chapter 11 (ibid.).

8. Use graphic organizers such as webbing or mapping before or after reading, described more fully in Chapter 11 (Farnan, Flood, and Lapp 1994, 145).

9. Use multiple texts on a variety of reading levels to accommodate different learners (ibid.). Incorporate such readings into thematic units when possible (Nurss and Hough 1992, 300).

10. Have students practice summarizing text (Farnan, Flood, and Lapp 1994, 148).

11. Have students write frequently, especially for functional uses such as messages and lists, and have them brainstorm before writing (Farnan, Flood, and Lapp 1994, 150; Nurss and Hough 1992, 307).

12. Provide instruction in the native language when feasible (ibid., 307), taking advantage of the bilingual materials now available (Allen 1994, 110).

13. Foster cooperative learning in the classroom (Wyman 1993, 26).

Technology and Comprehension

Imagine reading a book on a computer screen: You click the mouse to turn the page. If you wish to have it read aloud to you, you click on the audio "button." In some cases, you can choose to have the words highlighted as they are read aloud. Click on the illustration in the French story, *The Book of Lulu* (Victor-Pujebet, 1995), and the text disappears, while an animated video takes over the telling of Lulu's adventures with a robot. At the end of that episode, the video returns to book form for continued reading or exploring of the next chapter. Known as interactive storybooks, many of these products encourage users to "play" their way through the story. For example, the promotional material for the CD-ROM version of Brian Wildsmith's *A Christmas Story*, labeled a "multimedia nativity CD-ROM," proclaims that a key feature is "Point-and-click play to amuse and occupy your children."

The effectiveness of such products, as mentioned in Chapter 4, must be balanced within the entire program. As *The Book of Lulu* was field-tested, developers delightedly found that students who discovered the video component of the story usually returned to the beginning of that chapter to read it independently, checking the text against the video. The program that elicits that type of volunteer behavior can be especially helpful for the reluctant reader or second-language student who needs to have comprehension supported through hearing or, in this case, seeing the story in video form before reading it.

Many teachers use *Accelerated Reader*, a program that combines using the computer with reading picture or chapter books. After completing their reading, the students take a comprehension test on the computer. The scores show the questions they missed, giving them an opportunity to learn about their errors immediately. Teachers then have easy access to records on their students' comprehension scores and can counsel students who are reading material that is too difficult or too easy.

Involving Parents

A Russian psychologist, L. S. Vygotsky, believed that cognitive development begins with social interaction and is then internalized (1962). Generally, most of that early interaction occurs in the home. The teacher picks up that process in the school setting but should also work to encourage that the social interaction continues. Parents may not understand how to help with learning. Once again, the best way parents can help their children improve comprehension skills is to read aloud and discuss the key points of the book. Consider using the series of books by Anthony D. Fredericks, *Involving Parents through Children's Literature*, which has been prepared for varying grade levels. Alternatively, create your own activity sheets that contain questions and projects to explore and that can be sent home with students. It is important that such alternatives be fun for students and parents alike. Parents can be encouraged to be "buddy readers," reading the same book as their child is reading, discussing the key plot elements as the book unfolds. Encourage parents to set aside between 30 and 60 minutes a day where everyone reads and discusses their reading. The newspaper can be an excellent source for family reading, with the very youngest child reading the comics! (See Something to Try 2.)

something to try 2

Using the News

Plan for students to bring in a newspaper on a particular day. During the class, have each student choose a timely article to take home. The students' assign- ment will be to watch the nightly news with a parent or caregiver and compare the written news article with the television news. If possible, students with cable television could also compare the local stations with CNN. For students who do not have television at home, provide articles on the same topic from two different newspapers for comparison at home. Have students respond in writing regarding how the presentations were alike and how they differed. Part of the assignment should include differences that the parent notes. Your expectations for length of response will vary depending on the grade level of your students.

A Final Note

Early in this chapter you wrote a definition for comprehension. How would you define comprehension now? Has your definition changed? If you are like most active learners and serious teachers, you will continue to expand your understanding of how students learn, refining your definition of this process as you learn more. This is the very process that makes teaching and learning exciting!

Summary

Understanding how learners comprehend text is an important step to helping them improve their comprehension. Early textbook readers focused on recitation and memorization of materials. The translation view of learning emphasized the meanings implicit in the text. Students were viewed as vessels for instilling skills and facts with the transmission view of reading. An interactive view emphasizes the role of schema theory and active learning. Reading as a constructive process recognizes the reader's background, motivation, and response to the text. Teachers subscribing to the constructivist approach provide rich environments that support investigations and explorations. The various definitions of comprehension reflect the historical evolution of comprehension and learning theories.

Reading is purposeful and meaningful, with comprehension and appreciation serving as goals. Although there are various components to comprehension, children do not develop comprehension skills in an orderly fashion.

Listening comprehension should be developed along with reading comprehension. Reading aloud is an ideal activity to develop both skills.

Students bring a schema or a network of concepts to their reading, and this knowledge affects their interpretation of text. Building schemata develops more effective readers. Scaffolded Reading Experiences involve a series of activities that build appropriate background information and skills for successful reading.

Children's literature can be used to teach comprehension of phrases and sentences. To help students comprehend words, expand their understanding of individual words and encourage an interest in working and playing with words.

Prepare students for comprehending longer passages by developing connections and by providing models for comprehension and strategies for understanding text. Use appropriate questions, field trips, and concrete materials. Teach students to use text features, student-developed questions or teacher-provided monitoring questions, and typographical signals. Monitor comprehension through follow-up questions, activities, summaries, and discussions.

For second-language learners, choose materials appropriate for the level of development, culture, and instructional level. Support learning through discussions, conferences, and books that support reading-related activities. Provide direct instruction on reading text, use multiple texts, teach summarization, have students write frequently, teach in the native language, and use cooperative learning.

Interactive CD-ROM storybooks can provide diverse learners with opportunities to read with audio or language support. Finally, encourage parents to read and discuss literature with their children.

References

Allen, Virginia Garibaldi. "Selecting Materials for the Reading Instruction of ESL Children." In *Kids Come in All Languages: Reading Instruction for ESL Students*, edited by Karen Spangenberg-Urbschat and Robert Pritchard, 108–131. Newark, Del.: International Reading Association, 1994.

Barchers, Suzanne I., reteller and editor. *Wise Women: Folk and Fairy Tales from Around the World.* Illustrated by Leann Mullineaux. Englewood, Colo.: Libraries Unlimited, 1990.

Betts, Emmett Albert. *Foundations of Reading Instruction.* New York: American Book Company, 1957.

Buikema, Janice L., and Michael F. Graves. "Teaching Students to Use Context Cues to Infer Word Meanings." *Journal of Reading* 36, no. 6 (March 1993): 450–457.

Carle, Eric. *The Very Busy Spider.* New York: Philomel, 1985.

Clarke, John H. "Using Visual Organizers to Focus on Thinking." *Journal of Reading* 34, no. 7 (April 1991): 526–534.

Clément, Claude. *Musician from the Darkness.* Illustrated by John Howe. Boston: Little, Brown, 1989.

Conrad, Pam. *Animal Lingo.* Illustrated by Barbara Bustetter Falk. New York: HarperCollins, 1995.

Cooper, J. David. *Literacy: Helping Children Construct Meaning.* Boston: Houghton Mifflin, 1993.

Cox, James A. *Put Your Foot in Your Mouth and Other Silly Sayings.* Illustrated by Sam Q. Weissman. New York: Random House, 1980.

Davey, Beth. "Assessing Comprehension: Selected Interactions of Task and Reader." *The Reading Teacher* 42, no. 9 (May 1989): 694–697.

Dechant, Emerald. *Understanding and Teaching Reading: An Interactive Model.* Hillsdale, N.J.: Lawrence Erlbaum Associates, 1991.

_____. *Whole-Language Reading: A Comprehensive Teaching Guide.* Lancaster, Pa.: Technomic, 1993.

DeGross, Monalisa. *Donavan's Word Jar.* Illustrated by Cheryl Hanna. New York: HarperCollins, 1994.

Dole, Janice A., Sheila W. Valencia, Eunice Ann Greer, and James L. Wardrop. "Effects of Two Types of Prereading Instruction on the Comprehension of Narrative and Expository Text." *Reading Research Quarterly* 26, no. 2 (1991): 142–159.

Duffy, Gerald G., and Laura R. Roehler. *Improving Classroom Reading Instruction: A Decision-Making Approach,* 3rd ed. New York: McGraw-Hill, 1993.

Durkin, Delores. *Teaching Them to Read,* 5th ed. Boston: Allyn & Bacon, 1989.

Echo-Hawk, Roger C., and Walter R. Echo-Hawk. *Battlefields and Burial Grounds: The Indian Struggle to Protect Ancestral Graves in the United States.* Minneapolis, Minn.: Lerner, 1994.

Ediger, Marlow. "Reading: Skills Versus Ideas." *Reading Improvement* 32, no. 1 (Spring 1995): 60–62.

Eddy, Joyce. "Summaries and Sequence for Active Comprehension." In *Teacher to Teacher: Strategies for the Elementary Classroom,* edited by Mary W. Olson and Susan P. Homan, 69–71. Newark, Del.: International Reading Association, 1993.

Farnan, Nancy, James Flood, and Diane Lapp. "Comprehending through Reading and Writing: Six Research-Based Instructional Strategies." In *Kids Come in All Languages: Reading Instruction for ESL Students*, edited by Karen Spangenberg-Urbschat and Robert Pritchard, 135–157. Newark, Del.: International Reading Association, 1994.

Feelings, Muriel. *Moja Means One: Swahili Counting Book.* Illustrated by Tom Feelings. New York: Dial, 1972.

Fraser, Betty. *First Things First: An Illustrated Collection of Sayings Useful and Familiar for Children.* New York: Harper & Row, 1990.

Fredericks, Anthony D. *Involving Parents through Children's Literature.* Englewood, Colo.: Teacher Ideas Press, various dates.

Goble, Paul. *Love Flute.* New York: Bradbury Press, 1992.

Graves, Michael, and Bonnie Graves. *Scaffolding Reading Experiences: Designs for Student Success.* Norwood, Mass.: Christopher-Gordon, 1994.

Gwynne, Fred. *The King Who Rained.* New York: Simon & Schuster, 1970.

Hare, Victoria Chou, Mitchell Rabinowitz, and Karen Magnus Schieble. "Text Effects on Main Idea Comprehension." *Reading Research Quarterly* 24, no. 1 (Winter 1989): 72–87.

Hearne, Betsy. *Beauties and Beasts.* Phoenix, Ariz.: Oryx Press, 1993.

Hutchins, Pat. *Little Pink Pig.* New York: Greenwillow, 1994.

____. *Rosie's Walk.* New York: Macmillan, 1968.

Juster, Norton. *Otter Nonsense.* Illustrated by Eric Carle. New York: Philomel, 1982.

Konigsburg, E. L. *From the Mixed-up Files of Mrs. Basil E. Frankweiler.* New York: Dell, 1967.

Krashen, Stephen. *The Power of Reading: Insights from the Research.* Englewood, Colo.: Libraries Unlimited, 1993.

Levitt, Paul M., Douglas A. Burger, and Elissa S. Guralnick. *The Weighty Word Book.* Illustrated by Janet Stevens. Longmont, Colo.: Bookmakers Guild, 1987.

Lundsteen, Sara W. *Listening: Its Impact at All Levels on Reading and the Other Language Arts.* Urbana, Ill.: National Council of Teachers of English, 1979.

McConnell, Suzanne. "Talking Drawings: A Strategy for Assisting Learners." *Journal of Reading* 36, no. 4 (Dec. 1992/Jan. 1993): 260–269.

McKeown, Margaret G., Isabel L. Beck, Gale M. Sinatra, and Jane A. Loxterman. "The Contribution of Prior Knowledge and Coherent Text to Comprehension." *Reading Research Quarterly* 27, no. 1 (1992): 79–92.

McNeil, Heather. *Hyena and the Moon: Stories to Tell from Kenya.* Englewood, Colo.: Libraries Unlimited, 1994.

McNeil, John D. *Reading Comprehension: New Directions for Classroom Practice,* 3rd ed. New York: HarperCollins, 1992.

Merriam, Eve. *A Sky Full of Poems.* Illustrated by Walter Kafney-Kessell. New York: Dell, 1986.

Nabwire, Constance, and Bertha Vining Montgomery. *Cooking the African Way.* Minneapolis, Minn.: Lerner, 1988.

Nurss, Joanne R., and Ruth A. Hough. "Reading and the ESL Student." In *What Research Has to Say about Reading Instruction,* 2nd ed., edited by S. Jay Samuels and Alan E. Farstrup, 277–313. Newark, Del.: International Reading Association, 1992.

O'Donnell, Michael P., and Margo Wood. *Becoming a Reader: A Developmental Approach to Reading Instruction.* Boston: Allyn & Bacon, 1991.

Osseo-Asare, Fran. *A Good Soup Attracts Chairs: A First African Cookbook for American Kids.* Gretna, La.: Pelican, 1993.

Parrish, Peggy. *Play Ball, Amelia Bedelia.* Illustrated by Wallace Tripp. New York: Harper & Row, 1972.

Pearson, P. David, Laura R. Roehler, Janice A. Dole, and Gerald G. Duffy. "Developing Expertise in Reading Comprehension." In *What Research Has to Say about Reading Instruction,* 2nd ed., edited by S. Jay Samuels and Alan E. Farstrup, 145–199. Newark, Del.: International Reading Association, 1992.

Pearson, Tracey Campbell. *Old MacDonald Had a Farm.* New York: Dial, 1984.

Raphael, Taffy E. "Question-Answering Strategies for Children." *The Reading Teacher* 36 (Nov. 1982): 186–191.

_____. "Teaching Question-Answer Relationships, Revisited." *The Reading Teacher* 39, no. 6 (Feb. 1986): 516–522.

Renner, Sigrid M., and JoAnn M. Carter. "Comprehending Text—Appreciating Diversity through Folklore." *Journal of Reading* 34, no. 8 (May 1991): 602–604.

Rigg, Pat. "Language Experience Approach: Reading Naturally." In *When They Don't All Speak English: Integrating the ESL Student into the Reading Classroom*, edited by Pat Rigg and Virginia G. Allen, 65–76. Urbana, Ill.: National Council of Teachers of English, 1989.

Risko, Victoria J., and Marino C. Alvarez. "An Investigation of Poor Readers' Use of a Thematic Strategy to Comprehend Text." *Reading Research Quarterly* 21, no. 3 (Summer 1986): 298–316.

Rosenblatt, Louise M. *The Reader, the Text, the Poem: The Transactional Theory of the Literary Work.* Carbondale, Ill.: Southern University Press, 1978.

____. "The Reading Transaction: What For?" In *Literacy in Process*, edited by Brenda Miller Power and Ruth Hubbard, 114–127. Portsmouth, N.H.: Heinemann, 1991.

Rydell, Katy. *Wind Says Good Night.* Illustrated by David Jorgenson. Boston: Houghton Mifflin, 1994.

Schatz, Elinore Kress, and R. Scott Baldwin. "Context Clues Are Unreliable Predictors of Word Meanings." *Reading Research Quarterly* 21, no. 4 (Fall 1986): 439–451.

Schell, Leo M. "Dilemmas in Assessing Reading Comprehension." *The Reading Teacher* 42, no. 1 (Oct. 1988): 12–16.

Schwartz, Alvin. *Whoppers: Tall Tales and Other Lies Collected from American Folklore.* Illustrated by Glen Rounds. New York: HarperTrophy, 1990.

Shannon, George. *More Stories to Solve: Fifteen Folktales from Around the World.* Illustrated by Peter Sis. New York: Greenwillow, 1989, 1990.

____. *Stories to Solve: Folktales from Around the World.* Illustrated by Peter Sis. New York: Greenwillow, 1985.

Showers, Paul. *The Listening Walk.* Illustrated by Aliki. New York: Harper, 1991.

Sierra, Judy. *Cinderella.* Phoenix, Ariz.: Oryx Press, 1992.

Smith, Frank. *Understanding Reading: A Psycholinguistic Analysis of Reading and Learning to Read.* Hillsdale, N.J.: Lawrence Erlbaum Associates, 1988.

Stahl, Steven A., Michael G. Jacobson, Charlotte E. Davis, and Robin L. Davis. "Prior Knowledge and Difficult Vocabulary in the Comprehension of Unfamiliar Text." *Reading Research Quarterly* 24, no. 1 (Winter 1989): 27–43.

Terban, Marvin. *The Dove Dove: Funny Homograph Riddles.* Illustrated by Tom Huffman. New York: Clarion, 1988.

_____. *Funny You Should Ask: How to Make Up Jokes and Riddles with Wordplay.* Illustrated by John O'Brien. New York: Clarion, 1992.

_____. *Guppies in Tuxedos: Funny Eponyms.* Illustrated by Giulio Maestro. New York: Clarion, 1988.

_____. *Mad As A Wet Hen! And Other Funny Idioms.* Illustrated by Giulio Maestro. New York: Clarion, 1987.

Tierney, Robert J. "Redefining Reading Comprehension." *Educational Leadership* 47, no. 6 (March 1990): 37–42.

Tierney, Robert J., and P. David Pearson. "Learning to Learn from Text: A Framework for Improving Classroom Practice." In *Theoretical Models and Processes of Reading*, 4th ed., edited by Robert B. Ruddell, Martha Rapp Ruddell, and Harry Singer, 496–513. Newark, Del.: International Reading Association, 1994.

Van Leeuwen, Jean. *Going West.* Illustrated by Thomas B. Allen. New York: Dial, 1992.

Vygotsky, L. S. *Mind and Society: The Development of Higher Psychological Processes.* Cambridge, Mass.: MIT Press, 1962.

Waugh, Sylvia. *The Mennyms.* New York: Greenwillow, 1993.

Weaver, Constance. *Reading Process and Practice: From Socio-Psycholinguistics to Whole Language.* 2nd ed. Portsmouth, N.H.: Heinemann, 1994.

Wixson, Karen K., and Charles W. Peters. "Comprehension Assessment: Implementing and Interactive View of Reading." *Educational Psychologist*, 22, nos. 3 and 4 (1987) 333–356.

Wood, Audrey. *Heckedy Peg.* Illustrated by Don Wood. San Diego, Calif.: Harcourt Brace Jovanovich, 1987.

Wyman, Sarah LeBrec. *How to Respond to Your Culturally Diverse Student Population.* Alexandria, Va.: Association for Supervision and Curriculum Development, 1993.

CD-ROM AND SOFTWARE

Victor-Pujebet, Romain. *The Book of Lulu.* New York: Organa, 1995.

Wildsmith, Brian. *A Christmas Story.* Oxford: Oxford University Press, 1995.

7

Using Fiction and Folk Literature

FOCUS QUESTIONS

1. How can I use alphabet books?

2. How can I use counting and number books?

3. How can I use fictional picture books?

4. How can I use modern fantasy books?

5. How can I use historical, realistic, and science fiction?

6. How can I use folk literature?

The kindergarten teacher walked quietly through the classroom, observing her students. It was the day before Halloween and instead of working on the classification activity, the children were talking excitedly about their costumes and the next day's parade. The teacher walked over to the shelves, browsed for a moment, and then signaled to the students for quiet. "You have 5 minutes to finish sorting your shells. Then I want you to come to the rug. I have a book about a ghost to read to you." With singular purpose, the students returned to work, finishing quickly. They retrieved their throw pillows and sprawled out on the rug, waiting quietly until everyone had joined the group. The teacher sat on a small chair and opened a well-worn book. "This is one of my favorite stories. Its title is *Georgie and the Robbers* and the author is Robert Bright. . . ."

Introduction

This kindergarten teacher knows an important secret: Books have power. Books inform, instruct, enrage, amuse, motivate, and soothe. In this incident, a book became a useful distraction, giving the teacher an opportunity to focus the children using their natural excitement about Halloween. After the story, they recited a favorite Halloween fingerplay, "Five Little Jack-o'-lanterns," (see Figure 7.1 on page 222), and the students were ready to begin a math activity.

Kindergarten and primary teachers have used picture books in this way for years, but during the past two decades, literature has been used increasingly for instruction throughout all the primary, intermediate, and middle school grades. In *Children's Literature in the Elementary School*, Charlotte S. Huck, Susan Hepler, and Janet Hickman state that children's literature provides enjoyment, reinforces narrative as a way of thinking, develops the imagination, gives vicarious experiences, develops insight into human behavior, and presents the universality of experience (1979, 6–10). Increasingly, teachers recognize that literature also increases vocabulary, supports the writing program, fosters speaking and listening skills, and enhances research skills. In this chapter we explore the variety of fictional literature available and how it can be used in the primary, intermediate, and middle grades. Nonfiction books are discussed in Chapter 8. Consider applying the suggestions in the Spotlights to other titles found in this chapter or that you discover. Specific instructional strategies for managing the use of literature are given in Chapter 9.

Alphabet Books

Alphabet books teach and entertain. David L. Russell identifies three general organizational patterns: the theme book, which has a topical focus such as animals or food; the potpourri book, in which there are a variety of images, and the sequential-story book, which illustrates the alphabet through a continuous story line (1994, 62). Although primarily intended for the very young, the genre has expanded to include sophisticated, complex books such as Bruce Whatley and Rosie Smith's *Whatley's Quest: An Alphabet Adventure*, which is meant to be enjoyed by older readers and adults.

FIGURE 7.1

Halloween
Fingerplay

Five little Jack-o'-lanterns

Five little Jack-o'-lanterns sitting on a gate.
  [Hold up five fingers.]
The first one said, "My, it's getting late!"
  [Yawn and stretch.]
The second one said, "Who goes there?"
  [Shade eyes with hand and peer about.]
The third one said, "Ghosts are in the air!"
  [Shiver and look scared.]
The fourth one said, "We better run!"
  [Wiggle fingers in running motion.]
The fifth one said, "Ah, it's only Halloween fun."
  [Gesture with hand in a deprecating manner.]
Then up came the wind.
  [Make a howling wind sound.]
And out blew the lights.
  [Puff with cheeks and blow.]
And away ran those Jack-o'-lanterns on Halloween night.
  [Make running fingers or let students run to tables or a designated area.]

READING ALPHABET BOOKS ALOUD

The very youngest child enjoys sitting with an adult or sibling while identifying objects, letters, or numbers. Anita Lobel's *On Market Street*, inspired by seventeenth-century French trade engravings, explores the wares one might purchase at the market. Young readers will also enjoy Kathleen Hague's *Alphabears*, a book of bears and their activities, or Wanda Gág's classic *The ABC Bunny*. Older students will delight in Chris Van Allsburg's *The Z Was Zapped*, a book that combines drama with prediction, and the artistic power and humor in *Anno's Alphabet* by Mitsumasa Anno.

READING ALPHABET BOOKS SILENTLY

The Alphabet Parade by Seymour Chwast, a wordless alphabet book, is a fine example of a book that is meant to be explored silently. Appropriate for younger readers, the busy pages include a parade of animals, people, and objects that represent the letters; finding all the details requires a fair amount of examination. Laura Rankin's *The Handmade Alphabet* beautifully presents the alphabet in sign language, a fascinating topic for all ages. Older students are equally intrigued with *Anno's Magical ABC: An Anamorphic Alphabet*. This book uses a reflective cone to see the images in their usual perspective and can be appreciated by only one or two students at a time.

ALPHABET BOOKS IN CONTENT AREAS AND THEMATIC UNITS

Young students exploring fairy tales will enjoy the richly detailed *Macmillan Fairy Tale Alphabet Book* by Nancy Christensen Hall. Science teachers of older students will want to acquire *Astronaut to Zodiac: A Young Stargazer's Alphabet* by Roger Ressmeyer. Students studying Africa will enjoy *Ashanti to Zulu: African Traditions* by Margaret Musgrove.

ALPHABET BOOKS AS MODELS FOR WRITING

Although most of the aforementioned books are appropriate as writing models, young students enjoy creating simple alphabet books on familiar themes such as food, toys, or animals. (See Spotlight 1.) Students with limited artistic skills can use magazines for pictures or collaborate with older students who enjoy drawing. Because creating a 26-page book can be daunting, this is a fine project for an entire class or for small groups of students. Older students can use Ruth Well's *A to Zen* as a model for writing about a culture through its alphabet. Intermediate and middle school students will also enjoy the chal-

---

s p o t l i g h t 1

Creating an Alphabet Book

GRADE LEVELS: Kindergarten and up.

BOOK: *ABC: Musical Instruments from The Metropolitan Museum of Art* by Florence Cassen Mayers (New York: Harry N. Abrams, 1988).

ACTIVITY: Share this or others in this series of books based on artifacts in The Metropolitan Museum of Art. Schedule a trip to a nature, natural history, historical, art, or children's museum. Before attending, discuss with students what they might see while at the museum. Depending on the age of your students, plan to make a similar alphabet book in small groups, with several letters assigned to each group. Or, assign each student one letter. Before visiting the museum, decide how much text will be included. Young students could be responsible only for drawing or photographing the chosen artifact. Older students could be required to create a paragraph about the artifact, supplementing what they learn at the museum using a related CD-Rom or other library resources. Students should make two copies of the book, one for the class and one for the library.

lenge of creating a new version of *Q Is for Duck: An Alphabet Guessing Game* by Mary Elting and Michael Folsom, in which readers discover that Q is for duck because ducks quack. *Alphabatics* by Suse MacDonald challenges students to explore words from the inside out. Using alphabet books for a writing unit is an excellent way to begin the school year.

Counting and Number Books

Counting rhymes, such as "One, Two, Buckle My Shoe," have long been popular with children. As with alphabet books, counting books may simply feature numbers and objects, with little text (Russell 1994, 66). Counting books have also become quite sophisticated, addressing concepts far more complicated than counting. With books such as David Birch's *The King's Chessboard* or David Barry's *The Rajah's Rice*, older students can learn the effects of doubling numbers. A high school algebra teacher found that sharing George Shannon's *Stories to Solve: Folktales from Around the World* improved his students' problem-solving skills. Another book that is not a typical counting book but that intrigues students is *Math Curse* by Jon Scieszka and Lane Smith; it details the zany events in a girl's life when she wakes up and everything is a math problem. Resources such as the following books can enliven any math program.

READING COUNTING AND NUMBER BOOKS ALOUD

Eric Carle's *1, 2, 3, to the Zoo* and Brian Wildsmith's *1 2 3's* are favorite counting books. Primary students enjoy the illustrations and rhythm in *Roll Over! A Counting Song* by Merle Peek and appreciate counting backwards with *Ten, Nine, Eight* by Molly Bang. Although not a counting book, numbers are very important in *Another Mouse to Feed* by Robert Kraus, a story of a family of mice that struggles to add just one more mouse. Learning about coins is fun with Bruce McMillan's colorful *Jelly Beans for Sale*. Introduce original numbers with *Harriet Goes to the Circus* by Betsy and Giulio Maestro. Primary students can be introduced to multiplication with Stuart J. Murphy's *Too Many Kangaroo Things to Do!* and intermediate students appreciate the lively rhythm of *Counting by Kangaroos*, a multiplication book by Joy N. Hulme.

READING COUNTING AND NUMBER BOOKS SILENTLY

Tana Hoban's *Count and See* engages readers in thinking critically, and students enjoy the humor in *Bunches and Bunches of Bunnies* by Louise Mathews. Children will puzzle over all the animals in the cumulative story by Charlotte Hard, *One Green Island: An Animal Counting Game. How Many Snails* by Paul

Giganti draws the reader into the text by asking a series of "How many . . ." questions. Introduce students to Anno through *Anno's Math Games II*, which deals with volume and capacity, or *Anno's Math Games III*, which deals with geometry and spatial relationships.

COUNTING AND NUMBER BOOKS IN CONTENT AREAS AND THEMATIC UNITS

The study of many countries can be enhanced by integrating a book from the series entitled *Count Your Way through. . . .* Number words from "one" to "ten" describe key elements of the country's culture. Intermediate and middle school math teachers will enjoy teaching factorials with *Anno's Mysterious Multiplying Jar* or the concepts of million, billion, and trillion through *How Much Is a Million?* by David M. Schwartz. Introduce Chinese tangrams with *Grandfather Tang's Story* by Ann Tompert.

COUNTING AND NUMBER BOOKS AS MODELS FOR WRITING

In *Annie's One to Ten* by Annie Owen, illustrations show different combinations of objects that can be grouped together to equal 10, providing a model for new versions. *Counting Wildflowers* by Bruce McMillan uses photographs of wildflowers to illustrate the concepts of addition and subtraction up to 20. Lynne Bertrand's *One Day, Two Dragons* begins on one day with the two dragons going to Three Bug Street. Increasing numbers are incorporated into the story, bringing the total to 20 lollipops from their visit to the doctor. The cumulative nature of this counting book could inspire students to write stories that incorporate numbers sequentially. (See Spotlight 2.)

---

s p o t l i g h t   2

Creating a Counting Book

GRADE LEVELS:
2 and up.

BOOK: *Moja Means One: Swahili Counting Book* by Muriel Feelings, illustrated by Tom Feelings (New York: Dial, 1972).

ACTIVITY: This counting book includes information about the people, culture, and geography of Africa. After sharing the book, divide students into collaborative groups based on a country of interest. Use the library to find how to count from 1 to 10 in the country's language. Then have students find items from the country to count in the same style of *Moja Means One.* For example, *un* Eiffel Tower, *deux* loaves of French bread, *trois* francs, and so forth. Students should draw the items, write the text, and make an extra copy of each book for the library.

A student works on creating her book.

Fictional Picture Books

Think about your earliest reading experience. It was probably a picture book, perhaps Watty Piper's *The Little Engine That Could*, Virginia Lee Burton's *The Little House*, or *Goodnight Moon* by Margaret Wise Brown. David L. Russell defines a picture book as a book in which the text and pictures are equally important (1994, 31). Although considered a genre or distinctive literary category, picture books also include books from other genres, such as traditional stories (folktales, myths, legends, or fables); modern fantasies (*Where the Wild Things Are* by Maurice Sendak); realistic stories (*When I Was Young in the Mountains* by Cynthia Rylant); anthropomorphic stories (*The Little Engine That Could* by Watty Piper); or historical fiction (*Dakota Dugout* by Ann Turner). Some, such as *Bored—Nothing to Do!* by Peter Spier, combine elements of different genres.

Regardless of their content, good picture books are well-told stories. They may be simple, but they have a clear plot that is usually satisfactorily resolved. Characterization is often simple, with well-defined qualities. The setting, although simple, is an important element. The style is generally short, with vocabulary that ranges from extremely simple to relatively challenging. The art tells the story, representing the best uses of elements such as line, space, color, shape, texture composition, and perspective. The subject of a picture book may range from a simple story, such as *The Little House* by Virginia Lee Burton, to the nuclear holocaust as in *Hiroshima No Pika* by Toshi Maruki.

READING FICTIONAL PICTURE BOOKS ALOUD

Because of the range of subject matter and complexity, teachers should evaluate their choices of picture books carefully. Picture books are particularly meaningful to young children because they can "read" the story through the pictures, an important first step toward reading words. However, kindergarten children are not ready to listen to stories of the nuclear holocaust. While many picture books are excellent for reading aloud to a class, others, such as Raymond Briggs's *Father Christmas*, have so much visual detail that they are more appropriately shared with just one or two children.

One of the greatest joys of the primary teacher's day is reading aloud. Young students simply love being read aloud to, and their attention spans increase dramatically in a matter of weeks. Young students will chime right in with a favorite book, especially when books have rhythm and repetition such as found in *The Little Old Lady Who Was Not Afraid of Anything* by Linda Williams or Verna Ardema's *Why Mosquitoes Buzz in People's Ears.* Young children become passionately attached to books, connecting them to their home, friends, or belongings (Keifer 1989, 85). Some books help youngsters deal with growing up, such as Amy Hest's *In the Rain with Baby Duck,* Phyllis Root's *Contrary Bear,* or Harriet Lerner and Susan Goldhor's *What's So Terrible About Swallowing an Apple Seed?* Some children will act out the story or create their own interpretation using elements of the story. The very youngest will soon recognize the artistic styles of such distinctive author/illustrators as Eric Carle or Maurice Sendak and will squeal with delight when they discover a new book by a beloved author.

The wise intermediate teacher fosters this early love of picture books by continuing to share this genre with students. The wide variety of picture books provides ample opportunities to explore concepts, different points of view, cultures, history, and so forth. *Letting Swift River Go* by Jane Yolen introduces students to the dilemma faced by a town when a nearby city's needs for a reservoir force the people to relocate. *The Paddock: A Story in Praise of the Earth* by Lilith Norman demonstrates the effects of people and time on a patch of land in Australia. Judy Blume's *The Pain and the Great One* offers an older sister's and a younger brother's perspectives on each other. Marcia Brown's *Shadow* explores African beliefs through the shamans' stories. Each of these examples combines excellent illustrations with pertinent subject matter that students will want to discuss and explore.

Older students will appreciate longer and more complex picture books (Bishop and Hickman 1992, 9). There are picture books that present a new twist on the familiar, such as *The True Story of the 3 Little Pigs* by Jon Scieszka,

The Three Little Wolves and the Big Bad Pig by Eugene Trivizas, and *Snow White in New York* by Fiona French. These clever books are enjoyed by younger children, but they are also savored by middle and high school students who have the literary background to understand and appreciate the subtle nuances. David Macauley's *Black and White* is a complex presentation of four separate illustrations on each double-page spread that Macaulay says may or may not contain only one story. Middle school students and adults enjoy the challenge of interpreting the illustrations and discovering the historical link.

Some picture books are so complex that they take repeated readings and sophisticated knowledge. For example, most readers of *The Stinky Cheese Man and Other Fairly Stupid Tales* by Jon Scieszka will enjoy the spoof on traditional tales, but readers with a knowledge of publishing will especially appreciate how Scieszka and illustrator Lane Smith break with publishing traditions. For example, their table of contents is in the wrong place, the dedication is upside down, and the stories are often jumbled. Older readers will also appreciate the elegance of remembrances such as Christine Widman's *The Lemon Drop Jar*, a story of Great-Aunt Emma's crystal jar of lemon drops that brings the sun into her home. When selecting picture books for reading aloud to older readers, use the same criteria of outstanding pictures and text, but consider more sophisticated and complex possibilities along with simple, elegant stories.

READING FICTIONAL PICTURE BOOKS SILENTLY

A casual observer may wonder what a kindergarten student possibly learns from just paging through a picture book. However, the 5-year-old who loves looking at picture books is absorbing a variety of skills: left-to-right progression, the relationship of print to oral delivery, sequence, story structure, and appreciation of illustrations. With subsequent readings, the student may begin to read repeated words, identifying them in other books. The intermediate classroom teacher who fosters silent reading of picture books in addition to chapter books recognizes the challenging vocabulary such books include and understands that developing, or remedial, readers will benefit from reading familiar texts or books first heard as read-alouds. When discussing the use of picture books with adolescents, Linda Rief emphasizes that fine picture books have poetic language, filled with metaphor and crisp simplicity (1992, 71).

PREDICTABLE AND PATTERN PICTURE BOOKS

Predictable or pattern books are distinguished by repetitive or cumulative lines or text that are easily predicted by the listener or reader. They invite participation just by their very nature, especially if the reader pauses expectantly at key points. Most parents would agree that *Goodnight Moon* by Margaret Wise Brown is the classic predictable or pattern picture book. This is often the first

s p o t l i g h t   3

Writing a Variant

GRADE LEVELS:
Kindergarten and up.

BOOK: *The Wee Little Woman* by Byron Barton (New York: HarperCollins, 1995).

ACTIVITY: In this pattern book, the wee little woman's wee little cat gets in trouble for drinking milk from the wee little cow. After reading this aloud, brainstorm alternative word patterns such as *big huge man* and *big huge dog*. Create a story with the class and write it on chart paper. Have the students create a mural to illustrate the action in the story, using simple, bold pictures like Byron Barton's. Older students could add the words to the mural.

book the children "read," sometimes as early as they can talk. Students in preschool through early primary will enjoy familiar favorites such as *Old MacDonald Had a Farm* by Tracey Campbell Pearson, *Go Tell Aunt Rhody* by Aliki, or *The Three Billy Goats Gruff* by Marcia Brown. Traditional stories can be introduced with *Henny Penny* and *The Little Red Hen*, both by Paul Galdone. Few children will be able to resist acting out *Seven Little Rabbits* by John Becker, appreciating the repetition in *Home Sweet Home* by Jean Marzollo, or making the animal noises in Sue Hendra's *Oliver's Wood*. Mike Thaler's *In the Middle of the Puddle* describes what happens when it rains continually and a turtle and frog's puddle turns into a pond, lake, and sea. Both primary and intermediate children will appreciate the science incorporated into the story, especially if combined with Denise Fleming's *In the Small, Small Pond*. See Spotlight 3 for an activity using a repetitive book.

Primary and intermediate students also enjoy Joanna Cole's *This is the Place for Me*, a circular story of a bear who leaves his home in search of a better place to live, only to return to where he began. Though simple, the story also offers many opportunities to explore sequence, print conventions, punctuation, and story structure. Intermediate students will find Audrey Wood's *King Bidgood's in the Bathtub* (about a king who refuses to get out of the bathtub until a page solves the problem by pulling the plug) an enchanting pattern book. Another book with stunning illustrations, *The Heart of the Wood* by Marguerite W. Davol, explores the transformation of a tree into a fiddle. A totally different story about the use of a tree is Candace Christiansen's *The Mitten Tree*, where an old lady hangs mittens she knits for the neighbor children.

An especially beautiful cumulative picture book for older listeners is *The Rose in My Garden* by Arnold Lobel. Each page adds descriptive, alliterative lines, until a cat chasing a mouse wakes up a bee, which stings the cat on the nose. The amusing, but sophisticated, tale offers middle school students an opportunity to explore how this form could be applied to a writing assignments. *When I Was Young in the Mountains* by Cynthia Rylant is a much simpler story with the title serving as a repetitive line shaping the remembrances in episodic structure. Bishop and Hickman emphasize that although this is a short picture book, the text and pictures produce a harmonious whole that is especially enjoyable (1992, 8).

FICTIONAL PICTURE BOOKS IN CONTENT AREAS AND THEMATIC UNITS

Increasingly, teachers are incorporating picture books into content areas, such as science, math, music, or social studies. Picture books are also useful resources for 4-to-6-week-long immersions into subject areas such as insects or the

A student enjoys a picture book.

medieval period. They explore people's actions, sensitive issues, and can be used to pique curiosity (Farris and Fuhler 1994, 381). Primary students studying insects will pore over *The Grouchy Ladybug, The Very Busy Spider, The Very Hungry Caterpillar,* or *The Very Quiet Cricket,* simple picture books by Eric Carle. For a first experience with maps, share Sara Fanelli's *My Map Book.* Intermediate students studying the Aztecs can explore *The Flame of Peace: A Tale of the Aztecs* by Deborah Nourse Lattimore and *Spirit Child: A Story of the Nativity* translated from the Aztec by John Bierhorst. Middle or high school students studying European countries will be intrigued by Jörge Müller's *The Changing Countryside* or *The Changing City,* which show through wordless illustrations the effects of time on a typical European countryside or city.

FICTIONAL PICTURE BOOKS AS MODELS FOR WRITING

Picture books are perfect for inspiring writing activities. Younger students will respond to the message and style of easy picture books, and older students can examine the form and structure (Bishop and Hickman 1992, 7). In their article

"Scribbling Down the Pictures," eighth grade students Tricia Crockett and Sara Weidhaas describe the complex process of creating a picture book, concluding with the following paragraph:

We've been given our eyes to see and react to life, and words to pass what we've seen on to others. Picture books are able to combine both of these. When we're little, we like books for the pictures of animals and the stories. But when we get older, we can find more meaning in the words. The pictures don't just visualize what the words are saying, instead they go beyond the words giving clues to the depths of meaning in the words. These picture books can never be outgrown (1992, 67).

For initial book-inspired writing experiences, consider using any good predictable or pattern books at any grade level. Many first grade teachers use Bill Martin Jr.'s *Brown Bear, Brown Bear, What Do You See?* as a writing model. *The Fat Cat* by Jack Kent might prompt a student to create a similar cumulative tale in which a different animal swallows a variety of objects or characters. Older students might use *The Rose in My Garden* by Arnold Lobel or George Mendoza's *A Wart Snake in a Fig Tree*, a zany spin on *The Twelve Days of Christmas*. Pamela Duncan Edwards's *Four Famished Foxes and Fosdyke* serves as an outrageous model of the power of alliteration.

To teach letter writing, intermediate and middle school teachers can use Janet and Allan Ahlberg's *The Jolly Postman or Other People's Letters* or *The Jolly Christmas Postman*. (See Chapter 10, page 333, for a student example.) Byrd Baylor's *I'm in Charge of Celebrations*, a story of her observation of special days, provides excellent examples of how a writer uses print conventions to influence the mood and pace of the prose. After listening to new versions of nursery rhymes, fourth grade students wrote the examples in Figure 7.2.

FIGURE 7.2
Student versions of "Hickery, dickery dock!"

Hickery, dickery dock!

Hickery, dickery dock!
I see a hole in my sock.
I must be quick
To sew it back thick!
Hickery, dickery dock!

Hickery, dickery dock.
Twelve mice ran up the clock.
The clock struck two
The other ten declared war.

Modern Fantasy Books

"Fantasy may be defined as any story of the impossible . . ." (Russell 1994, 119). Although the commonly accepted laws of reality may be violated, these "impossible" stories succeed best when they are rooted in reality and presented as if they *were* possible. Therefore, it takes an excellent writer to maintain the impossible-as-plausible scenario without resorting to contrivances such as serendipitous meetings or dreams that explain away the entire story.

Although fantasy may be drawn from folktales, myths, or legends, it is distinguished from such traditional literature because it is not of the oral tradition. Madeleine L'Engle states that fantasy almost always starts in the familiar and real and moves to a deeper reality that is beyond ordinary human perception (1989, 130). Forms of modern fantasy include the literary fairy tale, animal fantasy, toy fantasy, eccentric and extraordinary characters, enchanted journeys and imaginary lands, heroic or quest fantasy, supernatural and time fantasy, and science fiction and space fantasy (Russell 1994, 120–126).

People of all ages love fantasy, whether the story is about an overworked hound dog who is head of Pawprints Inc. (Danny Shanahan's *Buckledown the Workhound*), an umbrella maker who discovers his ragged umbrella is magic (Odette Meyers's *The Enchanted Umbrella*), or a young boy who takes a magical train trip to the North Pole (Chris Van Allsburg's *The Polar Express*). Adolescents especially enjoy fantasy because they are actively involved in questioning right and wrong and are also on a quest to discover where they fit in society (Stelk 1989, 127). All readers of good fantasy will be entertained, bemused, enlightened, and enriched.

READING MODERN FANTASY BOOKS ALOUD

Perhaps the most beloved fantasy for young children is Maurice Sendak's *Where the Wild Things Are* in which Max misbehaves and is sent to his room, which transforms into the land of wild things. Young listeners enjoy Steven Kellogg's adventure about mice who travel to an island and face a fearful monster in *The Island of the Skog*. Another favorite read-aloud for young children is William Steig's *Doctor De Soto*, a tale of a mouse dentist who outwits a fox he is treating for toothache. Audrey Wood's *Heckedy Peg* has the sound and look of a traditional story, complete with a witch who transforms the children into food until their mother rescues them. Arthur Dorros's *Abuela* incorporates a variety of Spanish words into this tale of a grandmother and child who fly above Manhattan Island. In Patricia Polacco's *Rechenka's Eggs*, Babushka rescues an injured goose who ruins her painted eggs. *Some Fine Grandpa!* by Alan Arkin describes a grandfather who seems to be suffering from senility, until his friends—a gorilla, a polar bear that knits, a robot, and even the Queen of England—show up for his birthday party. Older children will find Audrey Wood's *Bright and Early Thursday Evening: A Tangled Tale* intriguing, particularly because Don Wood used the computer to create the illustrations. Explore the understanding of fantasy in Spotlight 4.

Students may be ready to listen to chapter books as early as first grade, perhaps listening to Roald Dahl's *James and the Giant Peach* or *Charlie and the Chocolate Factory* for their first experiences with fantasy. Use your judgment

s p o t l i g h t 4

Exploring Fantasy and Reality

GRADE LEVELS:
1 and up.

BOOK: *The Flute Player/La Flautista* by Robyn Eversole, illustrated by G. Brian Karas (New York: Orchard, 1995).

ACTIVITY: Presented in English and Spanish, this is the story of a flute player whose flute one day doesn't work. A little girl tries to play it and out comes marvelous things, such as an owl from the night song and fish from the sea songs. After reading the book aloud, preferably in both languages, discuss the music of the

words and pictures. Then discuss the mix of realism and fantasy. Listen to a recording of flute music and have a flutist visit and discuss how a flute works. Complete the exploration by creating art inspired by the fanciful illustrations: butterflies, fish, and so forth.

about deciding when to introduce longer read-alouds to your students. Listening to longer texts develops listening skills, vocabulary, and appreciation for literature. Many third grade teachers enjoy reading E. B. White's *Charlotte's Web* aloud. Another enjoyable transition book is *The Bear Nobody Wanted* by Janet and Allan Ahlberg, the story of a rather snobbish bear who has many adventures with his new family. Upper-intermediate listeners will enjoy Robert C. O'Brien's *Mrs. Frisby and the Rats of NIMH*, the story of a superintelligent community of mice. Anne Lindbergh's *Bailey's Window* describes a troubled boy who discovers he can draw a setting and step into it with his cousins. Elizabeth Winthrop created a riveting quest fantasy with *The Castle in the Attic*. One of the most beautifully written supernatural fantasies is Natalie Babbitt's *Tuck Everlasting*, the story of a family that never ages. Susan Cooper has written several fantasies based on the Arthurian legends, such as *The Grey King*, all enjoyed by upper-intermediate and middle school students. Lloyd Alexander's *Westmark* demonstrates the struggle between good and evil. An excellent example of a time slip is Philippa Pearce's *Tom's Midnight Garden*.

READING MODERN FANTASY BOOKS SILENTLY

Once students have listened to fantasy being read aloud, they will quite naturally want to read more independently. Young students will linger over Chris Van Allsburg's *Two Bad Ants*, enjoying the unusual perspectives in the illustrations. *Muskrat, Muskrat, Eat Your Peas* by Sarah Wilson delights early readers with its additional comments from the characters. They will also appreciate the detail in the colorful European setting in *The Flyaway Pantaloons* by Joseph

Sharples. *Wayfarers All* derived from *The Wind in the Willows* by Kenneth Grahame enchants young readers, who will also enjoy Grahame's *The Reluctant Dragon*. Upper-primary students find Jon Scieszka's *Knights of the Kitchen Table* an outrageous time slip.

Intermediate students who read C. S. Lewis's *The Lion, the Witch, and the Wardrobe*, often continue to read others from the Chronicles of Narnia, and J. R. R. Tolkien's *The Hobbit* is another favorite from this genre. Students who enjoy time slips will relish Anne Lindbergh's *The People in Pineapple Place* and its sequel, *The Prisoner of Pineapple Place*. Older readers enjoy Frances Hodgson Burnett's *The Secret Garden*, about a young girl who discovers a magical garden that brings her friends and happiness.

MODERN FANTASY BOOKS AS MODELS FOR WRITING

Writing fantasy is a challenging process and takes time to develop. However, a good place to start is with Chris Van Allsburg's *The Mysteries of Harris Burdick*. Each double page spread is a slightly eerie illustration accompanied by a title and a few words of text that inspire students to create their own short stories. Readers, old and young who still wish dinosaurs were alive, will enjoy James Gurney's *Dinotopia*, perhaps modeling their own writing after his journal entries. Mary Norton's *The Borrowers* may prompt students to create new adventures for these little people. Rachel Field's *Hitty, Her First Hundred Years* is an excellent model for a toy fantasy. Mature readers will appreciate Robin McKinley's kingdom of Damar presented in *The Hero and the Crown* and *The Blue Sword*. Compare these novels to McKinley's collection of short stories, *A Knot in the Grain and Other Stories*. For any fantasy writing, students need to experience a variety of examples in a particular area before they attempt their own versions. For more detailed information, consult *Scripted Fantasy in the Classroom* by Eric Hall, Carol Hall, and Alison Leech (1990).

Historical, Realistic, and Science Fiction

The most common categories of fiction are designated by the time period of the setting. Historical fiction takes place during a specific historical period, and specific details about the customs or characteristics of the period are often key components of this genre. Contemporary fiction focuses on the present, and the author may assume the reader has a certain degree of familiarity with the current features. Science fiction usually takes place in the future, either on earth or on another planet (Russell 1994, 125).

READING FICTION ALOUD

Teachers and librarians anxious to introduce historical fiction to their listeners cannot go wrong with Aliki's *A Medieval Feast*, about a king's feast in the 1400s, Ann Turner's *Dakota Dugout*, an illustrated book about a woman's early years on the Dakota prairie, or Patricia MacLachlan's *Sarah, Plain and Tall*, the story of a woman who answers an ad from a man who needs a wife and moves from the East Coast to the prairie. Upper-primary or intermediate students who listen to Bette Bao Lord's *In the Year of the Boar* and Jackie Robinson learn about a young immigrant's life in America. The novel, *my brother Sam is dead* by James and Christopher Collier, presents a family torn apart by the Revolutionary War and is only one of many fine historical fiction books by these authors. Older readers will also enjoy hearing Avi's *The True Confessions of Charlotte Doyle*, the story of a young girl who braves the seas during the summer of 1832.

Contemporary fiction is especially enjoyed by students because of the link to their everyday lives and the many challenges they face. Upper-primary and intermediate listeners will identify with the dilemma presented when Joel breaks his word to his parents and joins Tony in a swimming race in a dangerous river in Marion Dane Bauer's *On My Honor*. When Tony disappears, Joel must face up to the devastating truth. In Ivy Ruckman's *Night of the Twisters*, listeners are riveted by Dan's efforts to survive a series of tornadoes in a Midwestern town. Jerry Spinelli's *Maniac Magee* explores the gang-related challenges many kids face every day. Young adults will also appreciate Ivy Ruckman's *No Way Out*, the story of several teenagers caught in a flash flood.

Science fiction can be challenging for listeners because of the unfamiliarity of the settings and the ethical and moral messages they present. Perhaps the difficulty of this genre explains why there are so few of these novels available for young listeners and readers. Upper-primary students will enjoy hearing about Jeff Wells's robot in the series of books by Janet and Isaac Asimov that includes *Norby, the Mixed-Up Robot*. Older students will enjoy the interplanetary adventure presented in Frank Asch's *Journey to Terezor*.

READING FICTION SILENTLY

Primary students will pore over the amusing pictures in Helen Ketteman's *Aunt Hilarity's Bustle*, a rollicking story about Hilarity's attempts to create her own bustle. Clyde Robert Bulla offers upper-primary readers a variety of easy historical fiction chapter books such as *A Lion to Guard Us*, about two youngsters coming to America in the early 1600s. Pam Conrad's *Prairie Songs* tells of pioneer life on the Nebraska prairie. Intermediate readers will enjoy Patricia Beatty's work, including *The Coach That Never Came*, in which a boy visiting his grandmother in Colorado Springs becomes intrigued with a legend about a missing stagecoach and the gold it was carrying, or her post–Civil War novel, *Be Ever Hopeful, Hannalee*. Young adults will appreciate Emma Macalik Butterworth's portrayal of a young girl's struggle to survive World War II in *As the Waltz Was Ending* and the post–World War I novel, *After the Dancing Days*, by Margaret I. Rostkowski.

The very youngest readers will enjoy realistic fiction picture books such as *The Strawberry Dog* by Betty Paraskevas, Leslie Baker's *Morning Beach*, or Tomie dePaola's *Now One Foot, Now the Other*, the story of how a grandfather helped a boy learn to walk, who in turn helped the grandfather walk after his stroke. Mary Hoffman's *Boundless Grace* introduces young readers to the beauty of Africa, while exploring the challenges of getting to know a stepfamily. Intermediate students delight in the sibling problems presented in Judy Blume's *Tales of a Fourth Grade Nothing* and identify with Betsy Byars's story of foster children in *The Pinballs*. Young adult readers enjoy Patricia MacLachlan's *The Facts and Fictions of Minna Pratt*, agonize over the dilemma of a young girl trying to outwit terrorists in Robert Cormier's *After the First Death*, and experience vicariously the effects of hate in Bette Greene's treatment of prejudice against homosexuals in *The Drowning of Stephan Jones*.

Young readers of science fiction chapter books will enjoy Pamela F. Service's *Stinker from Space*, a fanciful story of a space warrior who must survive on earth, or Alfred Slote's *My Robot Buddy*, about a boy who gets a new robot on his birthday. Mature readers will enjoy the challenges in Madeleine L'Engle's *A Swiftly Tilting Planet*, *A Wind in the Door*, or *A Wrinkle in Time*, about the adventures of three youngsters who take fantastical journeys into space. Young adults will appreciate Paula Danziger's *This Place Has No Atmosphere*.

FICTION IN CONTENT AREAS AND THEMATIC UNITS

Historical fiction is usually the first choice for the reading teacher who wants to combine reading with social studies or history. Historical fiction helps students learn about change and crisis, common needs, and human dependency (Levstik 1989, 138). Reading a variety of novels in the same theme helps students see one event, such as a war, from different perspectives (Webb 1989, 150). Books such as Michelle Magorian's *Goodnight Mr. Tom* explore the effects of war in England on a young child far more effectively than a textbook can. Reading historical fiction can be combined with textbook reading (or it can replace the textbook); it also segues into related research on the book's setting. Realistic fiction may also be used during a theme. For example, students immersed in a unit on survival might read Gary Paulsen's *Hatchet* or Ivy

Ruckman's *Night of the Twisters* or *No Way Out.* (See Literature Contract in Appendix A for more examples.)

Intermediate students enjoy the touch of science fiction in Willo Davis Roberts's *The Girl with the Silver Eyes.* Older students studying energy sources can read Robert C. O'Brien's *Z for Zachariah,* the story of a young girl who believes she is the sole survivor of nuclear radiation. Any of these science fiction titles could be used in a thematic unit on space exploration.

FICTION AS MODELS FOR WRITING

Although immersion in any good fiction prepares students for writing fiction, certain books lend themselves well to further explorations through writing. Joan W. Blos's *A Gathering of Days: A New England Girl's Journal, 1830–32* and Karen Cushman's *Catherine Called Birdy* provide models of the journal form that intermediate and older students might replicate, and young adults learn the power of letters from Mary E. Lyons's *Letters from a Slave Girl: The Story of Harriet Jacobs.* Paul Fleischman's *The Borning Room* presents a farm girl's life through the births and deaths in the farmhouse's borning room. Writing historical fiction should involve research of the period, but in discussing her own writing, Mollie Hunter emphasizes that it also requires details that sharpen focus and develop real-life characters (1989, 158).

FIGURE 7.3
Student Writing
Inspired by
Science Fiction

The Extra-Terrestrial Others

I said nothing more. My feet left the land. Higher I flew until Westword was only a dot in the vast country. I had no idea where I was going. I felt a huge jolt forward. Then I lost control over my thoughts. I was thinking how I was going to take over the world. Sure I had thought that before, but I never really meant it. I felt another jolt and then I got control of my thoughts again. Had they taken me in their power? My stories had always gotten me into trouble, like the time I wrote about the jocks and I heard about it for the rest of the year. But never had I lived one of my stories.

I clutched my story tightly in my right hand knowing that it could be my one-way ticket to death. . . .

Christine

Avi's documentary contemporary novel, *Nothing But the Truth,* uses letters, journal entries, conversations, and articles to tell the story of a young boy whose humming of "The Star-Spangled Banner" leads inexorably to a devastating outcome. Students who enjoy science fiction sometimes find imaginative writing to be quite liberating. See Figure 7.3 for the beginning of a story about extraterrestrials.

Folk Literature

Readers of traditional literature, including folktales, tall tales, myths, legends, and fables, can choose from an abundance of individually illustrated stories, collections from many different countries, or treasuries on a variety of themes. Folktales include stories of talking beasts ("Puss in Boots"), noodlehead or simpleton tales ("Hans in Luck"), wonder tales ("Cinderella"), cumulative tales ("The Fat Cat"), and pourquoi tales (the French word for "why") ("How the Bear Got a Stumpy Tale"). Myths feature gods and goddesses, typified by Greek and Roman stories. Legends focus on mortal heroes rather than gods and goddesses. Fables are brief tales of animals that mirror human behavior, usually with a moral that summarizes the message.

READING FOLK LITERATURE ALOUD

Nearly every student knows at least one fairy tale and will appreciate the familiarity and comfort that comes with hearing that tale again. Beautifully illustrated tales such as *Cinderella* retold by Amy Ehrlich and illustrated by Susan Jeffers or Trina Schart Hyman's *Little Red Riding Hood* are ideal for beginning the year. The abundance of tales from other countries offers teachers and librarians the opportunity to find commonalities through books such as Judy Sierra's *Cinderella*, a collection of 25 variants. Margaret Read MacDonald's *Slop! A Welsh Tale* tells of an elderly Welsh family that helps out the wee folk who live next door. Caryn Yacowitz's *The Jade Stone*, an illustrated tale of China, introduces listeners to the Great Emperor of All China. In Oki S. Han's Korean tale, *Sir Whong and the Golden Pig*, Sir Whong handles treachery with wit and humor. Eric A. Kimmel's *Baba Yaga*, a story of a Russian witch, can be compared to the more familiar witch who captured Hansel and Gretel. Readers can learn about Mexico through Antonio Hernández Madrigal's *The Eagle and the Rainbow: Timeless Tales from Mexico* or about Micronesia through Bo Flood's *From the Mouth of the Monster Eel: Stories from Micronesia*. Audrey Wood provides a portrayal of the Paul Bunyan family in *The Bunyans*, and Steve Kellogg has done an illustrated version of *Pecos Bill*. Ingri and Edgar Parin D'Aulaire's *Book of Greek Myths* offers a large collection of myths for reading aloud or for individual reading. Fables can be introduced with collections such as Stephanie Calmenson's *The Children's Aesop* or individually illustrated versions such as Janet Stevens's *The Tortoise and the Hare*. Older students familiar with the genre will enjoy Arnold Lobel's contemporary treatments in *Fables*.

READING FOLK LITERATURE SILENTLY

The very youngest readers benefit from reading familiar or repetitive stories such as "The Little Red Hen" because their oral memory approximates the written text, bridging from the spoken to the written word. It isn't unusual for a first grader to read the same fairy tale repeatedly, finding comfort in the beloved story and success in the reading process. Jack Kent's *Fables of Aesop* is very easy to read and quite humorous and might inspire the reader to move on to Paul Galdone's *Three Aesop Fox Fables* or Eric Carle's *Twelve Fables from Aesop*. When young readers are ready to move on, they can tackle more complex tales, such as Deborah Apy's *Beauty and the Beast*. Intermediate students will appreciate Amy Tan's *The Moon Lady*, lavishly illustrated by Gretchen Schields. When they are ready for collections, there are many themed collections such as James Riordan's *The Woman in the Moon and Other Tales of Forgotten Heroines*, Suzanne Barchers's *Wise Women: Folk and Fairy Tales from Around the World*, Mary Helen Pelton's *Images of a People: Tlingit Myths and Legends*, Gail E. Haley's *Mountain Jack Tales*, or Margaret Read MacDonald's *Peace Tales: World Folktales to Talk About*. Children will enjoy reading *Whoppers: Tall Tales and Other Lies Collected from American Folklore* by Alvin Schwartz and Ann Bishop's *Wild Bill Hiccup's Riddle Book*. Students studying other countries will appreciate Geraldine Harris's *Gods and Pharaohs from Egyptian Mythology* or Douglas Gifford's *Warriors, Gods and Spirits from Central and South American Mythology* with their stories, illustrations, and information on exotic cultures.

FOLK LITERATURE AS MODELS FOR WRITING

Traditional literature is ideal for inspiring writing projects. Immersion in traditional stories, coupled with an analysis of the elements of the tales, leads naturally to students writing their own stories from grades 3 through high school. Begin a unit on writing folktales by reading traditional tales aloud, plus such unusual creations as Janet and Allan Ahlberg's *The Jolly Postman or Other People's Letters*, and George Shannon's *Stories to Solve: Folktales from Around the World* and *More Stories to Solve: Fifteen Folktales from Around the World*. Introduce the wonderful variety of modern folktales, such as Jon Scieszka's *The True Story of the 3 Little Pigs*, Eugene Trivizas's *The Three Little Wolves and the Big Bad Pig*, and Fiona French's *Snow White in New York*. To introduce writing a sequel, use Jon Scieszka's *The Frog Prince Continued*, or to illustrate how an author can combine old stories with new characters, use Stephen Sondheim and James Lapine's *Into the Woods*. Older readers will enjoy the zany interplay of folktale characters in Jon Scieszka's *The Stinky Cheese Man and Other Fairly Stupid Tales*. See Chapter 10 for an in-depth unit on reading and writing folk literature. Students can use the same model of this unit to write tall tales.

Summary

Children's and young adult literature is being used increasingly in primary, intermediate, and middle school grades. Teachers who read aloud to their students can increase both vocabulary and comprehension skills, and can focus a class.

Alphabet and counting books are enjoyed by the very youngest listener, and some complex books are useful for reading silently. The variety of themes allows their use in content areas and thematic units. Alphabet and counting books can be used as writing models for individuals or small groups.

Fictional picture books are well-told stories with fine illustrations that are integral to the story. All ages of students enjoy these stories and their illustrations, and older students also enjoy the more complex examples. Predictable and pattern books are especially useful for beginning readers or as writing models. Picture books can be used in thematic units or as extensions in the content areas and are especially useful as writing models for all ages.

Modern fantasy books are narratives of the impossible, moving from the known to the unknown. Primary students may first listen to and read fictional picture books and then progress to more challenging chapter books. Fantasy is a more challenging writing model, but experienced young writers often appreciate the freedom that writing fantasy offers.

Fiction includes historical fiction, contemporary fiction, and science fiction. Teachers who read fiction aloud acquaint students with a rich variety of styles that often prompts them to follow through with silent reading. Historical fiction is a favorite for extending reading to the content areas or for thematic units. Fiction provides a variety of formats that may inspire young writers to try their hands at creating fiction.

References: Literature

Ahlberg, Janet, and Allan Ahlberg. *The Bear Nobody Wanted.* New York: Viking, 1992.

_____. *The Jolly Christmas Postman.* Boston: Little, Brown, 1991.

_____. *The Jolly Postman or Other People's Letters.* Boston: Little, Brown, 1986.

Alexander, Lloyd. *Westmark.* New York: Dell, 1981.

Aliki. *Go Tell Aunt Rhody.* New York: Macmillan, 1974.

_____. *A Medieval Feast.* New York: Harper & Row, 1983.

Anno, Mitsumasa. *Anno's Alphabet.* New York: Harper & Row, 1974.

_____. *Anno's Math Games II.* New York: Philomel, 1982.

_____. *Anno's Math games III.* New York: Philomel, 1991.

Anno, Masaichiro, and Mitsumasa Anno. *Anno's Magical ABC: An Anamorphic Alphabet.* New York: Philomel, 1980.

_____. *Anno's Mysterious Multiplying Jar.* New York: Philomel, 1983.

Apy, Deborah, reteller. *Beauty and the Beast.* Illustrated by Michael Hague. New York: Holt, Rinehart & Winston, 1983.

Ardema, Verna. *Why Mosquitoes Buzz in People's Ears.* Illustrated by Leo and Diane Dillon. New York: Scholastic, 1975.

Arkin, Alan. *Some Fine Grandpa!* Illustrated by Dirk Zimmer. New York: HarperCollins, 1995.

Asch, Frank. *Journey to Terezor.* New York: Holiday House, 1989.

Asimov, Janet, and Isaac Asimov. *Norby, The Mixed-Up Robot.* New York: Walker, 1983.

Avi. *The True Confessions of Charlotte Doyle.* New York: Avon, 1990.

_____. *Nothing But the Truth.* New York: Orchard, 1991.

Babbitt, Natalie. *Tuck Everlasting.* New York: Farrar, Straus & Giroux, 1975.

Baker, Leslie. *Morning Beach.* Boston: Little, Brown, 1990.

Bang, Molly. *Ten, Nine, Eight.* New York: Greenwillow, 1983.

Barchers, Suzanne I. *Wise Women: Folk and Fairy Tales from Around the World.* Englewood, Colo.: Libraries Unlimited, 1990.

Barry, David. *The Rajah's Rice.* Illustrated by Donna Perrone. New York: W. H. Freeman, 1994.

Barton, Byron. *The Wee Little Woman.* New York: HarperCollins, 1995.

Bauer, Marion Dane. *On My Honor.* New York: Dell, 1986.

Baylor, Byrd. *I'm In Charge of Celebrations.* Illustrated by Peter Parnall. New York: Charles Scribner's, 1986.

Beatty, Patricia. *Be Ever Hopeful, Hannalee.* New York: William Morrow, 1988.

_____. *The Coach That Never Came.* William Morrow, 1985.

Becker, John. *Seven Little Rabbits.* Illustrated by Barbara Cooney. New York: Scholastic, 1973.

Bertrand, Lynne. *One Day, Two Dragons.* Illustrated by Janet Street. New York: Trumpet Club, 1992.

Biebow, Natascha. *Eleonora.* Illustrated by Britta Teckentrup. New York: W. H. Freeman, 1995.

Bierhorst, John, translator. *Spirit Child: A Story of the Nativity.* Illustrated by Barbara Cooney. New York: William Morrow, 1984.

Birch, David. *The King's Chessboard.* Illustrated by Devis Grebu. New York: Dial, 1988.

Bishop, Ann. *Wild Bill Hiccup's Riddle Book.* Chicago: Albert Whitman, 1975.

Blos, Joan W. *A Gathering of Days: A New England Girl's Journal, 1830–32.* New York: Atheneum, 1979.

Blume, Judy. *The Pain and the Great One.* Illustrated by Irene Trivas. Scarsdale, N.Y.: Bradbury Press, 1974.

_____. *Tales of a Fourth Grade Nothing.* New York: Dell, 1972.

Briggs, Raymond. *Father Christmas.* New York: Penguin, 1979.

Bright, Robert. *Georgie and the Robbers.* New York: Doubleday, 1963.

Brown, Marcia. *Shadow.* New York: Charles Scribner's, 1982.

_____. *The Three Billy Goats Gruff.* New York: Harcourt Brace & World, 1957.

Brown, Margaret Wise. *Goodnight Moon.* Illustrated by Clement Hurd. New York: Harper & Row, 1947.

Bulla, Clyde Robert. *A Lion to Guard Us.* Illustrated by Michelle Chessare. New York: Scholastic, 1981.

Burnett, Frances Hodgson. *The Secret Garden.* New York: Scholastic, 1987.

Burton, Virginia Lee. *The Little House.* Boston: Houghton Mifflin, 1942.

Butterworth, Emma Macalik. *As the Waltz Was Ending.* New York: Scholastic, 1982.

Byars, Betsy. *The Pinballs.* New York: Scholastic, 1977.

Calmenson, Stephanie, reteller. *The Children's Aesop.* Illustrated by Robert Byrd. Honesdale, Pa.: Caroline House, 1992.

Carle, Eric. *The Grouchy Ladybug.* New York: Thomas Y. Crowell, 1977.

_____. *1, 2, 3 to the Zoo.* Cleveland, Ohio: World, 1968.

_____, reteller. *Twelve Tales from Aesop.* New York: Philomel, 1980.

_____. *The Very Busy Spider.* New York: Philomel, 1985.

_____. *The Very Hungry Caterpillar.* New York: Putnam, 1986.

_____. *The Very Quiet Cricket.* New York: Putnam, 1990.

Christiansen, Candace. *The Mitten Tree.* Illustrated by Elaine Greenstein. Golden, Colo.: Fulcrum Kids, 1997.

Chwast, Seymour. *The Alphabet Parade.* San Diego, Calif.: Harcourt Brace Jovanovich, 1991.

Cole, Joanna. *This Is the Place for Me.* Illustrated by William Van Horn. New York: Scholastic, 1986.

Collier, James Lincoln, and Christopher Collier. *my brother Sam is dead.* New York: Scholastic, 1974.

Conrad, Pam. *Prairie Songs.* Illustrated by Darrel Zudeck. New York: Harper & Row, 1985.

Cooper, Susan. *The Grey King.* New York: Atheneum, 1975.

Cormier, Robert. *After the First Death.* New York: Avon, 1979.

Count Your Way Through . . . Minneapolis, Minn.: Carolrhoda, various dates.

Cushman, Karen. *Catherine Called Birdy.* New York: HarperTrophy, 1994.

Dahl, Roald. *Charlie and the Chocolate Factory.* Illustrated by Joseph Schindelman. New York: Bantam, 1979.

_____. *James and the Giant Peach.* Illustrated by Nancy Ekholm Burkert. New York: Viking Penguin, 1988.

Danziger, Paula. *This Place Has No Atmosphere.* New York: Dell, 1987.

D'Aulaire, Ingri and Edgar Parin. *Book of Greek Myths.* Garden City, N.Y.: Doubleday, 1962.

Davol, Marguerite W. *The Heart of the Wood.* Illustrated by Sheila Hamanaka. New York: Simon & Schuster, 1992.

de Paola, Tomie. *Now One Foot, Now the Other.* New York: G. P. Putnam's, 1980.

Dorros, Arthur. *Abuela.* Illustrated by Elisa Kleven. New York: Dutton, 1991.

Edwards, Pamela Duncan. *Four Famished Foxes and Fosdyke.* Illustrated by Henry Cole. New York: HarperCollins, 1995.

Ehrlich, Amy, reteller. *Cinderella.* Illustrated by Susan Jeffers. New York: Dial, 1985.

Elting, Mary, and Michael Folsom. *Q is for Duck: An Alphabet Guessing Game.* Illustrated by Jack Kent. New York: Clarion, 1980.

Eversole, Robyn. *The Flute Player/La Flautista.* Illustrated by G. Brian Karas. New York: Orchard, 1995.

Fanelli, Sara. *My Map Book.* New York: HarperCollins, 1995.

Feelings, Muriel. *Moja Means One: Swahili Counting Book.* Illustrated by Tom Feelings. New York: Dial, 1972.

Field, Rachel. *Hitty, Her First Hundred Years.* Illustrated by Dorothy P. Lathrop. New York: Macmillan, 1929.

Fleischman, Paul. *The Borning Room.* New York: HarperCollins, 1991.

Fleming, Denise. *In the Small, Small Pond.* New York: Henry Holt, 1993.

Flood, Bo. *From the Mouth of the Monster Eel: Stories from Micronesia.* Illustrated by Margo Vitarelli. Golden, Colo.: Fulcrum Kids, 1996.

French, Fiona. *Snow White in New York.* Oxford, England: Oxford University Press, 1986.

Gág, Wanda. *The ABC Bunny.* New York: Coward, McCann & Geoghegan, 1933.

Galdone, Paul. *Henny Penny.* New York: Scholastic, 1968.

_____. *The Little Red Hen.* New York: Scholastic, 1973.

_____. *Three Aesop Fox Fables.* New York: Houghton Mifflin, 1971.

Gifford, Douglas. *Warriors, Gods and Spirits from Central and South American Mythology.* Illustrated by John Sibbick. New York: Schocken, 1983.

Giganti, Paul. *How Many Snails?* Illustrated by Donald Crews. New York: Trumpet Club, 1988.

Grahame, Kenneth. *The Reluctant Dragon.* Illustrated by Michael Hague. New York: Holt, Rinehart & Winston, 1983.

_____. *Wayfarers All.* Illustrated by Beverly Gooding. New York: Charles Scribner's, 1981.

Greene, Bette. *The Drowning of Stephan Jones.* New York: Bantam, 1991.

Gurney, James. *Dinotopia.* Atlanta: Turner, 1992.

Hague, Kathleen. *Alphabears: An ABC Book.* Illustrated by Michael Hague. New York: Holt, Rinehart & Winston, 1984.

Haley, Gail E. *Mountain Jack Tales.* New York: Dutton Children's Books, 1992.

Hall, Nancy Christensen. *Macmillan Fairy Tale Alphabet Book.* Illustrated by John O'Brien. New York: Macmillan, 1983.

Han, Oki S., reteller. *Sir Whong and the Golden Pig.* New York: Dial, 1993.

Hard, Charlotte. *One Green Island: An Animal Counting Game.* Cambridge, Mass.: Candlewick Press, 1995.

Harris, Geraldine. *Gods and Pharaohs from Egyptian Mythology.* Illustrated by David O'Connor. New York: Schocken, 1982.

Hendra, Sue. *Oliver's Wood.* Cambridge, Mass.: Candlewick Press, 1996.

Hest, Amy. *In the Rain with Baby Duck.* Illustrated by Jill Barton. Cambridge, Mass.: Candlewick Press, 1995.

Hoban, Tana. *Count and See.* New York: Macmillan, 1972.

Hoffman, Mary. *Boundless Grace.* Illustrated by Caroline Binch. New York: Dial, 1995.

Horner, John R. and Don Lessem. *Digging Up Tyrannosaurus Rex.* New York: Crown, 1992.

Hulme, Joy N. *Counting by Kangaroos.* Illustrated by Betsy Scheld. New York: W. H. Freeman, 1995.

Hyman, Trina Schart. *Little Red Riding Hood.* New York: Holiday House, 1983.

Kellogg, Steven. *The Island of the Skog.* New York: Dial, 1973.

____. *Pecos Bill.* New York: William Morrow, 1986.

Kent, Jack. *Jack Kent's Fables of Aesop.* New York: Parents' Magazine Press, 1972.

____. *The Fat Cat.* New York: Scholastic, 1971.

Ketteman, Helen. *Aunt Hilarity's Bustle.* Illustrated by James Warhola. New York: Simon & Schuster, 1992.

Kimmel, Eric A., reteller. *Baba Yaga: A Russian Folktale.* Illustrated by Megan Lloyd. New York: Holiday House, 1991.

Kraus, Robert. *Another Mouse to Feed.* Illustrated by Jose Aruego and Ariane Dewey. New York: Trumpet Club, 1980.

Lattimore, Deborah Nourse. *The Flame of Peace: A Tale of the Aztecs.* New York: HarperTrophy, 1987.

L'Engle, Madeleine. *A Swiftly Tilting Planet.* Farrar, Straus & Giroux, 1978.

____. *A Wind in the Door.* New York: Dell, 1973.

_____. *A Wrinkle in Time.* New York: Dell, 1962.

Lerner, Harriet, and Susan Goldhor. *What's So Terrible About Swallowing an Apple Seed?* Illustrated by Catharine O'Neill. New York: HarperCollins, 1996.

Lewis, C. S. *The Lion, the Witch, and the Wardrobe.* Illustrated by Pauline Baynes. New York: Scholastic, 1950.

Lindbergh, Anne. *Bailey's Window.* Illustrated by Kinuko Craft. San Diego, Calif.: Harcourt Brace Jovanovich, 1984.

_____. *The People in Pineapple Place.* Illustrated by Kinuko Craft. San Diego, Calif.: Harcourt Brace Jovanovich, 1982.

_____. *The Prisoner of Pineapple Place.* Illustrated by Kinuko Craft. San Diego, Calif.: Harcourt Brace Jovanovich, 1988.

Lobel, Anita. *On Market Street.* New York: Greenwillow, 1981.

Lobel, Arnold. *Fables.* New York: Harper & Row, 1980.

_____. *The Rose in My Garden.* Illustrated by Anita. New York: Scholastic, 1984.

Lord, Bette Bao. *In the Year of the Boar and Jackie Robinson.* Illustrated by Marc Simont. New York: Harper & Row, 1984.

Lyons, Mary E. *Letters from a Slave Girl: The Story of Harriet Jacobs.* New York: Charles Scribner's, 1992.

Macaulay, David. *Black and White.* Boston: Houghton Mifflin, 1990.

MacDonald, Margaret Read. *Peace Tales: World Folktales to Talk About.* Hampden, Conn.: Linnet, 1992.

_____. *Slop! A Welsh Tale.* Illustrated by Yvonne Lebrun Davis. Golden, Colo.: Fulcrum Kids, 1997.

MacDonald, Suse. *Alphabatics.* New York: Bradbury, 1986.

MacLachlan, Patricia. *All the Places to Love.* Illustrated by Mike Wimmer. New York: HarperCollins, 1994.

_____. *The Facts and Fictions of Minna Pratt.* New York: Harper & Row, 1988.

_____. *Sarah, Plain and Tall.* New York: Harper & Row, 1985.

Madrigal, Antonio Hernández. *The Eagle and the Rainbow: Timeless Tales from Mexico.* Illustrated by Tomie dePaola. Golden, Colo.: Fulcrum Kids, 1997.

Maestro, Betsy, and Giulio Maestro. *Harriet Goes to the Circus.* New York: Crown, 1989.

Magorian, Michelle. *Good Night, Mr. Tom.* New York: Harper & Row, 1981.

Martin, Bill, Jr. *Brown Bear, Brown Bear, What Do You See?* Illustrated by Eric Carle. New York: Holt, Rinehart & Winston, 1983.

Maruki, Toshi. *Hiroshima No Pika.* New York: Lothrop, Lee & Shepard, 1980.

Marzollo, Jean. *Home Sweet Home.* Illustrated by Ashley Wolff. New York: HarperCollins, 1997.

Mathews, Louise. *Bunches and Bunches of Bunnies.* Illustrated by Jeni Bassett. New York: Scholastic, 1978.

Mayers, Florence Cassen. *ABC: Musical Instruments from The Metropolitan Museum of Art.* New York: Harry N. Abrams, 1988.

McKinley, Robin. *The Blue Sword.* New York: Greenwillow, 1982.

_____. *The Hero and the Crown.* New York: Greenwillow, 1984.

_____. *A Knot in the Grain and Other Stories.* New York: HarperCollins, 1994.

McMillan, Bruce. *Counting Wildflowers.* New York: Lothrop, Lee & Shepard, 1986.

_____. *Jelly Beans for Sale.* New York: Scholastic, 1996.

Mendoza, George. *A Wart Snake in a Fig Tree.* Illustrated by Etienne Delessert. New York: Dial, 1968.

Meyers, Odette. *The Enchanted Umbrella.* Illustrated by Margot Zemach. San Diego, Calif.: Harcourt Brace Jovanovich, 1988.

Müller, Jörge. *The Changing City.* New York: Atheneum, 1977.

_____. *The Changing Countryside.* New York: Atheneum, 1977.

Murphy, Stuart J. *Too Many Kangaroo Things to Do!* Illustrated by Kevin O'Malley. New York: HarperCollins, 1996.

Musgrove, Margaret. *Ashanti to Zulu: African Traditions.* Illustrated by Leo and Diane Dillon. New York: Dial, 1976.

Norman, Lilith. *The Paddock: A Story in Praise of the Earth.* Illustrated by Robert Roennfeldt. New York: Alfred A. Knopf, 1992.

Norton, Mary. *The Borrowers.* Illustrated by Beth and Joe Krush. San Diego, Calif.: Harcourt Brace Jovanovich, 1986.

O'Brien, Robert C. *Mrs. Frisby and the Rats of NIMH.* New York: Scholastic, 1971.

_____. *Z for Zachariah.* New York: Collier, 1974.

Owen, Annie. *Annie's One to Ten.* New York: Alfred A. Knopf, 1988.

Paulsen, Gary. *Hatchet.* New York: Puffin, 1987.

Paraskevas, Betty. *The Strawberry Dog.* New York: Dial, 1993.

Pearce, Philippa. *Tom's Midnight Garden.* New York: Dell, 1986.

Pearson, Tracey Campbell. *Old MacDonald Had a Farm.* New York: Dial, 1984.

Peek, Merle. *Roll Over! A Counting Song.* New York: Clarion, 1981.

Pelton, Mary Helen. *Images of a People: Tlingit Myths and Legends.* Englewood, Colo.: Libraries Unlimited, 1992.

Piper, Watty. *The Little Engine That Could.* New York: Platt & Munk, 1954.

Polacco, Patricia. *Rechenka's Eggs.* New York: Philomel, 1988.

Rankin, Laura. *The Handmade Alphabet.* New York: Dial, 1991.

Ressmeyer, Roger. *Astronaut to Zodiac: A Young Stargazer's Alphabet.* New York: Crown, 1992.

Riordan, James. *The Woman in the Moon and Other Tales of Forgotten Heroines.* Illustrated by Angela Barrett. New York: Dial, 1984.

Roberts, Willo Davis. *The Girl with the Silver Eyes.* New York: Atheneum, 1980.

Root, Phyllis. *Contrary Bear.* Illustrated by Laura Cornell. New York: HarperCollins, 1996.

Rostkowski, Margaret I. *After the Dancing Days.* New York: Harper & Row, 1986.

Ruckman, Ivy. *Night of the Twisters.* New York: Harper & Row, 1984.

_____. *No Way Out.* New York: HarperCollins, 1988.

Rylant, Cynthia. *When I Was Young in the Mountains.* Illustrated by Diane Goode. New York: E. P. Dutton, 1982.

Scieszka, Jon. *The Frog Prince Continued.* Illustrated by Steve Johnson. New York: Viking, 1991.

_____. *Knights of the Kitchen Table.* Illustrated by Lane Smith. New York: Puffin, 1991.

_____. *The Stinky Cheese Man and Other Fairly Stupid Tales.* Illustrated by Lane Smith. New York: Viking, 1992.

_____. *The True Story of the 3 Little Pigs.* Illustrated by Lane Smith. New York: Viking, 1989.

Scieszka, Jon, and Lane Smith. *Math Curse.* Illustrated by Lane Smith. New York: Viking, 1995.

Schwartz, Alvin. *Whoppers: Tall Tales and Other Lies Collected from American Folklore.* Illustrated by Glen Rounds. New York: Harper & Row, 1975.

Schwartz, David. *How Much Is a Million?* Illustrated by Steven Kellogg. New York: Lothrop, Lee & Shepard, 1985.

Sendak, Maurice. *Where the Wild Things Are.* New York: Harper & Row, 1963.

Service, Pamela F. *Stinker from Space.* New York: Macmillan, 1988.

Shanahan, Danny. *Buckledown the Workhound.* Boston: Little, Brown, 1993.

Shannon, George. *More Stories to Solve: Fifteen Folktales from Around the World.* Illustrated by Peter Sis. New York: Greenwillow, 1990.

_____. *Stories to Solve: Folktales from Around the World.* Illustrated by Peter Sis. New York: Greenwillow, 1985.

Sharples, Joseph. *The Flyaway Pantaloons.* Illustrated by Suse Scullard. Minneapolis, Minn.: Carolrhoda, 1990.

Sierra, Judy. *Cinderella.* Phoenix, Ariz.: Oryx Press, 1992.

Slote, Alfred. *My Robot Buddy.* Illustrated by Joel Schick. Philadelphia: J. B. Lippincott, 1975.

Sondheim, Stephen, and James Lapine. *Into the Woods.* Adapted by Hudson Talbott. New York: Crown, 1987.

Spier, Peter. *Bored—Nothing to Do!* Garden City, N.Y.: Doubleday, 1978.

Spinelli, Jerry. *Maniac Magee.* Boston: Little, Brown, 1990.

Steig, William. *Doctor DeSoto.* New York: Farrar, Straus & Giroux, 1982.

Stevens, Janet, adapter. *The Tortoise and the Hare.* New York: Holiday House, 1984.

Tan, Amy. *The Moon Lady.* Illustrated by Gretchen Shields. New York: Macmillan, 1992.

Thaler, Mike. *In the Middle of the Puddle.* New York: Harper & Row, 1988.

Tolkein, J. R. R. *The Hobbit.* Boston: Houghton Mifflin, 1938.

Tompert, Ann. *Grandfather Tang's Story.* Illustrated by Robert Andrew Parker. New York: Crown, 1990.

Trivizas, Eugene. *The Three Little Wolves and the Big Bad Pig.* Illustrated by Helen Oxenbury. New York: Margaret K. McElderry, 1993.

Turner, Ann. *Dakota Dugout.* Illustrated by Ronald Himler. New York: Macmillan, 1985.

Van Allsburg, Chris. *The Mysteries of Harris Burdick.* Boston: Houghton Mifflin, 1984.

____. *The Polar Express.* Boston: Houghton Mifflin, 1985.

____. *Two Bad Ants.* Boston: Houghton Mifflin, 1988.

____. *The Z Was Zapped.* Boston: Houghton Mifflin, 1987.

Wells, Ruth. *A to Zen.* Illustrated by Yoshi. Saxonville, Mass.: Picture Book Studio, 1992.

Whatley, Bruce, and Rosie Smith. *Whatley's Quest: An Alphabet Adventure.* New York: HarperCollins, 1994.

White, E. B. *Charlotte's Web.* Illustrated by Garth Williams. New York: Harper, 1952.

Widman, Christine. *The Lemon Drop Jar.* Illustrated by Christa Kieffer. New York: Macmillan, 1992.

Wildsmith, Brian. *Brian Wildsmith's 1 2 3's.* New York: Watts, 1965.

Williams, Linda. *The Little Old Lady Who Was Not Afraid of Anything.* Illustrated by Megan Lloyd. New York: HarperTrophy, 1986.

Wilson, Sarah. *Muskrat, Muskrat, Eat Your Peas!* New York: Simon & Schuster, 1989.

Winthrop, Elizabeth. *The Castle in the Attic.* New York: Bantam, 1985.

Wood, Audrey. *Bright and Early Thursday Evening: A Tangled Tale.* Illustrated by Don Wood. San Diego, Calif.: Harcourt Brace, 1996.

____. *The Bunyans.* Illustrated by David Shannon. New York: Blue Sky Press, 1996.

____. *Heckedy Peg.* Illustrated by Don Wood. San Diego, Calif.: Harcourt Brace Jovanovich, 1987.

____. *King Bidgood's in the Bathtub.* Illustrated by Don Wood. San Diego, Calif.: Harcourt Brace Jovanovich, 1984.

Yacowitz, Caryn, adapter. *The Jade Stone.* Illustrated by Ju-hong Chen. New York: Holiday House, 1992.

Yolen, Jane. *Letting Swift River Go.* Illustrated by Barbara Cooney. Boston: Little, Brown, 1992.

References

Bishop, Rudine Sims, and Janet Hickman. "Four or Fourteen or Forty: Picture Books Are for Everyone." In *Beyond Words: Picture Books for Older Readers and Writers*, edited by Susan Benedict and Lenore Carlisle, 1–10. Portsmouth, N.H.: Heinemann Educational Books, 1992.

Crockett, Tricia, and Sara Weidhaas. "Scribbling Down the Pictures." In *Beyond Words: Picture Books for Older Readers and Writers*, edited by Susan Benedict and Lenore Carlisle, 59–67. Portsmouth, N.H.: Heinemann Educational Books, 1992.

Farris, Pamela J., and Carol J. Fuhler. "Developing Social Studies Concepts through Picture Books." *The Reading Teacher* 47, 5 (Feb. 1994): 380–387.

Hall, Eric, Carol Hall, and Alison Leech. *Scripted Fantasy in the Classroom*. London: Routledge, 1990.

Huck, Charlotte S., Susan Hepler, and Janet Hickman. *Children's Literature in the Elementary School*, 4th ed. Orlando, Fla.: Holt, Rinehart & Winston, 1979.

Hunter, Mollie. "Living Close to History." In *Children's Literature in the Classroom: Weaving Charlotte's Web*, edited by Janet Hickman and Bernice E. Cullinan, 157–160. Needham Heights, Mass.: Christopher-Gordon, 1989.

Keifer, Barbara. "Picture Books for All the Ages." In *Children's Literature in the Classroom: Weaving Charlotte's Web*, edited by Janet Hickman and Bernice E. Cullinan, 75–88. Needham Heights, Mass.: Christopher-Gordon, 1989.

L'Engle, Madeleine. "Fantasy Is What Fantasy Does." In *Children's Literature in the Classroom: Weaving Charlotte's Web*, edited by Janet Hickman and Bernice E. Cullinan, 129–133. Needham Heights, Mass.: Christopher-Gordon, 1989.

Levstik, Linda. "A Gift of Time: Children's Historical Fiction." In *Children's Literature in the Classroom: Weaving Charlotte's Web*, edited by Janet Hickman and Bernice E. Cullinan, 135–145. Needham Heights, Mass.: Christopher-Gordon, 1989.

Rief, Linda. "Good Children's Literature Is for Everyone, ~~Even~~ Especially Adolescents." In *Beyond Words: Picture Books for Older Readers and Writers*, edited by Susan Benedict and Lenore Carlisle, 69–87. Portsmouth, N.H.: Heinemann Educational Books, 1992.

Russell, David L. *Literature for Children: A Short Introduction*, 2nd ed. New York: Longman, 1994.

Stelk, Virginia. "Fantasy in the Classroom." In *Children's Literature in the Classroom: Weaving Charlotte's Web*, edited by Janet Hickman and Bernice E. Cullinan, 121–127. Needham Heights, Mass.: Christopher-Gordon, 1989.

Webb, Lillian. "Teachers Using Historical Fiction." In *Children's Literature in the Classroom: Weaving Charlotte's Web*, edited by Janet Hickman and Bernice E. Cullinan, 147–156. Needham Heights, Mass.: Christopher-Gordon, 1989.

Poetry, Informational Books, and Biography

FOCUS QUESTIONS

1. How can I use poetry?

2. How can I use informational books?

3. How can I use biography and auto-biography?

4. How do I deal with censorship issues?

Jelly Fish

Slimy, wet, slithering in the water,
It stings the page JELLY FISH.
Don't touch the word,
Pain will be with you.
Good for lunch with a bit of peanut butter,
Or for breakfast on your toast.

Katy

Katy, a fourth grader, was inspired to write "Jelly Fish" after hearing a collection of poems, *Words with Wrinkled Knees* by Barbara Juster Esbensen. Poetry, in the form of nursery rhymes, is usually the first genre we experience as children, and we remember favorite poems all our lives. Poetry, biography, autobiography, and informational books are usually found on separate shelves from fiction and consequently may be overlooked by students and teachers. Yet these books can motivate students to read more examples or to write their own versions. This chapter provides a variety of suggestions for these books and their use. Because their primary use is in content areas or in thematic units, the following sections will integrate the use of such books in the discussions of reading and writing models. This chapter concludes with a brief discussion of censorship issues.

Poetry Books

Good poetry inspires reflection, speculation, and appreciation. The best poetry enlightens with its truths and delights with its use of words. Young children revel in the rhythms and rhymes of Mother Goose, even when it is nonsensical. Older children relish the offbeat and sometimes naughty poems of Shel Silverstein (*Where the Sidewalk Ends, A Light in the Attic,* and *Falling Up*) and Jack Prelutsky (*The New Kid on the Block* and *Rolling Harvey Down the Hill*). Middle school students savor the poems found in Naomi Shihab Nye's collection, *This Same Sky: A Collection of Poems from Around the World,* and *Reflections on a Gift of Watermelon Pickle . . . and Other Modern Verse* compiled by Stephen Dunning, Edward Lueders, and Hugh Smith.

READING POETRY ALOUD

"Good poetry is the effective combination of sound and sense" (Russell 1994, 87). Poetry includes such forms as Haiku, cinquain, diamante, concrete poetry, free verse, limerick, and acrostic. Narrative poems, such as ballads, tell a story. Poetry that requires the visual impact, such as acrostic or concrete poetry, will not be as effective for reading aloud as the lively poems that combine rhythm and rhyme. Any teacher or librarian will find an abundance of wonder-

A student enjoys
a collection
of poetry.

ful poems in *The Random House Book of Poetry for Children* selected by Jack Prelutsky. Intermediate students will savor Jeff Moss's *The Other Side of the Door* or *The Butterfly Jar*. Middle school students will appreciate the language in Jack Prelutsky's *Nightmares: Poems to Trouble Your Sleep* or *The Headless Horseman Rides Tonight: More Poems to Trouble Your Sleep*. Browse through such collections and mark favorites with sticky notes. For special occasions, use books such as Myra Cohn Livingston's *New Year's Poems* or Michael J. Rosen's *Food Fight*. Poems can fill an odd moment, introduce a read-aloud book, or extend a unit.

Once students have enjoyed a variety of poems, turn the responsibility over to them for reading aloud. Choral reading is "the oral art of a group sharing poetry by expressively speaking it together for enjoyment" (Anthony 1990, xiii). Students who read poetry aloud in a group need not worry about making a mistake, and they thus build confidence in their reading. Choral reading also develops articulation, memorization, and appreciation for the spoken word. At first, the teacher should lead choral reading, selecting poems with a strong rhythmic sense. The leader should direct the poems just as a conductor does, minimizing the motions as the students become more skilled. Eventually, students will need little direction and will be able to read and recite long poems. Once the process is familiar, small groups of students can work together to select and learn their readings independently.

READING POETRY SILENTLY

It is tempting to amend this heading to read "Reading Poetry *Somewhat* Silently" because students find it difficult not to share with a neighbor or friend what they have just discovered. Some teachers spend several weeks on a poetry unit. Others schedule a poetry reading day when everyone needs a break from the regular reading program. Either way, poetry is well received by children and the more variety, the better. So it will stand you in good stead to

Discovering Poets

GRADE LEVELS:
Kindergarten and up.

BOOKS: *Speaking of Poets: Interviews with Poets Who Write for Children and Young Adults* by Jeffrey S. Copeland (Urbana, Ill.: National Council of Teachers of English 1993).

Pauses: Autobiographical Reflections of 101 Creators of Children's Books by Lee Bennett Hopkins (New York: HarperCollins, 1995).

ACTIVITY: Choose a poet's interview to share with the students, choosing portions based on the grade and attention level of your students. Using Copeland's book, kindergarten students would enjoy Barbara Juster Esbensen's comments about the "whirling skirt" image after hearing her collection, *Dance with Me*, while older students would enjoy her discussion of the writing of *Words with Wrinkled Knees*. Discuss with students what processes they use as they write, encouraging them to notice things in their environment that might be viewed differently or with more attention. Choose several common objects around the room and experiment with a new spin on the mundane. For example, perhaps the chalk comes alive at night, covering the walls with graffiti and the eraser must clean up behind it. What other commonplace items could be seen differently?

assemble several collections of poetry, such as Bruce Lansky's *Kids Pick the Funniest Poems*, M. J. Wheeler's *First Came the Indians*, Michael Rosen's *Poetry*, and Arnold Adoff's *Sports Pages*. Students will admire the outstanding use of art with poetry in Joyce Carol Thomas's *Brown Honey in Broomwheat Tea* illustrated by Floyd Cooper, Ashley Bryan's *Sing to the Sun*, and Barbara Juster Esbensen's *Dance with Me* illustrated by Megan Lloyd. Use collections to enhance the content area, such as Jack Prelutsky's *Tyrannosaurus Was a Beast* or Sylvia Cassedy's *Zoomrimes: Poems about Things That Go*. Older students will find Ruth Gordon's selections useful: *Pierced by a Ray of Sun: Poems About the Times We Feel Alone*. Allow the students to browse through the collections, trading them with others as they finish. Invite them to read their favorite poems aloud to the class. (See also Spotlight 1.)

POETRY AS A MODEL FOR WRITING

One of the best choices for inspiring poetry writing is Eve Merriam's *A Sky Full of Poems*. This collection explores the craft of writing through poetry, with sections entitled "Poet's Play," "Poet's Tools," "Poet's Talk," "Poet's People," and "A Sky Full of Poems." Young writers will find Charlotte Zolotow's collection

spotlight 2

Creating Poems of Movement

GRADE LEVELS:
Kindergarten and up.

BOOK: *Zoomrimes: Poems about Things That Go* by Sylvia Casseday, illustrated by Michelle Chessare (New York: HarperCollins, 1993).

ACTIVITY: This collection includes 26 poems about things that move, from "Ark" to "Zeppelin." Ask your students to list all the things that help them move, move with them, or that they see move. After they have thought of a variety, begin sharing the poems that match their list. Some will be obvious: "Feet," "Limo," and "Subway." Others, such as "Vacuum Cleaner" or "Queue," will surprise students. Some are simple; other poems may need some discussion of the words. After they have heard several, challenge your students to think of an alphabet of things that move that need poems: computer mouse, heart, minute hand, wheelchair, and so forth.

helpful—*Snippets: A Gathering of Poems, Pictures, and Possibilities . . .* , as well as Lee Bennett Hopkins' *Good Rhymes, Good Times.* Intermediate students will chuckle over Arnold Lobel's *The Book of Pigericks,* and middle school students will be inspired by Barbara Juster Esbensen's *Words with Wrinkled Knees.* Paul Fleischman's *Joyful Noise: Poems for Two Voices* and *I Am Phoenix: Poems for Two Voices* both inspire collaborative writing and reading. (See Spotlight 2.)

Informational Books

Illustrated informational books represent one of the fastest growing segments of children's literature. David L. Russell defines this genre as works that deal exclusively with factual material that is intended to instruct (1994, 165) and identifies subjects such as lands and peoples, science and nature, fine and applied arts, human development and behavior. Illustrations or photographs are necessary for understanding or amplification, but they are not meant to stand alone like those found in picture books.

Pamela Green, a specialist on language and literacy from Australia, encourages the use of factual texts for the following reasons: They are authentic representations of everyday reading; they enable individuals to function within our society; and they provide information about the world. They also stimulate inquiry, show purposes for reading and writing, and demonstrate how language works. They extend writing options. They promote useful discussion, and they increase text repertoires as students become aware of language use in a range of contexts (1992, 15–19).

Some books combine information with a story line, such as Joan Knight's *Bon Appétit, Bertie!* with its labeling of objects in French or Zoe Hall's delightful *The Apple Pie Tree*. Doug Cushman's *Mouse and Mole and the All-Weather Train Ride* and Joanna Cole's *Magic Schoolbus* series may be classified as fiction, but they contain a strong element of nonfiction with the accompanying information. Such books provide a good introduction to informational books. When selecting informational picture books, consider the accuracy of the information in addition to content and perspective, style, quality of illustrations, and organization (Dowd 1992, 37).

READING INFORMATIONAL BOOKS ALOUD

In the past, teachers might pass over an informational book as a read-aloud, thinking it would be dull compared to a storybook. But today's authors and illustrators offer a wonderful variety of fascinating choices that relate to a thematic unit or unit of study. Ray Doiron suggests approaching nonfiction read-alouds by choosing books you enjoy. Preread the book; then you can give students any necessary background information. Discuss the topic and the features of the book. Sometimes reading only segments of a nonfiction book may be appropriate. Including other related nonfiction such as magazines and news articles can also enhance the students' early exposure to nonfiction (1994, 621–622). Primary teachers might look for nonfiction books that incorporate a story frame into the nonfiction format (Vardell and Copeland 1992, 80).

Many teachers begin the day reading aloud a nonfiction book that sets the stage for subsequent investigations. For example, the youngest students will enjoy *Boat Book* by Gail Gibbons, a colorful presentation of various boats. A natural follow-up is *Big City Port* by Betsy Maestro and Ellen DelVecchio. Another favorite by Gail Gibbons is *Check It Out! The Book About Libraries*, a useful orientation book. Youngsters like to know how things work and will appreciate Byron Barton's *Building a House* or Arthur Dorros' *This Is My House*, a description of materials used in countries around the world, accompanied by a pronunciation guide for 13 languages.

Younger students fascinated with science will enjoy hearing *Rain Forest Babies* by Kathy Darling, Seymour Simon's *Sharks*, and Aliki's *Wild and Woolly Mammoths*. Introduce students to the *One Small Square* series (see Spotlight 3) with an easy pop-up book by Donald M. Silver, *One Very Small Square: Busy Beaver Pond*, and progress to more difficult books for individual silent reading with Silver's *One Small Square: Cactus Desert*. A related book on deserts is Marianne Wallace's *America's Deserts* pictured on page 260. Capitalizing on children's interest in interactive books, Beverly K. Duncan has developed *Explore the Wild: A Nature Search-and-Find Book*.

During social studies, upper-primary teachers might share Peter Spier's *The Star-Spangled Banner* or Betsy and Giulio Maestro's *A More Perfect Union:*

spotlight 3

Backyard Explorations

GRADE LEVELS: Kindergarten and up.

BOOK: *One Very Small Square: Nighttime in My Backyard* by Donald Silver, illustrated by Patricia J. Wynne (New York: W. H. Freeman, 1994).

ACTIVITY: Share this book with your students, demonstrating the pop-up parts. Ask them what they have seen in their backyards at night and contrast their observations with what occurs in the book. For example, students in desert areas will not be familiar with fireflies. Let students check out the book on the weekends along with a letter of explanation to parents that they are invited to share some time after dark with their child, exploring nighttime in their backyard. (Be certain that this is a reasonable and safe expectation. A daytime substitute book and activity would be Silver's *One Very Small Square: Life on a Limb*.) Have students share their observations with the class.

The Story of Our Constitution, followed by Jean Fritz's *Shh! We're Writing the Constitution*. While older students will appreciate the detailed text, younger students will enjoy the excellent photographs in Frances King Koch's *Mariculture: Farming the Fruits of the Sea*, a fascinating overview of mariculture. Martin W. Sandler has written several Library of Congress books, such as *Inventors*. A wonderful read-aloud for older animal lovers is Gary Paulsen's *Woodsong*, an account of his experiences with his sled dog team and his running of the Iditarod.

During language arts, upper-primary and early-intermediate students will enjoy hearing Betty Fraser's amusing exploration of proverbs and idioms in *First Things First: An Illustrated Collection of Sayings Useful and Familiar for Children*. Older students will enjoy the books by Ruth Heller that deal with language, such as *Kites Sail High: A Book About Verbs*. Mary Blocksma's *Ticket to the Twenties: A Time Traveler's Guide* provides older readers with a light-hearted slice of history.

READING INFORMATIONAL BOOKS SILENTLY

Most informational books will be read silently, often for research, in the content areas, for thematic units, or for author studies. Judith W. Keck (1992) recommends the following nonfiction authors for subjects of author studies: Aliki, Jim Arnosky, Brent Ashabranner, Joanna Cole, Leonard Everett Fisher, Russell Freedman, Jean Fritz, Gail Gibbons, James Cross Giblin, Patricia Lauber, Milton Meltzer, Dorothy Hinshaw Patent, Helen Roney Sattler, and Seymour Simon.

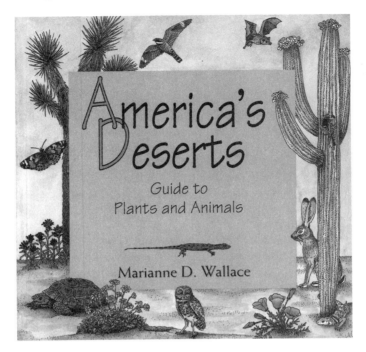

Primary students may only read portions of an informational book or may just study the illustrations or photographs. George Ancona's *Bananas: From Manolo to Margie* describes the journey of bananas from Honduras to the market and is enjoyed by kindergarten and primary students. Susan Ohanian's book on airplanes and the Dallas–Fort Worth airport, *747 * DFW* is one of a series of SRA books that offer many opportunities for learning math. Young readers interested in France will enjoy outstanding historical books such as Aliki's *The King's Day: Louis XIV of France* or Roxie Monro's *The Inside-Outside Book of Paris*. Older students studying the Pilgrims will appreciate *Eating the Plates: A Pilgrim Book of Food and Manners* by Lucille Recht Penner. Martin Sandler is becoming an important author of informational books that contribute to social studies with his lavishly illustrated Library of Congress books, *Immigrants* and *Civil War*. Russell Freedman is the author of many excellent informational books also useful for social studies, among them *An Indian Winter, Buffalo Hunt*, and *Children of the Wild West*.

Primary and intermediate students relish science books such as Joanna Cole's *The Magic Schoolbus: Lost in the Solar System*, one of a series that takes a school group on fanciful field trips, with scientific information interspersed. Intermediate and older readers will also enjoy the photographs and text in John R. Horner and Don Lessem's *Digging Up Tyrannosaurus Rex*, a factual accounting of a dinosaur dig. Horse lovers will appreciate Milton Meltzer's *Hold Your Horses! A Feedbag Full of Fact and Fable*. (See Spotlight 4.) Older stu-

s p o t l i g h t 4

Researching Fact and Fable

GRADE LEVELS:
4 and up.

BOOK: *Hold Your Horses: A Feedbag Full of Fact and Fable* by Milton Meltzer (New York: HarperCollins, 1995).

ACTIVITY: Share Meltzer's book as a model that combines a variety of information about horses in addition to a section on folklore, art, and myth. Have students work in small groups to choose a topic they would like to research. Collaborate with the librarian so that students can create a collection of individual essays for a resource on their topic, using Meltzer's book as inspiration. Retain one copy in the library.

dents will pore over *Castle, Cathedral, City: A Story of Roman Planning and Construction, Mill, Pyramid, Unbuilding,* and *The Way Things Work*—all by David Macaulay.

For older readers, series books, such as *Enchantment of the World* or *The Lands, Peoples, and Cultures Series,* explore a variety of countries. *Cooking the French Way* by Lynne Marie Waldee is one of a series of easy books on ethnic cooking. For more books about cooking or food, don't miss *The Amazing Apple Book* by Paulette Bourgeois, Fran Osseo-Asare's *A Good Soup Attracts Chairs: A First African Cookbook for American Kids,* or Karin Luisa Badt's *Good Morning, Let's Eat!*

Students and teachers who want to expand their language skills will enjoy browsing through *Guppies in Tuxedos: Funny Eponyms* or *Mad as a Wet Hen! And Other Funny Idioms,* both by Marvin Terban. An amusing treatment of grammar is offered in Mario Risso's *Safari Grammar.*

Youngsters interested in art will enjoy the history of colors in *Naming Colors* by Ariane Dewey. Jacob Lawrence's *The Great Migration: An American Story* will be appreciated by art students and researchers of immigration alike. Intermediate through adult readers will appreciate exploring the lavishly illustrated, oversize *Children's Book Illustration and Design,* edited by Julie Cummins.

INFORMATIONAL BOOKS AS MODELS FOR WRITING

After your students have had many opportunities to use informational books, Pamela Green recommends preparing them for a writing experience by immersing them in the experiences that build understanding and information for the writing (1992, 48). Next, consider formats that will inspire students to model their writing after an outstanding example (Salesi 1992, 90). A simple format for young students is the "How To" process, exemplified by Byron Barton's *Building a House.* A similar format can be found in Franklyn M. Branley's *What Makes a Magnet?* Budding cartoonists will enjoy modeling an informative book after any of Joanna Cole's *The Magic Schoolbus* series. Motivate letter writing with *Dear Laura: Letters from Children to Laura Ingalls Wilder*.

Any of the series books on cultures can inspire students to compile information in similar format. *City Kids in China* by Peggy Thomson is an excellent format for exploring and writing about one's own environment. Older students interested in photography will find a useful model in *Oh, Boy! Babies!* by Alison Cragin Herzig and Jane Lawrence Mali. Researchers will enjoy the use of text and historical illustrations and photographs found in *Food for the Settler* by Bobbie Kalman, part of the *Early Settler Life Series*. Older readers and writers might be inspired to use the interview format after reading *Talking with Artists*, compiled and edited by Pat Cummings.

Biography and Autobiography

Biography is a nonfictional work that describes a person's life in part or full (Russell 1994, 150). When a person writes their own story, the result is an autobiography. The authentic biography describes factual information about the subject. The fictionalized biography is essentially accurate, but dramatizes specific scenes, speculating on the details. Biographical fiction takes great liberties with the facts (ibid., 151). Russell emphasizes that readers should judge biographical writing on five elements: the subject of the biography; the accuracy of the information; the balance, which should reflect the human side of people; the style, which should be both interesting and appropriate; and the theme, which must be significant and sound (ibid., 153–155). Thanks to the efforts of fine writers such as Jean Fritz and Russell Freedman, we have many excellent biographies available for use in the classroom.

READING BIOGRAPHY AND AUTOBIOGRAPHY ALOUD

Alice and Martin Provensen's biography, *The Glorious Flight: Across the Channel with Louis Blériot*, is an excellent starting point for reading aloud to primary students. Students will also enjoy the brief text and rich paintings of Mattie Lou O'Kelley's *From the Hills of Georgia: An Autobiography in Paintings*. Intermediate and older students will chuckle at Jean Fritz's lighthearted treatment in *Where Do You Think You're Going, Christopher Columbus?* Her *What's the Big Idea, Ben Franklin?* can be paired with Robert Lawson's *Ben and Me*, which introduces students to biographical fiction through a mouse describing his experiences with Ben Franklin.

READING BIOGRAPHY AND AUTOBIOGRAPHY SILENTLY

Young students will pore over Alice and Martin Provensen's pop-up book, *Leonardo da Vinci*. Jill Krementz has created a series of photographic autobiographies of young people: *A Very Young Circus Flyer, A Very Young Musician, A Very Young Rider*, and *A Very Young Skier*. Intermediate readers will enjoy Jean Fritz's *The Double Life of Pocahontas*, Patricia Lauber's *Lost Star: The Story of Amelia Earhart*, or the journal form of Virginia Hamilton's *Anthony Burns: The Defeat and Triumph of a Fugitive Slave*. Intermediate and older students who are interested in the lives of favorite authors might read Betsy Lee's *Judy Blume's Story*, Beverly Cleary's memoir *A Girl from Yamhill*, or M. E. Kerr's *ME ME ME ME ME: Not a Novel*.

BIOGRAPHY AND AUTOBIOGRAPHY IN CONTENT AREAS AND THEMATIC UNITS

Many research projects or thematic units will be enhanced by coupling biography with other reading. Nancy DeVries Guth found that biography provided the springboard for the study of a decade; this work eventually led to studying the future with her at-risk, middle school students (1992). Martha Ward Plowden has collected a series of profiles in *Famous Firsts of Black Women*, and Willow Ann Sirch profiles women who led the fight to protect the environment in *Eco-Women: Protectors of the Earth*. Older readers will enjoy Ann Petry's *Harriet Tubman: Conductor on the Underground Railroad*. Emma Gelders Sterne's *They Took Their Stand* provides information about 12 people who struggled for equal rights, and Dee Brown offers *The Gentle Tamers: Women of the Old Wild West*. Ruth Minsky Sender's memoir, *The Cage*, describes her family's struggle to survive during Nazi rule for two years and can be combined with *Anne Frank: The Diary of a Young Girl*. Students studying China will appreciate Jean Fritz's *Homesick: My Own Story*. Intermediate and older science fans will enjoy Ellen R. Butts and Joyce R. Schwartz's *May Chinn: The Best Medicine* or Barbara Ford's *Howard Carter: Searching for King Tut*, both part of the *Science Superstars* series.

BIOGRAPHY AND AUTOBIOGRAPHY AS MODELS FOR WRITING

In *Lives of Promise: Studies in Biography and Family History*, Jerry Flack states that biography is the "key that unlocks the corridors of history for youth," and that biography should be appreciated through four R's: reflecting, responding, researching, and 'riting (1992, 1). All of the previously mentioned titles can serve as models for writing. Primary students will be amused by Robert Quackenbush's *Don't You Dare Shoot That Bear! A Story of Theodore Roosevelt*. They may use *Self Portrait: Trina Schart Hyman* as a model for creating an

Comparing Biography and Story

GRADE LEVELS:
2 and up.

BOOKS: *The Art Lesson* by Tomie dePaola (New York: Trumpet Club, 1989).

Pablo Picasso by Ibi Lepscky (New York: Trumpet Club, 1984).

ACTIVITY: Both books explore how teachers failed to encourage individuality in two budding artists. Picasso's story is told in traditional biographical form. Although truly autobiographical, dePaola's is presented as fiction. After reading each story aloud, discuss the meaning of biography, exploring how dePaola used a true incident in his life to create a story with an important message. Older students could use this as a model for writing stories based on their own life experiences.

autobiography with pictures and text. Russell Freedman's *Lincoln: A Photobiography* is an outstanding example of the interplay of text and pictures. Another memoir of life during Nazi rule, Nelly S. Toll's *Behind the Secret Window: A Memoir of a Hidden Childhood During World War Two*, also includes 29 of the author's wartime paintings. *Ryan White: My Own Story* is a moving account of his struggle to be accepted in school while he battled AIDS. For many ideas on writing biography and autobiographies, consult Jerry Flack's resource, *Lives of Promise: Studies in Biography and Family History*. (See Spotlight 5.)

The Challenge of Censorship

You may be surprised to know that at least 12 of the books mentioned in this chapter and in Chapter 7 have been challenged or criticized because of their content. Stop reading this section now and turn to the literature references at the end of these two chapters. Review the books and list ones you think could be controversial. Then review the books in Figure 8.1. How many did you identify? Perhaps you know of others from the references that have been challenged. Why were they challenged?

The following are typical challenges brought against books: the themes, plots, or characters are "too negative"; the book conflicts with religion; its materials are subversive; the book uses "bad language"; or it's "inappropriate" (Alexander 1992, 170–172). Also, books have been challenged for containing offensive illustrations, sexual content, or satanic overtones; as being racist or frightening; and for "brainwashing" children (Layne 1995, 195). In a review of the literature, Steven L. Layne found a consistent rise in both the number of complaints against titles and the variety of titles under attack (ibid., 103).

FIGURE 8.1
Challenged Books

Challenged Books

1. Janet and Allan Ahlberg. *The Jolly Postman or Other People's Letters.* The postman becomes a bit tipsy from drinking champagne on his rounds.
2. Marion Dane Bauer. *On My Honor.* Profanity.
3. Raymond Briggs. *Father Christmas.* Santa Claus is grumpy, sits on a toilet.
4. James Lincoln Collier and Christopher Collier. *my brother Sam is dead.* Profanity.
5. *Cinderella.* Secular humanist beliefs.
6. Anne Frank. *Anne Frank: The Diary of a Young Girl.* Secular humanist beliefs.
7. Bette Green. *The Drowning of Stephan Jones.* Homosexuality.
8. Trina Schart Hyman. *Little Red Riding Hood.* Grandma drinks wine.
9. Madeleine L'Engle. *A Wrinkle in Time.* Mixed signal about good and evil.
10. C. S. Lewis. *The Lion, the Witch, and the Wardrobe.* Mysticism and violence.
11. Jack Prelutsky. *Nightmares: Poems to Trouble Your Sleep.* Too frightening, occult.
12. Shel Silverstein. *Where the Sidewalk Ends.* Inappropriate.

What may be appropriate for one age level may be uncomfortable for another level. For example, I read aloud *The Kidnapping of Aunt Elizabeth* by Barbara Ann Porte to my fourth and fifth graders without prereading it. When the book discussed folktales about women with teeth in their vaginas, I decided to discontinue the reading. A friend whose eighth grade students had researched folktales said that she and her eighth graders would have been comfortable with the reference, because they had come across those tales in their research. I learned an important lesson: Preread everything. Further, I learned that what may be uncomfortable or inappropriate for one teacher or audience (students, parents, taxpayers, administrators, concerned citizens) might be acceptable for another. Therefore, especially now that teachers and students are so immersed in literature, it is important to have some strategies in mind for dealing with potential book challenges.

First, ask your librarian about the book selection procedures in place in the library and school. A written policy is considered an important defense against censorship (Pottorff and Olthof 1993, 73); therefore, become familiar with the established school district review procedures for book challenges. Although sometimes a parent just wants to have their opinion acknowledged, the challenge process can be costly in terms of time and resources. A second strategy is to preread every book that you assign or read aloud. You cannot possibly read every book your students encounter in the library, but the only way to ensure that you will be comfortable with the content of a required book is to read it carefully. A third strategy is to keep abreast of current issues in the areas of children's and young adult literature by reading periodicals such as *Hornbook*, *The Reading Teacher*, and *Language Arts*. You may miss details such as Little Red Riding Hood carrying a bottle of wine to her grandmother or not recognize other content that might make a book controversial to a particular audience. Read articles about challenged books, so you are aware of potential problems and can thus make an informed decision about what to include in your curriculum. For further assistance and background, Bantam Doubleday Dell Books for Young Readers offers the "First Amendment First Aid Kit," available by writing to them at BDD Books for Young Readers, Publicity Department, 1540 Broadway, New York, NY 10036.

One useful strategy is to send home at the beginning of the year a list of books you plan to include in your curriculum and invite parents to preread them. This might include novel sets that students will be reading or bibliographies for literature projects. Protect your reading program by considering what, if any, complaints might surface (Layne 1995, 104). Know your audience! And, if you choose to use a book that might be considered controversial, be sure to discuss this with your administrator. Ask your library media specialist for alternatives in case a parent objects to it.

A final strategy is to build student responsibility and decision making into every aspect of the classroom. When students and parents have choices, they will take ownership in the reading program. Once parents are committed, there will be fewer problems. However, respect the opinions parents have that might differ from your own. Finally, remember that discussing censorship is an important right, or "by default we will all become trapped in the reality that others will make the decisions about how we are going to live together without allowing us to discuss how we wish to live together. These are the high stakes with which we play if we ignore overt and covert censorship of children's books" (Shannon 1992, 71).

Summary

Poetry should be a regular part of the curriculum, interspersed throughout the program and the day. Students enjoy listening to and reading poetry and will be inspired to create their poems.

Informational illustrated books include factual materials, plus illustrations. Many teachers read these books aloud to their students, and individuals can read them silently for reports, thematic units, or enjoyment. Simple "how to" or series books can serve as writing models.

Biography and autobiography, written about an individual's life, are particularly useful when students are conducting research about people or a particular period of history. Many students enjoy writing profiles for content-area classes or writing an autobiography.

Because individuals can challenge the use of a particular book, teachers should become familiar with the district policies regarding book challenges. Keep abreast of the literature, read reviews, keep parents informed, and provide choices to readers.

References: Literature

Adoff, Arnold. *Sports Pages.* Illustrated by Steve Kuzma. New York: J. B. Lippincott, 1986.

Aliki. *The King's Day: Louis XIV of France.* New York: Thomas Y. Crowell, 1989.

____. *The Story of Johnny Appleseed.* New York: Simon & Schuster, 1963.

____. *Wild and Woolly Mammoths.* New York: HarperCollins, 1996.

Ancona, George. *Bananas: From Manolo to Margie.* New York: Clarion, 1982.

Badt, Karin Luisa. *Good Morning, Let's Eat!* Chicago: Childrens Press: 1994.

Barton, Byron. *Building a House.* New York: Greenwillow, 1981.

Blocksma, Mary. *Ticket to the Twenties: A Time Traveler's Guide.* Illustrated by Susan Dennen. Boston: Little, Brown, 1993.

Bourgeois, Paulette. *The Amazing Apple Book.* Illustrated by Linda Hendry. Reading, Mass.: Addison-Wesley, 1987.

Branley, Franklyn M. *What Makes a Magnet?* Illustrated by True Kelly. New York: HarperCollins, 1996.

Brown, Dee. *The Gentle Tamers: Women of the Old Wild West.* Lincoln, Nebr.: University of Nebraska Press, 1958.

Bryan, Ashley. *Sing to the Sun.* New York: HarperCollins, 1992.

Butts, Ellen R., and Joyce R. Schwartz. *May Chinn: The Best Medicine.* Illustrated by Janet Hamlin. New York: W. H. Freeman, 1995.

Cassedy, Sylvia. *Zoomrimes: Poems about Things That Go.* Illustrated by Michelle Chessare. New York: HarperCollins, 1993.

Cleary, Beverly. *A Girl from Yamhill: A Memoir.* New York: Dell, 1988.

Cole, Joanna. *The Magic Schoolbus: Lost in the Solar System.* Illustrated by Bruce Degan. New York: Scholastic, 1990.

Cooney, Barbara. *Miss Rumphius.* New York: Viking Press, 1982.

Copeland, Jeffrey S. *Speaking of Poets: Interviews with Poets Who Write for Children and Young Adults.* Urbana, Ill.: National Council of Teachers of English, 1993.

Cummings, Pat, compiler and editor. *Talking with Artists.* New York: Bradbury Press, 1992.

Cummins, Julie. *Children's Book Illustration and Design.* New York: PBC International, 1992.

Cushman, Doug. *Mouse and Mole and the All-Weather Train Ride.* New York: W. H. Freeman, 1995.

Darling, Kathy. *Rain Forest Babies.* Photographs by Tara Darling. New York: Walker, 1996.

Dear Laura: Letters from Children to Laura Ingalls Wilder. New York: HarperCollins, 1996.

de Paola, Tomie. *The Art Lesson.* New York: Trumpet Club, 1989.

Dewey, Ariane. *Naming Colors.* New York: HarperCollins, 1995.

Dorros, Arthur. *This Is My House.* New York: Scholastic, 1992.

Duncan, Beverly K. *Explore the Wild: A Nature Search-And-Find Book.* New York: HarperCollins, 1996.

Dunning, Stephen, Edward Lueders, and Hugh Smith. *Reflections on a Gift of Watermelon Pickle . . . and Other Modern Verse.* New York: Lothrop, Lee & Shepard, 1967.

Enchantment of the World. Chicago: Children's Press, various dates.

Esbensen, Barbara Juster. *Dance with Me.* Illustrated by Megan Lloyd. New York: HarperCollins, 1995.

_____. *Words with Wrinkled Knees.* Illustrated by John Stadler. New York: Thomas Y. Crowell, 1986.

Fleischman, Paul. *I Am Phoenix: Poems for Two Voices.* Illustrated by Ken Nutt. New York: Harper & Row, 1989.

_____. *Joyful Noise: Poems for Two Voices.* Illustrated by Eric Beddows. New York: Harper & Row, 1988.

Ford, Barbara. *Howard Carter: Searching for King Tut.* Illustrated by Janet Hamlin. New York: W. H. Freeman, 1995.

Frank, Anne. *Anne Frank: The Diary of a Young Girl.* New York: Washington Square Press, 1967.

Fraser, Betty. *First Things First: An Illustrated Collection of Sayings Useful and Familiar for Children.* New York: Harper & Row, 1990.

Freedman, Russell. *Buffalo Hunt.* New York: Holiday House, 1988.

_____. *Children of the Wild West.* New York: Clarion, 1983.

_____. *An Indian Winter.* New York: Holiday House, 1992.

_____. *Lincoln: A Photobiography.* New York: Scholastic, 1987.

Fritz, Jean. *The Double Life of Pocahontas.* Illustrated by Ed Young. New York: G. P. Putnam's, 1983.

_____. *Homesick: My Own Story.* New York: G. P. Putnam's, 1982.

_____. *Shh! We're Writing the Constitution.* Illustrated by Tomie dePaola. New York: Scholastic, 1987.

_____. *What's the Big Idea, Ben Franklin?* Illustrated by Margot Tomes. New York: Scholastic, 1976.

_____. *Where Do You Think You're Going, Christopher Columbus?* Illustrated by Margot Tomes. New York: G. P. Putnam's, 1980.

Gibbons, Gail. *Boat Book.* New York: Holiday House, 1983.

_____. *Check It Out! The Book About Libraries.* San Diego: Harcourt Brace Jovanovich, 1985.

Gordon, Ruth. *Pierced by a Ray of the Sun: Poems About the Times We Feel Alone.* New York: HarperCollins, 1995.

Hall, Zoe. *The Apple Pie Tree.* Illustrated by Shari Halpern. New York: Blue Sky Press, 1996.

Hamilton, Virginia. *Anthony Burns: The Defeat and Triumph of a Fugitive Slave.* New York: Alfred A. Knopf, 1988.

Heller, Ruth. *Kites Sail High: A Book About Verbs.* New York: Grosset & Dunlap, 1988.

Herzig, Alison Cragin, and Jane Lawrence Mali. *Oh, Boy! Babies!* Boston: Little, Brown, 1980.

Hopkins, Lee Bennett. *Good Rhymes, Good Times.* Illustrated by Frane Lessac. New York: HarperCollins, 1995.

_____. *Pauses: Autobiographical Reflections of 101 Creators of Children's Books.* New York: HarperCollins, 1995.

Horner, John R., and Don Lessem. *Digging Up Tyrannosaurus Rex.* New York: Crown, 1992.

Hyman, Trina Schart. *Trina Schart Hyman: Self Portrait.* Reading, Mass.: Addison-Wesley, 1981.

Kalman, Bobbie. *Food for the Settler.* New York: Crabtree, 1992.

Kerr, M. E. *ME ME ME ME ME: Not a Novel.* New York: Harper & Row, 1983.

Knight, Joan. *Bon Appétit, Bertie!* Illustrated by Penny Dann. New York: Dorling Kindersley, 1993.

Koch, Frances King. *Mariculture: Farming the Fruits of the Sea.* New York: Franklin Watts, 1992.

Krementz, Jill. *A Very Young Circus Flyer.* New York: Alfred A. Knopf, 1979.

_____. *A Very Young Musician.* New York: Simon & Schuster, 1991.

_____. *A Very Young Rider.* New York: Alfred A. Knopf, 1977.

_____. *A Very Young Skier.* New York: Penguin, 1990.

The Lands, Peoples, and Cultures Series. New York: Crabtree, various dates.

Lanksy, Bruce. *Kids Pick the Funniest Poems.* Illustrated by Steve Carpenter. Deephaven, Minn.: Meadowbrook Press, 1991.

Lauber, Patricia. *Lost Star: The Story of Amelia Earhart.* New York: Scholastic, 1988.

Lawrence, Jacob. *The Great Migration: An American Story.* New York: HarperCollins, 1993.

Lawson, Robert. *Ben and Me.* New York: Dell, 1939.

Lee, Betsy. *Judy Blume's Story.* New York: Scholastic, 1983.

Lepscky, Ibi. *Pablo Picasso.* New York: Trumpet Club, 1984.

Livingston, Myra Cohn. *New Year's Poems.* Illustrated by Margot Tomes. New York: Holiday House, 1987.

Lobel, Arnold. *The Book of Pigericks.* New York: Harper & Row, 1983.

Macaulay, David. *Castle.* Boston: Houghton Mifflin, 1977.

_____. *Cathedral.* Boston: Houghton Mifflin, 1981.

_____. *City: A Story of Roman Planning and Construction.* Boston: Houghton Mifflin, 1983.

_____. *Mill.* Boston: Houghton Mifflin, 1983.

_____. *Pyramid.* Boston: Houghton Mifflin, 1975.

_____. *Unbuilding.* Boston: Houghton Mifflin, 1980.

____. *The Way Things Work.* Boston: Houghton Mifflin, 1988.

Maestro, Betsy, and Ellen DelVecchio. *Big City Port.* New York: Four Winds Press, 1983.

Maestro, Betsy, and Giulio Maestro. *A More Perfect Union: The Story of Our Constitution.* New York: Mulberry, 1987.

Meltzer, Milton. *Hold Your Horses: A Feedbag Full of Fact and Fable.* New York: HarperCollins, 1995.

Merriam, Eve. *A Sky Full of Poems.* Illustrated by Walter Gafney-Kassell. New York: Dell, 1973.

Monro, Roxie. *The Inside-Outside Book of Paris.* New York: Dutton, 1992.

Moss, Jeff. *The Butterfly Jar.* Illustrated by Chris Demarest. New York: Bantam, 1989.

____. *The Other Side of the Door.* Illustrated by Chris Demarest. New York: Bantam, 1991.

Nye, Naomi Shihab. *This Same Sky: A Collection of Poems from Around the World.* New York: Four Winds Press, 1992.

Ohanian, Susan. *747 * DFW.* Columbus, Ohio: SRA/McGraw Hill, 1996.

O'Kelley, Mattie Lou. *From the Hills of Georgia: An Autobiography in Paintings.* Boston: Little, Brown, 1983.

Osseo-Asare, Fran. *A Good Soup Attracts Chairs: A First African Cookbook for American Kids.* Gretna, La.: Pelican, 1993.

Paulsen, Gary. *Woodsong.* New York: Penguin, 1990.

Penner, Lucille Recht. *Eating the Plates: A Pilgrim Book of Food and Manners.* New York: Macmillan, 1991.

Petry, Ann. *Harriet Tubman: Conductor on the Underground Railroad.* New York: HarperCollins, 1983.

Plowden, Martha Ward. *Famous Firsts of Black Women.* Illustrated by Ronald Jones. Gretna, La.: Pelican, 1993.

Porte, Barbara Ann. *The Kidnapping of Aunt Elizabeth.* New York: Greenwillow, 1985.

Prelutsky, Jack. *The Headless Horseman Rides Tonight: More Poems to Trouble Your Sleep.* Illustrated by Arnold Lobel. New York: Greenwillow, 1980.

____. *The New Kid on the Block.* Illustrated by James Stevenson. New York: Scholastic, 1984.

_____. *Nightmares: Poems to Trouble Your Sleep*. Illustrated by Arnold Lobel. New York: Greenwillow, 1976.

_____. *The Random House Book of Poetry for Children*. Illustrated by Arnold Lobel. New York: Random House, 1983.

_____. *Rolling Harvey Down the Hill*. Illustrated by Victoria Chess. New York: Greenwillow, 1980.

_____. *Tyrannosaurus Was a Beast*. Illustrated by Arnold Lobel. New York: Greenwillow, 1988.

Provensen, Alice, and Martin Provensen. *The Glorious Flight: Across the Channel with Louis Blériot*. New York: Viking, 1983.

_____. *Leonardo da Vinci*. New York: Viking, 1984.

Quackenbush, Robert. *Don't You Dare Shoot That Bear! A Story of Theodore Roosevelt*. Englewood Cliffs, N.J.: Prentice Hall, 1984.

Risso, Mario. *Safari Grammar*. Lincolnwood, Ill.: Passport, 1989.

Rosen, Michael J. *Food Fight*. San Diego, Calif.: Harcourt Brace, 1996.

_____. *Poetry*. New York: Simon & Schuster, 1985.

Sandler, Martin W. *Civil War*. New York: HarperCollins, 1996.

_____. *Inventors*. New York: HarperCollins, 1996.

_____. *Immigrants*. New York: HarperCollins, 1995.

Sender, Ruth Minsky. *The Cage*. New York: Bantam, 1986.

Silver, Donald M. *One Very Small Square: Busy Beaver Pond*. Illustrated by Patricia J. Wynne. New York: W. H. Freeman, 1994.

_____. *One Small Square: Cactus Desert*. Illustrated by Patricia J. Wynne. New York: W. H. Freeman, 1995.

_____. *One Very Small Square: Life on a Limb*. Illustrated by Patricia J. Wynne. New York: W. H. Freeman, 1994.

_____. *One Very Small Square: Nighttime in my Backyard*. Illustrated by Patricia J. Wynne. New York: W. H. Freeman, 1994.

Silverstein, Shel. *Falling Up*. New York: HarperCollins, 1996.

_____. *A Light in the Attic*. New York: Harper & Row, 1981.

_____. *Where the Sidewalk Ends*. New York: Harper & Row, 1974.

Simon, Seymour. *Sharks*. New York: HarperCollins, 1995.

Sirch, Willow Ann. *Eco-Women: Protectors of the Earth.* Golden, Colo.: Fulcrum, 1996.

Spier, Peter. *The Star-Spangled Banner.* New York: Doubleday, 1973.

Sterne, Emma Gelders. *They Took Their Stand.* New York: Crowell-Collier Press, 1968.

Terban, Marvin. *Guppies in Tuxedos: Funny Eponyms.* Illustrated by Giulio Maestro. New York: Clarion, 1988.

____. *Mad as a Wet Hen! And Other Funny Idioms.* Illustrated by Giulio Maestro. New York: Clarion, 1987.

Thomas, Joyce Carol. *Brown Honey in Broomwheat Tea.* Illustrated by Floyd Cooper. New York: HarperCollins, 1993.

Thomson, Peggy. *City Kids in China.* New York: HarperCollins, 1991.

Toll, Nelly S. *Behind the Secret Window: A Memoir of a Hidden Childhood During World War Two.* New York: Dial, 1993.

Waldee, Lynne Marie. *Cooking the French Way.* Minneapolis, Minn.: Lerner, 1982.

Wallace, Marianne. *America's Deserts.* Golden, Colo.: Fulcrum, 1996.

Wheeler, M. J. *First Came the Indians.* Illustrated by James Houston. New York: Atheneum, 1983.

White, Ryan, and Ann Marie Cunningham. *Ryan White: My Own Story.* New York: Dial, 1991.

Zolotow, Charlotte, *Snippets: A Gathering of Poems, Pictures, and Possibilities. . . .* Illustrated by Melissa Sweet. New York: HarperCollins, 1992.

References

Alexander, Francie. "The Censorship Challenge." In *Invitation to Read: Literature in the Reading Program,* edited by Bernice E. Cullinan, 166–176. Newark, Del.: International Reading Association, 1992.

Anthony, Rose Marie. *Fun with Choral Speaking.* Englewood, Colo.: Teacher Ideas Press, 1990.

Doiron, Ray. "Using Nonfiction in a Read-Aloud Program: Letting the Facts Speak for Themselves." *The Reading Teacher* 47, 8 (May 1994): 616–624.

Dowd, Frances Smardo. "Trends and Evaluative Criteria of Informational Books for Children." In *Using Nonfiction Trade Books in the Elementary Classroom: From Ants to Zeppelins*, edited by Evelyn B. Freeman and Diane Goetz Person, 34–43. Urbana, Ill.: National Council of Teachers of English, 1992.

Flack, Jerry. *Lives of Promise: Studies In Biography and Family History.* Englewood, Colo.: Teacher Ideas Press, 1992.

Green, Pamela. *A Matter of Fact: Using Factual Texts In the Classroom.* Armadale Vic, Australia: Eleanor Curtin, 1992.

Guth, Nancy DeVries. "Get Real, Teacher! What Happens when At-Risk Middle-School Readers Become Involved with Nonfiction." In *Using Nonfiction Trade Books in the Elementary Classroom: From Ants to Zeppelins*, edited by Evelyn B. Freeman and Diane Goetz Person, 113–122. Urbana, Ill.: National Council of Teachers of English, 1992.

Keck, Judith W. "Using a Nonfiction Author Study in the Classroom." In *Using Nonfiction Trade Books in the Elementary Classroom: From Ants to Zeppelins*, edited by Evelyn B. Freeman and Diane Goetz Person, 123–130. Urbana, Ill.: National Council of Teachers of English, 1992.

Layne, Steve L. "Censorship: The Best Defense Is a Strong Offense." *Contemporary Education* 66, no. 2 (Winter 1995): 103–105.

Pottorff, Donald D., and Kathleen Olthof. "Censorship of Children's Books on the Rise: Schools Need to Be Prepared." *Reading Improvement* 30, no. 2 (Summer 1993): 66–75.

Russell, David L. *Literature for Children: A Short Introduction.* New York: Longman, 1994.

Salesi, Rosemary. "Reading and Writing Connection: Supporting Content-Area Literacy through Nonfiction Trade Books." In *Using Nonfiction Trade Books in the Elementary Classroom: From Ants to Zeppelins*, edited by Evelyn B. Freeman and Diane Goetz Person, 86–94. Urbana, Ill.: National Council of Teachers of English, 1992.

Shannon, Patrick. "Overt and Covert Censorship of Children's Books." In *Becoming Political: Readings and Writings in the Politics of Literacy Education*, edited by Patrick Shannon, 65–71. Portsmouth, N.H.: Heinemann, 1992.

Vardell, Sylvia M., and Kathleen A. Copeland. "Reading Aloud and Responding to Nonfiction: Let's Talk about It." In *Using Nonfiction Trade Books in the Elementary Classroom: From Ants to Zeppelins*, edited by Evelyn B. Freeman and Diane Goetz Person, 76–85. Urbana, Ill.: National Council of Teachers of English, 1992.

Managing Instruction with Literature

People ask me: "What was the key to your survival?" And I struggle with that question. . . . But one thing I know for certain is that reading ran like a powerful thread through those years, keeping me in the world, stimulated and going. To read was to live, and, even today as a free man I live a fuller life with that reading done in captivity and all it meant as a part of my total experience. For I have forever in my mental bank the Old Testament Wars, the Yorkshire moors, the banks of the Seine, the Russian prison, the dark halls of Glamis Castle, the intrigues of William Casey's CIA, and all the rest that I can pull out at will to contemplate. For whatever it's worth, I feel somehow more of a man now than when that steel door clanged shut on me that June evening of 1985.

Excerpted from "Shackled Body, Free Mind," by Thomas M. Sutherland, in "Spotlight," *Rocky Mountain News* (March 27, 1994): 59A.

FOCUS QUESTIONS

1. How can I teach reading to individuals?

2. How do I use partner reading to enhance skills?

3. How can I teach using small groups?

4. How do I teach reading to learners with special needs?

5. How can technology help with the literature program?

6. How can I involve parents, college students, and other volunteers?

In his riveting essay, "Shackled Body, Free Mind," Thomas Sutherland describes how reading became his lifeline during his 2,354 days of captivity in Beirut. Guards would visit West Beirut bookshops and gather a hundred books at a time for the hostages to read. After devouring a book, Sutherland and fellow hostage Terry Anderson would spend hours discussing it.

And perhaps most importantly, we argued *about all the ideas set free from the page we read, argued and argued, honing and activating hourly our minds, interacting strongly and stridently and stimulating each other* (Sutherland 1994, 59A).

In this chapter we focus on the use of literature in the classroom because it is through reading and the discussion of reading that students hone their thinking skills, improve their writing skills, and become lifelong learners. A variety of instructional techniques is suggested for individuals and for small groups, and some, such as literature logs and partner reading, can be adapted to basal readers. Teachers who are required to use basal readers the majority of the time might choose one idea, such as the literature contract, use it for a month, and then return to the basal program. The various instructional strategies provide teachers with a program that can be changed and adapted to meet the needs of their students. See Chapter 15 for further discussion on integrating literature with basal reader instruction.

Individual Instruction

People of all ages love to discuss a good book they've just read. Book discussions begin when parents read aloud and discuss favorite books with their toddlers. They continue into the school setting with discussions with teachers and classmates and extend into adulthood with casual conversations about books or more formalized literary discussion groups. In *Learning to Read and Write Naturally*, Margaret Greer Jewell and Miles V. Zintz discuss the power of reading in an environment that values reading (1990, 124). They believe that reading and writing acquisition is a natural extension of oral language and use (ibid., 125).

In individualized instruction, personalized discussions naturally build on and develop oral language skills. Additionally, an individualized approach enables teachers to target reading concerns, to diagnose problems regularly, and to give immediate feedback on progress. Redirection can be implemented as necessary. Meaningful conversations spring from exciting or controversial readings, and students enjoy the social context individual instruction fosters. The challenge with individualized instruction is that it is time-consuming. With 25 or more students in our classes, this requires carefully organized activities. This section provides suggestions for organizing individual instruction that maximizes the benefits to children and minimizes the organizational challenges to the teacher.

INDIVIDUAL READING CONFERENCES

Book conferences with individual students can be a satisfying experience for both teacher and student. Central to a program that includes individual conferences are the student-selected readings. Such readings can come from the classroom, school, home, or public libraries. Students who are mature readers may need little or no guidance from the teacher. Those who are developing their reading skills may feel overwhelmed with the process of selecting books from the hundreds or thousands available, and they may need guidance in their choices. Teachers can narrow the scope by finding out which topics, genres, formats, or authors they enjoy, perhaps providing them with a selection of five or six books from which they can choose. Jane Hansen emphasizes that students who are allowed to choose what they read and how they respond grow confident and read more. She recommends that teachers build on reading comprehension by encouraging students to share what they know about the books, magazines, or other materials they have chosen to read (1987, 37).

Many teachers worry about how they will be able to discuss books with students if they haven't read the books themselves. Although it is certainly advisable to keep current by taking periodic refresher courses, attending conferences, reading professional literature, and reading new books regularly, it is not necessary to be an expert in children's or young adult literature to teach reading through literature, in part because students are usually eager to share their knowledge with an interested adult. In *Reading in the Elementary School* (1978), Jeannette Veatch recommends that the following four areas be explored in individual conferences:

1. *The personal involvement of the child*

   Why does a child prefer what he or she has chosen?

   Does the child have friends with the same preferences?

   Will the child recommend this story to others? To whom? Why?

   How does the story relate to the child's personality development?

2. *The ability to read and understand*

Does the child clearly understand the overall sense of the story?

Can the child read "between the lines"?

Can the child analyze the author's purposes?

Does the child catch the central thought of the material?

3. *The sheer mechanical ability of the child to read silently*

Does the child stumble over words that have no contextual clues?

Does the child show ability to use substitution when stuck on a word?

Has the child understood all of the more difficult words in the material?

4. *The ability of the child to hold an audience when reading aloud*

Do all within earshot stop what they are doing to listen?

Does the child like to "ham it up" when reading aloud?

Does the child like to prepare a story to read during sharing time—or to another grade? (1978, 68)

Students experienced in discussing books find this process enjoyable and stimulating. Those who have less experience will benefit from modeling from the teacher or another student. For example, if a conference seems to be going nowhere, the teacher might share why a book was especially enjoyable or read a favorite passage aloud and talk about the language therein. A teacher or discussion group leader can initiate wonderful discussions by merely saying, "What did you think of the book (chapter, passage, etc.)?" Students who are not yet accustomed to book discussion groups sometimes need prodding. In that event, teachers can use the list of reading conference questions in Figure 9.1 to generate discussion. These questions are not intended as a sequence of queries to assess comprehension or knowledge. Indeed, many teachers would find them confining and not suited to their philosophy. However, they can be used sparingly to "jump-start" a discussion.

A few thoughtful questions can indicate whether the student has indeed been reading and understanding the book, can elicit valuable information about the book, and can diagnose specific reading problems such as finding the main idea of a passage or chapter. It isn't always possible to have read the book, but the conversation will be more lively when both participants know the book. However, when the teacher is unfamiliar with the book, nothing is more flattering to the student than inspiring the teacher to read the book.

It can be challenging to manage 25 or 30 students, all of whom are reading different books. Managing successful literature conferences requires forethought and organization. The individual conference can be so enjoyable that

Background

What can you tell me about your book?
What kind of book is it?
What can you say about the setting?
What can you say about the characters?

Author Appreciation

Why do you think the author wrote the book?
Why do you think the author chose the title?
Does the author use any special literary devices? What are they?
Have you read other books by this author?
What would you ask the author about this book?

Comprehension

Is anything confusing to you?
What did you think about as you read the book?
What events moved the plot along?
What is the main point of the book?
Is there anything you would change about the book?
Was there a pivotal point in the book? If so, describe it.
Is there a character you would like to be?
Which characters contributed the most to the plot?
What have you learned from reading the book?

Evaluation

Is it a good book? Why or why not?
Did the book keep you reading, or did you get tired of it?
Can you compare this book to others you have read?
What was the best part?
What was the worst part?
What was the most important part?
What will you remember about the book?
Would you like to read another book like this one? Why or why not?
Would you recommend this to a friend? Why or why not?
Who might you recommend it to?

Extension

What does this book make you think about doing?
What could you do to show the best part of the book?
What could you do to show what you have learned?
What could you do to share this book with a friend without talking about it?
What could you do to compare this book to others you have read by the same author or on the same subject?

FIGURE 9.1
Reading Conference Questions

Excerpted from Suzanne I. Barchers, *Teaching Language Arts: An Integrated Approach* (Minneapolis, Minn.: West, 1994) 128.

it easily can exceed 15 minutes without careful attention to the time. Without a management system, some students may have five or six conferences in a month while others have none. Ideally, a teacher will try to meet with each primary student every day or two and with older students once or twice a week. Practically, this can be a challenging schedule to maintain.

One practice is to have a regular conference schedule whereby you see each student in a particular order, perhaps alphabetically. This assures that you see every student, but it may not be at an ideal time for discussion or when a student needs assistance. Another method is to have students sign up for conferences when they are ready. Although more personalized, this procedure does allow students to procrastinate or meet too frequently unless you monitor the schedule carefully. Some teachers combine these approaches, scheduling all students on a regular basis, while allowing some time each day for students who want to confer more frequently. Another combination approach involves having regularly scheduled conferences, plus informal, 1- or 2-minute conferences at each student's desk. Consider using a timer to keep the conference within a particular time frame, allowing for some flexibility to bring reasonable closure to the conference. An outside system, such as a timer, removes the burden from you to watch the clock so closely.

Whatever your favored system of conferences, do maintain a collaborative approach by sitting alongside rather than across from the student, by asking authentic questions, and by reacting with enthusiasm to the responses. Some teachers resist taking notes until after the conference, believing that students will be intimidated by notetaking. Other teachers believe that students recognize the diagnostic and evaluative component of any conference and accept notetaking as an important part of that process. Whatever your preference, maintain careful records to use in parent conferences and in writing reports or report cards. The notes could be placed in individual file folders or kept in a notebook with dividers until time for preparing report cards.

INSTRUCTION USING THEMES

Many teachers and entire schools often organize instruction around themes that may be related to a genre such as mysteries or to a content area such as the Revolutionary War. The theme may be limited to the language arts program or may connect two or more content areas. When limited to the reading or language arts class, students usually choose their reading selection from a bibliography prepared by the teacher or librarian. The students may have a series of individual, small-group, or whole-class assignments. The teacher may organize individual conferences in the fashion described previously or lead discussion groups that compare themes across the literature being read.

Patricia L. Roberts recommends initiating a unit through an artifact, book, video computer simulation, topical field trip, museum visit, current event, or problem to solve. In addition to reading a variety of books, students might use learning centers, read newspaper and magazine articles, listen to guest speakers, have simulated experiences, or role-play (1993, 2–10). Typical components of a thematic unit include the theme, focus, objectives, materials and resources, an initiating activity to open the unit, general activities, discussion questions, literature selections, a culminating activity, evaluation, and related works of literature (Fredericks, Meinbach, and Rothlein 1993, 64). When organizing for thematic approaches to literature, consider using one of the

something to try 1

Creating a Literature Log

Choose and read 10 children's books and complete a literature log for each one of them. What kind of questions did you enjoy answering? Did you want to do more logs? Consider creating a file of logs on 3 × 5 cards that could be stored in a recipe box. These could be the beginning of your classroom set that you and your students can add to over the years.

several processes—literature logs, literature contracts, paired reading, cross-age tutoring—that are described later in this chapter. (See Chapter 14 for more information on thematic teaching.)

LITERATURE LOGS

Literature log
Responses to reading literature.

A **literature log** encourages students to respond to the literature they are reading. Sometimes referred to as response journals, a log entry may be the starting point for the conference or merely be part of an ongoing record of responses. Carol J. Fuhler not only involves her students in responding to literature through journals, she also invites parents to participate in the journals (1994, 403). You can construct a log for students to use as a model that includes suggested lead-ins such as: "The best part was . . . ," "My favorite character was . . . ," "I laughed when . . . ," "Words I didn't understand were . . . ," and so on. Teachers generally suggest that students write one response per day. Once students are accustomed to writing responses to their reading, they can simply record their thoughts in a spiral-bound notebook. Figure 9.2 on page 282 shows Juan's week of entries about a collection of short stories he is reading. Encourage your students to augment this list with their own ideas for responses. (See Something to Try 1.)

LITERATURE CONTRACTS

Literature contract
A written agreement between the teacher and the student to complete a variety of activities related to reading a particular group of books.

A **literature contract** involves a 4- to 6-week immersion in a selected genre or theme. The teacher provides a bibliography and a variety of activities for developing receptive skills (reading, listening, vocabulary, and interpretation) and expressive skills (writing, speaking, and the arts). The key difference between this process and other units is that the student negotiates the reading and activities to be completed and signs a contract regarding those choices. The unit also includes a letter to the parents explaining the unit; student

FIGURE 9.2

Student-Prepared
Literature Log

Literature Log

Name: _Juan_

Title: _Local News_

Author: _Gary Soto_

Date: _October 15_

I laughed when I read about Weasel taking the picture of Angel when he was naked in the shower. That is something my brother would do to me if we had an instant camera.

Date: _October 16_

I will never forget when I went trick-or-treating and had my bag stolen. I wish someone like Alma would have helped me. I felt bad when she found out she wasn't invited to the party. I would have run away.

Date: _October 17_

I didn't like it that Mrs. Martinez' fence burned down. I don't think it was Alex's fault because she told him to go ahead and burn the leaves. How could he know that it would get worse?

Date: _October 18_

I liked the use of Spanish in this story, "El Radio." Patricia's parents reminded me of mine, kind of easy to get around if you're lucky.

Date: _October 19_

I didn't like how this story ended. How could Carmen let the cat bully the kitten? She seemed to care at first, but then seemed to be mean. The ending made me mad.

directions; a contract page for signatures (student, teacher, and parent); challenge options; sharing choices; and an evaluation process.

All the students read the same genre or theme, but their individual choices for books, activities, challenges, and evaluation may differ. The literature contract requires an investment in planning for the class, but during the period of the contract the students work independently, with the teacher serving as a guide and mentor. For a fully developed literature contract, see Appendix A beginning on page 520.

Partner Reading

There are many forms of reading with partners—some involve instruction and others emphasize the shared experience of enjoying a book. Paired reading emphasizes sharing the reading experience, rather than providing instruction. In contrast, peer tutoring emphasizes classmate assistance, and cross-age tutoring involves the help of an older student. Each of these programs is discussed in the following pages, and variations of them provide a wide range of support for the busy reading teacher.

PAIRED READING

Paired reading
When two students of approximately the same achievement read together collaboratively.

Paired reading, perhaps the easiest to institute, occurs in the self-contained classroom with a minimum of organization. Two students reading the same book plan their reading schedule together. The students may decide that one will read aloud one or two pages or a whole chapter to the other and then trade roles. After reading, the students might discuss the progress of the book or complete an activity. In one version, the listener summarizes the reading, and the reader clarifies the material as necessary. In another version, the listener jots down a series of questions during the reading. The listener asks the reader the questions, and they then evaluate how effectively the questions represented the events in that chapter. In still another variation, the listener jots down words or phrases that are important to the reading, using these notes to create a graphic representation of the chapter's sequence. Each of these practices applies equally well to nonfiction or fiction reading.

These practices offer the advantages of student-directed discussion and clarification of the story, characters, or plot that follow the reading. Students enjoy the socialization that accompanies paired reading, particularly as they approach the middle school years. Although paired reading most often involves students who are on approximately the same achievement level, occasionally a lower-achieving student will want to read with a stronger reader, often for social reasons. Usually, this arrangement is successful because the lower-achieving student will work extra hard to keep up, and the friend will provide assistance throughout the reading.

PEER TUTORING

Peer tutoring
When a more accomplished student tutors a younger student.

Keith Topping, an educational psychologist, has found that **peer tutoring** offers advantages to both participants, emphasizing that research demonstrates that the tutor accelerates as much, if not more, than the tutee (1989, 490). An achievement differential of approximately two years is most common; a wider differential may result in the tutor being understimulated.

Topping suggests that same-sex partners are preferable, but mixed-sex partnering does not affect results. In *Shared Reading in the Middle and High School Years*, Frank McTeague emphasizes the importance of preparing students for peer tutoring (1992, 82). He outlines the following steps for the tutor and recommends that the tutor keep a log of observations throughout the tutoring.

Notes for the Student Tutor

1. *Always approach tutees with the confident expectation that they can learn to read and write. After all, they understand spoken language, and they probably already know some things about how written language works and how it is used in everyday signs and situations. Think of the tutee as a co-reader and invite him or her to behave like a reader.*

2. *Select books that will provide an enjoyable experience for both of you. The books you choose at first may be picture books, Big Books, pattern books, or story books. These books may be found in your public library, your school library, or in the tutee's classroom. Teachers and librarians can help you in making good selections. In any case, you will want to bring along several books and allow the tutee to make a choice.*

3. *The third step in your role is called book sharing. Find a comfy place to sit together and make sure that the book is placed so either person can turn the pages easily. You begin by reading the title and author on the cover, by opening the book to the beginning and by starting to read. As you read, you are demonstrating how the print sounds, where the print is found on the page, how layout and direction works, and when pages are turned.*

4. *As you read, you should have some sense that the tutee is observing what you are doing, and is listening to where the story is going, how the text relates to the pictures, and that it is all making sense. You will know all is going well by the interest in the story, by the attentiveness to what you are doing, and by a general sense of concentration.*

5. *You may read all of the story by yourself, or you may prompt the tutee to join in, especially when you come to repeated parts, or to repeated words or predictable ones.*

6. *When you come to the end of the story, always invite tutees to tell you all about it in their own words. Just say, "Tell me all about the story in your own words." Then listen carefully and wait patiently for the tutee to tell you more. You may help the tutee to retell by using such prompts as, "What happened next?" "What else happened?" "Who else was in the story?"*

7. *Observe the retelling carefully, for it is a critical step for both you and the tutee. For the tutee, it is a satisfactory experience: It demands an ability to reconstruct the story. For you as tutor, it is important to discover what level of understanding the tutee is bringing to your shared experience. Remember, retelling is both an act of understanding and an act of composing. All of us can understand more easily than we compose.*

8. *The next step is to let the tutee guide you. Do you simply go on with other stories? Do you go back over some parts of the story you just finished? Do you, together, find key*

words or repeated words in the text? Do you go back to favorite parts, or funny parts, and read them again? Do you call it quits for the day?

9. *After several sessions together, you could invite the tutee to take turns reading back and forth with you. If you come to a tricky part (for the tutee), you take over and read it. There may now be some passages or parts the tutee can read quite well alone, even though not every word is right. The tutee may make mistakes or guesses. Be patient. Do not discourage the tutee by correcting every error. Assure the tutee that it is "okay to mess up," and remind him or her that the important thing is to "get the hang of it." The tutee should try to get the overall meaning of what you are reading together. You may be in this stage for some time, but both of you will have a sense of progress.*

10. *Whatever decisions you make now, always be careful to avoid anything which could give a sense of failure or discouragement. Your affirmation of progress is most important to the tutee's success.*

(© 1992 *Shared Reading* by Frank McTeague. Pembroke Publishers, 538 Hood Rd., Markham, Ontario L3R 3K9 Canada.)

Depending on the tutee's achievement level and the degree of progress, the procedures for the student tutor will vary. The tutor may also use the strategies for summarization, questioning, and notetaking mentioned in the previous section on paired reading. During peer tutoring, the teacher circulates and monitors the students' attention to the reading, their progress, their interest levels, and the interaction between the participants. Personality problems should be handled tactfully, but quickly. Back-up tutors or routine changes will alleviate difficulties between partners.

Parents may question the wisdom of peer tutoring, believing that their high-achieving youngster will not be challenged when working with a low-achieving student. Conversely, parents of low-achieving students may believe that their child should be taught by the teacher, not by a student. Although the research supports that the high-achieving students generally make greater gains in reading skills than the low-achieving students, progress for both participants is significant (Topping 1989, 492). Be prepared to discuss the benefits of these arrangements at conferences. Parents who have concerns should have opportunities to read articles about the process and to observe peer tutoring in action.

CROSS-AGE TUTORING

Cross-age tutoring When an older student instructs a younger one.

Martha D. Rekrut, a middle school English teacher, states that pupil-to-pupil teaching is probably as old as instruction, exemplified by the monitorial system developed in England in the early 1800s. In that system, the schoolmaster routinely trained older, more accomplished students to teach the younger children (1994, 356). **Cross-age tutoring** can involve students helping younger

A teenager reads with a young student.

students within the confines of the school or between a middle school and elementary school. Another successful model involves older siblings reading to youngsters in the home (Fox and Wright 1997). A university model of a Book Buddies program pairs education students with elementary students (Bromley, Winters, and Schlimmer 1994). Although most programs involve more accomplished, older students teaching younger, less accomplished readers, some successful programs involve older and less accomplished students helping significantly younger students (Labbo and Teale 1990, Leland and Fitzpatrick 1993/94). Connie Juel found that pairing college student athletes who had reading problems with first grade students proved successful for both tutors and tutees (1991). In any program it seems to be important to pair students of the same sex, although if necessary, older girls can be successfully paired with younger boys (Rekrut 1994, 359).

Connie Morrice and Maureen Simmons (1991), intermediate and primary teachers, began a program during which students worked with their buddies throughout the year, although sometimes in the context of larger groups or the whole class. Students extended the reading into the writing and publication of Big Books. Opportunities for informal interactions were linked to holidays and other special events. Student growth, documented through anecdotal observation in the context of their whole-language classroom, plus self- and peer-evaluations confirmed that the students had improved both reading and writing skills.

Because of the challenge of working with another classroom or school, organizing a cross-age program requires management skills and dedication. The teacher in charge must ensure that progress is steady, and that all partici-

something to try 2

Become a Reading Buddy

Volunteer to be a reading buddy in a neighborhood school. Contact the school office or work with a teacher you already know and volunteer to read with a student once or twice a week. Ask the teacher to set up an advance meeting with you to determine his or her expectations. If possible, spend some time observing the teacher working with reading students before you begin the reading. Work hard at being prompt and staying on schedule so that the experience is positive. You will learn a lot from working with a student!

pants continue to benefit from the process. (See Something to Try 2.) Training should include tips in the area of interpersonal skills, management skills, and content skills, such as those Frank McTeague provides. Some programs offer formal training that involves modeling, critiquing, and feedback (Rekrut 1994, 359).

Small-Group Instruction

In *Learning to Read and Write Naturally*, Margaret Greer Jewell and Miles V. Zintz emphasize the importance of reading in the social context of the classroom, noting how assignment to traditional groups might confer status upon good readers (1990, 124). Many of you may recall being in the "good" or "poor" reading group and how that felt. As you read through the section on working with small groups later in this chapter, you will learn of many grouping possibilities that avoid this potential problem.

TEACHER-PREPARED BOOK GUIDES

Many teachers prepare book guides that use short-answer questions to determine comprehension. Although they take time, they are relatively easy to create and can be saved for use in subsequent years. To develop a variety of questions, keep in mind Benjamin S. Bloom and David Krathwohl's taxonomy: knowledge, comprehension, application, analysis, synthesis, and evaluation (1956). Questions can be drawn from the following categories:

character motivation   *prediction*   *details*
character development   *important facts* *appraisal*
vocabulary clarification   *anticipation*   *plot direction*
understanding of figures of speech *opinion*   *inference*
understanding of expressive language *synthesis*   *reflection*
story structure

LITERARY DISCUSSION GROUPS

Discussion groups can be formed when students are reading the same book, reading books on similar topics, or reading books that have no thematic connection. Dorothy J. Leal found group discussion particularly effective when groups of six third graders discussed three different types of books: storybook, information book, and informational storybook (combining characteristics of fiction and nonfiction) (1993, 115). Cathy M. Roller emphasizes that students must initiate and be actively involved in the discussions (in contrast to teacher-directed discussions) for the students to create meaning from the text (1996, 63). When working with groups, the reading conference questions in Figure 9.1 can be used to stimulate discussion, but we should recognize that student talk is valuable and may be quite different than our preconceived expectations.

When working with a group that is reading unrelated books, you can begin by asking each student to share the title, author, illustrator, and one key event in their book. Alternatives include sharing a favorite part, the most important character, the setting, or how the book begins. Limit what students share in order to give all the students a turn. The next question might ask the students to rate their book on a scale from 1 to 5, explaining why they have given the score. A final question could be to whom they would recommend the book and why. Through these three simple questions, the teacher can quickly discover whether every student is completing the reading. A convenient record-keeping form is shown in Figure 9.3.

Some teachers initiate discussions by having students engage in literary analysis. Donita Covey suggests having students create a research map that shows the physical setting of a novel (1992, 42), conducting research in the library to learn more about the historical setting (ibid., 31), or researching

FIGURE 9.3
Recordkeeping
Form

Literary Discussion Record

Name	Brought book	Participated in discussion	Showed thoughtful response	Showed interest in other books	Comments

FIGURE 9.4
Student Literary
Analysis

Emotion Diagram

Title: _____

Author: _____

Directions: Take a close look at the main problem in the story. Notice the different characters involved. Notice the different emotions felt. Fill in the diagram below showing how the different characters feel about the main issue in the book.

Main Problem:

Character: Character:
Emotions: Emotions:

Character: Character:
Emotions: Emotions:

From *Novel Strategies for Young Adults* by Donita Covey. Teacher Ideas Press, 1992.

events that occurred during the time of the novel. To explore the characters' emotions, students can create an Emotion Diagram. Students fill in a chart like the one in Figure 9.4, either individually or in small groups, then discuss their opinions.

STUDENT-IMPLEMENTED BOOK GUIDES

Our goals as reading teachers include developing comprehension skills, vocabulary, discussion skills, and responsibility in the reading process, while simultaneously promoting continued interaction with the text being read. Student-implemented book guides (SIB Guides) structure students' daily reading of chapter books while giving them ownership in the aspects of their reading that need attention. In brief, small groups of 5–10 students read a book and write a set of responses for each chapter or for a designated number of pages. Each group gathers with the teacher in turn to discuss the chapter and the students'

responses from the previous day's reading. This process can be used in place of, or as a supplement to, commercial guides or teacher-prepared guides. An underlying premise is that students are the best judges of the questions they have about the content or vocabulary. The following discussion details how to teach reading using SIB Guides.

CREATING READING GROUPS

For a typical classroom of 25–30 students whose reading achievement ranges over three grade levels, collect approximately a dozen copies each of five or six different novels of varying difficulty. This method is most effective if the novels have a common theme, such as survival. A group of survival novels for fifth or sixth grade might include *Avalanche* by Arthur Roth, *Call It Courage* by Armstrong Sperry, *The Cay* by Theodore Taylor, *Hatchet* by Gary Paulsen, *Island of the Blue Dolphins* by Scott O'Dell, *The Sign of the Beaver* by Elizabeth George Speare, or *Trouble River* by Betsy Byars. A teacher of younger students who wants to use books featuring letters, might include *Dear Mr. Blueberry* by Simon James, *Dear Mr. Henshaw* by Beverly Cleary, *Dear Sarah* by Elizabeth Borchers, *The Jolly Postman or Other People's Letters* by Janet and Allan Ahlberg, or *Nettie's Trip South* by Ann Turner. Sometimes you will be unable to collect enough novels on a theme, and your choices will be limited to whatever sets of novels you have on hand or can borrow.

Arbitrarily divide the classroom into previewing groups of approximately 10 students, either by tables, rows, or sections. Hold up each novel and give a quick book talk, providing the author, title, and a brief summary of the book. After completing all the book talks, give each section of students a set of novels and encourage them to preview each novel by reading the blurb on the back cover, paging through the book, and reading the first one or two pages. When the groups have had a chance to explore a set of novels, pass that set to the next group. Keep rotating the novels through the groups until all students have had a chance to preview all the novels. Then ask them to list their first, second, and third choices for their reading groups. Write the titles on the board and ask for a show of hands for the students' first choices for each novel, recording their choices to create three reading groups of approximately equal size. Usually, all students will get either their first or second choices. If one or two students do not have any of the three final novels on their lists, plan to let them have their first choice the next time you use this process, or let them work independently, reading their selected novel.

STARTING THE GROUPS

After groups have formed, explain that students are to read one or two chapters (depending on the length of the chapters) and that, while reading, they are to use a piece of notebook paper to record three to five responses to the reading. Vary the number of responses based on your preferences, the grade level of your students, and the reading's difficulty. Then give them a model of the SIB Guide, show it on the overhead projector, or post copies around the room.

To model how to respond, read one or two pages aloud and demonstrate on the board how you might respond. For example, the first page of *The Sign of the Beaver* includes these words that might be unfamiliar: *reckon, pine boughs,* and *cedar splints.* The reader might wonder exactly why Matt was being left alone and where he was. Responses could include questioning unknown words, expressing appreciation or criticism of the story, raising questions, and recording personal reactions. (See Figures 9.5 and 9.6 on pages 292 and 293.)

A teacher of younger students modeling this process with *Dear Mr. Henshaw* might look at page 1 and exclaim, "Look, this book begins with a letter! Let's look through it—it's all letters! I've never read a book like this before. I think I'll write 'I've never read a book of letters before. I wonder if I'll like it. Page 1.' for my first response." Next, the teacher might read page 1 aloud, while the students read along, and then say, "Look at the last sentence. It says 'We licked it.' He must have meant 'liked.' I think I'll write down 'He misspelled liked. Page 1.'" The teacher might then have everyone read page 2 silently, writing on the board, "I don't know what 'tutch' means. Page 2."

Record a variety of thoughtful responses on the board, including effective criticisms, a difficult area for early readers and writers. Finally, emphasize the importance of including the page number, as this information is necessary for the follow-up discussion. For those students who dislike interrupting their

FIGURE 9.5
Student-
Implemented
Book Guide

Book Guide

Name: _____ Date: _____

Title of Book: _____

Directions:
1. Read the assigned chapter, chapters, or pages.
2. Record your name, the date, and title of the book.
3. Write down five statements about your reading on a piece of notebook paper. You can write questions about parts you don't understand, vocabulary words, compliments, or criticisms. You may want to write how you feel about the reading, problems, characters, or plot.
4. Give thoughtful responses.
5. Include the page number for each response.
6. Keep this form in your file or notebook.

1. _____
                                                    page #
2. _____
                                                    page #
3. _____
                                                    page #
4. _____
                                                    page #
5. _____
                                                    page #

Excerpted from Suzanne I. Barchers, *Creating and Managing the Literate Classroom* (Englewood, Colo.: Teacher Ideas Press, 1990) 77.

reading to write the responses, suggest they jot down the page numbers during the reading and return later to record their responses.

TEACHING THE NOVEL

After students have had a day to select their novels and read the first assignment, assemble one of the groups, asking students to bring their response papers. It usually takes a few minutes for a group to assemble, and you can suggest that students review the chapter from the day before to refresh their memories for the discussion. You can also use this time to grade the papers if letter grades are necessary. Read each paper and determine whether students provided thoughtful responses. Students who completed five responses in a

FIGURE 9.6

Sample Student-
Implemented
Book Guide

Book Guide

Name: _Anita_ _____   Date: _May 5_ _____

Title of Book: _The Sign of the Beaver_ _____

1. _Where is Matt?_ _____   _p. 1_
                                                          page #

2. _Why did his father leave him?_ _____   _p. 1_
                                                          page #

3. _I wonder what cedar splints are._ _____   _p. 1_
                                                          page #

4. _Why do they put pine boughs over the cedar splints?_   _p. 1_
                                                          page #

5. _I like the part about the silence. "It coiled around Matt and_
   reached into his stomach to settle there in a hard knot."   _p. 2_
                                                          page #

thorough manner would receive A's, with other grades awarded accordingly. Alternatively, grading can be a simple check-off that the work was actually accomplished.

Once you have graded or reviewed all the students' papers, you can use their responses to guide the discussion. Students can keep their papers, and you can lead the discussion page by page, asking for their comments, questions, or vocabulary words from each page in the book. Or, you can collect the papers and refer to the responses to guide the discussion.

For the discussion of unknown words, have students locate the words on the page and read the sentence or paragraph aloud to the group. This practice serves several purposes: (1) Students must give directions to the group regarding the location of the sentence containing the unknown word; (2) students read and hear the word in context; (3) the teacher can assess word-recognition skills and the fluency of the student who is reading aloud; and (4) dictionary use can be reinforced. Occasionally when a student reads aloud, you will discover that some word is being pronounced incorrectly; once the correct pronunciation is provided, the student recognizes the word and knows the meaning.

When students share criticisms of what they have read, differing opinions often surface, and lively discussions ensue. Students often share their own similar experiences, giving the teacher valuable insights into how students relate to their reading. In the case of *The Sign of the Beaver* or other survival stories, students sometimes discuss being alone, making poor choices, differences and similarities of cultures, and the importance of friendships. When discussing *Dear Mr. Henshaw*, students have shared their experiences with divorce, moving to a new school, or having a parent who rarely visits.

As you and your students read the novel, opportunities for in-depth responses or extensions will naturally develop. For example, there is a delightful episode in *Dear Mr. Henshaw* during which Leigh creates an alarm for his lunchbox. Students may want to discuss situations when they were frustrated and were tempted to create unusual solutions too. Another possible extension is to write letters to authors or keep journals. Of course, for responses to occur, the text must be readable, and the point of view, plot structure, and content presented therein should have relevance to the students and intrigue them as well. The readers' previous experiences, their cognitive development and developmental levels of moral judgment, their personalities, and their expectations for reading all come into play when they respond to the text. Group extensions provide an excellent opportunity for cooperative learning and should involve all students, but individual responses should also be encouraged.

After reviewing the chapter, the group can discuss what they think will happen next and plan their next reading. Once the first group is working on the reading and other assignments, the teacher works with other groups. Teaching three groups is manageable, but if more instructional groups are necessary, consider assigning reading for two days, with discussion groups meeting every other day. In practice, some teachers prefer to meet less frequently to allow for more uninterrupted silent reading.

The SIB Guides and responses developed through this process will be suited more to the individual student than those guides a teacher could produce. For the teacher who enjoys preparing reading guides, the responses given by the students could shape a teacher-prepared guide to be used with another class. However, it should be kept in mind that SIB Guides are best used occasionally, perhaps twice a year. Because written responses are generally brief, opportunities for extended periods of writing are limited unless a writing extension is pursued at the end of the reading. Also, some students require more structured reading experiences. However, SIB Guides do encourage discussions, so these skills and thus comprehension skills and vocabulary will naturally be enriched. The SIB Guide is an excellent method for those teachers making the transition from basal reader instruction to novels or for those who want to alternate basal readers with novels.

LITERATURE CIRCLES

Literature Circles involve small groups of students reading and discussing the same book, evaluating the group process, and following up with a project that extends the reading (Samway et al. 1991, 198–199). Mimi Neamen and Mary

Strong (1992), classroom teachers in New Mexico, discuss the use of Literature Circles as a method of reading instruction in grades 3–8. Similar to the use of SIB Guides, Literature Circles emphasize cooperative learning, group account-ability, and self-evaluation. The process will be described briefly here, but readers are encouraged to consult their resource, *Literature Circles: Cooperative Learning for Grades 3–8* (1992), for fully developed units for 30 novels.

CREATING READING GROUPS

First, present the novels students will be choosing from, providing five copies for each group. Give a book talk on the novels and then have students draw numbers. List each novel on the board with five slots for the group, and pro-vide one extra group of novels to allow the students who have drawn the highest numbers some choices. For example, if you have a class of 25 students, include six novels with five slots for each novel. Some groups will have fewer than five students, but they will still be able to work together successfully. Decide how many class days the students will have to finish their reading. Most novels can be read in 10 or 15 days.

STARTING THE GROUPS

Have the groups sit together and pass out numbered copies of the novels and a folder that contains five copies of the Individual Book Checklist (see Figure 9.7), the Group Novel Checklist (see Figure 9.8 on page 296), the Daily Checklist (see Figure 9.9 on page 297), a Group Worksheet (see Figure 9.10 on page 298), and five copies of the Group Projects list (a list of possible projects tailored to the book being read). Appoint a facilitator and a checker for the first day. Have students fill out their Individual Book Checklists. Each group then decides how many pages or chapters they'll read in the allotted time. The checker completes the Group Novel Checklist and the Daily Checklist, and the facilitator reads the Group Worksheet (which explains the functions and

FIGURE 9.7
Literature Circle
Individual Book
Checklist

Book Checklist

Name: _____

Title of book: _____

Book number: _____

Number of pages to be read each day: _____

Excerpted from Mimi Neamen and Mary Strong, *Literature Circles: Cooperative Learning for Grades 3–8* (Englewood, Colo.: Teacher Ideas Press, 800-237-6124, 1992) 9.

Novel Checklist

Title of book: _____

Names of group members:

1. _____

Book # _____

2. _____

Book # _____

3. _____

Book # _____

From Mimi Neamen and Mary Strong, *Literature Circles: Cooperative Learning for Grades 3–8* (Englewood, Colo.: Teacher Ideas Press, 800-237-6124, 1992) 10.

duties of the group) aloud. Finally, the facilitator reads the Group Projects aloud (see following discussion), the group discusses possible projects, and then decides how to proceed with the reading. Examine Figures 9.7 through 9.10 to understand the mechanics of setting up the process before proceeding to the next section.

INSTRUCTION WITH LITERATURE CIRCLES

A major component of preparing for Literature Circles is designing the list of group projects. Briefly, for *The Sign of the Beaver*, Mimi Neamen and Mary Strong suggest the group choose from among the following projects: review picture books that deal with extended families and tape a favorite for younger students; create a family tree; construct three-sided models of a log house and Indian lodge; prepare a meal representing the time and setting; or design a project (1992, 76). Recognizing that students often have more creative ideas than the teacher, the final suggestion, a student-designed project, is an option for every novel. Each project involves some research, and the librarian is especially valuable as the groups work on their projects. At the conclusion of the 2- or 3-week reading period, the students present their group project to other class members. Additional assignments might include vocabulary study, finding and illustrating descriptive phrases that are representative of the author's style, or writing about the reading in a journal.

Daily Checklist

Title of Book:_____

Names	Date	Date	Date	Date	Date
1.					
2.					
3.					
4.					
5.					
Checker's Initials					

Instructions for grading:

1. If the group member has read the assigned number of pages or chapters for the previous day, place a plus ($+$) in the upper right-hand corner of the appropriate box. If the group member has not completed the assigned reading, place a minus ($-$) in the upper right-hand corner of the appropriate box. Do this at the beginning of each work session.
2. Grade daily group participation in the following manner:

   3 = Good participation
   2 = Medium participation
   1 = Little participation
   0 = No participation

Place the assigned number in the appropriate box at the end of the group work session.

Excerpted from Mimi Neamen and Mary Strong, *Literature Circles: Cooperative Learning for Grades 3–8* (Englewood, Colo.: Teacher Ideas Press, 800-237-6124, 1992) 11.

Because choice and self-monitoring are strong elements of Literature Circles, the teacher's role is largely that of observer, mentor, and participant. In a group of 25–30 students, there will be six or seven novel groups. Just spending a bit of time observing or visiting with each group takes up a fair amount of time. Occasionally, there will be problems associated with a student who

FIGURE 9.10
Literature Circle
Group Worksheet

Group Worksheet

You will read your book individually. How you choose to read is up to you. You may choose to do all your reading at home, either with a parent or sibling. You may choose to read in class, either silently or aloud. You also may choose to do a combination of both.

All the work on the group projects will be done together. When discussing how the projects will be completed, you should follow three rules of good group discussion:

1. Give everyone a fair turn.

2. Give reasons for ideas.

3. Give different ideas.

Each group will have a facilitator and a checker to ensure that the criteria for good group discussion are met. The roles of the facilitator and checker will rotate on a daily basis. Each group member will probably fulfill each role at least three times during the span of the project.

Facilitator: The facilitator sees to it that everyone in the group has an equal amount of time to talk and to listen. The facilitator is also responsible for seeking answers to questions within the group. If the group is unable to answer a question, only the facilitator is permitted to ask the teacher or librarian for help.

Checker: The checker fills in the Daily Checklist appropriately each day.

Excerpted from by Mimi Neamen and Mary Strong, *Literature Circles: Cooperative Learning for Grades 3–8* (Englewood, Colo.: Teacher Ideas Press, 800-237-6124, 1992) 12.

doesn't complete the work or is disruptive. Usually, all it takes is for the group to vote to exclude the student, who then must complete the work alone, and the student is more cooperative in the future.

EVALUATING THE GROUPS

Evaluation is based on self-evaluation and the group's input. Students complete the Group Evaluation Form (see Figure 9.11) halfway through the project and also at the conclusion. After completing the forms, each student shares the assigned grades along with their reasons for the grades. The students discuss the results with the teacher and other group members, exploring why some self-assigned grades differ markedly from those assigned by other group members. Generally, performance increases markedly after the midpoint evaluation, and grades are more consistent by the end of the unit.

Group Evaluation Form

In the space provided below, list each member of your group. Evaluate each person according to the following criteria (use the Daily Checklists to help you in your evaluation):

1. Equal share of work (or extra)

2. Consistently a good group member

3. Dependable

4. Reading always completed on time

5. Contributed ideas to the group

6. Work done neatly and with pride

Give each person a grade and tell *why* you think the person deserves that grade. Be honest.

1. Name:_____Grade: _____

   Reason: _____

2. Name:_____Grade: _____

   Reason: _____

3. Name:_____Grade: _____

   Reason: _____

Excerpted from Mimi Neamen and Mary Strong, *Literature Circles: Cooperative Learning for Grades 3–8* (Englewood, Colo.: Teacher Ideas Press, 800-237-6124, 1992) 13.

Learners with Special Needs and Second-Language Learners

Many of the preceding instructional practices are effective with special students. The individual book conference provides opportunities for the finest personalized instruction, suiting both gifted and remedial students. Thematic units can be selected that suit the interests of students. Literature logs foster writing and can be personalized through teacher responses. Literature contracts foster modification for individual needs and interests. Paired reading, peer tutoring, and cross-age reading are useful for all students. Teacher-prepared book guides will be superior to commercial guides because they will be more sensitive to the individual needs of students. Through literary discussion groups, students reap social benefits as their conversation and comprehension skills rise. Student-implemented book guides may require more guidance until the students are independent readers.

Using Literature Circles with special education students is highly recommended by Neamen and Strong. All students, whether regular or mainstreamed, choose their books and are highly motivated to function successfully within the group. Because the projects require a variety of tasks, all students have an opportunity to select tasks that are of high interest. If the class has multigrade levels (for example, a grade 3/4 combination), students focus even less on grade levels and more on books they have chosen to read. Gail Whang's classroom included nine different languages; yet Literature Circles were found to be especially effective (Samway et. al, 1991). Students understood themselves and the world better, exploring topics such as racism through reading *The Cay* by Theodore Taylor (ibid., 199). Students also began to view themselves as readers and to appreciate the power of the language, finding the process of Literature Circles to be far more enjoyable than earlier classroom reading experiences (ibid., 201). Finally, the choice of a common goal through the project promotes successful collaboration, a powerful process for all.

Reluctant readers need strong motivation to tackle a process that has so far defeated them and that has affected their self-concept. Jo Worthy (1996) recommends using pattern books that foster successful reading through their predictability. Books of poetry provide short, finite reading opportunities that can be quite sophisticated and entertaining. Worthy describes one teacher's successful unit that involved seventh graders collecting jump rope and street rhymes. Students recorded rhymes they knew from their neighborhood and interviewed older relatives about their childhood rhymes. Worthy also recommends using speeches by historical heroes, readers theatre, comic books, cartoon collections, series books, magazines, sophisticated picture books, nonfiction books, authors who appeal because of their irreverent tone (Roald Dahl, Shel Silverstein), and adult books that appeal to adolescent readers.

Developing fluency as a reader is particularly challenging for second-language learners. Timothy Rasinski emphasizes the importance of strong modeling by the teacher who reads often and with good fluency. He also recommends paired reading and repeated readings (1997, Feb. 6 presentation). In a study conducted in Fairfax County to promote fluency, second-language first graders and regular students were given audio tapes to take home each day. The researchers determined that the audiotapes especially helped the second-language students read increasingly difficult texts with fluency. The repeated reading, supported by the tapes, also established a home reading habit that proved invaluable (Blum et al. 1996, 4–5). As discussed in Chapter 3, Carole Cox and Paul Boyd-Batstone also recommend the following for second-language learners: sustained silent reading, wide independent reading, talking, responding to questions, writing in journals, projects, reading related books, reading as writing models, story dramatization, readers theatre, storytelling, puppetry, artistic response, making media (such as slides or videos), using computers, making constructions, and making books (1997, 61–66).

Managing the Use of Technology

Although most school faculties favor increasing the amount of technology available to students, such additions come at a high cost. And unless the computer is linked to a liquid crystal display projection panel, large monitor, or television, the interaction is limited to one student or a small group. When a large-screen monitor is combined with a laser disc (videodisc), the user can easily access thousands of pictures, video sequences, and music instantaneously. With a large-screen monitor, one student or the teacher controls the keyboard and mouse; however, such equipment has great potential for large-group presentations. For example, a teacher can introduce a program that will be used by individuals, demonstrate the opportunities offered by online services, or model an activity, such as creating a report or finding information in the library.

Some schools create a computer lab and schedule classes for keyboarding instruction to give students the basic skills that will be useful with all their computer work. Others place computers on carts for check-out to teachers. Another alternative involves installing one or two classroom computers that are linked to a network housed in the library. These computers can be used to access the online library catalog, a CD-ROM encyclopedia, electronic mail, a reading management program such as *Accelerated Reader*, and so forth. Creating such a network requires the leadership of an individual dedicated to providing such opportunities, often a computer specialist or the librarian. For an easy literature activity, consider finding a partner school on the Internet and organize ongoing book discussion groups.

For those classrooms without computers, a television and VCR enables children to compare books with videos. Hundreds of children's books are available on video, and students who are second-language learners or reluctant readers often benefit from seeing the video version before they read the book. The class can discuss how the media differ, how video can enhance or detract from the author's creation, and other features of the video. Teachers have

something to try 3

Videotaping the School News

If possible, begin by visiting a local news studio. Explore events in the school community that might be newsworthy, either in the recent past or in the next few days. The tape could include stories about students receiving good grades, getting awards, finding a lost item, helping a friend, and so forth. Stories about teachers and other staff should also be considered. Have students work in small groups to prepare stories about these events. For future events, they should prepare how they will handle the feature. Perhaps they will need visuals, props, or narratives. After the tape is completed, make it available for parents to view at home. This activity could be modified so that it focuses on the events that occur during the beginning of the year and is then used at Back to School Night to orient parents.

found that video cameras allow students to create their own scripts, act them out, and videotape them for general viewing. Videotaping is a good way to record special events at the school, to share events or information with a home-bound student, or to promote a special program. (See Something to Try 3.)

Involving Parents and Volunteers

Having parents and volunteers available for instruction is particularly useful in the classroom that uses literature. With some training, volunteers can assist with individual book conferences, read with a partner, or serve as tutors. "Reading Together," a VISTA project in Philadelphia whose goal was to reach two generations at a time, involved community leaders in recruiting volunteers. The focus of the program was the use of literacy prop boxes containing a chant, jingle, or fingerplays, storybooks, play objects related to the theme of the stories, and blank writing books. The leaders recruited parent volunteers who were trained on how to work with children in this setting. They then met with the students, who were not their own children, twice a week during noninstructional class time (Neuman 1995).

Although some routine small-group activities require more training than most teachers can provide, extra adults can help with many of the activities associated with thematic units, literature contracts, or Literature Circles. Perhaps the best use of any extra help you may have is in having these volunteers listen to individual students read aloud. Because fluency is often a problem for developing or remedial readers, this extra practice might be just enough to foster improvement. When you prepare volunteers to help in your classroom, be sure that you communicate your expectations clearly, perhaps preparing a list of recommendations as well. For example, you may prefer that the reading partner supply unknown words quickly so that the student can concentrate on comprehension. At other times and with other students, you may want the students to use word-identification strategies to build independence. Depending on your motivation for having the student read aloud, you may want your volunteer to supply the missing word during one session to develop fluency and to work on word-identification strategies during another session. With clear-cut goals and practices, both volunteers and students will find the experience rewarding.

A Final Note

Managing a quality reading program takes commitment, energy, and a desire to continue to learn along with your students. Making decisions about instruction should be based on your personal philosophy, the district's philosophy and also your building's philosophy, and your students' needs. However, the realities of limited resources and time will also affect your decisions. A well-managed program can give you additional leeway as to how you can best meet the needs of your students. Chapter 15 examines combining literature instruction with basal readers.

Summary

Although challenging to provide, individualized instruction is often preferred by teachers and students. Students may choose their books from various libraries, with reading conferences scheduled during their reading time. In these individual conferences, teachers can explore each student's personal involvement in their reading, their ability to read silently and understand, as well as their ability to read aloud effectively.

Teachers or entire schools may develop thematic units in which students read a variety of books and discuss them in relation to the theme. Additionally, students complete writing or arts activities, work at centers, or validate their reading through activities such as literature logs.

A literature log or response journal allows students to write about their readings. A literature contract involves several weeks of immersion in a genre or related set of books. Students negotiate the reading, activities, and assignments they will complete during the contract.

Paired reading involves two students who plan to read and discuss a book together. Peer tutoring involves two students working together, with one student approximately two years ahead in achievement level. The tutor is trained on how to help the tutee. With cross-age reading, older students help younger students.

Teacher-prepared book guides are time-consuming to create but are useful for assessing comprehension and can be used in subsequent years. Literary discussion groups may have students reading the same or different books and are more informal. Student-implemented book guides allow students to determine the questions and vocabulary words. Literature Circles involve students in choosing their books and follow-up projects in a collaborative fashion.

Special education or second-language students can participate successfully in many of these practices. It is especially helpful to these students if the class works in cooperative groups such as Literature Circles. Computers can be used with a monitor to demonstrate lessons. Schools may use computers in a lab setting for instruction, provide computers on carts, or link computers to services in the library. Teachers can also use video cassette players and video cameras to enhance the program. Parents or volunteers can be trained to help with individual conferences, small-group instruction, or tutoring.

References

Ahlberg, Janet, and Allen Ahlberg. *The Jolly Postman or Other People's Letters.* Boston: Little, Brown, 1986.

Barchers, Suzanne I. *Creating and Managing the Literate Classroom.* Englewood, Colo.: Teacher Ideas Press, 1990.

_____. *Teaching Language Arts: An Integrated Approach.* Minneapolis, Minn.: West, 1994.

Bloom, Benjamin S., and D. R. Kratwohl. *Taxonomy of Education Objectives.* New York: Longman Green, 1956.

Blum, Irene H., Patricia S. Koskinen, Nancy Tennant, E. Marie Parker, Mary Straub, and Christine Curry. "Have You Heard Any Good Books Lately? Using Audiotaped Books to Extend Classroom Literacy Instruction into the Homes of Second-Language Learners." *NRRC News* (Oct. 1996): 4–5.

Borchers, Elizabeth. *Dear Sarah.* Illustrated by Wilhelm Slote. New York: Greenwillow, 1981.

Bromley, Karen, Deborah Winters, and Kerri Schlimmer. "Book Buddies: Creating Enthusiasm for Literacy Learning." *The Reading Teacher* 47, no. 5 (Feb. 1994): 392–400.

Byars, Betsy. *Trouble River.* Illustrated by Rocco Negri. New York: Scholastic, 1969.

Cleary, Beverly. *Dear Mr. Henshaw.* Illustrated by Paul O. Zelinsky. New York: Dell, 1983.

Covey, Donita. *Novel Strategies for Young Adults.* Englewood, Colo.: Teacher Ideas Press, 1992.

Cox, Carole, and Paul Boyd-Batstone. *Crossroads: Literature and Language in Culturally and Linguistically Diverse Classrooms.* Columbus, Ohio: Merrill, 1997.

Fox, Barbara J., and Maripat Wright. "Connecting School and Home Literacy Experiences through Cross-Age Reading." *The Reading Teacher* 50, no. 5 (Feb. 1997): 396–403.

Fredericks, Anthony D., Anita Meyer Meinbach, and Liz Rothlein. *Thematic Units: An Integrated Approach to Teaching Science and Social Studies.* New York: HarperCollins, 1993.

Fuhler, Carol J. "Response Journals: Just One More Time with Feeling." *Journal of Reading* 37, no. 5 (Feb. 1994): 400–405.

Gardiner, John. *Stone Fox.* Illustrated by Marcia Sewall. New York: Harper & Row, 1980.

Hansen, Jane. *When Writers Read.* Portsmouth, N.H.: Heinemann, 1987.

James, Simon. *Dear Mr. Blueberry.* New York: Macmillan, 1991.

Jewell, Margaret Greer, and Miles V. Zintz. *Learning to Read and Write Naturally*, 2nd ed. Dubuque, Iowa: Kendall/Hunt, 1990.

Juel, Connie. "Cross-Age Tutoring between Student Athletes and At-Risk Children." *The Reading Teacher* 45, no. 3 (Nov. 1991): 178–186.

Labbo, Linda D., and William H. Teale. "Cross-Age Reading: A Strategy for Helping Poor Readers." *The Reading Teacher* 43, no. 6 (Feb. 1990): 362–369.

Leal, Dorothy J. "The Power of Literary Peer-Group Discussions: How Children Collaboratively Negotiate Meaning." *The Reading Teacher* 47, no. 2 (Oct. 1993): 114–120.

Leland, Christine, and Ruth Fitzpatrick. "Cross-Age Interaction Builds Enthusiasm for Reading and Writing." *The Reading Teacher* 47, no. 4 (Dec. 1993/Jan. 1994): 292–301.

McTeague, Frank. *Shared Reading in the Middle and High School Years.* Portsmouth, N.H.: Heinemann, 1992.

Morrice, Connie, and Maureen Simmons. "Beyond Reading Buddies: A Whole Language Cross-Age Program." *The Reading Teacher* 44, no. 8 (April 1991): 572–577.

Neamen, Mimi, and Mary Strong. *Literature Circles: Cooperative Learning for Grades 3–8.* Englewood, Colo.: Teacher Ideas Press, 1992.

Neuman, Susan B. "Reading Together: A Community-Supported Parent Tutoring Program." *The Reading Teacher* 49, no. 2 (Oct. 1995): 120–129.

O'Dell, Scott. *Island of the Blue Dolphins.* Boston: Houghton Mifflin, 1960.

Paulsen, Gary. *Hatchet.* New York: Puffin, 1990.

Rasinski, Timothy. "Teaching Reading Fluency." Colorado Council on International Reading presentation, Feb. 6, 1997.

Rekrut, Martha D. "Peer and Cross-Age Tutor: The Lessons of Research." *Journal of Reading* 37, no. 5 (Feb. 1994): 356–362.

Roberts, Patricia L. *A Green Dinosaur Day: A Guide for Developing Thematic Units in Literature-Based Instruction, K–6.* Needham Heights, Mass.: Allyn & Bacon, 1993.

Roller, Cathy M. *Variability Not Disability: Struggling Readers in a Workshop Classroom.* Newark, Del.: International Reading Association, 1996.

Roth, Arthur. *Avalanche.* New York: Scholastic, 1979.

Samway, Katharine Davies, Gail Whang, Carl Cade, Melindevic Gamil, Mary Ann Lubandina, and Kansone Phommachanh. "Reading the Skeleton, the Heart, and the Brain of a Book: Students' Perspectives on Literature Study Circles." *The Reading Teacher* 45, no. 3 (Nov. 1991): 196–205.

Soto, Gary. *Local News.* San Diego, Calif.: Harcourt Brace Jovanovich, 1993.

Speare, Elizabeth George. *The Sign of the Beaver.* New York: Dell, 1983.

Sperry, Armstrong. *Call It Courage.* New York: Macmillan, 1971.

Sutherland, Thomas M. "Shackled Body, Free Mind." in "Spotlight," *Rocky Mountain News* (March 27, 1994): 59A.

Taylor, Theodore. *The Cay.* New York: Avon, 1969.

Topping, Keith. "Peer Tutoring and Paired Reading: Combining Two Powerful Techniques." *The Reading Teacher* 42, no. 7 (March 1989): 488–494.

Turner, Ann. *Nettie's Trip South.* Illustrated by Ronald Himler. New York: Macmillan, 1987.

Veatch, Jeannette. *Reading in the Elementary School,* 2nd ed. New York: John Wiley, 1978.

Worthy, Jo. "A Matter of Interest: Literature That Hooks Reluctant Readers and Keeps Them Reading." *The Reading Teacher* 50, no. 3 (Nov. 1996): 204–212.

Integrating Reading and Writing

FOCUS QUESTIONS

1. What are the principles of an integrated reading and writing program?

2. What are the features of the writing process?

3. How do I manage the writing program?

4. How do I manage conferences?

5. How can I use technology for reading and writing?

6. How can I connect reading and writing using folk literature?

7. How can I involve parents in the reading and writing program?

THE TRADE

There once was a vain queen who had to be better than anyone else. If someone wrote a poem, she had to write an even better poem. Queen Vivian could do almost anything except write stories.

One day she learned that Gabrielle had written a story that everyone liked.

"What shall I do? I can't write stories, let alone one better than this."

She went over to her window and looked out pensively at Gabrielle's pathetic hut, planning her revenge. She ordered her royal coach to take her to Gabrielle's hut and rapped on the door.

As Gabrielle opened the door, Queen Vivian's heart sank because Gabrielle was so beautiful. Her golden, wavy hair floated about her shoulders like billowy clouds. Her face was pale like the morning sun. Her lips shimmered like dew settling on a rose.

Queen Vivian said through clenched teeth, "Hello, I'm. . . ."

"Oh, I know who you are. Please come in."

"There is something I want you to do. It involves going to a faraway island to write a book about your adventures and how you survive. I'll give you until tomorrow to decide. Good day."

She stomped outside, climbed into her carriage, and went home.

Gabrielle was very excited at this opportunity. She didn't have to think about it. She wanted to go. She threw on her jacket and started for the castle to tell Queen Vivian right away.

Vivian was talking to her accomplice while Gabrielle unknowingly passed by the open window. "I want you to bring her to the island, and two months later I want you to get the story, but leave her there. Got it?"

Gabrielle ran home as fast as her legs could go. She had to think of a plan.

(continued)

aige wrote "The Trade" after reading and analyzing many fairy tales. She had clearly internalized the elements of a traditional fairy tale and had transformed her understanding of the form into her own story, demonstrating that "stories often are shaped by organizational features that guide writers and readers through an imaginary journey . . ." (Langer 1992, 33). As teachers have searched for more authentic language arts experiences, they have found that reading and writing support each other. People often respond to what they have read with writing—for students this may be through literature logs (Chapter 9) or through writing poetry, letters, or new stories. In response to a pressing issue, they may read, do research, or write a persuasive essay. In this chapter we examine the writing process and how it relates to reading and discuss management of the program. An example of how folk literature can be used in a writing-reading program unit is also included.

The next day, the queen's accomplice escorted Gabrielle to the island. She worked intensely on her story, day in and day out. After two months' time, the accomplice came to collect the story.

"You have to go get it. It's under my bed in the hut."

"Very well." He stepped out of the boat and went to her hut. She jumped in the boat and rowed off.

The queen was waiting. "What a pleasant surprise! What am I saying? It's not a surprise at all. Where is the story? Without it you are to die!"

"Oh Queen, I have no story. But I adore and envy you so much. May I have one last request?"

The queen was flattered and sort of dazed. "Anything."

"I want to be queen for just one day. I want to know what it feels like to be so powerful."

"Fine." Queen Vivian handed her crown to Gabrielle.

Late that night, Gabrielle called a meeting with her royal servants and ordered Vivian to be taken far away.

The next morning, Gabrielle was crowned the new, official queen because Vivian was nowhere to be found. Gabrielle lived happily ever after.

Paige, grade 5

Integrating Reading and Writing

efore you continue, take a moment and list the kinds of writing experiences you had as an elementary or middle school student. Did you fill in blanks on worksheets? Write an essay on what you did last summer when you started school in the fall? Write stories after being given story starters? Write research reports that you essentially paraphrased from the encyclopedia? If you are over 30, the chances are good that these practices comprised your writing instruction. If you are younger, you may have been fortunate enough to have had teachers who were knowledgeable about the writing process and who made it their business to provide authentic and personalized writing experiences.

Today's writing program can be characterized by two words—excitement and relief. Excitement on the part of students and parents, who like the results, and relief on the part of teachers, who badly wanted to get beyond mechanics and formulas but who didn't have the tools. Today the tools exist. Whether you or your school district has chosen to adopt programs built on the ideas of Nancie Atwell, Lucy Calkins, Donald Graves, or Jane Hansen, the tools, the approaches, and the programs are out there; they are being used; and the results are strong, accomplished, and confident student writers. These writing programs encompass various approaches, but they all strive to achieve these goals:

- Build on existing knowledge and experience
- Develop common knowledge and experience
- Involve students in authentic activities
- Teach in wholes
- Support initial learning efforts
- Build student responsibility
- Encourage students to take risks
- Encourage critical thinking
- Build a supportive environment

How do these goals get met? To give you an idea, let's look at them one at a time.

BUILD ON EXISTING KNOWLEDGE AND EXPERIENCE

Most children are curious about language—they show interest in reading and writing long before they attend school. Preschoolers recognize signs they see regularly, they try to write, and they know that people read books, newspapers, and magazines (Clay 1991, 28). Dolores Durkin found that reading aloud and having an adult support and reinforce an interest in writing plays an important role in early reading (1966).

Most children, no matter what their backgrounds, come to kindergarten fully expecting to have the mysteries of reading and writing revealed on the first day. Teachers of young children build on existing knowledge from the very first day of school by celebrating and using known words with their students. Teachers of older students usually need more time to find out what background knowledge the students hold in common, perhaps by taking a reading or writing inventory that explores students' interests and experiences. Simply asking students the titles of their favorite books or the names of their favorite authors will often reveal what students love to read and also what areas of interest are common to the group.

DEVELOP COMMON KNOWLEDGE AND EXPERIENCES

Providing common learning experiences not only builds knowledge, but also begins the development of a sense of community. Whether students are together for 45 minutes or 6 hours a day, they need to feel they are part of the group, this group that will spend 9 months together learning and growing. This initial learning community is part of a larger community that includes adults, friends, relatives, professional writers, and anyone else who contributes to the reading and writing process. When you are developing this community with younger students—especially those who have had limited early-literacy experiences—your first goal will be to provide rich learning adventures, perhaps through field trips, reading aloud, trips to the library, or learning centers such as a grocery store, veterinarian's office, or restaurant. Spotlight 1 is an example of a literacy experience that really gets children involved. Older students can help decide on topics of interest for their class; these can be as varied as environmental concerns, media manipulation, or substance abuse. Exploring such topics through speakers, research, and field trips develops common experiences that enable the students to build relationships and an appreciation for their expanding understanding and knowledge.

INVOLVE STUDENTS IN AUTHENTIC ACTIVITIES

Imagine that you show up at your college reading-methods class and your professor gives you a stack of worksheets to complete. Perhaps one worksheet directs you to look up a long list of words in the dictionary and write the definitions. Another worksheet has you filling in blanks such as "Teaching with _____ involves small groups of students reading and discussing the same book. . . ." In another worksheet, multiple-choice questions ask you to identify appropriate teaching strategies for various kinds of students. Your professor gives the class directions on how to complete these worksheets, and you "get to work." You are, of course, expected to keep yourself occupied until the end of the period.

This scenario is played out every day in thousands of classrooms across the country. Students who spend hours each day filling in the blanks or circling words in word-search puzzles quickly decide that school is tedious and boring. Some tolerate it well, marking time until they move on to more interesting work. But many do not tolerate it and express their boredom and frustration through inappropriate behavior. Others just give up.

s p o t l i g h t   1

Building the Reading and Writing Connection

GRADE LEVELS:
4 and up.

BOOK: *Jumanji* by
Chris Van Allsburg
(Boston: Houghton
Mifflin, 1981).

ACTIVITY: Peter and
Judy find a game that
comes frightfully alive in
their living room, with
events such as a lion
attack and a rhinoceros
stampede. The children
can only escape by fol-
lowing the rules exactly,
so they carefully play
out the game and
return it to where they
found it in the park.
The Budwing children,
known for not following
rules, find the game at
the end of the book,
and the reader is left to
guess what happened
next. After reading the
story aloud, speculate
on what happened next
and discuss what a
sequel is. Although writ-
ing sequels can be
overused, *Jumanji* pro-
vides the perfect impe-
tus for one about the
Budwings. For a com-
plete discussion of using
Jumanji for the writing
process, see Gina
Cowin's article,
"Implementing the
Writing Process with
Sixth Graders: *Jumanji*, a
Literature Unit."
Students may also com-
pare the book to the
movie version.

Jeannette Veatch (1978, 80) suggests that all learning activities

1. Absorb pupils so that there is little need for them to interrupt themselves or the teacher who is working with individuals and groups.

2. Are open-ended in the sense that they need not all start or finish at the same time.

3. Have a strong element of self-education and self-assignment.

4. Require little formal checking and much informal teacher approval through planning and time.

5. Are notable for encouraging the unique use of ordinary materials through the initiative, originality, creativity, and inventiveness of each pupil.

6. Are regarded with enthusiasm by children, as opposed to being considered a chore, even when the activity might normally be so considered.

The activity in Spotlight 2 on page 313 fits these criteria.

TEACH IN WHOLES

The teacher who first considers broad curricular goals and then searches for authentic activities will be comfortable with Kenneth Goodman's philosophy that literacy develops from whole to part (1986, 39). For example, the middle

school teacher who decides to collaborate with the social studies teacher to study the Civil War will seek out reading and writing activities that answer questions such as "How do you suppose the ordinary soldier lived day-to-day?" or "What and when did they eat?" (Mahood 1995, 19). The intermediate teacher who needs to teach state history may have students research materials on the Internet or at a local museum and then write answers to such questions as "What was it like to live in our state 100 years ago? 200 years ago?"

All readers and writers become better when they use their skills continually. Just as students learn phonics so they can recognize words, writers learn spelling so that others can recognize what they're writing. However, neither excellent grammar nor precise spelling are the end goals in a well-thought-out writing program. Rather, they are two of many skills in this ideal program, which emphasizes editing and polishing as only part of a total process that often ends in sharing the written work. (See Spotlight 3 on page 314.)

Many students begin to think analytically about letter-sound relationships when they begin to write. This process, in turn, supports their reading (Clay 1991, 291). Many of you have probably observed preschoolers laboriously sounding out words, analyzing which letters to use to represent the sounds. The word *little* may be represented solely by an *l* by the earliest writer. Later, the writer may write *ltl*, leaving out the vowels. Think back to the discussion about how difficult it is to separate the *uh* sound from *d*, and you will understand why early writers omit the vowels. Their next step might be to write *litl*, recognizing the first vowel, but omitting the second *t* and final *e*. Each example

s p o t l i g h t   2

Giving Context to Letter Writing

GRADE LEVELS:
All grades.

BOOK: *Mushy! The Complete Book of Valentine Words* by Lynda Graham-Barber, illustrated by Betsy

Lewin (New York: Avon, 1991).

ACTIVITY: This book includes an abundance of information about Valentine's Day and related words. The section on letters (93–95) includes a love letter written in 1599. After sharing this information, discuss the possible origins of Valentine's Day, tailoring your discussion

to the grade level. Have students write love letters to a favorite relative, revising them in the correct form of a friendly letter. With intermediate and middle school students, expand the activity by reading the readers theatre script "Esther's Lacy Valentine" from Charla Pfeffinger's *Holiday Readers Theatre* (1994, 32–35).

shows an increasingly sophisticated phonemic awareness. This functional spelling that approximates the correct form is called invented spelling or temporary spelling.

J. Richard Gentry writes about a first grader who was so concerned with correctness that he would write only words that he could copy correctly (1987, 13–14). His writing was uninspired and limited. Students who are encouraged to use temporary spelling are freed from the constraints of using only words they can spell. Their writing may be more challenging to read, but it is more creative and thoughtful, and the students actively strive to relate sounds to letters, confirming and refining their choices. For more information on how reading and writing interact, consult Jane Hansen's *When Writers Read*, a resource that brings reading and writing instruction together, emphasizing how recent approaches can be used in the teaching of reading.

SUPPORT INITIAL LEARNING EFFORTS

Do you remember your first efforts to learn a new computer program? Perhaps you began by reading the manual or by using the tutorial provided within the program. If you were learning to use a word processing program, perhaps you first just wrote a letter to friends, then you wrote a short essay or paper, and finally you learned how to use visual features, such as italics and boldface. If you liked the program, you probably tackled even more sophisticated features, such as creating text boxes or using graphic elements. You may have been highly motivated and learned on your own; more likely, you had a friend who helped you out when you felt confused or overwhelmed.

spotlight 3

Reading and Writing

GRADE LEVEL: 1–4.

BOOK: *A House Is a House for Me* by Mary Ann Hoberman, illustrated by William Van Horn (New York: Viking Press, 1978).

ACTIVITY: Many types of houses, such as a hill for an ant and even a shoe for a foot, are described. Share the book. Then encourage students to look around the room and brainstorm other "houses." Have them keep a pencil and paper handy for the next day or two, recording "houses" at home, at school, on the bus, and so forth. Have students work together to compile their writings in a class Big Book, complete with illustrations.

Everyone appreciates the comfort that comes with gradual understanding of a new task and the sense of accomplishment that comes with mastery. Your students are no different. They may be motivated because they crave learning, because their parents expect them to achieve, or because they know literacy is important to their future. However, unless you are a kindergarten teacher (kindergartners are almost always excited and eager), you will also have students with little or no motivation to learn. Their apathy can be very frustrating and even daunting. Today we are interested not only in teaching our students *how* to read and write but also in encouraging them to *want* to read and write (Spaulding 1992, 177). No student comes to school expecting to fail, yet by fourth grade many students have decided they can't learn. Whatever intrinsic motivation they had is gone. In some cases, these students truly need more help than you as the classroom teacher can provide, but in most cases, they have given up because they have encountered unrelenting failure from kindergarten forward.

Turning students around means finding out where they can be successful and building on those experiences. Sometimes a beginning can be as simple as sharing with a student who dislikes reading that you noticed how much she enjoyed listening to a particular book, suggesting that she reread it independently or with a friend. Then your challenge is to build on that first success until she realizes that she is truly a learner. To build on that first success, Cheryl L. Spaulding recommends that you assign appropriate and moderately challenging tasks, that you and classmates provide these students with instructional support, that you encourage these students to extend and internalize their learning through collaboration with others (1992, 192).

BUILD STUDENT RESPONSIBILITY

Teachers who follow the directives of a basal reading program allow the publisher to decide what skills and knowledge are important. Likewise, teachers who direct the majority of the learning experiences hold the primary responsibility for student accomplishments. Students in these classrooms have little choice in directing the course of their education. Every teacher would probably agree that developing lifelong learners is a critical goal. Yet achieving this goal requires an environment that encourages students to take increasing responsibility for their own learning. For example, just a few years ago, students who could use a dictionary, encyclopedia, and the card catalog were adequately equipped for most research needs for life. Now, as online information sources become more abundant and accessible, students need to know how to use these systems effectively and efficiently. Being knowledgeable about a few subjects is secondary to knowing how to find information about many topics.

In the effective reading and writing classroom, the teacher serves as "the guide on the side, rather than the sage on the stage" (Loertscher 1995). The major curriculum may be determined by the district, but students should share in deciding how the material will be researched, mastered, and shared. A context for learning that is shaped by the teacher and students working together to find answers, solve problems, and raise new questions gives students a much-needed sense of ownership.

ENCOURAGE STUDENTS TO TAKE RISKS

Just as readers skip words, make educated guesses, or reread, so do writers approximate, draft, and revise. Getting thoughts down on paper and communicating them effectively should be the initial focus; the tools of writing, such as spelling and punctuation, don't need to be stressed until the editing and polishing stages. As students' sense of community builds, they turn to peers for validation, support, and valuable criticism on their writing efforts. Ruth Ann Freedman, a second/third grade teacher, found that when her students formed a "club" to discuss similar writing topics, their focus improved and the time they spent writing increased (1995, 104).

ENCOURAGE CRITICAL THINKING

Students who use reading and writing to further their own understanding rather than to simply produce an end result are learning to think critically. They are the ones who observe that the illustration of a character on the front of a novel doesn't match the author's written description. They are the ones who notice that the story a classmate wrote about a pesky sibling reminds them of Judy Blume's *The Pain and the Great One* (1974). They are often the ones who notice when you've misspelled a word or forgotten to fulfill a promise. When students feel like they can challenge what they have read or what has been previously assumed to be "truth," they are learning that thinking critically can be rewarding.

One fine way to encourage students to think critically is for *you* to demonstrate that "it ain't necessarily so" as you deal with print materials. Be a role model for critical thinking, remembering to offer observations, such as "I wonder if I would think the same if I were [older, younger, poor, rich, hungry, ugly, beautiful, powerful, weak, and so forth]." For an excellent exercise on critical reading, gather a variety of books on dinosaurs dating from the 1950s and have students research a few facts about dinosaurs. They will soon see that the "facts" have changed as researchers have gained new information. Similarly, information from the recent *Voyager* and *Magellan* space probes have made relatively recent books hopelessly out of date.

Let students know that it's acceptable to question what they read and that what may be one person's truth may not be another's. Use discussion time to encourage divergent viewpoints. I recall a fifth grader in our social studies class who one day took an extreme point of view on an issue. The son of a judge, he not surprisingly was skilled in the verbal arts. Out of curiosity, I let him expound for several minutes until he jumped to his feet, making his concluding remarks to enthusiastic applause. At the end of the year when I had the students write on "the Bitter and the Best" of the year, he wrote that this was the best moment for him. Like me, he didn't remember exactly what the issue was, but he remembered how good it felt to be allowed to voice his opinion without censure.

Encourage students to

observe	make assumptions	criticize
compare	collect data	summarize
classify	organize data	evaluate
interpret	apply facts in new situations	design projects
imagine	make decisions	design investigations
hypothesize		

(Raths et al. 1986, 6–18).

Students need to be able to distinguish between facts and opinions, to verify factual information, and to recognize when words are used to confuse or slant the information. Given time and experience, they will distinguish persuasive language from objective language and assess the logic of conclusions. Use current events, especially issues that directly affect your students, to encourage critical thinking. When the local newspaper has articles on a neighborhood issue, such as building a nearby highway, have students assess the reliability of the media coverage. Thinking critically should not be relegated to the reading program, but should be a part of every subject.

BUILD A SUPPORTIVE ENVIRONMENT

Using literature, as discussed in Chapters 7 and 8, is the first step toward creating an environment that supports reading and writing. Additional reading materials include magazines, newspapers, charts, maps, student and teacher writings, a variety of reference materials, and computer information resources. The writing classroom should have a variety of appropriate materials available for any type of writing. Young children can write using finger paints, chalk, markers, and crayons. Older students also enjoy a break from the usual pencil or pen. Some teachers set up a writing center where their students can find materials and reference books. Others designate an area where students can store appropriate items as needed. The organizational structure is not important. Choose one that you like, but make sure that students have easy access to writing materials and instill in them the ongoing expectation that they will write in a variety of forms every day. See Chapter 13 for more information about creating the classroom environment.

The Writing Process

By now, you have read many Spotlights that include suggestions for using books, and you've probably noticed that many of them involve writing activities. This reflects a shift from 1970s practice, where reading and writing were taught separately, to 1990s practice, where the focus is on reading and writing being taught as an integrated, fluid process. Now, reading and writing programs, developed from skills and behaviors that apply to both processes, draw upon multiple texts for writing, reporting, synthesizing, and analyzing (Tierney 1992, 249). The teacher as writer is perhaps the most important common factor in the new programs.

How we feel about ourselves as writers influences our willingness to take risks. I occasionally reread the letter from my fifth grade teacher to my parents in which she praised my reading comprehension but added that my "written communications do not measure so high." Like many of today's teachers, I never thought of myself as a writer and was in my thirties before someone suggested that I could write. That professor not only encouraged me to submit a paper for publication, she invited me to write articles with her. At the same time, I began to write with my fifth-grade students, experimenting with poetry and stories right alongside them. I still wonder if I might have begun writing at age 10 if I'd had a mentor like my professor. Happily, many of today's teachers and students consider themselves writers.

Because reading and writing are inextricably intertwined and programs vary, it is difficult to describe a typical writing program, so perhaps it's best to take another tack: How are readers and writers similar? Andrea Butler and Jan Turbill draw some insightful parallels on this question. According to their research, the proficient reader and writer brings and uses knowledge about the topic, language, and sound-symbol system to the "before reading/writing" phases. The proficient reader and writer has certain expectations based on previous reading and writing experiences, their purpose for reading and writing, and the intended audience for the reading and writing (1987, 11). Readers "draft" their read-alouds by skimming and scanning the text, searching for sense, predicting outcomes, and redefining meaning. Writers draft their writing by writing notes and ideas, developing the lead, choosing outcomes, rereading, and revising. Readers reread to clarify; writers rewrite to clarify. Readers use writing cues, such as punctuation, to enhance the meaning, while writers reread to make sure their punctuation "sculpts" the meaning properly (ibid., 13). Finally, after completing their task, proficient readers and writers respond thoughtfully and critically to their work, reflect on it, admire their success, and then want to repeat the event (ibid., 14).

In a study of how his second graders used reading and writing, Peter J. Lancia found that his students successfully *borrowed* from their readings. They borrowed entire plots for retellings or wrote new material about known characters. Sometimes they borrowed plot devices such as setting, conflict, language patterns, and vocabulary. They also borrowed elements from a genre or information from nonfiction sources (1997, 472–473).

The following model is a composite of writing models described by Nancie Atwell; Lucy Calkins; Donald Graves; Roland Huff and Charles R. Kline, Jr.; Robert J. Marzano and Philip DiStefano; and Alan Ziegler (see References). Keep in mind that although there is a generally accepted sequence to the writing process, it is also a recursive process. Some students engage in several activities at once. Some projects are abandoned long before the sharing stage. So, rather than focus on sequential and precise steps, my composite model attempts to describe the "fuzzy logic" of writing with phases. Phases, defined as periods of change or development, are more in keeping with the dynamic, fluid nature of the writing process. See Figure 10.1 for a summary of this model.

PHASE ONE: PREWRITING

Prewriting activities vary widely. Sometimes writers know exactly what they want to say and waste no time getting it down on paper. Other times, the words come painfully and slowly. When I am wrestling with a writing problem, I may have a cup of coffee, read the paper, browse my bookshelves, talk

FIGURE 10.1
The Writing Process

Phase 1: Prewriting

Exploring
Identifying motivation
Determining purpose
Choosing topic
Choosing audience
Deciding form or format
Collecting information
Verbal activities such as
    brainstorming, reading
Written activities such as lists, maps,
    outlines, freewriting

Phase 2: Drafting

Creating content without concern
    for mechanics
Organizing or reorganizing content
    to some degree

Phase 3: Revising

Clarifying content
Sharing, discussing with peers or
    teacher

Phase 4: Editing

Proofreading by author:
    punctuation, spelling, grammar
Editing by peers or teacher

Phase 5: Publishing

Rereading for self
Creating a polished form: book,
    poster, display
Verbal sharing

with my husband, do laundry, or walk the dog. Procrastination? Perhaps. But usually while engaged in those activities, something comes to mind and a solution surfaces. Students are no different. Their styles vary, and what works today may not work tomorrow. Students need to be able to explore their topic to determine their purpose and the audience they want to reach, and also to decide what form or format their writing will take. They need to feel free to collect information, brainstorm, consult experts, make lists, make outlines, and doodle. They may want to "freewrite"—that is, write with no concern for punctuation, grammar, or organization. Some students will spend a long time in this phase, while others will move through it quickly.

PHASE TWO: DRAFTING

Drafting is the "get it down on paper" stage. In this stage, writers should focus on getting their thoughts written; it is important that they postpone concerns about spelling, punctuation, and grammar. More skilled writers will work from an outline or notes, organizing the entire piece as they go along. Other writers will delay the organization until they revise. Many students will share this first version with a trusted peer.

PHASE THREE: REVISING

During this phase, writers focus on revising content. In most writing classes, students will share their first draft with a peer or small group, noting suggestions or questions. Just as many professional writers have developmental editors who help them plan substantive changes, so do students rely on each other to respond to organization, content, and voice. The revision phase is usually rather messy, as writers cut and paste sections, add notes in the margins, experiment with synonyms, add details to build characterization, clarify portions, or rewrite major sections. Students working on computers particularly appreciate a word processor program during this phase. Writers may share their revisions with peers to see whether they have solved the problems before they move on to the fourth phase, editing.

PHASE FOUR: EDITING

Professional writers also have the benefit of a copy editor and a proofreader who check for grammar, punctuation, and spelling. After the writer has revised and proofread the project, a peer editor or the teacher might make additional suggestions. Revisions are generally minor at this stage.

PHASE FIVE: PUBLISHING

Not every written piece is destined to be published. Just as readers should be allowed to abandon a book that proves to be boring or inappropriate for the intended reading purpose, writers should be allowed to abandon a piece that is not working. Further, students should have opportunities to write for the pure pleasure of the act, with no eye on a "publishable" result. More often, however, writers will need to have an audience in mind, and reaching the intended audience occurs during this final phase. Occasionally, the piece is for the writer's enjoyment only; in that case, the audience is private. "Publication" may be as formal as a poster, a book, a collection of stories or poems, a sign, a report or display, or as simple as reading a piece aloud.

Managing the Writing Program

Most writing programs intertwine three ongoing "strands" of writing experiences: daily freewriting, writing connected to reading, and informational writing. Topics come from everywhere: hobbies, concerns, books, newspapers or magazine articles, friends, the teacher, or current events. When students work in a supportive environment with strong writing models, they quickly come to enjoy the process, looking forward to the next project. Now let's examine these strands in greater detail.

A student works
on her writing.

DAILY FREEWRITING

Interactive journals
Journals with
regular entries,
student-selected
themes, and teacher
responses.

Many teachers reserve a specific time period for students to pursue and write on any topic they wish. Some use **interactive journals** in which students write a regular entry for the teacher to read. The teacher writes brief responses, developing an ongoing dialogue with the student. Susan Ohanian found that writing "letters" in notebooks to her remedial middle school students improved both their fluency and their attitudes (1994, 8). Using questions to clarify the student's thoughts and feelings improves communication (Kirby and Liner 1981, 53).

Other teachers encourage students to keep journals but do not read them or respond to them in writing. Similar to a diary, these journals may inspire other writing efforts or simply be a record of private thoughts. A **class journal**, popular with primary students, goes home with different students, who add to the collective effort. A classroom mascot, such as Paddington Bear, may accompany the journal. The entries are shared with the class upon the bear and journal's return. **Parent journals**, dedicated to communication between home and school, are particularly useful with young students or special needs students. Students and the teacher may write messages home; the parents then respond, also in writing. These processes serve as important models for the power of written communication.

Class journal
A journal with
entries from all
students. It may
be accompanied
by a class mascot.

Parent journal
A journal dedicated
to communication
between school and
home.

CONNECTING WRITING AND READING

Will Hobbs wrote the following early draft while writing *Bearstone*:

> *He made a cut in the dozen or so peach trees, about a third of the way through. He didn't want them to die. He just wanted the leaves to wither and yellow, and the peaches to shrivel.*

Now read his final paragraph:

> *He cut through the skin of the nearest tree and winced as he withdrew the saw. Beads of moisture were forming along the edges of the fresh wound. From one to the next he ran with the saw roaring at full-throttle, and he cut each of the twenty-two peach trees most of the way through. Each time, as the saw's teeth bit into the thin bark, he hollered with hurt as if he felt the saw himself. He didn't want to cut them down, he wanted them to die slowly. Before they died, their leaves would yellow and the peaches shrivel, and they would look just like his grandmother's peaches.*

Will Hobbs comments on this process:

I used to hear that it was especially important in fiction writing to show, not tell, but for a long time I didn't know how to carry it through. Cutting the peach trees, I presumed, would show Cloyd's anger without telling it. But in the first version above, how involved can the reader become? As an example, most of us have heard a chain saw before, but does the first version bring that vivid sound to mind? What makes the difference between the two selections? Everything we experience comes through our five senses, and this is especially true when we're reading.

In the first version, the narrator mostly told *that Cloyd cut the trees. In the second, the narrator* showed *it. Showing means using the five senses as you write. In the second, we're in Cloyd's shoes, experiencing this awful moment through his senses. We see the teeth of the chain saw biting into the thin bark of the peach trees. We see the little beads of sap forming. We see and feel the cut as a wound in a living thing. Implicitly, we feel the saw in our own hands and feel the vibration running through our bodies. We hear the saw roaring at full throttle. We hear Cloyd hollering with hurt, and it feels as if we're hollering with hurt.*

When the reader is shown, that's when writing comes alive, and the reader becomes emotionally involved. The scene becomes so real, it's as if you were there. The writer doesn't need to overdo it, using all five senses like a shopping list. The readers' imaginations fill the scene in with associations from their own experience. Maybe some readers smell the gas fumes from the saw!

The part that I'd done well in the first version, I saved: "their leaves would yellow and the peaches shrivel." You learn to recognize what was good, and shouldn't be abandoned.

It's easy to assume that adjectives and adverbs are the key to writing with the five senses—they do contribute—but the verbs are even more important. Strong verbs convey images extremely well and reduce the need for piling on modifiers. Note for example "winced," "ran," "bit," "hollered," "yellow," "shrivel." "Yellow" made an effective strong verb here, though it's usually used as an adjective. Look for the words that convey images from the five senses in this paragraph from Chapter 17. Concentrate on the role that the verbs play:

The big fish flip-flopped against Cloyd's leg. He nudged it back into the water with his foot, then leaped across the Rincon stream and took off running in hopes of a second glimpse of the huge bear. Once in the trees Cloyd walked softly, looking all around, and tried to listen for the bear's passage. All he could hear was the furious pounding of his own heart.

The verbs ("flip-flopped," "nudged," "leaped," etc.) power the sentences and play a key role in the imagery. "Flip-flopped" may be an unusual verb, but I like it. It makes a picture full of motion. "Against Cloyd's leg" adds the sense of touch.

Remember, a first draft is only to get something on paper that you can work with. Then you apply what you know about good writing and work toward making those words come to life. Revision becomes downright enjoyable as you see that you're making great improvements. (Unpublished paper, 1989; Quotes from *Bearstone* reprinted with the permission of Athenum Books for Young Readers, an imprint of Simon & Schuster Children's Publishing Division by Will Hobbs. © 1989 Will Hobbs.)

Reading and writing support each other when students are inspired by fine writing, and particularly when they have insights into how a writer works, such as those shared by Will Hobbs. Teachers may involve students in a unit that fosters these connections: exploring genres, authors, illustrators, or themes. Because story reading may influence story writing, teachers often immerse students in a wide-ranging reading of the literature. In a review of research on the connections between story reading and writing, Jill Fitzgerald found that extended writing experiences in response to reading stories probably enrich students' interpretations of what they read (1992, 90). A more thorough discussion of using folk literature to make the reading and writing connection follows on page 327.

INFORMATIONAL WRITING

Students engage in informational writing when they summarize material, write research reports, label drawings, record observations, take lecture notes, make lists, or organize information. Practically speaking, this form of writing will be used by adults more than creative writing, yet it is often given less attention than writing stories or poetry. When you read Chapter 11 on content-area reading, you will discover many activities that connect reading and writing to support mastery of information.

WRITING CONFERENCES

Teachers who hold writing conferences with students find that instruction becomes more personalized and targeted as the conferences continue. Donald Graves, who has written extensively on the writing process, recommends that the teacher meet with each student a minimum of once a week until students have gained confidence. Of course, some students will need more frequent conferences (1983, 143). The following 65-minute schedule is one way to model writing and conferences:

- 5 minutes—once a week only writing with the class

- 10 minutes—circulating around the class with individuals

- 20 minutes—group conferences

- 5 minutes—circulating around the class

- 15 minutes—individual conferences

- 10 minutes—all-class share time (ibid., 36)

Here is another shorter schedule:

- 10 minutes—students who need immediate help

- 15 minutes—regularly scheduled conferences

- 12 minutes—individual conferences (ibid., 142)

A conference should be a supportive, intimate conversation about the writing piece underway. The teacher should sit next to the student, rather than across a desk, thereby fostering a spirit of collaboration. There should be adequate time for the conference. At first, you may need to ask open-ended questions to initiate the discussion (see Figure 10.2 for suggested questions), but in time students will come to the conference with specific issues and problems in mind.

The conference can also be used to record observations about a student's writing progress, although record keeping should not interfere with the discussion at hand. Information gained from conferences can help you form small instructional groups to tackle specific issues such as writing effective dialogue, using correct paragraphing, or solving punctuation problems. Often it takes

Background

What can you tell me about your writing?
What can you say about the setting?
What can you say about the characters?
What is the theme?
What inspired this idea?
What were you thinking about as you wrote this?

Evaluation

How is your work going?
What problems have you had?
Have you reread what you wrote aloud?
Are you pleased with what you wrote?
What is the best or favorite part?

What is the main point of your writing?
What do you want the reader to think?
Have you read this to any other students? What did they think?

Planning

What are you ready to share?
What are your next steps?
What changes do you plan to make?
Let's think of some new directions. What do you suggest?
You seem uncomfortable with this part. What could be done with it?
How can I help you?
How can another student help you?
What are your plans for polishing this?

FIGURE 10.2
Writing Conference Questions

Excerpted from *Teaching Language Arts: An Integrated Approach* by Suzanne I. Barchers (Minneapolis, Minn.: West, 1994).

only a minute or two to reteach a forgotten or misunderstood skill, and because the skill is immediately applied, the student is more likely to internalize the information.

Using Technology

Computers with word processing programs offer one of the most effective tools for supporting the reading-writing connection. Students can write their stories, reports, poems, or essays on the computer and return later to edit and revise them. Just as we dread laboriously erasing and correcting our mistakes and hand-copying a newly organized piece, so do students enjoy "instantly" creating a clean or reorganized copy of their writing on the computer. This is no small motivation to students to increase their efficiency on the computer.

Some educators argue that students should learn keyboarding skills before they use computers for writing activities. A typing class, traditionally taught in the high school, certainly improves a student's rate and accuracy. However, others argue that youngsters often use computers long before they come to school and that slowing them down to learn correct keyboard skills delays their using the computer as a word processor. Many educators resolve this dilemma by using one of the many available typing programs as an introductory computer experience. These programs are often gamelike, and students enjoy the challenges they present. They can then begin writing with a relatively easy word processor package, progressing to more complex programs in later years.

Prompted writing programs give students a structure that includes suggestions for, and advice about, writing. The exercises help writers include more detail and also assist them with writing such items as topic sentences, summaries, and so forth. Teachers and students can also use a template (which maintains basic format or text) to change details. For example, a newsletter could have all the basic formatting developed; the students simply enter specific articles into designated boxes and make other changes as appropriate. And, of course, we teachers can use these programs to record grades, write letters to parents, or create lesson plans—the time savings are tremendous.

When technology provides instructional support, students with physical challenges may be mainstreamed into the regular classroom for increasingly longer periods of time. For example, students with cerebral palsy who have limited speaking abilities or limited use of their hands can often use a specially designed word processing program, such as the Touch Talker available from the Prentke Romich Company (Erickson and Koppenhaver 1995, 680). Adaptive devices range from a voice-activated switch to dedicated communication devices to a strap-on pencil that allows a student to write more easily. Students who struggle with reading or writing may find word processing programs helpful to deal with the mechanics they are finding troublesome. In their work with tutors and at-risk students, Susanna Duckworth and Rhonda Taylor successfully combined reading and writing instruction using multimedia lessons and student-generated hypermedia assessment portfolios (1995).

With the increasing use of CD-ROMs, students now access information and use it in reading and writing reports at an astonishly young age. Interactive encyclopedias are available for preschoolers as well as for older students, with easy opportunities to move around and find more specific information on a topic (Wepner, Seminoff, and Blanchard 1995). Charles Kinzer and Donald J. Leu found that well-designed hypermedia programs that encourage students to click on additional information as needed help eliminate comprehension differences between high and low prior-knowledge readers (1997, 131). With some authoring programs, individuals or small groups of students can create their own on-screen reports that contain video, photographs, and text. Students can even create CD-ROMs with relatively inexpensive equipment, thanks to CD-R (compact disk-recordable) technology. With the arrival of CD-E (compact disk-erasable) products, students will be able to create their own CD-ROMs and reuse them even more economically (Seymour 1996).

Making the Reading-Writing Connection with Folk Literature

Students of every age love to explore the fascinating world of folktales and fairy tales. (*Note:* Because it is difficult to distinguish some folktales from fairy tales, the term *folk literature* is used in this chapter.) The very youngest students enjoy the repetitive folktales, such as "The Three Billy Goats Gruff" and "The Three Little Pigs." Older students appreciate the universal themes such as good versus evil, conquest, and rescue.

Because variants of many folktales occur in every culture, pursuing a folk literature unit in the multicultural classroom offers opportunities to compare and contrast similar stories. For the homogeneous classroom, a multicultural emphasis helps them see the differences and likenesses around the world. For example, students reading Michael Caduto's *Earth Tales from Around the World* learn that tales from dozens of countries address similar themes. One group of second-language fifth graders read folktales and legends, discussed legends from their native countries with their parents, shared the legends in class, and wrote first drafts of representative legends. Their carefully polished final versions were proudly presented in classrooms and school libraries. Students and community alike learned a great deal about these cultures in the process (Ernst and Richard 1995, 325).

Immersing students in folk literature prepares them for a variety of inspired writing experiences. The following activities hint at the variety of possibilities that can be explored during the reading and writing of folk literature. Although many of the examples were written by intermediate students, the unit is easily adapted for younger students. Further, the activities in this unit could be applied to other genres as well. Students usually think of additional writing activities during the unit and should be encouraged to find new ways to explore the topic.

EXPLORING BACKGROUND KNOWLEDGE

Conduct a survey, such as the one shown in Figure 10.3 on page 328, to discover what your students know about folk literature. With primary students, read the statements aloud and let them guess the answers. Consider sharing only the easier stories or substituting statements for more familiar tales. Make copies for intermediate and middle school students, or use an overhead transparency if all students can read comfortably from an overhead projector. Let students take the survey independently and then have them work in small groups to see what they know collectively. Finally, discuss the answers as a whole group. Although students may not seem to know many of them at first, more answers and other stories will come to mind with some group

Folk Literature Survey

Write the name of the tale you think of when you read these statements.

1. A wolf gets to grandmother's house before a young girl.
2. A fairy godmother helps a girl go to the ball.
3. A wealthy man's bride opens a locked closet.
4. A girl saves her brothers from a life as water birds.
5. Everyone in the castle sleeps till the princess is rescued.
6. A girl spins straw into gold.
7. A witch comes to a fiery end.
8. The youngest son is helped by a clever cat.
9. The youngest daughter drops a golden ball into the well.
10. A girl runs away to the home of several short miners.
11. A poor man gets a black pudding stuck on his nose.
12. Knights ride up a slippery hill to get the golden apple.
13. A tiny boy has adventures while he travels the world.
14. A boy's wishes are granted by a genie.
15. A prince climbs a girl's hair to get to the tower.
16. A poor man gives his daughter to the white bear.
17. A beast becomes a handsome prince.
18. Gerda rescues Kai from an icy future.
19. A girl's visit upsets a home of furry creatures.
20. Some musically talented animals scare off some robbers.

Answers

1. Red Riding Hood
2. Cinderella
3. Bluebeard
4. The Wild Swans
5. Sleeping Beauty
6. Rumpelstiltskin
7. Hansel and Gretel
8. Puss and Boots
9. The Frog Prince
10. Snow White and the Seven Dwarfs
11. The Foolish Wishes
12. The Princess on the Glass Hill
13. Tom Thumb
14. Aladdin's Lamp
15. Rapunzel
16. East of the Sun and West of the Moon
17. Beauty and the Beast
18. The Snow Queen
19. Goldilocks and the Three Bears
20. Bremen Town Musicians

FIGURE 10.3
Folk Literature Survey

The above survey was inspired by "How is Your F.Q. (Folklore Quotient)?" by Sister Margaret Mary Nugent. Excerpted from *Creating and Managing the Literate Classroom* by Suzanne I. Barchers (Englewood, Colo.: Teachers Ideas Press, 1990).

discussion. Occasionally, students will know a variant or a different title. For example, "The Foolish Wishes" may be known as "The Three Wishes." Make note of those titles and once you are immersed in the unit, compare the likenesses and differences of the tales. Try the survey yourself now. (Don't feel bad if you don't do well. Most adults correctly identify approximately half the tales.)

BEGINNING THE IMMERSION

Begin by visiting the school and public libraries; the goal is to gather enough individually illustrated tales for three or four tales per student, plus at least one collection per student. Encourage students to supplement this collection with books from home, especially if they have collections in other languages or from their native cultures. Because folk literature is an oral tradition, begin by reading familiar tales aloud, such as "Cinderella" or "Sleeping Beauty." Use the illustrated versions and share the pictures with the students. If you believe that your middle school students will find illustrated versions too juvenile, read from collections first. Then share illustrated tales that have particularly engrossing illustrations, such as Marilee Heyer's *The Weaving of a Dream*. Share tales from a variety of cultures, perhaps reading from Joanna Cole's *Best Loved Folk Tales of the World*, a collection of 200 tales from the remotest parts of the world. Jane Yolen's *Favorite Folktales from Around the World* is another fine resource for various cultures, with the added bonus of being organized thematically ("The Fool: Numbskulls and Noodleheads," "Shape Shifters," etc.) Older students can also listen to novel-length versions, such as Robin McKinley's *Beauty: A Retelling of the Story of Beauty and the Beast* or Eleanor Farjeon's *The Glass Slipper*.

Vary the reading by sharing filmstrips and cassettes such as James Marshall's amusing rendition of *Goldilocks and the Three Bears* or the filmstrip or tape for *La Gallinita Roja* by Paul Galdone, the Spanish version of *The Little Red Hen*. Videos, such as *The Emperor's New Clothes*, retold by Nadine Westcott, provide a convenient supplement to the read-aloud tales. Share *The Greedy Cat*, presented in American sign language, a version that both hearing and deaf students will enjoy (Nolan and Holman, 1987). Check with your librarian or at your video store for additional titles. (Be sure to preview videos before sharing them.) As you share a variety of stories, lead students to realize the common elements of folk literature listed in Figure 10.4 on page 330.

READING THE TALES

After several days of reading aloud and discussing the tales, students will be ready to read independently. If you need to formally evaluate your students for the purposes of report cards, or if you simply prefer an accounting of the stories they read, use a literature log as in Chapter 9 or use the form shown in Figure 10.5 on page 331. Consider the grade level of the students, their skills, and your purpose for the unit before you choose a particular system of accountability. If you are using a form, model the process with two or more tales before having students work independently. Continue to read other, increasingly unfamiliar stories aloud; discuss the elements and model your

What is Folk Literature?

STORY LENGTH: The tales are generally short and simple.

TIME: Tales often begin with "Once upon a time." The time of the tale may not be given, and time may even stand still, as in "Brier Rose."

CHARACTERS: Generally only a minimum of information is provided about the characters. Stereotypes are common, such as the beautiful princess, the handsome prince, and an evil antagonist. At times, the characters are not given names. They are described according to their relationships or station in life: daughter, son, prince, princess, witch. Characters are described simply: evil or good, weak or strong, beautiful or ugly.

SETTING: The setting often receives little description. It may include a castle or a forest. Few details are provided.

STYLE: The simple style of the tales make them appealing to early writers. Only necessary words appear in the tales.

ACTION: Adventure is important to folk literature. The action gives the tale its interest, is intertwined with and carries the theme, and builds quickly to a climax.

THEME: This is the main idea of a tale and is often hardest to articulate at first. In traditional tales, the theme is usually of journey, rescue, quest, and/or conquest. Often, tasks must be performed while on a journey or quest. Asking students to identify the problem in the story helps them understand the theme. When reading tales aloud, take time to summarize the theme so students develop an understanding of the message of the tale.

MAGIC: The presence of characters with magical powers often distinguishes a fairy tale from a folktale. Although this generalization is not consistent, the role of magic is often important to the resolution of the story.

ENDING: Nearly all traditional folk literature have happy endings with a solution to the problem. The endings often include marriage of the male and female heroes.

FIGURE 10.4

Elements of Folk Literature

expectations for record keeping. As students complete the forms, they can share them with you, compile a notebook for evaluation, or share them with other students. Offer support and redirection as necessary as they complete their forms.

A folk literature unit is especially valuable for remedial students because the stories are so familiar. Mary M. Gleason recommends that teachers review parts of a story with learning disabled students, discussing how they can find the same parts in their reading or writing. She also recommends examining models of writing, analyzing their critical features, and discussing how they can be improved (1995, 99). Students without strong independent reading skills will reread familiar tales at first, perhaps reading several versions of "Sleeping Beauty." Don't push these students too quickly. They will eventually run out of the familiar stories and begin to sample other stories, perhaps some that you read aloud. Encourage students who are reluctant to leave behind a favorite story to alternate reading familiar with unfamiliar tales.

FIGURE 10.5

Sample Folk
Literature Record

Folk Literature Record

Name:_____   Date: _____

Directions: As you finish reading your selected tale, complete the following
blanks. If your tale did not have a certain element, write "none" in the blank.

Title: _____

Setting: _____

Female Hero: _____

Male Hero: _____

Other Important Characters: _____

_____

Animals: _____

Theme (What was the problem?): _____

_____

Resolution (How was the problem solved?): _____

_____

Excerpted from *Creating and Managing the Literate Classroom* by Suzanne I. Barchers (Englewood, Colo.:
Teachers Ideas Press, 1990).

WRITING POETRY

To vary the reading and initiate the writing process, introduce fairy-tale poetry.
The acrostic and diamante forms are easy for first attempts at poetry writing.
Begin by sharing examples you have created. Because these poems have a definite visual element, show them on the board or use an overhead projector as
you read them aloud. Then brainstorm a variety of key words found in folk literature: castle, kingdom, king, queen, witch, and so on. Work with the class to
create examples, leaving poems on the board while students create their own.

ACROSTIC POEMS

An acrostic poem uses a key subject word vertically. Each line begins with the
vertical letters.

Examples:

Quite grandly is how she steps in
Unison with the king on the ballroom floor
Especially if she has just
Eaten—then she dances very
Nicely.

Emily, grade 4

King Caloban
Inspiring his queen
Nodding yes to his queen
Gazing at her with happiness

Atiba, grade 4

DIAMANTE POEMS

A more challenging poetic form, the diamante reinforces several grammatical terms. Before beginning this form, gather enough thesauri for at least half your students. Share a variety of examples, using this form:

Line one: a noun that indicates the topic

Line two: two adjectives

Line three: three participles

Line four: a four-word phrase

Line five: three participles

Line six: two adjectives

Line seven: a noun that is a synonym for the noun in line one

Examples:

Prince
Handsome, kind
Daring, sharing, caring
Always there when needed
Helping, giving, protecting
Strong, brave
Man

Atiba, grade 4

King
Royal, rich
Waiting, wanting, wishing
Always needing more money
Taxing, demanding, taking
Selfish, greedy
Figurehead

Bryce, grade 4

Practice with the students as you did with the acrostic poem, reminding them of the features of nouns, participles, adjectives, and synonyms. Teach the class how to use the thesaurus to find synonyms. Once they have learned this form, introduce a new twist. This form changes focus in the fourth line, ending with an antonym. Students can split the focus in the fourth line, as in the above poem, by dividing the four words, or they can introduce a new direction through the phrase. Discuss antonyms, such as *royalty* and *peasantry* and challenge students to write their own versions.

WRITING LETTERS

Three collections of letters from fairy-tale characters inspire students to create their own communiques. Janet and Allan Ahlberg's *The Jolly Postman or Other People's Letters* begins with an apology from Goldilocks to Baby Bear and an invitation to her birthday party. The postman continues on his rounds delivering advertisements, greetings, and announcements to various familiar characters. Each item can be removed from an envelope and examined. *The Jolly Christmas Postman* follows with even more delightful missives such as a puzzle, peep show, and game. In similar style, *Dear Peter Rabbit* by Alma Flor Ada includes a series of letters revolving around the pig's housewarming party, delayed repeatedly by the wolf. After reading one or more of these books, brainstorm other possible written projects; list on the board the characters they have discovered and discuss possibilities for new connections. Use this time to discuss the appropriate form for letters, cards, or advertisements. After students have completed and revised their projects, share the results.

Example:

October 15

Dear Cinderella,

We're sorry we treated you so bad, so to make it up to you, we would like you to come to a big party on June 22. Bring your husband. There will be a lunch and dinner and a dance contest. It is at 1430 Palace Road and it's the third palace on the left.

Love,
Your Sisters

P.S. Please dress nicely.

Chris, grade 5

SOLVING PROBLEMS

George Shannon created collections of folktales that pose a problem to solve, similar to "The Wise Woman" on page 186. For example, *Stories to Solve: Fifteen Folktales from Around the World* includes the fable of the thirsty crow that comes upon a pitcher with water at the bottom, out of its reach. The following page shows and explains how the crow dropped pebbles into the pitcher until the water came within reach. Intermediate students and middle school students enjoy listening to these tales, and, after hearing a few of the easier ones, become quite creative in thinking of possible solutions to the stories. Middle school or gifted elementary students could search for additional tales that can be rewritten into similar form, or they could create their own problem-solution tales. They could also search for tales that have no solution and rewrite those in problem form.

COMPARING AND CONTRASTING FEATURES

As was noted in Chapter 5, a semantic feature analysis can be used to compare different versions of the same fairy tale. Use this process first to compare characters within a story or across stories to note patterns of characterization. Students will soon begin to see that good characters are usually portrayed as beautiful and that bad characters are portrayed as ugly or stupid. See Figure 10.6 for an example using "Cinderella."

FIGURE 10.6
Semantic Feature
Analysis for
"Cinderella"

Semantic Feature Analysis

	Beautiful or Handsome	Good	Ugly	Bad
Cinderella	+	+	−	−
Prince	+	+	−	−
Stepsisters	−	−	+	+
Stepmother	−	−	+	+

USING READERS THEATRE

Readers theatre provides students with an opportunity to read aloud, practicing their oral-delivery skills, and this treatment works very well with folk literature. First, share a readers theatre script with the students. Use the sample script at the end of this chapter or consult Barchers's *Readers Theatre for Beginning Readers* or *Scary Readers Theatre* for other scripts based on folktales. After reading a variety of scripts aloud, have students write their own scripts. Consult Shirlee Sloyer's *Readers Theatre: Story Dramatization in the Classroom* for tips on writing scripts. If you wish to produce a play, consult Paul T. Nolan's collection, *Folk Tale Plays Round the World*.

WRITING TRADITIONAL STORIES

The previously described activities usually take 3–4 weeks to accomplish. Students should be immersed in many writing activities that are inspired by the stories, letters, and poems you have shared. Once they have had a variety of writing experiences with the poems and letters, discuss the elements of the story again, perhaps creating a story map, as in Figure 10.7. Have the students

FIGURE 10.7

Story Map
for "Cinderella"

Story Map

Title of Book: *Cinderella*

Setting(s): *Cinderella's home and Prince's castle.*

Character(s): *Cinderella, Stepmother, Stepsisters, Father, Prince, Fairy Godmother.*

Problem(s): *Getting Cinderella to the ball and finding Cinderella.*

Event(s):

1. *Invitation comes for the ball.*

2. *Everyone goes to the ball except Cinderella.*

3. *Fairy Godmother sends Cinderella to the ball.*

4. *Cinderella and Prince fall in love.*

5. *Cinderella runs away.*

Resolution: *Cinderella tries on the slipper. They get married.*

begin writing their versions, using the five-phase writing process noted earlier. Once tales have been revised and polished, publish them along with the poetry, letters, and any other writings inspired by the unit.

WRITING ANIMAL TALES

Many folk stories feature animals as the main characters. Consider having your students write tales using animals as the main characters. The story in Figure 10.8, written by a fifth grader, won inclusion in the *1987 Rainbow Collection: Stories and Poetry by Young People*.

WRITING ALTERNATIVE STORIES

By now, students should realize that many of the traditional tales feature stereotypes: passive women, brave men, evil witches, good fairy godmothers. Fortunately, we have many new collections that provide a more balanced

Sir Hopalot the Frog

FIGURE 10.8
Animal Tale Sample

Once upon a time a little frog hopped away from home. He acted like he wasn't afraid, but he was. He wanted to save a lady in trouble. All he could save was a nickel and penny from his allowance. Yes, it looked hopeless for him until he met his fairy-god-frog. He got three wishes to help him get going in the real world. He asked for some food, and some clothes, and a sword.

He saw a broken down shack and it looked deserted so he helped himself in. It was the best he could get, so this became his home now. The shack had cobwebs and a damp floor. He was hungry so he took out some meat and opened the window. Soon about ten flies flew in and the frog had supper and threw the meat out. Sir Hopalot (the frog) made a bed out of leaves and went to sleep on them.

When he woke up, he heard the croaking of a female frog in trouble. He got his sword and hopped as fast as he could to the noise.

When he got there he saw his school teacher in a huge spider web. He hesitated to save her because he hated school. Then he croaked, "I'll save you if (ribbit) you never give me any work (ribbit) again!"

"It's a (ribbit) deal!" So Sir Hopalot hopped up and cut the web so she fell to the ground, safe from the spider. He finally saved a female in trouble. He wasn't going to get married or anything, but it's a start!

Doug Kingsbury, grade 5

Excerpted from *1987 Rainbow Collection: Stories and Poetry by Young People* (McLean, Va: Young Writer's Contest Foundation, 1987).

view. Sample stories from James Riordan's *The Woman in the Moon and Other Tales of Forgotten Heroines*, Ethel Johnston Phelps's *The Maid of the North: Feminist Folk Tales from Around the World*, and Suzanne Barchers's *Wise Women: Folk and Fairy Tales from around the World*. Older students may be inspired to search for additional stories that break away from the stereotypes.

Authors, such as Jon Scieszka and his illustrator Lane Smith, have provided us with humorous twists to the traditional tales; this can motivate students who would like to treat the traditional structure creatively. To begin exploring new twists on old tales, share some poems from Roald Dahl's *Revolting Rhymes*, an outrageous collection of poems based on fairy tales. (Be sure to preread these; some editing may be appropriate.) Then introduce differing points of view by using Jon Scieszka's *The True Story of the 3 Little Pigs*, told from the wolf's perspective. For a recasting of roles, share Eugene Trivizas's *The Three Little Wolves and the Big Bad Pig* or Barbara Shook Hazen's *The Knight Who Was Afraid of the Dark*. Jon Scieszka's *The Frog Prince Continued* is excellent for discussing sequels. Explore the difference the setting makes through Fiona French's *Snow White in New York* or Frances Minters's *Cinder-Elly*. The "Time Warp Trio" series includes easy chapter books using fairy-tale themes, such as *Knights of the Kitchen Table* by Jon Scieszka.

To explore how traditional fairy-tale characters can interact with new characters, share the music and book from Stephen Sondheim and James Lapine's *Into the Woods*. Perhaps the most imaginative treatment of folk literature, Jon Scieszka and Lane Smith's *The Stinky Cheese Man and Other Fairly Stupid Tales*, demonstrates just how zany characters can become when writers put their minds to it. For a clever readers theatre script, see the sample from Anthony D. Fredericks' *Frantic Frogs and Other Frankly Fractured Folktales for Readers Theatre* on page 340.

CONCLUDING THE UNIT

Consider a variety of activities to bring closure to the unit. Put copies of all the writings from the students in a large book and keep it for the next year. Have the students perform readers theatre scripts. Have the students compile a list of fairy-tale or folktale titles that can be used in a game of charades. Use the following quotes and titles for a matching game, a variation on charades, or a quiz. After they have tried it, have them make up their own quotes using the new versions of folktales or fairy tales such as Jon Scieszka's *The Frog Prince Continued*. The answers follow, so you can try the quotes yourself.

Quotes:

1. "Magic beans!"

2. "What big teeth you have!"

3. "Don't worry, dear. I can spin the straw into gold."

4. "Not by the hair of my chinny chinny chin."

5. "You must never open the closet door."

6. "This porridge is too hot!"

7. "Who's that nibbling on my house?"

8. "Let down your hair."

9. "Pay me or I will play a different tune!"

10. "We can weave you some magical cloth!"

11. "Dog, where is that wicked girl? Why didn't you bark?"

12. "How cold you look. Let me warm you."

13. "Who will help me plant the grain?"

14. "I tossed and I turned all night."

15. "But I did what you wanted. I carried the cheese on my head."

16. "Who's that tramping over my bridge?"

17. "Hi ho, hi ho, it's off to work we go."

18. "Bring me some mice and a pumpkin."

19. "Stick, stick! Hit dog!"

20. "No thanks, cousin! I'm going back to the country where I belong!"

Answers:

1. *Mother or Jack in "Jack and the Beanstalk"*

2. *Little Red Riding Hood*

3. *Rumpelstiltskin*

4. *Pigs in "The Three Little Pigs"*

5. *Bluebeard*

6. *Goldilocks in "Goldilocks and The Three Bears"*

7. *Witch in "Hansel and Gretel"*

8. *Witch or prince in "Rapunzel"*

9. *Pied Piper of Hamelin*

10. *Weavers in "The Emperor's New Clothes"*

11. *Baba Yaga*

12. *Snow Queen*

13. *Little Red Hen*

14. *Princess in "The Princess and the Pea"*

15. *Lazy Jack*

16. *Troll in "Three Billy Goats Gruff"*

17. *Dwarves in "Snow White"*

18. *Godmother in "Cinderella"*

19. *Old Woman in "The Old Woman and Her Pig"*

20. *Country Mouse in "The Town Mouse and the Country Mouse"*

A Final Note

Implicit in all the recommendations throughout this chapter is the assumption that you the teacher are a writer. Indeed, you are perhaps the most important writer in the classroom—you are a powerful model for all of your students. You may protest that you can't write. If so, how can you justify requiring your students to write? There is no mystery to writing. It is not unlike learning to play a musical instrument. Once you unlock the relationship of the symbols on the music to the keys on the instrument, you have taken your first step. Then you simply have to practice. Just like learning any new skill, you may progress quickly, or you may find the progress painstakingly slow. No matter. You will improve over time and be the richer for it.

Summary

Writing programs vary, but most programs demonstrate several generally accepted principles. Children come to school with varying levels of literacy, and teachers should build on their existing knowledge and experiences. Developing common knowledge and experiences provides a basis for learning and develops a sense of community. Activities should be authentic, absorbing, open-ended, and regarded with enthusiasm. Students should use their skills in the context of meaningful, wholistic activities. Learning should occur in manageable chunks, with successes recognized and celebrated. Students should gradually assume more responsibility for learning and should feel empowered to take risks and think critically in a supportive environment.

The writing process generally includes five phases: prewriting, drafting, revising, editing, and publishing. However, not all writing goes through each of these phases. Writing programs should include three components: daily freewriting, such as journals; writing inspired by reading, such as a poem or fairy tale; and informational writing, such as lists or research reports. Writing conferences provide opportunities for individual instruction, support, and discussion. Word processing programs can enhance the reading-writing program, giving students opportunities to edit and revise their writing easily. Immersion in a reading and writing unit, such as the folk literature example, provides many reading and writing opportunities.

Sample Readers Theatre Script

THE BIG BAD WOLF GOES TO THE DOCTOR TO FIND OUT WHY HE CAN'T HUFF AND PUFF ANYMORE (READING LEVEL: GRADE 3)

SUMMARY

The wolf, having trouble with huffing and puffing, is ridiculed by other fairy-tale characters. After going to the doctor for help, a prescription solves his problem.

STAGING

The narrator should be seated on a stool in front of the audience. The other characters should all be standing as shown below. The wolf may move across the staging area during the course of the story.

Dr. Doolittle   Big Bad Wolf
      ✖   ✖

                                        Cinderella   Hansel
                                             ✖   ✖

                              Gretel   Snow White
                                ✖   ✖

                    Goldilocks
                        ✖

          Pharmacist
              ✖

Narrator
    ✖

NARRATOR: Once upon a time there was this wolf. Now, as you might expect, this was *the* Big Bad Wolf, but you'd never know it. See, the Wolf was having some real medical problems, breathing problems to be exact. He wasn't able to huff and he wasn't able to puff. In fact, he couldn't even blow out one candle on his birthday cake. So finally he decided it was time to go to the doctor to see what could be done.

DR DOOLITTLE: Good morning, Mr. Wolf. What can we do for you today?

BIG BAD WOLF: Well, you see, Doc, I'm having some real breathing problems. Every time I visit someone's house I try to huff and I try to puff, but nothing happens. Nothing, not even a whisper. Now I'm really starting to become worried. In a few months I'm going to be in a story in which I'm supposed to blow down these houses belonging to these three little porkers, and I don't even have enough breath to whistle.

DR DOOLITTLE: Well, well, well. We can't have that, can we? What would everyone say if the Bid Bad Wolf couldn't even blow down a house made of straw? You'd probably be the laughingstock of all the fairy-tale characters for miles around. Let's take a look down that throat of yours. Say "A-h-h-h-h-h-h."

BIG BAD WOLF: A-h-h-h-h-h-h-h.

DR DOOLITTLE: H-m-m-m-m-m-m-m. I think I see the problem. It looks like you've got something stuck in your throat. I can't operate on it, but I can give you this prescription for some medicine that should take care of it.

BIG BAD WOLF: Do I have asthma, or bronchitis, or emphysema, Doc?

DR DOOLITTLE: No, it's nothing as serious as that. It's just that you have a little something down in your throat that's causing you all those breathing problems. If you just get that medicine I prescribed, then you should be fine. Come back in a week or two, and we'll see how you're doing.

BIG BAD WOLF: Thanks, Doc. See ya around.

NARRATOR: Big Bad Wolf leaves the doctor's office and walks over to the drugstore on the other side of the forest. Along the way he has to pass by several characters' houses.

CINDERELLA: (*sarcastically*) Hey, guys, look. It's the Big Bad Wimp. Oh, *excuse me*, I meant the Big Bad Wolf. Ha, ha, ha. Having a little trouble huffing and puffing, Wolfie? Ha, ha, ha.

HANSEL: Hey, you big fur ball. I bet you couldn't even huff and puff your way out of a paper bag. Ha, ha, ha.

GRETEL: Hey look, guys. Look at Mr. Big Shot now. Why he's so big and mean and strong that I bet he could probably beat up a squirrel or a chipmunk or some really dangerous creature like that. Ha, ha, ha.

SNOW WHITE: What a wimp! How does it feel now, you overgrown river rat? You just think you can waltz into any story, scare and eat up all the characters, and live happily ever after? Fat chance. Ha, ha, ha.

GOLDILOCKS: (*sarcastically*) Yeah, I bet even Little Baby Bear could beat you up with both paws tied behind his back. Ha, ha, ha. Well, how does it feel, dog breath?

NARRATOR: And so it was. One character after another made fun of the not so Big Bad Wolf as he journeyed to the drugstore to get his medicine.

BIG BAD WOLF: Here, can you fill this prescription for me?

PHARMACIST: Hey look, guys, it's the old blowhard. He wants some medicine so he can huff and puff his way through some more flimsy houses. Ha, ha, ha.

BIG BAD WOLF: (*short-tempered*) Look, wise guy, just fill the prescription.

NARRATOR: The pharmacist fills the prescription, and the Big Bad Wolf takes it home. A week later he's back in the doctor's office.

DR DOOLITTLE: Well, well, well. Don't you sound a lot better today!

BIG BAD WOLF: (*excitedly*) The change is amazing, Doc! I can huff and I can puff and I can blow down almost every house in the entire neighborhood. I feel great. I can hardly wait to get back into that story with those stupid three little pigs and really do some damage to their homes. Say, by the way, what was it that was stuck in my throat?

DR DOOLITTLE: Actually, it was some of Granny's pajamas that you swallowed during the Little Red Riding Hood story. In the future, just stay away from flannel nighties and you'll be okay.

Excerpted from *Frantic Frogs and Other Frankly Fractured Folktales for Readers Theatre* by Anthony D. Fredericks (Englewood, Colo.: Teacher Ideas Press, 1993) 64–66.

References

Ada, Alma Flor. *Dear Peter Rabbit.* New York: Atheneum, 1994.

Ahlberg, Janet, and Allan Ahlberg. *The Jolly Christmas Postman.* Boston: Little, Brown, 1991.

_____. *The Jolly Postman or Other People's Letters.* Boston: Little, Brown, 1986.

Atwell, Nancie. *In the Middle: Writing, Reading, and Learning with Adolescents.* Portsmouth, N.H.: Boynton/Cook, 1987.

Barchers, Suzanne I. *Creating and Managing the Literate Classroom.* Englewood, Colo.: Teacher Ideas Press, 1990.

_____. *Readers Theatre for Beginning Readers.* Englewood, Colo.: Teacher Ideas Press, 1993.

_____. *Scary Readers Theatre.* Englewood, Colo.: Teacher Ideas Press, 1994.

_____. *Teaching Language Arts: An Integrated Approach.* Minneapolis, Minn.: West, 1994.

_____. *Wise Women: Folk and Fairy Tales from Around the World.* Illustrated by Leann Mullineaux. Englewood, Colo.: Libraries Unlimited, 1990.

Blume, Judy. *The Pain and the Great One.* Illustrated by Irene Trivas. Scarsdale, N.Y.: Bradbury Press, 1974.

Butler, Andrea, and Jan Turbill. *Towards a Reading-Writing Classroom.* Portsmouth, N.H.: Heinemann, 1987.

Caduto, Michael. *Earth Tales from Around the World.* Illustrated by Adelaide Murphy Tyrol. Golden, Colo.: Fulcrum, 1997.

Calkins, Lucy. *The Art of Teaching Writing.* Portsmouth, N.H.: Heinemann, 1986.

Clay, Maire. *Becoming Literate: The Construction of Inner Control.* Portsmouth, N.H.: Heinemann, 1991.

Cole, Joanna, ed. *Best Loved Folk Tales of the World.* Garden City, N.Y.: Anchor Press/Doubleday, 1983.

Cowin, Gina. "Implementing the Writing Process with Sixth Graders: *Jumanji,* a Literature Unit." *The Reading Teacher* 40, no. 2 (Nov. 1986): 156–161.

Dahl, Roald. *Revolting Rhymes.* Illustrated by Quentin Blake. New York: Bantam, 1986.

Duckworth, Susanna, and Rhonda Taylor. "Creating and Assessing Literacy in At-Risk Students through Hypermedia Portfolios." *Reading Improvement* 32, no. 1 (Sept. 1995): 26–31.

Durkin, Dolores. *Children Who Read Early.* New York: Teachers College Press, 1966.

Erickson, Karen A., and David A. Koppenhaver. "Developing a Literacy Program for Children with Severe Disabilities." *The Reading Teacher* 48, no. 8 (May 1995): 676–684.

Ernst, Gisela, and Kerri J. Richard. "Reading and Writing Pathways to Conversation in the ESL Classroom." *The Reading Teacher* 48, no. 4 (Dec. 1994/Jan. 1995): 320–326.

Farjeon, Eleanor. *The Glass Slipper.* New York: HarperTrophy, 1955.

Fitzgerald, Jill. "Reading and Writing Stories." In *Reading/Writing Connections: Learning from Research,* edited by Judith W. Irwin and Mary Anne Doyle, 81–95. Newark, Del.: International Reading Association, 1992.

Freedman, Ruth Ann. "The Mr. and Mrs. Club: The Value of Collaboration in Writer's Workshop." *Language Arts* 72, no. 2 (Feb. 1995): 97–104.

Fredericks, Anthony D. *Frantic Frogs and Other Frankly Fractured Folktales.* Englewood, Colo.: Teacher Ideas Press, 1993.

French, Fiona. *Snow White in New York.* New York: Oxford University Press, 1986.

Galdone, Paul. *La Gallinita Roja.* Filmstrip and cassette, 8 minutes. Weston, Conn.: Weston Woods, no date.

Gentry, J. Richard. *Spel . . . Is a Four-Letter Word.* Portsmouth, N.H.: Heinemann, 1987.

Gleason, Mary M. "Using Direct Instruction to Integrate Reading and Writing for Students with Learning Disabilities." *Reading and Writing Quarterly* 11 (Jan.–March 1995): 91–108.

Goodman, Kenneth. *What's Whole in Whole Language?* Portsmouth, N.H.: Heinemann, 1986.

Graham-Barber, Lynda. *Mushy! The Complete Book of Valentine Words.* Illustrated by Betsy Lewin. New York: Avon, 1991.

Graves, Donald. *Writing: Teachers and Children at Work.* Portsmouth, N.H.: Heinemann, 1983.

Hansen, Jane. *When Writers Read.* Portsmouth, N.H.: Heinemann, 1987.

Hazen, Barbara Shook. *The Knight Who Was Afraid of the Dark.* Illustrated by Tony Ross. New York: Dial, 1989.

Heyer, Marilee. *The Weaving of a Dream.* New York: Viking Kestrel, 1985.

Hobbs, Will. *Bearstone.* New York: Atheneum, 1989.

———. Unpublished paper. 1989.

Hoberman, Mary Ann. *A House Is a House for Me.* Illustrated by William Van Horn. New York: Viking Press, 1978.

Huff, Roland, and Charles R. Kline, Jr. *The Contemporary Writing Curriculum: Rehearsing, Composing, and Valuing.* New York: Teachers College Press, 1987.

Kinzer, Charles, and Donald J. Leu. "The Challenge of Change: Exploring Literacy and Learning in Electronic Environments." *Language Arts* 74, no. 2 (Feb. 1997): 126–136.

Kirby, Dan, and Tom Liner. *Inside Out: Developmental Strategies for Teaching Writing.* Montclair, N.J.: Boynton/Cook, 1981.

Lancia, Peter J. "Literary Borrowing: The Effects of Literature on Children's Writing." *The Reading Teacher* 50, no. 6 (March 1997): 470–475.

Langer, Judith. "Reading, Writing, and Genre Development." In *Reading/Writing Connections: Learning from Research*, edited by Judith W.

Irwin and Mary Anne Doyle, 32–54. Newark, Del.: International Reading Association, 1992.

Loertscher, David. "Curriculum Reform and the Library Media Program." American Association of School Librarians workshop, November 1995.

Mahood, Wayne. "Bringing the American Civil War to the Classroom: Suggestions and Sources." *Social Education* 59, no. 1 (Jan. 1995): 17–22.

Marshall, James. *Goldilocks and the Three Bears.* Filmstrip and cassette, 9 minutes. Weston, Conn.: Weston Woods, no date.

Marzano, Robert J., and Philip DiStefano. *The Writing Process: Prewriting, Writing, Revising.* New York: D. Van Nostrand, 1981.

McKinley, Robin. *Beauty: A Retelling of the Story of Beauty and the Beast.* New York: HarperTrophy, 1978.

Minters, Frances. *Cinder-Elly.* Illustrated by G. Brian Karas. New York: Viking, 1994.

Nolan, Paul T. *Folk Tale Plays Round the World.* Boston: Plays, Inc., 1982.

Nolan, Sheila, and Wendy Holman. *The Greedy Cat.* Seattle, Wash.: Sign A Vision Institute, 1987.

Nugent, Sister Margaret Mary. "How is Your F.Q. (Folklore Quotient)?" In "News Letter for Professors of Children's Literature," edited by Elliott D. Landau. *Elementary English* 45 (1068): 667–668.

Ohanian, Susan. *Who's In Charge?* Portsmouth, N.H.: Boynton/Cook, 1994.

Pfeffinger, Charla. *Holiday Readers Theatre.* Englewood, Colo.: Teacher Ideas Press, 1994.

Phelps, Ethel Johnston. *The Maid of the North: Feminist Folk Tales from Around the World.* Illustrated by Lloyd Bloom. New York: Holt, Rinehart & Winston, 1981.

Raths, Louis E., Selma Wassermann, Arthur Jonas, and Arnold Rothstein. *Teaching for Thinking: Theory, Strategies and Activities for the Classroom.* New York: Teachers College Press, 1986.

Riordan, James. *The Woman in the Moon and Other Tales of Forgotten Heroines.* Illustrated by Angela Barrett. New York: Dial, 1984.

Scieszka, Jon. *The Frog Prince Continued.* Illustrated by Steve Johnson. New York: Viking, 1991.

———. *Knights of the Kitchen Table.* Illustrated by Lane Smith. New York: Puffin, 1991.

_____. *The Stinky Cheese Man and Other Fairly Stupid Tales.* Illustrated by Lane Smith. New York: Viking, 1992.

_____. *The True Story of the 3 Little Pigs.* Illustrated by Lane Smith. New York: Viking, 1989.

Seymour, Jim. "Create Your Own CD." *PC Magazine* 15, no. 7 (April 9, 1996): 99–104.

Shannon, George. *Stories to Solve: Fifteen Folktales from Around the World.* Illustrated by Peter Sis. New York: Greenwillow, 1985.

Sloyer, Shirlee. *Readers Theatre: Story Dramatization in the Classroom.* Urbana, Ill.: National Council of Teachers of English, 1981.

Sondheim, Stephen, and James Lapine. *Into the Woods.* Adapted by Hudson Talbott. New York: Crown, 1987.

Spaulding, Cheryl L. "The Motivation to Read and Write." In *Reading/Writing Connections: Learning from Research,* edited by Judith W. Irwin and Mary Anne Doyle, 177–201. Newark, Del.: International Reading Association, 1992.

Tierney, Robert J. "Ongoing Research and New Directions." In *Reading/Writing Connections: Learning from Research,* edited by Judith W. Irwin and Mary Anne Doyle, 246–259. Newark, Del.: International Reading Association, 1992.

Trivizas, Eugene. *The Three Little Wolves and the Big Bad Pig.* Illustrated by Helen Oxenbury. New York: Margaret K. McElderry, 1993.

Van Allsburg, Chris. *Jumanji.* Boston: Houghton Mifflin, 1981.

Veatch, Jeannette. *Reading in the Elementary School,* 2nd ed. New York: John Wiley, 1978.

Wepner, Shelley B., Nancy E. Seminoff, and Jay Blanchard. "Navigating Learning with Electronic Encyclopedias." *Reading Today* 12, no. 6 (June/July 1995): 28.

Westcott, Nadine, reteller. *The Emperor's New Clothes.* VHS-animated, 9 minutes. Weston, Conn.: Weston Woods, no date.

Yolen, Jane, editor. *Favorite Folktales from Around the World.* New York: Pantheon, 1986.

Yorinks, Arthur. *Ugh.* Illustrated by Richard Egielski. New York: Farrar, Straus & Giroux, 1990.

Ziegler, Alan. *The Writing Workshop,* Vol. 1. New York: Teachers and Writers Collaborative, 1981.

11

Content-Area Reading

The divine wind protected Japan by sinking the fleet of invading Mongrels.

During the years 1933–38, there were domestic problems at home as well as abroad.

To collect sulphur, hold a deacon over a flame in a test tube.

Three kinds of blood vessels are arteries, vanes, and caterpillars.

When you breathe, you inspire. When you do not breathe, you expire.

The human is more intelligent than the beast because the human brain has more convulsions.

A fossil is an extinct animal. The older it is, the more extinct it is.

Excerpted from *Anguished English: An Anthology of Accidental Assaults upon Our Language*, copyright 1987 by Richard Lederer, published by Wyrick & Company.

FOCUS QUESTIONS

1. Why does reading need to be taught in the content areas?

2. What is expository text?

3. How do I use text-books effectively?

4. Can textbooks be enhanced with trade-books?

5. How can I use technology to teach content areas?

6. How can I help diverse learners?

7. What strategies work with content-area instruction?

As we saw in Chapter 5, a good vocabulary is important for success in school, but as the preceding examples show, the words must also be used in the appropriate context for the text to make sense. Most elementary school reading programs emphasize strategies for learning to read, such as decoding words, reading aloud fluently, and understanding a story. Similarly, students need sound strategies for reading and understanding important concepts in the content areas.

As readers gain skill, teachers shift the focus to strategies for successful reading in subject areas such as social studies, history, science, mathematics, English, music, art, health, technical arts, and physical education. Sometimes students have partial mastery of necessary skills, but their skills still need work. *Content reading* emphasizes strategies and activities in the various subject areas that help students read to learn. When working in the content areas, students need to do more than understand the essential content; they need to realize that reading helps them learn. Thus, they must be able to use their reading to learn, and they must be motivated to continue such reading beyond the classroom.

Much of content reading involves the use of textbooks, so teachers, of course, prefer that students have adequate reading skills so they can read expository text. This way teachers can focus on the content itself. However, not all students have the necessary skills. Most students encounter expository text in newspapers, nonfiction books, magazines, and other informative material early on. Unfortunately, the reality is that by fourth grade many of them have fallen behind in this area. Thus, specific instruction in successful content-area reading procedures is often required (Cochran 1993, 1). Sadly, students' failures to learn to read successfully often lead to negative attitudes toward reading that further complicate the challenges a content-area teacher faces. As the vocabulary becomes increasingly difficult in content areas and the lengths and formats of texts vary, students become even further disenfranchised. Therefore, students should receive direct and continual instruction in content reading as early as possible, a practice that benefits all students.

In this chapter we look at the following topics: suggestions for working with content-area textbooks; discussion, examples, and teaching models of expository text; the structures students will encounter in most textbooks; a discussion of tradebooks and the content area; strategies for teaching various skills; and recommended modifications for remedial readers. For additional content area teaching activities, consult *Reading in the Content Areas for Junior High and High School* by Judith A. Cochran, *Content Area Reading* by Richard T. and JoAnne L. Vacca, and *Reading Activities for Middle and Secondary Schools* by Carl B. Smith and Peggy G. Elliot. Although these books designate middle and high school as the target level for these activities, many of them are adaptable for upper elementary.

Working with Content-Area Textbooks

Finding an appropriate content-area textbook is a challenge for any teacher. Because textbook selection usually occurs at the district level or by committee, content-area teachers have little or no choice regarding which textbooks they may use. Textbooks vary widely in their use of visual aids, organization, and text aids such as headings, boldfaced words, or marginal notes. The elementary teacher who uses textbooks probably also teaches reading and is accustomed to helping students master all forms of reading, but the middle or secondary teacher may find it challenging to help students master the content, particularly if they are not competent readers.

The subject matter also affects the difficulty level. A science text will have more specialized vocabulary than a social studies textbook. A math textbook may have little expository text, but will have more graphics and symbolic information. Grammatical complexity (sentence length) and concept complexity add to the reading challenge, which is further affected by the writer's style and organization. Finally, the format (type size, white space surrounding the text, margins), illustrations (graphs, photos, charts, and figures), and mechanical aids (underlining, subheads, italics) affect the difficulty of the text (Fry 1972, 204).

In an effort to provide more readable and consistent texts, publishers aim their texts at specific reading levels using **readability** formulas. These formulas are usually based on two factors: syllable count and sentence length. Complex formulas were used in the past, but in his work with a group of Ugandan vocational and technical instructors on reading improvement, Edward Fry devised an easy readability formula that works quite well. Designed to supplement teacher judgment, his formula provides a quick way to assess the level of difficulty of prose (Fry 1995, 445). A version of the readability graph is included at the end of this chapter.

An easier way to assess readability involves using a word processing program that has a readabilty assessment as an option. Simply type or scan in several representative passages from the beginning, middle, and end sections of the text and obtain a score for each section. This will give you an idea of the complexity of the material according to that formula. However, readability

Readability
Refers to the difficulty of text as measured by a formula that quantifies the difficulty.

designations can be misleading because readability formulas don't take into account features that can provide "considerate text." These features include such components as author style, complexity of ideas, page layout, organization, use of headings, presence of visuals, reader motivation, and the reader's background knowledge (Armbruster, Osborn, and Davison 1985, 18; Anderson and Davison 1988, 23; Bruce and Rubin 1988, 7–8; Meese 1994, 347).

The use of readability formulas seems a worthwhile goal: Provide students with material they can read comfortably and thereby increase their opportunities for success. However, with content material that normally contains challenging vocabulary, publishers may be tempted to simplify the information until it is stultifying and even incomprehensible (Simonsen and Singer 1992, 204) or, as reported by Nobel prize–winning physicist Richard P. Feynman, create products that are hurried and inaccurate (Smith 1986, 57). To further complicate matters, districts with limited funding may be unable to stay current in rapidly changing content areas such as social studies.

For teachers who don't have appropriate textbooks, Judith A. Cochran (1993) suggests that they search for older, more suitable textbooks and for supplemental media and materials (films, videos, demonstrations, overhead transparencies, audio tapes). These can often be found by checking with other teachers or by poking around storage areas or the district's professional resource center, and by inquiring at other schools. Ask the post office for donations of "dead letter" tradebooks, newspapers, and journals to supplement textbooks. Use a variety of prereading, during reading, and postreading strategies to enhance existing materials. Jean Ciborowski emphasizes that for the student with low reading skills, the most critical phase is the before reading phase because students can draw upon previous experiences (1995, 90). Many of the activities in this chapter are useful for this phase. Judith A. Cochran also suggests setting clear and appropriate purposes for reading. Provide aids such as outlines. Vary assignment lengths to accommodate individual learning differences. Involve students in determining the best textbook or resources (1993, 37–38).

Expository Text

By now you have noticed that this textbook's chapters have a fairly predictable structure: focus questions, an anecdote or excerpt that sets the tone for the chapter, an introduction, sections and subsections with headings and related figures, boldfaced glossary words, summary, bibliographies, and occasionally additional lists. You have probably decided which sections you can skip or skim and which sections you must concentrate on. Perhaps you start by checking to see how long the chapter is, or you read the summary to decide whether you really need to read a particular chapter.

Perhaps you already have a highlighter in your hand to mark the passages you feel are important. Over the years, you have read many other examples of expository text, and you probably have definite opinions about the features that make reading such text easy or difficult. You've also developed your own strategies for using and mastering expository text.

Textbooks can be difficult for students who have become used to the narrative style typified by a plot or theme, characters that may move the plot, descriptive writing, and a readable, entertaining style. Expository writing found in textbooks features informational or factual writing, technical vocabulary, new or abstract concepts, and often a specialized text structure. The best textbooks have interesting, comprehensible content that is relevant for today's students, but students will also need to be able to read textbooks that are less than ideal. The question is, how do we help them do this?

Dolores Durkin notes that students in the primary grades should be given more experience in reading expository text instead of primarily reading stories (1989, 436). As students move through the early years, those who are hampered by not knowing the subject matter need particular assistance in obtaining that information through a textbook or other resources. They also need to understand the organization of the prose, such as cause/effect or problem/solution. In addition, they need assistance recognizing how signal words, such as *first, second, more importantly*, and *finally*, aid in the comprehension of expository prose (Garner 1987, 300; Spyridakis and Standal 1987, 293). Once students understand the components of, and word cues in, expository text structure, they can use this knowledge for structured notetaking (Smith and Tompkins 1988). Fortunately, easier informational books, which can be used as early introductions to expository text, are being published each year, so the primary teacher can and should strive to find ways to support students' use of expository text.

GENERAL ORGANIZATION OF EXPOSITORY TEXT

Well-developed text is organized to help readers maneuver efficiently through the text. The table of contents, for example, includes the heading structure of the text, thus giving an overview of the text's organization. Most textbook chapters include introductory paragraphs that signal purpose or important ideas, the body of the text, transitional paragraphs, and concluding paragraphs that usually enumerate or summarize (Camperell 1991, 108). The text may also include questions; organizers such as webs; headings that signal the topic; and graphic aids such as charts, figures, captioned photographs, and maps with references that help the reader use the aids. The end of the chapter may include a chapter summary, follow-up questions, additional material, and extensions. A well-developed index and glossary may be especially beneficial.

Before reading on, take a few minutes to examine other books that have expository text, and decide what features you find most helpful. For example, you may prefer books that have an outline at the beginning of the chapter to books with focus questions. You may favor books with a lot of white space (extra space on the page) that allows room for making marginal notes, and if you read with bifocals, you probably appreciate shorter lines, preferring double-column text. Check to see whether the general organization is consistent from chapter to chapter. Finally, get a sense of whether the content is clear and interesting.

When teaching expository text, have the students begin as you did by examining books with expository text. They should learn how expository text differs from narrative in style and structure. Once they see how the writing differs in general, they can begin to utilize specific features effectively, such as outlines, questions, headings, graphic aids, and summaries.

INTERNAL ORGANIZATION OF EXPOSITORY TEXT

Once students determine the overall structure of the text they are reading, they are ready to look at how the author has organized the text internally. In expository text, authors typically use a highly defined internal structure—smaller segments or paragraphs that are organized into identifiable, predictable patterns. Typical patterns include identifying a problem and the solution(s) or presenting a cause-and-effect relationship. Some paragraphs, such as the sequential paragraph, use key or signal words such as *then*, *next*, *before*, *after*, or *finally*. Signal words relate and organize facts and concepts (a relationship among facts) and are helpful in establishing a pattern. To enhance students' understanding of text patterns, have them analyze and write paragraphs using common text structures.

Jo Anne Piccolo, a Colorado teacher/researcher, suggests that teachers instruct students on the following six structures (1987, 839). She notes that effective paragraphs have both a topic sentence (which represents the main idea of the paragraph) and a "clincher sentence" (a strong, logical conclusion to the paragraph).

■ **Descriptive paragraph** Addresses attributes of a topic.

1. The **descriptive paragraph** presents a topic and addresses its attributes. There are no signal words (see Figure 11.1).

■ **Enumerative paragraph** Lists examples to support topic.

2. The **enumerative paragraph** usually states its main thesis or idea in the topic sentence, then lists supporting examples in the body of the paragraph (see Figure 11.2 on page 354).

■ **Sequential paragraph** Lists supporting details in a specific order.

3. In the **sequential paragraph**, the details that support the main topic are presented in a specific order to build the reader's understanding in a logical manner. Signal words include words such as *first*, *second*, *third*, *then*, *next*, *before*, *after*, *finally* (see Figure 11.3 on page 355).

FIGURE 11.1

Descriptive
Paragraph

Turtles

Questions: Do you want to present the properties or critical attributes of something? Do you want to tell what something is?
Signal words: none.

> Turtles are fascinating creatures. They are 200 million years old, as old as the dinosaurs. Turtles developed hard shells that protected them from predators. Turtles can live all over the world in forests, seas, rivers, jungles and even in deserts. Turtles can weigh from 220 grams to 680 kilograms. There are more than 200 species in the world. No doubt having their own roofs have helped turtles survive for so many years.

Topic Sentence: Turtles are fascinating creatures.

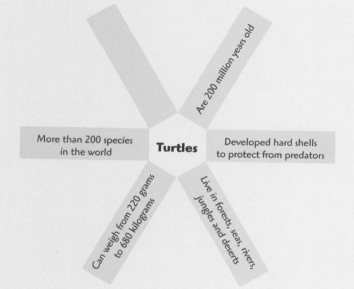

Clincher sentence: No doubt having their own roofs have helped turtles survive for so many years.

■ **Cause/effect paragraph**
Gives the results of an event or action.

4. In the **cause/effect paragraph,** the "cause" is usually stated in the topic sentence; supportive details explain the results—that is, the effects. Examples of signal words or phrases include *so, so that, because of, as a result of, since, in order to* (see Figure 11.4 on page 356).

■ **Compare/contrast paragraph**
Shows similarities and differences.

5. The topic sentence in a **compare/contrast paragraph** states whether two things are alike or different. Supporting details follow in sentences that use sig-

Four Kinds of Turtles

FIGURE 11.2
Enumerative
Paragraph

Questions: Do you want to present a list of examples, instances, or illustrations related to your topic and tell about each one?
Signal words: first, second, third, in addition to, additionally, next, last, finally, for example, another, also.

> There are four kinds of turtles. First, the most familiar are freshwater turtles, which live in rivers or ponds. They have webbed feet and flat shells. The second kind, sea turtles, live in the sea and have strong flippers for swimming long distances. Another kind, tortoises, live on dry land and have thick heavy legs for walking. The last kind, semiterrestrial turtles, spend some time on land and some in fresh water. You can probably find some kind of turtle living near you.

Topic Sentence: There are four kinds of turtles.

Freshwater Turtles — Live in rivers or ponds — Have webbed feet and flat shells
Sea Turtles — Live in sea — Have strong flippers for swimming
Tortoises — Live on land — Have thick, heavy legs for walking
Semi-terrestrial — Spend some time on land — Spend some time on water

Clincher sentence: You can probably find some kind of turtle living near you.

nal words or phrases such as *different from, same as, alike, similar to, resembles, compared to, unlike* (see Figure 11.5 on page 357).

- **Problem/solution paragraph** States a problem, proposes a solution.

6. The topic sentence in a **problem/solution paragraph** states a problem. The remainder of the paragraph describes the problem and its causes, and then presents a solution(s). The signal phrases include *a problem is, a solution is, the problem is solved by* (see Figure 11.6 on page 358).

WRITING EXPOSITORY TEXT

Writing expository text is a natural partner of reading expository text. In the past, writing research reports was reserved for intermediate and middle school students. With the emphasis on using a variety of materials in the classroom,

FIGURE 11.3

Sequential
Paragraph

How a Turtle is Born

Questions: Do you want to tell the reader how to do something? Do you want to tell the reader how to make something? Do you want to tell the reader how something happens?

Signal words: first, second, third, and all other ordinal numbers, then, next, before, after, finally, following.

It isn't easy being a newborn turtle. First, its mother digs a hole in the ground. Next, she lays the eggs and covers them. Then she leaves them to hatch by themselves. Sometimes the eggs are found and eaten by people or predators. When the newborns hatch, they must dig out alone. Finally, they must hurry to the safety of water. If turtles make it to water, they may live for many years.

Topic Sentence: It isn't easy being a newborn turtle.

Mother digs a hole.

Mother lays the eggs.

Mother leaves the eggs.

Predators sometimes eat eggs.

Turtles hatch alone.

Turtles must hurry to water.

Clincher sentence: If turtles make it to water, they may live for many years.

students now create minireports in the early primary grades. The report may only contain one short paragraph on an intriguing topic, but the student is engaged in reading and writing expository text.

Begin teaching expository writing by having students analyze the kind of paragraphs they are reading by first identifying the structure. Use the diagrams found in Figures 11.1 through 11.6 to help students organize examples of

FIGURE 11.4
Cause/Effect
Paragraph

The Future of Turtles

Questions: Do you want to tell what happens as a result of an event or action?
Signal words: because of, as a result of, reasons for.

> Turtles face an uncertain future. Because of overhunting, giant tortoises are only found in two places in the world. As a result of pollution, rivers and streams are no longer healthy for freshwater turtles. Another reason is the destruction of forests where wood turtles and box turtles lived. A final reason is that habitats are being destroyed to make way for beach resorts. People are now working to protect turtles with new laws.

Topic Sentence (Cause): Turtles face an uncertain future.

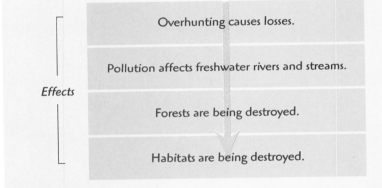

Effects

Overhunting causes losses.

Pollution affects freshwater rivers and streams.

Forests are being destroyed.

Habitats are being destroyed.

Clincher sentence: People are now working to protect turtles with new laws.

expository text that are easy to read; perhaps you can find examples in textbooks from earlier grade levels. Ask questions that will help the students explore why the author used the structure: What kind of signal words did the author use? Could the author have used words like *first, second,* and *third* in this paragraph? Does this paragraph talk about a problem? Is a solution provided?

Choose a topic that the students have a common interest in and brainstorm with them on what they know about it. Make lists and then diagrams on the board. For example, primary students often have a wealth of knowledge about dinosaurs and enjoy listing their characteristics. A natural next step would be to compare the dinosaurs to well-known animals, such as elephants or lizards. Shape a compare/contrast paragraph with the entire class, pointing out the signal words during the process. For primary students, create examples of such paragraphs over the course of several days before you have them create their own examples on topics of their choice. For older students, use examples from

Turtle Shells and Human Skeletons

FIGURE 11.5
Compare/Contrast
Paragraph

Questions: Do you want to show the similarities or differences between two topics?

Signal words: same, same as, like, similar to, resembles, compared to, different from, unlike, in contrast to, on the other hand, both, either, yet, as well as.

> You have much in common with a turtle's shell. The turtle's shell is part of its skeleton. Just like your skeleton, the shell cannot be removed from its body. The turtle's ribs and backbone are attached to the flat, bony plates that form the shell, while your bones are connected by ligaments. Its hard scales are made of keratin, just like your fingernails. Both skeletons shape the body. Your legs are long and straight, but a turtle's stick out sideways to fit under the shell. Unlike your shoulders, which are outside your ribs, the turtle's shoulders are inside their ribs. The turtle may look different, but it is very similar to you.

Topic Sentence: You have much in common with a turtle's shell.

Turtle Shell Differences	Similarities	Human Skeleton Differences
Ribs and backbone are attached to a shell.	Skeleton cannot be removed.	Skeleton connected by ligaments.
Legs stick out sideways.	Scales and fingernails made of keratin.	Legs are long and straight.
Shoulders are inside ribs.	Skeletons shape the body.	Shoulders are outside ribs.

Clincher sentence: The turtle may look different, but it is very similar to you.

textbooks or draw material from informational books on the topic to create examples. Be certain that students have ample opportunities to see and analyze models while they write their own paragraphs.

Provide many opportunities to talk about the text and how the writing should be developed. A structured use of dialogue to teach expository writing is referred to as a dialogical approach. This is a useful technique where small groups of students tape and transcribe their conversations about a topic; they then use the transcriptions to write dialogical books. First, the teacher engages the students in the topic and encourages them to elaborate on what background knowledge they have. Students then work in small groups, recording

FIGURE 11.6
Problem/Solution
Paragraph

Box Turtles as Pets

Questions: Do you want to state some sort of problem related to your subject and offer some solutions?
Signal phrases: a problem is, a solution is, the problem is solved by.

Turtles can be rewarding but challenging pets. They prefer a natural environment, but can adapt to indoor life. It may be hard to find a healthy one. To avoid this problem, look for an active turtle that responds to being picked up. Be sure it is also at least five inches long. A box turtle needs dry and wet areas. Buy a 10-gallon aquarium and put a plastic dish of water in it along with pebbles from the pet shop. Turtles can be finicky eaters. For this problem, be sure the turtle is warm enough. Offer it small bits of meat, worms, fruit, and vegetables. If you have a problem with your turtle sleeping all the time, it may be hibernating. Keep a light on it during the day and take it out for exercising or a swim in the sink. By thinking about these challenges, you can help your turtle live a long and healthy life.

Topic Sentence: Turtles can be rewarding but challenging pets.
Problem (Effect): Turtles can be challenging as pets.

	Problems	Solutions
Cause: Turtles prefer a natural environment.	Hard to find a healthy turtle.	Look for an active turtle. Make sure the turtle is five inches long.
	Needs dry and wet areas.	Buy an aquarium, add a dish of water and pebbles.
	Can be finicky eaters.	Be sure it is warm enough. Feed it meat, worms, fruits, or vegetables.
	May hibernate.	Keep a light on it; give it exercise or a swim.

Clincher sentence: By thinking about these challenges, your turtle should live a long and healthy life.

their conversations and keeping written notes. They begin to revise their notes and make outlines, and they also continue to tape their conversations; sometimes the recorded conversations can be transcribed by volunteer adults. As students revise the transcriptions, they begin to clarify information they have found in the text. Eventually, they revise, polish, and edit the material; then they "publish" and present the books to the class (Reutzel, Larson, and Sabey 1995, 100–106). Although this process requires a well-organized group of volunteers to transcribe the recorded conversations, teachers have found this to be a particularly effective process for students with special needs (ibid., 108).

Figures 11.1 through 11.6 provide examples of how expository text can be structured and also how it can be organized graphically to illustrate the six paragraph styles. The graphics are adapted from texts on expository writing by Jo Anne Piccolo (1996). In the next section we will examine specific strategies that promote student success with expository text.

Trade Books in the Content Areas

You may decide to use a variety of textbooks when you teach topics such as science or social studies. Alternatively, you may use a variety of informational or fictional tradebooks to replace or supplement your textbooks. For example, your second graders might read a chapter in the science book about the human body and also explore the *3-D Kid* by Roger Culbertson and Robert Margulies, which is a life-size pop-up book that shows how the body systems work. While your fifth graders read a chapter on the Civil War, they might also read *A Separate Battle: Women and the Civil War* by Ina Chang, *The Boys War: Confederate and Union Soldiers Talk about the Civil War* by Jim Murphy, or *Charley Skedaddle* by Patricia Beatty.

Such auxiliary readings expose students to the same vocabulary but in different contexts. These readings present different perspectives (which helps to breathe life into the topic) and fleshes out both important concepts and the backgrounds against which the events took place (Alvermann 1994, 56). Louise M. Rosenblatt points out that "In an efferent reading of a text, the attention is focused on abstracting out, analyzing, and structuring what is to be retained after the reading, as—for example, information, logical argument, or instructions for action. In an aesthetic reading, attention is focused on what is being lived through, the ideas and feelings being evoked and organized during the transaction" (1991, 60).

Using tradebooks allows second-language learners and remedial readers to explore the topic with easier text or with information supported by numerous illustrations, labels, and graphics. Finally, tradebook presentations help students see the relationships of their own lives to those in the past, understanding their place in history (Johnson and Ebert 1992, 489). See Chapter 8 for more ways to use informational books. A sample unit on the Civil War that supplements a textbook is included in Chapter 14, and recommended resources for supplementing textbooks with literature are listed at the end of this chapter.

Strategies for Teaching in the Content Area

In their review of 10 texts on content-area reading methods, Ned Ratekin, Michele L. Simpson, Donna E. Alvermann, and Ernest K. Dishner (1985, 434) emphasize that teachers need to

Students use their reading and writing skills in a science class.

- Vary organizational settings and instructional methods.

- Plan activities for developing students' readiness for learning, acquisition of information, and internalization of concepts.

- Use a variety of instructional resources to help students develop concerns.

The following strategies provide content-area teachers with tools for using textbooks effectively. When selecting a strategy, be certain that it is appropriate for the topic, is adaptable and transferable to other areas, and provides for high- and low-achieving students. It should require minimal preparation time, match existing student skills, and provide for depth and breadth of content coverage. Also ask yourself whether it promotes independence and fits your time limitations (Radencich, Beers, and Schumm 1993, 83). Once you have chosen a strategy, be sure your students understand why the strategy is important (Garner 1987, 305). For specific vocabulary strategies, refer to Chapter 5, Teaching Vocabulary.

PREVIEWING A TEXTBOOK

Mature readers take time to look through a textbook chapter before they set out to read it, particularly if the subject matter is difficult. Because textbooks are often used as early as the primary grades, previewing should be taught and reinforced from the beginning. That is, whenever students use informational material, have them first search out reading aids such as heads, subheads, and boldfaced words.

When you introduce students to a new textbook, ask them what they think it will be about based on the title, cover, and also from what they already know about the subject. Review the major components of the book with them, especially those that will be helpful to them as they use the book, such as the table of contents, chapter divisions, glossary, and index. Review the table of contents and invite responses as to how well the table of contents matches earlier predictions about what the textbook covers. (An overhead transparency of the table of contents is useful for this discussion.) Does the subject match expectations of the students for the course content? Are major topics omitted? Will supplementary materials be necessary or helpful?

Invite students to participate in a preliminary critique of the text; keep a record of their comments, which you will discuss and review with them after they've read the book. Spend time discussing how the book will be used, especially if some chapters will be reorganized or omitted. This discussion may comprise your entire first lesson. Don't hurry it: When presented thoroughly and thoughtfully, this introduction to the text can set the stage for a successful unit.

When you are ready to begin a chapter, lead the students in a discussion of what they already know about the topic. Consider using K-W-L—identifying what students *Know*, what students *Want* to know, and later identifying what they *Learned* (Ogle 1986). (See page 362 for more details and variations of this technique.) Think about what the students have shared and determine whether you need to develop more schemata, as discussed in Chapter 6, before the class examines the topic through the textbook.

Once students have enough background information, have them use the table of contents to focus on the first chapter. Turn back to this book's table of contents and note how this chapter includes heads and subheads. Lead students to discover how their textbook's organization is reflected in the table of contents and speculate on the usefulness of this for finding information, for answering questions, and for rereading.

Make an overhead or handout of the following suggestions for the students, and model and discuss each step the first few times with them.

HOW TO PREVIEW A CHAPTER

1. Read the title. What question does it raise? Can you turn it into a question?

2. Read the introduction at the beginning of the chapter. Think of at least three questions you have about the chapter.

3. Read the summary of the chapter. If your questions won't be answered, decide what questions will probably be answered.

4. Read the first few heads and subheads for the chapter. Think of at least three questions they will probably answer.

5. Look for several examples of words or phrases that are boldfaced, italicized, or treated differently. Speculate on what the treatment means and try to confirm your theories.

6. Look at charts, maps, or other figures. What information do they provide?

7. Skim the chapter, reading the heads, subheads, words or phrases that are treated differently, and any other information that stands out. Make a quick list of what you have learned and discuss it with another student.

PREVIEWING A PASSAGE

Stephen B. Kucer and Jerome C. Harste (1991, 133) describe a lesson on previewing that helps students use text aids to predict and understand a passage. Begin by using a selection that includes a variety of text aids such as headings and visuals. Tell students they will have time to read only the text aids. Stop the previewing when the time is up. Make two columns on the blackboard labeled "Predictions" and "Parts of the text used." Have students share what they think the text will be about based on their preview, and list this information on the board under "Predictions." Then list the text aids the students used in the second column. Discuss how the aids helped them organize meaning. Next, have the students read the passage and verify or revise their predictions, noting that not all predictions will be accurate. Finally, discuss the process and how it helped their comprehension (ibid., 133).

After students are familiar with this process, Kucer and Harste suggest preparing an expository text passage with the text aids removed. Review the purpose of text aids with the students and have them read the passage. Have the students work individually or in small groups to decide what kind and where text aids are needed. Students can then cut the article apart and insert the text aids, pasting their version onto another piece of paper. Compare the students' results and discuss their efforts before contrasting them with the original article (ibid., 135).

K-W-L

Students can prepare for and evaluate their reading or research by determining what they *Know*, what they *Want to know*, and what they *Learned* (Ogle 1986). During this prereading and postreading activity, students analyze the knowledge they are acquiring. Here are the steps of K-W-L:

1. Teacher or students discuss the topic.

2. Small groups or the whole class discusses what they know, listing the information under "What I know."

3. The class creates categories of information about what they might encounter during their reading.

4. The students list what they want to know in the next column.

5. The students discuss the ideas they have generated.

6. The teacher adds important vocabulary, concepts, or information.

7. The students read the text.

8. The class discusses the reading.

9. Students list what they have learned.

Variations include adding "What I still want to know" or inserting "How I find out" after "What I want to know."

Although generally considered a strategy for elementary students, Eileen Carr and Donna Ogle discuss the advantages of K-W-L–Plus for remedial secondary students, adding the steps of mapping and summarizing (1987). To construct a map, students look at each item under "What I have learned" and ask what each statement describes; they categorize the information and arrange it in a diagram (or map) with the topic in the center. See Figure 11.7 for an example. Carr and Ogle note that remedial readers benefit from mapping because it helps them summarize what they have learned. Their learning is enhanced when they number the categories on the map in an appropriate sequence and then write the information in complete sentences. Paragraphs then evolve easily. This is a good approach to paragraphing for regular intermediate students as well.

FIGURE 11.7
Turtles Map

Description
• reptiles
• more than 200 million years old
• cold-blooded
• weigh between 1/2 and 1500 pounds
• more than 200 kinds

Locations
• sea turtles in oceans
• freshwater turtles in rivers or ponds
• tortoises on land
• some tortoises on both

Turtles

Raising turtles
• female digs a hole
• lays up to 200 eggs
• covers eggs
• babies hatch, dig out, look for water

Dangers for future
• pollution
• lack of food
• overhunting

something to try 1

Creating an Attitude Inventory

An attitude inventory can be used when the class is working with current events, in addition to textbooks. Review the newspaper or a current news magazine and choose a controversial topic. Make a list of all the related controversial issues. Develop sentences that can be responded to using a gradient, such as in Figure 11.8. Try out the inventory yourself or with another adult, and refine it accordingly. Then present it to the students on an overhead or have them respond in small groups. Discuss the responses as a whole class. If time allows, discuss where they could find further information. Research the topic and repeat the inventory to determine whether the students' attitudes have changed. Alternatively, bring in subsequent related articles that affect the topic and repeat the process to determine whether their attitudes have changed.

ATTITUDE INVENTORY

Students read expository text more successfully when they are curious about the topic, so it is important to involve them in the topic before they read the text. Taking an attitude inventory is one way to do this. For example, before a class of middle school students read about the bombing of Hiroshima, they completed and discussed the inventory in Figure 11.8. The discussion was lively, making the students eager to explore the topic further. Repeating the inventory after the reading brings closure and demonstrates how opinions can change. (See Something to Try 1.)

ANTICIPATION GUIDES

■ **Anticipation guide**
A series of statements that students respond to before they read a text.

An **anticipation guide** is another effective way to jump-start discussions (Vacca and Vacca 1996, 194). Students can read and respond to their statements on the board, in a handout, or on an overhead transparency. Afterward, they discuss their predictions in small groups or with the whole class. Be sure to discuss their guides again after they read the text. What would they change?

To create an anticipation guide, review the material and outline the major ideas. Write a sentence outline in clear, short statements. Then consider a format that will elicit responses and discussion from students. The form of the responses can vary; in Figure 11.9, note that instead of *old* and *new*, the response could be *likely* and *unlikely*.

Hiroshima

Directions: Read the following statements and place an X on the line indicating if you agree or disagree.

	Agree	Disagree
1. A nation has the right to defend itself.		_____
2. A nation has the right to defend itself in another country.		_____
3. A nation has the right to retaliate against a country.		_____
4. A nation has the right to invade another country.		_____
5. A nation has the right to kill innocent people in defense.		_____
6. A nation has the right to kill innocent people in retaliation.		_____
7. A nation has a responsibility to defend other countries.		_____

Old and New Korea

Directions: You will be reading about old and new Korea. Before reading your textbook, place an O in front of those statements you think apply to old Korea and place an N by those that apply to new Korea. Place an O and an N by those statements that you think apply to both.

1. _____ Men wear a topknot.
2. _____ The favorite color for clothing is white.
3. _____ Parents or matchmakers arrange marriages.
4. _____ Houses are made of clay.
5. _____ Roofs are made of thatch of rice stalks.
6. _____ Houses are heated by pipes carrying smoke from fires.
7. _____ Korean children play soccer after school.
8. _____ Korean girls often play on swings and seesaws.
9. _____ Education is highly valued.
10. _____ Women are allowed to call on each other during the evening when men must stay home.
11. _____ Korea is a patriarchal society.
12. _____ Korea has a primarily agricultural economy.

FIGURE 11.10

Anticipatory
Problem Solving

The Netherlands

You live in the village of Colijnsplaat, which is very close to the sea. Your town's only protection from the sea is a dike. Each villager takes turns walking along the dike checking for leaks. During your turn, you notice that there is a small leak and you place a sandbag there to stop the leak. But that evening a storm comes up, and you hear church bells and sirens warning the danger. What do you and the villagers do? Write your answer here.

_____

_____

_____

_____

ANTICIPATORY PROBLEM SOLVING

Students will become more invested in their reading if they are actively engaged in solving a real or hypothetical problem. Figure 11.10 presents an alternative introduction for a unit on The Netherlands. Note that it encourages students to think about problems the Dutch have faced for centuries.

POSSIBLE SENTENCES

Without an understanding of the content-area vocabulary, students will not make much headway on their reading, so learning vocabulary must be an integral part of the unit. One effective activity, recommended by Steven A. Stahl and Barbara A. Kapinus, is **possible sentences** (1991, 36–37). The teacher reviews the reading and selects six to eight key concept words that might present difficulty. An additional six to eight familiar words are chosen to help with the development of the possible sentences. For a discussion of sharks, for example, the key target words might be _undulations, navigate, viviparous, parasite, migrate, camouflage._ The contrast (or more familiar) words might be _waves, move, live, freeloader, disguise._ The words are placed on the chalkboard or on an overhead transparency, and the students provide definitions. Students are then asked to think about what they are going to read and to create possible sentences that contain at least two of the words. After their reading, the class can discuss whether the sentences are true or whether they need revision. Using this activity before reading activates prior knowledge and encourages students to verify understanding during and after their reading. (See Something to Try 2.)

Possible sentences
An activity using target and familiar words to make sentences that might be appropriate in a reading activity.

Preparing for Chapter 12

Your next chapter is on reading evaluation and assessment. Use the following words and create definitions without consulting this text or other sources. Then create possible sentences that contain at least two of the words. Save your possible sentences and review them before reading Chapter 12. Afterward, determine whether they helped you understand some of the concepts.

TARGET WORDS: assessment, checklists, reliability, rubric, validity.

RELATED WORDS: accurate measurement, informal records, consistency, scoring guide, data gathering.

FINDING DETAILS

Carl B. Smith and Peggy G. Elliot believe that one way to teach middle and high school students how important a content book can be as a source of information is to have them find information in it that can't be found elsewhere. For example, social studies students might use the index or table of contents to determine why the Israeli raid on Entebbe was an important international event (1986, 8). This strategy is useful for all ages of learners, and youngsters enjoy the discovery process. Review your content-area book and choose several interesting questions whose answers can be found through the table of contents or index. If map or graph reading is important to the text, be sure to include questions that require interpreting such graphics. Once students have located the information, discuss how much can be learned quickly and how they can use this skill in the future.

SQ3R

SQ3R
Survey, question, read, review, and recite.

SQ3R is a long-standing recommended practice for students to employ in their textbook readings. Using it successfully, however, requires modeling and frequent reinforcement by the teacher. The steps are briefly outlined here:

1. *Survey.* Student previews the material, noting the title, introduction, heads, subheads, boldfaced or italicized words or phrases, and summary.

2. *Question.* Student predicts the questions the text will answer.

3. *Read.* Student reads to answer the questions raised in step 2.

4. *Recite.* Reader discusses or writes answers found through the reading.

5. *Review.* Student rereads as needed to confirm questions or to locate information.

VISUAL READING GUIDE

Visuals, such as photographs, charts, graphs, and maps, contribute important information to the content of a text, but they are often ignored because students don't always perceive their importance (Moore, Readence, and Rickelman 1989, 32). In preparing a Visual Reading Guide, a teacher should determine the critical visuals and explain to the students why some visuals are more important than others. Students then analyze each visual to determine the content, its organization, and its accuracy. Finally, students discuss the graphic to come to consensus about its main idea. Once the teacher has modeled this process, the students should be encouraged to follow it independently or in small groups (ibid.).

STRUCTURED OVERVIEW

As discussed in Chapter 5, this graphic organizer is a hierarchical arrangement of words that represent concepts. It is especially useful for analyzing content-area reading because the text often includes boldfaced words that can serve as the source for the overview. Students may organize information differently based on their background knowledge, leading to lively discussions. Refer to pages 169–170 for more information on constructing a structured overview.

FOLLOWING A FLOW CHART

If students must understand textbook flow charts, which are similar to structured overviews, Carl B. Smith and Peggy G. Elliot (1986, 216) suggest creating a situation where students need to get a message to everyone in the class, perhaps to communicate a schedule change. The teacher can only contact one student from four classes of 30 students each, so students create a calling tree in which the teacher contacts the first four students who in turn call two other classmates, who then call others, and so forth. Students may devise several variations, but they will soon understand how a flow chart works.

DIRECTED READING-THINKING ACTIVITY

The DRTA, developed by Russell Stauffer (1969), has students predict, question, and refine their purposes as they read. Begin by directing students to review the title, heads, subheads, and visuals in the text. Ask them to predict what the section is about, frequently asking why they think this will be true, perhaps recording the information on the chalkboard. Students then read that section, using context to define unknown words. When they are finished, review the questions and their predictions and have students verify or refine the predictions through class or small-group discussion. Unfamiliar vocabulary can be discussed and clarified at this time. Generate new predictions about the next section and continue reading in the same fashion. As the reading progresses, some students will need to continue using DRTA throughout the entire reading, and some will move to independent reading and evaluation.

SEMANTIC FEATURE ANALYSIS

As discussed in Chapter 5, the semantic feature analysis analyzes the features of the chosen words or concepts. Try constructing one that compares features of vegetables. This process is also appropriate for kindergarten students. Then contrast the features of classical, romantic, and jazz music. You may need to research the meaning of the terms related to the periods. For more information on semantic feature analysis, consult *Semantic Feature Analysis: Classroom Applications* by Susan D. Pittelman, Joan E. Heimlich, Roberta L. Berglund, and Michael P. French.

BACKTRACKING

Backtracking
Rereading text
to clarify under-
standing or to
find information.

According to Ruth Garner at the University of Maryland, **backtracking**, also called text reinspection or text lookbacks, is another valuable strategy for reading expository text (1987, 301). Students often think that such deliberate rereading is "cheating," but Garner and her colleagues found that remedial readers trained in backtracking experienced success in locating answers they could not recall (ibid., 302). To teach backtracking, prepare a passage of expository text, breaking it up into chunks with three or four central, factual questions following each chunk. Have the students read each section and then have them reread it immediately to locate the answers. Urge the students to reread *only* to locate the information necessary to answer the questions. Some students will quickly decide to skim the text, read the questions, and reread for the answers. Point out that this strategy is useful for taking standardized tests.

"SAY SOMETHING" SUMMARIZATION

Summarizing enables students to monitor their understanding of expository text by paraphrasing it (Garner 1987, 302). To introduce an easy form of summarization, select an interesting, short passage of expository text for a "Say Something" strategy lesson (Kucer and Harste 1991, 144). Place numbered dots throughout the text where you anticipate students will have something to say. Tell the students to read silently to the first dot. Then have each say something about what they have read. Encourage them to expand from a basic restatement to a personal response to the reading. Continue in this fashion

Turtles

F I G U R E   1 1 . 1 1
Hierarchical
Summary Writing

1. *Turtles are reptiles.* Turtles are like dinosaurs. There are more than 200 species of turtles.
2. *A turtle's shell is like a skeleton.* The shell provides protection. The skeleton shapes the turtle's body.
3. *Most turtles live in fresh water.* They may live in cold or warm water. They breathe air, but can stay under water for hours.

throughout the reading. Vary the process by having students work in pairs or small groups, perhaps writing their responses. Eventually encourage them to choose their own reaction points by placing dots and numbers where they want to respond to the text.

HIERARCHICAL SUMMARY WRITING

When a textbook has headings, students can use hierarchical summary writing, which can increase understanding and recall of major ideas (Taylor 1992, 223). Model this process by displaying the information contained under one heading on an overhead transparency. Read the information aloud and ask students to suggest the most important idea, plus one or two additional ideas from the passage. Paraphrasing, write the most important idea first, followed by the others. Repeat the process with each section until the material has been read. Once students have learned the process, have them work in pairs, comparing their summaries. Their summaries will differ, but they will soon learn when they have omitted major ideas. Students should review their summaries after several pages to further enhance their learning and to improve retention. See Figure 11.11 for an example.

PRÉCIS WRITING

Précis writing is a summarization strategy that emphasizes paraphrasing, develops vocabulary and critical thinking, and improves comprehension (Bromley and McKeveny 1987, 392). Suggested for intermediate grades and up, Bromley and McKeveny recommend the practice for both content-area teachers and reading specialists. A related process, writing short essays after reading content text, can be equally useful according to Judith Langer (1986). She found that following content-area reading with essay writing provided long-term and more reasoned learning than answering study questions or taking notes. The following steps outline the process of précis writing.

PREWRITING

1. Establish purpose by telling students that précis writing will help them improve their vocabulary, comprehension, and study skills. This skill is particularly useful when researching and reporting.

2. Make a commitment for long-term usage of the process, preferably twice a week throughout a semester.

3. Demonstrate the process using an overhead transparency of a prepared passage and a blank for summarizing.

4. Provide copies of the prepared passage to students, encouraging students to underline or write on the passage as they work.

5. Practice the process orally, identifying key words, supplying synonyms, and paraphrasing the content of the passage. Bromley and McKeveny recommend introducing the thesaurus at this time. Students enjoy the challenge, and they also like to find new ways to say things (1987, 394).

WRITING

1. Invite the class to work together to dictate the précis as you write it on the overhead transparency. Revise the summary until it reflects the consensus of the group. Once the class has done a few group summaries, they can do this step in small groups and compare the results. This allows them to see that there is more than one way to construct a précis.

2. Adapt and revise the process, especially when working with disabled readers. Bromley and McKeveny found that remedial readers were more successful when allowed to start the process by combining sentences they copied with those they paraphrased (ibid.).

POSTWRITING

1. Provide models of acceptable summaries to compare with and evaluate their own summaries.

2. Use folders to collect and store précis. These collections can be used to demonstrate how summaries provide the main idea and to answer questions. They also allow you to track progress over time.

3. Provide study time for students to review their précis as necessary, perhaps for tests.

READING TEST DIRECTIONS

Do you recall a time when you scored lower on a test because you misread or skipped test directions? This is a problem for today's readers also. Carl B. Smith and Peggy G. Elliot (1986) recommend teaching students to read directions effectively by providing them with copies of an old standardized test or a sample you have constructed. Have students circle every direction and example. Then have a volunteer put the directions and an example on the board, explaining how it should be worked or answered. Next, students should identify the most important words in the directions, list them on the board, and discuss their meaning and any possible misinterpretations. Examine test items that could be missed without a careful reading of the directions. Discuss these key essay-test words: *clarify, compare, contrast, describe, discuss, explain, outline*. Additional important words are *alike, antonym, eliminate, opposite, related, synonym* (ibid., 36).

Technology in the Content Areas

As mentioned in previous chapters, students benefit from using electronic encyclopedias, online services, and content-specific CD-ROMs such as *History of the World* (Dorling Kindersley 1995). Schools that have networks with CD-ROM stacks in the library enable users to conveniently access many research sources from the classroom-based computer. Where teachers may have previously required a report to include information from three different forms of print (magazine, encyclopedia, book, newspaper), now they also require information from one or more electronic sources.

Some CD-ROMs combine a game element with a story line and information. For example, users of *Stowaway!* (Biesty 1995) can discover what life was like on an 18th-century warship through authentic drawings, realistic animation, sound effects, narrations, and a game. Some CD-ROMs focus on content areas without a game scenario, such as *The Viking Opera Guide on CD-ROM* (Holden, 1995), which uses music, text, pictures, and maps to explore operatic form. *You Be the Reporter!* (Ridgeway) provides an interactive journalism workshop that can be used to explore a variety of subjects as students create a newspaper. *Ride Like the Wind Bike Rally* (Barchers 1996) provides second-language learners with a simulated bike trip through South America, teaching users map-reading skills. Virtual reality products, such as *Bird* (Dorling Kindersley 1995/1996), allows the user to enter a museum to explore videos, photographs, exhibits, songs, and animations of bird families.

Two students work on a CD-ROM program.

When choosing materials for the content areas, consider whether the CD-ROM or software truly supports the curriculum. Often, simulations teach significant concepts and have supporting materials that further enhance the experience. When materials are not available, content-area teachers can gather materials that support or explain the simulation's concepts (Blanchard and Mason 1985). Because of the proliferation of such programs in the educational marketplace, products increasingly come with supportive auxiliary materials. As mentioned in Chapter 10, teachers can also capitalize on the advantages of technology, both with word processing and authoring programs, for student-generated, high-tech research reports.

Working with Diverse Learners

Although students with reading problems may be receiving specialized instruction for their reading or language arts class, teachers generally have to teach all students in the content areas, often relying heavily on textbooks that may be at an inappropriate reading level or that have information too dense for special students to read successfully. Second-language learners may also need support when faced with content-saturated textbooks.

When planning instruction and work using textbooks, consider how your classroom activities can accommodate the strengths of individual learners. Try to step inside that learner's shoes for a moment and ask yourself how you would want to tackle the book or materials. Would a graphic organizer help? Perhaps you would be better able to demonstrate your understanding of the material through drawings, charts, and labels instead of through an essay. Would an oral presentation be intimidating? Perhaps you would want to read an informational book or historic fiction instead of the textbook. Adult learners appreciate a variety of assignments and options for learning; so do youngsters.

Sometimes having everyone use the same textbook is the only practical option; in this event, recognizing prior knowledge is strongly recognized by Jean Ciborowski. Students then see the connections between what they know and what they will be learning (1995, 90). Many of the prereading activities in this chapter address this need for all students. Ciborowski also recommends during reading activities, such as having students construct maps, having them reconstruct the meaning of the text, and having frequent discussions about related activities as students use them. Be sure to make the connections between the activity and the content of the text clear because students need to know why they are doing something (ibid., 98). In the postreading phase, complete or repeat any prereading activities that apply to postreading, analyze end-of-chapter questions, extend maps, and analyze text structure (ibid., 99–100).

Discussion is an important component of learning content information for all learners, but especially for remedial readers and second-language learners. Anna Uhl Chamot and J. Michael O'Malley recommend that instead of choosing easier textbooks for second-language students, you should work closely with their support teachers to develop common goals. When teaching the less-than-fluent student, base your evaluations on the content and ideas expressed, not on the fluency of the learner (1989, 114). Use strategies that will help students organize information and foster the transfer of their new organizational skills to other learning situations (ibid.).

Many teachers have students read in pairs or small groups, or they **jigsaw** the information. This process increases the conversational opportunities, particularly important for second-language learners. For second-language learners, consider brainstorming activities, using literature to enhance the content area, and previewing lessons orally. Choral reading, reading with partners, visual aids, and manipulatives are helpful, as are the activities found in this chapter (Tinajero 1994, 263) Second-language learners also benefit from having a variety of supplementary materials available in their primary language as well.

When taping textbooks, another useful support strategy, Ruth Lyn Meese makes the following suggestions:

Jigsaw
When a heterogeneous group of three to six students share responsiblity for content by learning a portion of the information and sharing it with other group members.

1. Enlist the aid of student, parent, or community volunteer groups as readers.

2. Use clear directions on the tape so that students will know when to move from one page to the next or from one paragraph/section to the next.

3. Use colors or symbols to highlight important information or to indicate movement through the text.

4. Periodically pause and insert questions to keep the listener actively engaged with the text.

5. Give students an advance organizer (that is, a topical outline or study guide) to structure the reading selection (ibid., 349–350).

When asked, a reading or bilingual specialist will often help a student work on content-area assignments, but time constraints limit direct help.

Many good teaching strategies useful for second-language learners, average, and above-average students are equally important for remedial readers: Discuss texts and assignments before reading begins (Conley 1992, 72), set clear purposes, provide essential background information, provide appropriate motivation, set up an organized structure, and suggest strategies that will prove useful for reading the text (ibid.). Be sure to provide regular feedback and reinforcement, and always summarize their accomplishments.

To adapt assignments for remedial readers, consider extending deadlines, giving shorter assignments, substituting verbal assignments for written ones, allowing aids such as calculators or word processors, and allowing students to suggest or devise their own adaptations. Carl B. Smith and Peggy G. Elliot suggest giving remedial readers the study questions before they read the chapter. Remedial readers can use these questions as organizers. Having them beforehand helps students read selectively, and they can also serve as a source for the tutor (1986, 16). Be specific; Eunice N. Askov suggests giving the remedial reader a guide that identifies exactly which paragraphs to read, which to summarize or respond to, and which to skip (1991, 88).

The following strategies for helping remedial readers in the regular classroom, suggested by S. B. Cohen and D. K. Lynch, are organized into categories and can be helpful for all students.

PHYSICAL ARRANGEMENTS

- Use study carrels.
- Use room dividers.
- Provide headsets to muffle noise.
- Seat child away from doors/windows.
- Seat child near a model (student or teacher).

- Put desks close to blackboard.
- Provide a time-out area.
- Vary working surfaces (for example, use the floor and vertical surfaces such as blackboards).

ORGANIZING

- Use timers to show allocated time.
- Use clock faces to show classroom routine times.
- Provide daily and weekly assignment sheets.
- Post daily/weekly schedules.
- Establish routines for handing in work, heading papers.
- Provide organizers (cartons/bins) for desk material.
- Collect notebooks weekly (periodically) to review student notes.
- Establish rules and review frequently.

GROUPING

- Rearrange student groups (according to instructional needs, role models, etc.).
- Group for cooperative learning.

PROVIDING SUPPORTS

- Have student repeat lesson objectives.
- Use manipulatives.
- Provide functional tasks (related to child's environment).
- Have a peer-tutor program.
- Use a study guide.
- Provide critical vocabulary list for content material.
- Provide essential fact lists.
- Use self-teaching materials.
- Use self-correcting materials.

- Adapt test items for differing response modes.
- Provide visual cues (posters, desktop number lines).
- Tape-record student responses.
- Use dotted lines to line up math problems or show margins.
- Use graph paper for place value or when adding/subtracting two-digit numbers, or turn notebook paper horizontally.
- Color-code place-value tasks.
- Provide pencil grips.
- Tape paper to desk.

GUIDING INSTRUCTION

- Provide discussion questions before reading.
- Use word markers to guide reading.
- Teach varied reading rates (scanning, skimming, etc.).
- Repeat major points.
- Use physical cues while speaking (1, 2, 3, etc.).
- Pause during speaking.
- Use verbal cues ("Don't write this down."; "This is important.").
- Change tone of voice (whisper, etc.).
- Have student summarize at end of lesson.
- Provide mnemonic devices.
- Provide content/lecture summaries.

GIVING DIRECTIONS

- Simplify/shorten directions.
- Teach key direction words.
- Provide transition directions.
- Segment directions.
- Provide sequential directions (label as first, second, etc.).
- Have student repeat directions.

- Tape-record directions.
- Use rebus (picture) directions.

QUESTIONING

- Ask frequent questions.
- Change question level.
- Change response format (for example, from verbal to physical, from saying to pointing).
- Increase your wait-time (time allowed for student responses).

ADAPTING TASKS

- Reduce number of items on a task.
- Do only odd- or even-numbered items.
- Assign only one task at a time.
- Shorten project assignment into daily tasks.
- Number (order) assignments to be completed.
- Reorganize tests to go from easy to hard.
- Alter sequence of presentation.
- Highlight relevant words/features.
- Use a primary typewriter or large print to create written material.
- Change far-point material (material that is far away) to near-point material (material that is close) for copying or review.
- Block out extraneous stimuli on written material.
- Enlarge or highlight key words on test items.

PROVIDING PRACTICE

- Provide guided practice.
- Provide more practice trials.
- Use distributed practice.
- Increase allocated time.

- Provide frequent review.
- Provide error drill.

MOTIVATING

- Change reinforcers.
- Provide tangible reinforcers.
- Increase reinforcement frequency.
- Delay reinforcement.
- Use specific rather than general praise.
- Incorporate currently popular themes/characters into assignments.
- Teach self-monitoring.

From "Effective Instruction: Principles and Strategies for Programs," by S. B. Cohen and D. K. Lynch. In *Program Leadership for Serving Students with Disabilities* by B. Billingsley (ed.), 1993, 201–203. Copyright 1993 by the State Department of Education, Commonwealth of Virginia.

A Final Note

When you are working in the content areas, remember that teaching reading is everyone's responsibility. Teaching reading in the content areas can be particularly enjoyable because of the wide variety of materials and the high level of interest in the topics. The strategies in this chapter can not only enhance both reading and writing in the content areas but can also give students skills that will prove useful throughout their adult lives, a most satisfying consequence.

Summary

Because many students lack the necessary skills for successful content-area reading, teachers will want to use a variety of strategies that assist students as they read textbooks. The readability of a textbook is an all-important criterion. The most common form of writing style in textbooks, expository writing, often requires direct instruction. General organization may include features such as organizers, headings, graphic aids, chapter summaries, follow-up questions, and so forth. Paragraphs in expository writing fall into the following categories: descriptive, enumerative, sequential, cause/effect, compare/contrast, and problem/solution. Many teachers supplement textbooks with tradebooks in order to provide additional contexts for the information. Other strategies for teaching content areas include the following:

previewing a textbook	*previewing a passage*
K-W-L	*attitude inventory*
anticipation guides	*anticipatory problem solving*
possible sentences	*finding details*
SQ3R	*visual reading guide*
structured overview	*following a flow chart*
Directed Reading-Thinking Activity	*semantic feature analysis*
backtracking	*"Say Something" summarization*
hierarchical summary writing	*précis writing*
reading test directions	

Teachers and students can take advantage of a wide variety of CD-ROMs and software products that relate directly to content areas. Students with lower achievement levels may benefit from using hypertext on CD-ROMs. Diverse learners may need aids such as adapted reading assignments, special assistance, advance organizers, or study guides.

Readability Formula That Saves Time

Directions for using the readability graph (see example on page 382):

1. Randomly select three sample passages and count out exactly 100 words each, beginning with the beginning of a sentence. Do count proper nouns, initializations, and numerals.

2. Count the number of sentences in the 100 words, estimating the length of the fraction of the last sentence to the nearest one-tenth.

3. Count the total number of syllables in the 100-word passage. If you don't have a hand-counter available, an easy way is to simply put a mark above every syllable over one in each word, then when you get to the end of the passage, count the number of marks and add 100. Small calculators can also be used as counters by pushing numeral 1, then push the + sign for each word or syllable when counting.

4. Graph the *average* sentence length and *average* number of syllables; mark a dot where the two lines intersect. The area where the dot is plotted will give you the approximate grade level.

Average number of syllables per 100 words

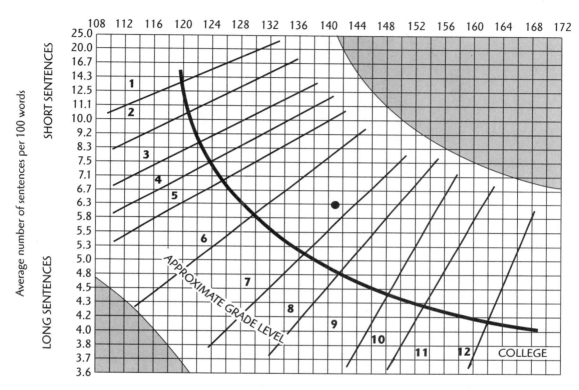

SHORT WORDS   LONG WORDS

FIGURE 11.12

Fry's Readability Graph

From "Fry's Readability Graph: Clarifications, Validity, and Extension to Level 17." by Edward Fry, *Journal of Reading* 21, 3 (Dec. 1977): 249. *Note:* This extended graph does not outmode or render the earlier (1968) version inoperative or inaccurate; it is an extension. Reprinted with permission.

5. If a great deal of variability is found in syllable count or sentence count, putting more samples into the average is desirable.

6. A word is defined as a group of symbols with a space on either side; thus, *Joe, IRA, 1945,* and *&* are each one word.

7. A syllable is defined as a phonetic syllable. Generally, there are as many syllables as vowel sounds. For example, *stopped* is one syllable and *wanted* is two syllables. When counting syllables for numerals and initializations, count one syllable for each symbol. For example, *1945* is four syllables, *IRA* is three syllables, and *&* is one syllable.

Example:

	SENTENCES PER 100 WORDS	SYLLABLES PER 100 WORDS
100-word sample page 5	*9.1*	*122*
100-word sample page 89	*8.5*	*140*
100-word sample page 150	*7.0*	*129*
Total	*24.6*	*391*
Divide total by 3 (average)	*8.2*	*130*

Plotting these averages on the graph, we find they fall in the fifth grade area; hence the book is at about a fifth grade difficulty level. If great variability is encountered either in sentence length or in syllables, count for the three selections, then randomly select several more passages and average them in before plotting.

Resources for Integrating Literature with Textbooks

Angell, Carole S. *Celebrations Around the World: A Multicultural Handbook.* Golden, Colo.: Fulcrum, 1996.

Barchers, Suzanne I., and Patricia C. Marden. *Cooking Up U.S. History.* Englewood, Colo.: Teacher Ideas Press, 1991.

Braddon, Kathryn L., Nancy J. Hall, and Dale Taylor. *Math through Children's Literature.* Englewood, Colo.: Teacher Ideas Press, 1993.

Butzow, Carol M., and John W. Butzow. *Science through Children's Literature.* Englewood, Colo.: Teacher Ideas Press, 1989.

Caduto, Michael J., and Joseph Bruchac. *Keepers of the Earth: Native American Stories and Environmental Activities for Children.* Golden, Colo.: Fulcrum, 1988. (Also see others in series.)

Fredericks, Anthony D. *Social Studies through Children's Literature.* Englewood, Colo.: Teacher Ideas Press, 1991.

Fredericks, Anthony D., Anita Meyer Meinbach, and Liz Rothlein. *Thematic Units: An Integrated Approach to Teaching Science and Social Studies.* New York: HarperCollins, 1993.

Freeman, Evelyn B., and Diane Goetz Person, eds. *Using Nonfiction Trade Books in the Elementary Classroom from Ants to Zeppelins.* Urbana, Ill.: National Council of Teachers of English, 1992.

Green, Pamela. *A Matter of Fact: Using Factual Texts in the Classroom.* Armadale, Vic, Australia: Eleanor Curtin, 1992.

Heltshe, Mary Ann, and Audrey Burie Kirchner. *Multicultural Explorations: Joyous Journeys with Books.* Englewood, Colo.: Teacher Ideas Press, 1991.

Laughlin, Mildred Knight, and Patricia Payne Kardaleff. *Literature-Based Social Studies: Children's Books and Activities to Enrich the K–5 Curriculum.* Phoenix, Ariz.: Oryx Press, 1991.

Levene, Donna. *Music through Children's Literature.* Englewood, Colo.: Teacher Ideas Press, 1993.

Marden, Patricia C., and Suzanne I. Barchers. *Cooking Up World History: Multicultural Recipes and Resources.* Englewood, Colo.: Teacher Ideas Press, 1994.

McGlathery, Glenn, and Norma J. Livo. *Who's Endangered on Noah's Ark? Literary and Scientific Activities for Teachers and Parents.* Englewood, Colo.: Teacher Ideas Press, 1992.

Ramsey, Diane P. *Voyage to Discovery: An Activity Guide to the Age of Exploration.* Englewood, Colo.: Teacher Ideas Press, 1992.

Ray, Robert D., and Joan Klingel Ray. *Integrating Aerospace Science into the Curriculum: K–12.* Englewood, Colo.: Teacher Ideas Press, 1992.

Roberts, Patricia L. *A Green Dinosaur Day: A Guide for Developing Thematic Units in Literature-Based Instruction, K–6.* Boston: Allyn & Bacon, 1993.

References

Alvermann, Donna. "Tradebooks and Textbooks: Making Connections across Content Areas." In *Integrated Language Arts: Controversy to Consensus,* edited by Lesley Mandel Morrow, Jeffrey K. Smith, and Louise Cherry Wilkinson, 51–69. Boston: Allyn & Bacon, 1994.

Anderson, Richard C., and Alice Davison. "Conceptual and Empirical Bases of Readability Formulas." In *Linguistic Complexity and Text Comprehension: Readability Issues Reconsidered,* edited by Alice Davison and Georgia M. Green, 23–53. Hillsdale, N.J.: Lawrence Erlbaum Associates, 1988.

Armbruster, Bonnie B., Jean H. Osborn, and Alice L. Davison. "Readability Formulas May Be Dangerous to Your Textbooks." *Educational Leadership* 42, no. 7 (April 1985): 18–20.

Askov, Eunice N. "Teaching Study Skills." In *Effective Strategies for Teaching Reading*, edited by Bernard L. Hayes, 85–102. Needham Heights, Mass.: Allyn & Bacon, 1991.

Beatty, Patricia. *Charley Skedaddle.* New York: Morrow Junior Books, 1987.

Blanchard, Jay S., and George E. Mason. "Using Computers in Content Area Reading Instruction." *Journal of Reading* 29, no. 2 (Nov. 1985): 112–117.

Bromley, Karen D'Angelo, and Laurie McKeveny. "Précis Writing: Suggestions for Instruction in Summarizing." *Journal of Reading* 29, no. 5 (Feb. 1987): 392–395.

Bruce, Bertram, and Andee Rubin. "Readability Formulas: Matching Tool and Task." In *Linguistic Complexity and Text Comprehension: Readability Issues Reconsidered*, edited by Alice Davison and Georgia M. Green, 5–22. Hillsdale, N.J.: Lawrence Erlbaum Associates, 1988.

Camperell, Kay. "Teaching Reading in Content Area Materials." In *Effective Strategies for Teaching Reading*, edited by Bernard L. Hayes, 103–122. Needham Heights, Mass.: Allyn & Bacon, 1991.

Carr, Eileen, and Donna Ogle. "K-W-L Plus: A Strategy for Comprehension and Summarization." *Journal of Reading* 30, no. 7 (April 1987): 626–631.

Chamot, Anna Uhl, and J. Michael O'Malley. "The Cognitive Academic Language Learning Approach." In *When They Don't All Speak English: Integrating the ESL Student into the Regular Classroom*, edited by Pat Rigg and Virginia G. Allen, 104–125. Urbana, Ill.: National Council of Teachers of English, 1989.

Chang, Ina. *A Separate Battle: Women and the Civil War.* New York: Lodestar, 1991.

Ciborowski, Jean. "Using Textbooks with Students Who Cannot Read Them." *Remedial and Special Education* 16, no. 2 (March 1995): 90–101.

Cochran, Judith A. *Reading in the Content Areas for Junior High and High School.* Boston: Allyn & Bacon, 1993.

Cohen, S. B., and D. K. Lynch. "Effective Instruction: Principles and Strategies for Programs." In *Program Leadership for Serving Students with Disabilities* edited by B. Billingsley, 201–203. Copyright 1993 by the State Department of Education, Commonwealth of Virginia.

Conley, Mark W. *Content Reading Instruction: A Communication Approach.* New York: McGraw Hill, 1992.

Culbertson, Roger, and Robert Margulies. *3-D Kid.* New York: W. H. Freeman, 1995.

Durkin, Dolores. *Teaching Them to Read,* 5th ed. Needham Heights, Mass.: Allyn & Bacon, 1989.

Fry, Edward. "African Reading Stories." *The Reading Teacher* 48, no. 5 (Feb. 1995): 444–445.

———. *Reading Instruction for Classroom and Clinic.* New York: McGraw Hill, 1972.

Garner, Ruth. "Strategies for Reading and Studying Expository Text." *Educational Psychologist* 22, nos. 3 & 4, (1987): 299–312.

Johnson, Nancy M., and M. Jane Ebert. "Time Travel Is Possible: Historical Fiction and Biography—Passport to the Past." *The Reading Teacher* 45, no. 7 (March 1992): 488–495.

Kucer, Stephen B., and Jerome C. Harste. "The Reading and Writing Connection: Counterpart Strategy Lessons." In *Effective Strategies for Teaching Reading,* edited by Bernard L. Hayes, 123–152. Needham Heights, Mass.: Allyn & Bacon, 1991.

Langer, Judith A. "Learning through Writing: Study Skills in the Content Areas." *Journal of Reading* 29, no. 5 (Feb. 1986): 400–406.

Lederer, Richard. *Anguished English: An Anthology of Accidental Assaults upon Our Language.* Charleston, S.C.: Wyrick, 1987.

Meese, Ruth Lyn. *Teaching Learners with Mild Disabilities: Integrating Research & Practice.* Belmont, Calif.: Brooks Cole, 1994.

Moore, David W., John E. Readence, and Robert J. Rickelman. *Prereading Activities for Content Area Reading and Learning,* 2nd ed. Newark, Del.: International Reading Association, 1989.

Murphy, Jim. *The Boys' War: Confederate and Union Soldiers Talk About the Civil War.* New York: Clarion, 1990.

Ogle, Donna. "K-W-L: A Teaching Model That Develops Active Reading of Expository Text." *The Reading Teacher* 39, no. 6 (Feb. 1986): 564–670.

Piccolo, Jo Anne. "Expository Text Structure: Teaching and Learning Strategies." *The Reading Teacher* 40, no. 9 (May 1987): 838–847.

———. *Reading, Writing, and Thinking: Book One.* San Antonio, Texas: ECS Learning Systems, 1996.

_____. *Reading, Writing, and Thinking: Book Two*. San Antonio, Texas: ECS Learning Systems, 1996.

Pittelman, Susan D., Joan E. Heimlich, Roberta L. Berglund, and Michael P. French. *Semantic Feature Analysis: Classroom Applications*. Newark, Del.: International Reading Association, 1991.

Radencich, Marguerite C., Penny G. Beers, and Jeanne Shay Schumm. *A Handbook for the K–12 Reading Resource Specialist*. Boston: Allyn & Bacon, 1993.

Ratekin, Ned, Michele L. Simpson, Donna E. Alvermann, and Ernest K. Dishner. "Why Teachers Resist Content Reading Instruction." *Journal of Reading* 28, no. 5 (Feb. 1985): 432–437.

Reutzel, D. Ray, Cynthia Middleton Larson, and Brenda L. Sabey. "Dialogical Books: Connecting Content, Conversation, and Composition." *The Reading Teacher* 49, no. 2 (Oct. 1995): 98–109.

Rosenblatt, Louise M. "Literary Theory." In *Handbook of Research on Teaching the English Language Arts*, edited by James Flood, Julie M. Jensen, Diane Lapp, and James R. Squire, 57–62. New York: Macmillan, 1991.

Simonsen, Stephen, and Harry Singer. "Improving Reading Comprehension in the Content Areas." In *What Research Has To Say about Reading Instruction*, 2nd ed., edited by S. Jay Samuels and Alan E. Farstrup, 200–219. Newark, Del.: International Reading Association, 1992.

Smith, Carl B., and Peggy G. Elliot. *Reading Activities for Middle and Secondary Schools: A Handbook for Teachers*, 2nd ed. New York: Teachers College Press, 1986.

Smith, Patricia L., and Gail E. Tompkins. "Structured Notetaking: A New Strategy for Content Area Readers." *Journal of Reading* 32, no. 1 (Oct. 1988): 46–53.

Smith, Frank. *Insult to Intelligence: The Bureaucratic Invasion of Our Classrooms*. New York: Arbor House, 1986.

Spyridakis, Jan H., and Timothy C. Standal. "Signals in Expository Prose: Effects on Reading Comprehension." *Reading Research Quarterly* 22, no. 33 (Summer 1987): 285–298.

Stahl, Steven A., and Barbara A. Kapinus. "Possible Sentences: Predicting Word Meanings to Teach Content Area Vocabulary." *The Reading Teacher* 45, no. 1 (Sept. 1991): 36–43.

Stauffer, Russell G. *Directing Reading Maturity as a Cognitive Process*. New York: Harper & Row, 1969.

Taylor, Barbara M. "Text Structure, Comprehension, and Recall." In *What Research Has To Say about Reading Instruction*, 2nd ed., edited by S. Jay Samuels and Alan E. Farstrup, 220–235. Newark, Del.: International Reading Association, 1992.

Tinajero, Josefina Villamil. "Are We Communicating? Effective Instruction for Students Who Are Acquiring English as a Second Language." *The Reading Teacher* 48, no. 3 (Nov. 1994): 260–264.

Vacca, Richard T., and JoAnne L. Vacca. *Content Area Reading*. 5th ed., New York: HarperCollins, 1996.

CD-ROMS

Barchers, Suzanne I. *Ride Like the Wind Bike Rally*. Denver, Colo.: Intercomm International, 1998.

Biesty, Stephen. *Stowaway!* New York: Dorling Kindersley, 1995.

Bird. New York: Dorling Kindersley, 1995/1996.

History of the World. New York: Dorling Kindersley, 1995.

Holden, Amanda, editor. *The Viking Opera Guide*. New York: Penguin Electronic Publishing, 1995.

Ridgeway, George. *You Be the Reporter!* Freeport, N.Y.: Educational Activities, no date.

Reading Assessment and Evaluation

FOCUS QUESTIONS

1. What is the impact of national education goals and standards on assessment and evaluation?

2. What is formal assessment and what are typical tests?

3. How can I help students take formal tests?

3. What is informal assessment and what are typical measures?

4. How can I build an evaluation program that blends formal and informal assessments?

5. How can I involve and educate parents and students regarding assessment and evaluation?

6. What is the role of assessment with special students?

The midyear reading test scores returned just in time for report cards, and two of my best students had extremely low scores. I didn't need to check their records; I knew that last fall these students had scored 99 percent on the long form of this test, drawn from the basal reading program. I had asked why they needed to take the identical test again and had been told it was district policy. This time they had taken only the first half of the same test and done poorly. How could they take the first half of the test and have a score of less than 60 percent when they previously had scored 99 percent on the whole test? Knowing that the test scores would devastate these students, I requested that their tests be rescored, with the same results. I stubbornly returned them again. This time they came back with 99 percent and photocopies of the computer-read test forms so that I could see what had happened. When administering the test, I was required to read much of it aloud and had stopped at the midpoint of the test. These two bright students quite naturally worked ahead, going beyond the stopping point and completing a few more answers. Their additional pencil marks triggered the computer to read the entire form, thereby giving them the low scores.

Introduction

Striking a balance between required district test procedures and day-to-day knowledge about a student's performance can be challenging. During my recent years teaching, although I was not using the basal readers, I was required to use the full form of this test during the fall and spring and a short form at midyear. Despite performance levels, every student was required to take the same test three times, certainly a waste of time for students who had already demonstrated proficiency. In the opening anecdote, the tests, had I left them unchallenged, would have presented a distorted picture of these students' achievement.

The public has become increasingly concerned about reading performance. For more than 20 years, the National Assessment of Educational Progress (NAEP), also known as the Nation's Report Card, has conducted assessments in the areas of reading, writing, mathematics, and science, summarizing accomplishments by race and ethnicity, gender, community type, and region. The results of the 1990 NAEP in reading suggested that the reading performance of 9-, 13-, and 17-year-olds had not changed much in the previous 20 years (Hiebert and Kapinus 1992, 732). Yet citizens remain convinced that student achievement is deteriorating (Farr 1992, 27).

America 2000, a strategy developed by the President and the 50 governors to improve education by setting national goals, laid out three basic objectives:

- Encourage every community to adopt the national goals, develop its own local strategy, and prepare an annual community report card on its progress toward the goals.

- Stimulate the creation of thousands of "break-the-mold schools" that would approach education in totally new ways to meet the needs of today's children and families.

- Develop voluntary "world-class" standards and American Achievement Tests (Ravitch 1993, 767).

Content standards
What a student should know and be able to do.

Curriculum standards
What should take place in the classroom.

Benchmarks
Expected or anticipated performance at various developmental levels.

With this mandate, local districts and national organizations, such as the International Reading Association and the National Council of Teachers of English, have striven to define standards for reading. The results were the creation of **content standards**; **curriculum standards**, sometimes referred to as program standards; and **benchmarks** (Kendall and Marzano 1994, 10). In their efforts to meet these standards, school districts are turning to a variety of assessment measures that will give a valid picture of an individual's progress.

Diane Ravitch asserts that "standards are the starting point of education reform. You can't design an assessment unless you have agreement about what children should learn" (1993, 772). Presumably, additional and alternative assessment measures would determine whether attempts at innovation are making a difference (ibid., 768). However, Ken Goodman cautions that standards sought by the Department of Education are precise and tangible, more consistent with standard outcomes than the process learning that many educators prefer today (1994, 20).

An educator's primary goal should be that the curriculum meets the highest standards. First, the content or subject matter should be appropriate for teaching and learning, according to the norms of the community in authority (Newmann, Secada, and Wehlage 1995, 3). Second, the material in the texts and the statements of the teachers and students should be consistent with authoritative knowledge and competence in the subject area (ibid.). Third, a lesson or assessment task should have some value beyond the context of school success (ibid., 4).

Once standards are developed for content, teachers then need additional standards to guide assessment. Thus we have documents such as *Standards for the Assessment of Reading and Writing* (IRA/NCTE 1994), produced collaboratively by the International Reading Association and National Council of Teachers of English. As the variety of assessment measures expands, teachers must take ownership of the process of assessment. Testing terminology can be complex and confusing, and the sheer number of options can be overwhelming. This chapter provides basic information about assessment and evaluation measures, looks at a variety of assessment examples, and examines the impact of national and local standards on reading programs. However, before we begin, do you remember your "possible sentences" activity from Something to Try 2 in Chapter 11, page 367? Review the sentences you constructed now so that you can keep them in mind as you read this chapter.

Assessment and Evaluation

Assessment
The gathering of data that provides information for evaluation.

Many terms are used to discuss assessment and evaluation. Some are often confused with others, and some are (correctly) used interchangeably. **Assessment** is usually quantitative and based on tests, but it may also include interviews and observation. This information is used to evaluate students' progress (Bertrand 1991, 17). To fully understand assessment, we need to put it in the context of current learning models. Education has shifted from a knowledge transmission model, where teachers using prescribed materials deliver knowledge to learners, to an inquiry model where inquiry forms the basis of teaching and learning. It is within this latter model that we will look at assessment.

Within an inquiry model (typical examples are whole language, integrated language arts, and interdisciplinary programs), knowledge is dynamic rather than static, and learning is social and collaborative (Crafton and Burke 1994, 3). Students identify areas of inquiry and investigation, and the curriculum is built around these interests. In this framework, assessment explores how "the educational environment and the participants in the educational community support education as [the] process of learning to become independent thinkers and problem solvers" (IRA/NCTE 1994, 6). Students, followed by teachers, are held accountable for their learning. Such accountability relies on centers of inquiry where everyone—students, teachers, administrators, and citizens—investigate effective learning processes through quality assessment (ibid., 7).

Teachers may use formal or informal assessment, and various measures have come to be associated with these terms. For example, the test discussed in the opening anecdote was a **formal assessment**, a process that usually occurs at the end of a unit or school term (Farr and Beck 1991, 489). These are usually districtwide, standardized tests or teacher-created, multiple-choice or true-and-false tests that are easily scored. When a teacher tries to help a student read or write better through observation, conferences, or other processes that are not "tests," the teacher is making an **informal assessment** (ibid.). In informal assessment, teachers use checklists, inventories, questioning, interviews, conferences, portfolios, learning logs, observations, anecdotal records, self-evaluations, and peer-evaluations. These practices will be described more fully later in this chapter.

Evaluation, the process of collecting and using information to determine how a student learns, includes assessments and is a process you are no doubt familiar with, both as a student and as a teacher. Because formal assessments such as standardized tests usually occur at the end of a substantial undertaking or time period, they are often referred to as **summative evaluation** (Huff and Kline 1987, 159).

Many teachers use informal assessment measures, such as conferences, observations, or checklists, to conduct **formative evaluation**, perhaps during a personalized reading conference or during a basal reading lesson (Lipson and Wixson 1989, 118). However, it is important to note that these same assessment measures are also used for summative evaluation.

Formal assessment Determines how much students have learned and is generally based on criterion- or norm-referenced tests.

Informal assessment Determines why students perform or learn as they do, rather than how well they perform.

Summative evaluation Tests on, or judgments made about, a finished project or upon completion of a particular unit of study.

Formative evaluation A process of evaluation that provides feedback and redirection during the learning process.

Formal Assessment

Any reading program, whether it uses basal readers or literature, should make a variety of assessments to fully evaluate student progress. Formal assessment is often criticized for relying on

A student takes a standardized test.

numerical scores without knowing a student's underlying reasoning (Harman 1992, 250), driving curriculum (IRA/NCTE 1994, 17; Marzano, Pickering, and McTighe 1993, 11), causing undue teacher and student anxiety, and not accurately reflecting individual achievement. However, our society continues to rely on formal assessment, so teachers need to know how to provide instruction that supports successful performance on commercial tests.

NORM-REFERENCED TESTS

Norm-referenced tests
Tests that relate results to other students with predetermined performance indicators or scales, generally by student's age, grade, or gender.

Norm-referenced tests provide a way to compare large groups of students. The Iowa Test of Basic Skills and the California Achievement Test are familiar norm-referenced tests that assess word recognition, vocabulary, comprehension, and other topics. Typically covering a broad area of achievement, these tests are administered to large numbers of students across a region or country. The scores are based on the normal curve (see Figure 12.1) and indicate comparative performance levels. For example, a student who scores at the 50th percentile on the comprehension portion of a reading test has performed as well as approximately half the students taking that test. A grade-equivalent score may be assigned by relating the score to the average scores obtained by students at a given grade level (Slavin 1988, 586).

FIGURE 12.1
The Normal Curve
with Percentile
Equivalents

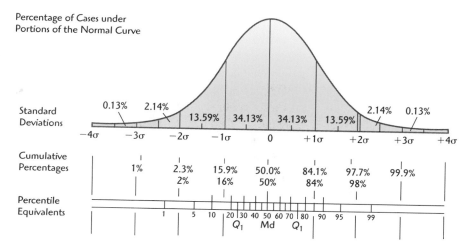

Percentage of Cases under
Portions of the Normal Curve

Standard
Deviations

| 0.13% | 2.14% | 13.59% | 34.13% | 34.13% | 13.59% | 2.14% | 0.13% |

-4σ -3σ -2σ -1σ 0 $+1\sigma$ $+2\sigma$ $+3\sigma$ $+4\sigma$

Cumulative
Percentages

1%   2.3%   15.9%   50.0%   84.1%   97.7%   99.9%
     2%   16%   50%   84%   98%

Percentile
Equivalents

1   5   10   20 30 40 50 60 70 80   90   95   99
                    Q_1 Md Q_1

These tests are referred to as *standardized* tests because of the rigorous procedures used to develop them and because they are usually scored by computers. Computer scoring allows districts to compute a variety of scores such as raw scores, percentile ranks, and grade equivalents.

Standardized reading tests sample reading performance, typically focusing on word recognition, sound blending, punctuation, and spelling (Rhodes and Dudley-Marling 1988, 35). Reading-comprehension passages are often short, using narrative or expository writing. Because standardized tests only sample a student's performance on a given day on a particular test, the results may provide a very narrow view of an individual's reading achievement. Students unfamiliar with the test's format may perform more poorly than they would given a more comfortable test form. Because evaluation is an important component of the educational process, additional measures should be included, such as teacher observation and an understanding of the student's mastery of the reading process (Levande 1993, 127).

CRITERION-REFERENCED TESTS

The test mentioned in the opening anecdote, which compared the students' scores to accepted levels of achievement in a basal reader program, is an example of a criterion-referenced test. Rather than test large groups of students to determine a statistical expectation of achievement ranges, a criterion-referenced test typically focuses on a limited set of learning tasks. For example, a publisher or district may develop a test that determines whether a student has mastered the reading skills taught in a basal reading program. A specific level of mastery may be expected, such as being able to identify the main idea in 8 out of 10 questions following a reading.

BASAL SERIES TESTS

Basal series tests generally feature multiple-choice questions because they are scored more easily. Tied directly to the program's scope and sequence of skills, the tests emphasize decoding and comprehension, with 80 percent correct serving as the usual passing criterion. Because of the many skills taught in basal programs, only three or four test items may be dedicated to a single skill, thus reducing the passing criterion to 67 or 75 percent (Shannon 1989, 99).

In a review of three major basal series, Eunice Ann Greer found that basal-series assessment measures include more choices, more support for using measures such as portfolios, longer passages for reading from a wider range of genres, and improved comprehension questions (1992, 650–651). Although Sharon Murphy believes that many problems remain, she appreciates the basal test formats that are more consistent with the reading formats and welcomes the open-ended questions that require more complex responses (1994, 112–113).

Basals sometimes provide Informal Reading Inventories (IRIs), which can be used to approximate reading levels. Word lists assess word recognition, and short oral reading selections followed by 6–10 questions test comprehension. IRIs, administered individually, can be time-consuming for the teacher who rarely has uninterrupted blocks of time, but they can also provide valuable insights into miscues and reading strategies. Some teachers schedule several days of quiet independent projects or use paraprofessionals to help monitor other students during testing.

Criterion-referenced tests found at the end of basal units can be used as formative evaluation. Teachers can determine which of the supplementary reteaching materials to use before a student moves on to the next unit. If unit pretests are not available, a teacher can use posttests as pretests to determine whether a student needs to complete all the skill-related assignments in the next unit. If the student already achieves an 80 percent mastery level, worksheets or lessons can be skipped, or novels can replace the basal.

ISSUES IN FORMAL ASSESSMENT

Although many teachers prefer informal assessments to standardized tests, commercial tests are here to stay, particularly when organizations such as the NAEP rely on their scores to assess national trends. Few people would argue against the stance taken by many educators that teachers are better at assessing achievement than machine-scored, multiple-choice questions. Tests cannot diagnose why or how a child chose a particular answer, but through discussion and questions, teachers can and do. Taking standardized tests requires only passive recognition on the part of the child, rather than active engagement. Adding insult to injury, students may be drilled on how to choose among a, b, c, or d to prepare for a standardized test (Barthe and Mitchell 1992, 88). When educational decisions are made using test results that only assess how a student does on that particular day, important factors such as motivation, health, and lack of sleep are ignored. Standardized tests do not adequately measure critical thinking, nor do they measure student potential (Bartoli and Botel 1988, 175). John J. Pikulski asserts that the greatest misuse of standardized tests may be their *overuse*. If standardized tests were used to sample achievement selectively, districts could save money and time, using these savings to purchase literature or more meaningful assessment measures (1990, 686).

Notwithstanding these criticisms, schools continue to use standardized tests. Some schools test selected grade levels annually, minimizing the pressures inherent in wide-range testing. Other school districts publish scores or use scores to determine instructional groups or evaluate teaching ability. Publishers of commercial materials systematically analyze achievement tests, using similar formats and content to ensure success on commercial tests (Durkin 1989, 485).

Schools, and thereby teachers, are increasingly pressured to be accountable (Hiebert and Calfee 1992, 74). When school test scores are published in community newspapers, teachers may be tempted to teach to the test. When student test scores are used to determine merit pay, the system becomes severely stressed (Glass 1990, 238). By definition, norm-referenced tests follow a normal or bell curve distribution, as seen in Figure 12.1. By careful design, when 100 randomly selected students take the test, 50 will score above and 50 below the 50th percentile. Essentially, it is unrealistic to increase everyone's test scores unless the entire program is devoted to preparing students for the test. And then the results would only show that the students could be taught the test, not whether they were truly achieving at the indicated levels. It is certainly prudent to help students perform at optimal levels, but the assessment process should be kept in perspective (Barchers 1994, 374; Pikulski 1990, 686–687).

When considering formal assessment practices, teachers can explore the following questions:

■ **Validity**
The degree to which a test assesses what it purports to measure.

1. What is the purpose of the test?

2. Do the tests influence the curriculum?

■ **Reliability**
The consistency of scores obtained when persons are reexamined with the same test on different occasions or with tests composed of parallel sets of items.

3. Do the tests have **validity**? Do they assess what ought to be taught or what is actually being taught? Does the test measure what you want it to?

4. Do the tests have **reliability**? For example, if you used the test repeatedly on different occasions or used tests composed of parallel sets of items, would a student achieve at or near the same level?

5. Is testing overemphasized by the educational community?

6. Should students be evaluated based on the factual knowledge typically assessed by standardized tests?

7. Is formal assessment the sole form of evaluation?

8. Does the existence of formal measures displace teacher evaluation, particularly the use of informal measures?

9. Does product, as assessed by formal measures, become more important than process?

10. Are the tests fair to minority groups, students with special needs, limited English students, or other individuals? (Excerpted from *Teaching Language Arts: An Integrated Approach* by Suzanne I. Barchers, 374. Minneapolis, Minn.: West, 1994.)

RECOMMENDATIONS FOR USING FORMAL ASSESSMENTS

You may have decided that students should never have to take formal assessments. Although most districts and states will disagree with you, fortunately they are beginning to recognize the importance of a variety of assessments, and many are seeking better measures and giving more choices regarding the frequency or type of assessments to be used (Hiebert and Calfee 1992, 74–75). Yet standardized tests are going to be part of your reading program. As a teacher, you have a responsibility to prepare your students for a world that continues to use formal assessments as partial criteria for obtaining scholarships or admittance into college or graduate school. The following recommendations can help you prepare them for the world of formal assessments:

1. Become familiar with test terminology. (See terminology list at the end of this chapter.)

2. Become familiar with the test form. Most standardized tests are multiple choice, but some tests offer more open-ended or complex questions.

3. Become familiar with the general information that will be tested. If a criterion-referenced test is based on the district's basal language arts program, become familiar with the information that is expected to be mastered at your grade level. A criterion-referenced test based on a basal program may be similar in content to a norm-referenced test.

4. Integrate test-related terms and skills into your teaching throughout the year. If sixth graders need to know how to identify a main idea or sequence, be certain that even if you don't use basal materials that you have taught these skills.

5. Teach test-taking strategies throughout the year. Help students become famil-iar with test formats and how to follow written and verbal directions. Help them become familiar with typical test items. Teach how to preview the test, and how to plan for efficient use of time, such as answering easy questions first. Demonstrate how to check answers if there is time. Encourage students to be rested and to stay both relaxed and alert (Orr 1986, 104, 52). Specific strategies include using the process of elimination, recognizing resemblances between a test item stem and its options, using information from other parts of the test, and using grammatical cues (Woodley 1978, 20–29). Some schools take two weeks or more to teach an intensive course on test-taking skills. Though it is valuable to teach such survival skills, it is more effective to inte-grate them into the curriculum.

6. If practice tests are provided by the publisher, use them. They give you and the students an opportunity to familiarize yourselves with the nature and for-mat of the test.

7. Be supportive of test-taking. Consider tests not as a necessary evil, but as a necessary tool. Support your students, giving them as much useful informa-tion about the process as possible, without creating undue anxiety.

8. Modify your program so that students are not under pressure to complete assignments during the testing period.

9. When test scores are distributed, explain what scores mean, while providing perspective. Remind students that test scores give only a small amount of information about what they have achieved and that your other assessment measures are also important.

10. Be willing to discuss test results with parents. Be prepared to refer parents to re-sources such as test-taking guides, tutors, or specialized resources if necessary.

11. Make notes for next year's testing period. Though tests cannot be copied or kept from year to year, it is acceptable to make note of general needs for sub-sequent years.

12. Consider informal, as well as formal, assessments when making decisions about students. Remember that formal tests assess how well students respond to multiple-choice test items on a particular day. Informal tests provide infor-mation about the process, about how students learn.

13. If you are using tests provided by a basal series, consider using them as a pretest to assist with determining what skills have already been mastered. In short, make the tests work *for* you and *for* your students.

14. When test scores are overemphasized and the pressure to improve scores in-creases, it is tempting to teach to the test, emphasizing the facts or skills that

you know will be tested. Instead of spending time drilling students in this way, try having them construct their own simple tests. Use easy reading or language arts material and model how you might construct a specific test, say on identifying the main idea of a selection. Have the students work in small groups to prepare tests and then administer them to other groups. Discuss the results, the reasoning behind the test construction, the answers chosen, and any other issues that develop. For intermediate students and middle school students, explain and use appropriate terms such as *reliability* and *validity*. If students develop mock tests routinely through the year, they will reinforce the skills being learned and in the process will also alleviate possible test anxiety. This activity also develops critical thinking skills, provides more student insights into testing, and lends some authenticity to the testing process.

15. Educators must work toward more authentic assessment and evaluation (Lipson and Wixson 1989, 137). If possible, take an active role in the school or district's testing policy, working toward improved and appropriate test measures, both formal and informal. (Adapted from *Teaching Language Arts: An Integrated Approach* by Suzanne I. Barchers, 375–376. Minneapolis, Minn.: West, 1994.)

Informal Assessment

When considering testing measures, the term *informal* is not synonymous with "casual." Indeed, Kenneth P. Wolf makes a strong case for changing this designation to *informed* assessment, emphasizing that knowledgeable teachers provide the foundation for informed assessment (1993, 519). Teachers who are intimately involved with their students every day are more likely to give a true assessment of students' accomplishments than a test that does not delve into students' reasoning or learning strategies (Johnston 1992).

Ken Goodman advocates forms of evaluation that are holistic, authentic, relevant, interesting, functional, and accurate. They should respect learners and their differences, encourage independence, use natural language, and reveal competence in the users. Finally, they should be open-ended and allow for variation and modification (1989, xi–xii). Good assessment should look like good instruction, with authentic contexts for engaging activities and opportunities for social interaction. Further, good assessment should allow for reflection (Kapinus 1994, 579).

Authentic assessment
Assessments that engage students in applying knowledge and skills in the same way they are used outside of school.

Authentic assessment, the idea that assessments should have some relevance to students' lives (Marzano, Pickering, and McTighe 1993, 13), requires authentic content (Peters 1991 and Valencia 1990). Charles Peters suggests the following guidelines for selecting authentic content: Material should reflect important themes and ideas, be consistent with the goals of the district's curriculum, be rooted in real-world experiences and have real-world applications, be sensitive to students' developmental progression, and encourage higher-order thinking (1991, 590–591). Authentic assessments are often called alternative assessments because they differ from the norm- or criterion-referenced assessments discussed previously.

Performance assessment acknowledges that students have many opportunities to demonstrate reading mastery in life (Marzano, Pickering, and McTighe 1993, 13). Thus the idea of **outcome-based education**, which uses performance assessment, is consistent with the informal measures described in this chapter. These measures evolved from a philosophy that advocates Ken Goodman's points and are favored by many teachers and administrators over traditional test measures.

Each example used in performance assessment should be viewed as one version of many that teachers have developed and customized for their students and programs. When considering any assessment measure, consider what you want to measure, the effectiveness of a measure, your audience, time limitations, and how to integrate assessment with instruction (Winograd 1994). Good assessments should be based on high standards with clear expectations (Valencia 1990, 61). See Figure 12.2 on page 400 for a summary of the IRA/NCTE standards for reading and writing assessment.

- **Performance assessment**
  The variety of opportunities that students have to demonstrate understanding and apply their knowledge, skills, and habits in varying contexts.

- **Outcome-based education**
  A program that relies on performance assessment.

OBSERVATION AND ANECDOTAL RECORDS

- **Observation**
  A systematic effort to watch a student and record learning behaviors and progress.

Observation is the basis of much of the informal assessment that occurs daily. Yetta Goodman calls this "kid watching," and it occurs as you circulate through the room, during small- and large-group interactions, or while your students are working independently. Linda J. Pils, a first grade teacher, uses a clipboard and mailing labels to record her notes (with dates) as she discusses work with the students. She places the labels in a notebook at the end of each day, rereading her notes for behavior patterns, problems, and achievements (1991, 48). Some teachers use the computer to generate peel-and-stick labels with student names on them. This method, as well as photocopying classroom sets, ensures that regular notes are recorded.

- **Anecdotal records**
  An informal collection of observations over a period of time.

Notes can include such information as what your students are reading, comments about their reading and writing, how they approach and use reading, how they respond to instruction, and your questions and comments (Siu-Runyon 1991, 115). These notes become the basis for your **anecdotal records**, which may include particularly thoughtful responses to problems, difficulties a student has had with a novel, or concerns that you wish to discuss with a parent or caregiver. You can use these observations to find patterns of success and difficulty, to plan individual or small-group instruction and minilessons, and to record progress (Rhodes and Nathenson-Mejia 1992, 507).

FIGURE 12.2
IRA/NCTE
Assessment
Standards

Standards for the Assessment of Reading and Writing

1. The interests of the student are paramount in assessment.
2. The primary purpose of assessment is to improve teaching and learning.
3. Assessment must reflect and allow for critical inquiry into curriculum and instruction.
4. Assessments must recognize and reflect the intellectually and socially complex nature of reading and writing and the important roles of school, home, and society in literacy development.
5. Assessment must be fair and equitable.
6. The consequences of an assessment procedure are the first, and most important, consideration in establishing the validity of the assessment.
7. The teacher is the most important agent of assessment.
8. The assessment process should involve multiple perspectives and sources of data.
9. Assessment should be based in the school community.
10. All members of the educational community—students, parents, teachers, administrators, policy makers, and the public—must have a voice in the development, interpretation, and reporting of assessment.
11. Parents must be involved as active, essential participants in the assessment process.

Excerpted from *Standards for the Assessment of Reading and Writing* by IRA/NCTE (Peter Johnston, Committee Chair): Copyright 1987 by the National Council of Teachers of English. Reprinted with permission.

STAIR (System for Teaching and Assessing Interactively and Reflectively) is a more structured approach to observation. With STAIR, the teacher makes regular entries based on observations, related hypotheses about a student's strengths and needs, and regular revisions of these hypotheses. Records include information about the texts the student reads, the context of the reading, and related activities. Teachers then use the records to plan reading instruction, assess progress against district or school benchmarks, or develop reports to parents (Afflerbach 1993a). In a simple example, a teacher might notice that a student has trouble sustaining interest in a chosen book. The teacher records this observation and a hypothesis, perhaps that the student lacks the background information to read the entire selection. An alternative hypothesis might be that the student lacks the appropriate sight-word vocabulary. After noting the hypothesis, the teacher plans instruction and opportunities for further observations to confirm or disconfirm the hypothesis. STAIR can also help teachers in content areas such as science or social studies (Hager and Gable

1993, 270). Through a cycle of observation, planning, teaching, observing, and reflecting, the teacher can guide learning experiences and refine instruction.

REFLECTION

The inquiry-based learning model demonstrates a major philosophical shift that affects assessment: Instead of teachers and administrators thinking about what students *don't* know, the community of learners begins with what students *do* know. Reflection, an important feature of an inquiry-based reading program, capitalizes on this emphasis on knowledge, encouraging both students and teachers to actively notice and document everyday signs of learning and achievement (Crafton and Burke 1994, 6; Silvers 1994, 26). Active discussion and personal writing about the learning process help students become skilled at self-evaluation. Linda K. Crafton and Carolyn Burke (1994, 6) use collaboration and conversation to encourage learners to ask each other such questions as, Did I fulfill my intent? What did I learn? How did I learn it? And, most important, how have my values and perspective on the world changed as a result of this experience?

To get in the habit of reflecting on your observations, begin by actively observing students and recording *their* thoughts about their knowledge and learning. Students will spontaneously offer thoughts such as "I just can't get long division." Perhaps such a statement reflects momentary frustration, but consistent expressions of ignorance or poor performance indicate that the student needs to begin thinking about accomplishments instead of failures.

Penny Silvers suggests using observation and anecdotal records to build a profile of a student's achievements. She documents these in a list headed with "What Leni Can Do as a Reader and Writer" and builds a narrative from these observations. Jane Hansen recommends that teachers encourage students to take ownership in their reading and writing programs, helping them realize that they do have options. Sixth graders in one study interacted freely with teachers and peers to discuss their reading and writing, worked more collaboratively, shared their work with each other, and gave direct input on their report-card grades (Hansen 1992c, 103–104).

The entire class can begin to reflect more actively while pursuing a unit of inquiry. K-W-L, discussed in more detail in Chapter 11 on content-area reading, can be a good starting point. Briefly, before beginning an investigation, students in small groups or the whole class discuss and record what they *Know* about a topic. Then they record what they *Want* to know. After the research or project, they record what they *Learned*. Variations on K-W-L include adding a section labeled "Where I find out" after "What I want to know" or adding "What I still want to know" after "What I learned." This process reinforces the value of contemplating and evaluating their learning.

FIGURE 12.3
Evaluation for
Independent
Inquiry

Self-Evaluation

Directions: Mark your response to each statement with a number ranging from 1 to 5 (1 indicating "Below Average," 3 indicating "Average," and 5 indicating "Above Average").

I have recorded what I know about my topic.   _____

I have asked three or more questions about my topic.   _____

I have consulted a variety of resources.   _____

I have answered all my questions.   _____

I have created a project that shows what I have learned.   _____

If my project is written, I have checked spelling and punctuation. _____

I have new questions or an idea for a new project.   _____

Peer-Evaluation

This project answered the questions.   _____

This project shows understanding of the topic.   _____

This project is interesting.   _____

I learned from the project.   _____

_____   _____
Signature of student   Date

_____   _____
Signature of evaluator   Date

_____   _____
Signature of teacher   Date

SELF-EVALUATION AND PEER-EVALUATION

A more formalized process of reflection occurs when students use a form or checklist to record progress on their reading or with a project. Once students are accustomed to thinking about what they have learned and accomplished, providing a detailed form is a natural next step. The checklist (see Figure 12.3), an informal assessment that combines self-evaluation and peer-evaluation, could be used by upper-primary or older students who are investigating a topic of interest.

CHECKLISTS OR INVENTORIES

The checklist allows teachers to check off student accomplishments, skills, interests, and progress. The checklist can be labeled "developmental" if it

Quarters:	1	2	3	4
Reading Attitudes				
Enjoys books				
Shows interest in books				
Uses classroom library				
Uses school library				
Brings books from home				
Talks about books				
Reads variety of materials				
Appreciation for Story				
Appreciates author style				
Appreciates figurative language				
Recognizes genre				
Appreciates variety of genres				
Relates story to self				
Identifies authors				
Book Knowledge				
Uses table of contents				
Uses glossary				
Uses index				
Uses dictionary				
Uses encyclopedia				
Uses atlas				
Uses card catalog				
Uses computer				
Uses librarian, peers, teacher				

addresses the stages of language development that accompany maturation, or the checklist itself may be in a developmental stage (Bailey et al. 1988). These instruments take time to develop and refine, and they should not be the sole form of assessment. However, they are easy to use, and parents understand them. Once developed, a regular administrative time should be designated, perhaps monthly or quarterly. The sample fifth grade checklists in Figures 12.4 and 12.5 could be adapted for a variety of grade levels.

	Quarters:	1	2	3	4
Oral and Silent Reading					
Reads with fluency					
Varies reading speed					
Previews, skims					
Uses organizational text cues					
Reads for sustained periods					
Chooses oral versus silent reading appropriately					
Reading Comprehension Strategies					
Rereads for meaning					
Skips or substitutes words					
Uses punctuation for meaning					
Uses pictures or graphs					
Uses reference sources					
Accesses help from adults					
Accesses help from peers					
Works on developing vocabulary					
Comprehending Story					
Can retell story					
Understands plot					
Understands main idea					
Understands characterization					
Understands setting					
Understands climax					
Distinguishes fact from opinion					
Sequences events					
Predicts outcomes					
Understands cause and effect					
Word-Recognition Strategies					
Self-corrects for pronunciation					
Uses word structure cues					
Uses appropriate sight words					

PORTFOLIOS

As language arts teachers focus on authentic content for their programs, they are turning to portfolios as a particularly useful performance-based assessment tool. Portfolios "contain multiple stories of what individuals can do—within the language arts of reading, writing, listening, and speaking, and across the curriculum" (Kieffer and Morrison 1994, 417). Although usually a collection of a student's best work, some teachers instead use portfolios to collect samples that are not necessarily the best, but that represent particular tasks over a period of time (Hiebert 1991, 514). Jane Hansen recommends that portfolios also include nonschool items, demonstrating the value of students' out-of-school lives (1994, 31–32). Some portfolios include work chosen only by the teacher, and some include a combination of student- and teacher-chosen items. District or school purposes may vary, but portfolios are now found in many classrooms.

Generally, reading portfolios include dated samples of students' reading, plus items such as logs, book reports, tapes of oral reading, checklists, and research. Sometimes referred to as "artifacts" (Lamme and Hysmith 1991, 629), samples may also include writings from a variety of projects. For the very youngest learner, consider creating literacy albums. Similar to scrapbooks, the representative samples chosen by the child may include name-writing attempts, photographs of play constructions, drawings and dictated stories, scribble messages, lists of favorite books, and so forth (Roskos and Neuman 1994, 81).

Teachers can generate items for specific inclusion in the portfolios, such as an assessment of the number of words read aloud in one minute (Pils 1991, 49) or a reading questionnaire that asks such questions as "Are you a good reader?" or "Do you enjoy reading?" (Paris 1991, 681). These measures may be repeated regularly to assess change throughout the year. Penny Silvers emphasizes that the portfolio assessment process is particularly effective when students are actively involved in the portfolio's selection and interpretation (1994, 25). By asking themselves why they are including certain samples or why a particular piece is important, students become more thoughtful about the portfolio's meaning and the work therein. A teacher could begin the year by sharing a portfolio of selected artifacts of the teacher's own work, inviting students to think about how they will construct their own portfolios (Hansen 1992a, 607).

To involve students more directly in sharing their accomplishments, consider instituting student-led parent conferences. Susan B. Mundell and Karen DeLario (1994, 11) recommend teaching students how to share the contents of their portfolios with parents or other interested adults. Several students meet with their parents in the classroom at one time, and the teacher circulates among them. The first conference familiarizes parents with the portfolio format. Parents are involved in completing various response forms. Because

Parents review their child's portfolio during a conference.

parents often have specific questions in the fall, the teacher may schedule personalized conferences to coincide with the student-led conferences. This process requires teaching the students through modeling and practice how to lead the conferences before the actual parent-student conferences occur. For more detailed information, consult *Practical Portfolios: Reading, Writing, Math, and Life Skills, Grades 3–6* by Susan B. Mundell and Karen DeLario, 1994.

Assessment, a cumulative process, provides a wealth of detail about students' development over time (McGregor 1991, 58). In a survey of 150 users of student portfolios, Robert C. Calfee and Pam Perfumo found that teachers usually combined alternative assessment with whole language and practices such as **cooperative instruction** and school-based curriculum decisions, the process by which schools take control of factors such as the budget, personnel, and curriculum choices (1993, 536). Portfolios can be a fine example of a cumulative process that represents authentic instructional choices; they also can be a great source of pride as students take ownership of where they have been and where they are headed. Portfolios may be sent home at the end of the year, or selections may be photocopied for a cumulative portfolio amassed over the years.

■ **Cooperative instruction**
Any pattern of classroom organization that encourages students to work together to achieve individual goals.

RUBRICS

■ **Rubric**
A scoring guide that provides criteria that describe student performance at various levels of proficiency.

A **rubric** is a scoring guide. It can provide criteria to assess student proficiency levels (O'Neil 1994, 4), or it can provide a hierarchy of acceptable responses or qualities (Garcia and Verville 1994, 238). See Figure 12.6 for an example of a rubric for student-led parent conferences. Well-written rubrics help teachers evaluate progress and work more fairly. They also communicate to students

FIGURE 12.6
Rubric for
Student-Led
Parent Conferences

Exceeds Standard	I follow the conference agenda, and I check off each item as it is completed. I make appropriate introductions. I answer parent questions with thoughtful answers. I give a full explanation for each agenda item. I write two or more goals with my parent.
Standard	I follow the conference agenda. I make appropriate introductions. I answer parent questions satisfactorily. I briefly explain each agenda item. I write one goal with my parent.
Emerging	I follow the agenda some of the time. I make introductions with help. I am unsure of answers for parent questions. I explain about half of the agenda items. My parent writes the goal for me without my help.
Novice	I am not sure how to follow the agenda. I make introductions with help and reminders. I need help to answer parent questions. I explain one or two of the agenda items. I do not write goals.

Excerpted from *Practical Portfolios: Reading, Writing, Math, and Life Skills, Grades 3–6* by Susan B. Mundell and Karen DeLario (Englewood, Colo.: Teacher Ideas Press, 800-237-6124, 1994), 103.

what qualities their work should demonstrate (O'Neil 1994, 4). They give more information than a letter grade might give, although rubrics can be used as the basis for a numerical score or letter grade by assigning a numerical value to the response choices. The sample rubric in Figure 12.7 on page 408, drawn from items in the checklist in Figure 12.5, can be used by an intermediate teacher to assess reading comprehension progress throughout the year. Each of the 16 items can be worth 1 point (for seldom or never) to 3 points (for always and easily), with a possible total score of 48 points. Grades could be allocated as follows:

GRADE	POINTS
A	41–48 (consistently)
B	32–40 (consistently for most areas)
C	26–31 (consistently for some areas)
D	17–25 (inconsistently for most areas)
F	1–16 (inconsistently for all areas)

	Seldom or Never	Some-times	Always and Easily
Reading Comprehension Strategies			
Rereads for meaning, recognizing when rereading is necessary			
Recognizes miscues and self-corrects			
Skips or substitutes words as needed			
Uses punctuation as an aid to meaning			
Uses text aids, such as pictures, charts, and graphs			
Uses reference sources, such as a dictionary, glossary, thesaurus			
Comprehending Text			
Can retell story with understanding			
Understands plot			
Understands and identifies main idea			
Understands characterization			
Understands setting, description			
Understands and recognizes climax			
Distinguishes fact from opinion			
Can sequence events			
Predicts outcomes			
Understands cause and effect			

Try constructing another rubric from other information in the checklists in Figures 12.4 and 12.5.

Involving Parents in Evaluation

P arents are always interested in how students are doing in school but may need help understanding formal assessments, especially if test scores on standardized tests provide only a partial achievement profile. Although most parents understand letter grades on a report card, they will benefit from additional information that can be shared at conferences.

FIGURE 12.8
Checklist for
Parents of
Kindergarten and
Primary Students

Parent Checklist

Student name: _____   Date: _____

I can be a better teacher if I know more about your child's interest in reading. Please answer the following questions. You may use the back for more comments.

	Yes	No
1. My child liked to look at picture books as a toddler.	___	___
2. My child likes to look at picture books now.	___	___
3. My child likes to have someone read aloud.	___	___
4. My child likes to talk about books and stories.	___	___
5. My child corrects me if I read a familiar story differently.	___	___
6. My child likes to look at magazines.	___	___
7. My child has a library card.	___	___
8. We go to the library every week or two.	___	___
9. We have a home library.	___	___
10. We read aloud or my child reads to us nearly every day.	___	___

What can you tell me about your child that will help me be a better teacher?

_____

_____

_____

Parents may need help in understanding newer assessments, such as portfolios. Teachers can use the checklists found in Figures 12.8 and 12.9 to involve parents in assessment. As parents become familiar with the form, they begin to think about important learning issues. The parent letter in Figure 12.10 on page 411 is also useful. Of course, modifications may be necessary so you can use it with parents for whom English is not their primary language.

Learners with Special Needs and Second-Language Learners

Some educators worry that students in schools that use informal assessments may be overlooked for remediation because administrators are accustomed to using traditional measures to identify students for special help. To avoid this potential problem, teachers should be alert to three areas of assessment for children with special needs: (1) *Preventative assessment*

Parent Checklist

Student name: _____   Date: _____

I can be a better teacher if I know more about your child's interest in reading. Please answer the following questions. You may use the back for more comments.

	Yes	No
1. My child likes to read books.	_____	_____
2. My child reads for uninterrupted periods of time.	_____	_____
3. My child likes to be read to.	_____	_____
4. My child likes to read magazines and the newspaper.	_____	_____
5. My child gets information from a variety of reading sources.	_____	_____
6. My child likes to talk about books.	_____	_____
7. My child likes to talk about newspaper or magazine articles.	_____	_____
8. We have a home library or go to the library often.	_____	_____
9. My child likes to read to me.	_____	_____
10. We have a set time for homework, reading, or studying.	_____	_____

What can you tell me about your child that will help me be a better teacher?

_____

_____

identifies young children who may be late to develop literacy; (2) *surveillance assessment*, used to look at progress over time, identifies students who may need special help; and (3) *corrective assessment* measures the effect of the special help a student has received (Kemp 1989, 136). The classroom teacher should take primary responsibility for developing a total picture of a student's performance through ongoing, *cumulative assessment*. The special student should be comfortable with the procedures and materials for assessment, and the assessment should track individual progress rather than compare the student with others or with a standard (ibid., 137).

A student referred for special help is usually subjected to a wide battery of specialized tests, administered by the psychologist, nurse, and reading specialist. Both formal and informal measures should be selected to provide as much information about the student as possible. One advantage of using informal assessments, such as portfolios, is that they give students with special needs an opportunity to demonstrate their accomplishments and progress over time.

FIGURE 12.10
Parent Letter

Dear Parents:

We use several assessments in our classroom: observation, portfolios, and peer-evaluation. Together with standardized tests required by the district, we can provide a more complete profile of your child's progress. You play an important role in your child's success. Think about adopting some of the following suggestions:

· Provide a quiet and comfortable place to study. Consider having a reading hour, perhaps after dinner, when the entire family reads or does homework.

· Ask your child specific questions about school, such as:
What is the best thing that happened today?
What is the first thing your teacher talked about today?
Who is the (silliest, smartest, most irritating) person in your class?
What did you dislike about today?

· Become involved in school activities. Be sure you know about grades, the parent–teacher organization, conferences, fundraisers, or social events.

· Let your children know how important education is to their future. If you take courses, talk about your teachers and studies.

· Require your child to participate in family responsibilities, such as chores, but do not let a part-time job interfere with school success.

· Set a good example: read, read, read. Have a dictionary, atlas, and thesaurus. Build a home library or go to the public library often.

· Visit school regularly. Become acquainted with the teacher, principal, secretary, counselor, and other key staff members. Communicate with the appropriate person when problems occur.

· When tests are given, encourage your children to be serious about them, but don't put undue pressure on them. Avoid family conflicts and outside pressures.

· Try to send a well-rested and healthy child to school.

Yours truly,

With students who are second-language learners, Carole Cox and Paul Boyd-Batstone emphasize the importance of using authentic assessment, listing the following principles:

1. Information is gathered by teachers and students.

2. Ongoing, daily observations are made.

3. Multiple sources of information are used.

4. Information is considered in the context of process.

5. Artifacts (writing, art, journals, tapes) and rich descriptions (anecdotal records, checklists) are used.

6. Teachers and students make decisions about assessment.

7. Information is gathered as part of the classroom schedule (1997, 55).

Using authentic assessment with all students reinforces the fact that the special students and second-language learners do indeed have a place in the regular classroom and that they too have accomplishments worthy of note.

Assessment and Report Cards

Report cards generally provide a limited amount of information about a student's reading progress. Often developed at the district level and without much input from teachers, report cards seldom meet the needs of the teacher or the students. Peter Afflerbach recommends that report cards be developed by representatives from all groups who read and write report cards, and that they provide useful feedback to both students and parents. Further, they should be both flexible and manageable to the users (1993b, 459–460). He recommends the following five questions:

1. *What is the audience and purpose of the reading report card?* Perhaps more detail should be provided through a checklist.

2. *Who will participate in the design of the report card?* A report card developed collaboratively by students, teachers, parents, and administrators will better represent the people using it.

3. *What is the context of communicating reading assessment?* When the report card is part of a context that includes portfolios, conversations, or other informal measures, it is only part of the information provided about the student's progress and thus does not take on disproportionate importance.

4. *What are the responsibilities related to the new report card?* The committee should consider how it will communicate report card changes or the use of other assessments to everyone involved.

5. *Will the new reading report cards be understood?* Parents and other readers of the report card should understand why it has changed and what is contained in the new one. They should have an opportunity, perhaps through a section on the report card, to respond with comments or concerns (ibid., 460–464).

Many teachers prefer to use report cards as only one component of the evaluation process. Portfolios or checklists may replace report cards, especially in the primary grades, if they are evaluative in nature. Portfolios are perhaps the best source of information for report card grades, especially when students are involved in selecting the examples they feel best represent their achievements. Rubrics, such as the one in Figure 12.7, can be translated into scores for grades.

The most important component of the grading process is the student's involvement. Grades should be earned by students, not magically conferred. Many teachers plan an absorbing activity a week before report cards and have individual conferences with students to collaborate on grade assignment. All assessment measures can be reviewed, and the report cards can be completed during the conference. In this way, students develop a clear understanding of their progress and of future expectations.

A Final Note

As mentioned in the introduction to this chapter, meaningful assessment is a skillful balancing act. With so many choices in assessment measures (besides those required by the district), it can seem to the busy teacher that an undue amount of time is devoted to assessment and evaluation. However, with the increasing emphasis on standards and national goals, many districts are working hard to find or develop appropriate assessments that are sensitive to their needs. Noteworthy statewide efforts at achieving authentic, large-scale reading assessments include California's New English-Language Arts Assessment, the Arizona Student Assessment Program, and the Maryland School Performance Assessment Program (Afflerbach 1994).

To achieve balance, Peter Afflerbach and Barbara Kapinus recommend that experts as well as parents, teachers, and students help with the development and use of reading assessments. Once selected, the nature, purpose, and results of an assessment should be communicated to parents. There should be both formative and summative reading assessments, plus student *and* external evaluations that use various texts, tasks, and contexts. It is important that everyone involved in the assessment process keep the purpose of tests in perspective, especially when the test scores are published. Finally, choices of reading assessments should be flexible in light of developing changes in reading and literacy (1993). With these recommendations in mind, schools and districts can develop sound assessment and evaluation programs that will motivate and inform learners and the community.

Now about your possible sentences on page 367. . . . Although limited to just a few words, did they preview some aspects of this chapter? Take a minute to evaluate how this process could be even more effective in the classroom.

Summary

The public has become increasingly concerned about reading achievement. National goals have given rise to content standards, curriculum standards, and benchmarks. Educators are designing a variety of assessment measures that provide better insight into student achievement.

Formal assessment measures usually include norm- and criterion-referenced tests produced commercially to specific standards. Basal Series Tests can include Informal Reading Inventories, plus pre- and posttests. Commercial tests provide only a small amount of information about an individual's performance, and they are sometimes overused. Yet, standardized testing continues for a variety of purposes and should be carefully evaluated for appropriateness. Teachers should prepare students for testing without placing undue emphasis on test results.

Informal assessments include wholistic measures based on authentic content. Observation, a systematic effort to watch students and record their behaviors and progress, can be used by both classroom and content-area teachers. Reflection involves active contemplation of accomplishments and goals. Self-evaluation and peer-evaluation, a more formalized process of reflection, can be recorded on a form or checklist. Checklists or inventories record student accomplishments, skills, interests, and progress.

Portfolios contain samples of student work and can be used for long-term assessment. A rubric is a scoring guide that describes student performance at varying proficiency levels. Rubrics can be converted to numerical scores or letter grades.

Parents often need help understanding standardized test scores and appreciate teachers taking the time to familiarize them with assessment measures that are different from report cards.

Students with special needs benefit from having assessment measures that are consistent with tests taken by other students in the regular classroom. Traditional assessments used in special education placement should supplement classroom assessment to obtain a complete profile of the student's achievement and instructional needs.

Report cards should be thoughtfully designed by the users and should be one component of the evaluation process. Portfolios or rubrics can be used to develop grades. Grading is enhanced when students are directly involved in the process.

Achieving a balanced evaluation process requires considering a variety of assessment measures. Standardized tests should be viewed as one component of this process that should remain flexible as programs and needs change.

Testing Terminology

Authentic assessment: The idea that assessments should engage students in applying knowledge and skills in the same way they are used outside of school. The use of portfolios is an example.

Assessment: "The gathering of data, usually quantitative in nature and based on testing, that provide the information for evaluation to take place" (Bertrand 1991, 17).

Checklists: Informal records that allow teachers to check off student accomplishments, skills, interests, and progress.

Criterion-referenced tests: Tests that compare performance to a standard, such as demonstrating mastery at the 80 percent level.

Evaluation: A process of collecting and using information to determine both how a student learns, and the student's progress and achievement.

Formal assessment: A process of determining how much students have learned, generally based on criterion- or norm-referenced tests.

Formative evaluation: Provides feedback and redirection during the learning process.

Holistic scoring: In reading, an assessment with four interrelated parts: (1) comprehension/construction meaning, (2) metacognition/reading strategies/ knowledge about reading, (3) topic familiarity/prior knowledge, and (4) attitudes/self-perceptions/literary experiences (Farr and Beck 1991, 497). In writing, an assessment that involves teachers agreeing on rating standards, rating papers together, and agreeing on a single score (Dyson and Freeman 1991, 758).

Informal assessment: A process of determining why students perform or learn as they do, rather than how well they perform (Farr and Beck 1991, 489).

Norm-referenced tests: Tests that relate results to other students with predetermined performance indicators or scales, generally by students' age, grade, or gender. A student scoring at the 80th percentile on a subtest has a score higher than 80 percent of the other students.

Outcome-based education: A program that relies on performance assessment.

Performance assessment: The variety of opportunities students have to demonstrate understanding and apply knowledge, skills, and habits of mind in varying contexts (Marzano, Pickering, and McTighe 1993, 13).

Reliability: "The consistency of scores obtained when persons are reexamined with the same test on different occasions or with tests composed of parallel sets of items" (Farr and Beck 1991, 492).

Rubric: A scoring guide that uses criteria to describe student performance at various levels of proficiency.

Summative evaluation: Tests or judgments made about a finished project or upon completion of a particular unit of study.

Validity: The degree to which a test assesses what it purports to measure.

References

Afflerbach, Peter. "Large-Scale Authentic Assessment." In *Authentic Reading Assessment: Practices and Possibilities*, edited by Sheila W. Valencia, Elfrieda H. Hiebert, and Peter P. Afflerbach, 193–196. Newark, Del.: International Reading Association, 1994.

_____. "Report Cards and Reading." *The Reading Teacher* 46, no. 6 (March 1993): 458–465.

_____. "STAIR: A System for Recording and Using What We Observe and Know About Our Students." *The Reading Teacher* 47, no. 3 (Nov. 1993): 260–263.

Afflerbach, Peter, and Barbara Kapinus. "The Balancing Act." *The Reading Teacher* 47, no. 1 (Sept. 1993): 62–64.

Bailey, Janis, Phyllis E. Brazee, Sharyn Chiavaroli, Joyce Herbeck, Thomas Lechner, Debra Lewis, Ann McKittrick, Lorraine Redwine, Kris Reid, Betty Robinson, and Harry Spear. "Problem Solving Our Way to Alternative Evaluation Procedures." *Language Arts* 65 (April 1988): 364–373.

Barchers, Suzanne I. *Teaching Language Arts: An Integrated Approach.* Minneapolis, Minn.: West, 1994.

Barthe, Patte, and Ruth Mitchell. *Smart Start: Elementary Education for the 21st Century.* Golden, Colo.: North American Press, 1992.

Bartoli, Jill, and Morton Botel. *Reading/Learning Disability: An Ecological Approach.* New York: Teachers College Press, 1988.

Bertrand, John E. "Student Assessment and Evaluation." In *Assessment and Evaluation in Whole Language Programs*, edited by Bill Harp, 17–33. Norwood, Mass.: Christopher-Gordon, 1991.

Calfee, Robert C., and Pam Perfumo. "Student Portfolios: Opportunities for a Revolution in Assessment." *The Journal of Reading* 36, no. 7 (April 1993): 532–537.

Cox, Carole, and Paul Boyd-Batstone. *Crossroads: Literature and Language in Culturally and Linguistically Diverse Classrooms.* Columbus, Ohio: Merrill, 1997.

Crafton, Linda K., and Carolyn Burke. "Inquiry-Based Evaluation: Teachers and Students Reflecting Together." *Primary Voices K–6* 2, no. 2 (April 1994): 2–7.

Durkin, Dolores. *Teaching Them to Read*, 5th ed. Boston: Allyn & Bacon, 1989.

Dyson, Anne Hass, and Sarah Warshauer Freeman. "Writing." In *Handbook of Research on Teaching the English Language Arts*, edited by James Flood, Julie M. Jensen, Dianne Lapp, and James R. Squire, 754–774. New York: Macmillan, 1991.

Farr, Roger. "Putting It All Together: Solving the Reading Assessment Puzzle," *The Reading Teacher* 46, no. 1 (Sept. 1992): 29.

Farr, Roger, and Michael Beck. "Formal Methods of Evaluation." In *Handbook of Research on Teaching the English Language Arts*, edited by James Flood, Julie M. Jensen, Dianne Lapp, and James R. Squire, 489–501. New York: Macmillan, 1991.

Garcia, Mary W., and Kathy Verville. "Redesigning Teaching and Learning: The Arizona Student Assessment Program." In *Authentic Reading Assessment: Practices and Possibilities*, edited by Sheila W. Valencia, Elfrieda H. Hiebert, and Peter P. Afflerbach, 228–246. Newark, Del.: International Reading Association, 1994.

Glass, Gene V. "Using Student Test Scores to Evaluate Teachers." In *The New Handbook of Teacher Evaluation: Assessing Elementary and Secondary School Teachers*, edited by Jason Millman and Linda Darling-Hammond, 229–240. Newbury Park, Calif.: Corwin Press, 1990.

Goodman, Kenneth S. "Preface." In *The Whole Language Evaluation Book*, edited by Kenneth S. Goodman, Yetta M. Goodman, and Wendy J. Hood, xi–xv. Portsmouth, N.H.: Heinemann, 1989.

_____. "Standards—NOT!" *The Council Chronicle* 4, no. 2 (Nov. 1994): 20 and 17.

Greer, Eunice Ann. "Basal Assessment Systems: 'It's Not the Shoes.'" *The Reading Teacher* 45, no. 8 (April 1992): 650–652.

Hager, Jane Meeks, and Robert A. Gable. "Content Reading Assessment: A Rethinking of Methodology." *The Clearing House* 66, no. 5 (May/June 1993): 269–272.

Hansen, Jane. "Literacy Portfolios: Windows on Potential." In *Authentic Reading Assessment: Practices and Possibilities*, edited by Sheila W. Valencia, Elfrieda H. Hiebert, and Peter P. Afflerbach, 26–40. Newark, Del.: International Reading Association, 1994.

_____. "Literacy Portfolios Emerge." *The Reading Teacher* 45, no. 8 (April 1992): 604–607.

_____. "Students' Evaluations Bring Reading and Writing Together." *The Reading Teacher* 46, no. 2 (Oct. 1992): 100–105.

Harman, Susan. "Snow White and the Seven Warnings: Threats to Authentic Evaluation." *The Reading Teacher* 46, no. 3 (Nov. 1992): 250–252.

Hiebert, Elfrieda H. "Teacher-Based Assessment of Literacy Learning." In *Handbook of Research on Teaching the English Language Arts*, edited by James Flood, Julie M. Jensen, Dianne Lapp, and James R. Squire, 510–520. New York: Macmillan, 1991.

Hiebert, Elfrieda H., and Robert C. Calfee. "Assessing Literacy: From Standardized Tests to Portfolios and Performances." In *What Research Has to Say about Reading Instruction*, 2nd ed., edited by S. Jay Samuels and Alan E. Farstrup, 70–100. Newark, Del.: International Reading Association, 1992.

Hiebert, Elfrieda H., and Barbara Kapinus. "National Assessment of Educational Progress: What Do We Know and What Lies Ahead?" *The Reading Teacher* 45, no. 9 (May 1992): 730–734.

Huff, Roland, and Charles R. Kline, Jr. *The Contemporary Writing Curriculum: Re-hearsing, Composing and Valuing.* New York: Teachers College Press, 1987.

IRA/NCTE. Peter Johnston, Committee Chair. *Standards for the Assessment of Reading and Writing.* International Reading Association and National Council of Teachers of English, 1994.

Johnston, Peter H. "Nontechnical Assessment." *The Reading Teacher* 46, no. 1 (Sept. 1992): 60–62.

Kapinus, Barbara. "Looking at the Ideal and the Real in Large-Scale Reading Assessment: The View from Two Sides of the River." *The Reading Teacher* 47, no. 7 (April 1994): 578–580.

Kemp, Max. "The Wholistic Classroom: Assessment of Children with Special Needs." In *Monitoring Children's Language Development: Holistic Assessment in the Classroom*, edited by Elizabeth Daly, 133–139. Portsmouth, N.H.: Heinemann, 1989.

Kendall, John S., and Robert J. Marzano. *The Systematic Identification and Articulation of Content Standards and Benchmarks: Update.* Aurora, Colo.: Mid-Continent Regional Educational Laboratories, 1994.

Kieffer, Ronald D., and Linda S. Morrison. "Changing Portfolio Process: One Journey Toward Authentic Assessment." *Language Arts* 71, no. 6 (Oct. 1994): 411–418.

Lamme, Linda Leonard, and Cecilia Hysmith. "One School's Adventure into Portfolio Assessment." *Language Arts* 68, no. 8 (Dec. 1991): 629–640.

Levande, David. "Standardized Reading Tests: Concerns, Limitations, and Alternatives." *Reading Improvement* 30, no. 2 (Summer 1993): 125–127.

Lipson, Marjorie Y., and Karen K. Wixson. "Student Evaluation and Basal Instruction." In *Improving Basal Reader Instruction*, edited by Peter N. Winograd, Karen K. Wixson, and Marjorie Y. Lipson, 109–139. New York: Teachers College Press, 1989.

Marzano, Robert. J., Debra Pickering, and Jay McTighe. *Assessing Student Outcomes: Performance Assessment Using the Dimensions of Learning Model.* Alexandria, Va.: Association for Supervision and Curriculum Development, 1993.

McGregor, Robert. "Criteria for Kidwatching: A Secondary Perspective." In *Monitoring Children's Language Development: Holistic Assessment in the Classroom*, edited by Elizabeth Daly, 55–81. Portsmouth, N.H.: Heinemann, 1991.

Mundell, Susan B., and Karen DeLario. *Practical Portfolios: Reading, Writing, Math, and Life Skills, Grades 3–6.* Englewood, Colo.: Teacher Ideas Press, 1994.

Murphy, Sharon. "Neither Gone nor Forgotten: Testing in New Basal Readers." In *Basal Readers: A Second Look*, edited by Patrick Shannon and Kenneth S. Goodman, 103–113. Katonah, N.Y.: Richard C. Owen, 1994.

Newmann, Fred M., Walter G. Secada, and Gray G. Wehlage. *A Guide to Authentic Instruction and Assessment: Vision, Standards and Scoring.* Madison, Wis.: Wisconsin Center for Education Research, 1995.

O'Neil, John. "Making Assessment Meaningful." *ASCD Update* 36, no. 6 (August 1994): 1–5.

Orr, Fred. *Test-Taking Power.* New York: Prentice-Hall, 1986.

Paris, Scott G. "Portfolio Assessment for Young Readers." *The Reading Teacher* 44, no. 9 (May 1991): 680–681.

Peters, Charles W. "You Can't Have Authentic Assessment Without Authentic Content." *The Reading Teacher* 44, no. 8 (April 1991): 590–591.

Pikulski, John J. "The Role of Tests in a Literacy Assessment Program." *The Reading Teacher* 43, no. 9 (May 1990): 686–688.

Pils, Linda J. "Soon Anofe You Tout Me: Evaluation in a First-Grade Whole Language Classroom." *The Reading Teacher* 45, no. 1 (Sept. 1991): 46–50.

Ravitch, Diane. "Launching a Revolution in Standards and Assessments." *Phi Delta Kappan* 74, 10 (June 1993): 767–772.

Rhodes, Lynn K. and Curtis Dudley-Marling. *Readers and Writers with a Difference.* Portsmouth, N.H.: Heinemann, 1988.

Rhodes, Lynn K., and Sally Nathenson-Meija. "Anecdotal Records: A Powerful Tool for Ongoing Literacy Assessment." *The Reading Teacher* 45, no. 7 (March 1992): 502–509.

Roskos, Kathleen A., and Susan B. Neuman. "Of Scribbles, Schemas, and Storybooks: Using Literacy Albums to Document Young Children's Literacy Growth." *Young Children* 49, no. 2 (Jan. 1994): 78–85.

Shannon, Patrick. *Broken Promises: Reading Instruction in Twentieth-Century America.* New York: Bergin & Garvey, 1989.

Silvers, Penny. "Everyday Signs of Learning." *Primary Voices K–6* 2, no. 2 (April 1994): 20–29.

Siu-Runyon, Yvonne. "Holistic Assessment in Intermediate Classes: Techniques for Informing Our Teaching." In *Assessment and Evaluation in Whole Language Programs*, edited by Bill Harp, 109–136. Norwood, Mass.: Christopher-Gordon, 1991.

Slavin, Robert. *Educational Psychology: Theory into Practice.* Englewood Cliffs, N.J.: Prentice-Hall, 1988.

Valencia, Sheila W. "Alternative Assessment: Separating the Wheat from the Chaff." *The Reading Teacher* 44, no. 1 (Sept. 1990): 60–61.

Winograd, Peter. "Developing Alternative Assessments: Six Problems Worth Solving." *The Reading Teacher* 47, no. 5 (Feb. 1994): 420–423.

Wolf, Kenneth P. "From Informal to Informed Assessment: Recognizing the Role of the Classroom Teacher." *The Journal of Reading* 36, no. 7 (April 1993): 518–523.

Woodley, Katheryn K. *Testwiseness: Test-Taking Skills for Adults.* New York: McGraw-Hill, 1978.

The Literate Environment

Rules for Teachers 1872

1. Teachers each day will fill lamps, clean chimneys.

2. Each teacher will bring a bucket of water and a scuttle of coal for the day's session.

3. Make your pens carefully. You may whittle nibs to the individual taste of the pupils.

4. Men teachers may take one evening each week for courting purposes, or two evenings a week if they go to church regularly.

5. After ten hours in school, the teachers may spend the remaining time reading the Bible or other good books.

6. Women teachers who marry or engage in unseemly conduct will be dismissed.

7. Every teacher should lay aside from each pay a goodly sum of his earnings for his benefit during his declining years so that he will not become a burden on society.

8. Any teacher who smokes, uses liquor in any form, frequents pool or public halls, or gets shaved in a barber shop will give good reason to suspect his worth, intention, integrity and honesty.

9. The teacher who performs his labor faithfully and without fault for five years will be given an increase of twenty-five cents per week in his pay, providing the Board of Education approves.

(Source unknown.)

FOCUS QUESTIONS

1. How important is the classroom environment?

2. How can I support an effective home environment?

3. How can I assess the classroom environment?

4. How can I organize an effective physical and intellectual environment?

5. How do I accommodate learners with special needs?

6. What are effective ways to incorporate different cultures into the environment?

7. How can I use libraries effectively?

8. What are the best first resources for the literate classroom?

9. How can I use informal learning environments effectively?

In 1872, only the first three rules for teachers addressed the importance of providing a productive environment. For those pioneers, education was a luxury that few communities provided. Children learned to read in the home or in church until the community had the time and resources to build a school. According to Bobbie Kalman in *Early Schools*, the first schoolhouses were made of logs with dirt floors and windows covered with greased paper. Students sat on benches at narrow tables. A smoky fire might provide some heat, but it could get so cold ink froze in the inkwells (1982, 10). As the rules indicate, teachers were responsible for bringing in the coal and gathering wood. Because paper was expensive and scarce, students wrote on chalk slates. The teacher would mend and sharpen the quill pens, but each family provided the homemade ink (ibid., 14). In some towns and cities, poor children attended "ragged schools," where children worked at the school making shoes, furniture, and clothes in exchange for their lessons. They also served food, swept the floors, and chopped the firewood (ibid., 56).

Today's environments are dramatically different from our country's early schools, but we teachers still have the primary responsibility for providing an effective learning climate. Because learning can be positively enhanced by creating a thoughtful environment, this is an important task (Strickland and Morrow 1989, 178). The classroom environment has a strong influence on student behaviors, and wise teachers use it to their advantage. For example, open space provides the flexibility necessary to form and change learning groups frequently. The presence of books communicates an expectation that students will succeed at learning to read, and the presence or absence of materials reflects the philosophy driving the curriculum (Dempsey and Frost 1993, 306). This chapter addresses how we as teachers can create and manage an exceptional in-school environment and also how we can effectively utilize additional environments such as libraries, museums, and the outdoors.

The Importance of the Literate Environment

Today we recognize the importance of providing an environment that encourages students to explore and learn in comfort. The literate environment is not merely an attractive environment with abundant resources, it is also a "deep" environment that defines the intellectual climate of the classroom (Tway 1991, 425). Sadly, schools still exist with extremely limited resources and with environments that impede learning and alienate students. I began teaching in the late 1960s, and I have taught in many settings. One year, I taught remedial reading in the back portion of a janitor's closet, and my students walked past cleaning supplies to reach our small table and book shelves. In a private school, I tested students in what was the bomb shelter of a formerly luxurious home. I have also had the more typical classrooms, complete with sinks, storage, movable tables, and desks. The best environment accommodated my large collection of books: the former library of a 100-year-old building, complete with three walls of floor-to-ceiling oak bookshelves and one wall of windows that let in an abundance of natural light and air.

In each setting, I was faced with the challenge of making the best of the resources available. I learned early in my career that I could not rely on a school district to provide me with all that I needed to create even a basic environment for my students. The most dismal setting was in one inner-city school where the students sat in bolted-down desks, the room had no glass in the windows, and the resources included only dated books and a ream of newsprint. I offered to teach summer school that year with no salary in exchange for getting materials for my class in the fall. I wrote letters to family members, who spread the word, raising money so that my fourth graders could have a four square ball, toilet paper, and, in some cases, shoes and clothes. I obtained the only piano in the K–8 building of more than 1,000 students by offering to direct a choir before and after school. During that year I learned that although I couldn't do much about the bolted-down desks, I could improve the conditions by asking for support from others. Although my most miserable school settings were in the late 1960s and early 1970s, many school districts still struggle to provide adequate environments for learners. Sadly, some districts continue to sorely neglect needy populations, as described by Jonathan Kozol in *Savage Inequalities* (1992).

When children do not have breakfast at home, toilet paper at school, and safety on the streets, it is difficult to concentrate on learning. The classroom can be a haven, however, or it can reinforce a general feeling of helplessness. It is critical that we teachers recognize that we must take an active role in providing environments that support and further learning. Whether a school has an abundance or a dearth of resources, we are ultimately responsible for collaborating with our students to provide an effective learning environment suitable for them, regardless of their learning styles, cultures, or physical limitations.

Supporting the Home Environment

As we saw in Chapter 3, the home environment is the critical beginning point for early literacy experiences. The importance of Brian Cambourne's conditions of learning (immersion, demonstration, expectation, responsibility, approximation, use, and response) do not diminish

A child enjoys reading a favorite book at home.

as a child matures (1988, 83). However, it is realistic to assume that some children will come to school without a supportive, nurturing environment. Although it may be impossible to change the past, one can influence the home environment by educating parents and students. Most parents have high hopes for their children, especially that they will go on to a more successful lifestyle. Such parents benefit from, and appreciate, guidance on how to create a more supportive home environment.

For middle school teachers, it may be impossible to visit every student's home, but many elementary classroom teachers plan home visits a week or two before school. During this visit, the teacher can engage in a nonthreatening discussion about the student by asking to see baby photos, to hear favorite family stories, or take a walk through the immediate neighborhood. A letter should go home in advance giving parents and caretakers a clear idea of what will happen during the visit so that everyone will be comfortable. Information about the individual's learning conditions is invaluable and provides insights into providing a more thoughtful learning experience. Distributing a handout such as that in Figure 13.1 will be appreciated by many parents.

Assessing the Environment

Enter any classroom, and you will immediately get a feel for the personalities of the teacher and students. Visual clues include such items as the arrangement of the tables or desks, the use of print, the presence or absence of books, and the accessibility of student materials. Depending on your personal experiences and your teaching philosophy, you may have definite ideas about appropriate classroom environments. Try to visit a classroom soon and answer the questions in the list on page 426. If you can't visit a classroom, think about one you have been in recently as you respond to the questions.

FIGURE 13.1
Creating a Literate
Home Environment

You can be a powerful force in your child's education by trying out some or all of the following suggestions.

1. Develop a home library containing books, magazines, and a dictionary. Find bargains at used book sales, garage sales, and discount houses.

2. Provide a good reading model. Reading with your child may mean reading the same book or cartoons or magazines to each other in turns or merely sharing the same couch while you read different materials.

3. Even if you share reading as above, and especially if you don't, always try to spend some time reading aloud to your child. Buy or borrow from the library Jim Trelease's *The New Read Aloud Handbook*, or see your child's teacher for good read-aloud books. Bedtime is a fine time for this quiet activity. An even better idea from Trelease's book is to let your child clean up the kitchen while you read aloud from a favorite book.

4. Get a library card for your child and make regular visits.

5. Show the utility of reading by having your child look up numbers or addresses in the phone book, prepare recipes, or find the weather forecast or horoscope in the newspaper.

6. For the younger child, read aloud billboards, street signs, and signs on buildings as you drive.

7. Subscribe to a children's monthly magazine such as *Odyssey* or *Ranger Rick*, or browse through magazines at the public library.

8. Leave notes for your children to read. If they are to come home after school before you, write out directions for special chores or privileges. Slip messages into sack lunches or pockets.

9. Teach children how to answer the phone, write messages, and politely ask a caller to repeat information (an intimidating request for a child).

10. Have children write thank you notes, letters, or messages.

11. Dictate your shopping list or memos for your child to write.

12. Encourage your child to keep a diary. A spiral notebook is adequate.

13. Take time to listen to your child. Set aside time to converse and find out what has happened in school.

14. Teach your child how to use a calculator and have him or her help with adding grocery prices, clothing costs, or estimating total bills.

Excerpted from *Creating and Managing the Literate Classroom* by Suzanne I. Barchers (Englewood, Colo.: Teachers Ideas Press, 1990), 48.

FURNITURE

1. Does the classroom have desks or tables?

2. Are the desks or tables arranged in rows or clusters?

3. Where is the teacher's desk? Is it facing the class, off to the side, in the back, or not in evidence?

4. Is there space for whole-group and small-group instruction?

PRINT DISPLAYS

5. Are bulletin boards prepared by teachers or students?

6. Is print displayed in more than one language?

7. Is student work displayed? Where?

8. How many chalkboards are available?

9. Is group written work such as group stories or poetry displayed? Where?

10. Does the print help with the organization of the room, such as labels for storing materials or books?

11. Does the print help with learning, such as providing tips for figuring out an unknown word or editing a story?

12. Does the print record events, such as a log for plant growth?

13. Does the print help with everyday organization, such as assignment of chores, attendance, lunch count, and so forth?

CENTERS

14. Is there a reading center, perhaps with a relaxed place to read?

15. Is there a writing center?

16. Are there centers for content or interest areas, such as science, art, or history?

TRAFFIC PATTERNS

17. Is it easy to move about in the room?

18. Does the room accommodate students using wheelchairs or walkers?

19. Does the traffic flow past other students, allowing for interruptions or conversation?

20. Does the traffic encourage use of books and materials?

SOUND

21. Is the room quiet, moderately noisy, or annoyingly noisy?

22. If it is quiet, is it a comfortable quiet? If it is noisy, is it purposefully noisy?

23. Is equipment, such as earphones or tape recorders, contained in a specified area?

24. Are quiet areas available to individuals or small groups of students?

OTHER PHYSICAL FEATURES

25. Is the temperature comfortable?

26. Is the lighting natural, florescent, or a combination?

27. Does the room allow for flexibility and changing needs?

28. Is storage accessible to teacher and students?

29. Does the class use unusual spaces for learning, such as the hallway or coat room?

30. Is the classroom inviting to students and adults?

CLASSROOM CLIMATE

31. Are students at their desks or tables, or are they scattered throughout the room?

32. Are students working alone, in small groups, or as one class?

33. Are students engaged in different tasks or all working on the same task?

34. Does the classroom appear to be dominated by the teacher?

35. Do students appear to have choices?

36. Is the teacher the only other adult in the classroom?

37. Do the students appear to be productively busy?

38. Do the students appear to be content?

39. Do the students greet visitors?

40. Do you feel comfortable in the classroom?

Depending on the grade level, community, building, and personalities of the teacher and students, every classroom will and should be somewhat different. As you read through this chapter, think about how the different features support an effective reading program, and begin to determine what you believe would be the ideal classroom environment.

The Physical Environment

Answering the preceding questions about a classroom you have visited will give you clues regarding the school's curriculum and the teacher's philosophy. The physical arrangement sends strong messages to class members and encourages certain behaviors (Loughlin and Martin 1987, 7). Most new and many experienced teachers spend several days before school begins experimenting with various classroom arrangements, only to change nearly everything once school has been in session for a few weeks. One courageous teacher removed everything, including furniture, from his classroom shortly after school began and let the students choose what would be returned. He was quite gratified when the first choice was books! Although your classroom will change, consider the following factors as you determine your ideal reading classroom. See Figures 13.2 and 13.3 on pages 429 and 430 for sample classroom floor plans.

FURNITURE

The teacher often has little control over whether the classroom has desks or tables. Usually, primary classrooms will have tables; intermediate classrooms may have either; and middle school classrooms have desks. Teachers who organize instruction through small groups choose to have the desks or tables arranged in small groups to foster discussion and collaboration. If a classroom has students all facing the front of the room, it is fairly safe to assume the teacher lectures frequently and students work independently. The placement of the teacher's desk can also indicate the teacher's philosophy; many teachers are never at their desks, relegating them to the back of the room. Others sit at or on their desks to lecture. Gay Fawcett, a former classroom teacher, gradually moved her "big desk" from a place of prominence by the door to a far corner of the room and found that moving the desk became a symbol of the changes she instituted as she allowed students to have more ownership in their learning (1992, 185).

No matter what your style, students should be able to see the chalkboard, screen, or overhead projector from their desks or tables. Check the levels of lighting throughout the day to ensure that it is adequate for students from all seating areas. A small cluster of tables can be useful for small-group instruction or projects. Another essential feature is an area where the entire class can gather in a more relaxed fashion for reading aloud. This area can also be used for whole-class meetings or other informal interactions.

Many primary teachers use components of the room to create spatial boundaries. Physical cues may be used; for example, bookshelves may set off the reading area or a portable chalk board or bulletin board may designate an

FIGURE 13.2

Primary classroom

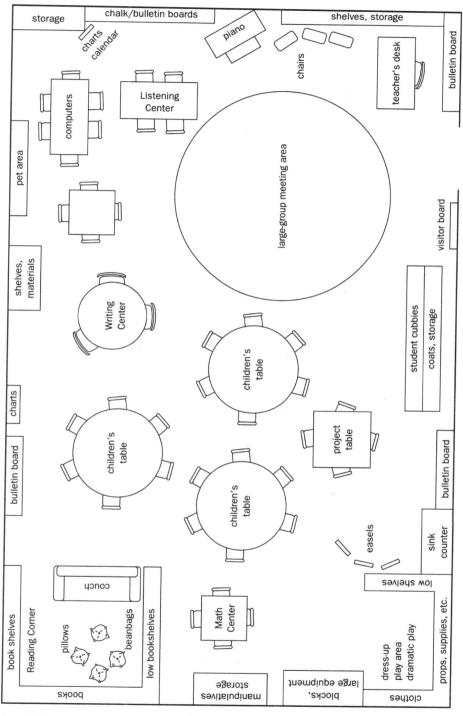

From *Teaching Language Arts: An Integrated Approach* by Suzanne Barchers (Minneapolis, Minn.: West, 1994), 56.

FIGURE 13.3
Intermediate/
middle school
classroom

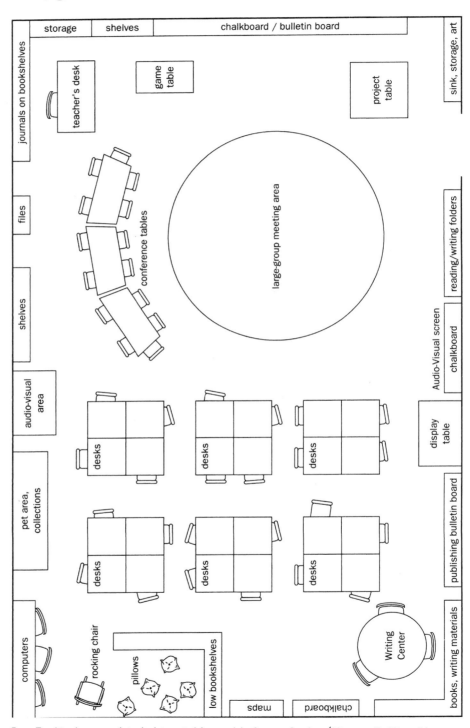

From *Teaching Language Arts: An Integrated Approach* by Suzanne Barchers (Minneapolis, Minn.: West, 1994), 57.

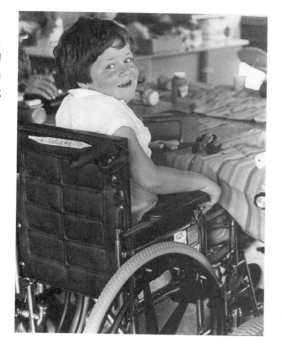

A young child
enjoys a rich
learning
environment.

art area. Symbolic cues, such as print and symbols, may further define a space (Neuman and Roskos 1993, 105). Intermediate teachers may have fewer areas, but may retain a reading area or writing center. Middle school teachers have been less likely to deviate from the traditional desks in rows with the teacher's desk in the front. There are a number of reasons for this; they may share a classroom with one or more other teachers, or their students may move to various classrooms throughout the day. Gradually, however, middle school teachers are experimenting with room arrangements, as they see how the environment can shape behaviors. The fortunate middle school teacher who is the sole occupant of a classroom should take time to visit elementary classrooms and analyze physical arrangements, such as centers or other informal learning spaces, that could be adopted or adapted to advantage.

PRINT DISPLAYS

The successful use of print on walls, bulletin boards, or other areas is a vital feature of the reading classroom and supports Brian Cambourne's condition of immersion in print. There should be an abundance of print, but it should be functional and appropriate. A room with labels on everything is confusing and overwhelming. Labels, posters, or charts that organize materials, guide behaviors, and provide information is useful for everyone. When students take ownership by creating the print or bulletin boards, it increases their responsibility and reinforces reading and writing. Catherine E. Loughlin and Mavis D. Martin (1987, 47–49) outline three kinds of print display:

Readable display Print that is easy to read.

1. For **readable display** (Loughlin and Martin 1987, 47), the teacher or the students may make the signs, posters, or charts, but they are easy to read and pertinent. They may label bins, shelves, baskets, or areas. They may provide schedules, assignments, checklists, or a news bulletin board (Strickland and Morrow 1988, 156).

■ **Appreciative display**
Student work that can be enjoyed by others.

2. **Appreciative display** encourages "awareness of writing as a medium for reflection, expression, and pleasure" (ibid., 48). Samples, such as poetry or stories, should be placed where students can enjoy them, perhaps above the water fountain.

■ **Visitor display**
Useful information for adult visitors to the classroom.

3. **Visitor display** includes useful information about the class or schedule and may be posted by the door (ibid., 49).

CENTERS

Primary classrooms often have a variety of centers: play (blocks, housekeeping, art); reading; writing; math manipulatives; and so forth. The science center will probably change with each new topic, while the art center will be more stable as it is primarily a source of materials in an easily cleaned area. The reading center may include a casual seating area, perhaps with beanbag chairs, a rocking chair, or even a bathtub. Shelves or bins help organize the permanent and rotating classroom library. Labels help organize the books for easy management. Teachers may assign tasks for students to complete at each center. Claire Staab describes how a teacher provides whole-group instruction and then dismisses the group to seven centers (language, math, science, writing, home, construction, and art) while she provides small-group instruction and observes (1991, 109). Other teachers use centers to supplement the curriculum.

Intermediate and middle school teachers are less likely to use centers for assignments; instead, centers serve to organize activities. A writing or publishing center and a reading center are the most common choices. Another center may be a multipurpose work area where small groups can tackle special projects. As computers become more common in the classroom, teachers may organize a computer or audio-visual equipment center. Computers may also be linked to a network in the library that provides access to CD-ROMs or online services.

TRAFFIC PATTERNS

Determining appropriate traffic patterns through a classroom takes careful assessment and thought. Susan B. Neuman and Kathleen A. Roskos recommend creating spatial boundaries in preschool classrooms through partitions, such as book shelves and dividers and labels of print and pictures (1993, 105–108). Such arrangements encourage focused activity and careful organization, but they make visual monitoring by the teacher more difficult. Further, when students with physical limitations are mainstreamed into the classroom, such arrangements may be an additional challenge. Rena B. Lewis and Donald H. Doorlag recommend that traffic patterns be direct, providing easier access and fewer distractions (1987, 143). Think carefully about your population and be ready to make changes throughout the year. For example, sixth graders take up a lot of space and are at an awkward and distractible stage. If you have no students using wheelchairs or walkers, you may want to create traffic patterns that slow movement just to calm the room. You may want direct access to heavily used items such as pencil sharpeners or waste baskets. Place critical information, such as assignments for chores or take-home handouts, prominently in the traffic flow or by the door.

SOUND

When many of us grew up, a quiet classroom was considered a good classroom because the teacher evidently had control and the students were productively busy. While talking was possibly acceptable in the kindergarten, it was methodically squelched as students moved through the grades. We now know how closely linked speaking is to reading, vocabulary development, problem solving, and writing. Wise teachers also recognize that by the time students reach middle school, many come to school primarily for the social interaction. Therefore, today's classrooms are often noisier than those of just a decade ago. Students discuss assignments, work in formal or informal small groups, or read aloud in pairs.

Recognizing the importance of talk is challenging to teachers, parents, and administrators who still assume that noise equals chaos. To assure yourself that noise levels are appropriate and productive, rotate through the classroom, listen to the conversations, and interact with the students frequently. Redirect the groups who are off track and guide those who need refocusing. Be sensitive to those students who may not function well in a noisy room because of their learning style or disabilities. Provide a quieter area with fewer distractions, perhaps allowing students to use earphones to shield noise. Recognize that it is acceptable to occasionally announce that *you* need a time-out, declaring a 15-minute quiet time or asking students to use their "indoor" rather than their "outdoor" voices.

The Intellectual Environment

The physical setting provides the setting for learning, but the intellectual environment is even more critical. Just as parents expect their infants to talk and walk eventually, teachers and students must expect they will all learn in the classroom. Establishing appropriate expectations becomes an ongoing challenge, and this process requires open communication and trust. High expectations are often intermingled with responsibility; every teacher's goal is to have responsible students who complete their work satisfactorily and on time.

At one back-to-school night, I listened to my son's fifth grade teachers discuss how it was time that students took over responsibility for their assignments and grades. Their message came across loud and clear: Students would get one chance at fulfilling their obligations and there would be no further chances. Because I had a son who needed his share of second chances, I reacted as many parents would, with fear that my son would struggle with such a rigid style. Fortunately, these were caring, experienced teachers who recognized when students were indeed trying their best, and they were very supportive.

Listening to those teachers discuss responsibility crystallized my thoughts on helping fifth graders, which I refer to as the five *R*s of responsibility: Rehearse, Risk, Rescue, Reteach, and Release. The steps, summarized in Figure 13.4, are simple.

1. *Rehearse.* Rehearse expectations frequently, especially at the beginning of the year. This involves Brian Cambourne's second and fifth conditions of learning, demonstration and use. Learners need many demonstrations throughout their schooling, both of an academic and social nature. Don't assume that telling students, even older students, something once is enough. Assume that students must practice a desired behavior or skill before it is mastered. Even something as simple as how to use a book or walking quietly to the bathroom must be reinforced for youngsters at the beginning of the school year.

2. *Risk.* Encourage students to take risks. Brian Cambourne's approximation condition is a key element in this model. If students know they can make mistakes, get close to the right answer, or have differing opinions, they will grow and learn. As he emphasizes, when adults respond supportively to children, children continue to grow.

3. *Rescue.* An environment that encourages risk taking must be a safe and trusting one. It is therefore sometimes prudent to "rescue" students who are floundering. At the end of each year I asked students to write about the "Bitter and the Best" of the year. One fifth grader wrote that the long-term projects made him feel like he never got done. He was an excellent student, and I never suspected he was frustrated. If I had known of his feelings, I could have helped him with a rescue—some intermediate goals or a checklist to help him stay on track.

4. *Reteach.* Be prepared to teach the concept differently or to allow students to explore the topic or process differently. Retain some flexibility, and continually explore better ways to reach your students. Often, asking your students how they would teach a difficult concept to a friend gives you excellent ideas.

5. *Release.* Release the responsibility back to the student once it is clear that mastery is imminent. This may mean eliminating rescues or giving students choices about whether they still need such help, but at this point they own the "help," which may be in the form of a daily assignment book or checklist.

FIGURE 13.4
Responsibility

The Five *R*'s of Responsibility

1. *Rehearse.* Make sure expectations are clear and provide regular practice.

2. *Risk.* Ensure that the environment is safe enough for risk taking.

3. *Rescue.* For students who need help, provide support. This may be extra help or time, checklists, an assignment book, more communication with parents, tutoring, and so forth.

4. *Reteach.* Provide alternative ways of learning, as necessary.

5. *Release.* Return the responsibility to the student. This may mean eliminating the rescue or giving the students choices about using the rescues.

The Environment for Learners with Special Needs

Students with mild learning disabilities or those who are easily distracted may need quiet work spaces with minimal distractions. Their desks or tables should be away from windows, doors opening into hallways, or other heavy traffic areas. Sometimes students with behavioral problems benefit from having limited space, and sometimes they need more work space (Hammill and Bartel 1990, 371). Providing two or three study carrels gives any student an opportunity to work in a quiet area. The downside to having isolated work spaces is that students who are easily distractible can also take advantage of being out of your line of sight (Meese 1994, 76). This problem is minimized if you circulate frequently through the classroom or if you use low room dividers.

Students with physical limitations or who use wheelchairs need a room that is free of clutter and architectural barriers. Evaluate whether the environment encourages independence or dependence. For example, if the water fountain is out of reach, the student using a wheelchair will have to ask someone to help with a cup. Although you might not be able to change a water fountain, you can be sure that materials are within reach, perhaps on lower shelves or counters (Lewis and Doorlag 1987, 139). Students with hearing or visual limitations benefit from being at the front of the room or from having a buddy assigned to make sure they are receiving accurate information.

Occasionally, you may arrange with a teacher of special students to have them join your class for one or more hours each day. For example, one year a high-functioning mentally retarded sixth grader joined my language arts class. More commonly, students with special learning challenges will be in your regular classroom most of the day, but will leave for special help with a remedial reading teacher or other specialist. It is particularly important that the environment accommodates these students so that they remain integrated in the classroom, with smooth departures and returns.

When integrating students with special needs, take time to analyze how the environment can support their learning. Sometimes, a simple modification such as giving a clip board to a student who has mild arm spasms provides just the bit of independence that child needs for successful writing. When I first worked with remedial reading students, I remember wishing I had seat belts on their chairs. After observing them at work, I realized that sitting down was *my* expectation, not their need: Their work was quite acceptable even though they stood at their desks for seemingly hours at a time. When analyzing environments, try to set aside your learning style or preferences and decide what is best for your students. Finally, don't forget to ask the individuals what *they* think would be the most effective accommodations. Once their ideas are honored, they will often be more invested in the learning process.

The Multicultural Environment

Just as a home provides a child's first environment, the community provides a secondary, broader environment. The community has its own culture, characterized by locale, social class, ethnicity, values, beliefs, and shared interests about language (Wolfram 1991, 470). In a culturally diverse neighborhood, the school should reflect the community of learners, whether students come from the immediate neighborhood or arrive on buses. Print displays and pictures should reflect the cultural mix of the student community. In schools where the population is predominantly from one culture, the teacher must work to ensure that a variety of cultures are represented.

The library should be similarly developed to reflect a wide variety of cultures. Fortunately, new multicultural children's and young adult literature is continually being published, enabling teachers to surround their students with the ideas and flavors of various cultures. Folktales from around the world provide opportunities to share cultural differences and similarities. I remember the delight expressed by one student as I read "Cinderella" aloud one September. He had just arrived from Vietnam the previous month; the next day he brought in his family's version of the tale, carefully and lovingly transported thousands of miles from his home country. Judy Sierra has collected 25 "Cinderella" tales from around the world in *Cinderella*; this is a convenient resource for comparing variants from many cultures. (See Appendix C, Recommended Multicultural Literature.) Teachers should also seek out newspapers, magazines, and other materials from different cultures, particularly if they have second-language students (Crawford 1993, 110).

The classroom should also reflect the everyday and special occurrences from related cultures. These can include community events, national observances, lists of birthdays or historical events, and so forth. To reinforce the everyday utility of literacy, provide practical experiences for students that relate to their cultures. For example, students can research creating a meal or a single dish—studying newspapers for sale prices, shopping for the groceries, and preparing the item for sharing. This activity involves reading, writing, speaking, math, research, and collaboration. Consult *Cooking Up World History: Multicultural Recipes and Resources* (Marden and Barchers 1994) or *The Multicultural Cookbook for Students* (Albyn and Webb 1993) for representative recipes. For more in-depth experiences, consider immersing the class in thematic units that explore a culture. See *Multicultural Explorations: Joyous Journeys with Books* (Heltshe and Kirchner 1991) for thematic units for a round-the-world tour that includes Hawaii, Australia, Japan, Italy, Kenya, and Brazil.

Theme or Role-Playing Environments

Educators are increasingly recognizing the importance of play for young learners. Preschool and kindergarten classrooms have had special play environments for years, such as a housekeeping or dress-up area, and many teachers believe that play is a "window into children's minds" (Pellegrini and Boyd 1993, 117). When discussing the use of games and play to foster literacy, James Moffett and Betty Jane Wagner state, "Just as lion cubs gambol and tumble to develop the agility they will need as predators, human children invent kinds of play that exercise their minds" (1993, 35).

The wise primary teacher doesn't relegate play experiences to preschool and kindergarten, but considers creating play environments in the classroom also, infusing these environments with opportunities for many reading and writing experiences. Creating a generic area that can be refocused with a minimum of effort offers opportunities for a variety of themes, and Susan B. Neuman and Kathy Roskos found that children use literacy as they play in an assortment of environments (1990, 220).

An office environment, for example, is appealing to many primary- or intermediate-age children because they have relatives who work in offices and they have been in offices. An office space can be equipped with numerous basics: a desk, table, waiting area, telephone, typewriter or computer, adding machine, writing materials, charts, posters, calendar, file folders, note cards, message board, reference books, shelves, storage areas, counters, telephone book, paper clips, and so forth. With a few changes, this office can become an office for a veterinarian, nurse, reporter, writer, cartographer, or an architect.

For a science lab, equip the space with the appropriate investigative tools and props, such as lab coats, and rotate the theme: rocks, fossils, shells, outer space, plants, shells, or small animals. A housekeeping theme found in a primary classroom can be the home of the Three Bears, Cinderella's castle, or the setting for any number of popular children's picture books. The theme can be changed with a minimum of effort and timed to relate to the curriculum.

Teachers who work with upper primary and older students are less likely to have role-playing areas. Some teachers develop thematic units for 4–6 weeks of immersion in a topic. Bess Altwerger and Barbara Flores discuss theme cycles rather than theme units, characterizing these experiences as a recursive and spiral process of knowledge construction in which the subject areas serve the topic (1994, 4).

Temporary immersion in themed environments can enhance such studies and stimulate interest, particularly when related to other cultures. For example, Mary Ann Heltshe and Audrey Burie Kirchner suggest the following items for a trunk: chopsticks, rice bowl, tea cups, tea box, a Japanese doll and kite, fortune cookies, mandarin oranges, and Japanese songs. They suggest using a folding room divider to make a Japanese teahouse screen, creating kimonos and obis, learning Japanese symbol writing, playing Japanese games, learning origami, and participating in a tea ceremony (1991, 66–101). Middle school teachers may collaborate with the social studies or history teacher to create similar temporary environments while researching a particular country or theme.

Library Environments

For the reading teacher, the most important sources of support are libraries: classroom, school, public, and professional. Each library makes a valuable contribution to the literate classroom, but utilizing them effectively requires effort, organization, and collaboration with the librarian.

THE CLASSROOM LIBRARY

Students usually favor a well-developed classroom library over the school or public libraries, perhaps because it is a familiar, comfortable place, and indeed you want your classroom library to be inviting and cozy. I've seen classroom libraries as simple as pillows and an area rug and as elaborate as a loft. What is important is the message conveyed—that you value books and literacy enough to dedicate considerable resources, space, and time to it.

Unfortunately, few districts have adequate funding to provide elaborate libraries for each classroom, and centralized school libraries allow for more efficient use of resources. When considering what you want in your classroom library, ask your students what they love to read. Then ask yourself the following questions:

1. What books are always in use?

2. What books are always hidden in students' desks because they hate to return them to the shelves or library?

3. What books do I use year after year for certain lessons or units?

4. What books are favorites for reading aloud?

5. What books of poetry are useful for inspiring writing or for reading aloud during odd moments?

6. What reference books are necessary for routine reading, writing, and research?

7. What reference books would eliminate frequent trips to the library?

8. What teacher resources do I use frequently?

9. What books win awards, both local, state, and national? (For up-to-date information, consult the Children's Book Council's Web site at www.cbcbooks.org.)

FIRST CHOICES FOR THE LITERATE CLASSROOM

We teachers today are fortunate to have an abundance of books choices available to us. This profusion, however, can be overwhelming when you begin to gather resources for the literate classroom. The lists at the end of the chapter include my favorite teacher resources and resources for primary, intermediate, and middle school grades: picture books, short stories, poetry collections, novels, and folktales. I think of these resources as my "jewels"—I would always choose them even if my funds were severely limited, and I would rescue them first in the event of a disaster. Some have been popular for many years; others are relatively new. All stand up to repeated readings or use. Your list may include some of these titles or be very different, and it will likely change from year to year.

SOURCES OF MATERIALS

Creating a literate environment requires ingenuity and an investment in time as you seek to acquire materials. Garage sales, used book stores, and library sales are excellent sources for books, magazines, games, records, tapes, posters, and other materials. Popular paperback books are often available for very little cost at garage sales, and many sellers will negotiate lower prices for teachers. Ask your public librarian to keep you posted on upcoming library sales where most books are less than one dollar.

Book clubs for school children are a convenient source of inexpensive books, resource materials, and equipment. For each order, teachers earn points that can be exchanged for books, tapes, posters, or other equipment. Special offers throughout the year provide books for as little as 50 cents per book. Ordering these books requires an investment of time, but the free and inexpensive materials are worth it. (Check out Scholastic Book Clubs, Inc., P.O. Box 3745, Jefferson City, MO 65102-9838 or The Trumpet Club, P.O. Box 6003, Columbia, MO 65205-9888.)

A classroom book exchange can help build your classroom library. It is fun and your students get invested in the process. Students bring in two paperback books and trade them for one book. The extra book stays in the classroom library for student use. Some schools have a book exchange on a one-to-one basis just to encourage circulation of books; others may combine a book exchange with a Reading Is Fundamental (RIF) distribution. The RIF program, often funded by a service organization, provides a free book to each student. (For information, contact Reading Is Fundamental, Inc., Smithsonian Institution, Room 500, 600 Maryland Avenue, S.W., Washington, D.C. 20560, or call 202-287-3220.) Many families donate books on a student's birthday or for other special occasions.

For those teachers in large metropolitan areas, book wholesalers sometimes offer discounts to schools or teachers for classroom purchases. Some wholesalers organize book fairs for the school, and a percentage of the profit can be used for purchasing books. Book store chains often have tables of discounted books, with substantial seasonal discounts, and independent book stores may offer a small discount for teachers.

Teachers who attend local, regional, or national conferences can obtain free posters, pamphlets, information about authors, and other materials while visiting the exhibits. Vendors often offer substantial discounts or give away the books just before the exhibits close, reducing their inventory that would otherwise have to be returned. These conventions or conferences vary in location throughout the region or country. Consider joining an organization that deals with language arts, such as the International Reading Association or the National Council of Teachers of English. College students receive a discounted rate and a subscription to the journal.

Parents can be encouraged to provide an annual subscription as a class gift or to bring in used magazines in a variety of subject areas. Occasionally parent-teacher organizations publish a "wish list," requesting donations from parents. These lists can include magazine subscriptions, books, records, cassettes, book ends, shelving, or any other needs. Lobby your principal to let you use money that might be spent on basal materials for your classroom library.

Finally, let everyone know you want to acquire books. If you don't enjoy garage or estate sales, ask a friend who does to look for you. My relatives know that I especially appreciate books from countries they visit. If others make purchases for you, some mistakes may be made regarding content. Be sure to review any unfamiliar books before placing them on the classroom shelves. When there is no time to preread a book, set it aside until you can read it or until you can consult a library media specialist or published book review. A parent or volunteer who is familiar with quality materials could assist with screening materials.

SCHOOL, PUBLIC, AND PROFESSIONAL LIBRARIES

With or without a well-established classroom library, your school, public, and professional libraries will be major sources of materials for your reading program, and librarians should be your most important allies.

SCHOOL LIBRARIES

Despite the move by many districts to develop programs that use literature in place of basal textbooks, library funding is often one of the first budget cuts. In some districts, a library media specialist has few interactions with students and teachers, and instead may supervise several paraprofessionals who essentially maintain the collections in several schools. In schools fortunate to have a full-time library media specialist, their job description has grown to reflect an increasingly important collaborative role. This professional organizes and maintains the environment, acquires and processes materials, manages the collection's circulation, and organizes and repairs a variety of audio-visual equipment. In addition, the library media specialist keeps current through constant reading of new books, attending professional meetings, and reading professional journals, and may supervise use of technology.

In the past, the library media specialist's job was more passive, but today good library media specialists actively seek out their "customers," pursuing collaboration by supporting classroom research projects, teaching critical library skills, or team-teaching for thematic units. A good library media specialist is an essential and integral member of the educational team who has chosen the profession out of a love of books and people. Ask your librarian for help at the early stages of planning for a theme or research project. You may need to change the focus of a unit because there are few materials available or because another teacher has that topic underway.

Libraries can be a catalyst for change in the public schools. The Library Power Project, funded by the DeWitt Wallace-Reader's Digest Fund, stresses including every child in the program (Goldfarb and Salmon 1993, 568). Members of the school community in New York City have collaborated to determine how best to serve special needs students, and these efforts have triggered adaptations that fully integrate students with limitations. In general, the teachers and librarians have found that the good teaching practices that work with the general population also work with specialized populations with some modifications. Librarians and teachers share their adaptations with others in the

schools. Liz Goldfarb and Sheila Salmon note that an important mile-
stone is the realization that there is little to fear in serving special populations
(1993, 571).

PUBLIC LIBRARIES

Your local public librarian should be one of your closest off-campus professional associates. The public library is not only a source for books, films, and
videos, but can also be a destination for field trips for special programs. One
teacher in a small town in western Colorado told me that the library is her first
and favorite field trip for her kindergartners. The students not only get to learn
how to check out books, but for many, it is also the first time in their lives that
they ride on an elevator, the only one in town!

Public librarians have access to an immense informational system, and
given enough time, they can locate books from other libraries to complete a
set of novels for group instruction or to enhance a theme. Judith Volc, a librarian in Boulder, Colorado, holds monthly acquisition meetings for teachers and
school librarians who lack the time to review new books for purchase. She
regularly hosts classes for research, special programs, or collaborative efforts.
Like many public librarians, she provides programs during the summer that
will support the classroom teacher's efforts to keep students reading year-
round.

Ms. Volc also regularly searches for ways to develop literate learners. Concerned with those intermediate students who are not fluent readers, she trains
them to read aloud to younger students. They select easy-to-read picture
books, and she models the process of good storytelling. They analyze the plot,
characterization, and setting of each book, thus guaranteeing a full understanding of the book. The students practice using a tape or video recorder,
receive coaching, and then read to young students. Those who remain uncomfortable after this process learn to read aloud a filmstrip script, secure in a
semidarkened room behind the projector (Barchers 1990, 15).

PROFESSIONAL LIBRARIES

Most school districts maintain professional libraries that provide teachers with
the latest in educational resources, textbooks, samples of textbook series, curriculum, and current journals. Classroom materials might include films, videos,
picture books, sets of novels, and artifacts. Many professional libraries collect
baskets or trunks of books organized by themes or genres. Many also provide
teachers with information through specialized data bases and will assist with
computer research. Many have monthly or quarterly publications that help
teachers keep abreast of new acquisitions or trends in literature. Because these
libraries are supported by taxes, the public can use the facilities. They are par-

ticularly useful for education students because they conveniently house a cross section of sample textbooks, curriculum, and educational resources.

Informal Learning Environments

Learning does not stop when students leave the classroom or library. Before coming to school, students begin learning in the home and then expand their learning to informal environments in the community. Fortunate youngsters may already have had their first experiences with dinosaurs in a museum, with mammals in a zoo, or with exotic foods at a marketplace or festival. Experiential education was a buzzword in the 1970s, when people believed that students needed to have hands-on experiences in order to learn successfully. Although the pendulum has swung closer to center again, it is true that thematic cycles, research projects, interviews, and natural curiosity can take students to a variety of settings that enhance the learning process.

Every environment inspires behaviors that students need to learn; conduct appropriate in an interactive science center may not be suitable in a natural history museum. Because of tight budgets, teachers and students must make the best of increasingly rare field trips. To maximize visits to informal learning environments, contact the institution well in advance of the visit to determine their expectations regarding the adult-student ratio and preparation. Many museums have inexpensive or complimentary curriculum available that provides background information for the visit or extends it afterward. If your school's budget cannot support field trips, contact institutions about bringing the program to your school or obtaining sponsored admissions for schools with limited funds. If you are in a rural area without access to special facilities, ask parents to share any special expertise they have or to show slides of trips they have taken. Finally, consider your immediate neighborhood for sources for field trips. Take a walk around the school's area as if you were a stranger trying to discover everything you could: architecture, markets, businesses, flora, fauna, and so forth. Sometimes, the best learning opportunities are within five minutes of your classroom.

A Final Note

You and your students will spend a significant portion of your lives in your classroom. In many cases, your students will spend more waking hours in the classroom than in their homes. This all-important environment should reflect your philosophy and your instructional practices, and therefore, its creation deserves thoughtful consideration. Now that you have read this chapter, consider the philosophies reflected in classrooms you have visited and return to the list of questions on assessing the environment (page 426). Think about how you might organize your classroom in the future. Remember that the classroom also belongs to your students; they will often have revealing insights into how it can be more comfortable and functional. Make creating a literate environment important and enjoyable for everyone in your classroom.

Summary

Teachers continue to influence the school environment, just as they did 100 years ago. The environment should be a "deep" one that promotes literacy. Teachers can support the home environment by recommending literacy activities.

The school environment and climate can be assessed by observing and asking a series of questions. The physical arrangement should allow for large- and small-group instruction, spatial boundaries, quiet areas, and flexibility. Print displays should reflect the community and include readable display, appreciative display, and visitor display.

Primary classrooms may have a variety of centers for assignments or informal exploration. Intermediate and middle school classes may develop reading, writing, or computer centers. Traffic patterns should accommodate the needs of the population and guide behaviors. The classroom should have noise levels that appropriately reflect ongoing learning.

The intellectual environment is driven by expectations for learning. Students should rehearse skills and behaviors, be encouraged to take risks, and assume more responsibility, with "rescues" offered as necessary. Students with special needs may need environmental modifications or adaptations. The room should be barrier-free for students or visitors. The environment should be analyzed to determine how it can support successful mainstreaming.

The classroom should reflect the community's culture and the cultures of the world. Books, magazines, and newspapers will support various cultures. Consider using folktales, cooking activities, and community events to support the multicultural climate.

Preschool and kindergarten teachers often use role-playing environments, and research supports the idea that such enriched play environments increase literacy. Older students enjoy temporary immersion in environments during theme units or cycles.

The classroom library is an important source of books and materials and demonstrates the value placed on reading. The school library and librarian should be a vital part of the reading program. Public libraries have access to a broader resource base, and professional libraries provide teachers with opportunities to review and borrow textbooks, curriculum, films, and other materials. Informal learning environments, such as museums, the zoo, or immediate community, provide another extension to the school environment.

My Favorite Resources

PRIMARY FIRST CHOICES

Ahlberg, Janet, and Allan Ahlberg. *The Jolly Postman or Other People's Letters.* Boston: Little, Brown, 1986. Picture/toy book.

Aliki. *How a Book Is Made.* New York: Thomas Y. Crowell, 1986. Nonfiction.

Carle, Eric. *The Very Busy Spider.* New York: Philomel, 1985. Picture book.

Dorros, Arthur. *Abuela.* Illustrated by Elisa Kleven. New York: Dutton, 1991. Picture book.

Gwynne, Fred. *The King Who Rained.* New York: Simon & Schuster, 1970. Wordplay.

Lobel, Arnold. *Fables.* New York: Harper & Row, 1980. Modern fables.

McPhail, David. *Lost!* Boston: Little, Brown, 1990. Picture book.

Prelutsky, Jack, ed. *The Random House Book of Poetry for Children.* Illustrated by Arnold Lobel. New York: Random House, 1983. Poetry.

Scieszka, Jon. *The True Story of the 3 Little Pigs.* Illustrated by Lane Smith. New York: Viking, 1989. Picture book.

Wood, Audrey. *King Bidgood's in the Bathtub.* Illustrated by Don Wood. New York: Harcourt Brace Jovanovich, 1985. Picture book.

INTERMEDIATE FIRST CHOICES

Baylor, Byrd. *I'm in Charge of Celebrations.* Illustrated by Peter Parnall. New York: Charles Scribner's, 1986. Picture book.

McKinley, Robin. *Beauty: A Retelling of the Story of Beauty and the Beast.* New York: Pocket, 1979. Novelized folktale.

Moss, Jeffrey. *The Butterfly Jar.* Illustrated by Chris Demarest. New York: Bantam, 1989. Poetry.

Paulsen, Gary. *Hatchet.* New York: Puffin, 1987. Realistic fiction.

____. *Woodsong.* New York: Puffin, 1990. Nonfiction.

Scieszka, Jon. *The Stinky Cheese Man and Other Fairly Stupid Tales.* Illustrated by Lane Smith. New York: Viking, 1992. Picture book/folktales.

Shannon, George. *Stories to Solve: Folktales from Around the World.* Illustrated by Peter Sis. New York: Greenwillow, 1985. Folktales.

Spinelli, Jerry. *Maniac Magee.* Boston: Little, Brown, 1990. Realistic fiction.

Trelease, Jim, ed. *Hey! Listen to This: Stories to Read Aloud.* New York: Penguin, 1992. Folktales and excerpts from chapter books.

Van Allsburg, Chris. *The Mysteries of Harris Burdick.* Boston: Houghton Mifflin, 1982. Picture book.

MIDDLE SCHOOL FIRST CHOICES

Avi. *Nothing But the Truth.* New York: Orchard, 1991. Realistic fiction.

Cormier, Robert. *After the First Death.* New York: Avon, 1979. Realistic fiction.

Creech, Sharon. *Chasing Redbird.* New York: HarperCollins, 1997. Fiction.

Gallo, Donald R., ed. *Center Stage: One-Act Plays for Teenage Readers and Actors.* New York: Harper & Row, 1990. Plays.

____. *Sixteen: Short Stories by Outstanding Writers for Young Adults.* New York: Dell, 1984. Short stories.

Lyons, Mary E. *Letters from a Slave Girl: The Story of Harriet Jacobs.* New York: Charles Scribner's, 1992. Fiction.

Macaulay, David. *Black and White.* Boston: Houghton Mifflin, 1990. Picture book.

Magorian, Michelle. *Good Night, Mr. Tom.* New York: Harper & Row, 1981. Historical fiction.

Müller, Jörg. *The Changing City.* New York: Atheneum, 1976. Picture portfolio.

Nye, Naomi Shihab. *This Same Sky: A Collection of Poems from Around the World.* New York: Four Winds Press, 1992. Poetry.

O'Brien, Robert C. *Z for Zachariah.* New York: Macmillan, 1974. Science fiction.

TEACHER RESOURCES

Angell, Carole S. *Celebrations Around the World: A Multicultural Handbook.* Golden, Colo.: Fulcrum, 1996.

Atwell, Nancie. *In the Middle: Writing, Reading, and Learning with Adolescents.* Portsmouth, N.H.: Boynton/Cook, 1987.

Bohning, Gerry, Ann Phillips, and Sandra Bryant. *Literature on the Move: Making and Using Pop-Up and Lift-Flap Books.* Englewood, Colo.: Teacher Ideas Press, 1993.

Canavan, Diane D., and LaVonne H. Sanborn. *Using Children's Books in Reading/Language Arts Programs.* New York: Neal-Schuman, 1992.

Covey, Donita. *Novel Strategies for Young Adults.* Englewood, Colo.: Teacher Ideas Press, 1992.

Frank, Marjorie. *If You're Trying to Teach Kids How to Write, You've Gotta Have This Book.* Nashville, Tenn.: Incentive, 1979.

Krashen, Stephen. *The Power of Reading: Insights from the Research.* Englewood, Colo.: Libraries Unlimited, 1993.

Lies, Betty Bonham. *The Poet's Pen: Writing Poetry with Middle and High School Students.* Englewood, Colo.: Teacher Ideas Press, 1993.

McElmeel, Sharron. *The Latest and Greatest Read-Alouds.* Englewood, Colo.: Libraries Unlimited, 1994.

Neamen, Mimi, and Mary Strong. *Literature Circles: Cooperative Learning for Grades 3–8.* Englewood, Colo.: Teacher Ideas Press, 1992.

Trelease, Jim. *The New Read-Aloud Handbook.* New York: Penguin, 1989.

References

Albyn, Carole Lisa, and Lois Sinaiko Webb. *The Multicultural Cookbook for Students.* Phoenix, Ariz.: Oryx Press, 1993.

Altwerger, Bess, and Barbara Flores. "Theme Cycles: Creating Communities of Learners." *Primary Voices K–6* 2, no. 1 (Jan. 1994): 2–6.

Barchers, Suzanne I. *Creating and Managing the Literate Classroom.* Englewood, Colo.: Teacher Ideas Press, 1990.

Cambourne, Brian. *The Whole Story: Natural Learning and the Acquisition of Literacy in the Classroom.* Auckland, New Zealand: Ashton Scholastic, 1988.

Crawford, Leslie. *Language and Literacy Learning in Multicultural Classrooms.* Boston: Allyn & Bacon, 1993.

Dempsey, James D., and Joe L. Frost. "Play Environments in Early Childhood Education." In *Handbook of Research on the Education of Young Children*, edited by Bernard Spodek, 306–321. New York: Macmillan, 1993.

Fawcett, Gay. "Moving the Big Desk." *Language Arts* 69, no. 3 (March 1992): 183–185.

Goldfarb, Liz, and Sheila Salmon. "Enhancing Language Arts for Special Populations: Librarians and Classroom Teachers Collaborate." *Language Arts* 70, no. 7 (Nov. 1993): 567–572.

Hammill, Donald D., and Nettie R. Bartel. *Teaching Students with Learning and Behavior Problems.* Boston: Allyn & Bacon, 1990.

Heltshe, Mary Ann, and Audrey Burie Kirchner. *Multicultural Explorations: Joyous Journeys with Books.* Englewood, Colo.: Libraries Unlimited, 1991.

Kalman, Bobbie. *Early Schools.* New York: Crabtree, 1982.

Kozol, Jonathan. *Savage Inequalities.* New York: HarperPerennial, 1992.

Lewis, Rena B., and Donald H. Doorlag. *Teaching Special Students in the Mainstream.* Columbus, Ohio: Merrill, 1987.

Loughlin, Catherine E., and Mavis D. Martin. *Supporting Literacy: Developing Effective Learning Environments.* New York: Teachers College Press, 1987.

Marden, Patricia C., and Suzanne I. Barchers. *Cooking Up World History: Multicultural Recipes and Resources.* Englewood, Colo.: Teacher Ideas Press, 1994.

Meese, Ruth Lyn. *Teaching Learners with Mild Disabilities: Integrating Research and Practice.* Belmont, Calif.: Brooks/Cole, 1994.

Moffett, James, and Betty Jane Wagner. "What Works Is Play." *Language Arts* 70, no. 1 (Jan. 1993): 32–36.

Neuman, Susan B., and Kathleen A. Roskos. *Language and Literacy Learning in the Early Years: An Integrated Approach.* Orlando, Fla.: Harcourt Brace Jovanovich, 1993.

_____. "Play, Print, and Purpose: Enriching Play Environments for Literacy Development." *The Reading Teacher* 44, no. 3 (Nov. 1990): 214–221.

Pellegrini, A. D., and Brenda Boyd. "The Role of Play in Early Childhood Development and Education: Issues in Definition and Function." In *Handbook of Research on the Education of Young Children*, edited by Bernard Spodek, 105–121. New York: Macmillan, 1993.

Sierra, Judy. *Cinderella.* Phoenix, Ariz.: Oryx Press, 1992.

Staab. Claire. "Classroom Organization: Thematic Centers Revisited." *Language Arts* 68, no. 2 (Feb. 1991): 108–113.

Strickland, Dorothy S., and Lesley Mandel Morrow. "Emerging Readers and Writers: Creating a Print Rich Environment." *The Reading Teacher* 42, no. 2 (Nov. 1988): 156–157.

_____. "Emerging Readers and Writers: Environments Rich in Print Promote Literacy Behavior During Play." *The Reading Teacher* 43, no. 2 (Nov. 1989): 178–179.

Tway, Eileen. "The Elementary School Classroom." In *Handbook of Research on Teaching the English Language Arts*, edited by James Flood, Julie M. Jensen, Dianne Lapp, and James R. Squire, 425–437. New York: Macmillan, 1991.

Wolfram, Walt. "The Community and Language Arts." In *Handbook of Research on Teaching the English Language Arts*, edited by James Flood, Julie M. Jensen, Dianne Lapp, and James R. Squire, 470–476. New York: Macmillan, 1991.

14

Building Reading and Writing Units

FOCUS QUESTIONS

1. What does it mean to teach using units?

2. What are interdisciplinary units?

3. What are the current models of reading and writing units?

4. How do I decide when to use a unit?

5. How do I choose a unit?

6. How do I plan a unit?

7. How can I involve parents and volunteers?

A Soldier's Daily Camp Ration

12 ounces of pork or bacon—or 20 ounces salt or fresh beef

22 ounces soft bread or flour—or 16 ounces hard bread—or 20 ounces corn meal

A Soldier's Daily Marching Ration

1 pound hard bread
3/4 pound salt pork or 1 1/4 pound fresh meat
Sugar
Coffee
Salt

Excerpted from *Hardtack and Coffee: The Unwritten Story of Army Life* by John D. Billings (Boston: George M. Smith, 1887) 111–112.

Students who learn that soldiers often dipped their hardtack into coffee so they could scoop out the weevils that floated to the top gain a perspective on the Civil War that rarely occurs when they only read textbooks. Students who then make and eat hardtack and coffee or barley water, a coffee substitute, will never forget the importance of food to soldiers during this war. Teachers dedicated to providing authentic, absorbing learning experiences have always turned to immersion in units based on common themes or problems, such as the Civil War unit included at the end of this chapter. The one-room schoolhouse provides our earliest model, where students of every age worked together to learn about such topics as their region's history. Older students helped younger students master material while learning practical skills that would be useful for a lifetime. When my mother attended the 50-year reunion of the students she taught in a one-room schoolhouse, their memories were not of the subjects they studied, but of learning to cook and sew.

In this chapter we discuss the different types of units found in many schools and how to plan and implement a unit. Though rewarding and stimulating, teaching and learning through units is challenging. To choose the appropriate unit, consider the needs of your students, the resources available to you, the structure of your school, and your energy level.

Kinds of Units

Discipline-based content design
The traditional practice of teaching each subject during a specific instructional period.

Interdisciplinary instruction
Consciously applying methodology and language from more than one discipline to examine a central theme, issue, problem, or experience.

In the traditional model for teaching, **discipline-based content design**, subject matter is clearly defined and presented as separate topics. This model will be quite familiar to parents, who were usually taught in this fashion. In contrast, **interdisciplinary instruction** integrates subject matter such as history, math, and science in order to create a wholistic approach to learning (Jacobs 1989, 8). These units are commonly referred to as thematic units or theme cycles, with the latter term reflecting the recursive nature of the questioning and problem solving that occurs during such investigations (Altwerger and Flores 1994, 2).

"A thematic unit is multidisciplinary and multidimensional; it knows no boundaries" (Fredericks, Meinbach, and Rothlein 1993, 6). When creating a unit based on a theme, you need to develop a point of view or a position to explore. For example, reading Barbara Cooney's *Miss Rumphius* inspires the topic of planting lupines, but could be used to explore the theme of making the world a better place (Shanahan, Robinson, and Schneider 1995, 718). Teachers who use this format find that they require more preparation and that students may at first be reluctant to take on the extra involvement this type of learning requires since this approach to learning moves children outside the comfort of passive learning. However, students soon see the connections, and they become empowered as they develop confidence in their abilities to take risks and take ownership in their learning (Andrews-Sullivan and Negrete 1994, 17). The following interdisciplinary instructional models demonstrate applications from preschool through high school.

PARALLEL DISCIPLINE DESIGN

■ **Parallel discipline design**
When two teachers of different disciplines collaborate on the same topic.

Parallel discipline design (Jacobs 1989, 15) occurs when the language arts teacher has students reading mythology, while the history teacher explores Greek history. Perhaps the easiest to institute, many teachers first integrate curriculum using this model. Because the teachers still teach during their respective periods, integration is not as fully realized as when they work as a team. This model may occur at any grade level.

COMPLEMENTARY DISCIPLINE UNITS

■ **Complementary discipline units**
When related disciplines are studied together.

With **complementary discipline units** or courses, teachers team-teach related disciplines (ibid., 16). For example, a secondary humanities course may include history, literature, music, and art. Usually two or more middle school or secondary teachers work together for an extended time period. Students may focus on a theme or issue, drawing upon the strengths of the individual teachers' subject areas.

INTERDISCIPLINARY UNITS

■ **Interdisciplinary units**
Combining disciplines for a unit of study.

Usually found in elementary and middle schools, **interdisciplinary units** (ibid.) often feature teachers of all subjects working together on a theme or problem during a specified time period. During the study of Medieval times, for example, the physical education teacher may teach games or dances of the period; the art teacher may help students research and design appropriate clothing; the music teacher may share folk music and the role of troubadours; the language arts teacher may require reading of historical fiction; the science teacher may have students study the spread of disease through rodents; and the history teacher may explore the government of the period. Interdisciplinary units are effective when the topic naturally lends itself to a broad investigation and when teachers dedicate themselves to working as a team. Without careful planning, however, the unit can suffer from the "potpourri problem," where the unit lacks focus and depth (ibid., 2). In elementary schools without specialists, the classroom teacher can use this model more easily, bringing in community experts to enhance the investigation.

INTEGRATED-DAY MODEL

■ Integrated-day model
An instruction problem based on student-selected themes.

Originating in the British Infant School, the **integrated-day model** (ibid., 17) is based on themes the children choose to explore. Usually found in private or alternative preschools, kindergartens, and primary schools, this student-centered program is highly motivating. Because students essentially drive the program, teachers must be diligent, continually reviewing accomplishments to determine whether students are mastering required content and skills.

COMPLETE PROGRAM

■ Complete program
An instructional program in which students live in the school environment and determine their own curriculum.

Typified by a school such as A. S. Neil's Summerhill, where students live at the school and create the curriculum from their interests and daily events, the **complete program** is rarely found (ibid., 18). Students take complete responsibility for their learning program, totally immersing themselves in an investigation.

PROBLEM-BASED UNITS

■ Problem-based thematic unit
Learning based on simulation of a problem.

The **problem-based thematic unit**, described by Patricia Cordeiro, begins with a problem statement. When she challenged her students to get their families by wagon train to a new site in the western United States, they found they needed to use math and learn about geology, meteorology, geography, map reading, and survival techniques. They discovered the value of diaries and the need for careful planning (1990, 27).

Students might want to investigate topics with more unknowns, such as why the dinosaurs became extinct or why the Virginia Colony didn't survive. Such topics lend themselves to forming hypotheses and determining whether the theories have validity. Similarly, be watchful for current events that could trigger an authentic investigation that would be of high interest to your students. For example, a man out with his dog came upon what he believed to be some dinosaur bones in an undeveloped Denver suburban lot. This prompted great interest in the community as experts worked to determine the kind of bones, if there were additional bones, and so forth. Such occurrences provide imaginative teachers with the perfect opportunity to instigate meaningful problem-based units.

Reading and Writing Units

Many language arts teachers immerse their students in units that involve primarily reading and writing rather than a variety of topic areas. More easily managed in the context of a language arts period, they are usually implemented by one or two teachers. The following units are commonly found in elementary and middle school classrooms, but variants abound.

GENRE UNITS

A genre unit is based on a type of literature generally regarded as having a recognizable style, such as the folk literature unit found in Chapter 10. The unit, appropriate for any grade level, may be limited to reading activities that explore the common elements in the genre or may be expanded to include writing activities. Other examples of possible genres include autobiography, biography, mystery, fantasy, science fiction, poetry, short story. Other areas for exploration include specific forms, such as alphabet or counting books.

AUTHOR AND ILLUSTRATOR STUDIES

Authors write books to entertain, inform, express opinions, and persuade (Wildberger 1993, 2). When a class or group studies the work of an author or illustrator, they become experts at recognizing connections between the originator's corpus of works. The students and teacher can work together to decide which author and illustrator to study. Once books, biographical information, articles, and films have been collected, students can begin reading materials. A display about the author might include a photograph and background information of the author or illustrator, critiques or book reviews, and projects that the students are completing during the study. Activities might include reading aloud and silently, comparing the person's work over time, and comparing the work to other authors or illustrators. Students can explore art techniques used by an illustrator, write biographical information or a newsletter about the author or illustrator, and share their work with the author or illustrator. They can also dramatize a story or event or create a culminating activity that summarizes the study. For ready-made author studies, consult Sharron McElmeel's titles in the References.

THEMATIC UNITS

Similar to interdisciplinary units, these units explore a theme that cuts across a variety of books. For example, the survival unit found in Appendix A, organized for independent reading using individual literature contracts, suggests using the survival theme with a variety of reading levels. Middle school students could select books ranging in difficulty from *Trouble River* by Betsy Byars to the more challenging reading and content levels of *After the First Death* by Robert Cormier. Discussion groups can investigate how the theme is explored in different contexts, time periods, genres, and styles. Asking a few pertinent questions will spark comparisons: What is a pivotal point in the plot? What role does the setting play in the advancement of the plot? What is the author's message or motivation? Other questions can be used to explore issues: How would you behave when faced with the same or similar challenges? What defines courage?

Deciding When to Use Units

Using units has distinct advantages for teachers. You gain more flexible time usage, encourage logical connections across subjects, and promote more fluid and continuous learning. This learning is certainly more student-centered, places more emphasis on collaboration, and also more emphasis on multiple possible answers. The learning is holistic and authentic. And there are opportunities—for reading, writing, and use of literature; for critical thinking and problem solving with a topic; and for your individual growth as a teacher.

There are also advantages for students. Students focus on the process rather than on the product of learning. They encounter fewer artificial barriers between disciplines. The curriculum is student-centered. They themselves direct discovery and investigations. Comprehension and appreciation of the topic is enhanced through their development of relationships between ideas and concepts. Students build on existing knowledge, and their individual interests, home experiences, and cultural backgrounds come into play in rewarding ways. Discoveries are first-hand and self-initiated. Risk taking is supported, and independence is encouraged. Students pay attention to the *why* instead of the *what* of learning. The learning is focused on Brian Cambourne's approximation condition, and there is more time to investigate topics thoroughly (Meinbach, Rothlein, and Fredericks 1995, 3–4).

Teachers who have seen educational practices come and go may view thematic units as another passing fad. As mentioned previously, such units can become a scattered collection of activities with little or no cohesion. This is less likely to happen when studying authors, illustrators, or genres; however, when you implement an interdisciplinary unit, consider the following guidelines suggested by David B. Ackerman (1989, 27–30):

1. Base the inclusion of any one subject, such as art or math, on its validity for the project. Do not include topics that are only tangentially related.

2. Consider whether students will truly learn more effectively through the unit or whether a traditional model would be more valid.

3. Consider whether the integrated unit ties the disciplines together, thereby stimulating a deeper understanding of how the subject areas relate.

4. Consider whether the unit improves the learning process by encouraging problem solving and flexible thinking.

In addition to Ackerman's guidelines, consider whether you and potential teammates have the resources and energy to pursue such a unit. Many teachers begin with a self-contained unit, such as a genre or author study, and progress to an interdisciplinary unit. As the enthusiasm spreads, departments or entire schools may decide to implement one interdisciplinary unit during the year, adding a second unit the following year.

Choosing a Unit

When you decide to implement a unit, your first major decision is to determine whether the unit is going to be curriculum-, teacher-, or student-driven. Sometimes a unit grows out of a required topic, such as studying the Revolutionary War or the short story in eighth grade. In other cases, the unit grows out of a teacher's interests, perhaps from a hobby, talent, or favorite country. Finally, the unit may be suggested by the students, perhaps through a special interest, holiday, or special event such as Black History Month.

Elena Castro, a third grade bilingual teacher, asked her students what they wanted to learn during the year. The class brainstormed, Castro interjected some topics she was required to teach, and the class then voted on one topic per month for the entire year: natural disasters, music, the Imperial Valley, cultures, wild animals, insects, inventions, and the human body (1994, 7). Clearly experienced in using thematic units, Ms. Castro also recognized the power of allowing students to follow their interests. However, even when a unit is curriculum- or teacher-driven, instruction should always allow for choices from the students, plus opportunities to explore unplanned topics or activities.

A History Fair, used to culminate a year-long study of U.S. history in the fifth grade, provided one class with an opportunity to integrate their learning through historical fiction, nonfiction, and the textbook. Students then chose the topic they wanted to explore more fully, using a variety of resources while reading and conducting research. Students then completed the process by participating in a fair attended by parents and friends. Information was shared in a variety of displays and presentations. Report reading was banned, so students found other (interesting and surprising) ways to present their topic (Nelson and Nelson 1994).

Deciding to embark on any topical or thematic unit requires dedication to active, involved learning. A project such as a History Fair also requires energy, hard work, and abundant resources. Before finalizing your choices, consult with the librarian to ensure that adequate resources are available and that another teacher won't be competing for materials. In either event, you may need to reorganize your schedule or adapt the unit.

Planning a Unit

Planning a unit can be an exciting task the first time. The following description of the planning process assumes that the unit will involve several disciplines. Keep in mind that a reading and writing unit may be more focused on language arts activities, such as that found in the literature contract example on the theme of survival in Appendix A.

DETERMINING CONCEPTS

Once the topic or theme has been selected, determine the concepts to be learned. Concepts for topics drawn from required curriculum may be designated by the district or state. However, when developing a unit from teacher or student interests, this stage requires more planning. It can be useful to work with another teacher to brainstorm concepts. Most importantly, this is the time to involve the students. Even with a required topic, they will have ideas regarding specific concerns and interest areas. Think about the essential questions you hope the unit will answer and ask other teachers and students to raise other essential questions. Simply allowing students to browse through books on the topic and listening to their conversations will provide you with an abundance of information about their background and previous experiences with the information, plus help them determine the questions that remain.

DETERMINING GOALS

Your unit's goals should relate to the skills developed through the unit. Again, work with the students and other teachers to think about possible outcomes from the unit. A unit on insects requires attention to vocabulary development. A unit on deserts will involve mapping activities. Keep in mind the need to avoid the potpourri problem, limiting subjects to those that logically fit in the unit.

PLANNING FOCUS AND ACTIVITIES

Once you have brainstormed concepts and goals, begin to plan activities that support the unit. You may have some specific ideas or favorite activities

A teacher begins
a unit by sharing
an artifact.

already in mind. Lynn Rhodes of the University of Colorado at Denver suggests four types: group activities and lessons, individual activities and lessons, learning centers, and student-initiated extensions.

GROUP ACTIVITIES

The first lesson in any unit should be a whole-group activity that sets the stage for the weeks of investigation to follow. Possible activities for implementing the unit include the K-W-L or attitude inventories discussed in Chapter 11, a powerful read-aloud book, or a guest speaker. Patricia L. Roberts also suggests using artifacts, audio-visual presentations, computer simulations, themed display table, centers, newspaper articles, paintings, problems, questions, replicas, resource people, role-playing, and social actions such as decision making (1993, 3–13). Ongoing large- and small-group activities could include read-alouds, speakers, discussions, or keeping a log. A culminating activity should draw the unit together, perhaps through student reports, a field trip, or sharing projects with other classes and parents. Sometimes a unit begins without a culminating activity in mind, and ideas emerge throughout the investigation.

INDIVIDUAL ACTIVITIES AND LESSONS

Many independent activities can be drawn from this textbook or the required curriculum: silent reading from a prepared bibliography, related book projects, or vocabulary activities. Writing activities might include reports, stories, poetry, logs, research reports (see Appendix B), or journal entries. Some activities might combine the work of individuals with that of small groups, such as writing individual short reports that become part of a small group's longer report.

LEARNING CENTERS

Organizing centers allows students opportunities for individual or small-group investigations. Some centers, such as one for listening to tapes, may already be in place, with appropriate materials added during the unit. The publishing or writing center can be used for writing reports. A hands-on center might allow students to experiment with materials or construct related projects. Videos, picture files, magazines, and artifacts could be organized into a resource center.

STUDENT-INITIATED EXTENSIONS

Students should have the opportunity to contribute to the unit throughout the planning stage. Students will have many ideas at the beginning of the unit, but will have even more exciting suggestions as the unit unfolds. The unit should be flexible, allowing for new directions and inquiries. Encourage students to raise additional questions and to find new ways to solve problems throughout the unit.

GATHERING RESOURCES

Enlist the aid of your school, professional, and public librarians as you pull the unit together. Consider the following resource categories:

trade books	*textbooks*
films	*filmstrips*
pictures	*videos*
magazines	*students' work*
records, CDs	*manipulatives*
newspaper articles	*parents*
other teachers	*community people and organizations*
field trips	*museums*
businesses	*experts, speakers*

ORGANIZING THE UNIT

At this point, you have a wealth of information about the content and activities you and your students will pursue. You may decide, based on the available resources, that you want to limit, revise, or expand some of the proposed activities. Consider using a theme map to organize the unit. See Figure 14.1 on page 464 for a map developed from the Civil War unit included at the end of this chapter. Once you have created the map, you will begin to see gaps in the unit. Perhaps you will need to work with the class to think of additional writing activities. Finally, you can plan the calendar, specifying the day-to-day group and individual activities. The calendar will give you a general guide to the unit, but you won't know until you implement the unit exactly how long everything will take. Speakers and field trips should be scheduled as soon as possible. Organize volunteers for special activities. Revise expectations as you proceed. The dynamic nature of units almost guarantees that the activities will change; therefore, it is almost more important to record your accomplishments rather than your plans.

ASSESSING STUDENT WORK

At some point, you will need to translate the students' work throughout the unit into report card grades. Grades can be determined by assessing the completion of many of the individual components of the unit and by determining how well the goals were met. Students can also contract to read a certain number of books or complete a number of activities as seen in the literature contract model in Appendix A. Evaluating a research report can involve letter grades for evidence of research; quality of the report; and mechanics (organization, punctuation, spelling, and grammar). Consider other assessment techniques, such as observation, checklists, inventories, and rubrics (see Chapter 12).

EVALUATING THE UNIT

Notes you keep throughout the unit will be invaluable. Students should also be directly involved in evaluating their accomplishments and the overall success of the unit. Students can be asked to evaluate how well they understand the concepts or how much they improved their skills. Ask open-ended questions:

What was the best feature of the unit?

What did you enjoy the most?

What did you enjoy the least?

What helped you learn the most?

What didn't help you learn much?

What was confusing to you?

Which activities were most fun?

Which lessons should be dropped next time?

What should be added for next time?

Using Parents and Volunteers

Teaching through units provides an excellent opportunity to involve adults in the classroom. Consider recruiting volunteers for special activities at Back-to-School night. Supplement this list by sending home a letter about the unit, explaining the focus and soliciting help from experts or for field trips. For lengthy units, provide periodic updates on the progress of the unit, perhaps inviting parents to become involved at home through reading related materials. Some parents may be able to provide artifacts or realia. For more specifics on involving parents, consult *The Complete Guide to Thematic Units: Creating the Integrated Curriculum* by Anita Meyer Meinbach, Liz Rothlein, and Anthony D. Fredericks, pages 85–89.

A Final Note

Teaching through units can be exhilarating and exhausting. Planning the unit requires an investment of time, and many units don't progress as planned. When deciding whether to instigate a unit, consider the flexibility of the school staff, even if you are in a self-contained classroom. You will need moral support at the very least. Depending on the climate of the school, you may want to change gradually. Think about your schedule's flexibility, a feature necessary for increasing student choices. Be sure that you can cover the curriculum as required by the district or state, analyzing how a unit can enliven the required program (Jacobs 1989, 19). Finally, be prepared to learn a lot about your chosen topic!

Summary

Units offer teachers and students an opportunity to explore a variety of topics, issues, or problems through immersion in an investigation. Models of integrated instruction include the parallel discipline design, the complementary discipline unit, interdisciplinary units, integrated-day model, the complete program, and the problem-based thematic unit. Reading and writing units include the genre unit, author and illustrator studies, and thematic units.

Using units has advantages and disadvantages, and teachers should consider the validity, effectiveness, possibilities for extensions, and possible effects on students. Units can be curriculum-, teacher-, or student-driven. Students should be involved in planning the unit. Concepts and goals should be defined. Planning should include group and individual activities, learning centers, resources, the proposed calendar, and evaluation. Parents and volunteers should be used as much as possible.

Upper Intermediate/Middle School Unit on the Civil War

INTRODUCTION

This Civil War unit exemplifies a thematic unit for upper intermediate and middle school learners that integrates language arts and social studies. The unit concentrates on reading and writing in the context of social studies, rather than on a fully interdisciplinary unit. The model is not complete, but demonstrates how one unit might begin. The entire class should collaborate on the major focus and on suggesting additional activities. Activities are organized to allow adaptation to the needs of the class. The social studies textbook can be used where appropriate.

RATIONALE

The Civil War is often studied in the upper intermediate grades or middle school. There is a wealth of excellent information on the subject, including nonfiction and fiction titles that present a range of reading difficulty so that all levels of readers can be successful. Artifacts, such as letters, scrapbooks, and journals, can be found in libraries or through historical societies, providing rich repositories of information that bring the war to life.

FOCUS QUESTIONS

The following questions could be considered when determining the theme of the unit:

- Which side of the war would you join?
- Would you lie about your age to join the military?
- Would you lie about your sex to join the military?
- Would you be willing to risk your life to be a drummer at age 12?

- Is war justified on domestic soil? On foreign soil? On any soil?

- Is war justified to preserve an ideal (preserving the union, abolishing slavery)?

TOPICS

Sample topics include:

- Significant events leading up to the Civil War

- Slavery issues

- Role of Abraham Lincoln and other political leaders

- Significant battles

- Military leaders

- Conditions of war (food, protection, clothing)

- General issue of war

- Role of children in the war

GOALS

- To develop vocabulary

- To participate in cooperative research activities

- To improve research skills

- To develop skill in using strategies to read nonfiction

- To become familiar with reading portions of nonfiction as an aid to research

- To read or listen to historical fiction

- To explore food from the period

THEME MAP

The map in Figure 14.1 provides an overview of the activities that will occur throughout the unit. Creating a map helps teachers and students determine concepts that need further exploration. The map can be expanded as the unit continues, serving as an informal record of accomplishments.

FIGURE 14.1
Civil War
Activities Map

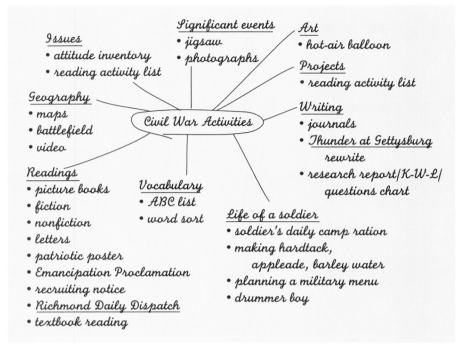

GATHERING RESOURCES

Gather a variety of fiction and nonfiction titles from the list of recommended books that follows and the bibliography at the end of this unit. Use the parent letter (page 480) to find experts and to ask for artifacts, books, or other information about the Civil War. Order Jackdaw F-106, an envelope of primary source materials about the Civil War that contains letters, a recruiting notice, President Lincoln's Emancipation Proclamation, pages from the *Richmond Daily Dispatch*, a patriotic poster, and photographs. (Order from Jackdaw Publications, Division of Golden Owl Publishing, P.O. Box AO3, Amawalk, NY 10501.)

Plan how you will incorporate any required textbook reading into the unit. The text could be used as an overview, as a springboard to the unit, as a research source, or as assigned reading. See Group Lesson 3 for suggestions.

Obtain maps of North America showing the changes before and after the Civil War. Display them in the room.

GROUP AND INDIVIDUAL ACTIVITIES

Review and choose the group and individual lessons you wish to include in the unit. Some activities are introductory, others are appropriate throughout the unit, and some provide closing activities. Though lessons are labeled as

FIGURE 14.2

Organization Chart
for Civil War Unit

	Concepts (list here)										Goals (list here)									
Group Lessons																				
1. ABC																				
2. Reading																				
3. Nonfiction																				
4. Attitude																				
5. Events																				
6. Rations																				
7. Hardtack																				
8. Menu																				
9. Gettysburg																				
10. Video																				
11. Word Sort																				
Individual Lessons																				
1. Journal																				
2. Research																				
3. Activities																				
4. Drummer Boy																				
5. Hot-Air Balloon																				
Culminating																				

group or individual, some will involve both individual work and group activities, such as the sharing of research. Many of the individual lessons will require group instruction or introduction before individual work can begin. Plan a schedule, but allow flexibility, as some lessons may take more or less time than allowed in the sample calendar that follows the unit. A chart such as Figure 14.2 organizes the activities, demonstrating which concepts and goals they address.

GROUP LESSONS

GROUP LESSON 1: ABC LIST

Introduce the topic by passing out a copy of the ABC list on the Civil War in Figure 14.3. Tell the students that the list includes words they may or may not

How do these words relate to the Civil War?

Appomattox _____

Blockade runners _____

Confederates, carpetbaggers _____

Dred Scott Decision _____

Exposure _____

Food processing _____

Grant _____

Gettysburg _____

Homestead Act _____

Icehouse _____

Juice _____

Kearney, General Phil _____

Little Round Top _____

Mules _____

Naval warfare _____

Oil _____

Profiteers _____

Quantrill, William C. _____

Railroads _____

Sherman _____

Transportation _____

Underground Railroad _____

Vegetable preservation _____

Wagons _____

Yankees _____

Zoaves _____

Excerpted from *Cooking Up U.S. History: Recipes and Research to Share with Children* by Suzanne I. Barchers and Patricia C. Marden, illustrated by Leann Mullineaux (Englewood, CO: Teacher Ideas Press, 1991), 70.

know. Tell them to decide how the words relate to the Civil War based on what they know about the war. Since many students will have had limited exposure to the topic, encourage them to make educated guesses. Share and discuss their responses.

This is a good activity for cooperative groups. It is a preresearch activity and should not be graded. It can be kept in the students' notebooks and added to

A student shares her project.

throughout the thematic unit, or it can be reproduced again at the end of the unit and used as a follow-up activity instead of the suggested word sort activity. Students could also use the list and alternative words to create an alphabet book of the Civil War.

GROUP LESSON 2: READING ALOUD

Begin reading aloud a fiction book drawn from the following book list. Irene Hunt's *Across Five Aprils*, Patricia Beatty's *Charley Skedaddle*, and Scott O'Dell's *The 290* are all recommended. Each book gives a different perspective on the war. Some of the titles on the book list are simple books, such as Patricia Lee Gauch's *Thunder at Gettysburg*, and can be read during one short period.

Alternatively, the students can be given the nonfiction and fiction booklist with an assignment to complete the book and a project from the activity list on pages 478–479. This project would then be shared with the class toward the end of the unit.

RECOMMENDED BOOKS (See Bibliography on page 484 for annotations.)

Across Five Aprils by Irene Hunt.

The Boys' War: Confederate and Union Soldiers Talk about the Civil War by Jim Murphy.

Charley Skedaddle by Patricia Beatty.

The First Book of the Civil War by Dorothy Levenson.

Runaway Balloon: The Last Flight of Confederate Air Force One by Burke Davis.

Thunder at Gettysburg by Patricia Gauch.

The 290 by Scott O'Dell.

Vicksburg Veteran by F. N. Monjo.

GROUP LESSON 3: READING NONFICTION OR THE TEXTBOOK

Choose a nonfiction book about the Civil War to read aloud in preparation for the individual research reports. Dorothy Levenson's *The First Book of the Civil War* (see Bibliography) is a good choice. If the social studies textbook has a comprehensive discussion of the Civil War, consider using the textbook. Read the materials aloud to give students an overview of the major events leading up to and during the war. This will take several days to complete and should be paced according to the needs of the class.

GROUP LESSON 4: ATTITUDE INVENTORY

Students in the middle school may have little knowledge of, or numerous misconceptions about, the Civil War. Use the attitude inventory in Figure 14.4 to determine their prior knowledge and to initiate discussion about the Civil War or war in general. Provide concrete examples for the students so that they understand the statements. For example, for statement 2, raise the issue of slavery, but also bring out the more current issues facing people today such as driving laws. Discuss the responses.

The statements can be duplicated or prepared on an overhead transparency. The same statements should be presented at the end of the unit with a discussion regarding any changes in attitude that have resulted from knowing more about the Civil War.

GROUP LESSON 5: EVENTS LEADING UP TO THE CIVIL WAR

The following questions can be used with the students in a "jigsaw" activity. It is an excellent way to develop group cooperation and responsibility. To use this process, divide the students into equal groups—for example, five groups of five students. Give each group one question to research. Students will need to use the library to find the answers. After the groups have found the answers, label the groups as group 1, group 2, and so forth. Then regroup the students so that each group contains a 1, 2, 3, 4, and 5. Each of the students then shares the answer with the rest of the group. This process can be used with four groups of four, six groups of six, and so on. Two questions can be given to each group to accomplish more research. If the class is an odd number, keep the

FIGURE 14.4

Attitude Inventory

Civil War

Directions: During the next few weeks, you will be studying the Civil War. Read the following statements and examine your beliefs about war. For each statement, put a check mark along the continuum to indicate the extent to which you agree or disagree.

Agree   Disagree

1. A state has the right to place its needs ahead of the greater needs of the entire country.   _____

2. A state has the right to control the lives of people living within that state.   _____

3. Even though a person might not believe in the position taken by the state, each person must fully support the state once war is declared.   _____

4. Individuals should be prepared to sacrifice for war. Sacrifices may include giving up one's life.   _____

5. Sometimes war is the only solution.   _____

6. When war is declared, there should be no distinction between civilian and military populations.   _____

7. It is acceptable to break the law during war.   _____

8. The government has the right to force people to fight in times of war.   _____

9. Governmental leaders have a responsibility to the country as a whole rather than to their individual state.   _____

10. It is acceptable for individuals or governments to profit from war.   _____

Adapted from *Content Area Reading* by Richard T. Vacca (Boston: Little, Brown, 1981), 101.

groups larger rather than smaller so that everyone receives the information. For example, divide a class of 28 in groups of five, five, six, six, and six. Have 5 or 10 different questions, giving each group 1 or 2 questions to research. When you regroup the students to share their answers, three groups will have extra members who will share the responsibility.

The questions in Figure 14.5 should be shared in the chronological order of the list as it approximates the timeline of the years preceding the Civil War.

GROUP LESSON 6: A SOLDIER'S DAILY CAMP RATION

Prepare the information in Figure 14.6 on an overhead transparency, or duplicate it for the students. Before giving them the information, have them list all

FIGURE 14.5

Jigsaw Questions

Events Leading Up to the Civil War

1. What was the Compromise of 1850? Why was it significant prior to the war?
2. What was the abolitionist movement and who were the leaders?
3. What was the significance of the book *Uncle Tom's Cabin* by Harriet Beecher Stowe? Include information about the number of books sold, the impact of the play, and other important details.
4. Find out about the Kansas-Nebraska Bill and the impact it had on the Missouri Compromise of 1820. Be sure to include information about the role geography played.
5. What was the Emigrant Aid Society? Why was it important to America? Include information about Congressman Preston Brooks's attack on Senator Charles Sumner.
6. Who was John Brown? What effect did his actions have on the country?
7. Who was Dred Scott? Describe the importance of his court case.
8. Research the Lincoln-Douglas debates and the subsequent election. How did the results affect the movement toward war?
9. The South relied on agriculture and the North relied on an industrial society. Discuss the conflict this caused.
10. Find out what happened at Fort Sumter on April 12, 1861.

the food they eat on a normal day. Then have them list all the food they eat when they are especially active, such as during field day or when they are camping.

Have the students list what they think would be an appropriate day's ration for a soldier. Have them consider the more rigorous environment, similar to rugged camping, and the periods of strenuous fighting contrasted with imposed periods of inactivity.

Share the prepared ration list with the students. Divide the responsibility for bringing in as many items on the list as possible. Bring in 1 pound of rice or coffee rather than 10 pounds. Measure out the daily camp ration of the meat and bread. Then divide 1 pound of rice or coffee into 10 portions. Work with the ration until the students have a good idea of what a soldier would receive in a day.

During the study of the Civil War, have students keep in mind the challenge of having adequate food. Read aloud Chapter 5, "A Long and Hungry War" from *The Boys' War* by Jim Murphy. Then have the students consider some of the complications of the war:

FIGURE 14.6

Civil War
Camp Rations

A Soldier's Daily Camp Ration

12 ounces of pork or bacon or 20 ounces salt or fresh beef
22 ounces soft bread or flour or 16 ounces hard bread or 20 ounces corn meal

With every 100 such rations, there should be:

1 peck of beans or peas
10 pounds of rice or hominy
10 pounds of green coffee or 8 pounds of roasted and ground coffee or
1½ pounds of tea
15 pounds of sugar
20 ounces of candles
4 pounds of soap
2 quarts of salt
4 quarts of vinegar
4 ounces pepper
½ bushel potatoes
1 quart molasses

Marching Ration:

1 pound hard bread
¾ pound salt pork or 1¼ pound fresh meat
Sugar
Coffee
Salt

Excerpted from *Hardtack and Coffee: The Unwritten Story of Army Life* by John D. Billings, illustrated by Charles W. Reed (Boston: George M. Smith, 1887), 111–112.

- Supplies had to be brought by wagons that were often delayed during inclement weather.

- Often, meat was not available; General Robert E. Lee ate meat on the average of only twice a week.

- The fields of the South were exhausted from cotton production and were not adequate for the increased agricultural demands of the war.

- The North was more industrialized and thus better prepared to handle the increased demands for production.

- Preservatives were not available.

GROUP LESSON 7: PREPARING HARDTACK AND APPLEADE OR BARLEY WATER

Soldiers relied on hardtack as a staple. It is an easy recipe to make. If you don't have access to an oven, bring the ingredients to class and divide the recipe into thirds and place the flour and salt into bags that seal. Give each student a bag, a nail that has been boiled, and a copy of the second set of directions. Have the students bake the hardtack at home, bringing in the results on the following day for sharing.

Barley water or appleade can be prepared in the classroom using a hot plate. Prepare one of the beverages to serve with the hardtack. See Figures 14.7, 14.8., 14.9, and 14.10 for recipes.

GROUP LESSON 8: PLANNING A MILITARY MENU

Food was a critical issue during the Civil War. The lack of crops in the South was problematic from the beginning of the war, and the destruction wrought by William Tecumseh Sherman's march to the sea hastened the end of the war. One of the first efforts by the North at the close of the war was to bring food and supplies to the south.

Duplicate the information about food during the Civil War in Figure 14.11 on page 474 and distribute to the students. Their assignment is to plan meals that would be appropriate for military use today.

Hardtack: Full Recipe

FIGURE 14.7
Recipe for
Civil War Soldiers

Ingredients	Steps
3 cups flour	1. In a large bowl, mix flour and salt.
2 teaspoons salt	2. Add water and stir or work with hands to blend.
1 cup water	3. Knead dough, adding more flour if mixture becomes
boiled nail	sticky.
	4. Roll the dough into a rectangle ½ inch thick.
Makes 12.	5. Using a sharp knife, cut the dough into 3-inch squares.
	6. Using a large nail, poke 16 holes through each square.
	7. Bake in a 375° oven for 25 minutes or until brown.
	8. Store in an airtight container.

Adapted from *Cooking Up U.S. History: Recipes and Research to Share with Children* by Suzanne I. Barchers and Patricia C. Marden, illustrated by Leann Mullineaux (Englewood, Colo.: Teacher Ideas Press, 1991), 73.

Hardtack: Individual Recipe

FIGURE 14.8

Recipe for
Civil War Soldiers

Ingredients

1 cup flour
$\frac{2}{3}$ teaspoons salt
$\frac{1}{3}$ cup water
boiled nail

Makes 4.

Steps

1. Empty bag of flour and salt into a large bowl.
2. Add water and stir or work with hands to blend.
3. Knead dough, adding more flour if mixture becomes sticky.
4. Roll the dough into a rectangle $\frac{1}{2}$ inch thick.
5. Using a sharp knife, cut the dough into 3-inch squares.
6. Using a large nail, poke 16 holes through each square.
7. Bake in a 375° oven for 20 minutes or until brown.
8. Store in an airtight container.

Appleade

FIGURE 14.9

Recipe for
Civil War Soldiers

Ingredients

2 large apples
1 quart water
sugar to taste

Serves 6.

Steps

1. Cut apples into slices. Do not peel. Place in a pan.
2. Boil the water.
3. Pour boiling water over apple slices.
4. Let mixture sit for 30 minutes.
5. Strain mixture well.
6. Sweeten to taste.
7. Chill and then drink.

Barley Water

FIGURE 14.10

Recipe for
Civil War Soldiers

Ingredients

$\frac{1}{2}$ cup barley
3 pints water
peel of 1 lemon
sugar to taste

Serves 6.

Steps

1. Put barley, water, and lemon peel in a saucepan.
2. Simmer for 30–45 minutes.
3. Add sugar to taste.
4. Strain and drink while hot.

Figures 14.8–14.10 adapted from *Cooking Up U.S. History: Recipes and Research to Share with Children* by Suzanne I. Barchers and Patricia C. Marden, illustrated by Leann Mullineaux (Englewood, Colo.: Teacher Ideas Press, 1991), 73, 77, and 78.

FIGURE 14.11
Planning a
Military Menu

Planning a Military Menu

The canning industry was just developing when the Civil War began. Gail Borden was dedicated to providing food that would travel. He developed condensed milk, and his factory was commandeered by the government to produce condensed milk for the soldiers. Soldiers became very fond of condensed milk, ensuring its continued use after the war. Borden also produced canned blackberry juice, which was a favorite with convalescing soldiers in hospitals.

Keeping baked goods fresh was difficult. Weevils, a slim brown bug ⅛ inch in length, infested hardtack, boring through it. Soldiers would dip the hardtack in coffee to drown the weevils and skim them off the top of their coffee, or they would simply eat the hardtack at night when they couldn't see the weevils.

Spices such as ginger were often added to meat (when it was available) to disguise the taste. Ginger was imported from Jamaica, India, and the African countries of Sierra Leone and Nigeria.

Soldiers loved coffee, but it was often unavailable, and substitutes, including barley, parched corn, peanuts, chicory, sweet potatoes, and rye, were used instead.

Plan a military menu, keeping in mind the need to provide food that will travel, remain unspoiled, and provide nutrition. Research could include your local grocery store, a nearby military base, or the library.

GROUP LESSON 9: RESPONDING TO GETTYSBURG

Read aloud *Thunder at Gettysburg* by Patricia Lee Gauch. After the first reading, point out how the book is written in the third person. Tell the students you are going to read each section again and then together the class will rewrite the book as if Tillie were keeping a diary. Use chart paper to record the class's thoughts. The book's five sections accommodate completing this activity over two days.

GROUP LESSON 10: BATTLEFIELDS VIDEO

Obtain from your librarian or SVE (a video source) a copy of the 1-hour video *Touring Civil War Battlefields*, which shows modern-day reenactments of the battles, plus memorials. Discuss the video and the differences between reading about battlefields and seeing them on film. Obtain a catalog from SVE (1345 Diversey Parkway, Chicago, IL 60614-1299, 1-800-829-1900).

Word Sort List

Ulysses S. Grant	Robert E. Lee	Henry Clay
Compromise of 1850	Charles Sumner	John Brown
Fugitive Slave Law	Preston Brooks	Dred Scott
Harriet Beecher Stowe	Abraham Lincoln	Slavery
Kansas–Nebraska Act	Harpers Ferry	Secession
Missouri Compromise	Reconstruction	Fort Sumter
Emigrant Aid Society	Jefferson Davis	Charleston
Stephen A. Douglas	Confederate	Fort Henry
William Tecumseh Sherman	Merrimack	Shiloh
Emancipation Proclamation	Sherman's march	Monitor
Ambrose E. Burnside	Missionary Ridge	Navy
Observation balloons	Richmond	Union
George B. McClellan	Big Round Top	Animals
Underground Railroad	Little Round Top	Weather
Treatment of wounded	Chattanooga	Telegraph
Shenandoah Valley	Jeb Stuart	Weather
Battle of First Manassas	Appomattox	Food
Stonewall Jackson	Industry	Bayonets
Thirteenth Amendment	Cannons	Rifles
Gettysburg Address	Blockades	Budgets
Ford's Theater	Atlanta	Uniforms

GROUP LESSON 11: WORD SORT

Use this activity to close the unit. Prepare three or four sets of cards with one each of the words in Figure 14.12 on a card. Omit any words that were not covered during the course of the unit. Divide the class into three or four groups. Give each group a set of cards and have them sort the words in any way they feel is logical. Have the groups share their decisions and their reasons.

INDIVIDUAL LESSONS

INDIVIDUAL LESSON 1: JOURNAL WRITING

Read aloud *The Vicksburg Veteran* by F. N. Monjo, a fictionalized journal of the 13-year-old son of Ulysses S. Grant. Share the journal form with the students and letters ordered from the Jackdaw set.

Have the students reflect on the text that is being read aloud each day through writing in a journal or log, expressing their reactions to the book.

INDIVIDUAL LESSON 2: RESEARCH REPORTS

A major portion of this unit is an individual research report (see Appendix B). After reading *The Vicksburg Veteran* or the textbook, have the students brainstorm topics on the board. Discuss the possible topics with them, allowing students to choose their own topics. Plan deadlines, library time, and sharing time with the students.

Evaluation of the research unit should be planned in the early stages. If your school requires grading, three grades can be assigned: the first for the quality of the report; the second for evidence of research; the third for punctuation and mechanics. The research process outlined in Chapter 9 can be used for the students' independent work. Additional strategies for beginning the research follow.

Looping　To help students focus on a topic, follow this process:

1. Have the students write for two minutes on a topic that is of interest.

2. Have them circle something that looks promising.

3. Have the students put the phrase or word on another piece of paper.

4. Have the students write for another three minutes.

5. Have them circle something that looks promising.

6. Repeat until three rounds are completed. Students should have narrowed their topic to a manageable area for research.

Modified K-W-L Chart　The chart in Figure 14.13 is an adaptation of the "What I know. What I want to know. What I learned." investigation process. The change is the inclusion of the sentence "How I find out." This additional step allows students to plan their research process.

Questions Chart　An alternative strategy for the beginning researcher is to use the questions chart in Figure 14.14. Have the students put the topic in the upper-left-hand box and their questions in the top boxes. Next have the students go to the library and find three appropriate sources, listing them in the source boxes. Information from each source should be entered in the appropriate intersecting boxes. Some boxes may remain empty. The bottom row of boxes should be used to summarize the information. See Figure 14.15 for research suggestions.

INDIVIDUAL LESSON 3: READING ACTIVITIES

The projects or activities listed on pages 478–479 can be completed by individual students or in small groups. A fiction or nonfiction book can be read in conjunction with an activity instead of completing the preceding research report.

FIGURE 14.13
Modified
K-W-L Chart

What I Know	What I Want to Know	How I Find Out	What I Learned

FIGURE 14.14
Questions Chart

Topic	Question	Question	Question
Source			
Source			
Source			

FIGURE 14.15
Research
Suggestions

Decisions, acts, laws
Ground battles
Naval battles
Role of foreign
   countries
Role of animals
Naval ships
Underground Railroad
Role of weather
Role of food
Role of industry
Slavery issues

Transportation
Division of states
Political leaders
Communication
Division of territories
Military leaders
Elections
Newspaper accounts
Important women
Weapons
Role of children in
   armies

Sherman's march
Blockades
Slavery opponents
Hot-air balloons
Budgets
Slavery proponents
Speeches
Forts
Treatment of wounded
Cities
Uniforms

1. Research foods enjoyed by civilians during the Civil War. Prepare a sample day's meals (breakfast, lunch, and dinner) and have a tasting party at school. This works better with a small class.

2. Prepare a chart of the major land battles fought during the Civil War. Include the date of the battle, location, leaders, number of soldiers lost, and other pertinent information.

3. Prepare a map that illustrates the major land battles. If you are using a commercial U.S. map, use sticky notes to list the information given in item 2 and place the notes on each battle site. If you are drawing the map, the information can be included on the map.

4. Prepare a timeline of the major events of the war. A role of white shelf paper is convenient to use.

5. Prepare a chart of important governmental decisions that occurred before, during, and after the Civil War, such as the Compromise of 1850.

6. Find important fiction or essays from the period and share excerpts with the class.

7. Prepare a map that illustrates the role of rivers in the establishment of states and territories.

8. Find important speeches and share them with the class.

9. Find information about famous slaves. Share biographical information with the class.

10. Find poetry written during the Civil War (Ralph Waldo Emerson, Henry David Thoreau, and William Cullen Bryant) and share it with the class.

11. Prepare a map that illustrates the division between the North and the South as well as the uncommitted territories.

12. Find newspaper accounts of the war and share them with the class.

13. Choose a battle and write an account as if you were a news reporter.

14. Find music from the war period and share it with the class.

15. Replicate the flags used in the war.

16. The telegraph was used as communication during the war. Find the Morse code and prepare a message about a conflict.

17. Prepare a replica of a hot-air balloon used for observation during the war.

18. Choose a battleground such as Big Round Top and Little Round Top and prepare a topographical map.

19. Prepare a map showing William Tecumseh Sherman's march through the South.

20. Reenact a water battle with model ships.

21. Prepare a display of products that affected the outcome of the war. (Cotton and condensed milk are two examples.)

22. Prepare drawings of the uniforms worn by the soldiers.

23. Construct a replica of Ford's Theater, where Abraham Lincoln was assassinated.

24. Construct a replica of one of the forts.

25. Prepare a map that highlights the important cities during the war.

26. Write an editorial supporting or opposing any single issue.

27. Research the trial of John Brown. Assume the role of the defending or prosecuting attorney and prepare your case.

28. Prepare a survey that includes questions about Civil War issues. Ask teachers, students, parents, and neighbors the questions. Compile the results.

29. Create a journal that a drummer boy might have kept. Refer to *The Boys' War* by Jim Murphy for information.

30. Create replicas of money used by the North and South during the Civil War.

INDIVIDUAL LESSON 4: DRUMMER BOY

Read aloud Chapter 4, "Drumbeats and Bullets," from *The Boys' War* by Jim Murphy. One of the boys is only 11 years old. Have the students respond to this chapter in any form: written, artistic, or poetic. Encourage students to put themselves in the role of the young boys who found themselves in the middle of fighting.

INDIVIDUAL LESSON 5: HOT-AIR BALLOONS

Read aloud *Runaway Balloon: The Last Flight of Confederate Air Force One* by Burke Davis. According to the author's note, the balloon was constructed of the southern women's dresses. Have the students draw their own balloon designs. Patterns from favorite shirts, sweaters, or dresses could be used for inspiration.

CULMINATING ACTIVITY

Arrange for parents or other classes to participate in sampling hardtack, coffee, or other foods of the period. Students could also share their research reports or reading activities at this time. An alternative activity detailed in a *Teaching*

PreK–8 article, "Putting the Civil War on Trial" by Joyce Charleston (April 1995, 46–48), suggests putting John Wilkes Booth on trial. Students prepare by reading background information to choose their part in the drama. After competing for parts through a written and oral presentation, class members are chosen for the roles of attorneys, jurors, Booth, and other appropriate historical figures. The students plan the trial, rehearse the trial several times, and proceed with a presentation for parents followed by a question-and-answer period. Charleston suggests that this process could be used for any key event in history. Also consider using Paul Fleischman's *Bull Run*, a powerful novel that can be performed as readers theatre.

EVALUATION OF UNIT

It is important to evaluate the success of the unit on an ongoing basis. Keep notes regarding problems or future changes weekly. Refer to Chapter 12 for a variety of assessment tools, or use the forms in Figures 14.16 and 14.17 on pages 483 and 484.

PARENT LETTER

ABC School
Date

Dear Parents,
    Next month we will begin a thematic unit on the Civil War. During this unit, we will study the following:

The events leading up to the Civil War

Slavery issues

Role of Abraham Lincoln and other political leaders

Significant battles

Military leaders

Conditions of war (food, protection, clothing)

Role of children in the war

    We will be using books and materials from our curriculum. However, we want to use a variety of other resources. We need your help as we plan the various components. Please let us know if you can suggest or provide any of the following resources about the Civil War:

books

newspaper or magazine articles

tapes

slides

speakers

models

videos

help with making food from the period

field trip help or suggestions

anything else that would be useful

If you send any items that you wish to have returned, please be sure that they are clearly marked.

Your child will be reading both nonfiction and fiction books and will be required to complete a research report. More information on these projects will be sent later.

Thanks for your help, and please call if you have any questions or suggestions.

Yours truly,

CIVIL WAR UNIT CALENDAR

The following schedule should be adapted to the needs of your class. Although the activities and readings are presented sequentially, certain readings may need to be timed differently depending on the amount of time devoted to reading nonfiction information on the war.

Day 1   Group Lesson 1: Do activity using "ABC List."

Group Lesson 2: Begin reading fiction aloud.

Day 2   Group Lesson 3: Begin reading nonfiction aloud.

Continue reading fiction.

Group Lesson 4: Complete "Attitude Inventory."

Day 3   Group Lesson 5: Begin jigsaw on "Events Leading Up to the Civil War."

Continue reading fiction and nonfiction.

Day 4   Group Lesson 5: Continue with jigsaw research and sharing.

Continue reading fiction and nonfiction.

Individual Lesson 1: Read aloud *The Vicksburg Veteran* by F. N. Monjo and introduce journal or log responses.

Day 5   Group Lesson 6: Complete activity, "A Soldier's Daily Camp Ration."

Continue reading fiction and nonfiction.

Continue journal or log responses.

Day 6   Individual Lesson 2: Research Reports, Looping, Modified K-W-L Chart or Questions Chart. Or assign Lesson 3.

Individual Lesson 3 (optional): Selected reading and choice of activity.

Group Lesson 7: "Preparing Hardtack, Appleade, or Barley Water."

Continue reading fiction and nonfiction.

Continue journal or log responses.

Days 7–11   Schedule the following as appropriate:

Assist with research in the library or classroom.

Group Lesson 8: Do "Planning a Military Menu."

Individual Lesson 4: Do "Drummer Boy" activity.

Individual Lesson 5: Do "Hot-Air Balloon" activity.

Group Lesson 9: Responding to Gettysburg.

Group Lesson 10: Video on Gettysburg.

Continue reading fiction and nonfiction as appropriate.

Continue journal or log responses.

Days 12–15   Share research reports or activity projects.

Continue reading fiction and nonfiction as appropriate.

Continue journal or log responses.

Group Lesson 11: Conclude unit with Word Sort.

Culminating Activity   Sharing food, research reports, readers theatre as appropriate.

FIGURE 14.16

Civil War Evaluation

Rubric for Student Evaluation

Exceeds Standards

I increased my vocabulary beyond the words presented in the activities.

I have a strong understanding of the issues.

I can explain several significant events that led up to the Civil War.

I read a variety of artifacts and documents.

I read several fiction and nonfiction books.

I completed several projects related to the reading.

I completed all the writing activities.

I prepared a thorough research report.

I participated fully in all other activities.

Standard

The activities increased my vocabulary.

I understand the issues better than before.

I can explain two significant events that led up to the Civil War.

I read a few artifacts and documents.

I read one fiction and one nonfiction book.

I completed two projects related to the reading.

I completed two writing activities.

I prepared an acceptable research report.

I participated fully in some other activities.

Emerging

I know a few more new words.

I understand some issues.

I can explain one significant event that led up to the Civil War.

I read one artifact and one document.

I read one book.

I completed one project related to the reading.

I completed one writing activity.

I did some research.

I participated in a few other activities.

Novice

I don't know any more new words.

I really don't understand many of the issues.

I'm not sure what events led up to the war.

I didn't read any artifacts or documents.

I didn't read any books.

I didn't complete any reading projects.

I didn't complete any writing activities.

I didn't do any research.

I didn't participate in many other activities.

FIGURE 14.17

Teacher Evaluation

Civil War Unit Teacher Evaluation

Were the concepts appropriate for the unit? _____

Did students increase their conceptual knowledge? _____

Were the goals appropriate for the unit? _____

Did students meet the goals of the unit? _____

Did the vocabulary activities increase vocabulary? _____

Did students understand the issues better after the unit? _____

Did the students read a variety of materials? _____

Were the book lists appropriate and useful? _____

Did the students complete a variety of reading projects? _____

Did the students fully participate in the writing activities? _____

Did the students enjoy the art and food activities? _____

Did the students fully immerse themselves in the research? _____

Did the students enjoy the unit? _____

Was the length of time appropriate for the unit? _____

Was the culminating activity enjoyable and useful? _____

What activities should be eliminated or added? _____

_____

_____

Additional comments: _____

_____

_____

BIBLIOGRAPHY

BIOGRAPHY AND NONFICTION BOOKS

Barchers, Suzanne I., and Patricia C. Marden. *Cooking Up U.S. History: Recipes and Research to Share with Children.* Illustrated by Leann Mullineaux. Englewood, Colo.: Teacher Ideas Press, 1991. Grades 3 and up.
    Recipes drawn from U.S. history and regional America combine with research questions for children and teachers.

Chang, Ina. *A Separate Battle: Women and the Civil War.* New York: Dutton, 1991. Grades 4 and up.
    Teachers, nurses, spies, couriers, and disguised soldiers made up the ranks of the women waging their own battles during the Civil War.

Photographs enhance this important account of the contributions of women.

Coffey, Vincent J. *The Battle of Gettysburg.* Morristown, N.J.: Silver Burdett, 1985. Grades 4 and up.

Photographs and maps illustrate the text that describes the events leading up to, during, and following the battle at Gettysburg.

D'Aulaire, Ingri, and Edgar D'Aulaire. *Abraham Lincoln.* Garden City, N.Y.: Doubleday, 1957. Grades 2 and up.

Lincoln's youth is emphasized in this colorful, oversize biography.

Davis, Burke. *The Civil War: Strange and Fascinating Facts.* New York: Crown, 1982. Grades 4 and up.

Contains trivia from the whimsical to the tragic.

_____. *Runaway Balloon: The Last Flight of Confederate Air Force One.* Illustrated by Salvatore Murdocca. New York: Coward, McCann & Geoghegan, 1976. Grades 3 and up.

The Yankees were spying on the Confederates from a hot-air balloon, motivating the Confederates to create their own balloon. Reluctantly, Lieutenant Bryan flew in the balloon, only to be shot at. His second voyage ended in his losing his clothing and returning to earth naked. The line drawings add interest to this amusing war story.

Freedman, Russell. *Lincoln: A Photobiography.* New York: Scholastic, 1987. Grades 4 and up.

Photographs, posters, portraits, and text provide an enlightening biography of Lincoln. This is a Newbery Medal book.

Freeman, Fred. *Duel of the Ironclads.* New York: Time-Life Books, 1969. Grades 3 and up.

Freeman's maps, charts, and illustrations tell the story of the battle between the Merrimack and the Monitor. Though the confrontation was considered a standoff, it affected the future of naval warfare.

Fritz, Jean. *Harriet Beecher Stowe and the Beecher Preachers.* New York: G. P. Putnam's, 1994. Grades 5 and up.

Lyman Beecher, a famous preacher, raised seven preachers. The most famous, to his surprise, was his daughter Harriet, author of *Uncle Tom's Cabin.* Fritz's biography brings Harriet Beecher Stowe alive.

Glass, Paul. *Singing Soldiers: A History of the Civil War in Song.* New York: Grosset & Dunlap, 1964. Grades 4 and up.

A collection of songs representing both sides, plus appropriate notes.

Horgan, Paul. *Citizen of New Salem.* Illustrated by Douglas Gorsline. New York: Farrar, Straus & Cudahy, 1961. Grades 5 and up.

Lincoln's years in New Salem, Illinois, from age 21 to 28, are described in this acclaimed biography. The story and line drawings provide the reader with intriguing insights into frontier times.

Jordan, Robert Paul. *The Civil War.* Washington, D.C.: National Geographic Society, 1969. Grades 4 and up.

An abundance of colorful photographs, maps, charts, and illustrations give the reader a broad understanding of the agonies of the Civil War. The text provides the research student with a wealth of material.

Katz, William Loren. *An Album of the Civil War.* New York: Franklin Watts, 1974. Grades 3 and up.

The liberal use of original prints and photographs makes this album an intriguing resource. Text is provided primarily to explain the photographs, yet it provides a wealth of background information about the war.

Kent, Zachary. *John Brown's Raid on Harpers Ferry.* Chicago: Childrens Press, 1988. Grades 3 and up.

John Brown intended to provide slaves with weapons, and he led a raid on the arsenal at Harpers Ferry. The 36-hour raid resulted in the loss of 17 lives. Photographs illustrate his raid, capture, and execution.

_____. *The Story of the Battle of Bull Run.* Illustrated by David J. Catrow III. Chicago: Childrens Press, 1986. Grades 3 and up.

Black-and-white and brown-line drawings illustrate the story of this famous battle. The contrast between the sightseeing crowds and the reality of 900 dead and thousands injured is clearly described.

_____. *The Story of Ford's Theater and the Death of Lincoln.* Chicago: Childrens Press, 1987. Grades 3 and up.

Photographs of the theatre, historical paintings, and the room where Lincoln died enhance this recounting of the events surrounding Lincoln's assassination.

_____. *The Story of Sherman's March to the Sea.* Illustrated by Ralph Canaday. Chicago: Childrens Press, 1987. Grades 3 and up.

General William Tecumseh Sherman led his soldiers on a 300-mile march of destruction, demonstrating the strength of the Union army.

_____. *The Story of the Surrender at Appomattox Court House.* Chicago: Childrens Press, 1987. Grades 3 and up.

The surrender of General Lee at Appomattox is described through text and reproductions of a variety of prints. The humane treatment of the Confederates and the dignity and courage of all the soldiers is described with compassion.

Latham, Frank B. *Lincoln and the Emancipation Proclamation, January 1, 1863: The Document That Turned the Civil War into a Fight for Freedom.* New York: Franklin Watts, 1969. Grades 4 and up.

    The Emancipation Proclamation, the Lincoln-Douglas Debates, and the events leading up to the beginning of the Civil War are illustrated through the use of prints, posters, and text.

Levenson, Dorothy. *The First Book of the Civil War.* New York: Franklin Watts, 1968. Grades 4 and up.

    Original Civil War drawings and photographs provide the reader with an intimate look at the horrors of the Civil War. The text provides a good overview of the war, and the index assists the beginning research student.

Marrin, Albert. *Virginia's General: Robert E. Lee and the Civil War.* New York: Atheneum, 1994. Grades 5 and up.

    Details the life of Robert E. Lee and his military skills, still admired today. Photographs and maps add interest.

Mettger, Zak. *Till Victory Is Won: Black Soldiers in the Civil War.* New York: Dutton, 1994. Grades 5 and up.

    Artifacts, line drawings, and photographs tell the story of the little-known efforts made by Black Americans determined to contribute to the Civil War.

Monjo, F. N. *The Drinking Gourd.* Illustrated by Fred Brenner. New York: HarperCollins, 1969. Grades 2 and up.

    A young white boy helps a family escape to freedom. The words to the song are included.

_____. *Gettysburg: Tad Lincoln's Story.* Illustrated by Douglas Gorsline. New York: E. P. Dutton, 1976. Grades 3 and up.

    This is the fictionalized account of the three-day battle of Gettysburg as Tad Lincoln might have told it.

_____. *Me and Willie and Pa: The Story of Abraham Lincoln and His Son Tad.* Illustrated by Douglas Gorsline. New York: Simon & Schuster, 1973. Grades 4 and up.

    Tad Lincoln tells the story of his life with his brother Willie and his father, Abraham Lincoln. Tad's perspective and the numerous portraits bring this era alive.

Murphy, Jim. *The Boys' War: Confederate and Union Soldiers Talk about the Civil War.* New York: Clarion, 1990. Grades 4 and up.

    Using graphic photographs and firsthand accounts from the war's youngest soldiers, Murphy provides a startling perspective on the Civil War.

Richards, Kenneth. *The Story of the Gettysburg Address.* Illustrated by Tom
    Dunnington. Chicago: Childrens Press, 1969. Grades 3 and up.
        The devastation at the Battle of Gettysburg was extensive. Lincoln
    prepared only 268 words for his memorable speech at the Soldier's
    National Cemetery. Black, white, and tan drawings blend beautifully
    with the text to tell this famous story.

Root, Waverly, and Richard de Rochemont. *Eating in America: A History.* New
    York: The Ecco Press, 1976. Resource book.
        Chapter Twenty-two, "War and Food," deals with the Civil War.
    Other chapters are of general interest.

Sandler, Martin W. *Civil War.* New York: HarperCollins, 1996. Grades 3 and up.
        Featuring an abundance of color photographs, artifacts, and simple
    text, this provides readers with a rich background on the Civil War.

FICTION BOOKS

Ackerman, Karen. *The Tin Heart.* Illustrated by Michael Hays. New York:
    Atheneum, 1990. Grades 1 and up.
        People who live near the Ohio River face the start of the Civil War in
    this illustrated book.

Archer, Myrth. *The Young Boys Gone.* New York: Walker, 1978. Grades 5 and up.
        A family struggles to survive in the Ozark wilderness during the Civil
    War. Thad tries to reconcile the war, slavery, and the environment.

Beatty, Patricia. *Be Ever Hopeful, Hannalee.* New York: Morrow Junior Books,
    1988. Grades 5 and up.
        The Civil War is finally over, and instead of returning home to stay,
    Hannalee must join her brother in Atlanta where she faces hard work
    and danger. See *Turn Homeward, Hannalee*, following.

_____. *Charley Skedaddle.* New York: Morrow Junior Books, 1987. Grades 4
    and up.
        Charley's brother is killed, and Charley enlists in the Union Army as
    a drummer boy. When he experiences his first battle, he flees to the
    mountains where he resolves his feelings of cowardice.

_____. *A Long Way to Whiskey Creek.* New York: Morrow Junior Books, 1971.
    Grades 4 and up.
        Two boys grapple with the hostility between Northern and Southern
    supporters.

_____. *Turn Homeward, Hannalee.* New York: William Morrow, 1984. Grades 5
    and up.

Hannalee is a 12-year-old textile mill hand when she is forced from her Georgia home to work in the Yankee mills during the Civil War. See *Be Ever Hopeful, Hannalee* above.

Burchard, Peter. *The Deserter: A Spy Story of the Civil War.* New York: Coward, McCann & Geoghegan, 1973. Grades 4 and up.

This is the story of Levi Blair, who chose to be a deserter in order to spy. Based in part on fact.

_____. *Jed.* New York: Coward, McCann & Geoghegan, 1960. Grades 5 and up.

Sixteen-year-old Jed fights at Shiloh on the Yankee side, but befriends an injured Confederate boy.

_____. *North by Night.* New York: Coward, McCann & Geoghegan, 1962. Grades 4 and up.

Two Yankee soldiers escape from a Confederate prison.

Clapp, Patricia. *The Tamarack Tree.* New York: Lothrop, Lee & Shepard, 1986. Grades 5 and up.

As a 13-year-old orphan, Rosemary left England and came to Vicksburg. The conflicts of the Civil War are presented through her unbiased point of view, but the siege of Vicksburg becomes a test of her courage.

Crane, Stephen. *Red Badge of Courage.* Illustrated by Herschel Levit. New York: Macmillan, 1962. Grades 5 and up.

The horror of war is experienced in this moving novel about Henry Fleming, a young farm boy who enlists to fight in the Union Army.

Fleischman, Paul. *Bull Run.* New York: HarperTrophy, 1993. Grades 5 and up.

Sixteen participants in the Civil War describe their experiences in this moving novel, which can also be used as readers theatre.

Gauch, Patricia Lee. *Thunder at Gettysburg.* Illustrated by Stephen Gammell. New York: Coward, McCann & Geoghegan, 1975. Grades 2 and up.

The Battle of Gettysburg promises to provide great entertainment, but Tillie quickly discovers just how devastating war can be.

Hall, Anna Gertrude. *Cyrus Holt and the Civil War.* Illustrated by Dorothy Bayley Morse. New York: Viking Press, 1964. Grades 5 and up.

The Civil War begins when Cyrus is 9 years old. The impact of the war on his family and friends is seen through Cyrus's eyes.

Hamilton, Virginia. *Anthony Burns: The Defeat and Triumph of a Fugitive Slave.* New York: Alfred A. Knopf Books for Young Readers, 1988. Grades 6 and up.

Anthony Burns, an escaped slave from Virginia, was captured in Boston, tried, and returned to slavery. His biography is a poignant reminder of the challenges faced by slaves.

_____. *The House of Dies Drear.* New York: Macmillan, 1968. Grades 5 and up.
This mystery is set in a house that was once a station on the Underground Railroad.

Hansen, Joyce. *Out from This Place.* New York: Walker, 1988. Grades 4 and up.
A 14-year-old black girl searches for a fellow ex-slave during the turbulent period after the Civil War.

_____. *Which Way to Freedom.* New York: Walker, 1986. Grades 4 and up.
Obi is a slave who escapes to fight in a black Union regiment. This important book addresses the black contributions to the war effort.

Haynes, Betty. *Cowslip.* Nashville, Tenn.: Thomas Nelson, 1973. Grades 4 and up.
The Civil War had begun when Cowslip was on the auction block. After being sold, she is profoundly affected by her new friends who strive for freedom.

Houston, Gloria. *Mountain Valor.* New York: Philomel, 1994. Grades 5 and up.
While Valor's father is fighting in the Civil War, the family must face threats from renegade soldiers in addition to the hardships of the war. Based on the true story of Matilda Houston, Valor dresses as a boy to save her family's livestock.

Hiser, Berniece T. *The Adventure of Charlie and His Wheat-Straw Hat: A Memorat.* Illustrated by Mary Szilagyi. New York: Dodd, Mead, 1989. All ages.
Charlie's dad had left to fight in the Civil War, leaving him with the family in their Appalachian mountain home. When soldiers come to steal Squire McIntosh's animals, Charlie's treasured straw hat is almost lost. Based on a true incident.

Hunt, Irene. *Across Five Aprils.* New York: Berkley, 1986. Grades 5 and up.
Jethro's life is disrupted when he must take over the work of the farm while the men fight in the Civil War. The historical details of this rich novel make it ideal for the study of the Civil War.

Hurmence, Belinda. *Tancy.* New York: Clarion, 1984. Grades 4 and up.
The Civil War is over, and Tancy leaves the plantation in search of her mother Lulu during the difficult time of the Reconstruction period.

Keith, Harold. *Rifles for Watie.* New York: Thomas Y. Crowell, 1967. Grades 5 and up.
When a full-blooded Cherokee, Watie, obtains rifles for the Confederates, Jefferson Davis Busey, a Union soldier, must spy on the Rebels.

Lester, Julius. *Long Journey Home: Stories from Black History.* New York: Dial Press, 1972. Grades 5 and up.

Lester has created six short stories of historical fiction. Each contributes to the reader's understanding of the issues of the day.

Levy, Mimi Cooper. *Corrie and the Yankee*. Illustrated by Ernest Crichlow. New York: Viking, 1959. Grades 4 and up.

Corrie is a young black girl on a southern plantation. She becomes involved in the war when she rescues a wounded Yankee soldier.

Lunn, Janet. *The Root Cellar*. New York: Charles Scribner's, 1981. Grades 5 and up.

Rose is unhappily spending the summer with Canadian relatives. Taking refuge in a root cellar, she finds herself thrust into the 1860s and the Civil War.

Lyons, Mary E. *Letters from a Slave Girl: The Story of Harriet Jacobs*. New York: Scribner, 1992. Grades 5 and up.

Based on Jacobs' autobiography, this is a fictionalized account of her life told through letters.

McKissack, Patricia C., and Fredrick L. McKissack. *Christmas in the Big House, Christmas in the Quarters*. New York: Scholastic, 1994. Grades 3 and up.

Christmas is celebrated before the Civil War begins, with plantation owners anxious about the future and slaves whispering of freedom.

Monjo, F. N. *The Vicksburg Veteran*. Illustrated by Douglas Gorsline. New York: Simon & Schuster, 1971. Grades 2 and up.

Twelve-year-old Fred Grant is with his father, Ulysses S. Grant, during the Battle of Vicksburg. With simple text and black-and-white illustrations, the reader learns how Fred becomes the Vicksburg veteran.

Moore, S. E. *Secret Island*. Illustrated by Judith Gwyn Brown. New York: Four Winds Press, 1977. Grades 4 and up.

To cheer up young John, Captain Gray gives him an assignment as a special agent looking for escaped Rebel prisoners. Surprisingly, John becomes involved with secret codes, spies, and mystery.

O'Dell, Scott. *The 290*. Boston: Houghton Mifflin, 1976. Grades 4 and up.

Jim Lynne signed on with the crew of the *290*, which unexpectedly became the *Alabama*, an important Confederate Civil War vessel.

Paulsen, Gary. *Nightjohn*. New York: Dell, 1993. Grades 5 and up.

Nightjohn, a courageous older slave, risks beatings and death to teach others to read. (Graphic description of mutilation.)

Polacco, Patricia. *Pink and Say*. New York: Philomel, 1994. Grades 2 and up.

A gravely injured young white Union soldier is taken by a young black Union soldier to his mother's home deep in Confederate territory.

The mother hides the soldiers when marauders come, but they shoot her. The young men try to reunite with their troops, but are captured and taken to Andersonville, where the black soldier is hanged. Based on a family story, Polacco has created rich illustrations to accompany the text.

Reeder, Carolyn. *Shades of Gray.* New York: Macmillan, 1989. Grades 4 and up.

Will Page has lost his entire family to the Civil War, and now he must live with his Uncle Jed, who refused to fight the hated Yankees. Will must come to grips with his growing respect for Uncle Jed, while resenting his noninvolvement with the war.

Reit, Seymour. *Behind Civil Lines: The Incredible Story of Emma Edmonds, Civil War Spy.* San Diego, Calif.: Harcourt Brace Jovanovich, 1988. Grades 3 and up.

Emma Edmonds disguises herself as a man, joins the Union Army, and infiltrates the Confederate Army.

Ruby, Lois. *Steal Away Home.* New York: Macmillan, 1994. Grades 5 and up.

Dana discovers a skeleton and a diary in a hidden room in their old house in Kansas. Through alternating chapters, the reader learns of the Quaker family who helped fugitives on the Underground Railroad, while Dana pieces the truth together in contemporary times.

Steele, William O. *The Perilous Road.* New York: Harcourt, Brace & World, 1958. Grades 4 and up.

Though Chris's brother joined the Northern army and his parents maintain neutrality, Chris continues to hate the Yankees. His report of a Yankee supply train endangers his brother, bringing home the futility of the war.

Stolz, Mary. *Cezanne Pinto: A Memoir.* New York: Alfred A. Knopf, 1994. Grades 5 and up.

In his old age, Cezanne Pinto recalls his harrowing escape on the Underground Railroad.

Turner, Ann. *Nettie's Trip South.* Illustrated by Ronald Himler. New York: Macmillan, 1987. Grades 2 and up.

A young white girl travels to the South and recounts her horror at the treatment of slaves through letters to a friend.

Wormser, Richard. *The Black Mustanger.* Illustrated by Don Bolognese. New York: William Morrow, 1971. Grades 4 and up.

Set in the post–Civil War period in Texas, this is the story of a boy and his half-black, half-Apache mentor.

VIDEOS

Across Five Aprils: A Time to Change. Columbus, Ohio: MTI/Coronet, 1990. 33 minutes. Grades 5 and up.

Burns, Ken. *The Civil War.* 13 hours. Available through PBS and video stores.

American Civil War Series. Creative Adventures. Distributed by United Learning, 1996. 18–20 minutes. *Causes of the War; The War Years; Reconstruction.* Grades 5–9.

Follow the Drinking Gourd. Worthington, Ohio: SRA, 1990. 11 minutes. Grades 2 and up.

The Quest for Freedom: The Harriet Tubman Story. Richardson, Tex.: Grace Products, 1994. 41 minutes. Grades 5 and up.

War and Hope. Columbus, Ohio: MTI/Coronet, 1990. 33 minutes. Grades 5 and up.

CD-ROMS

The Civil War: Two Views. Society for Visual Education, Z60329–CDR. Macintosh, Windows, and DOS. Presents the issues from both views. This comprehensive program includes link to student encyclopedia, dictionary, plus questions for students.

Reconstruction. Society for Visual Education, Z60343-CDR. Macintosh, Windows, and DOS. Explores the rebuilding after the Civil War. Includes text, link to student encyclopedia, dictionary, plus questions for students.

Twelve Roads to Gettysburg. Society for Visual Education, Z60385-CDR. Macintosh. Includes maps, biographical sketches, illustrations, photographs, music, and so forth.

U.S.A. Wars: Civil War. Society for Visual Education, Z60023-CDR. MPC (Windows). Covering the years 1850–1865, it includes biographies, chronologies, battles, photographs, statistics, music.

GAME

Civil War Game. Charlottesville, Va.: Educational Materials Associates. Covers campaigns, locations, dates, commanders, battle results, balance of power, opposing forces, North and South data.

References

Ackerman, David B. "Intellectual and Practical Criteria for Successful Curriculum Integration." In *Interdisciplinary Curriculum: Design and Implementation*, edited by Heidi Hays Jacobs, 25–38. Alexandria, Va.: Association for Supervision and Curriculum Development, 1989.

Andrews-Sullivan, Marty, and Esther Orono Negrete. "Our Struggles with Theme Cycle." *Primary Voices K–6* 2, no.1 (Jan. 1994): 15–18.

Altwerger, Bess, and Barbara Flores. "Theme Cycles: Creating Communities of Learners." *Primary Voices K–6* 2, no.1 (Jan. 1994): 2–6.

Billings, John D. *Hardtack and Coffee: The Unwritten Story of Army Life.* Boston: George M. Smith, 1887.

Byars, Betsy. *Trouble River.* New York: Scholastic, 1969.

Castro, Elena. "Implementing Theme Cycle: One Teacher's Way." *Primary Voices K–6* 2, no.1 (Jan. 1994): 7–18.

Cooney, Barbara. *Miss Rumphius.* New York: Viking Press, 1982.

Cordeiro, Patricia. "Problem-Based Thematic Instruction." *Language Arts 67*, no. 1 (Jan. 1990): 26–34.

Cormier, Robert. *After the First Death.* New York: Avon, 1979.

Fredericks, Anthony D., Anita Meyer Meinbach, and Liz Rothlein. *Thematic Units: An Integrated Approach to Teaching Science and Social Studies.* New York: HarperCollins, 1993.

Jacobs, Heidi Hayes. "Design Options for an Integrated Curriculum." In *Interdisciplinary Curriculum: Design and Implementation*, edited by Heidi Hays Jacobs, 13–24. Alexandria, Va.: Association for Supervision and Curriculum Development, 1989.

Jacobs, Heidi Hayes. "The Growing Need for Interdisciplinary Curriculum Content." In *Interdisciplinary Curriculum: Design and Implementation*, edited by Heidi Hays Jacobs, 1–12. Alexandria, Va.: Association for Supervision and Curriculum Development, 1989.

McElmeel, Sharron. *An Author a Month (for Dimes).* Englewood, Colo.: Teacher Ideas Press, 1990.

_____. *An Author a Month (for Pennies).* Englewood, Colo.: Teacher Ideas Press, 1988.

_____. *An Author a Month (for Nickels).* Englewood, Colo.: Teacher Ideas Press, 1990.

_____. *Bookpeople: A First Album.* Englewood, Colo.: Teacher Ideas Press, 1989.

_____. *Bookpeople: A Second Album.* Englewood, Colo.: Teacher Ideas Press, 1989.

Meinbach, Anita Meyer, Liz Rothlein, and Anthony D. Fredericks. *The Complete Guide to Thematic Units: Creating the Integrated Curriculum.* Norwood, Mass.: Christopher-Gordon, 1995.

Nelson, Lynn R., and Trudy A. Nelson. "The History Fair: Multiple Resources and Activities Create Understanding and Enthusiasm." *Social Studies and the Young Learner* 7, no. 2 (Nov./Dec. 1994): 12–16.

Roberts, Patricia L. *A Green Dinosaur Day: A Guide for Developing Thematic Units in Literature-Based Instruction, K–6.* Needham Heights, Mass.: Allyn & Bacon, 1993.

Shanahan, Timothy, Bonita Robinson, and Mary Schneider. "Avoiding Some of the Pitfalls of Thematic Units." *The Reading Teacher* 48, no. 8 (May 1995): 718–719.

Wildberger, Mary Elizabeth. *Approaches to Literature through Authors.* Phoenix, Ariz.: Oryx Press, 1993.

15

Putting the Reading Program Together

Best of All
A Poem

I like art,
and music
and reading,
and spelling,
and math,
and Charlie,
and journals,
and freetime,
and lunch,
and recess,
and Fri. afternoon club,
and Wed. morning club.
But best of all I
like at home.

Josh

FOCUS QUESTIONS

1. What programs are teachers using?

2. What are the advantages of using commercial reading programs?

3. How can I use and adapt commercial reading programs?

4. How do I prepare for the first week in the primary classroom?

5. How do I prepare for the first week in the intermediate or middle school classroom?

6. How can I involve parents and adults in my reading program?

Introduction

Most students would prefer to stay home, just as this first grader did. Developing a program that meets the needs of all students *and* makes them excited about school can be challenging, especially when faced with the myriad choices in reading practices. How does a teacher begin to build a successful program?

With the wide variety of resources and options available today, the reading teacher has many decisions to make. As mentioned in the introduction, nearly 75 percent of teachers surveyed use basals, but 75 percent also use whole language, with basals serving as a guide. More than 90 percent include themes in their teaching (Resnick 1996). Clearly, many teachers use components of basal programs, but most do not limit themselves to a basal program. Making sound decisions about developing a program takes careful thought. Many teachers find that they enjoy using the commercial program in combination with other practices described in previous chapters. Therefore, in this chapter we look at practical suggestions for beginning with basal readers and for adapting them. You will often find that just as a program feels comfortable and successful to you, chances are your next group of students will need different strategies. Therefore, no matter how you choose to structure your reading program, keep in mind that teaching reading is a continually evolving process. Consider the questions in Figure 15.1 as you think about how you want to develop your reading program.

Advantages of Commercial Reading Programs

Most teachers, administrators, and parents of today's students have grown up with basals. The system served the vast majority of learners with a fair amount of effectiveness. There is definitely an underlying attitude of "Well, it worked for me, so it's good enough for my kid!" and certainly there is some truth to this point of view. Large numbers of students did learn to read, write, and spell effectively with traditional materials. Further, basal publishers continually assess the needs of the marketplace, and the inclusion of literary wholes is one of the most promising features of the newest series. In a study of five basal reader publishers, researchers, including students in grades K–2, found that significant improvements had

FIGURE 15.1
Questions about
My Reading
Program

1. What is my definition of reading?
2. Do I think children should guess at words?
3. Do I think children should carefully sound out words?
4. Do I think children should master letters and sounds before trying to read text?
5. Do I think children should learn the vocabulary before reading new text?
6. Do I prefer a quiet environment?
7. Do I believe that students benefit from talking in the classroom?
8. Do I prefer a highly structured environment?
9. Do I prefer polished print displays or the work of students?
10. Do I prefer desks or tables in rows or in groupings?
11. Do I prefer to work with small groups or individuals?
12. Do I prefer teacher-selected or student-selected groups?
13. Do I prefer a carefully sequenced program or am I comfortable with teaching spontaneously?
14. Do I prefer detailed plans or general guidelines?
15. Do I believe that students should work independently so they are accountable for their own work?
16. Do I believe that some students who work with others will use the opportunity to "coast"?
17. Do I believe that most students who work with others will benefit, whether they are stronger or weaker students?
18. Do I believe that most students need careful guidance regarding their education?
19. Do I believe that most students want to learn and will make good choices about educational activities?
20. Do I feel it is important for students to be tested regularly so I know how they are doing?
21. Do I believe that all students should be tested frequently because our society judges students based on how well they perform on standardized tests?
22. Do I believe that standardized tests provide only a small part of the picture of an individual?
23. Do I prefer informal test measures to standardized tests?
24. Do I believe that special students would do better in programs designed specifically for their needs?
25. Do I believe that special students can learn along with regular learners given the right conditions?

been made when comparing 1986/87 texts and manuals to 1993 programs (McCarthey and Hoffman 1995, 74). More diverse children's literature was included, and fewer stories were adapted. Although they contained fewer words, they included more unique words. Further, the stories included more complex plots and idiomatic language. The researchers felt that the basals were generally more engaging, that the teachers' editions were less directive, and that the skills were more integrated (ibid.).

UNIFORMITY OF CURRICULUM

School districts largely favor the use of commercial reading programs for a variety of reasons that relate to the uniformity of curriculum. Such consistency allows for improved management. Principals can learn the designated curriculum and support the teachers in their classroom instruction through their own familiarity with the materials. Students and teachers can more easily manage the assignments to new schools because they know that although the setting may have changed, the curriculum has remained constant.

TEACHER TRAINING

Probably the most important role of reading programs is that they "provide on-the-job training for teachers. Such programs are source books for reading instruction" (McCallum 1988, 207). A basal program provides a vast array of materials for instruction, practice, review, remediation, supplementary instruction, and evaluation. The materials also include management techniques and systems, support for teachers, and research. With limited courses during teacher training programs, basals provide a common starting point for new teachers. Given time, new teachers can adapt, delete, replace, or expand assignments as appropriate.

WORKSHEETS FOR TEACHING SKILLS

Worksheets can provide a systematic method for teaching skills. Ongoing assessment of progress can be easily documented through the assignments. Seatwork can be modified to fit individual needs. Assignments can be eliminated or extra practice provided. Worksheet assignments also provide the student with directions and assignments similar to that found in standardized tests. Good worksheets can provide practice on needed skills, following directions, working independently, and using a variety of formats for test taking. Worksheets can provide review and a sense of accomplishment (Osborn 1984, 50).

Deborah Keller-Cohen and Janet Heineken conducted a study on the relationship of mastery of workbook assignments to the completion of forms such as applications, registration materials, and request forms. Forms generally have a question-and-answer format and resemble an interview in that the respondent must answer predetermined questions. Deborah Keller-Cohen and Janet Heineken define a form as a structured question-and-answer exchange in which the questions are predetermined and written and the kinds of written responses permitted are highly constrained. Though there are basic differences between workbooks and forms (especially forms with several complex sections), they noted many similarities in structure and organization. They concluded that teachers should use workbooks effectively to help students with the skill of completing forms (1987, 288).

Robert C. Aukerman concludes his discussion of basal readers and his review of 15 basal reading series in *The Basal Reader Approach to Reading* with the following statements of their advantages:

1. Beautiful, exciting format of stories and art interwoven in full color—each story presented in a different layout.

2. A carefully selected anthology of stories, biography, poems, and informational articles, written at high-interest grade-level readability.

3. A sequential program of vocabulary development.

4. A developmental plan of word-analysis techniques.

5. Teacher's manuals embodying the best classroom practices oriented directly to each story, poem, and article.

6. Coordinated pupil study-books, filmstrips, independent reading bibliographies, and enrichment materials.

7. An extensive collection of fine children's literature and informational articles appropriate for children in the intermediate grades, together with suggested strategies for transferring basic reading skills to those materials.

8. A developmental sequence of comprehension skills throughout the entire elementary grades.

9. A well-developed management system that assures mastery learning (1981, 333).

Using a Basal Reader

Teachers who use a basal as their primary resource will probably include instruction on phonic analysis; word recognition; sight words; use of word patterns; literature (excerpts, poetry, expository text); reading strategies; and skills. The teacher receives guidance from a detailed teacher's manual that includes recommendations for all instruction and a wide variety of resources to draw from. The basal program may also offer CD-ROMs; a classroom library of trade books; Big Books; equipment such as pocket charts; audiotapes; and so forth.

USING AND ADAPTING THE BASAL AS THE PRIMARY RESOURCE

As we saw in the preceding discussion, there can be many advantages to using a basal. Beginning teachers often feel more comfortable using the basal reader program as the primary instructional focus. Many experienced teachers prefer basals because they have learned to glean the very best from them while adapting or ignoring unnecessary materials.

Despite the wealth of materials, the fourth grade classroom that has all 30 students reading at the fourth grade level probably does not exist; this classroom more likely has students achieving at grades 2, 3, 4, 5, and 6. Therefore, teachers must find a way to accommodate the variety of achievement levels.

In past years, teachers have divided their classes into three instructional groups, meeting with each group daily. It is challenging to meet with each group every day and keep the other students busy. Often, students' time is taken up with completing worksheets that may keep them busy but are not promoting active learning. Some teachers collaborate with other classroom teachers to regroup students across a grade level into more homogeneous levels. During the designated language arts period, students from two or more classrooms may travel to another classroom where they will work together. Three teachers can comfortably handle two disparate groups, giving a wide range of opportunities for instruction. The instructional management is somewhat easier with this arrangement.

When teachers collaborate to regroup students for basal instruction, one concern that emerges is how to help low-achieving students who may need additional instruction at a particular grade level. If they have already had limited success with a particular program, repeating that instruction is usually not a solution. Therefore, many schools offer two distinctly different basal programs to accommodate individual differences. Using two basals can be a good compromise, especially when reading resource teachers are not available. However, it is important that the lower-achieving students do not perceive that they are relegated to a different basal because they are "dumb." Having a varied program, as discussed in the next section, can help create a classroom climate that supports diverse learners.

The teacher's manual can be a new teacher's best resource. However, manuals must be used critically. Adhering to the scientific, assembly-line theory of the turn of the century, teacher manuals continue to leave little to the teacher's imagination. In a review of three 1993 reading programs (Houghton Mifflin,

Macmillan/McGraw Hill, and Scott, Foresman), Patricia Crawford and Patrick Shannon concluded that although the readers included more quality children's literature, fewer altered selections, and some progressive philosophical statements, the teacher's manuals, which provide the framework for learning, remained essentially the same (1994, 18).

Although the basal programs provide many advantages, adhering to each step in a manual can be deadly. Every stage of instruction from readiness to extension is carefully scripted for the user. The teacher is told exactly how to teach the lessons and often what to say to the students. The language is frequently directive, although some manuals are gentler, using phrases such as "You might ask . . ." (ibid., 14). Many activities are labeled "additional" or "extension," but in general, the teacher need only progress through the many discrete steps of the lesson, minimizing the need for lesson plans or systems of accountability.

Teachers often lament, "How will I cover everything?" My mother, who taught first grade with Scott Foresman basals for more than two decades, is now in her eighties and says that she still dreams that it is December and she hasn't taught all the first graders how to read! Teachers take this responsibility seriously, and the excessive materials in a basal program can add undue pressure to "get everything done." However, with a bit of intuition and some practice, teachers learn what activities work well and which ones can be discarded. Good teachers continue to use the manuals to their and the students' advantage, adapting, augmenting, and omitting activities as appropriate. Consider trying the adapted basal lesson format in Something to Try 1.

Although the use of quality literature is welcome in the new programs, critics are dismayed by the preponderance of exercises that take away time that could be spent reading and writing (Edelsky 1994, 33). When writing about the best and worst of the year, one fifth grader stated that she understood the need to complete the grammar worksheets, but it seemed that correctly completing 10 examples demonstrated competency and completing 50 examples seemed unnecessary. Such criticisms are not new. In 1957, Emmett Albert Betts stated, "Some workbooks appear to be constructed on the assumption that sheer repetition fixes learning" (531). He cautioned that workbooks should not be used in place of instruction and that their indiscriminate use tends to overemphasize the mechanics of reading (ibid.). All seatwork must be evaluated in terms of its ability to educate with an appropriate amount of practice. The purpose of any assignment is to keep children learning, not to keep them busy. Consider the following strategies for adapting the basal skills assignments:

1. *Give the unit posttest first.* Eliminate skills lessons and worksheets that address skills the students have mastered. Target those skills in need of instruction.

2. *Provide skills instruction before instead of after reading.* Link the skill to the reading, demonstrating to the students how mastery of the skill will help during the

something to try 1

Adapting a Basal Reader Lesson

PREREADING: Read aloud an easy or harder book, poem, article, or essay on a related topic. Build background through a common experience, such as an experiment or the use of manipulatives. Examine the postreading activities. Can any be used as a prereading activity more effectively? Perhaps it could also be repeated as a postreading activity. Choose and teach a skill that links to the passage and will help with its reading. Be certain that students know *why* they are reading and that their purpose for reading *is meaningful.*

DURING READING: This portion of the lesson is generally silent reading. However, when more than one student has a question about something, it may be appropriate to take time to clarify or explain something confusing to readers.

DIAGNOSIS: Have brief individual conferences during which students read aloud passages they have preread. Use this time to take note of minilessons they may need on word recognition or other skills. Plan to group several students who need direct instruction together.

SKILLS: Elaborate on the skill introduced previously. Replace a skill with a strategy, such as creating an attribute chart that compares features or literary elements. Instead of using a worksheet, have students construct activities that explore the con-

cept. For example, have students choose passages and determine the main idea, testing their ideas on other students. Teach minilessons using alternative materials from the basal or other sources.

POSTREADING: Connect the reading to meaningful writing activities. Create activities or strategies that take students back into the reading to clarify ideas or apply their learning. Perhaps a prereading activity could be repeated to see whether their opinions have changed. Read aloud related picture books, poetry, newspaper or magazine articles, excerpts from chapter books, and so forth.

reading. If the skill doesn't link to the reading, teach it when it does relate. For example, a typical worksheet will have the students explore a topic such as distinguishing fact from opinion after reading a selection. First be sure that the reading selection does indeed include facts and opinions. If it does, instead of delaying the discussion until after the reading, discuss the differences before reading the story, telling students that they should watch for examples while they read. Discuss what they have found, perhaps using the worksheet as a small- or whole-group discussion point. If the reading selection does not include facts and opinions, teach the skill at a more appropriate time.

spotlight 1

Sequencing

GRADE LEVELS:
3 and up.

BOOK: *Jumanji* by Chris Van Allsburg (Boston: Houghton Mifflin, 1981).

ACTIVITY: Have the students write the directions on how to play their favorite board game. Then have them bring in their games and try to play them according to their written directions. Next read *Jumanji* aloud and discuss the importance of following directions. Students can then try to rewrite their game directions, checking their success by playing the games.

3. *Use skills more appropriate for writing in the context of meaningful writing assignments.* For example, teach sequence in the context of writing and testing a recipe or provide directions for an activity instead of having students complete a worksheet that asks students to number the events in order from a story they have just read. As adults, we rarely sit down and number the events of a story in order; however, we do find occasion to write recipes or provide directions. In other words, make the learning authentic. (See Spotlight 1.)

4. *Learn which pages in the workbook address the same skills by examining the index of the workbook's teacher's manual.* Cluster those worksheets together for mini-lessons and immersion. Dorothy S. Strickland suggests reviewing the curriculum guides and collapsing a list of many skills into a more general statement, such as "Students make use of a variety of word-recognition strategies to aid reading comprehension" (1994/1995, 298).

5. *Instead of having the students complete the worksheet independently (and having 30 papers to grade), work in small groups or as a class to determine the answers.* This process eliminates grading and provides opportunities to discuss exceptions, misconceptions, alternative strategies, and so forth.

6. *Evaluate the skill in terms of its usefulness.* For example, one district's first grade curriculum requires all first graders to learn that no word in the English language ends in the letter *v*. Instead of having students master a rather obscure rule through worksheets, address such an issue by observing the characteristic in the context of need. For example, when a first grader writes *uv* (a logical spelling choice) for *of*, point out that *of* happens to be one of those words you just have to memorize because no word in our language ends in the letter *v*. (At that point, however, someone will pipe up with, "But what about *rev* teacher?" And yes, *rev* does indeed occur in the dictionary, but not as a standard word.)

Students enjoy
board games as a
sequencing activity.

7. *Remain aware of the skills that relate to standardized tests.* Be alert to opportunities to reinforce a skill throughout all content areas and activities. For example, when writing poetry, a student may use several particularly good adjectives and adverbs. Point this out, reminding students that they need to know the difference between an adjective and an adverb when taking tests. This only takes a minute, but it reinforces key elements necessary for successful test-taking.

8. *Be sure that the purposes for a skill or activity are meaningful.* Carole Edelsky cites instances of contrived purposes for activities such as writing a letter that is not sent to someone or having a debate that functions as an exercise (1994, 30). Save that activity for a more meaningful context.

9. *Establish the practice of having students read silently when they finish worksheets so that time is used efficiently.* Students should never ask, "What do I do now?" They should use every spare minute to read.

10. *Use worksheets that encourage creativity, allow for individuality, and foster independence.* They should also transfer to other learning situations, foster critical thinking, and develop a useful skill.

COMBINING THE BASAL WITH OTHER PRACTICES

When I taught one of three fifth grades in an urban school, I regularly volunteered to take the lowest-achieving readers if I could also have the highest-achieving readers. I found that having two distinct basal groups gave me a lot of leeway in adapting and enriching instruction at both levels. Only one basal program was available, and I knew that to date none of these low-achieving students had fared well with it. Therefore, I felt justified in exploring other practices, such as allowing students to read individually selected novels and to form literature circles, even though that particular faculty had not yet embraced literature-based practices.

I used many of the practices discussed in the previous section so that we could move as quickly as possible through the basics in the basal. Then I would take approximately one month to use an alternative practice, such as those described in Chapters 9 and 10. I found that when we explored thematic units or when students read books they had selected, we focused on individual accomplishments rather than how the two disparate groups progressed. The lower-achieving or remedial readers worked alongside the others, and there was a nice sense of community. Further, when we used literature circles or literature discussion groups, many of the lower-achieving students would tackle a harder book with better-than-expected success, even if it meant getting extra help at home. Higher-achieving students occasionally chose an easier book, enjoying an opportunity to coast a bit, but this was never a long-term problem. Consider alternating the basal program with one or more of the following combinations.

BASALS AND LITERATURE

Many basal readers contain excerpts, chapters, or entire stories drawn from the best of children's literature. If the story has been adapted, read the original aloud or have students silently read it and compare the changes. If the story has been excerpted, compare the excerpt to the entire work. Use this opportunity to combine the work with skills instruction that directly relates to the entire work.

A basal story may serve as the beginning point for immersion in a unit about a genre, such as fairy tales or fables. Read several trade book examples aloud as an introduction, adapt the basal lessons as appropriate, and have students continue reading other examples. Combine the reading with authentic writing activities, such as those described in Chapter 10.

Many basal stories, articles, and poetry are organized by theme. After reading the selections in the basal, the class could explore a wider variety of texts on that particular theme. For example, after reading an essay about Martin Luther King, you might share *Kente Colors* by Debbi Chocolate, and the students might explore poetry by Langston Hughes and Eloise Greenfield and read *Famous Firsts of Black Women* by Martha Ward Plowden.

When students discover an author they enjoy in the basal, the class might pursue a two- or three-week author study. Kindergartners and first graders especially enjoy Eric Carle's work and would appreciate seeing the video *Eric Carle: Picture Writer* to learn how he creates the art. Students could then compare Carle's work to another favorite artist, such as Tomie dePaola, analyzing the likenesses and differences. Teachers of young children have found that they too can follow Carle's use of tissue paper and paints in a comfortable exploration of making pictures. Older students enjoy an author study with a writer who writes chapter books as well as picture books, such as Eve Bunting. This wide variety of literature gives every level of reader an opportunity to contribute to the understanding of that author's corpus of works.

Units inspired by basal stories can be short. A modified version of the thematic unit can be used on a two- or three-day basis. The theme may only use two or three books and yet include a variety of language activities, skills, and extensions. The following points outline the elements of such a unit, inspired by a basal article about rabbits in a second grade reader.

1. After reading an article in the basal about rabbits, you could use a predictable book (see more below) or a catchy song or poem. For example, you could read or play the record *Seven Little Rabbits* by John Becker. The text is predictable and lively, describing the rabbits as they walk down the road. A rabbit becomes tired, and they turn around, going to mole's hole, where the tired rabbit falls asleep. The six continue, with another rabbit tiring. They again return to mole's hole, repeating the verses until all the rabbits are asleep and the last rabbit dreams they are going to toad's house. The musical version is lively and easily sung by the children.

2. After the predictable book has been read, you could introduce *The Tale of Peter Rabbit* by Beatrix Potter and read it aloud to the class. This story includes words that are particularly fun for their sounds: *Flopsy, Mopsy, kertyschoo* (when Peter sneezes), *lippity-lippity, scr-r-ritch*. You would next return to various parts of the story to teach a minilesson that includes a quick discussion of how writers match words to images (*Flopsy, Mopsy*) or the usage of onomatopoeia for *kertyschoo, lippity,* and *scritch*. Another lesson could include listing all the items eaten by Peter (lettuce, French beans, radishes) and a brainstorming session on everything that could be grown in a garden. This list could be left on the board or chart paper for students who might use the words in one of the following extension activities.

3. The students could next pursue an independent activity, perhaps creating their own garden in picture form with labels of the items included. Perhaps they would draw the garden and label all the places Peter stopped, retracing his route and eventual escape. Students who are writing might create a new version in which Peter gets caught by Mr. McGregor for an extended period of time and has to contrive a new escape. In the spring, the students might plant seeds in paper cups or outside.

4. A period would be devoted to sharing the children's extension activities. This period might also include another minilesson based on the children's work.

For example, a discussion on sequence logically precedes or follows the reconstruction of Peter's route through the garden.

5. The final activity in this unit might include a return to the first book, *Seven Little Rabbits*. This predictable book lends itself well to a dramatization activity requiring little preparation. Children could take turns reading the text as others act it out, or the record could be played while children take turns reenacting the story.

Among the advantages of this unit are that it takes only a day or two, it provides ample opportunities for skills lessons, and it supports the earliest readers through the predictable books. It also introduces more traditional literature, it allows for choices through the extension activities, and, finally, it provides for exciting closing activities such as the dramatization. A primary teacher with a strong children's literature background or a helpful librarian can link literature to the basal and pair two or more books without devoting extended amounts of planning time to the project that the more involved thematic units demand.

BASALS AND READING ALOUD

The benefits of reading aloud have been extolled several times throughout this book. Reading aloud to the students every day remains one of the easiest ways to combine literature with the basal program. Use related picture books to introduce the basal reading *at every level, including middle school*. Students at the upper levels can learn about all literary elements by listening to and seeing picture books every day. By modeling the pleasure of reading picture books, you sanction reading a variety of materials. You may begin your teaching career with a basic knowledge of children's literature, and this provides an excellent method to expand your knowledge with the students. However, always take time to preread everything you choose to read aloud.

BASALS AND SUSTAINED SILENT READING

Many schools have a period of silent reading. This provides the class with an excellent opportunity to read literature instead of texts. Model reading a wide variety of literature during this time period. If you teach middle school and you read picture books during Sustained Silent Reading, your reluctant readers might decide it's alright to read an easy book—and improve their reading skills in the process. Conversely, if you are a kindergarten teacher, read adult books occasionally in the classroom. Your students will be interested in what you are reading, and you will be demonstrating that reading can be enjoyed throughout one's lifetime. Try to schedule informal literature discussion groups after the silent reading, even if you can only meet for 5 or 10 minutes.

USING BASALS TO SUPPORT YOUR LITERATURE PROGRAM

Some teachers may be comfortable with using alternatives to basals except in the area of skills instruction. Because basal skills programs often reflect items on standardized tests, some teachers use the skills components to ensure they are covering the standard expectations for that grade. Basal programs provide a detailed scope and sequence chart that details the skills taught across and within the grade levels. Many also provide a matrix that details the themes, stories, articles, poetry, and other elements found in the lessons. These resources can be invaluable in your planning. You might notice that one basal unit has an article about an author you are using, plus worksheets that explore related literary elements. These can be incorporated into the literature activities already underway. Skills sheets can be clustered, as mentioned previously, or can be used to support appropriate minilessons.

Preparing for the First Week in the Primary Classroom

Much of the first week or two of school is devoted to orienting students to the routines. Simple directions, such as "line up at the door," can bewilder a group of kindergarten children. Create a list of topics you will want to begin establishing routines for and ease the students into them. Consider the following procedures:

How children can get your attention.

How to enter and leave the room.

How to move within the room.

How to take care of bathroom and washing needs.

How to get around the building.

How to distribute and collect materials.

How to use equipment and supplies.

How to clean up.

How to store coats and bags.

How to collect lunch money.

What to do when work is done.

How to store work, finished and unfinished.

How to use books.

How you will gain their attention.

How to use writing materials.

How to use play areas or centers.

How to talk with other students.

How to take turns.

Where the playground is.

Determine a theme for the first week of school that includes a wide variety of reading and writing experiences and that will be fun. Kindergartners and first graders come to school expecting to be readers and writers. Don't disappoint them. Collect a variety of books with predictable text or patterns that they can read with little practice.

Consider developing a reading and writing theme that will continue through the year. A classroom library is usually a first priority. Enhance the library area by adding date stamps for marking books, bookmarks or materials to make them, writing implements, sign-out/sign-in records, card file, calendar, posters advertising books (commercial and student produced), appropriate office supplies, return trays, reference books.

Charla R. Pfeffinger, a former kindergarten teacher, began her year with a card writing center. She assembled a variety of interesting kinds of paper plus pens, markers, crayons, ribbon, string, paint, and so forth. She added a calendar that included all the birthdays of the students and staff members. A chart listed possible occasions for making cards: birthdays, illness, anniversaries, cheering up, thank you notes, congratulations, and so forth. Related easy reference books and books that might inspire ideas were included. Students were encouraged to add dates to the calendar for special occasions for family members. The card center was in use almost daily, with an endless variety of messages, and the school community often expressed their appreciation at the thoughtfulness of the students. This sort of ongoing activity is particularly admirable because it not only supports authentic literacy activities, it also fosters a most desirable lifelong habit of recognizing another person's special occasions or accomplishments.

Aggregating
The gathering together of related materials or objects, generally in the context of a topical investigation.

A similar focus for a yearlong center is a post office theme. Collecting the related provisions, referred to as **aggregating**, not only provides a network of related materials or objects (Neuman and Roskos 1993, 111), it also is a fun activity for students, who begin to take ownership in the process. For the post office theme, gather together posters and signs about mailing, stationery, envelopes, sorting trays, calendar, tote bag for mail, large mailbox, individual mailboxes, stamp pads and stamps, stickers, writing utensils, various office supplies (ibid.). Check with your post office for field trips and related supportive programs and materials.

Memory Long Schorr, an experienced teacher of young children and physically handicapped children, recommends beginning the year with a table of

s p o t l i g h t   2

The Body Center

GRADE LEVELS:
Preschool–1.

BOOK: *3-D Kid: A Life-Size, Pop-Up Guide to Your Body and How It Works* by Roger Culbertson and Robert Margulies (New York: W. H. Freeman, 1995).

ACTIVITY: This intriguing fold-out book becomes a 40-inch model of a child's body, complete with pop-ups. It can be used in book form to explore parts of the body, or folded out as a display. After sharing the book, show students how to work in pairs to outline their bodies with butcher paper, adding details. Memory Long Schorr recommends using their drawings at Back to School Night, adding new clothing as the seasons change, adding toothy mouths during the dental unit and removing teeth when they lose them (1995, 100). Bring in plastic models of the body to give another perspective of how it works. Provide clay so students can create their own brains, heart, liver, and so forth. Have students label and display their models. Small books can be compiled of drawings of their bodies, with appropriate labels.

---

science inquiry titled "What in the World?" She places a variety of items on the table: a bird's nest, feathers, animal bones, seed pods, rocks, nuts, bolts, gears, shells, magnets, a broken wristwatch, magnifying glasses, mealworms, and so forth. Schorr notes that she never knows where their interests will lead them, but this table sets the tone for science investigations throughout the year (1995, 99–100). Another possibility focuses on the human body and can be used throughout the year. (See Spotlight 2.)

Young children are still learning a sense of time, particularly in relation to changing seasons. Another theme for the beginning of the year could be investigating signs of autumn, with students bringing in evidence, such as leaves or fall flowers, to add to the center. Other artifacts could include fall vegetables, gourds, newspaper photographs or articles, lists of signs seen on autumn walks, a record of changing temperatures, books about autumn, and so forth. Plan art work, read-alouds, science investigations, and other activities to complement the theme.

After the first week or two, develop a learning center with input from the students. This is the time to use what you have observed regarding their interests to date and to incorporate their ideas into the direction you wish to take. For example, one kindergarten class may take an unusual interest in the block area, playing there almost exclusively. Build on this interest by developing a unit on buildings, beginning with an easy book such as Byron Barton's *Building a House*, discussing how blocks can be used to create a house. Gail Gibbons's

Up Goes the Skyscraper! gives another view of buildings, and children may decide they want to try building skyscrapers next. Other related building projects include doll houses, Lincoln logs, castles, office buildings, malls, and so forth. Planning buildings or entire communities can involve measurement, drawing and labeling plans, and cooperative work. Charla Pfeffinger's kindergarten class created the school and the individual students' houses out of graham crackers and frosting, asking the bus driver (with no prompting from their teacher) to determine the distances from the school for the houses so they could make the project to scale. Keep in mind that the class might begin with one focus and move in an unexpected direction as the investigation evolves. This is what makes teaching and learning exciting!

Preparing for the First Week in Intermediate and Middle School Classrooms

Many of the strategies in the preceding section can be applied to the intermediate classroom. Students appreciate knowing what the rules are, where to find supplies, and what materials they will be using. Many students will be familiar with the basics of getting around the school and will require less general orientation than younger students. However, there will often be a few new students, and a review of all routines can be useful for everyone. Be sure your expectations are clear and remember the five *R*'s of teaching for intermediate students, as discussed in Chapter 13:

1. *Rehearse* your expectations.

2. Encourage students to take *risks*.

3. *Rescue* students who need help, perhaps with more structure, checklists, organizational tips, or other aids.

4. *Reteach* as necessary.

5. *Release* responsibility for learning to the students.

Establishing a Sustained Silent Reading period on the first day can help set the tone for a reading classroom. Before school begins, gather a wide variety of reading materials from the library. Include magazines, newspapers, fiction, and nonfiction. Give students an opportunity to select something to read from the classroom library and ease them into reading silently for 15 minutes or more. One of the best rules you can establish on the first day is the answer to "I'm finished. What do I do now?" The response, worthy of posting on the board, is "Read!" Ensure that all students have something to read in their desks and reinforce this habit from the first day.

Consider having students read independently and respond in literature logs for the first few weeks while you get to know their interests and levels, perhaps using prompts such as those found in Chapter 9. Marcia Blake recommends that older students use logs in a variety of subjects, with entries prompted by questions such as "What do you already know about . . . ?" In addition to response entries, logs can be used for lists, webs, brainstorming, or collections of data (1990).

Prepare for journal writing by requesting that students bring spiral-bound notebooks, or purchase them yourself during the back-to-school sales. The latter has the advantage of ensuring that all students have notebooks on the first day. Until students become accustomed to writing in journals, suggest some optional topics. Barbara Steiner and Kathleen C. Phillips suggest the following ideas, which will get students writing and provide you with background information (1991, 23–25):

1. Write a journal entry that introduces yourself.

2. Write about your name: why you have it; where it came from; how you feel about it; what it means.

3. List 10 words that describe you best, ranking them from 1 to 10, with the most descriptive as number 1.

4. Identify all the individuals that make up your whole (dreamer, artist, musician, friend, daughter, uncle, and so forth).

Plan for an engaging read-aloud. Intermediate and older students will enjoy Gary Paulsen's *Hatchet*, Michelle Magorian's *Good Night, Mr. Tom*, Willo Davis Roberts' *The Girl with the Silver Eyes*, Ivy Ruckman's *Night of the Twisters*, or Martin Waddell's *The Kidnapping of Suzie Q*. Read the book yourself before sharing it with the class. Although these represent engaging literature, the concepts and the difficulty vary. Plan to fill short periods of time with high-quality picture books that may be related to content areas found in the textbooks or themes you plan to investigate. Establish from the beginning that you honor reading a wide variety of literature, and model this by reading aloud from various materials yourself. Choose two or three collections of poetry that you keep on your desk at all times for planned and unplanned reading. *This Same Sky: A Collection of Poems from Around the World* selected by Naomi Shihab Nye, *The Butterfly Jar* by Jeff Moss, and *Kids Pick the Funniest Poems* compiled by Bruce Lansky provide a good variety of entertaining, thoughtful, and inspiring poetry.

Create a reading-interest inventory that you can have the students complete during the first week. Review the following questions and choose 10 or 15 that fit your needs. Some students may find it difficult to answer some of them. Complete your own first, modeling the process, with some questions skipped. Students will find they can be forthcoming if your examples include

Students work together on a project.

comments such as your favorite part of the newspaper is the comics or Ann Landers! Allow them to skip some questions, or have students discuss theirs in small groups before turning them in. Often, the discussion will trigger additional ideas.

1. My favorite books are about _____.

2. My favorite book is _____.

3. My favorite author is _____.

4. My favorite place to read is _____.

5. I don't like reading about _____.

6. My favorite magazine is _____.

7. My favorite part of the newspaper is _____.

8. My favorite cartoon is _____.

9. My favorite musician is _____.

10. My favorite sports star is _____.

11. When I have free time, I _____.

12. My favorite television show is _____.

13. My favorite movie is _____.

14. When I feel tired, I like to _____.

15. My favorite place to visit is _____.

16. I talk about books with _____.

17. _____ recommends good books to me.

18. When I feel sad, I _____.

19. My favorite video is _____.

20. The best story I ever heard was _____.

21. _____ reads aloud to me.

22. This year I want to read about _____.

23. This year I don't want to read about _____.

24. I like to write _____.

25. Most people think I am a _____ reader.

Involving Parents and Adults

Before the beginning of school, plan how you want to involve parents. If you will be teaching writing, think about how you might use volunteers to type students' stories or poems. If you want parents to serve as reading partners, plan a training program for communicating your expectations. Assume that you will have to recruit parents, even if you will be teaching in a neighborhood where parents actively volunteer. They will need to feel that they are contributing positively to the program. One school offered a coupon book, with each coupon listing a different task. Some were ongoing, such as coming to school and helping with photocopying. Some tasks, such as typing, could be completed at home. Others, such as helping judge a writing contest or playing the piano for graduation, occurred only once a year and required a special interest or talent. Parents could browse through the coupon book and choose how they could contribute to the class.

Plan for a back-to-school event that will draw your families into your classroom. Some teachers prepare a slide show that shows the students in a variety of school activities, using the slides to give an overview of the program. Middle schools often have the parents move through the classes on an abbreviated schedule so that they get a taste of each class. Be sure you give a sample of what happens in a normal class, so that parents know the context of the learning.

A wise principal once urged his teachers to call every parent to welcome their child within the first two weeks of school so that the first contact would be positive. This may feel overwhelming, especially given the busy time at the beginning of the year. However, most parents are so disarmed by a friendly call that they don't prolong conversation, especially if you say something like the following: "This is Mrs. _____, Juan's third grade teacher. I just called to let you know how much I am looking forward to a good year. We are all learning about each other and I hope to see you at the school soon. Please call me at school if you have any questions about the program." This principal also suggested keeping a calling log, recording the date and a notation about the reason for each call. He recommended that when the calls of a negative nature exceed the calls of a positive nature, it is time to make some positive calls to keep the balance.

A Final Note

Teaching reading can be the most frustrating challenge you will face. It usually proves to be the most exhilarating and rewarding too, especially to those who love reading. Sometimes, however, the problems seem persistent. This is the time to step back and decide which priorities need to be addressed and which can be ignored. Try to periodically revisit the questions in Figure 15.1 as you grow and change as a teacher. Finally, to be an effective teacher, you first need to take care of yourself. Consider these final thoughts:

1. Laugh—collect and share jokes.
2. Exercise—walk, dance, stretch.
3. Be friends—with your students, adults, nonteachers.
4. Reward yourself—with treats, new books, flowers, naps.
5. Enjoy—music, art, books, movies, conversation.

Summary

The majority of today's teachers use basals as part of their language arts program, often in combination with other instructional practices. Research shows that commercial reading programs have responded to the marketplace, with more literary wholes, less directive manuals, and more engaging formats. Advantages include the uniformity of curriculum, the training they provide for teachers, the developmental skills sequence, and the management program.

Basal reading programs contain a wide variety of materials with most including phonic analysis, word-recognition instruction, sight-word and word-patterns instruction, literature, reading strategies, and a skills program.

Teachers may group their students across grade levels to accommodate differing achievement levels and to minimize management challenges. Teachers can use the manual to reorganize and adapt lessons for more efficient teaching. Skills instruction can be reorganized or clustered to link the learning more closely to the reading.

Teachers can combine using basals with literature, can use basals as part of a short thematic unit, or can relate the read-aloud to the basal. The basal can be supplemented through self-selected reading during a silent reading period. The basal skills program can be used to support a literature-based program.

Prepare for the first week in the classroom by determining the rules and routines that need teaching. Choose a beginning-of-the year theme and a continuing reading and writing theme. Plan an intriguing learning center to be in place when school starts and later involve students in creating one or more centers.

Consider establishing a Sustained Silent Reading period, using literature logs for independent reading, writing in journals, choosing an engaging read-aloud, reading high-quality picture books, and using a reading-interest inventory. Plan how you can use volunteers and how you will involve parents in your reading program.

References

Aukerman, Robert C. *The Basal Reader Approach to Reading.* New York: John Wiley, 1981.

Barton, Byron. *Building a House.* New York: Greenwillow, 1981.

Becker, John. *Seven Little Rabbits.* Illustrated by Barbara Cooney. New York: Scholastic, 1973.

Betts, Emmett Albert. *Foundations of Reading Instruction.* New York: American, 1957.

Blake, Marcia. "Learning Logs in the Upper Elementary Grades." In *Coming to Know: Writing to Learn in the Intermediate Grades,* edited by Nancie Atwell, 53–60. Portsmouth, N.H.: Heinneman, 1990.

Chocolate, Debbi. *Kente Colors.* Illustrated by John Ward. New York: Walker, 1996.

Crawford, Patricia, and Patrick Shannon. "I Don't Think These Companies Have Much Respect for Teachers: "Looking at Teacher's Manuals." In *Basal Readers: A Second Look,* edited by Patrick Shannon and Kenneth S. Goodman, 19–33. Katonah, N.Y.: Richard C. Owen, 1994.

Culbertson, Roger, and Robert Margulies. *3-D Kid: A Life-Size, Pop-Up Guide to Your Body and How It Works.* New York: W. H. Freeman, 1995.

Edelsky, Carole. "Exercise Isn't Always Healthy." In *Basal Readers: A Second Look*, edited by Patrick Shannon and Kenneth S. Goodman, 19–33. Katonah, N.Y.: Richard C. Owen, 1994.

Gibbons, Gail. *Up Goes the Skyscraper!* New York: Four Winds Press, 1986.

Harlow, Joyce. *Story Play: Costumes, Cooking, Music, and More for Young Children*, Englewood, Colo.: Teacher Ideas Press, 1992.

Johnston, Tony. *The Vanishing Pumpkin.* Illustrated by Tomie dePaola. New York: G. P. Putnam's, 1983.

Keller-Cohen, Deborah, and Janet Heineken. "Workbooks: What They Can Teach Children about Forms." In *Literacy and Schooling*, edited by David Bloome, 258–288. N.J.: Ablex, 1987.

Kimmel, Eric. *The Gingerbread Man.* New York: Holiday House, 1993.

Lansky, Bruce. *Kids Pick the Funniest Poems.* Illustrated by Stephen Carpenter. Deephaven, Minn.: Meadowbrook Press, 1991.

Magorian, Michelle. *Good Night, Mr. Tom.* New York: Harper & Row, 1981.

McCallum, Richard D. "Don't Throw the Basals Out with the Bath Water." *The Reading Teacher* 42, no. 3 (Dec. 1988): 204–208.

McCarthey, Susan J., and James V. Hoffman. "The New Basals: How Are They Different?" *The Reading Teacher* 49, no. 1 (Sept. 1995): 72–75.

Moss, Jeff. *The Butterfly Jar.* Illustrated by Chris Demarest. New York: Bantam, 1989.

Neuman, Susan B., and Kathleen A. Roskos. New York: Harcourt Brace Jovanovich, 1993.

Nye, Naomi Shihab. *This Same Sky: A Collection of Poems from Around the World.* New York: Four Winds Press, 1992.

Osborn, Jean. "The Purposes, Uses, and Contents of Workbooks and Some Guidelines for Publishers." In *Learning to Read in American Schools: Basal Readers and Content Texts*, edited by Richard C. Anderson, Jean Osborn, and Robert J. Tierney, 45–111. Hillsdale, N.J.: Lawrence Erlbaum Associates, 1984.

Paulsen, Gary. *Hatchet.* New York: Puffin, 1982.

Plowden, Martha Ward. *Famous Firsts of Black Women.* Illustrated by Ronald Jones. Gretna, La.: Pelican, 1993.

Potter, Beatrix. *The Tale of Peter Rabbit.* New York: Frederick Warne, 1902.

Resnick, Robert M. *National Survey of Reading/Language Arts: Whole Language and Multimedia Product Needs, Grades K–6.* Rockaway Park, N.Y.: Education Market Research, 1996.

Roberts, Willo Davis. *The Girl with the Silver Eyes.* New York: Atheneum, 1980.

Ruckman, Ivy. *Night of the Twisters.* New York: Thomas Y. Crowell, 1984.

Schorr, Memory Long. *A Handbook for First Year Teachers: Ready! Set! Go!* Englewood, Colo.: Teacher Ideas Press, 1995.

Steiner, Barbara, and Kathleen C. Phillips. *Journal Keeping with Young People.* Englewood, Colo.: Teacher Ideas Press, 1991.

Strickland, Dorothy S. "Reinventing Our Literacy Programs: Books, Basics, Balance." *The Reading Teacher* 48, no. 4 (Dec. 1994/Jan. 1995): 294–302.

Titherington, Jeanne. *Pumpkin Pumpkin.* New York: William Morrow, 1986.

Van Allsburg, Chris. *Jumanji.* Boston: Houghton Mifflin, 1981.

Waddell, Martin. *The Kidnapping of Suzie Q.* Cambridge, Mass.: Candlewick Press, 1994.

Zemach, Margot. *The Little Red Hen: An Old Story.* New York: Farrar, Straus & Giroux, 1983.

VIDEO

Eric Carle: Picture Writer. New York: Philomel, 1993.

Appendix A: Survival Unit

PART ONE

GENERAL DESCRIPTION

This literature contract includes a variety of books that have a survival theme. The books range across a variety of settings: Nebraska, an island off Baja California, London, Auschwitz, and others. In every book, a young person must face and survive a variety of challenges.

GRADE LEVEL

This literature contract is intended for middle school students, although the books range in difficulty from fourth grade through high school.

OBJECTIVES

Appreciation

For students to understand the themes of survival literature.

For students to be inspired by reading about other young people who face unusual challenges.

For students to discover commonalities in the various books.

For students to appreciate written characterizations.

For students to appreciate descriptive narrative.

For students to compare and contrast the elements found in the various books.

Skills

For students to improve their reading skills.

For students to improve their writing skills.

For students to improve their speaking skills.

For students to improve their listening skills.

For students to increase their vocabulary.

For students to improve their research skills.

For students to become better at solving problems.

For students to be inspired to express themselves through the arts.

For students to improve their expressive skills through sharing.

STRATEGIES FOR STUDENTS WITH SPECIAL NEEDS

Modifications in student expectations are integral to the literature contract. Remedial reading or mainstreamed students may read fewer books or may be given an extension for the completion of their activities. Peer or adult tutors, paraprofessionals, or resource teachers may be available for paired reading, read-alouds, or direct support. Students may also read books not found on the bibliography. Gifted students may be required to complete additional projects, to help students who require extra assistance, or to identify and read more challenging materials. Students with limited English may use a combination of materials in their native language and English and may substitute extra projects for reading if bilingual books are not available.

OTHER INFORMATION

All students should be encouraged to identify additional examples of books with a survival theme. The librarian should be consulted prior to the literature contract regarding availability of books.

PART TWO

WEB

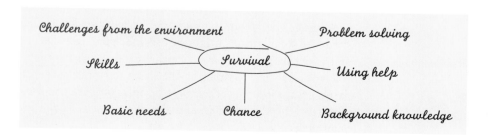

ESSENTIAL QUESTIONS

1. What do you need to survive a threatening situation?

2. What role does decision making play in survival?

3. What problems do characters in survival novels face?

4. What role does the character's emotions play in the plot?

5. How does an author effectively develop a character?

6. What qualities do heroes have?

7. How does an author advance the story line?

8. How does an author enhance the narrative?

9. How does an author effectively describe a setting?

10. How do novels with similar themes compare?

INTRODUCTORY LESSON PLAN

Before class, think about all the things you would pack in a backpack if you had to be on your own for one week in a setting that is unfamiliar to you: the woods, the mountains, the ocean, the city, a cave, and so forth. Fill a backpack with your choices. Bring it to class and also enough large grocery bags so that each student can have one bag. Without opening your backpack, explain to the students that you have packed it so you could survive for one week in your designated area.

Distribute the bags and tell students they have about this much space to fill their "backpack" with their choices for survival. If you want this activity to be done at home, send students home with the bags with instructions to fill them and to make a list of what they were able to fit in. If this is done in class, students could write the items they would choose directly on the bag. Compare the lists in small groups and then with the whole class. Then share what is in your backpack. Have the students revise their lists using the ideas they have gotten from listening to other students.

Alternatively, have the students fill their bags thematically in groups. For example, small groups might be assigned such settings as the desert, a sailboat on the ocean, the wilderness, or the mountains in winter.

Plan that after completing the literature unit, students will fill a backpack based on the reading they have done. Compare the lists with students who have read the same books, and also compare the lists with those created at the beginning of the unit.

PART THREE

COVER PAGE

Prepare a decorative cover page for the components of Part Three, which is given to students.

LETTER TO PARENTS

The following letter explains the purpose of a literature contract and can be modified before it is sent to parents.

Date

Dear Parent(s):

Our class will be spending the next six weeks working on individual literature contracts on the theme of survival. Each student will negotiate with me regarding how many books to read, how many activities to complete, how to share the work with the class, and a form of evaluation. The activities will involve using both receptive skills (reading, listening, vocabulary, and interpretation) and expressive skills (writing, speaking, and the arts).

After the students and I have negotiated the terms of the contract, you will be asked to sign the contract page. The students should fully understand their responsibilities, but if you have any questions, be sure to call me.

Yours truly,

STUDENT DIRECTIONS

The students need clear directions regarding the expectations of the literature contract. This may be in the form of a letter or a list of responsibilities. The following example can be used as a guide.

LITERATURE CONTRACT DIRECTIONS

During the next six weeks, you will be reading a variety of books using the theme of survival. You will be required to negotiate every section of the literature contract; therefore read these directions thoroughly:

1. Review the student bibliography, which lists books with the survival theme. You will negotiate with me the number of books you plan to read during the

next six weeks. Use our classroom, school, and the public libraries to review the books on the bibliography before you negotiate how many books you will read. If you wish to read alternative books, consult with the librarian or book resources to identify additional books and obtain my approval.

2. You will need to choose activities from the enclosed lists: reading activities, listening activities, vocabulary activities, interpretation activities, writing activities, speaking activities, and arts activities. If you have additional ideas now or during the course of the contract, we will negotiate those alternatives.

3. To receive an A for the contract, you will be required to complete a minimum of one challenge activity. Review the list and be prepared to discuss these choices or your alternative ideas.

4. Near the end of the six weeks, you will be required to share a completed activity. Activities that can be shared are starred (*) in the activities lists. Although you do not have to specify the activity at this time, be thinking about what you might do.

5. Near the end of the six weeks, you will evaluate yourself on your completion of the unit. This will conclude the contract.

CONTRACT PAGE

Prepare a contract page like the one shown on page 525 that students and parents can sign. Include all components of the unit requirements.

STUDENT BIBLIOGRAPHY

Burnfurd, Sheila. *The Incredible Journey.* Illustrated by Carl Burger. New York: Bantam, 1961.
>Three family pets cross 250 miles of wilderness to return home.

Byars, Betsy. *Trouble River.* New York: Scholastic, 1969.
>Dewey and Grandma must escape from Indians on a raft down a dangerous river.

Cole, Brock. *The Goats.* New York: Farrar, Straus & Giroux, 1987.
>A boy and girl are stripped of their clothes and left on a small island for the night. They decide they won't be the "goats" of the prank and escape from the island.

Cormier, Robert. *After the First Death.* New York: Avon, 1979.
>When a bus full of preschool campers is hijacked by terrorists, Kate, Miro, and Ben play out a tragic and suspenseful game of survival.

_____. *The Chocolate War.* New York: Dell, 1974.

Literature Contract

I, _____(student's name)_____ , agree to complete the following items for my literature contract.

I will read (number) books from the bibliography.

I will complete (number) reading activities.

I will complete (number) listening activities.

I will complete (number) vocabulary activities.

I will complete (number) interpretation activities.

I will complete (number) writing activities.

I will complete (number) speaking activities.

I will complete (number) arts activities.

I will complete (number) challenge activities.

I will share one activity at the end of the unit. (See starred items throughout the unit.)

I will complete a self-evaluation activity.

_____   _____
Signature of student   Date

_____   _____
Signature of teacher   Date

_____   _____
Signature of parent   Date

Jerry, who attends a private school, refuses to participate in the annual chocolate sale. Seen at first as a hero, Jerry becomes an outcast and faces isolation and danger.

George, Jean Craighead. *Julie of the Wolves.* New York: Harper & Row, 1972.
    When Julie escapes an arranged marriage, she must survive an Alaska winter among the wolves.

____. *My Side of the Mountain.* New York: Dutton, 1988.
    A young boy leaves New York City and lives in the Catskill Mountains for a year. Written in journal form.

Hill, Kirkpatrick. *Toughboy and Sister.* New York: Margaret McElderry, 1990.
   When their father dies, Toughboy and his sister must survive along Alaska's Yukon River.

Hinton, S. E. *The Outsiders.* New York: Dell, 1967.
   Since the deaths of Ponyboy's parents, he has had to cope with gang warfare, more deaths, and learning how to survive.

Magorian, Michelle. *Good Night, Mr. Tom.* New York: Harper & Row, 1981.
   A frightened, young Willie Beech is sent from London to Mr. Tom's home in the country during World War II. Just when he begins to feel safe, he is returned to his abusive mother where his life is again endangered.

Moeri, Louise. *Save Queen of Sheba.* New York: Avon, 1981.
   During a Sioux Indian attack, a brother and sister are separated from the wagon train. With few provisions, they must try to find their family along the Oregon Trail.

O'Brien, Robert C. *Z for Zachariah.* New York: Collier, 1974.
   Sixteen-year-old Ann believes that nuclear radiation has destroyed everything in the world except her valley. When John Loomis arrives in his safe suit, Ann must choose how she will continue to survive.

O'Dell, Scott. *Island of the Blue Dolphins.* Boston: Houghton Mifflin, 1960.
   Karana stays on an island with her brother, only to lose him to wild dogs. Drawing on her internal strength, she survives alone for 18 years.

Paulsen, Gary. *Hatchet.* New York: Puffin, 1987.
   Brian is flying to the Canadian wilderness in a small plane when the pilot dies of a heart attack. Brian lands the plane and must survive with only his clothes and a hatchet.

_____. *The Voyage of the Frog.* New York: Orchard, 1989.
   David takes the sailboat he has inherited out to sea to scatter his uncle's ashes. A storm forces him to survive with meager supplies.

Roth, Arthur. *Avalanche.* New York: Scholastic, 1979.
   Buried in an avalanche while cross-country skiing, Chris confronts the events leading up to his predicament while struggling to survive.

Ruckman, Ivy. *Night of the Twisters.* New York: Harper & Row, 1986.
   Inspired by true events in Nebraska, this is the story of Dan Hatch who desperately strives to save his baby brother during a series of tornadoes.

_____. *No Way Out.* New York: HarperCollins, 1988.
   Amy, her boyfriend, her brother, and several friends are hiking in the Zion Narrows when a flash flood threatens their lives.

Sender, Ruth Minsky. *The Cage.* New York: Bantam, 1986.
> Riva helps her brothers survive in the Lodz ghetto, but then is separated and deported to Auschwitz in this true story of faith and courage.

Speare, Elizabeth George. *The Sign of the Beaver.* New York: Dell, 1983.
> Matt is left alone in the Maine wilderness but is befriended by an Indian chief and his grandson, Attean. When his family fails to return, Matt must decide between trying to survive alone in the hope that his family will return or moving on with his new friends.

Sperry, Armstrong. *Call It Courage.* New York: Collier, 1940.
> Mafatu fears the sea because it killed his mother. Finally he decides to face his fears, earning the meaning of his name, Stout Heart.

Taylor, Theodore. *The Cay.* New York: Avon, 1969.
> Young Phillip and a West Indian, Timothy, are castaways on a Caribbean island. Phillip learns many lessons about people, prejudice, and survival.

READING ACTIVITIES

1. *Decision Rating.* As you read your book, keep a list of the decisions the main character makes throughout the story on one side of a piece of paper. On the other side of the paper, rate the decisions on a 1 to 5 scale, with 1 indicating a poor decision and 5 indicating a good decision. When you have finished the book, rate the decisions again in a different colored pen. Does the outcome of the book change your perceptions of the effects of the character's decisions? Give your character an overall rating regarding decision-making abilities.

2. *Problem Solving.* Characters in survival stories usually have many problems to solve. Prepare a chart that describes the problems, the character's action or solution, and alternative actions or solutions. Your chart might look like this example:

Character's Problem	Character's Action	Alternative Action

3. *Setting Descriptors.* Think about the setting in the book and create a list of descriptors or quotations that make the setting especially vivid. Be sure to record the page numbers where you found these descriptors. When you finish the book, place asteriks by those descriptors that are critical to the plot and influence the outcome of the story.

4. *Plot Graph.* Create a plot graph that rates the main events of the story. List each main event across the bottom of the page and then create a bar graph by rating each event from 1 to 10 with 10 the most exciting. (From *Novel Strategies for Young Adults* by Donita Covey. Englewood, Colo: Teacher Ideas Press, 1992, 38.)

*5. *Timeline.* Keep a detailed timeline of events as your novel evolves. Create a method that demonstrates the importance of each event on the timeline. This could include highlighting key events with a different color or any other method you devise. Your timeline should be a fully developed representation of the unfolding of the novel.

6. Create your own activity and have it approved by your teacher.

LISTENING ACTIVITIES

Note: For each activity, you will need one or more partners. Complete each activity by evaluating and summarizing the effectiveness of the process with your partner. Then write a short paragraph about your conclusions.

1. *Radio Reading.* Form a group with five other students. Each student can be reading a different book. Schedule five meetings during which you will take turns reading aloud a passage from your book that you have practiced reading. During each session, one student reads the prepared passage aloud. The listeners give a quick summary of the reading. If the summary includes misinformation or ambiguities, the reader rereads pertinent sections to clarify the reading.

2. *Paired Reading.* This process is similar to radio reading. Find one other student reading the same book as you. Schedule daily sessions during which one of you reads aloud for at least 10 minutes. The other person then summarizes the reading, and the reader clarifies the material as necessary. The next day, reverse the roles, so the reader becomes the listener. The remainder of the reading can be done silently.

3. *Paired Questioning.* Find one other student reading the same book as you, or ask a relative or friend to help you. Have your partner read a chapter aloud. While you are listening, jot down a series of questions that represent the most important points of the book. Ask your partner the questions. Together, evaluate

how effectively the questions represented the events in that chapter. Repeat this process at least four times with other chapters.

4. *Paired Notetaking.* Find one other student reading the same book as you, or ask a relative or friend to help you. Have your partner read a chapter aloud. While you are listening, jot down words or phrases that are important to the story. Use your list to create a graphic representation of that chapter's sequence. Repeat this process at least four times with other chapters.

5. *Partner Read-Aloud.* Find another student who will tape-record a chapter of your novel in exchange for you doing the same. Listen to the tape. Then read the chapter silently. Evaluate how effective each process was for comprehension: reading aloud, listening, or reading silently.

6. Create your own activity and have it approved by your teacher.

VOCABULARY ACTIVITIES

1. *Emotions.* Keep a log of all the words that describe the emotions of the main character in your novel. Be sure to add to it daily. At the end of the book, review the list. Do you see any patterns or changes over the course of the novel? Write a paragraph describing any observations you can make.

2. *Structured Overview.* As you read, keep a list of key words or concepts from your novel. When you are finished, arrange them in a structured overview using the following example as a model.

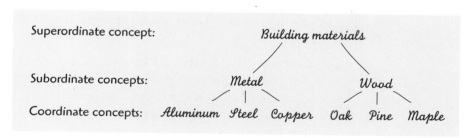

Superordinate concept:	*Building materials*	
Subordinate concepts:	*Metal*	*Wood*
Coordinate concepts:	*Aluminum Steel Copper*	*Oak Pine Maple*

3. *Semantic Feature Analysis.* As you read your novel, complete an analysis of the characters. List the characters on the left side of the grid. Add characteristics across the top as you read. When completed, write a paragraph with any observations you have about the characters and their attributes. This is not an appropriate activity for a novel that has only one main character. The following example is partially completed for "Cinderella." An alternative application is to use the same process with settings and their attributes.

	Attractive	Ugly	Wise	Stupid
Cinderella	+	−	+	−
Stepmother	−	+	−	+
Stepsisters	−	+	−	+
Prince	+	−	+	−

*4. *Paragraph Rewrites.* Find a minimum of three passages in your novel that are especially eloquent. Rewrite the passage using simple language. Read all versions aloud to another student or adult. Write a short paragraph with your observations regarding the process of creating well-written prose.

5. *Venn Diagram.* Create a Venn diagram that compares the likenesses and differences between two books you have read. Think about the characters, settings, problems, emotions, events, and so forth.

6. Create your own activity and have it approved by your teacher.

INTERPRETATION ACTIVITIES

*1. *Bag It.* Collect a variety of artifacts that represent the book you are reading. Put the items in a bag and challenge a friend to guess the book based on the items in the bag.

2. *Literature Report Card.* Create a report card that assesses at least two characters' traits. For example, the subjects could include bravery, problem solving, compassion, or thoughtfulness. Each subject should have a grade assigned. Be sure to include a comments section and write a brief narrative on the character's overall performance.

3. *Journey.* Most of the survival novels involve a journey. Make a word map of the journey that the main character took. Add "signposts" along the way that indicate challenges the character met. Then indicate the consequences of the choices the character made.

4. *Personality Comparison.* Make a comparison chart for the positive and negative personality characteristics of the main character. The following example is based on "Little Red Riding Hood."

Little Red Riding Hood	
Positive	Negative
Independent	Willful
Adventurous	Disobedient
Courageous	Foolish
Thoughtful	Careless

5. *Qualities of a Hero.* Think about what qualities are found in someone who is a hero. Then think about the main character in your story. In what ways is the main character a hero? List the qualities you choose on the left side of a chart and your evidence from the story on the right side of the chart. (From *Novel Strategies for Young Adults* by Donita Covey. Englewood, Colo: Teacher Ideas Press, 1992, 38.)

Qualities of a Hero	Evidence

6. Create your own activity and have it approved by your teacher.

WRITING ACTIVITIES

1. *Research.* Use the library to research the setting of your novel. Prepare a minimum of one typed page that describes information pertinent to the setting.

2. *Résumé.* Imagine a job that the main character in your novel might apply for and make a résumé that could be taken to an interview. Include the character's name, address, phone number, education, skills, experiences, hobbies, and references.

3. *Notebook.* While you read your novel, keep a notebook that you think the main character would find useful. You might record observations, facts, important lessons, memoirs, and so forth.

*4. *Travel Brochure.* Create a detailed travel brochure that describes the setting of the novel. Include enough information from the book so that the reader will be able to make an informed decision about visiting there.

5. *Story Map.* Create a story map that summarizes your novel. A frame for a story map may look like the following examples with more space allowed for your answers. You should customize your story map to fit your novel.

Story Map

Title of Book: _____

Setting(s): _____

Character(s): _____

Problem(s): _____

Goal: _____

    Event 1 _____

    Event 2 _____

    Event 3 _____

    Event 4 _____

Resolution: _____

Story Map (Alternative version)

Title of Book: _____

Setting(s): _____

Character(s): _____

Problem(s): _____

Action: _____

Outcome: _____

6. Create your own activity and have it approved by your teacher.

SPEAKING ACTIVITIES

*1. *News Story.* Write a news story based on the culminating event in the book you are reading. Prepare to read it to the class as a 60-second news piece that succinctly captures the essence of this event.

2. *Sharing the Best.* As you read, mark the passages that you believe represent the best writing in the book. Prepare a taped book talk that gives a brief overview of the book and includes passages you have selected for reading aloud.

3. *Partner Comparison.* Find a student who is reading a different book. Discuss your books and make lists of similarities and differences. Present a short oral report to the teacher regarding your findings.

*4. *Interview.* Find an adult who has had an experience similar to that in your book (such as seeing the results of a tornado or flood) or who lived during the time period of your book. Prepare a minimum of 10 questions to ask the adult. Tape-record the interview and share it with the class.

5. *Tape.* Your goal is to prepare a tape recording that will convince other students to read this book. Prepare a short introduction that describes the book, including the title, author, setting, and characters. Then tape-record the first chapter of your book, reading it as expressively as possible. Before preparing this tape, listen to commercially prepared tapes available from the library.

6. Create your own activity and have it approved by your teacher.

ARTS ACTIVITIES

*1. *Word Theater.* Find a student who has read the same book as you. You should each select a variety of words from your reading that can be pantomimed as in Charades. Trade your lists and take turns dramatizing them for a group of players.

*2. *Menu and Meal.* Create a menu representative of the book and prepare the foods included. Bring the meal to class for students to sample.

3. *Map.* Create a detailed map that represents the setting(s) of the book you have read. Label all the important places, perhaps including key events that occurred at those sites. Include a legend.

4. *Photo Album.* Create a photo album that represents the important events in the main character's life. You may draw the pictures, use pictures from magazines,

or enlist help from other students to act out scenes you photograph. Label and date each photo in the album.

*5. *Musical Setting.* Create a tape of music to play as the background to a chapter in your book. The music can be played on any instrument, sung, clapped, or rapped, but must be original. Practice your presentation before sharing it so that the music supports the narrative.

6. Create your own activity and have it approved by your teacher.

CHALLENGE ACTIVITIES

1. *Semantic Feature Analysis.* Create a semantic feature analysis that compares a minimum of three books. It should be a detailed representation of the settings, characters, or events in each book.

*2. *Script.* Select at least one chapter that can be revised into a readers theatre script. (Obtain examples from your teacher.) When you have completed the script, find several other students who will rehearse and present it to the class.

3. *Book on Tape.* Tape-record your entire book for use in the school library or for use by blind students. Read clearly and expressively.

4. *Hero Chart.* Refer to the "Qualities of a Hero" activity in the Interpretation section. Create a chart that compares the qualities of all the heroes in all the books you read. After completing the chart, write a summary of the common characteristics found in the books.

5. *Survival Chart.* Prepare a chart that details all the survival items used by the main characters in all the books you read. Your chart could be organized like the following example.

Hatchet	Avalanche	Trouble River	No Way Out
Brian	Chris	Dewey	Amy
Items:	Items:	Items:	Items:

6. Create your own activity and have it approved by your teacher.

SHARING ACTIVITIES

Note: The following sharing activities are a repetition of the starred items in the preceding lists. Choose one to share with the class. You may have already completed the activity, or it may be an additional activity.

1. *Timeline.* Keep a detailed timeline of events as your novel evolves. Create a method that demonstrates the importance of each event on the timeline. This could include highlighting key events with a different color or any other method you devise. Your timeline should be a fully developed representation of the unfolding of the novel.

2. *Paragraph Rewrites.* Find a minimum of three passages in your novel that are especially eloquent. Rewrite the passage using simple language. Read all versions aloud to another student or adult. Write a short paragraph with your observations regarding the process of creating well-written prose.

3. *Bag It.* Collect a variety of artifacts that represent the book you are reading. Put the items in a bag and challenge a friend to guess the book based on the items in the bag.

4. *Travel Brochure.* Create a detailed travel brochure that describes the setting of the novel. Include enough information from the book so that the reader will be able to make an informed decision about visiting there.

5. *News Story.* Write a news story based on the culminating event in the book you are reading. Prepare to read it to the class as a 60-second news piece that succinctly captures the essence of this event.

6. *Interview.* Find an adult who has had an experience similar to that in your book (such as seeing the results of a tornado or flood) or who lived during the time period of your book. Prepare a minimum of 10 questions to ask the adult. Tape-record the interview and share it with the class.

7. *Word Theater.* Find a student who has read the same book as you. You should each select a variety of words from your reading that can be pantomimed as in Charades. Trade your lists and take turns dramatizing them for a group of players.

8. *Menu and Meal.* Create a menu representative of the book and prepare the foods included. Bring the meal to class for students to sample.

9. *Musical Setting.* Create a tape of music to play as the background to a chapter in your book. The music can be played on any instrument, sung, clapped, or rapped, but must be original. Practice your presentation before sharing it so that the music supports the narrative.

10. *Script.* Select at least one chapter that can be revised into a readers theatre script. (Obtain examples from your teacher.) When you have completed the script, find several other students who will rehearse and present it to the class.

11. Create your own activity and have it approved by your teacher.

PART FOUR

TEACHER AND STUDENT LITERATURE CONTRACT EVALUATIONS

Teacher Literature Contract Evaluation

Did students meet the objectives of the unit? _____

_____

Were the essential questions answered adequately? _____

_____

Were the objectives and essential questions appropriate for the unit? _____

_____

Were the student directions appropriate? _____

_____

Does the contract page need revisions? _____

_____

Did the reading list allow for adequate choices? _____

_____

Did students understand the activities? _____

_____

Which activities should be eliminated or added? _____

_____

Did students complete the activities in a timely fashion? _____

_____

Were the challenge activities adequately challenging? _____

_____

Were the sharing activities appropriate for individuals and the group? _____

_____

Was six weeks adequate for the unit? _____

_____

What changes should be made for the next time? _____

_____

Additional comments: _____

Student Literature Contract Evaluation

Name: _____

Books you read:

Book 1 _____

Book 2 _____

Book 3 _____

Book 4 _____

Directions: Rate the activities in each category on a scale from 1 to 5, with 5 indicating your highest level of interest.

Reading activities _____

Listening activities _____

Vocabulary activities _____

Interpretation activities _____

Writing activities _____

Speaking activities _____

Arts activities _____

Challenge activities _____

Sharing activities _____

OTHER INFORMATION

Closure Activities

1. Complete all sharing activities.

2. Review the opening web. Create a new one that reflects additional information.

3. Repeat the backpack activity. Compare how the contents change after reading the books.

4. Discuss the similarities of the literature. Draw out generalizations about the characters, settings, and events of the examples of survival literature.

5. Collect input on the success of the literature unit using the evaluation forms. Ask for recommendations on how to improve the unit next time.

Appendix B: Research Reports

Research reports link the curriculum directly to the library. Designed for intermediate and middle school students, this method of research can be adapted for capable primary students. Research reports can also be used to temporarily replace or supplement textbooks.

PLANNING THE RESEARCH PROJECT

When planning a research unit, your first stop should be the library. School libraries often have a variety of materials; by investigating available materials before planning your unit, you can save time by letting the materials help shape your plans. Don't automatically exclude older materials, unless having current information is necessary. Ask for films, filmstrips, videos, CD-ROMs, books, magazines, articles—anything related to your unit.

With the current trend to cut back funding in many school and public libraries, the classroom teacher may have to operate without much support. Be sure to obtain whatever support is available while you are planning. Librarians or paraprofessionals who know what you're working on can keep an eye out for materials for you. If you have a full-time librarian who will work with you, solicit collaboration from the very start. Also, make a call to your professional library. The librarian in the district's library may gather a basket of books and materials and send them directly to your classroom through school mail.

If you have no support, spend time determining whether students can complete the project successfully. You will save time and frustration by determining the availability of resources before you introduce the subject or project. You might discover that another class is working on the same topic, which will deplete available resources.

Look for adult resources by sending a letter home about your project. Parents may have reference materials to loan or may know of speakers.

THE RESEARCH PROCESS

The research tip sheet (Figure B.1) provides step-by-step guidance for the students. It may seem difficult for upper primary; however, it is assumed that any grade-level teacher will thoroughly introduce and discuss the information. The research tip sheet provides you and students with guidance and a permanent record of the process, and you avoid having to repeat expectations. This process also builds student accountability and enables parents to help their children at home. Spend time thoroughly discussing the research tip sheet, and students will be off to an excellent start.

The research report worksheet (Figure B.2) on page 540 replaces the standard bibliography, yet provides practice in recording bibliographic information. The research worksheets function like the more traditional note card, and subsequent teaching of the bibliography is a natural extension.

FIGURE B.1
Student Research
Tip Sheet

How to Fill Out the Research Report Worksheet

1. Complete the blanks for topic, name, and date on every page.
2. Put the name of the book, magazine, or encyclopedia in the blank for "title of resource."
3. Mark which type of resource it is. If it isn't one of these resources, write what it is in the blank after "other."
4. Books usually have an author. Encyclopedias or magazines often have editors. If a book has both, include both.
5. The publisher is the company that created the book. Its name is usually on the page with the title and the author's name. It often looks something like this: A. B. Smith & Co.
6. The place of publication is usually a city's name and is on the same page as the publisher. If there are several cities listed, use the first city in the list.
7. The date is harder to find. It may be on the same page with the publisher and city or on another page in small print. Scan the page for numbers. The word *copyright* is often nearby.
8. Once you have found some facts you want to remember, write them in the information section. Use your own words. Often, you don't need all that the author says anyway. If you do copy from the book, put the words in quotation marks.
9. Write the page or pages where you found the information. This saves time if you need to go back to it later. The page number is necessary if you include a quote.

FIGURE B.2
Student Research
Report Worksheet

Research Report Worksheet

Name: _____ Date: _____

Topic: _____

_____

_____

Title of resource: _____

Book? _____ Magazine? _____ Other? _____

Encyclopedia?_____ If yes, what volume number is it? _____

Author or editor: _____

Publisher: _____

Place of publication: _____ Date: _____

Information: _____

In general, follow the outline below for teaching research reports, adapting the list as appropriate.

RESEARCH REPORT OUTLINE

Teacher Planning

1. Choose a topic. It could be on a subject, seasonal topic, special event, or holiday.

2. Investigate resources in the school library and ascertain whether there are adequate materials.

3. Order additional resources from professional or public libraries.

4. Select a film, filmstrip, or other audiovisual material for your introduction, if appropriate.

5. Determine the requirements of the project. A short report is appropriate for a student's first experience with research. Decide whether students can collaborate. How many resources do you want them to consult? (For students new to research, consider limiting resource requirements to one encyclopedia and one nonfiction book.) Students get uneasy about new learning experiences; work out plans in advance and answer all questions thoroughly.

6. Schedule work sessions in the library.

7. Prepare a letter to send home with students describing the project, asking for resources and recommendations for speakers. Include requirements, deadlines, and other pertinent information.

TEACHING THE RESEARCH REPORT TO YOUR STUDENTS

1. Introduce the topic to the class.

2. Brainstorm components of the topic. Use a web or a similar activity to show topical connections. Ask students what they know and what they want to know about the subject, perhaps using the K-W-L (see Chapter 11).

3. Make assignments or allow for topic selection.

4. Provide the research report outline (Figure B.3) and discuss what types of questions are appropriate for the report, avoiding questions that can be answered in one word. There are 10 blanks for questions on the reproducible. Assign only what is reasonable for your group. Have students fill in the due date for the report.

5. Give students time to generate questions. They might collaborate with others, exchanging lists, or preparing webs.

FIGURE B.3
Research Report
Outline

Research Report Outline

Name: _____ Date: _____

Topic: _____ Due Date: _____

Questions about my topic:

1 _____

2. _____

3. _____

4. _____

5. _____

6. _____

7. _____

8. _____

9. _____

10. _____

Ask your teacher to check your questions before you begin your research.

6. Review questions before moving on. Some questions will be too broad and will need revision. Others will be obvious, brief, or unnecessary. Remind students that they may not find answers to all their questions and that they may need to revise or create new ones.

7. Hand out the research tip sheet (Figure B.1) and the research report worksheet (Figure B.2) and review the steps carefully. Have students record the due date on the research tip sheet.

8. Take the class to the library and provide an overview of references, the nonfiction section, and other resources.

9. Guide students through the scheduled work periods in the library. Once they have begun their research and are familiar with the resources, they will retrieve resources and work with minimal help.

10. Provide support as needed throughout their research.

11. When students are nearing completion of their research, hand out the guide sheet, "How to Write Your Report" (Figure B.4), and discuss it in detail. Make certain that students understand that they are to rewrite the information they have collected into an organized report. Amplify certain points based on the needs of your group.

12. When the deadline arrives, collect and evaluate papers and worksheets. Three grades can be assigned: content, research based on the attached sheets, and mechanics such as punctuation and spelling. Skim the research sheets, checking for completion of the required information. Vary evaluation based on student needs.

13. Plan a sharing time. Have students read their reports aloud, or ask permission to share portions of their work. The collective knowledge is the purpose of the report; therefore, sharing is an important step.

14. Gather copies of the papers into a central folder and bind or staple them, making them available for reference. (Make these copies before adding evaluative comments.)

FIGURE B.4
Student
Guide Sheet

How to Write Your Research Report

Once you have completed several research worksheets, you have done the hardest part of the report. You are now ready to organize and prepare to write your report. Follow these directions.

1. Read through your worksheets. Check for publication information, page numbers, spelling, and so forth. Go back to your sources if you have left out anything.
2. Check to see if you answered all your questions. If you didn't, try again, find more resources, or ask different questions.
3. Spread out your papers and decide on the order of your report. Number the pages or paragraphs in the order you want them to appear. If you need to reorganize paragraphs, use a colored pencil to number the paragraphs.
4. Read through the numbered pages or paragraphs in order. Decide if you have enough information and if it makes sense.
5. If you need more material, go back to the library and use more research worksheets to record the information.
6. Write your report using the research sheets as your guide. Put quotation marks around anything you have copied. **Do not** write the information from one source, followed by information from another source. Your information should be grouped by the questions or topic of the paragraph, not by the sources you used.
7. Reread your paper, checking for spelling, punctuation, and indentation of paragraphs. Make sure your writing makes sense.
8. Have a friend read and check your paper.
9. Make changes.
10. Gather together all your research worksheets.
11. Be sure your name is on every page.
12. Turn in your report with your outline and research worksheets stapled or clipped together.

Research report process adapted from *Creating and Managing the Literate Classroom* by Suzanne I. Barchers (Englewood, Colo: Teacher Ideas Press, 1989) 86–92.

Appendix C: Multicultural Literature

Note: These books were selected from published, critical reviews and subsequently reviewed by the author.

AFRICAN LITERATURE

Aardema, Verna. *Bringing the Rain to Kapiti Plain: A Nandi Tale.* Illustrated by Beatriz Vidal. New York: Dial Books for Young Readers, 1981. Grades kindergarten and up.
   Ki-pat uses an eagle feather for an arrow that pierces the clouds, bringing rain to parched Kapiti Plain.

_____. *Traveling to Tondo: A Tale of the Nkundo of Zaire.* Illustrated by Will Hillenbrand. New York: Alfred A. Knopf, 1991. Grades 1 and up.
   Bowane, a civet cat, takes too long to return to his intended, losing her to another cat. The brief glossary and pronunciation guide are especially useful.

_____. *What's So Funny, Ketu? A Nuer Tale.* Illustrated by Marc Brown. New York: Dial , 1982. Grades kindergarten and up.
   A snake rewards Ketu's kindness with a secret magical gift, the ability to hear the animals' thoughts, that threatens everything Ketu loves.

_____. *Who's in Rabbit's House?* Illustrated by Leo and Diane Dillon. New York: Dial , 1977. Grades 1 and up.
   This Masai tale of Rabbit, who is prevented from entering his house by the Long One, is perfect for dramatic interpretation.

_____. *Why Mosquitoes Buzz in People's Ears.* Illustrated by Leo and Diane Dillon. New York: Scholastic, 1975. Grades 2 and up.
   This West African cumulative tale explains why mosquitoes are swatted.

Alexander, Lloyd. *The Fortune-Tellers.* Illustrated by Trina Schart Hyman. New York: Dutton, 1992. Grades kindergarten and up.

Set in Cameroon, a carpenter learns he will marry his true love and be happy if he avoids misery.

Appiah, Sonia. *Amoko and Efua Bear.* Illustrated by Carol Eastmon. New York: Macmillan, 1988. Grades preschool and up.
  Amoko, a 5-year-old girl who lives in Ghana, temporarily loses her beloved teddy bear.

Bryan, Ashley. *Beat the Story-Drum, Pum-Pum.* New York: Atheneum, 1980. Grades 1 and up.
  Five African tales are illustrated with striking woodcuts.

Case, Diane. *Love, David.* Illustrated by Dan Andreason. New York: Lodestar, 1991. Grades 4 and up.
  The harsh realities of life in South Africa are portrayed through the day-to-day lives of Ann and her beloved half-brother, David.

Chocolate, Debbi. *Kente Colors.* Illustrated by John Ward. New York: Walker, 1996. Grades preschool and up.
  Bright illustrations celebrate the Kente colors.

Dee, Ruby. *Tower to Heaven.* Illustrated by Jennifer Bent. New York: Henry Holt, 1991. Grades 1 and up.
  Onyankopon, the sky god, gets tired of Yaa and returns to the sky. When the villagers build a tower to heaven out of mortars, it is one mortar short.

Feelings, Muriel. *Jambo Means Hello: Swahili Alphabet Book.* Illustrated by Tom Feelings. New York: Dial Books for Young Readers, 1974. Grades 1 and up.
  The simple text explains the letters of the Swahili alphabet.

_____. *Moja Means One: Swahili Counting Book.* Illustrated by Tom Feelings. New York: Dial, 1971. Grades preschool and up.
  Children not only learn to count in Swahili, they also explore East African life.

Grifalconi, Ann. *Darkness and the Butterfly.* Boston: Little, Brown, 1987. Grades kindergarten and up.
  Osa's fear of the dark is diminished when the Wise Woman tells her that the butterfly flies in the dark.

_____. *The Village of Round and Square Houses.* Boston: Little, Brown, 1986. Grades kindergarten and up.
  A child relates why the village has round houses for women and square houses for men. Cameroon.

Isadora, Rachel. *The Crossroads.* New York: Greenwillow, 1991. Grades 1 and up.

In South Africa, everyone rejoices when the fathers return from the mines.

_____. *Over the Green Hills.* New York: Greenwillow, 1992. Grades kindergarten and up.
As Zolani and his mother cross the Transkei countryside, the reader learns about South Africa.

Lewin, Hugh. *Jafta—The Journey.* Illustrated by Lisa Kopper. Minneapolis, Minn.: Carolrhoda, 1984. Grades preschool and up.
Jafta journeys from his rural South African village to the town where his father works in the factory.

Mollel, Tololwa M. *The Orphan Boy.* Illustrated by Paul Morin. New York: Clarion, 1990. Grades 2 and up.
In this African story, Venus is embodied in a young boy who comes to earth to help an old man.

AFRICAN-AMERICAN LITERATURE

Adler, David A. *Martin Luther King, Jr.: Free at Last.* Illustrated by Robert Casilla. New York: Holiday House, 1986. Grades 2 and up.
Black-and-white drawings highlight the story of King's life.

Adoff, Arnold. *Black Is Brown Is Tan.* Illustrated by Emily Arnold McCully. New York: Harper & Row, 1973. Grades preschool and up.
A story poem about a family with black, tan, brown, and white members.

_____. *Malcolm X.* Illustrated by John Wilson. New York: Thomas Y. Crowell, 1970. Grades 2 and up.
The story of Malcolm X's difficult life and death is told simply but bluntly.

Barrett, Joyce Durham. *Willie's Not the Hugging Kind.* Illustrated by Pat Cummings. New York: Harper & Row, 1989. Grades kindergarten and up.
Willie realizes that everyone benefits from hugs.

Caines, Jeannette. *I Need a Lunch Box.* Illustrated by Pat Cummings. New York: Harper & Row, 1988. Grades kindergarten and up.
When Doris gets shoes, crayons, and a lunch box for school, her little brother yearns for his own lunch box.

Collier, James Lincoln, and Christopher Collier. *Jump Ship to Freedom.* New York: Delacorte Press, 1981. Grades 4 and up.
Daniel tries to claim his rights to freedom after his father dies in the Revolution, and is forced on a ship bound for the West Indies and slavery.

_____. *War Comes to Willy Freeman*. New York: Dell, 1983. Grades 4 and up.
  Willy disguises herself as a boy after her father is killed by the Redcoats and her mother is taken prisoner.

Fields, Julia. *The Green Lion of Zion Street*. Illustrated by Jerry Pinkney. New York: Margaret K. McElderry, 1988. Grades 1 and up.
  Children who tire of waiting for the bus in the fog begin to explore, only to be scared by a lion that turns out to be stone.

Flourney, Valerie. *The Patchwork Quilt*. Illustrated by Jerry Pinkney. New York: Dial Books for Young Readers, 1985. Grades kindergarten and up.
  When grandmother becomes ill, Tanya decides to help finish the quilt.

Gray, Nigel. *A Balloon for Grandad*. Illustrated by Jane Ray. New York: Orchard, 1988. Grades preschool and up.
  When Sam's balloon floats away, he hopes it will fly to Grandad Abdulla's home across the sea.

Greene, Bette. *Get On Out of Here, Philip Hall*. New York: Dial, 1981. Grades 4 and up.
  Beth Lambert is crushed when Philip Hall wins a coveted award, but she recovers with style.

_____. *Philip Hall Likes Me. I Reckon Maybe*. New York: Dial, 1974. Grades 4 and up.
  Beth Lambert is the irrepressible heroine of this story of a young African-American girl and her up-and-down relationship with Philip Hall.

Greenfield, Eloise. *Grandpa's Face*. Illustrated by Floyd Cooper. New York: Philomel, 1988. Grades 1 and up.
  Tamika, who loves her grandpa's expressive face, worries after seeing his tight mouth and cold eyes when he is rehearsing for a play.

_____. *Honey, I Love and Other Love Poems*. Illustrated by Diane and Leo Dillon. New York: HarperCollins, 1978. Grades 1 and up.
  A child shares love through 16 poems.

_____. *Nathaniel Talking*. Illustrated by Jan Spivey Gilchrist. New York: Black Butterfly Children's Books, 1990. Grades kindergarten and up.
  Nathaniel's poems reveal his life and thoughts.

_____. *Night on Neighborhood Street*. Illustrated by Jan Spivey Gilchrist. New York: Dial Books for Young Readers, 1991. Grades 1 and up.
  The warmth of a neighborhood is illustrated through poetry.

_____. *Paul Robeson*. Illustrated by George Ford. New York: Thomas Y. Crowell, 1975. Grades 1 and up.
  Explores Paul Robeson as an actor, singer, and activist.

_____. *Rosa Parks.* Illustrated by Eric Marlow. New York: Thomas Y. Crowell, 1973. Grades 1 and up.
    This is an easy-to-read account of Rosa Parks's life.

Hale, Sarah Josepha. *Mary Had a Little Lamb.* New York: Scholastic, 1990. Grades preschool and up.
    Mary, a young African-American girl, and her lamb are lovingly photographed in this recreation of the famous poem.

Hamilton, Virginia. *Cousins.* New York: Philomel, 1990. Grades 3 and up.
    Cammy dislikes her "perfect" cousin, Patty Ann, but when tragedy strikes, Cammy must cope with her emotions and fears.

_____. *The House of Dies Drear.* New York: Macmillan, 1968. Grades 4 and up.
    This mysterious house, with its underground passages, tales of murder, and history with the Underground Railroad, holds danger for the Small family.

_____. *M. C. Higgins, the Great.* New York: Macmillan, 1974. Grades 5 and up.
    Mayo Cornelius Higgins observes and dreams from a 40-foot pole hovering over Sarah's Mountain and his home.

_____. *The People Could Fly: American Black Folktales.* New York: Alfred A. Knopf, 1985. Grades 4 and up.
    This collection includes tales of animals, the supernatural, freedom, and of the real, the extravagant, and the fanciful.

_____. *The Planet of Junior Brown.* New York: Macmillan, 1971. Grades 5 and up.
    Instead of attending classes, Junior Brown and his friend Buddy Clark hide out in the cellar of their school—until they are caught.

_____. *Zeely.* New York: Macmillan, 1967. Grades 3 and up.
    Eleven-year-old Geeder Perry finds a picture of an African queen who looks like Zeely and decides Zeely must also be a queen.

Hoffman, Mary. *Amazing Grace.* Illustrated by Caroline Bench. New York: Dial Books for Young Readers, 1991. Grades kindergarten and up.
    Grace loves to act out stories. When she is told she can't play Peter in *Peter Pan* because she is a girl and African-American, she proves she can be anything she wants to be.

Hooks, William H. *The Ballad of Belle Dorcas.* Illustrated by Brian Pinkney. New York: Alfred A. Knopf, 1990. Grades 3 and up.
    Belle Dorcas, a free-issue mixed woman, consults a conjure woman to help her keep her man; the results are unexpected.

Howard, Elizabeth Fitzgerald. *Chita's Christmas Tree.* Illustrated by Floyd Cooper. New York: Bradbury Press, 1989. Grades preschool and up.

Rich illustrations and lilting prose describe Chita's Christmas season.

Johnson, Angela. *Tell Me a Story, Mama.* Illustrated by David Soman. New York: Orchard, 1989. Grades preschool and up.

A mother and child share stories of the past.

Johnson, Dolores. *What Will Mommy Do When I'm at School?* New York: Macmillan, 1990. Grades preschool and up.

When a little girl worries how her mother will manage without her, her mother tells her she is beginning a new job.

Johnson, Herschel. *A Visit to the Country.* Illustrated by Romare Bearden. New York: Harper & Row, 1989. Grades preschool and up.

Mike and his grandpa enjoy the chickens, passing trains, and their care of a baby bird.

Lester, Julius. *The Tales of Uncle Remus: The Adventures of Brer Rabbit.* New York: Dial, 1987. Grades 3 and up.

Forty-eight tales are highlighted with color and black-and-white illustrations.

Mathis, Sharon Bell. *The Hundred Penny Box.* Illustrated by Diane and Leo Dillon. New York: Viking Penguin, 1975. Grades 1 and up.

As Great-Great Aunt Dew counts the hundred pennies that represent her life, she shares her stories with Michael.

McKissack, Patricia. *Mirandy and Brother Wind.* Illustrated by Jerry Pinkney. New York: Alfred A. Knopf, 1988. Grades 1 and up.

Mirandy consults with a conjure woman in her efforts to capture Brother Wind for her partner at the cakewalk.

———. *Nettie Jo's Friends.* Illustrated by Scott Cook. New York: Alfred A. Knopf, 1989. Grades 1 and up.

Nettie Jo helps Miz Rabbit, Fox, and Panther, who in turn help her find a sewing needle to make a new dress for her doll.

Monjo, F. N. *The Drinking Gourd.* Illustrated by Fred Brenner. New York: Harper & Row, 1970. Grades 1 and up.

This is an easy-to-read account of escaping slaves before the Civil War.

Petry, Ann. *Tituba of Salem Village.* New York: Thomas Y. Crowell, 1964. Grades 5 and up.

Petry tells the story of Tituba, one of the first three "witches" condemned during the Salem witch trials.

Ringgold, Faith. *Tar Beach.* New York: Crown, 1991. Grades kindergarten and up.

Using a story quilt form, Ringgold describes when the stars fall around a little girl who flies over Harlem, claiming all she sees for herself.

Saller, Carol. *The Bridge Dancers.* Illustrated by Gerald Talifero. Minneapolis, Minn.: Carolrhoda, 1991. Grades 3 and up.

Maisie is afraid of the bridge from the mountain, but when her sister Callie is hurt, she must face her fears.

Sanfield, Steve. *A Natural Man: The True Story of John Henry.* Boston: David R. Godine, 1986. Grades 2 and up.

John Henry is portrayed as the legendary steel driver.

San Souci, Robert D. *The Talking Eggs.* Illustrated by Jerry Pinkney. New York: Dial Books for Young Readers, 1989. Grades kindergarten and up.

This adaptation of a Creole folktale is of two sisters, one of whom is rewarded for her kindness.

Schroeder, Alan. *Ragtime Tumpie.* Illustrated by Bernie Fuchs. Boston: Little, Brown, 1989. Grades 1 and up.

It's the summer of 1915 in St. Louis, and Tumpie, who grows up to be the legendary Josephine Baker, can only think about dancing.

Slote, Alfred. *Finding Buck McHenry.* New York: HarperCollins, 1991. Grades 4 and up.

In need of a baseball coach for his team, Jason decides that the school custodian must be Mack Henry, a former baseball player.

Smalls-Hector, Irene. *Irene and the Big, Fine Nickel.* Illustrated by Tyrone Geter. Boston: Little, Brown, 1991. Grades 2 and up.

Irene's pleasant day in 1957-era Harlem becomes even more delightful when she finds a nickel that will buy a big raisin bun to share with her three best friends.

Steptoe, John. *Stevie.* New York: Harper & Row, 1969. Grades preschool and up.

Robert thinks his foster brother Stevie is a big pest until Stevie leaves with his parents.

Taylor, Mildred. *The Gold Cadillac.* Illustrated by Michael Hays. New York: Dial Books for Young Readers, 1987. Grades 3 and up.

When father brings home a new Cadillac, the family is nearly torn apart by the trouble that comes with it.

_____. *Let the Circle Be Unbroken.* New York: Dial, 1981. Grades 5 and up.

In this sequel to *Roll of Thunder, Hear My Cry*, the Logan family copes with falling cotton prices, the Depression, and prejudice.

_____. *Roll of Thunder, Hear My Cry.* New York: Dial, 1976. Grades 5 and up.

Cassie courageously copes with prejudice against African-Americans and with the hardships of the Depression.

Wahl, Jan. *Tailypo!* Illustrated by Wil Clay. New York: Henry Holt, 1991. Grades preschool and up.

A creature torments an old man who ate its tail. Deliciously scary with wonderful illustrations of the Tennessee woods.

Williams, Karen Lynn. *When Africa Was Home.* Illustrated by Floyd Cooper. New York: Orchard, 1991. Grades 1 and up.

Peter, a young white boy, loves living in an African village while his father works there and misses his friends and the country when he must return to America.

Yarbrough, Camille. *The Shimmershine Queens.* New York: G. P. Putnam's, 1989. Grades 5 and up.

Cousin Seatta tells Angie that the "shimmershine feeling" comes when she does her best, but Angie continues to prefer her dreams until a new drama teacher arrives at school.

ASIAN LITERATURE

Barry, Dave, adapter. *The Rajah's Rice: A Mathematical Folktale from India.* Illustrated by Donna Perrone. New York: W. H. Freeman, 1994. Grades 1 and up.

When Chandra saves the Rajah's life, she tricks him into giving her a fortune in rice.

Birdseye, Tom. *A Song of Stars.* New York: Holiday House, 1990. Grades 2 and up.

When Princess Chauchau, a weaver, and Newlang, a herdsman, fall in love, they neglect their work. The Emperor of the Heavens decrees that they will be allowed to meet only on the seventh night of the seventh moon. Asian.

Clément, Claude. *The Painter and the Wild Swans.* Illustrated by Frederic Clément. New York: Dial Books for Young Readers, 1986. Grades 1 and up.

Telling the story through Japanese, English, and exquisite paintings, Clément tells of Teiji, a painter who goes in search of his beloved swans.

Demi. *The Magic Boat.* New York: Henry Holt, 1990. Grades 2 and up.

Chang is rewarded for his unselfish bravery, but greedy Ying tricks Chang into giving him the magic boat. With the help of his many friends, Chang regains his prize. China.

Goldstein, Peggy. *Lóng Is a Dragon: Chinese Writing for Children.* San Francisco: China Books and Periodicals, 1991. Grades 2 and up.

Goldstein introduces 75 Chinese characters.

Ho, Minfong. *The Clay Marble.* New York: Farrar, Straus & Giroux, 1991. Grades 4 and up.

 Dara and her family flee Cambodia for a border refugee camp. When shelling begins along the border, she is separated from her family and must rely on her inner strength to survive.

Hong, Lily Toy. *How the Ox Star Fell from Heaven.* Morton Grove, Ill.: Albert Whitman, 1991. Grades preschool and up.

 When Ox Star garbles the message from the emperor of the Heavens to the hungry people, oxen are sent to earth to labor in the fields. China.

Lobel, Anita. *The Dwarf Giant.* New York: Holiday House, 1991. Grades 1 and up.

 When a dwarf enchants the prince and threatens the kingdom, the princess seeks help from a farmer and his wife. Japan.

Miller, Moira. *Moon Dragon.* New York: Dial Books for Young Readers, 1989. Grades 1 and up.

 When Ling Po brags that he can make a kite that will fly to the moon, he finds he must try to make good on his boast. China.

Paek, Min. *Aekyung's Dream.* San Francisco: Children's Book Press, 1988. Grades 1 and up.

 After a special dream, Aekyung tries harder to master English. This simple story is presented in English and Korean.

Paterson, Katherine. *The Tale of the Mandarin Ducks.* Illustrated by Leo and Diane Dillon. New York: Dutton, 1990. Grades 2 and up.

 After being captured, a drake pines for his mate. Yasuko, the kitchen maid, saves the drake; but she and Shozo face the lord's wrath. Japan.

Pittman, Helena Clare. *The Gift of the Willows.* Minneapolis, Minn.: Carolrhoda, 1988. Grades 3 and up.

 In this beautifully illustrated tale, Yukiyo lives with his wife by the Okayama River, nurturing the willows and yearning for a baby. After their baby's birth, the willows repay Yukiyo's devotion. Japan.

Rodanas, Kristina. *The Story of Wali Dâd.* New York: Lothrop, Lee & Shepard, 1988. Grades 1 and up.

 An old grasscutter in India has his generosity repaid manyfold.

Snyder, Dianne. *The Boy of the Three-Year Nap.* Illustrated by Allen Say. Boston: Houghton Mifflin, 1988. Grades 1 and up.

 Taro, the laziest boy in a Japanese village, uses his wits to gain a better home and a wife, but he cannot stay lazy after his marriage.

Thomson, Peggy. *City Kids in China.* New York: HarperCollins, 1991. Grades 2 and up.

The Chinese city of Changsha is the site for this fascinating glimpse of life in China.

Wang, Rosalind. *The Fourth Question: A Chinese Tale.* Illustrated by Ju-hong Chen. New York: Holiday House, 1991. Grades 2 and up.

When Yee-Lee journeys to ask the wise man why he is hardworking yet poor, three people he meets on the journey have a question as well. Upon Yee-Lee's arrival, he learns he can have only three questions answered and must make a difficult choice.

Wisniewski, David. *The Warrior and the Wise Man.* New York: Lothrop, Lee & Shepard, 1989. Grades 3 and up.

Striking illustrations of cut paper combine with text for this tale of twin brothers of Japan who compete to become emperor.

Xiong, Blia. *Nine-in-One, Grr! Grr!* Illustrated by Nancy Hom. San Francisco: Children's Book Press, 1989. Grades preschool and up.

In this Hmong tale, when Bird hears tiger sing that she'll have nine cubs in a year, Bird tricks her into saying she'll have one cub in nine years.

Yacowitz, Caryn. *The Jade Stone: A Chinese Tale.* Illustrated by Ju-hong Chen. New York: Holiday House, 1992. Grades 1 and up.

Chan Lo risks the Emperor's displeasure by carving jade into a fish instead of a dragon. China.

Yen, Clara. *Why Rat Comes First: A Story of the Chinese Zodiac.* Illustrated by Hideo C. Yoshida. San Francisco: Children's Book Press. Grades 1 and up.

The Jade King invites the animals to become the 12 months' symbols, but the children choose the rat to be the first.

Young, Ed. *Lon Po Po: A Red Riding Hood Story from China.* New York: Philomel, 1989. Grades kindergarten and up.

Clever children outwit the wolf in a variant of this traditional folktale.

ASIAN-AMERICAN LITERATURE

Chang, Heidi. *Elaine, Mary Lewis, and the Frogs.* New York: Crown, 1988. Grades 2 and up.

With some help from a new friend, Elaine Chow adjusts to her new home in Iowa.

Yee, Paul. *Tales from Gold Mountain: Stories of the Chinese in the New World.* Illustrated by Simon Ng. New York: Macmillan, 1989. Grades 4 and up.

These original stories, with a folktale flavor, tell of the struggles of the Chinese who came to North America.

Yep, Laurence. *The Rainbow People.* Illustrated by David Wiesner. New York: Harper & Row, 1989. Grades 3 and up.

    Yep retells stories of tricksters, fools, virtues and vices, Chinese America, and love.

_____. *The Star Fisher.* New York: Morrow Junior Books, 1991. Grades 3 and up.

    Joan Lee and her family encounter prejudice and challenges when, in 1927, they move from Ohio to a small town in West Virginia to open a laundry.

AUSTRALIA

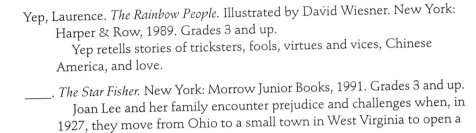

Barbalet, Margaret. *The Wolf.* Illustrated by Jane Tanner. New York: Macmillan, 1992. Grades 1 and up.

    Tal and his family cope with an ongoing nightmare, the threat of a howling wolf. Finally, Tal overcomes his fears through acceptance of the wolf.

Beatty, Patricia. *Jonathan Down Under.* New York: William Morrow, 1982. Grades 5 and up.

    Jonathan and his father change from a ship bound to China to a ship full of hopeful gold miners heading to Australia.

Cox, David. *Bossyboots.* New York: Crown, 1985. Grades preschool and up.

    Abigail's bossiness comes to the rescue when a stagecoach is being robbed.

Fox, Mem. *Possum Magic.* Nashville, Tenn.: Abingdon Press, 1987. Grades preschool and up.

    Grandma Poss makes Hush invisible, but she struggles to make him visible again.

Klein, Robin. *All in the Blue Unclouded Weather.* New York: Viking, 1991. Grades 4 and up.

    Four sisters enjoy the Australian summer during the late 1940s.

_____. *Tearaways.* New York: Viking, 1990. Grades 5 and up.

    This collection of short stories, peopled with interesting, sinister, and clever characters, is excellent for reading aloud.

Park, Ruth. *Playing Beatie Bow.* New York: Atheneum, 1982. Grades 6 and up.

    While Abigail deals with family difficulties in the present, she discovers life and love from 100 years ago.

Pople, Maureen. *The Other Side of Family.* New York: Henry Holt, 1986. Grades 5 and up.

Until the second World War ends, Kate must stay with relatives in Australia where she makes surprising discoveries about her family.

Roughsey, Dick. *The Rainbow Serpent.* Milwaukee, Wis.: Gareth Stevens, 1975. Grades kindergarten and up.

This creation story features Goorialla, a huge rainbow serpent.

Thiele, Colin. *Shadow Shark.* New York: HarperCollins, 1985. Grades 5 and up.

Joe is living with his cousin on an island off southern Australia when they join fishermen in pursuit of a huge shark.

Trezise, Percy. *The Peopling of Australia.* Milwaukee, Wis.: Gareth Stevens, 1987. Grades kindergarten and up.

The development of this ancient civilization is explored in art and simple text.

Trezise, Percy, and Mary Haginikitas. *Black Duck and Water Rat.* Milwaukee, Wis.: Gareth Stevens, 1988. Grades kindergarten and up.

When Water Rat takes Black Duck for his wife, their children are two strange creatures, the platypuses.

Trezise, Percy, and Dick Roughsey. *Gidja the Moon.* Milwaukee, Wis.: Gareth Stevens, 1988. Grades kindergarten and up.

This tale explains the moon's origin and its role in the world.

———. *Turramulli the Giant Quinkin.* Milwaukee, Wis.: Gareth Stevens, 1982. Grades 1 and up.

This is an aboriginal myth about a family that is pursued by the fierce Turramulli.

Vaughan, Marcia D. *Wombat Stew.* Illustrated by Pamela Lofts. Englewood Cliffs, N.J.: Silver Burdett Press, 1984. Grades preschool and up.

In this rollicking tale, the animals outsmart a dingo that is trying to make stew from a captured wombat.

Wrightson, Patricia. *The Nargun and the Stars.* New York: Atheneum, 1974. Grades 5 and up.

Young orphan Simon must live with relatives on a sheep farm in northern Australia, where he is challenged by the country's spirits.

———. *Moon Dark.* Illustrated by Noela Young. New York: Margaret K. McElderry, 1987. Grades 5 and up.

This is the story of the effect settlers have on a community of animals: kangaroos, bush rats, bandicoots, goanna, possums, fly foxes, and a dog.

_____. *An Older Kind of Magic.* Illustrated by Noela Young. San Diego, Calif.: Harcourt Brace Jovanovich, 1972. Grades 4 and up.

Three children encounter fantasy and magic when they try to save the botanical gardens from being turned into a parking lot.

COMMONWEALTH OF INDEPENDENT STATES

Afanasyev, Alexander Nikolayevich. Retold by Lenny Hort. *The Fool and the Fish.* Illustrated by Gennady Spirin. New York: Dial, 1990. Grades 1 and up.

A fish grants Ivan the Fool's every wish, and soon he marries the Tsar's daughter.

_____. *Russian Fairy Tales.* Translated by Norbert Guterman. Illustrated by Alexander Alexeieff. New York: Pantheon, 1945. Grades 3 and up.

This large volume provides a fascinating variety of Russian tales.

Asch, Frank, and Vladimir Vagin. *Here Comes the Cat!* New York: Scholastic, 1989. Grades preschool and up.

In Paul Revere style, a mouse warns the others of a cat's arrival. The Russian/English text repeats the warning, "Here comes the cat!" leading the reader to a surprise ending.

Black, Algernon D., reteller. *The Woman of the Wood.* Illustrated by Evaline Ness. New York: Holt, Rinehart & Winston, 1973. Grades 1 and up.

A woodcarver, tailor, and teacher argue over who should own a jointly made creation.

Bogard, Larry. *The Kolokol Papers.* New York: Farrar, Straus & Giroux, 1981. Grades 6 and up.

Sixteen-year-old Lev speaks out against the Soviet government after his father's arrest and faces pressures from the officials. Lev tells his story in *The Kolokol Papers* for release in the West.

Brett, Jan, adapter. *The Mitten.* New York: G. P. Putnam's, 1989. Grades kindergarten and up.

Nicki drops his white mitten in the snow, and a variety of animals share it as a temporary home.

Brown, Marcia. *The Bun.* New York: Harcourt Brace Jovanovich, 1972. Grades kindergarten and up.

In this variant of "The Gingerbread Boy," a bun is eaten by the fox.

Cole, Joanna. *Bony-Legs.* Illustrated by Dirk Zimmer. New York: Macmillan, 1983. Grades kindergarten and up.

Sasha outwits the witch with help from a gate, dog, and cat.

Croll, Carolyn, adapter. *The Little Snowgirl.* New York: G. P. Putnam's, 1989. Grades 1 and up.
 A childless couple is delighted with their daughter of snow and almost lose her through their devotion.

Dolphin, Laurie. *Georgia to Georgia: Making Friends in the U.S.S.R.* Photographs by E. Alan McGee. New York: Tambourine, 1991. Grades 2 and up.
 Leslie Schulten's letter writing campaign from students in Georgia to the Soviet Republic of Georgia resulted in a trip to Tbilisi, which is depicted in text and colored photographs.

Ginsburg, Mirra, adapter. *Striding Slippers.* Illustrated by Sal Murdocca. New York: Macmillan, 1978. Grades 1 and up.
 A clever shepherd's magic slippers are repeatedly stolen, to the dismay of the thieves.

Gogol, Nikolai. *Sorotchintzy Fair.* Illustrated by Gennadij Spirin. Translated by Daniel Reynolds. Boston: David R. Godine, 1990. Grades 2 and up.
 Paraska goes to the fair for the first time and encounters exciting adventures.

Hastings, Selina, reteller. *Peter and the Wolf.* Illustrated by Reg Cartwright. New York: Henry Holt, 1987. Grades kindergarten and up.
 In this pictorial version of Sergei Prokofiev's musical tale, Peter disobeys his grandfather and must defeat the wolf.

Helprin, Mark. *Swan Lake.* Illustrated by Chris Van Allsburg. Boston: Houghton Mifflin, 1989. Grades 3 and up.
 Colorful illustrations enhance this classic ballet.

Kimmel, Eric A. *Baba Yaga: A Russian Folktale.* Illustrated by Megan Lloyd. New York: Holiday House, 1991. Grades 1 and up.
 Like Cinderella, Marina is mistreated by her stepmother and must also escape from Baba Yaga, a witch in the forest.

———. *Bearhead.* Illustrated by Charles Mikolaycak. New York: Holiday House, 1991. Grades 1 and up.
 Madame Hexaba is so frustrated by Bearhead's literal interpretation of her directives that she sends him home with a wagon full of gold.

Levine, Arthur A. *All the Lights in the Night.* Illustrated by James E. Ransome. New York: Tambourine, 1991. Grades 2 and up.
 When the tsar makes life difficult for Jews, two young boys keep their spirits up with tales of Hanukkah as they travel to Palestine.

Mintz, Mary, translator. *The Millstones.* Illustrated by T. Berezenskaya. U.S.S.R.: Minsk Yunatstva, 1985. Grades 2 and up.

The landlord steals a couple's magic millstones in this Byelorussian folktale.

Morgan, Pierr. *The Turnip.* New York: Philomel, 1990. Grades preschool and up.
It takes all the family plus the animals to help pull up the turnip.

Murphy, Claire Rudolf. *Friendship Across Arctic Waters: Alaskan Cub Scouts Visit Their Soviet Neighbors.* Photographs by Charles Mason. New York: Lodestar, 1991. Grades 3 and up.
Eleven Cub Scouts from Nome, Alaska, visit with Young Pioneers of Provideniya, where they live with Soviet families, celebrate the Fourth of July, and learn about Russia.

Polacco, Patricia. *Rechenka's Eggs.* New York: Philomel, 1988. Grades kindergarten and up.
Babushka rescues an injured goose, Rechenka, which ruins her beautifully painted eggs. But the next morning she discovers the first of several miracles.

Pushkin, Alexander. *The Tale of Czar Saltan or The Prince and the Swan Princess.* Translated and retold by Patricia Tracy Lowe. Illustrated by I. Bilibin. New York: Thomas Y. Crowell, 1975. Grades 3 and up.
Despite the treachery of her sisters, the czarina and her son are rewarded for their faithfulness.

_____. *The Tale of the Golden Cockerel.* Translated and retold by Patricia Tracy Lowe. Illustrated by I. Bilibin. New York: Thomas Y. Crowell, 1975. Grades 3 and up.
An aging czar makes desperate promises to keep peace and must sacrifice all he loves.

Sherman, Josepha, reteller. *Vassilisa the Wise: A Tale of Medieval Russia.* Illustrated by Daniel San Souci. San Diego, Calif.: Harcourt Brace Jovanovich, 1989. Grades 1 and up.
Vassilisa uses her intelligence to save her husband from imprisonment.

Small, Ernest. *Baba Yaga.* Illustrated by Blair Lent. Boston: Houghton Mifflin, 1966. Grades 1 and up.
Marusia and her hedgehog friend take on Baba Yaga, a traditional Russian folk character.

Tate, Carole. *Pancakes and Pies.* New York: Peter Bedrick, 1989. Grades kindergarten and up.
An old man and his wife acquire a magic handmill that produces pancakes and pies. When a rich man steals the handmill, their cockerel rescues it.

Tompert, Ann. *The Tzar's Bird.* Illustrated by Robert Rayevsky. New York: Macmillan, 1990. Grades 1 and up.

    When Baba Yaga isn't invited to the tzar's coronation, she arrives and commands him to care for her firebird. The lesson he learns is important for all readers to share.

Vernon, Adele, reteller. *The Riddle.* Illustrated by Robert Rayevsky and Vladimir Radunsky. New York: Dodd, Mead, 1987. Grades 1 and up.

    A king is intrigued by a charcoal maker's riddle: how can he make enough to pay back a debt, survive, save for his old age, and have money to throw out the window?

Voight, Erna. *Peter and the Wolf.* Boston: David R. Godine, 1979. Grades kindergarten and up.

    The musical phrases highlight the illustrations of Sergei Prokofiev's musical tale of Peter's capture of a wolf.

Weiss, Pola. *Russian Legends.* Translated by Alice Sachs. New York: Crescent, 1980. Grades 4 and up.

    Photographs of Russian art, people, and country enhance this collection of 19 tales.

Winthrop, Elizabeth, adapter. *Vasilissa the Beautiful.* Illustrated by Alexander Koshkin. New York: HarperCollins, 1991. Grades 2 and up.

    In this Cinderella variant, Vasilissa is protected from her evil stepmother and stepsisters by a magic doll.

Zemach, Harve, reteller. *Salt.* Illustrated by Margot Zemach. New York: Farrar, Straus & Giroux, 1965. Grades kindergarten and up.

    Ivan the Fool finds an island of salt and shows his true abilities.

LATIN AND SOUTH AMERICAN LITERATURE

Aardema, Verna. *The Riddle of the Drum: A Tale from Tizapan Mexico.* Illustrated by Tony Chen. New York: Four Winds Press, 1979. Grades 1 and up.

    A king announces that no man may marry his daughter unless he can guess the kind of leather used in a drum.

Ada, Alma Flor. *The Gold Coin.* Illustrated by Neil Waldman. Translated by Bernice Randall. New York: Atheneum, 1991. Grades 2 and up.

    Set in Central America, this is the tale of Juan, who is determined to steal a gold coin.

Alexander, Ellen. *Llama and the Great Flood: A Folktale from Peru.* New York: Thomas Y. Crowell, 1989. Grades 1 and up.

After a llama tells his owner of his dreams of a great flood, the animals and people climb atop a mountain and are safe.

Anderson, Joan. *Spanish Pioneers of the Southwest.* New York: Dutton, 1989. Grades 3 and up.
   Photographs, taken at El Rancho de las Golondrinas, near Sante Fe, and text recreate life in a family in the mid-1700s.

Ashabranner, Brent. *Children of the Maya: A Guatemalan Indian Odyssey.* Photographs by Paul Conklin. New York: Dodd, Mead, 1986. Grades 4 and up.
   Mayan Indians struggling to survive are helped by residents of Indiantown, Florida.

Baden, Robert, reteller. *And Sunday Makes Seven.* Illustrated by Michelle Edwards. Niles, Ill.: Albert Whitman, 1990. Grades 1 and up.
   Carlos and Ana are poor in Costa Rica, until Carlos is rewarded for his rhyme by a group of witches. When Ricardo also tries to get some gold, the witches reward him with two moles on his nose.

Bierhorst, John, translator. *Spirit Child: A Story of the Nativity.* Illustrated by Barbara Cooney. New York: William Morrow, 1984. Grades 3 and up.
   This is an Aztec version of Mary and her spirit child.

Carlson, Lori M., and Cynthia L. Ventura. *Where Angels Glide at Dawn: New Stories from Latin America.* Illustrated by Jose Ortega. New York: J. B. Lippincott, 1990. Grades 4 and up.
   Ten tales from Latin America are illustrated with woodcuts.

Delacre, Lulu. *Arroz con Leche: Popular Songs and Rhymes from Latin America.* New York: Scholastic, 1989. Grades preschool and up.
   Charming songs are presented in English and Spanish.

_____. *Las Navidades: Popular Christmas Songs from Latin America.* New York: Scholastic, 1990. Grades preschool and up.
   Old and new Christmas songs are presented in Spanish and English.

dePaola, Tomie. *The Lady of Guadalupe.* New York: Holiday House, 1980. Grades 3 and up.
   Juan Diego, a poor Indian, carries a miraculous sign from the Lady of Guadalupe to the Bishop. Mexico.

Dorros, Arthur. *Abuela.* Illustrated by Elisa Kleven. New York: Dutton Children's Books, 1991. Grades 1 and up.
   Rosalba imagines a wonderful trip with her grandmother, flying over Manhattan. Spanish words are interspersed throughout the text.

_____. *Tonight Is Carnaval.* New York: Dutton Children's Books, 1991. Grades 1 and up.

The excitement of Carnaval for people of the Andes is highlighted by *arpilleras,* wall hangings created for the book by members of the Club de Madres Virgen del Carmen, of Lima, Peru.

Ehlert, Lois. *Moon Rope: A Peruvian Folktale.* Translated by Amy Prince. San Diego, Calif.: Harcourt Brace Jovanovich, 1992. Grades preschool and up.

Mole and Fox want to go to the moon in this boldly illustrated oversize folktale presented in English and Spanish.

Frost, Abigail. *Myths and Legends of the Amazon.* Illustrated by Jean Torton. New York: Marshall Cavendish, 1989. Grades 3 and up.

Color illustrations enhance 10 stories plus background information of South America.

Gelman, Rita Golden. *Dawn to Dusk in the Galapagos: Flightless Birds, Swimming Lizards, and Other Fascinating Creatures.* Photographs by Tui De Roy. Boston: Little, Brown, 1991. Grades 3 and up.

Color photographs explore a day in the life of the unusual animals found on the Galápagos Islands west of Ecuador.

George, Jean Craighead. *One Day in the Tropical Rain Forest.* Illustrated by Gary Allen. New York: Thomas Y. Crowell, 1990. Grades 3 and up.

Tepui loves the rain forest of Venezuela, but his world is threatened by bulldozers coming to level the forest. He endeavors to stop the destruction by searching for a nameless butterfly.

Gifford, Douglas. *Warriors Gods and Spirits from Central and South American Mythology.* Illustrated by John Sibbick. New York: Schocken, 1983. Grades 4 and up.

This impressive collection of myths includes striking illustrations and a discussion of the symbols used in the myths.

Griego, Margot C., Betsy L. Bucks, Sharon S. Gilbert, and Laurel H. Kimball. *Tortillitas Para Mama and Other Nursery Rhymes/Spanish and English.* New York: Holt, Rinehart & Winston, 1981. Grades preschool and up.

Nursery rhymes and lullabies collected from Spanish communities in the Americas.

Krumgold, Joseph. *. . . and now Miguel.* New York: Thomas Y. Crowell, 1953. Grades 5 and up.

Miguel, the middle child, yearns to go to the Sangre de Cristo Mountains to guard his family's sheep.

Lattimore, Deborah Nourse. *Why There Is No Arguing in Heaven: A Mayan Myth.* New York: Harper & Row, 1989. Grades 2 and up.
Intricate illustrations enhance this creation myth about the Maize God who proves his worthiness to be seated at Kunab Ku's side.

Lewis, Richard. *All of You Was Singing.* Illustrated by Ed Young. New York: Macmillan, 1991. Grades 1 and up.
In simple style, Lewis tells an Aztec myth of the earth's creation and how music comes to earth.

Madrigal, Antonio Hernández. *The Eagle and the Rainbow: Timeless Tales of Mexico.* Illustrated by Tomie dePaola. Golden, Colo.: Fulcrum, 1997.
Five tales representing ancient tribes.

O'Dell, Scott. *Carlotta.* Boston: Houghton Mifflin, 1977. Grades 4 and up.
A courageous young woman rides with the men to ambush Kit Carson in the Battle of San Pasqual.

____. *The Feathered Serpent.* Boston: Houghton Mifflin, 1981. Grades 5 and up.
A young student finds himself embroiled in the adventures of a Mayan legend.

Pino-Saavedra, Yolando, ed. *Folktales of Chile.* Translated by Rockwell Gray. Chicago: University of Chicago Press, 1967. Grades 4 and up.
This collection includes animal, wonder, religious, romantic, trickster, and cumulative tales.

Pitkänen, Matti A., Ritva Lehtinen, and Kari E. Nurmi. *The Grandchildren of the Incas.* Minneapolis, Minn.: Carolrhoda, 1991. Grades 3 and up.
Brilliantly colored photographs enhance the text about the lives of the Incan children.

Shetterly, Susan Hand. *The Dwarf-Wizard of Uxmal.* Illustrated by Robert Shetterly. New York: Atheneum, 1990. Grades 3 and up.
In this Yucatan Maya legend, a boy hatched from an egg becomes ruler.

Taha, Karen T. *A Gift for Tia Rosa.* Illustrated by Dee deRosa. Minneapolis, Minn.: Dillon Press, 1986. Grades kindergarten and up.
Carmela is sad when her elderly friend, Tia Rosa, dies but she plans a gift for Tia Rosa's new grandchild.

Vaughn, Marcia. *Tingo Tango Mango Tree.* Illustrated by Yvonne Buchanan. Morristown, N.J.: Silver Burdett, 1995.
An iguana named Sombala Bombala finds and plants a giant mango seed. When it grows, she needs help getting it down.

MIDDLE EAST

Abodaher, David J. *Youth in the Middle East: Voices of Despair.* New York: Franklin Watts, 1990. Grades 4 and up.
Black-and-white photographs of people in Lebanon, Israel, and Egypt enhance the essays about life in these war-torn areas.

Banks, Lynne Reid. *One More River.* New York: Morrow Junior Books, 1973, 1992. Grades 5 and up.
Lesley has the perfect teenage life until her parents announce they will be moving from Canada to Israel. Lesley not only survives the war in 1967 but also becomes a self-reliant young woman.

Bergman, Tamar. *The Boy from over There.* Translated by Hillel Halkin. Boston: Houghton Mifflin, 1988. Grades 4 and up.
Avramik and Rina struggle to adjust to a kibbutz after WW II.

Carrick, Carol. *Aladdin and the Wonderful Lamp.* Illustrated by Donald Carrick. New York: Scholastic, 1989. Grades 1 and up.
Aladdin learns to use the power of the lamp and its genie wisely as he matures in the Carricks's boldly illustrated version of the traditional tale.

Climo, Shirley. *The Egyptian Cinderella.* Illustrated by Ruth Heller. New York: HarperTrophy, 1989. Grades kindergarten and up.
Rhodopis, a slave girl, eventually becomes the Pharaoh's queen.

Dewey, Ariane, reteller. *The Fish Peri.* New York: Macmillan, 1979. Grades 1 and up.
Ahmed catches a fish that turns into a young woman who helps him achieve impossible feats.

Edwards, Michelle. *Chicken Man.* New York: Lothrop, Lee & Shepard, 1991. Grades kindergarten and up.
Chicken Man loves working in the chicken coop at the kibbutz, but he must rotate through other jobs until the chickens ensure his permanent return.

Giblin, James Cross. *The Riddle of the Rosetta Stone: Key to Ancient Egypt.* New York: Thomas Y. Crowell, 1990. Grades 3 and up.
Giblin discusses how the Rosetta stone led to an understanding of the Egyptian hieroglyphs.

Gold, Sharlya, and Mishael Maswari Caspi. *The Answered Prayer and Other Yemenite Folktales.* Illustrated by Marjory Wunsch. Philadelphia: The Jewish Publication Society, 1990. Grades 4 and up.

In addition to the 12 folktales, the authors provide background information, a glossary, and a pronunciation guide to the Yemenite names.

Harris, Geraldine. *Gods and Pharaohs from Egyptian Mythology.* Illustrated by David O'Connor. New York: Schocken, 1982. Grades 4 and up.
Stories of Egypt, line drawings, colorful illustrations, maps, and background information make this a useful resource.

Heide, Florence Parry, and Judith Heide Gilliland. *The Day of Ahmed's Secret.* Illustrated by Ted Lewin. New York: Lothrop, Lee & Shepard, 1990. Grades kindergarten and up.
Ahmed treasures his secret as he works in the fascinating city of Cairo.

Hiçyilmaz, Gaye. *Against the Storm.* Boston: Little, Brown, 1990. Grades 5 and up.
Mehmet expects their move from the Turkish village to Ankara will bring the family comfort and abundance, but finds only misery.

Hort, Lenny. *The Tale of Caliph Stork.* From the tale by Wilhelm Hauf. Illustrated by Friso Henstra. New York: Dial Books for Young Readers, 1989. Grades 1 and up.
In Arabia, when the Caliph of Baghdad and his Grand Vizier are tricked into becoming storks, they have troubling undoing the spell.

Ludwig, Warren, adapter. *Old Noah's Elephants.* New York: G. P. Putnam's, 1991. Grades preschool and up.
In this amusing tale, Noah has to convince the elephants that they can't eat all the food on the ark.

MacQuitty, William. *Tutankhamun: The Last Journey.* New York: Crown, 1978. Grades 5 and up.
Photographs and text tell the story of Tutankhamun, from ancient history to excavation.

Mayers, Florence Cassen. *ABC: The Alef-Bet Book, The Israel Museum, Jerusalem.* New York: Harry N. Abrams, 1989. Grades preschool and up.
The Hebrew alphabet is illustrated with art photographed in the Israel Museum in Jerusalem.

Travers, P. L., reteller. *Two Pairs of Shoes.* Illustrated by Leo and Diane Dillon. New York: Viking Press, 1980. Grades 2 and up.
In "Abu Kassem's Slippers," a rich but miserly merchant in Baghdad struggles to rid himself of old slippers. In "The Sandals of Ayaz," the king's trusted Treasurer uses his tattered sandals to prove his loyalty.

Walker, Barbara K., reteller. *A Treasury of Turkish Folktales for Children.* Hamden, Conn.: Linnet, 1988. Grades 2 and up.

Thirty-four tales are accompanied by a Turkish pronunciation guide, a glossary, notes, and riddles.

Walker, Barbara K., and Ahmet E. Uysal. *New Patches for Old.* Illustrated by Harold Berson. New York: Parents' Magazine Press, 1974. Grades kindergarten and up.

In honor of a holiday, Hasan buys presents for his family and new trousers for himself. The trousers are in need of hemming, which leads to an amusing sequence of events.

Zemach, Margot. *It Could Always Be Worse.* New York: Scholastic, 1976. Grades kindergarten and up.

In this Yiddish tale, a rabbi helps a man appreciate his crowded hut.

NATIVE AMERICAN LITERATURE

Ashabranner, Brent. *Morning Star, Black Sun: The Northern Cheyenne Indians and America's Energy Crisis.* New York: Dodd, Mead, 1982. Grades 4 and up.

Photographs and text tell the history and contemporary story of how the Northern Cheyenne are coping with the coal crisis.

Baker, Betty. *Rat Is Dead and Ant Is Sad.* Illustrated by Mamoru Funai. New York: Harper & Row, 1981. Grades kindergarten and up.

In this easy-to-read tale, ant thinks rat is dead and spreads the sad news until a wise horse rescues rat.

Baker, Olaf. *Where the Buffaloes Begin.* Illustrated by Stephen Gammell. New York: Frederick Warne, 1981. Grades 2 and up.

Little Wolf searches for the lake where the buffaloes begin.

Baylor, Byrd. *And It Is Still That Way: Legends Told by Arizona Indian Children.* New York: Charles Scribner's, 1976. Grades 2 and up.

Children's individual and group stories of animals, people, and the world are presented by Baylor.

____. *Before You Came This Way.* Illustrated by Tom Bahti. New York: E. P. Dutton, 1969. Grades kindergarten and up.

Baylor provides a poetic exploration of prehistoric Indian petroglyphs.

____. *The Desert Is Theirs.* Illustrated by Peter Parnall. New York: Charles Scribner's, 1975. Grades kindergarten and up.

Baylor writes of the desert, its animals, and its people.

____. *A God on Every Mountain Top.* Illlustrated by Carol Brown. New York: Charles Scribner's, 1981. Grades 1 and up.

Baylor's poems tell stories of the Southwest Mountains.

_____. *Hawk, I'm Your Brother.* Illlustrated by Peter Parnall. New York: Charles Scribner's, 1976. Grades 1 and up.

Rudy Sato, who yearns to fly, works with a hawk to become its brother.

Bierhorst, John. *A Cry from the Earth: Music of the North American Indians.* New York: Four Winds Press, 1979. Grades kindergarten and up.

Melody lines are accompanied by photos, history, and information about the songs.

_____, ed. *Songs of the Chippewa.* New York: Farrar, Straus & Giroux, 1974. Grades kindergarten and up.

These engaging traditional Chippewa songs are arranged for piano and guitar.

Coatsworth, Emerson, and David Coatsworth. *The Adventures of Nanabush: Ojibway Indian Stories.* Illustrated by Francis Kagige. New York: Atheneum, 1980. Grades 3 and up.

Nanabush's adventures are captured in 16 tales, as told by Ojibway tribal elders.

dePaola, Tomie. *The Legend of the Bluebonnet.* New York: G. P. Putnam's, 1983. Grades kindergarten and up.

In this Comanche tale, a young girl makes the ultimate sacrifice, bringing the bluebonnets to Texas.

Dodge, Nanabah Chee. *Morning Arrow.* Illustrated by Jeffrey Lunge. New York: Lothrop, Lee & Shepard, 1975. Grades 2 and up.

Morning Arrow, a young Navaho boy, wants to replace his blind grandmother's tattered shawl.

Echo-Hawk, Roger C., and Walter R. Echo-Hawk. *Battlefields and Burial Grounds: The Indian Struggle to Protect Ancestral Graves in the United States.* Minneapolis, Minn.: Lerner, 1994. Grades 4 and up.

The authors describe various efforts to rebury Indian remains from museums and historical societies.

Esbensen, Barbara Jester. *Ladder to the Sky: How the Gift of Healing Came to the Ojibway Nation.* Illustrated by Helen K. Davie. Boston: Little, Brown, 1989. Grades kindergarten and up.

This is the legend of how the Ojibway people, who once enjoyed good health, had to deal with sickness and death.

Freedman, Russell. *Buffalo Hunt.* New York: Holiday House, 1988. Grades 3 and up.

Paintings from nineteenth-century artists highlight Freedman's account of the role of the buffalo in our history.

_____. *Indian Chiefs*. New York: Holiday House, 1987. Grades 3 and up.
> Famous chiefs are profiled: Red Cloud of the Oglala Sioux, Quanah Parker of the Comanches, Washakie of the Shoshonis, Joseph of the Nez Perce, Sitting Bull of the Hunkpapa Sioux, and others.

_____. *An Indian Winter*. New York: Holiday House, 1992. Grades 4 and up.
> Prince Alexander Philipp Maximilian's journal and Bodmer's portraits, landscapes, and drawings tell the story of a winter spent among the Mandan Indians in North Dakota.

Goble, Paul. *Beyond the Ridge*. New York: Bradbury Press, 1989. Grades 3 and up.
> An Indian grandmother takes her last journey, joining those who died before her.

_____. *The Girl Who Loved Wild Horses*. Scarsdale, N. Y.: Bradbury Press, 1978. Grades 2 and up.
> An Indian girl who has a special relationship with wild horses eventually joins the herd.

_____. *Her Seven Brothers*. New York: Bradbury Press, 1988. Grades 2 and up.
> This Cheyenne legend of the creation of the Big Dipper tells of a girl who searches for her seven brothers.

_____. *Iktomi and the Berries: A Plains Indian Story*. New York: Orchard, 1989. Grades preschool and up.
> Iktomi nearly dies in his pursuit of bright red berries he thinks he sees in the river.

_____. *Iktomi and the Boulder: A Plains Indian Story*. New York: Orchard, 1988. Grades preschool and up.
> When a boulder pins Iktomi, he convinces the bats to attack the boulder, breaking it into tiny pieces.

_____. *Iktomi and the Buffalo Skull: A Plains Indian Story*. New York: Orchard, 1991. Grades preschool and up.
> Iktomi gets into trouble when he puts his head in a buffalo skull.

_____. *Iktomi and the Ducks: A Plains Indian Story*. New York: Orchard, 1990. Grades preschool and up.
> Iktomi tries to feast on ducks, but is outsmarted by the coyote.

Highwater, Jamake. *Anpao: An American Indian Odyssey*. Illlustrated by Fritz Scholder. Philadelphia: J. B. Lippincott, 1977. Grades 5 and up.
> Readers learn of Indian tradition through Anpao's journeys.

Hobbs, Will. *Bearstone*. New York: Atheneum, 1989. Grades 4 and up.
> A troubled youth spends a summer with an elderly rancher in the Colorado mountains.

Hoyt-Goldsmith, Diane. *Pueblo Storyteller.* Photographs by Lawrence Migdale. New York: Holiday House, 1991. Grades 3 and up.
> Ten-year-old April tells the story of her life and the Pueblo traditions preserved by her family members.

Hudson, Jan. *Sweetgrass.* New York: Philomel, 1989. Grades 5 and up.
> Sweetgrass, a 15-year-old Blackfoot girl, who is anxious to marry Eagle-Sun, must endure a difficult year of waiting.

Locker, Thomas. *The Land of Gray Wolf.* New York: Dial, 1991. Grades 1 and up.
> Locker's stunning paintings tell the story of Running Deer and the white settlers' destruction of Indian lands.

Martin, Bill, and John Archambault. *Knots on a Counting Rope.* Illustrated by Ted Brand. New York: Henry Holt, 1987. Grades 1 and up.
> Each time Grandfather tells the dramatic story of his blind grandson's birth, he ties another knot on the counting rope.

Miles, Miska. *Annie and the Old One.* Illustrated by Peter Parnall. Boston: Little, Brown, 1971. Grades 1 and up.
> Annie tries to delay the death of the Old One by stopping her mother's weaving of a rug.

Norman, Howard. *How Glooskap Outwits the Ice Giants and Other Tales of the Maritime Indians.* Illustrated by Michael McCurdy. Boston: Little, Brown, 1989. Grades 2 and up.
> Woodcuts enhance these five tales of Glooskap, the first great teacher and hero.

O'Dell, Scott. *Sing Down the Moon.* Boston: Houghton Mifflin, 1970. Grades 5 and up.
> The tragic story of the Navaho's forced march to Fort Sumner is told by Bright Morning.

Ortiz, Simon. *The People Shall Continue.* Illustrated by Sharol Graves. San Francisco: Children's Book Press, 1988. Grades 2 and up.
> This story of Native American people teaches responsibility for life.

Robinson, Gail, and Douglas Hill. *Coyote the Trickster: Legends of the North American Indians.* Illustrated by Graham McCallum. New York: Crane, Russak, 1976. Grades 3 and up.
> These 12 trickster tales entertain and educate readers.

Rohmer, Harriet, and Mary Anchondo. *How We Came to the Fifth World.* Illustrated by Graciela Carrillo. San Francisco: Children's Book Press, 1988. Grades 3 and up.
> An ancient Mexican creation myth. Spanish and English.

Sneve, Virginia Driving Hawk. *Dancing Teepees: Poems of American Indian Youth.* Illustrated by Stephen Gammell. New York: Holiday House, 1989. Grades 2 and up.

    Traditional songs and poems enhanced by rich illustrations.

REGIONAL NORTH AMERICA

Ammon, Richard. *An Amish Christmas.* Illustrated by Pamela Patrick. New York: Atheneum, 1996. Grades 1 and up.

    The gentle life of the Amish traditions is described with beautiful illustrations and informative text.

Damjan, Mischa. *Atuk.* Illustrated by Jozef Wilkon. New York: North-South Books, 1990. Grades 1 and up.

    Atuk plans to avenge his dog's death by a wolf, but after each attempt, he learns that revenge is not satisfying. Northern America.

Davis, Deborah. *The Secret of the Seal.* Illustrated by Judy Labrasca. New York: Crown, 1989. Grades 3 and up.

    Instead of killing a seal with his harpoon, Kyo befriends the animal. Northern America.

Faber, Doris. *The Amish.* New York: Doubleday, 1991. Grades 2 and up.

    With its index, oversize illustrations, and detail about everyday life, this account of Amish life is useful for research as well as general reading.

George, Jean Craighead. *Shark Beneath the Reef.* New York: Harper & Row, 1989. Grades 5 and up.

    In Baja California, Tomas struggles with the life of a fisherman and his dream of catching a shark.

Houston, Gloria. *The Year of the Perfect Christmas Tree.* Illustrated by Barbara Cooney. New York: Dial Books for Young Readers, 1988. Grades 1 and up.

    In this story of Appalachia, Ruthie and Papa pick the perfect Christmas tree one summer. When Papa is called away to war, Ruthie and Mama must make Christmas happen.

Lewis, Richard. *In the Night, Still Dark.* Illustrated by Ed Young. New York: Atheneum, 1988. Grades kindergarten and up.

    Drawn from the *Kamulipoo*, a traditional Hawaiian creation chant, this book has simple text and striking illustrations.

Milnes, Gerald. *Granny Will Your Dog Bite and Other Mountain Rhymes.* Illustrated by Kimberly Bulckenroot. New York: Alfred A. Knopf, 1990. Grades preschool and up.

Milnes collected these entertaining rhymes from the Appalachia region in West Virginia. A cassette tape is available.

O'Dell, Scott. *Black Star, Bright Dawn.* Boston: Houghton Mifflin, 1988. Grades 5 and up.

Bright Dawn unexpectedly must take her father's place in the Alaskan Iditarod.

Paulsen, Gary. *Dogsong.* New York: Bradbury Press, 1985. Grades 5 and up.

A fourteen-year-old boy takes a team of dogs north through Alaska during a rite of passage to learn about the old ways.

Shetterly, Susan Hand. *Raven's Light: A Myth from the People of the Northwest Coast.* Illustrated by Robert Shetterly. New York: Atheneum, 1991. Grades 1 and up.

The trickster Raven creates and populates the world, stealing the light so that he can enjoy his creation.

Sloat, Teri. *The Eye of the Needle.* New York: Dutton Children's Books, 1990. Grades 1 and up.

Sloat illustrated this Yupik tale of an Alaskan boy who swallows a variety of fish—including a whale.

Smucker, Anna Egan. *No Star Nights.* Illustrated by Steve Johnson. New York: Alfred A. Knopf, 1989. Grades 2 and up.

Children who live in a steel mill town must cope with the smoke and graphite that fill the air, but they also enjoy the daily events.

LITERATURE FROM OTHER COUNTRIES

Adoff, Arnold. *Flamboyan.* Illustrated by Karen Barbour. San Diego, Calif.: Harcourt Brace Jovanovich, 1988. Grades 1 and up.

In lilting prose, Adoff tells the story of Flamboyan, a girl born in the Caribbean and named for the red tree near her window, who dreams of swimming with the fish and flying.

Bernier-Grand, Carmen T., reteller. *Juan Bobo: Four Folktales from Puerto Rico.* Illustrated by Ernesto Ramos Nieves. New York: HarperCollins, 1994. Grades 1 and up.

Four humorous tales of Juan Bobo's adventures.

Conrad, Pam. *Animal Lingo.* Illustrated by Barbara Bustetter Falk. New York: HarperCollins, 1994. Grades preschool and up.

Animal sounds from around the world are presented.

Donehower, Bruce. *Miko: Little Hunter of the North.* Illustrated by Tom Pohrt. New York: Farrar, Straus & Giroux, 1990. Grades 3 and up.

Miko searches for the truth about King Winter and Ravna in this story from Lapland.

Dooleyk, Norah. *Everybody Cooks Rice.* Illustrated by Peter J. Thornton. Minneapolis, Minn.: Carolrhoda, 1991. Grades kindergarten and up.
As Carrie searches for her little brother, she samples rice at each neighbor's house in her wonderfully multicultural neighborhood. Recipes are included at the back of the book.

Greenfield, Eloise. *Under the Sunday Tree.* Illustrated by Amos Ferguson. New York: Harper & Row, 1988. Grades 1 and up.
Life in the Bahamas is portrayed through poetry and paintings.

Morris, Ann. *On The Go.* Photographs by Ken Heyman. New York: Lothrop, Lee & Shepard, 1990. Grades kindergarten and up.
Color photographs from around the world illustrate how people move.

Pomerantz, Charlotte. *Chalk Doll.* Illustrated by Frane Lessac. New York: J. B. Lippincott, 1989. Grades preschool and up.
Mother tells Rose stories about growing up in Jamaica.

Temple, Frances, reteller. *Tiger Soup: An Anansi Story from Jamaica.* New York: Orchard, 1994. Grades kindergarten and up.
Anansi tricks tiger into leaving his soup and blames the monkeys for eating it.

Wisniewski, David. *Elfwyn's Saga.* New York: Lothrop, Lee & Shepard, 1990. Grades 1 and up.
A curse causes Elfwyn's blindness, but her second sight and internal vision help save her people. Cut-paper illustrations enhance this tale from Iceland.

Appendix D: Readers Theatre

R eaders theatre is an excellent vehicle for reinforcing reading, listening, and speaking skills. Rather than memorizing and dramatizing a play, students read a script aloud, conveying the drama through oral delivery. A readers theatre script usually includes a narrator and two or more other characters who stand or sit on stools while they read the script placed in folders or on music stands. The delivery is relatively formal, with the readers wearing simple clothes that do not distract from the reading, although occasionally readers may choose to use a simple prop such as a hat or coat. Once students are familiar with this process, the logical next step is for students to create their own scripts.

Susan Carlson, a second grade teacher in Denver Public Schools, introduced readers theatre to her students by reading aloud two picture book versions of a script selected from *Readers Theatre for Beginning Readers* (Barchers, 1993). The students formed small groups and read the scripts aloud. Next, they discussed how to organize for the reading and decided among themselves who should read the various parts. After each group presented the play, the group compared and contrasted the features of the picture book versions with the script, displaying their findings in a chart. A sample script with presentation suggestions follows. The student's lines begin on page 574 and can be copied for easy use.

THE FOX AND THE CROW

SUMMARY

The fox tricks a crow into dropping its piece of cheese in this fable by Aesop. Reading level: 1.

PRESENTATION SUGGESTIONS

This is a very short, simple tale that is especially appropriate for beginning readers. Because there are only three characters, it could be presented with other short fables. Staging could include the crow perched on a stool with the fox looking up.

PROPS

For a whimsical treatment, the crow could have a piece of cheese in its mouth until it speaks, and the fox could have a "fur" felt tail.

DELIVERY

Because the crow's role is so small, it could shake its head in response to the fox's requests. The fox should sound alternatively pleading, flattering, and pompous.

BOOKLIST

Calmenson, Stephanie, reteller. "The Fox and the Crow." In *The Children's Aesop*, illustrated by Robert Byrd (Honesdale, Penn.: Caroline House, 1992) 22.
   Each tale is beautifully illustrated in this large collection.

Carle, Eric, reteller. "The Fox and the Crow." In *Twelve Tales from Aesop* (New York: Philomel, 1980) 12.
   Discusses not only how Carle portrays the crow with plate and beverage but also the perspective of the crow in the tree.

Galdone, Paul. "The Fox and the Crow." In *Three Aesop Fox Fables* (Boston: Clarion, 1971) unpaged.
   Large, colorful illustrations highlight Galdone's simple retellings.

Kent, Jack. "The Fox and the Crow." In *Jack Kent's Fables of Aesop* (New York: Parents' Magazine Press, 1972) 18.
   Kent's version is in simple language, with amusing illustrations.

THE FOX AND THE CROW

CHARACTERS

Narrator
Fox
Crow

NARRATOR: One day a fox saw a crow fly by. It had a piece of cheese in its beak. Seeing the cheese made the fox very hungry. The crow came to rest on the branch of a tree.

FOX: Good morning, Miss Crow. Will you share your cheese with me?

NARRATOR: The crow looked at the fox. It slowly shook its head.

FOX: You look so kind. I am so hungry. Please share with me.

NARRATOR: The crow looked at the fox. Again it slowly shook its head.

FOX: You are the finest crow I have ever seen. Your feathers are so black and glossy. You also have good luck by getting that cheese. Won't you share your good fortune with me?

NARRATOR: The crow looked at the fox. Again it slowly shook its head.

FOX: Your eyes are so bright. I am sure your voice must be every bit as beautiful. Won't you sing for me? Then I will greet you as the Queen of Birds.

NARRATOR: The crow could not resist such flattery.

CROW: Caw, caw, caw.

NARRATOR: As the crow sang, the cheese dropped to the ground. The fox gobbled it up.

CROW: You are a sneaky beast. One day your trickery will get you into trouble. You should be taught a lesson.

FOX: That may be true. But you have learned a valuable lesson, Miss Crow. Do not trust flatterers.

Excerpted from *Readers Theatre for Beginning Readers* by Suzanne I. Barchers (Englewood, Colo.: Teacher Ideas Press, 1993).

Appendix E: Storytelling for Children

WHY ANANSI THE SPIDER HAS A SMALL WAIST

A story from West Africa retold by Martha Hamilton and Mitch Weiss, Beauty and the Beast Storytellers.

This story about Anansi (pronounced a-NON'-see) the spider is told in many countries of West Africa. Anansi is a sly trickster who often fools other animals and people as well. Sometimes, however, as in this story, Anansi gets into trouble because of his ambitious plans.

Nowadays,
if you look closely at a spider,
you will see
that he has a **big** head
and a **big** body
and a **tiny** waist inbetween.
But long ago
spiders **did not** have small waists.
I'll tell you the story
of how this came to be.

Make a big round circle with both hands as you say, "big head" and again when you say, "big body." Then make a gesture to show a tiny waist.

Anansi the spider
LOVED to eat more than
anything. And he could smell
good cooking from a **mile** away.
One day when he was in the
forest he noticed
a **delicious** smell in the air.

Say this with a lot of enthusiasm.

Raise your eyebrows up and down a bit and look as if you smell a delicious smell.

Sniff! Sniff! Sniff!
Where was the wonderful smell
coming from?

Sniff in three different directions as if you're trying to find which direction the smell is coming from. Don't say the word "sniff" but instead pretend to actually sniff the air.

Just then Anansi remembered
that today was the festival of the
harvest.
The two villages nearby—
one to the **east**,
the other to the **west**—

would **both** be having feasts!
Anansi's mouth began to water.
He thought,
"There will be **SO** much food!
I'll be able to eat
as much as I want!"

But,
Anansi wondered,
which village
would be serving the **best** food,
the one to the **east**
or the one to the **west**?

Anansi thought,
I'll go to *both* feasts!
I'll find out
who will be serving food first.

**I'll go there,
eat my fill,
and then go to the other village.**

But
when Anansi went to
the two villages and asked
when the feasts would begin,
no one would tell him.

The people of **both** villages
knew that Anansi **never** did **any**
work to deserve a feast,
but **always** appeared
just when the food was served.

Look as if you just had a brilliant idea.

Point to the right as you say "east" and to the left as you say "west."

Look very excited as you say this. You could rub both hands together to show how pleased Anansi is.

Get very excited and pat your stomach as you say this.

As you say "but," have a look of concern on your face.

Look confused as you say this.
Point to the right as you say "east" and to the left as you say "west."

Get even more excited at the thought of two feasts.

Say this fast and excitedly. Try to show how brilliant Anansi thinks he is.

Slowly.

Sound very upset.

Say this with suspicion and disgust.

Anansi knew that if he showed up,
he could have
all the food he wanted
since it was the custom
of the villagers
not to refuse **anyone**
who came to their door hungry.

As you say "all," make a circular gesture with both hands.

Before long
Anansi came up
with what he **thought**
was a *very* clever plan.
First he called his eldest son.
Anansi tied a very long rope
around his **own** belly
and said to his son,

Again, look and sound as if you had a brilliant idea.

Pretend to tie a rope around your stomach as you say this.

"Take the other end of this rope
to the **east** village.
When the food is served,
give a **hard** pull
so that I'll know it's time
for me to come and eat."

Pretend to hand a rope to someone with both hands. Then point to the right as if pointing east.

Pretend to pull hard on a rope as you say this.

Then he called his youngest son.
Anansi took **another** long rope
and tied it around his belly also,
and told **that** son
to take the **other** end of the rope
toward the **west** village
and give a **hard** pull
when the food was ready.

Pretend to hand a rope to someone with both hands.

Then point to the left as if pointing west.
Pretend to pull hard on a rope as you say this.

Anansi **waited** and **waited**
for the feasts to begin.

Say this as if you're very impatient.

Suddenly
he felt a **hard pull** to the east.
Anansi was **very** excited.

Say this quickly, with a lot of excitement. Jerk your waist to the right as you say "hard pull."

But just then

Slowly, with concern on your face.

there was a **hard pull** to the west.

Jerk your waist to the left as you say "hard pull," or at the end of the sentence.

Anansi realized that the **two villages** must have served their feasts at the *same time*!

Look very upset as you say this.

His two sons were **pulling SO** hard on their ropes that Anansi

As you say "pulling so," make a pulling gesture with your hands, and show great strain in your voice.

was caught *right* in the middle.

Have a look of dread on your face.

He couldn't go to the **east** and he couldn't go to the **west**.

Point to the right as you say "east" and to the left as you say "west."

The two sons kept pulling **as hard as they could** on their ropes until the feasts were **over**

Say this with strain in your voice.

and *all* the food **was gone**.

Say this with great disappointment.

When they went to find their father to see why he hadn't come when they pulled, they found that he now had a **tiny** waist where the ropes had gone around his big belly.

Show great surprise on your face and in your voice as you say this.

And that is why to **this** day all spiders have a **big** head and a **big** body and a **tiny little waist**.

Make a big round circle with both hands as you say, "big head" and again when you say "big body." Then make a gesture to show a tiny waist.

"Why Anansi the Spider Has a Small Waist" from *Stories in My Pocket: Tales Kids Can Tell* by Martha Hamilton and Mitch Weiss. (Golden, Colo.: Fulcrum, 1996.) Reprinted by permission of the authors.

Appendix F: Newbery & Caldecott Winners

1922 Van Loon, Hendrik. *The Story of Mankind*. Boni and Liveright.

1923 Lofting, Hugh. *The Voyages of Doctor Dolittle*. Stokes.

1924 Hawes, Charles Boardman. *The Dark Frigate*. Little, Brown.

1925 Finger, Charles J. *Tales from Silver Lands*. Illustrated by Paul Honoré. Doubleday.

1926 Chrisman, Arthur Bowie. *Shen of the Sea*. Illustrated by Else Hasselriis. Dutton.

1927 James, Will. *Smoky, the Cowhorse*. Charles Scribner's.

1928 Mukerji, Dhan Gopay. *Gay Neck*. Illustrated by Boris Artzybasheff. Dutton.

1929 Kelly, Eric P. *Trumpeter of Krakow*. Illustrated by Angela Pruszynska. Macmillan.

1930 Field, Rachel. *Hitty, Her First Hundred Years*. Illustrated by Dorothy P. Lathrop. Macmillan.

1931 Coatsworth, Elizabeth. *The Cat Who Went to Heaven*. Illustrated by Lynd Ward. Macmillan.

1932 Armer, Laura Adams. *Waterless Mountain*. Illustrated by Sidney Armer and author. Longmans, Green.

1933 Lewis, Elizabeth Foreman. *Young Fu of the Upper Yangtze*. Illustrated by Kurt Wiese. Winston.

1934 Meigs, Cornelia. *Invincible Louisa*. Little, Brown.

1935 Shannon, Monica. *Dobry*. Illustrated by Atanas Katchamakoff. Viking.

1936 Brink, Carol Ryrie. *Caddie Woodlawn*. Illustrated by Kate Seredy. Macmillan.

1937 Sawyer, Ruth. *Roller Skates*. Illustrated by Valenti Angelo. Viking.

1938 Seredy, Kate. *The White Stag*. Viking.

1939 Enright, Elizabeth. *Thimble Summer*. Farrar & Rinehart.

1940 Daugherty, James H. *Daniel Boone*. Viking.

1941 Sperry, Armstrong. *Call It Courage*. Macmillan.

1942 Edmonds, Walter D. *The Matchlock Gun*. Illustrated by Paul Lantz.

1943 Gray, Elizabeth Janet. *Adam of the Road*. Illustrated by Robert Lawson. Viking.

1944 Forbes, Esther. *Johnny Tremain*. Illustrated by Lynd Ward. Houghton Mifflin.

1945 Lawson, Robert. *Rabbit Hill*. Viking.

1946 Lenski, Lois. *Strawberry Girl*. Lippincott.

1947 Bailey, Carolyn Sherwin. *Miss Hickory*. Illustrated by Ruth Gannett. Viking.

1948 DuBois, William Pène. *The Twenty-One Balloons*. Viking.

1949 Henry, Marguerite. *King of the Wind*. Illustrated by Wesley Dennis. Rand McNally.

1950 de Angeli, Marguerite. *The Door in the Wall*. Doubleday.

1951 Yates, Elizabeth. *Amos Fortune, Free Man*. Illustrated by Nora Unwin. Aladdin.

1952 Estes, Eleanor. *Ginger Pye*. Viking.

1953 Clark, Ann Nolan. *Secret of the Andes*. Illustrated by Jean Charlot. Viking.

1954 Krumgold, Joseph. *And Now Miguel*. Illustrated by Jean Charlot. Crowell.

1955 DeJong, Meindert. *The Wheel on the School*. Illustrated by Maurice Sendak. Harper & Row.

1956 Latham, Jean Lee. *Carry On, Mr. Bowditch*. Houghton Mifflin.

1957 Sorensen, Virginia. *Miracles on Maple Hill*. Illustrated by Beth Krush and Joe Krush. Harcourt Brace.

1958 Keith, Harold. *Rifles for Watie*. Illustrated by Peter Burchard. Crowell.

1959 Speare, Elizabeth George. *The Witch of Blackbird Pond*. Houghton Mifflin.

1960 Krumgold, Joseph. *Onion John*. Illustrated by Symeon Shimin. Crowell.

1961 O'Dell, Scott. *Island of the Blue Dolphins*. Houghton Mifflin.

1962 Speare, Elizabeth George. *The Bronze Bow.* Houghton Mifflin.

1963 L'Engle, Madeleine. *A Wrinkle in Time.* Farrar, Straus.

1964 Neville, Emily. *It's Like This, Cat.* Illustrated by Emil Weiss. Harper & Row.

1965 Wojciechowska, Maia. *Shadow of a Bull.* Illustrated by Alvin Smith. Atheneum.

1966 de Treviño, Elizabeth Borten. *I, Juan de Pareja.* Farrar Straus.

1967 Hunt, Irene. *Up a Road Slowly.* Follett.

1968 Konigsburg, E. L. *From the Mixed-Up Files of Mrs. Basil E. Frankweiler.* Atheneum.

1969 Alexander, Lloyd. *The High King.* Holt, Rinehart & Winston.

1970 Armstrong, William H. *Sounder.* Harper & Row.

1971 Byars, Betsy. *Summer of the Swans.* Viking.

1972 O'Brien, Robert C. *Mrs. Frisby and the Rats of NIMH.* Atheneum.

1973 George, Jean Craighead. *Julie of the Wolves.* Harper & Row.

1974 Fox, Paul. *The Slave Dancer.* Bradbury.

1975 Hamilton, Virginia. *M. C. Higgins the Great.* Macmillan.

1976 Cooper, Susan. *The Grey King.* Atheneum.

1977 Taylor, Mildred D. *Roll of Thunder, Hear My Cry.* Dial.

1978 Paterson, Katherine. *Bridge to Terabithia.* Crowell.

1979 Raskin, Ellen. *The Westing Game.* Dutton.

1980 Blos, Joan W. *A Gathering of Days: A New England Girl's Journal, 1830–32.* Charles Scribner's.

1981 Paterson, Katherine. *Jacob Have I Loved.* Crowell.

1982 Willard, Nancy. *A Visit to William Blake's Inn: Poems for Innocent and Experienced Travelers.* Harcourt Brace Jovanovich.

1983 Voight, Cynthia. *Dicey's Song.* Atheneum.

1984 Cleary, Beverly. *Dear Mr. Henshaw.* Morrow.

1985 McKinley, Robin. *The Hero and the Crown.* Greenwillow.

1986 McLachlan, Patricia. *Sarah, Plain and Tall.* Harper & Row.

1987 Fleischman, Sid. *The Whipping Boy.* Greenwillow.

1988 Freedman, Russell. *Lincoln: A Photobiography.* Clarion.

1989 Fleischman, Paul. *Joyful Noise: Poems for Two Voices.* Harper & Row.

1990 Lowry, Lois. *Number the Stars.* Houghton Mifflin.

1991 Spinelli, Jerry. *Maniac Magee.* Little, Brown.

1992 Naylor, Phyllis Reynolds. *Shiloh.* Atheneum.

1993 Rylant, Cynthia. *Missing May.* Jackson/Orchard.

1994 Lowry, Lois. *The Giver.* Houghton Mifflin.

1995 Creech, Sharon. *Walk Two Moons.* HarperCollins.

1996 Cushman, Karen. *The Midwife's Apprentice.* Clarion.

1997 Konigsburg, E. L. *The View from Saturday.* Atheneum.

CALDECOTT AWARD WINNERS

1938 Text selected from the King James Bible by Helen Dean Fish. *Animals of the Bible, A Picture Book.* Illustrated by Dorothy O. Lathrop. Stokes.

1939 Handforth, Thomas. *Mei Li.* Doubleday.

1940 d'Aulaire, Ingrid, and Edgar Parin d'Aulaire. *Abraham Lincoln.* Doubleday.

1941 Lawson, Robert. *They Were Strong and Good.* Viking.

1942 McCloskey, Robert. *Make Way for Ducklings.* Viking.

1943 Burton, Virginia Lee. *The Little House.* Houghton Mifflin.

1944 Thurber, James. *Many Moons.* Illustrated by Louis Slobodkin. Harcourt Brace.

1945 Field, Rachel. *Prayer for a Child.* Illustrated by Elizabeth Orton Jones. Macmillan.

1946 Petersham, Maud, and Miska Petersham. *The Rooster Crows.* Macmillan.

1947 MacDonald, Golden. *The Little Island.* Illustrated by Leonard Weisgard. Doubleday.

1948 Tresselt, Alvin. *White Snow, Bright Snow.* Illustrated by Roger Duvoisin. Lothrop.

1949 Hader, Berta, and Elmer Hader. *The Big Snow.* Macmillan.

1950 Politi, Leo. *Song of the Swallows.* Charles Scribner's.

1951 Milhous, Katherine. *The Egg Tree.* Charles Scribner's.

1952 Will (William Lipkind). *Finders Keepers.* Illustrated by Nicolas (Mordvinoff). Harcourt Brace.

1953 Ward, Lynd. *The Biggest Bear.* Houghton Mifflin.

1954 Bemelmans, Ludwig. *Madeline's Rescue.* Viking.

1955 Perrault, Charles. *Cinderella.* Illustrated by Marcia Brown. Harper & Row.

1956 Langstaff, John. *Frog Went a-Courtin'.* Illustrated by Feodor Rojankovsky. Harcourt Brace.

1957 Udry, Janice May. *A Tree Is Nice.* Illustrated by Marc Simont. Harper & Row.

1958 McCloskey, Robert. *Time of Wonder.* Viking.

1959 Cooney, Barbara. *Chanticleer and the Fox.* Crowell.

1960 Ets, Marie Hall, and Aurora Labastida. *Nine Days to Christmas.* Viking.

1961 Robbins, Ruth. *Baboushka and the Three Kings.* Illustrated by Nicolas Sidjakov. Parnassus.

1962 Brown, Marcia. *Once a Mouse.* Charles Scribner's.

1963 Keats, Ezra Jack. *The Snowy Day.* Viking.

1964 Sendak, Maurice. *Where the Wild Things Are.* Harper & Row.

1965 de Regniers, Beatrice Schenk. *May I Bring a Friend?* Illustrated by Beni Montresor. Atheneum.

1966 Leodhas, Sorche Nic. *Always Room for One More.* Illustrated by Nonny Hogrogian. Holt, Rinehart & Winston.

1967 Ness, Evaline. *Sam, Bangs and Moonshine.* Holt, Rinehart & Winston.

1968 Emberley, Barbara. *Drummer Hoff.* Illustrated by Ed Emberley. Prentice-Hall.

1969 Ransome, Arthur. *The Fool of the World and the Flying Ship.* Illustrated by Uri Shulevitz. Farrar, Straus.

1970 Steig, William. *Sylvester and the Magic Pebble.* Windmill/Simon & Schuster.

1971 Haley, Gail E. *A Story—A Story: An African Tale.* Atheneum.

1972 Hogrogian, Nonny. *One Fine Day.* Macmillan.

1973 Mosel, Arlene. *The Funny Little Woman.* Illustrated by Blair Lent. Dutton.

1974 Zemach, Harve. *Duffy and the Devil.* Illustrated by Margot Zemach. Farrar, Straus.

1975 McDermott, Gerald. *Arrow to the Sun.* Viking.

1976 Aardema, Verna. *Why Mosquitos Buzz in People's Ears.* Illustrated by Leo and Diane Dillon. Dial.

1977 Musgrove, Margaret. *Ashanti to Zulu: African Traditions.* Illustrated by Leo and Diane Dillon. Dial.

1978 Spier, Peter. *Noah's Ark.* Doubleday.

1979 Goble, Paul. *The Girl Who Loved Wild Horses.* Bradbury.

1980 Hall, Donald. *Ox-Cart Man.* Illustrated by Barbara Cooney. Viking.

1981 Lobel, Arnold. *Fables.* Harper & Row.

1982 Van Allsburg, Chris. *Jumanji.* Houghton Mifflin.

1983 Cendrars, Blaise. *Shadow.* Illustrated by Marcia Brown. Charles Scribner's.

1984 Provensen, Alice, and Martin Provensen. *The Glorious Flight: Across the Channel with Louis Blériot, July 25, 1909.* Viking.

1985 Hodges, Margaret, adapter. *Saint George and the Dragon.* Illustrated by Trina Schart Hyman. Little, Brown.

1986 Van Allsburg, Chris. *Polar Express.* Houghton Mifflin.

1987 Yorinks, Arthur. *Hey Al.* Illustrated by Richard Egielski. Farrar, Straus & Giroux.

1988 Yolen, Jane. *Owl Moon.* Illustrated by John Schoenherr. Philomel.

1989 Ackerman, Karen. *Song and Dance Man.* Illustrated by Stephen Gammell. Knopf.

1990 Young, Ed. *Lon Po Po: A Red Riding Hood Story from China.* Philomel.

1991 Macaulay, David. *Black and White.* Houghton Mifflin.

1992 Wiesner, David. *Tuesday.* Clarion.

1993 McCully, Emily Arnold. *Mirette on the High Wire.* Putnam.

1994 Say, Allen. *Grandfather's Journey.* Houghton Mifflin.

1995 Bunting, Eve. *Smoky Night.* Illustrated by David Diaz. Harcourt Brace.

1996 Rathman, Peggy. *Officer Buckle and Gloria.* Putnam.

1997 Wisniewski, David. *Golem.* Clarion/Houghton Mifflin.

Glossary

ACTIVE LEARNING: The theory that learners need to determine purposes and strategies for successful reading.

AGGREGATING: The gathering together of related materials or objects, generally in the context of a topical investigation.

ALPHABETIC STAGE OF PHONICS: When children use individual letters and sounds to identify words.

ALPHABETIC WRITING: A system of writing in which each character represents a unit speech sound.

ANALOGY: A comparison of two similar relationships.

ANALYTIC PHONICS: The practice of having students find sounds in the context of words (for example, finding all the words that start like *dog*). Usually coupled with implicit teaching of phonics.

ANECDOTAL RECORDS: An informal collection of observations over a period of time.

ANTICIPATION GUIDE: A series of statements that students respond to before they read a text.

APPRECIATIVE DISPLAY: Student work that can be enjoyed by others.

APPROXIMATION: According to Cambourne, a condition of learning where one comes close to mastery.

ASSESSMENT: According to Bertrand, the gathering of test data that provides information for evaluation.

AUDITORY DISCRIMINATION: The ability to distinguish among sounds.

AUTHENTIC ASSESSMENT: The idea that assessments should engage students in applying knowledge and skills in the same way they are used outside of school. The use of portfolios is an example of authentic assessment.

BACKTRACKING: Rereading text to clarify understanding or to find information.

BASAL TEXTBOOKS: Readers prepared for elementary grade levels that provide the basic system for reading instruction. A basal reading program includes student texts and workbooks, teacher's manuals, and supplemental materials.

BENCHMARKS: According to Marzano, statements that describe expected or anticipated performance at various developmental levels.

CAUSE/EFFECT PARAGRAPH: States the event or action in the topic sentence, then gives the results.

CHECKLISTS: Informal records that allow teachers to check off student accomplishments, skills, interests, and progress.

CLASS JOURNAL: A journal with entries from all students. It may be accompanied by a class mascot.

CLASSIFICATION SORT: A vocabulary activity in which students sort words into possible categories.

CLOZE: A test of reading comprehension in which the student is asked to supply words that have been systematically deleted from the text.

COMPARE/CONTRAST PARAGRAPH: Uses supporting details to show how two (or more) things are alike and how they are different.

COMPLEMENTARY DISCIPLINE UNITS: When related disciplines are studied together, for example, in a humanities course.

COMPLETE PROGRAM: An instructional program in which students live in the school environment and determine their own curriculum.

CONNECT TWO: A vocabulary activity in which students decide on relationships between words and then justify their connection.

CONTENT STANDARDS: According to Kendall and Marzano, they describe what a student should know and be able to do.

CONTEXTUAL ANALYSIS: The use of words, sentence structure, or other features to understand an unknown word.

COOPERATIVE INSTRUCTION: Any pattern of classroom organization that encourages students to work together to achieve individual goals.

CORRECTIVE READING INSTRUCTION: Integrates diagnosis with teaching to eliminate skill deficiencies that could become problematic. Often occurs in the regular classroom.

CRITERION-REFERENCED TESTS: Tests based on comparing performance to a standard, such as demonstrating mastery at the 80 percent level.

CROSS-AGE TUTORING: When an older student instructs a younger one.

CURRICULUM: All planned learning experiences.

CURRICULUM STANDARDS: According to Kendall and Marzano, they describe what should take place in the classroom.

DECODE: Literally meaning to break the code, it has come to mean identifying words through a letter-sound relationship.

DEMONSTRATION: According to Cambourne, modeling what is to be learned; also an artifact.

DESCRIPTIVE PARAGRAPH: Presents a specific topic and addresses its attributes.

DEVELOPMENTAL READING: Sequential reading instruction given by regular classroom teachers to the average or near average grade-level children and in the content areas.

DIRECTED LISTENING-THINKING ACTIVITY: Develops critical listening and thinking skills by having students listen to part of a story read aloud and then predict what will happen next based on the illustrations, what they have heard, and their own experiences and knowledge.

DIRECTED READING ACTIVITIES: According to Betts, reading instruction that includes readiness for reading, silent reading, discussion to develop comprehension and word-recognition skills, rereading, and follow-up activities.

DISCIPLINE-BASED CONTENT DESIGN: The traditional practice of teaching each subject during a specific instructional period.

DURING READING: Questions, activities, and discussion that encourage comprehension.

ELABORATION: Active use of prior knowledge.

EMERGENT LITERACY: The time before formal reading instruction when children build concepts about reading. This process can begin as early as 14 months of age.

ENUMERATIVE PARAGRAPH: States its main topic in the topic sentence followed by a supporting list of examples in the body of the paragraph.

ENVIRONMENTAL PRINT: Words found in children's environments that they recognize, such as names of toys, food, fast-food establishments, and street signs.

EVALUATION: Collecting and using information to determine how a student learns and to monitor the student's progress and achievement.

EXPECTATION: According to Cambourne, a condition of learning where we assume that children can indeed learn.

EXPOSITORY TEXT: Text that informs; usually features highly structured text, graphs and tables, and visual cues such as boldfaced or italicized words, and headings.

FORMAL ASSESSMENT: A process of determining how much students have learned, generally based on criterion-referenced or norm-referenced tests.

FORMATIVE EVALUATION: A process of evaluation that provides feedback and redirection during the learning process.

FREE VOLUNTARY READING: The practice of allowing students to choose their own reading materials and then to read for extended time periods.

GENRE: A distinctive literary category.

GRAPHEME: The graphic representation of a unit of sound.

GRAPHIC ORGANIZER: A diagram or scheme for showing the relationships among words and concepts.

GRAPHOPHONICS: According to Ken Goodman, a combination of cues that readers and writers use, including sound system (phonology), graphic system (orthography), and the system that relates them (phonics).

HYPERMEDIA: The use of more than one medium of communication, such as video, sound, graphics, and photography, to deliver a message. Also referred to as *multimedia*.

HYPERTEXT: A process of organizing or stacking information for easy computer access.

IMMERSION: According to Cambourne, a condition of learning that involves surrounding children with language to the point where they are practically inundated.

INDIVIDUALIZED READING: An approach to reading that emphasizes student selection of reading materials, self-pacing, small-group work, and conferences.

INFLECTIONAL ENDINGS: Word elements, such as *-s*, *-d*, or *-ing*, that change the meaning.

INFORMAL ASSESSMENT: According to Farr and Beck, a process of determining why students perform or learn as they do, rather than how well they perform.

INFORMAL READING INVENTORY (IRI): Graded passages of reading that can be used to determine students' strengths and weaknesses in recognizing words and comprehending text.

INTEGRATED-DAY MODEL: An instructional program based on student-selected themes.

INTERACTIVE JOURNAL: Journals with regular entries, student-selected themes, and teacher responses.

INTERDISCIPLINARY INSTRUCTION: A knowledge view and curriculum approach that consciously applies methodology and language from more than one discipline to examine a central theme, issue, problem, topic, or experience.

INTERDISCIPLINARY UNITS: Combining disciplines for a unit of study, such as a unit on the Civil War, where social studies, geography, reading, and writing will all be taught.

INVENTED SPELLING: Functional spelling that approximates the correct form. Also called *temporary spelling*.

IRE MODEL: The teacher **i**nitiates through a question, the student **r**esponds, and the teacher **e**valuates.

JIGSAW: When a heterogeneous group of three to six students share responsibility for content by learning a portion of the information and sharing it with other group members.

LANGUAGE EXPERIENCE APPROACH (LEA): An early language arts approach based on students' experiences.

LAW OF EFFECT: The belief of Edward L. Thorndyke that an increased level of satisfaction improves the effect of exercise.

LAW OF EXERCISE: The belief of Edward L. Thorndyke that exercise strengthens the relationship between a situation and the response.

LAW OF READINESS: The belief of Edward L. Thorndyke that readiness for learning must be present for effective instruction.

LEXICON: A personal dictionary or body of terms relating to a topic, profession, or style.

LIMITED-ENGLISH-PROFICIENT (LEP) STUDENTS: Children whose home language is not English; children who need to acquire English as a second language.

LINGUISTICS: The study of sounds that humans make when speaking to each other.

LITERARY WHOLES: Complete stories, poems, and articles rather than excerpts or adaptations.

LITERATURE CONTRACT: A written agreement between the teacher and student to complete a variety of activities related to reading a particular group of books.

LITERATURE LOG: Written responses to reading literature.

LOGOGRAPHIC STAGE OF PHONICS: The first stage of word learning, when children learn words as whole units.

MAINSTREAMING: Placing students with special learning needs in a regular classroom.

METACOGNITION: Awareness of, and knowledge about, one's thinking processes.

MORPHEME: The smallest unit of meaning, such as a prefix, suffix, or root word, that cannot be divided into a smaller meaningful unit.

MORPHEMIC ANALYSIS: The determination of a word's meaning by analyzing its prefix, root, and/or suffix.

MULTIMEDIA: The use of more than one medium of communication, such as video, sound, graphics, and photography, to deliver a message. Also referred to as *hypermedia*.

NARRATIVE TEXT: Written material that tells a story, as found in novels and short stories.

NORM-REFERENCED TESTS: Tests that relate results to other students with predetermined performance indicators or scales, generally by student's age, grade, or gender. A student scoring at the 50th percentile on a subtest has a score higher than 50 percent of the comparable students.

OBSERVATION: A systematic effort to watch a student and record learning behaviors and progress.

ONSET: The initial consonant or consonant cluster of a word.

OPIN: A vocabulary strategy that involves selecting words that best fit in a sentence.

ORTHOGRAPHIC STAGE OF PHONICS: The last stage of learning words, when children see and use patterns to recognize words.

OUTCOME-BASED EDUCATION: A program that relies on performance assessment.

PAIRED READING: When two students of approximately the same achievement level read together collaboratively.

PARENT JOURNAL: A journal dedicated to communication between school and home.

PARALLEL DISCIPLINE DESIGN: When two teachers collaborate on the same topic, such as language arts and social studies.

PEER TUTORING: When a more accomplished student tutors a less accomplished student.

PERFORMANCE ASSESSMENT: The variety of opportunities students have to demonstrate understanding and apply knowledge, skills, and habits of mind in varying contexts.

PHONEME: The smallest speech sound that can be distinguished.

PHONEMIC AWARENESS: The ability to recognize that a spoken word comprises a sequence of individual sounds.

PHONICS: An approach to reading instruction that teaches students to recognize the relationships between letters or letter combinations and the speech sounds they represent.

PHONOLOGY: The sound system of an oral language.

PORTFOLIO: A collection of a student's best work gathered over a period of time.

POSSIBLE SENTENCES: An activity using target and familiar words to make sentences that might be appropriate in a reading passage.

POSTREADING: All lessons and activities that follow the reading.

PREFIX: A word element that precedes a root word.

PREREADING: All lessons and activities that prepare and motivate students to read.

PROBLEM-BASED THEMATIC UNITS: Learning based on simulation of a problem.

PROBLEM/SOLUTION PARAGRAPH: States a problem in the topic sentence with supporting details describing the problems, its causes, and solutions.

PROCEDURAL TEXT: Material that describes the processes for doing something, such as directions for assembling a toy or a recipe.

RATING SCALE: A grid for rating the degree of presence of a characteristic.

READABILITY: The difficulty of text as measured by a formula that quantifies the difficulty.

READABLE DISPLAY: Print that is easy to read.

REBUSES: Words that combine letters and pictures.

RECODE: To attach pronunciation to the written representation of a word.

RELIABILITY: According to Farr and Beck, "The consistency of scores obtained when persons are reexamined with the same test on different occasions or with tests composed of parallel sets of items."

REMEDIAL READING INSTRUCTION: For students who need intensive diagnosis and tutoring. Usually taught by a resource or remedial reading teacher who works with small groups of children or who works collaboratively with the classroom teacher.

RESPONSE: According to Cambourne, a condition of learning where children are given feedback.

RESPONSIBILITY: According to Cambourne, a condition of learning where children take ownership of their learning.

RIME: The vowel or vowel-plus-consonant element of a word.

RUBRIC: A scoring guide that provides criteria that describe student performance at various levels of proficiency.

SCAFFOLDING: The process of using prereading, during-reading, and postreading activities to assist students to successfully comprehend, learning from, and enjoy a reading selection.

SCHEMA: A related network of concepts or existing conceptual background for learning new words.

SCHEMA THEORY: Building new connections and knowledge on existing experience.

SEMANTIC FEATURE ANALYSIS: A chart that analyzes features of a chosen category of terms or concepts.

SEMANTIC GRADIENT: A classification scheme that arranges related words on a continuum.

SEMANTIC MAP: This graphic organizer emphasizes the nuances of meanings of vocabulary words and is similar to a web.

SEMANTICS: Meaning of text.

SEQUENTIAL PARAGRAPH: Has a main topic that is supported by details that must be presented in a specific order to build the reader's understanding in a logical manner.

SQ3R: Survey, Question, Read, Review, and Recite.

STANDARDS: See *content standards* and *curriculum standards*.

STRATEGIES: Specific systems or approaches to reading.

STRUCTURED OVERVIEW: A scheme for organizing vocabulary words while analyzing concepts. Also referred to as a graphic organizer.

SUFFIX: A word element that follows the root word.

SUMMATIVE EVALUATION: Tests on, or judgments made about, a finished project or upon completion of a particular unit of study.

SUSTAINED SILENT READING (SSR): A period of independent silent reading. Synonymous to SQUIRT (sustained quiet uninterrupted individualized reading time), DEAR (drop everything and read), and USSR (uninterrupted sustained silent reading).

SYLLABLE: A group of letters forming one unit of pronunciation.

SYNTAX: Patterns of phrases and sentences.

SYNTHETIC PHONICS: The isolation of each sound of a letter followed by the sounds being blended together as they are pronounced. Usually coupled with explicit teaching.

TEMPORARY SPELLING: Functional spelling that approximates the correct form. Also called *invented spelling*.

USE: According to Cambourne, a condition of learning that involves employment of language.

VALIDITY: The degree to which a test assesses what it purports to measure.

VENN DIAGRAM: Overlapping circles that demonstrate relationships.

VISITOR DISPLAY: Useful information for adult visitors to the classroom.

VOCABULARY RATING: A list of vocabulary words with an opportunity to respond with "can define," "have seen or heard," or "not sure."

WEB: An informal map that shows the relationships between concepts and important terms.

WHOLE LANGUAGE: A philosophy that language is acquired through use and that advocates using authentic materials and genuine literacy events, such as writing letters.

WORD RECOGNITION: The process of identifying printed symbols with correct pronunciation and the association of meaning with the pronounced word.

WORD THEATER: Acting out the meanings of vocabulary words.

Photo Credits

Index